Cultural Heritage Rights

The International Library of Essays on Rights
Series Editor: Tom Campbell

Titles in the Series:

Sexual Orientation and Rights
Nicholas Bamforth

Rights: Concepts and Contexts
Brian Bix and Horacio Spector

Disability Rights
Peter Blanck

The Right to a Fair Trial
Thom Brooks

Global Minority Rights
Joshua Castellino

Cultural Heritage Rights
Anthony J. Connolly

Indigenous Rights
Anthony J. Connolly

Migrants and Rights
Mary Crock

Refugees and Rights
Mary Crock

Civil Rights and Security
David Dyzenhaus

Democratic Rights
Ran Hirschl

Group Rights
Peter Jones

Human Rights and Corporations
David Kinley

Prisoners' Rights
John Kleinig

Genocide and Human Rights
Mark Lattimer

Language Rights
Stephen May

Animal Rights
Clare Palmer

Gender and Rights
Deborah L. Rhode and Carol Sanger

Economic, Social and Cultural Rights
Manisuli Ssenyonjo

Health Rights
Michael J. Selgelid and Thomas Pogge

Citizenship Rights
Jo Shaw and Igor Štiks

Theories of Rights
C.L. Ten

Bills of Rights
Mark Tushnet

Environmental Rights
Steve Vanderheiden

The Right to Bodily Integrity
A.M. Viens

Labour Rights
Marley S. Weiss

Religious Rights
Lorenzo Zucca

Cultural Heritage Rights

Edited by

Anthony J. Connolly

Australian National University

ASHGATE

© Anthony J. Connolly 2015. For copyright of individual articles please refer to the Acknowledgements.

All rights reserved. No part of this publication may be reproduced, stored in a retrieval system or transmitted in any form or by any means, electronic, mechanical, photocopying, recording or otherwise without the prior permission of the publisher.

Wherever possible, these reprints are made from a copy of the original printing, but these can themselves be of very variable quality. Whilst the publisher has made every effort to ensure the quality of the reprint, some variability may inevitably remain.

Published by
Ashgate Publishing Limited
Wey Court East
Union Road
Farnham
Surrey GU9 7PT
England

Ashgate Publishing Company
Suite 3-1
110 Cherry Street
Burlington
VT 05401-3818
USA

www.ashgate.com

British Library Cataloguing in Publication Data
A catalogue record for this book is available from the British Library.

Library of Congress Control Number: 2015932172

ISBN 9781472423245

Printed in the United Kingdom by Henry Ling Limited,
at the Dorset Press, Dorchester, DT1 1HD

Contents

Acknowledgements   *ix*
Series Preface   *xiii*
Introduction   *xv*
Bibliography and Further Reading   *xxxii*

PART I FOUNDATIONS

The Concept of Cultural Heritage
1 John Henry Merryman (2005), 'Cultural Property Internationalism', *International Journal of Cultural Property*, **12**, pp. 11–39.   3
2 Janet Blake (2000), 'On Defining the Cultural Heritage', *International and Comparative Law Quarterly*, **49**, pp. 61–85.   33

The Politics of Cultural Heritage Rights
3 Rosemary J. Coombe (2009), 'The Expanding Purview of Cultural Properties and Their Politics', *Annual Review of Law and Social Science*, **5**, pp. 393–412.   59
4 Jonathan S. Bell (2013), 'The Politics of Preservation: Privileging One Heritage over Another', *International Journal of Cultural Property*, **20**, pp. 431–50.   79

PART II TYPES OF CULTURAL HERITAGE RIGHTS

Natural Heritage as Cultural Heritage
5 Shabnam Inanloo Dailoo and Frits Pannekoek (2008), 'Nature and Culture: A New World Heritage Context', *International Journal of Cultural Property*, **15**, pp. 25–47.   101
6 Gonzalo Oviedo and Tatjana Puschkarsky (2012), 'World Heritage and Rights-Based Approaches to Nature Conservation', *International Journal of Heritage Studies*, **18**, pp. 285–96.   125

Urban Landscapes as Cultural Heritage
7 Lindsay M. Weiss (2014), 'Informal Settlements and Urban Heritage Landscapes in South Africa', *Journal of Social Archaeology*, **14**, pp. 3–25.   137

Artefactual Cultural Heritage Rights
8 Michael L. Dutra (2004), 'Sir, How Much is that Ming Vase in the Window? Protecting Cultural Relics in the People's Republic of China', *Asian-Pacific Law and Policy Journal*, **5**, pp. 62–100.   161

Underwater Cultural Heritage Rights

9 Sarah Dromgoole (2003), '2001 UNESCO Convention on the Protection of the Underwater Cultural Heritage', *International Journal of Marine and Coastal Law*, **18**, pp. 59–91. 201

Intangible Cultural Heritage Rights

10 Michael F. Brown (2005), 'Heritage Trouble: Recent Work on the Protection of Intangible Cultural Property', *International Journal of Cultural Property*, **12**, pp. 40–61. 235

11 Thomas M. Schmitt (2008), 'The UNESCO Concept of Safeguarding Intangible Cultural Heritage: Its Background and *Marrakchi* Roots', *International Journal of Heritage Studies*, **14**, pp. 95–111. 257

Indigenous Cultural Heritage Rights

12 Rosemary J. Coombe with Joseph F. Turcotte (2012), 'Indigenous Cultural Heritage in Development and Trade: Perspectives from the Dynamics of Cultural Heritage Law and Policy', in Christoph B. Graber, Karolina Kuprecht and Jessica C. Lai (eds), *International Trade in Indigenous Cultural Heritage: Legal and Policy Issues*, Cheltenham: Edward Elgar, pp. 272–306. 275

13 Melissa F. Baird (2013), 'Indigenous Cultural Landscapes and the Politics of Heritage', *International Journal of Heritage Studies*, **19**, pp. 327–40. 311

PART III CONTEMPORARY ISSUES IN CULTURAL HERITAGE RIGHTS LAW

Repatriation of Cultural Heritage

14 Robert K. Paterson (2006), 'Resolving Material Culture Disputes: Human Rights, Property Rights and Crimes against Humanity', *Willamette Journal of International Law and Dispute Resolution*, **14**, pp. 155–74. 327

Illicit Trade in Cultural Heritage

15 Patty Gerstenblith (2007), 'Controlling the International Market in Antiquities: Reducing the Harm, Preserving the Past', *Chicago Journal of International Law*, **8**, pp. 169–95. 347

Armed Conflict and Cultural Heritage Protection

16 Hirad Abtahi (2001), 'The Protection of Cultural Property in Times of Armed Conflict: The Practice of the International Criminal Tribunal for the Former Yugoslavia', *Harvard Human Rights Journal*, **14**, pp. 1–32. 375

17 Francesco Francioni and Federico Lenzerini (2006), 'The Obligation to Prevent and Avoid Destruction of Cultural Heritage: From Bamiyan to Iraq', in B. Hoffman (ed.), *Art and Cultural Heritage: Law, Policy, and Practice*, Cambridge: Cambridge University Press, pp. 28–40. 407

Tourism, Economic Development and Cultural Heritage Protection

18 Tim Winter (2008), 'Post-Conflict Heritage and Tourism in Cambodia: The Burden
    of Angkor', *International Journal of Heritage Studies*, **14**, pp.524–39.   421

PART IV FUTURE DIRECTIONS IN CULTURAL HERITAGE RIGHTS LAW

Cultural Heritage Protection and the Challenge of Climate Change

19 Hee-Eun Kim (2011), 'Changing Climate, Changing Culture: Adding the Climate
    Change Dimension to the Protection of Intangible Cultural Heritage', *International
    Journal of Cultural Property*, **18**, pp. 259–90.   439

Cultural Expressions as Cultural Heritage

20 Rachael Craufurd Smith (2007), 'The UNESCO Convention on the Protection and
    Promotion of Cultural Expressions: Building a New World Information and
    Communication Order?', *International Journal of Communication*, **1**, pp. 24–55.   471

The Human Genome and Cultural Heritage

21 Pilar N. Ossorio (2007), 'The Human Genome as Common Heritage: Common
    Sense or Legal Nonsense?', *Journal of Law, Medicine and Ethics*, **35**, pp. 425–39.   503

Beyond Rights? Rethinking the Cultural Heritage Protection Paradigm

22 Ian Hodder (2010), 'Cultural Heritage Rights: From Ownership and Descent to
    Justice and Well-Being', *Anthropological Quarterly*, **83**, pp. 861–82.   519

Name index   541

Acknowledgements

Ashgate would like to thank our researchers and the contributing authors who provided copies, along with the following for their permission to reprint copyright material.

Annual Reviews for the essay: Rosemary J. Coombe (2009), 'The Expanding Purview of Cultural Properties and Their Politics', *Annual Review of Law and Social Science*, **5**, pp. 393–412. Copyright © 2009 by Annual Reviews. All rights reserved.

Anthropological Quarterly for the essay: Ian Hodder (2010), 'Cultural Heritage Rights: From Ownership and Descent to Justice and Well-Being', *Anthropological Quarterly*, **83**, pp. 861–82. Copyright © 2010 by the Institute for Ethnographic Research (IFER), a part of the George Washington University. All rights reserved.

Asian-Pacific Law and Policy Journal for the essay: Michael L. Dutra (2004), 'Sir, How Much is that Ming Vase in the Window? Protecting Cultural Relics in the People's Republic of China', *Asian-Pacific Law and Policy Journal*, **5**, pp. 62–100.

Brill Academic Publishers for the essay: Sarah Dromgoole (2003), '2001 UNESCO Convention on the Protection of the Underwater Cultural Heritage', *International Journal of Marine and Coastal Law*, **18**, pp. 59–91. Copyright © 2003 Kluwer Law International.

Cambridge University Press for the essays: John Henry Merryman (2005), 'Cultural Property Internationalism', *International Journal of Cultural Property*, **12**, pp. 11–39. Copyright © 2005 International Cultural Property Society, published by Cambridge University Press, reproduced with permission; Janet Blake (2000), 'On Defining the Cultural Heritage', *The International and Comparative Law Quarterly*, **49**, pp. 61–85. Copyright © 2000 British Institute of International and Comparative Law, published by Cambridge University Press, reproduced with permission; Jonathan S. Bell (2013), 'The Politics of Preservation: Privileging One Heritage over Another', *International Journal of Cultural Property*, **20**, pp. 431–50. Copyright © 2013 International Cultural Property Society, published by Cambridge University Press, reproduced with permission; Shabnam Inanloo Dailoo and Frits Pannekoek (2008), 'Nature and Culture: A New World Heritage Context', *International Journal of Cultural Property*, **15**, pp. 25–47. Copyright © 2008 International Cultural Property Society, published by Cambridge University Press, reproduced with permission; Michael F. Brown (2005), 'Heritage Trouble: Recent Work on the Protection of Intangible Cultural Property', *International Journal of Cultural Property*, **12**, pp. 40–61. Copyright © 2005 International Cultural Property Society, published by Cambridge University Press, reproduced with permission; Francesco Francioni and Federico Lenzerini (2006), 'The Obligation to Prevent and Avoid Destruction of Cultural Heritage: From Bamiyan to Iraq', in B. Hoffman (ed.), *Art and Cultural Heritage: Law, Policy, and Practice*, Cambridge: Cambridge University Press, pp. 28–40. Copyright © 2006 Cambridge University Press, © 2006 Introduction and Compilation, Barbara T. Hoffman, reproduced with permission; Hee-Eun Kim (2011), 'Changing Climate, Changing Culture: Adding the Climate Change Dimension to the Protection of Intangible Cultural Heritage', *International Journal of Cultural Property*, **18**, pp. 259–90. © 2011 International Cultural Property Society, published by Cambridge University Press, reproduced with permission.

Chicago Journal of International Law for the essay: Patty Gerstenblith (2007), 'Controlling the International Market in Antiquities: Reducing the Harm, Preserving the Past', *Chicago Journal of International Law*, **8**, pp. 169–95.

Edward Elgar Publishing for the essay: Rosemary J. Coombe with Joseph F. Turcotte (2012), 'Indigenous Cultural Heritage in Development and Trade: Perspectives from the Dynamics of Cultural Heritage Law and Policy', in Christoph B. Graber, Karolina Kuprecht and Jessica C. Lai (eds), *International Trade in Indigenous Cultural Heritage: Legal and Policy Issues*, Cheltenham: Edward Elgar, pp. 272–306.

Harvard University Law School for the essay: Hirad Abtahi (2001), 'The Protection of Cultural Property in Times of Armed Conflict: The Practice of the International Criminal Tribunal for the Former Yugoslavia', *Harvard Human Rights Journal*, **14**, pp. 1–32.

International Journal of Communication for the essay: Rachael Craufurd Smith (2007), 'The UNESCO Convention on the Protection and Promotion of Cultural Expressions: Building a New World Information and Communication Order?', *International Journal of Communication*, **1**, pp. 24–55. Copyright © 2007 Rachael Craufurd Smith.

John Wiley and Sons for the essay: Pilar N. Ossorio (2007), 'The Human Genome as Common Heritage: Common Sense or Legal Nonsense?', *Journal of Law, Medicine and Ethics*, **35**, pp. 425–39. Copyright © 2007, John Wiley and Sons.

SAGE Publications for the essay: Lindsay M. Weiss (2014), 'Informal Settlements and Urban Heritage Landscapes in South Africa', *Journal of Social Archaeology*, **14**, pp. 3–25. Copyright © 2014 The author. Reprinted by permission of SAGE.

Taylor and Francis for the essays: Gonzalo Oviedo and Tatjana Puschkarsky (2012), 'World Heritage and Rights-Based Approaches to Nature Conservation', *International Journal of Heritage Studies*, **18**, pp. 285–96. Copyright © 2012 Taylor & Francis. Reprinted with permission of the publisher (Taylor & Francis Ltd, http://www.tandfonline.com); Thomas M. Schmitt (2008), 'The UNESCO Concept of Safeguarding Intangible Cultural Heritage: Its Background and *Marrakchi* Roots', *International Journal of Heritage Studies*, **14**, pp. 95–111. Copyright © 2008 Taylor & Francis. Reprinted with permission of the publisher (Taylor & Francis Ltd, http://www.tandfonline.com); Melissa F. Baird (2013), 'Indigenous Cultural Landscapes and the Politics of Heritage', *International Journal of Heritage Studies*, **19**, pp. 327–40. Copyright © 2013 Taylor & Francis. Reprinted with permission of the publisher (Taylor & Francis Ltd, http://www.tandfonline.com); Tim Winter (2008), 'Post-Conflict Heritage and Tourism in Cambodia: The Burden of Angkor', *International Journal of Heritage Studies*, **14**, pp. 524–39. Copyright © 2008 Taylor & Francis. Reprinted with permission of the publisher (Taylor & Francis Ltd, http://www.tandfonline.com).

Every effort has been made to trace all the copyright holders, but if any have been inadvertently overlooked the publishers will be pleased to make the necessary arrangement at the first opportunity.

Publisher's Note

The material in this volume has been reproduced using the facsimile method. This means we can retain the original pagination to facilitate easy and correct citation of the original essays. It also explains the variety of typefaces, page layouts and numbering.

Series Preface

Much of contemporary moral, political and legal discourse is conducted in terms of rights and increasingly in terms of human rights. Yet there is considerable disagreement about the nature of rights, their foundations and their practical implications and more concrete controversies as to the content, scope and force of particular rights. Consequently the discourse of rights calls for extensive analysis in its general meaning and significance, particularly in relation to the nature, location and content of the duties and responsibilities that correlate with rights. Equally important is the determination of the forms of argument that are appropriate to establish whether or not someone or some group has or has not a particular right, and what that might entail in practice.

This series brings together essays that exhibit careful analysis of the concept of rights and detailed knowledge of specific rights and the variety of systems of rights articulation, interpretation, protection and enforcement. Volumes deal with general philosophical and practical issues about different sorts of rights, taking account of international human rights, regional rights conventions and regimes, and domestic bills of rights, as well as the moral and political literature concerning the articulation and implementation of rights.

The volumes are intended to assist those engaged in scholarly research by making available the most important and enduring essays on particular topics. Essays are reproduced in full with the original pagination for ease of reference and citation.

The editors are selected for their eminence in the study of law, politics and philosophy. Each volume represents the editor's selection of the most seminal recent essays in English on an aspect of rights or on rights in a particular field. An introduction presents an overview of the issues in that particular area of rights together with comments on the background and significance of the selected essays.

TOM CAMPBELL
Series Editor
Professorial Fellow, The Centre for Applied Philosophy and Public Ethics (CAPPE),
Charles Sturt University, Canberra

Introduction

Cultural Heritage Rights: Conceptual, Legal and Political Foundations

The first decade of the twenty-first century saw an increase in the prominence of cultural heritage rights globally – in public discourse, in academic writings, and in law.[1] By cultural heritage rights, I mean the legal rights of individuals, peoples, nations and even humanity at large, to the recognition, preservation and enjoyment of certain distinctive elements of human culture.[2] Because legal rights necessarily subsist within a broader economy of legal rules, the rise of cultural heritage rights implicates the rise of cultural heritage law more generally. The causes of this recent increase in prominence are many and complex. Part of it may be traced to the widespread concern generated by global media coverage of the destruction and looting of vast quantities of heritage phenomena in a number of civil and military conflicts in the 1990s and early 2000s – those in Yugoslavia, Afghanistan and Iraq being among the most notable. The names Dubrovnik, Bamiyan, and Baghdad these days all connote not only a dreadful toll of human death and suffering but also the loss of countless artefacts, monuments, buildings and other items of cultural value to local and national communities and to the world at large (see the essays by Abtahi (Chapter 16) and Francioni and Lenzerini (Chapter 17) in this collection).

It would not be unreasonable to speculate that the concern for cultural heritage generated by these conflicts is informed by a wider sensitivity to the finitude and vulnerability of both our natural and cultural resources which has emerged of late in the contemporary world. Just as the disappearance of animal species and ecosystems in the face of human activity has caused many to pause and respond with legal solutions, so too has the recognition of a gradually declining stock of distinctive cultures and their artefacts. Cultural heritage law, like environmental law, has become a front line response for those who care about the

---

[1] Coombe, in this collection (Chapter 3), construes this rise as part of 'a recent acceleration of global policymaking with respect to culture' (p. 61). Of course, as Blake (Chapter 2) points out, '[e]xamples can be found from ancient times of concern for the protection of cultural artefacts and early legislation to protect monuments and works of art first appeared in Europe in the 15th century' (p. 33).

[2] Though there may be (and, indeed, are) extra-legal moral rights to cultural heritage, the essays collected in this volume are, for the most part, not concerned with these. Their focus is primarily legal. Moral rights to cultural heritage may figure in a discussion of legal rights by grounding a claim for a corresponding legal right or by serving as a basis for critiquing and calling for the reform of a presently operative set of legal rights to cultural heritage. See Hart (1961) on the distinction between legal and moral rights. Note also here that it is possible for an agent to have legal rights to elements of someone else's culture and not merely their own.

physical, ethical and ideological damage wreaked not only by war but by modernization, industrialization, and the cultural homogenization which is thought to attend these.[3]

This, in turn, points us to another important factor in the rise of cultural heritage rights – namely, the relatively recent emergence of a global discourse of the rights of peoples – particularly, minority and indigenous rights.[4] Cultural heritage rights have become a key part of an expanding worldwide political movement and human rights agenda.[5] The importance of culture and heritage to the identity and political integrity of indigenous peoples and other minority groups has long been recognized within international, regional and national law.[6] Cultural difference has become a prime value in the contemporary world and cultural heritage has been recognized as a key marker of this difference. As a number of contributors to this volume point out, in the last two decades or so, the international law of cultural heritage has been overtly and increasingly integrated with and oriented towards the ends and values of international human rights law (see Blake, Chapter 2; Coombe, Chapter 3; Oviedo and Puschkarsky, Chapter 6; and Coombe and Turcotte, Chapter 12). So too, as regional confederations and individual nation states work towards aligning their legal systems with international human rights law, the cultural heritage rights of indigenous peoples and other minority groups within those jurisdictions – as well as the cultural heritage rights of majority peoples within those jurisdictions – have found expression in regional and national law (see, for example, Blake, Chapter 2; see also Niezen, 2003 and Anaya, 2004). At the heart of this increasingly global body of cultural heritage law, then, lies the modern ideal of the cultural, political and economic self-determination of all the world's peoples (Coombe and Turcotte, Chapter 12; Paterson, Chapter 14). In this sense, cultural heritage law is a profoundly political kind of law.[7]

Law around the world is changing in response to this increased sensitivity to the importance of cultural heritage – at the national, regional and international levels. Concurrently, thinkers,

---

[3] And, of course, cultural heritage law has also become a key tool for those who benefit from these global forces and who don't care about the damage caused by them. 'Changing practices, behaviors, attitudes, and protocols regarding cultural heritage both index and reflect transformations in social relationships that are indicative of larger patterns of late modernity and decolonization' (Coombe, Chapter 3, p. 62).

[4] See Crawford (1988). Niezen (2003) and Morgan (2011) trace the emergence of a global indigenous rights discourse and movement to the 1970s. Coombe and Turcotte (Chapter 12) claim that for indigenous peoples, cultural heritage rights are 'often linked to a broader project of decolonisation that stresses the inextricable link between cultural heritage and the maintenance, strengthening, transmission and renewal of indigenous peoples' identity, knowledge, laws and practices' (p. 282).

[5] See Morgan (2011). Coombe and Turcotte (Chapter 12) claim that, '[t]he right of communities, minorities and indigenous peoples to participate in the process of determining how cultural heritage of significance to them will be protected is arguably the most important issue of cultural heritage law and policy today' (p. 279).

[6] In contemporary international law, this recognition extends back to the 1948 Universal Declaration of Human Rights and includes, most notably, the 1966 International Covenant on Economic, Social and Cultural Rights and the 2007 United Nations Declaration on the Rights of Indigenous Peoples. See Craufurd Smith (Chapter 20, p. 475). See also Crawford (1988), Thornberry (1991) and Anaya (2004). For a discussion of regional (EU) law on this, see Malloy (2005).

[7] I will have more to say about the politics of cultural heritage rights below.

practitioners, advocates and citizens around the world are developing and refining their ideas about this topic and the legal changes associated with it. The aim of this book is to give readers a sense of both the state of the law globally in relation to cultural heritage rights and the state of contemporary thinking about these rights and this law. The 22 essays in this collection comprise an up-to-date overview of the key legal, philosophical, political and economic themes and issues presently associated with cultural heritage rights in legal and academic discourse around the world. They have been curated with a view to providing those readers unfamiliar with this topic with an understanding of its general contours. The collection has also been designed to stimulate and refine the thought of those readers more familiar with the topic by providing them with access to the most important recent developments in the law and theory surrounding cultural heritage rights.

The collection commences with four essays on the key conceptual and political issues informing cultural heritage discourse today (Merryman, Chapter 1; Blake, Chapter 2; Coombe, Chapter 3; and Bell, Chapter 4). It continues with a series of essays which identify and discuss six notable kinds of cultural heritage presently subject to legal regulation around the world today (Dailoo and Pannekoek, Chapter 5; Oviedo and Puschkarsky, Chapter 6; Weiss, Chapter 7; Dutra, Chapter 8; Dromgoole, Chapter 9; Brown, Chapter 10; Schmitt, Chapter 11; Coombe and Turcotte, Chapter 12; and Baird, Chapter 13). The essays in this second part of the book are designed to provide readers with a sense of the issues and regulatory challenges peculiar to those kinds of heritage, as well as those issues and challenges they have in common. Part III of the collection explores four key issues in the contemporary literature on cultural heritage – the repatriation of cultural heritage, the looting of and illicit trade in cultural heritage, the effects of armed conflict on cultural heritage and the relationship between tourism, economic development and cultural heritage (Paterson, Chapter 14; Gerstenblith, Chapter 15; Abtahi, Chapter 16; Francioni and Lenzerini, Chapter 17; and Winter, Chapter 18). The last part of the book presents a series of essays exploring a number of issues likely to become increasingly important in the years and decades ahead – climate change, cultural globalization, human genomic science and the shift to a post-liberal, post-rights politics and law of cultural heritage (Kim, Chapter 19; Craufurd Smith, Chapter 20; Ossorio, Chapter 21; and Hodder, Chapter 22).

Readers with a specific interest in the field – say, indigenous cultural heritage rights or world heritage law – might find it useful to turn directly to the essays dealing with that interest. However, there is, I think, much to be gained in the understanding of any particular aspect of cultural heritage law by critically and comparatively reading all the essays in this collection. The collection is designed to provide a multifaceted understanding of the field as a whole. Care has been taken to utilize the work of both established and highly influential authors, as well as early-career, up and coming thinkers across a range of disciplines, including law, political theory, anthropology, cultural studies, heritage studies, environmental policy and urban planning. These authors hail from around the world, including the United States, the United Kingdom, Australia, Canada, New Zealand, Switzerland, Germany, Italy, Iran and South Africa. All of the essays are recent, extending no further back than the early twenty-first century. As a result, this book comprises one of the most significant, comprehensive and contemporary collection of writings about cultural heritage rights presently in print.

At this point, let me set the scene and provide those readers unfamiliar with the topic of cultural heritage rights with some foundational discussion in light of which they might better understand and engage with the essays in the collection.

What Is Cultural Heritage?

Cultural heritage rights are legal rights to cultural heritage. Cultural heritage law is law regulating cultural heritage. What, though, is the nature of the class of phenomena these rights and this law are about? What is cultural heritage? As a number of the essays in this collection make clear, there is no unanimously agreed definition of cultural heritage – either at law or in the wider practical and theoretical literature on the topic (see the essays in this collection by Merryman, Chapter 1; Blake, Chapter 2; and Coombe and Turcotte, Chapter 12; see also Prott and O'Keefe, 1984). Indeed, even the terminology used to refer to the class of phenomena in question has varied over the years.[8] The category is a heterogeneous one. It is difficult to make generalizations over all the various phenomena which are comprehended by it.[9] At international law, for example, phenomena falling under the category (as defined by various international legal conventions) include the Mona Lisa, seventeenth-century Polynesian headdresses, the languages of the Karen people of southern Burma, the recently destroyed Bamiyan statues of Afghanistan, the botanical knowledge of Amazonian tribal peoples, the urban landscapes of Soweto's townships, the museum-based human remains of nineteenth-century Australian Aborigines, the underwater wreck of the Titanic, New Zealand's Tongariro National Park and the Francophonic television industry. What is it, if anything, these things share which render them instances of the same kind of thing, cultural heritage?

As a way forward, and drawing on certain common strands of both the law and the academic literature on the topic,[10] let me offer a conception according to which cultural heritage comprises a category of phenomena which meet certain criteria involving the four notions of culture, inheritability, value and identity.

Culture

First – and, perhaps, most obviously – cultural heritage is a subset of all the phenomena that comprise the *culture* of some human group or society.[11] It comprises some of the elements of the cultural matrix of a group of people – namely, those elements of culture which meet the other criteria of my definition (inheritability, value and identity). The social sciences have, for over a century, been the site of disputes about the definition of culture. I do not propose

---

[8] A number of terms are used in the law and academic literature for what I will be referring to in this introduction as cultural heritage. These terms include cultural objects, cultural property and cultural patrimony. See the essays by Merryman (Chapter 1), Blake (Chapter 2) and Coombe (Chapter 3).

[9] Merryman (Chapter 1, p. 3). In the indeterminacy of the concept of cultural heritage lies the seeds of much of the theoretical dispute and political conflict which surrounds the topic.

[10] Including the essays in this collection.

[11] What the precise boundaries of any such subset are, and indeed, whether *all* the elements of a society's culture may be conceived of as cultural heritage may be open to debate.

to rehearse those here.[12] For our purposes, culture may be defined as the totality of shared ideas, beliefs and practices which a community of people (a society) maintain both at any given time and over generational iterations of that community, together with the physical artefacts generated by that thought and practice.[13] More controversially, perhaps, we might also include under the rubric of culture, elements of the physical environment within which and in relation to which that thought and practice generally take place.[14]

Culture includes, then, tangible phenomena such as artefacts (tools, clothing, artworks and religious objects, for example), monuments, buildings and built environments, as well as observable and interpretable human activities such as religious rituals, leisure activities, performances of story and song, subsistence and economic practices and spoken and written language. It also includes intangible phenomena such concepts, beliefs, knowledge claims, scientific explanations of the world, religious myths and kinship systems.[15] Further, pre-existing natural phenomena – rocky outcrops, forests, mountains, an entire landscape even – may be given a pseudo-artefactual and, therefore, cultural quality by coming to figure meaningfully in the thought and practice of a society (see Dailoo and Pannekoek, Chapter 5 and Oviedo and Puschkarsky, Chapter 6; see also Lowenthal, 2005).

As a subset of culture, cultural heritage comprises these kinds of phenomena.[16] Whatever forms it might take, as culture, cultural heritage is a collective or social phenomenon arising

---

[12] Historically influential theorists here include Tylor, Malinowski, Boas, Benedict, Levi-Strauss, Geertz and Clifford. See Kroeber and Kluckhohn (1952) for a dated but still useful critical overview of the history of anthropological definitions. See also Geertz (1973) and Clifford (1988).

[13] See Connolly (2010, ch. 1). The OED defines culture as 'The distinctive ideas, customs, social behaviour, products, or way of life of a particular nation, society, people, or period. Hence: a society or group characterized by such customs, etc.' The cognitive anthropologist Roy D'Andrade says, '[o]ne can conceive of a society's culture ... as "whatever it is one has to know or believe in order to operate in a manner acceptable to its members"' (1995, p. xiii quoting Goodenough, 1953).

[14] See the essays by Dailoo and Pannekoek (Chapter 5), Oviedo and Puschkarsky (Chapter 6) and Baird (Chapter 13) in this collection. Recent developments in the international law surrounding the World Heritage Convention are significant here.

[15] Craufurd Smith (Chapter 20) points out that the 2001 Universal Declaration on Cultural Diversity states that 'culture should be regarded as the set of distinctive spiritual, material, intellectual and emotional features of society or a social group, and that it encompasses, in addition to art and literature, lifestyles, ways of living together, value systems, traditions and beliefs' (p. 479) and that the 2005 UNESCO Convention on the Protection and Promotion of the Diversity of Cultural Expressions 'adopts a broad approach to its subject matter, encompassing not just artistic expressions but all expressions that reflect distinct cultures. It consequently covers film and television programmes, classic cinema and tacky game shows, web logs and websites, as well as man-made landscapes, food and culinary practices, sport and other forms of recreation' (p. 479).

[16] In this volume I have chosen to include essays not only on standard examples of tangible heritage such as ethnographic artefacts, archaeological and historical antiquities, fine art, shipwrecks, monuments and buildings, but also on phenomena that have more recently and more controversially come into the frame here – culturally significant *natural* phenomena (often referred to as cultural landscapes), contemporary urban landscapes and human genetic material. Likewise, I have selected essays not only on commonly recognized intangible heritage such as bodies of traditional medicinal knowledge, the plots of creation myths, rules of kinship and customary laws of trade, but also contemporary pop music, television and film scripts and human genetic code.

out of and finding a place in the lived experience and existence of a community or society.[17] Cultural heritage is the heritage of some or other social group.[18] Though legal rights to it may be held by individuals, ontologically, at least, cultural heritage is a collective phenomenon transcending the interests and practices of any individual.

Inheritability

Second, drawing on the etymology of its latter term, cultural heritage comprises those elements of culture that are *inheritable*. By this I mean not only that they have been inherited by the present generation of a society from previous generations but also that they are considered worthy of being transmitted or handed on by the present generation to future generations of the society, who will in turn be said to have inherited them.[19] Cultural heritage, then, is a profoundly temporal class of phenomena. It subsists over the duration of a society. It is intergenerational in this distinctive and important sense. Further, though, it characteristically subsists *within human thought and practice*. It must be handed on and received by people in order to be maintained temporally, in order to exist *as heritage*. As Silverman and Ruggles assert, '[c]ultural heritage requires memory. It is not enough for things and monuments to exist in a landscape: in order to be cultural heritage they must be remembered and claimed as patrimony even if their original meaning is lost or poorly understood' (2007, p. 12).[20] Though the common meaning of the term 'heritage' connotes items of some antiquity, an emergent strand of cultural heritage law and theory is concerned to bring under the concept relatively new and novel phenomena – phenomena presently recognized as having the potential to be transmitted to future generations of the society in question. And that which motivates this transmission is a sense of the *value* of the heritage in question. Cultural heritage maintains its status as such over time because it comprises those things thought to be of sufficient value to justify being handed on to subsequent generations of a society.

Value

This last point brings us to the third element of the concept of cultural heritage – namely that the category comprises those things that are of particular value or significance to a social group, including, possibly, a group which has not been responsible for its creation or primary

---

[17] 'The term "culture" as a qualifier to the concept of heritage acknowledges a social collective to whom the forms have significance' (Coombe and Turcotte, Chapter 12, p. 278).

[18] Of course, it may comprise the heritage of more than one social group. For example, the monolith of Uluru in the centre of Australia has long been part of the cultural heritage of the local indigenous peoples of that region. More recently, it has been considered by the wider population of Australia to be part of the cultural heritage of the nation. And more recently still, as a declared World Heritage Site, it has been recognized by the international community as being part of the cultural heritage of humanity.

[19] A number of essays in this collection note this element of cultural heritage, including Merryman (Chapter 1), Blake (Chapter 2) and Coombe and Turcotte (Chapter 12).

[20] They go on to make the point that, '[i]n this sense cultural heritage is always to some degree intangible' (2007, p. 12).

use.[21] Cultural heritage is collectively valued. Cultural heritage *matters* to societies, to human groups and not merely to individuals (though, of course, it may also matter to individuals). Only social groups can maintain the cultural matrix, the intergenerational temporality and the collective valuing required for the instantiation of cultural heritage. Another way of putting this is to say that cultural heritage has a certain kind of shared *meaning* for people.[22] It means something to them, not merely in the sense that it represents or symbolizes some state of affairs for them (as it may), but also in the sense that it matters to them. Cultural heritage has no intrinsic value independent of its being valued by some community.[23] As a social construct, its value may change over time, positively or negatively. Cultural heritage is such at any given time by virtue of being valued as such at that time.[24] On this approach, cultural heritage may be seen to be more than just the tangible or intangible things themselves but to include also the surrounding discourse and value system associated with those things – 'the meanings, values and practices by which people engage with' those things (Smith, 2006, p. 1 quoted in Baird, Chapter 13, p. 312).

Its collective value explains why cultural heritage is inherited from past generations and transmitted to future generations. People care about their own cultural heritage – and potentially that of others – enough to want to pass it on to future generations. And they care in a quite distinctive way and for quite distinctive reasons.[25] These reasons may be manyfold. Heritage may be valued because it serves as a link with revered ancestors, or because it is the only surviving trace of an earlier time or generation of the group, or because it represents an important stage in the history of an art form, or it symbolizes a group's identity or historical experience, or because it serves as a means of subsistence and survival for the group. Because people care about cultural heritage, they want it to feature in their lives as they believe it should. They want access to it, they want to be able to interact with it, they want it protected

---

[21] Any human artefact can qualify as cultural property. 'Most people, however, will discriminate, reserving the "cultural property" title for a more limited range of objects that are distinguishable from the ordinary run of artifacts by their special cultural significance and/or rarity' (Merryman, Chapter 1, p. 11). In his essay, Merryman discusses how the cultural heritage of a given people or nation may become valued by other peoples and nations and thereby become part of humanity's cultural heritage. See also Blake (Chapter 2) and Joyner (1986) on this.

[22] 'Meaning is not intrinsic to a work of art or a monument, but is actively defined by those who experience it, with each stakeholder group and, arguably, each individual adding a new layer of significance and meaning' (Bell, Chapter 4, p. 81).

[23] 'The concept of cultural heritage reflects the fact that goods of cultural significance, unlike properties per se, are not separate from the social processes that sustain their values' (Coombe and Turcotte, Chapter 12, p. 281). 'For tangible and intangible cultural heritage to have meaning and potency, the heritage must be active dynamic used and performed, rather than existing inert and static …' (Silverman and Ruggles, 2007, p. 12).

[24] 'Johnson observes that "landscapes sites and monuments are always emergent and processable, whose meanings and significance are continually being remade through various material and discursive practices"' (Silverman and Ruggles, 2007, p. 12).

[25] Coombe and Turcotte (Chapter 12) say that cultural heritage 'may have expressive value that is aesthetic, religious or moral in nature, it may have historical and scientific value, and it may have economic value, to consider three forms of value that have received particular emphasis' (p. 278).

from interference.²⁶ Because it matters to them, people may be willing to fight for rights to it or, for that matter, to fight against the rights of others to it. Thus, the value dimension of cultural heritage may inform a *politics* of cultural heritage.²⁷

Identity

Some part of this value may have to do with the fourth criterion of cultural heritage – that it contributes to the *identity* of the society which values and transmits it.²⁸ That is, cultural heritage may be held to be valuable because it represents, expresses, reproduces or otherwise serves to maintain the collective and distinctive identity of a group over time.²⁹ It may contribute in an important way to making a group the group it is, as well as making individuals within the group the individuals they are. This is a common reason why cultural heritage is valuable to people. This is often why it is considered worthy of being transmitted to future generations as an inheritance for them. Cultural heritage is implicated in the recovery and transmission into the future of social or collective identity. Cultural heritage engages not merely temporally but also symbolically with the past, present and future of human societies.³⁰ It connects current members of the group to past and future members. It is in this regard that a significant part of the *meaning* of heritage referred to earlier operates.

A number of essays in this collection point to the role that cultural heritage plays when group identity is in question or threatened for some reason or other (see, in particular, the essays by Weiss, Chapter 7; Schmitt, Chapter 11; Baird, Chapter 13; Winter, Chapter 18; and Kim, Chapter 19). For example, the identity-serving role of cultural heritage explains to some degree why in times of war or civil conflict items of a group's cultural heritage may come under deliberate attack with a view to impairing the identity and associated morale of the group under attack.³¹ It also explains the key role that cultural heritage and cultural

---

²⁶ All of these desires find their expression in the idea that we have *interests* in heritage we care about. I take this point further below.

²⁷ I will also have more to say on this point below.

²⁸ 'Heritage is important because it provides symbolic and economic sustenance, meaning, and dignity to human lives. It legitimises territorial and intellectual ownership and it is a critical factor in the formation of social identity' (Silverman and Ruggles, 2007 p. vi). 'Art and cultural heritage are two pillars on which a society builds its identity, its values, its sense of community and the individual' (Hoffman, 2006, p. 17). See also Blake (Chapter 2, p. 48); Coombe (Chapter 3, p. 62); and Coombe and Turcotte (Chapter 12, pp. 277–78).

²⁹ See Baird (Chapter 13) on the role played by World Heritage site classification on the identity of both settler and Maori communities in New Zealand. See also Winter (Chapter 18) on how the ancient site of Angkor informs the identities of both the Cambodian nation and the site's local peoples. Finally, Kim (Chapter 19) describes the threat to communal and national identity posed by the impact of climate change on cultural heritage in the Pacific.

³⁰ '... the material culture is understood to be symbolic of cultural identity on a deeper level' (Blake, Chapter 2, p. 48).

³¹ A number of contributors to this collection discuss this issue, most notably Abtahi (Chapter 16) and Francioni and Lenzerini (Chapter 17). Blake (Chapter 2) argues that: 'The deliberate destruction of cultural monuments and artefacts during periods of armed conflict, particularly between groups who define their opposition in ethnic terms, serves to illuminate the nature of the cultural heritage itself and its role in the construction of identity. Indeed, it could be seen that it is the intangible heritage – the

heritage rights play in the formation and development of ideologies of national identity by national governments,[32] as well as contemporary law and public discourse concerning the self-determination of indigenous and other colonized or oppressed minority peoples (see Blake, Chapter 2; Coombe and Turcotte, Chapter 12; Baird, Chapter 13; and Paterson, Chapter 14 on this).

Cultural Heritage and Cultural Property

One last point on this definitional issue. The concept of cultural heritage I have outlined here is consistent with the spirit if not the letter of an increasing number of contemporary legal definitions at work in the world today. However, this has not always been the case. A number of essays in this collection outline the shift that occurred over the course of the second half of the twentieth century in both the law and academic literature surrounding cultural heritage from a narrow and, arguably, ethnocentric *property-based* conception to a broader, more political, and more culturally versatile conception (Blake, Chapter 2, p. 39; Coombe, Chapter 3, p. 73; and Coombe and Turcotte, Chapter 12, p. 277; as well as Loulanski, 2006, p. 211; and Hoffman, 2006, p. 15). At international law, for example, there has been a shift from the use of the term 'cultural property' (used in the 1954 Hague Convention for the Protection of Cultural Property in the Event of Armed Conflict) to the term 'cultural heritage' (used in the 2003 UNESCO Declaration Concerning the Intentional Destruction of Cultural Heritage). This change in terminology has reflected a change in the concept of cultural heritage in a number of respects, rendering it less materially oriented and economically commodifiable and more comprehensive of the wide range of heritage phenomena and the range of relationships – spiritual, political, existential – which can be maintained with heritage. Key here has been the recognition that property is an historically and culturally specific notion, not readily applicable to the heritage concerns and practices of many of the world's peoples – nor, for that matter, to a range of phenomena even Western property-based cultures might wish to include in the category of cultural heritage.[33]

Cultural Heritage Law and Rights

The Anatomy of Cultural Heritage Rights

Those who consider cultural heritage phenomena to be of value to them[34] will generally possess an *interest* in that heritage which reflects a desired state of affairs conducive to the

---

relationship of a people to their cultural heritage – which is really under attack in such conditions' (p. 48).

[32] See especially Weiss (Chapter 7) and Winter (Chapter 18) on this. Coombe (Chapter 3) says, '[a] concern with cultural heritage emerged from modern state anxieties around national social cohesion and identity and the need to inculcate national sentiment and civic responsibility' (p. 62).

[33] Such as natural and certain intangible phenomena.

[34] We can term such parties stakeholders in relation to the heritage in question. Stakeholders are those for whom that heritage is of value – though not necessarily for identity-based reasons. The generic

value the heritage holds for them.[35] So, a local group who values a religious monument because it contributes to their collective identity may have an interest in the preservation of that monument, or in there being ready access to the monument for group members, or in the group being compensated by the state for past damage to the monument. Alternatively, a national government or commercial cartel may value the monument purely for financial reasons, without its very identity being tied up with that heritage in any way.[36] In light of this, it might maintain an interest in controlling access to the monument to the exclusion of others, or in being able to establish a tourism operation in relation to the monument and to profit exclusively from that operation and so on.[37]

Often interests such as these translate into *claims* that those interests be appropriately recognized in law. In such cases, claimants generally believe their claim is justified by virtue of the value the cultural heritage holds for them. A legal system[38] may or may not recognize such a claim and associated interests through the enactment of laws providing for the satisfaction of the claim and the realization of the interests served by the claim.[39] Where laws enable those with an interest in cultural heritage to make legally justified demands on others within the jurisdiction – including the state itself – to recognize and otherwise accommodate that interest then we may conceive of there being a *legal right* to cultural heritage in operation within the jurisdiction. Those with such a legally recognized interest may be conceived of as holders of that cultural heritage right – that is, as cultural heritage rights-holders. The existence of rights to cultural heritage entails that there be correlative legal obligations or duties on others in relation to the interests of the rights-holders and the heritage in question.[40] Rights implicate a set of consequences in the world, generally to the benefit of the rights-holders. Legal rights of this kind make available the resources of the state in the service of the interests of the rights-holders. It is in access to these resources – that is, to state power – that much of the value of these rights lies. It is also in relation to accessing this power that political conflict between claimants, rights-holders, the state and others under legal obligations flowing from cultural heritage rights becomes a real possibility.

---

purpose of cultural heritage rights is the recognition, protection and facilitation of the interests of legally recognized stakeholders in cultural heritage.

[35] I adopt here a simple version of what is termed an interest theory of rights. See Raz (1986), MacCormick (1977) and Kramer (2001) for sophisticated elaborations of this way of thinking about rights.

[36] Of course, on our definition of heritage as identity-linked, some group or other must have their identity tied up with the heritage in order for it to be heritage at all. This is to say that a government or business may have a financial interest in someone else's heritage.

[37] Merryman (Chapter 1) says that the most basic interest rights-holders have in relation to cultural heritage is 'preservation: protecting the object and its context from impairment' (p. 13).

[38] Which is to say, those who make the law and the constituency those law-makers represent.

[39] The legal system may recognize that interest whether or not the legal system (or anyone else for that matter) considers the interest to be a morally legitimate one.

[40] For example, an indigenous group's legal right to non-interference with a significant cultural site entails obligations on others not to interfere with that site, contravention of which may lead to the exercise of state power on those others. Likewise, such a right may entail obligations on the state to ensure no interference takes place – to provide fencing and signage around the site, for example, or to resource the rights-holders in monitoring the site themselves, and so on.

Within this analytic framework there can be (and are) many kinds of cultural heritage rights. These kinds may be classified by a number of criteria – including on the basis of the kind of heritage phenomenon in question (the object of the right), the kind of stakeholder holding the rights (the holder of the right), the particular outcomes aimed at or interest protected by the right (the effects of the right) and the kind of law or legal system within which the right subsists (the form and jurisdiction of the right).[41] First, there can be as many kinds of cultural heritage rights as there are kinds of cultural heritage. Thus, there can be legal rights to the protection of ethnographic artefacts or of historic monuments or of urban landscapes.[42] The essays in this collection cover a number of kinds of heritage phenomena. In Part II of this collection, particular attention is paid to a number of common as well as controversial kinds of cultural heritage – natural heritage, urban landscapes, artefacts, underwater heritage and intangible heritage.

Likewise, there can be as many kinds of cultural heritage rights as there are kinds of stakeholders. There can be a legal right to access an historic monument possessed by a specific local tribe or by any local tribe with longstanding cultural links to the monument. So, too, there may be a legal right to access the same monument possessed by a cartel of local tourism operators or by a single operator,[43] or the right may be possessed solely by the government of the nation state. Cultural heritage law is highly versatile on this score. Any group with a publicly recognized interest in a given instance or kind of cultural heritage may be granted legal rights of some kind to that heritage. In this collection a range of rights holders and the relations between them is discussed, from national governments, to local peoples and communities, to economic developers, to the international community at large.[44] Due the recent prominence of indigenous rights globally and due to the distinctive importance which cultural heritage plays in the political being of indigenous groups, a number of the essays in this collection place particular emphasis on indigenous cultural heritage rights and the issues surrounding these (see Coombe, Chapter 3; Brown, Chapter 10; Coombe and Turcotte, Chapter 12; Baird, Chapter 13; Paterson, Chapter 14; and Kim, Chapter 19).

Further, cultural heritage rights may vary in relation to the kind of interests or claims they recognize and protect and the kinds of obligations they impose – which is to say they may be classified according to the kind of consequences or effects they result in. A local group's right in relation to a monument may be to non-interference with that monument by others (including the state), it may be to access and maintain the monument, it may be to control the economic exploitation of that monument and any tourism benefits relating to that monument, it may be to compensation by the state or others for past damage to that monument and so on. At a wider level, a set of rights may manifest in a complex regulatory regime of management of cultural heritage involving rights-holders, the state and other interested parties such as

---

[41] These criteria may operate at greater or lesser degrees of generality.

[42] Many legal instruments will specifically identify those categories of phenomena which fall into the applicable legal definition of cultural heritage.

[43] Though cultural heritage is always the heritage of some group and not of any single individual, legal rights to some group's cultural heritage may be held by a single individual.

[44] There is an important question here as to the very idea of the international community having a legitimate interest in the cultural heritage of a local people or nation and, as a result, being able to hold rights to that heritage – perhaps even rights that trump those of the local people or nation state. See Merryman (Chapter 1) and Merryman (1986). See also Prott and O'Keefe (1984), Chapter 1.

museums, tourism operators, mining companies and so on (see the essays by Weiss, Chapter 7; Baird, Chapter 13; and Winter, Chapter 18). These are all different kinds of right though they may all be comprehended by a more general right – say, to outright ownership or some analogy.[45]

And, finally, a cultural heritage right can be characterized by the form of law it takes and kind of jurisdiction it subsists within. There can be statutory heritage rights, common law heritage rights and even constitutional heritage rights within a national legal system.[46] Cultural heritage rights may also be found in conventions, declarations, bilateral treaties and other instruments of international and regional law, including important human rights instruments.[47] Private international law also plays a role in relation to some cultural heritage matters (Hoffman, 2006). Finally, cultural heritage rights may be found within the traditional law and custom of subnational peoples[48] or within the growing systems of international, regional and national soft law operative around the world.[49] The essays in this collection involve cultural heritage rights of many legal forms across a range of jurisdictions.

---

[45] A right to own may implicate narrower rights to access, use or control.

[46] Indigenous cultural heritage rights in Australia, for example, are to be found in statutory form within both federal and state jurisdictions, as well as within the Australian common law of native title. See McRae et al., 2003, chs 7 and 8. Dutra (Chapter 8) and Paterson (Chapter 14) discuss the national cultural heritage regimes of China and the United States, respectively.

[47] Key international instruments directly recognizing cultural heritage rights discussed in this collection include the 1954 Hague Convention on the Protection of Cultural Property in the Event of Armed Conflict, the 1970 UNESCO Convention on the Means of Prohibiting and Preventing the Illicit Import Export and Transfer of Ownership of Cultural Property, the 1972 World Heritage Convention, the 2001 UNESCO Convention on the Protection of Underwater Cultural Heritage, the 2003 UNESCO Convention for the Safeguarding of Intangible Cultural Heritage, the 2003 UNESCO Declaration Concerning the Intentional Destruction of Cultural Heritage and the 2005 UNESCO Convention on the Protection and Promotion of Cultural Expressions. In her essay in this collection, Craufurd Smith (Chapter 20) identifies a number of international and regional human rights documents which incidentally establish cultural heritage rights. These include the 1948 Universal Declaration of Human Rights, the 1966 International Covenant on Economic, Social and Cultural Rights, the 1966 International Covenant on Civil and Political Rights and the 1995 Council of Europe Framework Convention on National Minorities. Mention should also be made here of the 2007 United Nations Declaration on the Rights of Indigenous Peoples. In this collection, Abtahi (Chapter 16) and Francioni and Lenzerini (Chapter 17) discuss the international law relating to the protection of cultural heritage under conditions of armed conflict, Dromgoole (Chapter 9) discusses the international law relating to underwater heritage, Ossorio (Chapter 21) discusses elements of international law relating to common heritage rights in the human genome.

[48] The indigenous peoples of Australia for example, maintain within their own traditional law and custom complex sets of norms regulating the engagement of their members and others with sacred sites and objects, as well as other elements of their cultural heritage. See Keen (1994). Of course, whether these traditional indigenous norms are in turn recognized by the non-indigenous Australian legal system through native title or some other statutory regime is another question altogether.

[49] Soft law is a term used to describe norms without any legal force which nonetheless are effective in regulating some or other sphere of activity, largely by voluntary compliance. Soft law may take a variety of forms, including guidelines, recommendations, principles and so on. In the international cultural heritage arena, examples include UNESCO's Operational Guidelines for the Implementation of the World Heritage Convention and its Recommendation on the Historic Urban Landscape (discussed by

The Politics of Cultural Heritage Rights

As has been mentioned, cultural heritage *matters* to some social group or other. Indeed, it might matter a great deal to certain groups because of the role which that heritage plays in maintaining the identity and survival of those groups over time. It might also matter to others outside this primary interest group because of some potential benefit, financial or otherwise, the heritage in question might offer them. Cultural heritage might matter enough for any interested party, primary or otherwise, to seek legal rights to the heritage in question, recognizing and protecting their particular interests in it. Further, it might matter to other agents – individuals, groups, governments – who might be subject to potentially onerous obligations if such claims were ever realized as legal rights. When things like this matter for competing interests in a society, the grounds are laid not merely for agreement and compromise on those things but also for disagreement and conflict. Such has been and continues to be the case with cultural heritage around the world. And such is the stuff of politics.

Like many areas of human rights law, cultural heritage rights law is deeply political in this sense.[50] It is a political matter as to what is (and what is not) cultural heritage within a jurisdiction. It is a political matter as to who within the jurisdiction should possess such rights. It is a political matter as to the content and form any such rights should take. Cultural heritage rights – actual or potential – together with their correlative legal obligations, generating costs and benefits to different parties within a legal jurisdiction, will often engender the conditions for disagreement of various kinds to emerge between those parties. The potential for political discussion, struggle and conflict lies within every situation of a claim or right to cultural heritage.[51] Such conflict may be quite intense given the high value certain groups may attach to cultural heritage – particularly where their very identity is at stake.

Disagreement may arise at a preliminary level in relation to whether or not a given phenomenon is or is not cultural heritage (and, therefore, even be eligible for recognition and protection by way of a rights regime). This, in turn, may be the result of disagreement about the content of the operative concept (or legal definition) of cultural heritage that is to be applied to the situation (for example, to what extent, if any, must the phenomenon in question contribute to the very identity of a group in question in order to be cultural heritage?). Alternatively, it may be about whether the phenomenon in question actually meets the criteria inherent in an agreed concept of cultural heritage (does this item actually

---

Weiss in her essay (Chapter 7)). In her essay, Weiss also points out that the International Law Association (ILA) has been working to prepare a set of Principles for Cooperation in the Mutual Protection and Transfer of Cultural Material which are aimed at providing a degree of regulation of certain spheres of the global cultural heritage marketplace.

[50] 'Heritage, the retrospective expression of culture, is ... a highly politicized commodity' (Brown, Chapter 10, p. 238). Coombe also makes this point in her essay (Chapter 3), '[t]he subject of cultural heritage, scholars now widely recognize, is not a group of tangible things from the past – sites, places, and objects – with inherent historical values that can be properly owned, controlled, and managed. Rather, it is a set of values and meanings that are contested and negotiated in a wider field of social practices' (p. 64).

[51] '[C]ompeting claims and conflicts of interest on national and international level are endemic to any discussion of cultural heritage' (Blake, Chapter 2, p. 40).

have the requisite collective value to constitute an item of heritage?) (Blake, Chapter 2, p. 40). A number of essays in this collection are concerned with this kind of conceptual and classificatory disagreement and conflict – particularly those by Merryman (Chapter 1), Blake (Chapter 2), Coombe (Chapter 3) and Bell (Chapter 4).

One particular issue in this context, mentioned by a number of essays in this collection, concerns how the law, in its design of a legal definition of what heritage is or in its evaluation of whether a given phenomenon falls under that definition, may come to be informed by dominant authoritative discourses about these things in the wider society. According to some of the contributors to this collection, public discourse about the nature of cultural heritage may be appropriated by governments or other powerful sectors of a society to the detriment of less powerful, often local or indigenous, groups. Various kinds of expert agent – archaeologists, anthropologists, museum conservators, art experts and so on – may become powerful players in the struggle over what cultural heritage is, articulating and authorizing the claims of one or other set of interested parties (commonly the nation state which is often the only interested party with the resources to engage such experts).[52] This is to say that the relative political power of a given party within a heritage dispute may determine whether, to what extent and how the values and interests of that party are recognized. Coombe and Turcotte (Chapter 12) maintain that as far as the international law of cultural heritage is concerned, '[m]inority groups and indigenous peoples with little formal authority in an international system dominated by nation states as the sole sources of legitimate political authority have limited capacities to define the scope of their relevant heritage or to object to heritage claims made by others' (p. 278).[53] Additionally, developing nation states may face similar challenges in the international arena in dealing with developed nations.[54]

Even if there is agreement on what cultural heritage is and whether a given phenomenon falls under the category of cultural heritage, there may be disagreement as to whether any legal rights in relation to that phenomenon or to cultural heritage generally should be granted within the legal system, and if so, who should possess those rights and, correlatively, who should be subject to any attendant obligations. There may be disagreement as to what the actual nature and extent of those rights and attendant obligations should be. A related issue here is how *prima facie* legitimate competing interests in or rights to cultural heritage should be balanced or reconciled. How, for example, should we balance the economic use of a heritage site by a local indigenous group with the preservation of that site for the benefit of the wider society or world community? A number of essays in this collection address this question – notably Bell (Chapter 4), Baird (Chapter 13) and Winter (Chapter 18).[55] Further,

---

[52] See Coombe (Chapter 3) and Winter (Chapter 18). Bell (Chapter 4) quotes Meskell saying, 'the "creation of heritage is a culturally generative act that is intrinsically political. Heritage consultants and archaeologists could be said to invent culture, and, in the process, constitute heritage"' (p. 83).

[53] Bell (Chapter 4) says, 'a dominant interpretation of a heritage site can simply overwhelm other interpretations and discourses integral to its layered significance but not "authorized" as valid or valuable. The result is a disempowerment and disenfranchisement of the other "subaltern" ... viewpoints or associations' (p. 82).

[54] Blake (Chapter 2) makes this point.

[55] Bell's essay (Chapter 4) is particularly illuminating on this question. But see also the essays by Dailoo and Pannekoek (Chapter 5), Oviedo and Puschkarsky (Chapter 6), Weiss (Chapter 7) and Winter (Chapter 18).

disagreement might also surround the question of the legal form any such rights should take – whether customary, statutory or constitutional within a national legal system, or part of some regional or international legal instrument, or as merely soft law. A number of essays in this collection are concerned with this kind of operational disagreement and conflict.[56]

Ultimately, of course, those with power over the law surrounding cultural heritage in the jurisdiction in question will decide any such disputes. Law is not merely political but authoritatively so, in this sense. As such, the law formalizes, operationalizes and stabilizes – provisionally, at least – the dynamic raw politics of cultural heritage at both the conceptual and practical levels. Notwithstanding a better moral claim, identity-based stakeholders may in fact be (and often are) trumped in law by financially motivated governments and corporations. Of course, though we should recognize the role that brute political power plays in the creation and design of cultural heritage rights regimes around the world, we should not overstate the extent to which the powerful inevitably prevail. Though governments and economic agents often get a legal regime that serves their interests, there are many examples worldwide of marginalized and less powerful groups having their own interests recognized in law despite it not serving the interest of their opponents. The politicization of cultural heritage need not always work to the detriment of marginalized groups. Schmitt's essay (Chapter 11) nicely illustrates how local politics can collaborate with global politics in gaining legal recognition for local interests – even in the grand realm of international law.[57]

One important mode of the politics of cultural heritage rights discussed by a number of essays in this collection is the economic mode. It is obvious that cultural heritage may be of economic value in a variety of ways. Artefacts and antiquities may be sold on the international market for these things (see the essays by Merryman, Chapter 1; Dutra, Chapter 8; and Gerstenblith, Chapter 15); sites and landscapes may attract a lucrative tourism industry;[58] the traditional botanical knowledge of indigenous peoples may open new and lucrative lines of inquiry for pharmaceutical companies (see the essays by Brown, Chapter 10 and Coombe and Turcotte, Chapter 12); the very maintenance and management of cultural heritage objects and sites may attract government funding and support a local economy (see the essays by Weiss, Chapter 7; Coombe and Turcotte, Chapter 12; Baird, Chapter 13; and Winter, Chapter 18). Economic stakeholders may include local people whose identity is tied up in the heritage and who see it as a source of sustainable development; governments who see a lucrative tourism trade linked to heritage;[59] independent developers and business people who see a range of economic opportunities associated with heritage – whether a specific instance or generally;

---

[56] Those by Dutra (Chapter 8), Brown (Chapter 10), Paterson (Chapter 14) and Gerstenblith (Chapter 15).

[57] Niezen (2003) and Morgan (2011) tell a similar story in relation to indigenous rights.

[58] See the essays in this collection by Weiss (Chapter 7), Schmitt (Chapter 11), Baird (Chapter 13) and Winter (Chapter 18). Bell (Chapter 4) describes heritage tourism as 'an inherently political power struggle that results in the domination of tourists over the indigenous population, and examples abound of the negative impact of tourism on the lives of residents. This domination further accords tourists a simplified or "flattened" history that supersedes all others for the sake of presentation. The interpreted heritage site tends to tell the story of the local elite, often overlooking the underclasses intimately involved in the processes of creation, rediscovery, or present-day activity' (p. 83).

[59] See Dutra (Chapter 8) on China's interest in this.

and NGOs and international organizations (UNESCO) charged with cultivating sustainable development as part of their human rights or justice agenda.[60]

We have already seen that one kind of struggle that can take place within the context of cultural heritage rights is that between those who hold an identity-based set of interests in an item of heritage and those who hold a purely financial interest. A number of essays in this collection provide case studies involving such conflicts – particularly in the contexts of the licit and illicit trade in heritage phenomena and of heritage tourism.[61] However, other kinds of economic struggle may occur in relation to cultural heritage rights. For example, we have already noted how such rights comprise an important part of the global human rights agenda in international law, as well as in regional, and (increasingly) national legal systems. As such, cultural heritage rights may serve the growing movement towards the self-determination of colonized and otherwise disempowered peoples worldwide. They have become legal vehicles through which political claims are pursued. But, of course, self-determination is not solely a matter of political institutions. Importantly, it includes an economic dimension. It is synonymous with the economic security of the group in question and, where such security does not presently exist, with the economic development of that group.[62]

This is to say that the self-determination dimension of cultural heritage rights is linked to the economic development of those cultural heritage claimants and rights-holders whose very identity is tied up with the heritage in question.[63] To the extent that the self-determination of a claimant group is opposed by some agent – a national government, for example – then we may find a concomitant resistance by that agent to the provision of cultural heritage rights which provide economic benefits to a claimant group.[64] Likewise, where an agent – say a commercial corporation – is opposed to economic benefits flowing

---

[60] Coombe (Chapter 3), Weiss (Chapter 7) and Winter (Chapter 18) discuss this.

[61] See Merryman (Chapter 1), Dutra (Chapter 8) and Gerstenblith (Chapter 15) on illicit trade in heritage. See Bell (Chapter 4) and Winter (Chapter 18) on heritage tourism.

[62] A number of key international human rights instruments recognize the economic dimensions of self-determination, including the International Covenant on Civil and Political Rights and the International Convention on Economic, Social and Cultural Rights. Article 1 of both of these instruments states, '(1) All peoples have the right of self-determination. By virtue of that right they freely determine their political status and freely pursue their economic, social and cultural development. (2) All peoples may, for their own ends, freely dispose of their natural wealth and resources without prejudice to any obligations arising out of international economic co-operation, based upon the principle of mutual benefit, and international law. In no case may a people be deprived of its own means of subsistence.'

[63] See Coombe (Chapter 3), Oviedo and Puschkarsky (Chapter 6) and Coombe and Turcotte (Chapter 12). Coombe (Chapter 3) says, '[n]ew forms of cultural or ethnodevelopment, for instance, which may include ecotourism and the cultivation of culturally distinctive export goods, have been implemented as a means for realizing rural economic revitalization, social cohesion, human security, and political autonomy ... This is a distinctive area of neoliberal governmentality, involving both multilateral institutions and NGOs that seek to empower local communities, recognize traditions as sources of social capital ... and otherwise encourage people to adopt a possessive and entrepreneurial attitude toward their culture and the social relations of reproduction that have traditionally sustained them' (p. 61).

[64] Oviedo and Puschkarsky (Chapter 6) discuss such a situation in their essay.

to a claimant group (wanting them to flow to it instead, in a zero sum calculation), we may find a resultant obstruction of political autonomy for that group (see Weiss's essay (Chapter 7)). More positively, though, a number of essays in this collection provide case studies of situations where local peoples, commercial corporations and national governments have been able to craft a cooperative regime of cultural heritage rights which result in beneficial outcomes for all – both political and economic.[65] In such cases the political and economic benefits to the parties – especially local peoples – may be closely intertwined. Cultural heritage rights, then, may not merely address a deficit in the political power of certain sectors of a society but may also address poverty and facilitate sustainable development in those sectors.[66]

What is apparent when one reads through the analyses of the politics of cultural heritage rights offered by the various commentators in this collection is the *ambivalence* of cultural heritage rights regimes around the world in relation to the various kinds of stakeholders who maintain an interest in cultural heritage. No one category of stakeholder consistently wins or loses within such regimes. Coombe nicely captures this ambivalence in her essay (Chapter 3). Commenting on the relationship that may obtain between the political and economic dimensions of cultural heritage rights, she says,

> [local] stakeholders see cultural expressions, cultural distinctions, and cultural diversity as sources of meaning and value that promote social cohesion, prevent rural-to-urban migration, offer new livelihood opportunities, and, of course, have the potential to provide new sources of income ... If culture is increasingly seen as a new basis for capital accumulation, however, it may also be deployed in strategic interventions in the accumulation of mutual respect, recognition, and dignity. (p. 68)

She goes on,

> One might well argue that the enormous intensity of interest in traditional knowledge and its preservation in international policymaking circles has more to do with identifying and tapping into reservoirs of insight, technique, and systemic knowledge that hold promise for future developments in science and technology than it does with the maintenance of local people's livelihoods, the alleviation of their poverty, or the promotion of their political autonomy. Nonetheless, to the extent that the discourse provides grounds for recognition and valorization of cultural differences, it also thereby provides a means of making linkages to other human rights associated with cultural distinction and thus a covert ground for pressing more political claims. (pp. 69–70)

The English legal positivist philosopher, H.L.A. Hart, maintained that it was in the very nature of law to have such moral and political ambivalence (1961, p. 114). 'It is in no

---

[65] See Baird (Chapter 13) and Winter (Chapter 18). We should take note, though, of Coombe's warning that mixed motives may apply in such cases. In her essay (Chapter 3) she says, '[t]he growing interest in protecting traditional cultural expression, however, is at least as indicative of state interests in locating and cultivating new investments, cultural export products, and tourism opportunities as it is evidence of concern with the livelihoods and well-being of those indigenous peoples and minority communities most likely to harbor distinctive cultural resources' (p. 71).

[66] Hodder (Chapter 22) looks to construe such a feature of the law of cultural heritage in terms of a justice model, along the lines of Nussbaum and Sen.

sense a necessary truth that laws reproduce or satisfy certain demands of morality', he said (1961, p. 181). Law may be used for good or for ill – or, perhaps, for both simultaneously. No necessity one way or the other applies. As a component of law, the same may be said for cultural heritage rights. There is a (perhaps, surprising) contingency at work in them, which may partly explain their increasing prominence globally. It might be that people of all kinds around the world perceive in the discourse and practice of cultural heritage rights an opportunity to achieve things they might not otherwise be able to achieve.

Bibliography and Further Reading

Anaya, J. (2004), *Indigenous Peoples in International Law* (2nd edn), Oxford: Oxford University Press.
Anderson, J.E. (2009), *Law, Knowledge, Culture: The Protection of Indigenous Knowledge in Intellectual Property Law*, Cheltenham: Edward Elgar.
Bhabha, H. (1994), *The Location of Culture*, New York: Routledge.
Bell, C. and Napoleon, V. (eds) (2008), *First Nations Cultural Heritage and Law: Case Studies, Voices, and Perspectives*, Vancouver: UBC Press.
Bell, C and Paterson, R.K. (eds) (2009), *Protection of First Nations Cultural Heritage*, Vancouver: UBC Press.
Borelli, S. and Lenzerini, F. (eds) (2012), *Cultural Heritage, Cultural Rights, Cultural Diversity: New Developments in International Law*, Leiden: Brill Nijhoff.
Brown, M. (2003), *Who Owns Native Culture?*, Cambridge, MA: Harvard University Press.
Clifford, J. (1988), *The Predicament of Culture: Twentieth-Century Ethnography, Literature, and Art*, Cambridge, MA: Harvard University Press.
Connolly, A.J. (ed.) (2009), *Indigenous Rights*, Farnham: Ashgate.
Connolly, A.J. (2010), *Cultural Difference on Trial: The Nature and Limits of Judicial Understanding*, Farnham: Ashgate.
Coombe, R.J. (1998), *The Cultural Life of Intellectual Properties: Authorship, Appropriation, and the Law*, Durham, NC: Duke University Press.
Crawford, J. (ed.) (1988), *The Rights of Peoples*, Oxford: Clarendon Press.
D'Andrade, R. (1995), *The Development of Cognitive Anthropology*, Cambridge: Cambridge University Press.
Donnelly, J. (2003), *Universal Human Rights in Theory and Practice*, Ithaca, NY: Cornell University Press.
Dromgoole, S. (2013), *Underwater Cultural Heritage and International Law*, Cambridge: Cambridge University Press.
Forrest, C. (2010), *International Law and the Protection of Cultural Heritage*, Abingdon: Routledge.
Geertz, C. (1973), *The Interpretation of Cultures*, New York: Basic Books.
Geertz, C. (1983), *Local Knowledge: Further Essays in Interpretive Anthropology*, New York: Basic Books.
Graber, C.B., Kuprecht, K. and Lai, J.C. (eds) (2012), *International Trade in Indigenous Cultural Heritage: Legal and Policy Issues*, Cheltenham: Edward Elgar.
Halpin, A. (1997), *Rights and Law – Analysis and Theory*, Oxford: Hart Publishing.
Handler, R. (2003), 'Cultural Property and Cultural Theory', *Journal of Social Archaeology*, **3**, pp. 353–65.
Harding, S. (2003), 'Defining Traditional Knowledge – Lessons from Cultural Property', *Cardozo Journal of International and Comparative Law*, **11**, pp. 511–18.
Hart, H.L.A. (1961), *The Concept of Law* (1st edn), Oxford: Clarendon Press.

Hoffman, B.T. (2006), *Art and Cultural Heritage: Law, Policy, and Practice*, Cambridge: Cambridge University Press.

Joyner, C. (1986), 'Legal Implications of the Concept of the Common Heritage of Mankind', *International and Comparative Law Quarterly*, **35**, pp. 190–99.

Keen, I. (1994), *Knowledge and Secrecy in an Aboriginal Religion: Yolngu of North-East Arnhem Land*, Melbourne: Oxford University Press.

Kramer, M. (2001), 'Getting Rights Right', in M. Kramer (ed.), *Rights, Wrongs, and Responsibilities*, London: Macmillan, pp. 28–95.

Kroeber, A.L. and Kluckhohn, C. (1952), *Culture: A Crucial Review of Concepts and Definitions*, New York: Vintage Books.

Kukathas, C. (1992), 'Are There Any Cultural Rights?', *Political Theory*, **20**, pp. 105–39.

Kymlicka, W. (ed.) (1995a), *The Rights of Minority Cultures*, Oxford: Oxford University Press.

Kymlicka, W. (1995b), *Multicultural Citizenship: A Liberal Theory of Minority Rights*, Oxford: Oxford University Press.

Langfield, M., Logan, W. and Nic Craith, M. (eds) (2010), *Cultural Diversity, Heritage and Human Rights: Intersections in Theory and Practice*, Abingdon: Routledge.

Lenzerini, F. (ed.) (2008), *Reparations for Indigenous Peoples: International and Comparative Perspectives*, Oxford: Oxford University Press.

Loulanski, T. (2006), 'Revising the Concept for Cultural Heritage: An Argument for a Functional Approach', *International Journal of Cultural Property*, **13**, pp. 207–33.

Lowenthal, D. (1998), *The Heritage Crusade and the Spoils of History*, Cambridge: Cambridge University Press.

Lowenthal, D. (2005), 'Natural and Cultural Heritage', *International Journal of Heritage Studies*, **11**, pp. 81–92.

MacCormick, D.N. (1977), 'Rights in Legislation', in P. Hacker and J. Raz (eds), *Law, Morality and Society: Essays in Honour of H.L.A Hart*, Oxford: Oxford University Press, 1977, pp. 189–209.

Malloy, T.H. (2005), *National Minority Rights in Europe*, Oxford and New York: Oxford University Press.

McRae, H., Nettheim, G., Beacroft, L. and McNamara, L. (2003), *Indigenous Legal Issues: Commentary and Materials*, Sydney: Lawbook Company.

McGrane, B. (1989), *Beyond Anthropology: Society and the Other*, New York: Columbia University Press.

Merryman, J.H. (1986), 'Two Ways of Thinking about Cultural Property', *American Journal of International Law*, **80**, pp. 831–53.

Meskell, L. (2002), 'The Intersection of Identity and Politics in Archaeology', *Annual Review of Anthropology*, **31**, pp. 279–301.

Meskell, L. (2012), *The Nature of Heritage: The New South Africa*, Oxford: Blackwell.

Morgan, R. (2011), *Transforming Law and Institution: Indigenous Peoples, the United Nations and Human Rights*, Farnham: Ashgate Publishing.

Nafziger, J.A.R., Paterson, R.K. and Renteln, A.D. (eds) (2010), *Cultural Law: International, Comparative, and Indigenous*, New York: Cambridge University Press.

Niezen, R. (2003), *The Origins of Indigenism*, Berkeley, CA: University of California Press.

Niezen, R. (2009), *The Rediscovered Self: Indigenous Identity and Cultural Justice*, Montreal: McGill-Queens University Press.

Prott, L.V. and O'Keefe, P.J. (1992), '"Cultural Heritage" or "Cultural Property"?', *International Journal of Cultural Property*, **1**, pp. 307–20.

Prott, L.V. and O'Keefe, P.J. (1984), *Law and the Cultural Heritage: Volume 1, Discovery and Excavation*, Abingdon: Professional Books.

Raz, J. (1986), *The Morality of Freedom*, Oxford: Oxford University Press.

Schmidt, P.R. and McIntosh, R.J. (eds) (1996), *Plundering Africa's Past*, Bloomington, IN: Indiana University Press.
Sen, A. (2009), *The Idea of Justice*, Cambridge, MA: Belknap Press.
Silverman, H. and Ruggles, D.F. (eds) (2007), *Cultural Heritage and Human Rights*, New York: Springer.
Smith, L. (2004), *Archaeological Theory and the Politics of Cultural Heritage*, London: Routledge.
Smith, L. (2006), *Uses of Heritage*, New York: Routledge.
Smith, L. and Akagawa, N. (eds) (2009), *Intangible Cultural Heritage*, London: Routledge.
Sperber, D. (1996), *Explaining Culture: A Naturalistic Approach*, Oxford: Blackwell Publishers.
Thornberry, P. (1991), *International Law and the Rights of Minorities*, Oxford: Clarendon Press.
Toman, J. (1996), *The Protection of Cultural Property in the Event of Armed Conflict*, Aldershot: Dartmouth Publishing; Paris: UNESCO.
Tsosie, R. (2002), 'Reclaiming Native Stories: An Essay on Cultural Appropriation and Cultural Rights', *Arizona State Law Journal*, **34**, pp. 299–358.
Wagner, R. (1975), *The Invention of Culture*, Englewood Cliffs, NJ: Prentice Hall.
Weatherall, K. (2001), 'Culture, Autonomy and *Djulibinyamurr*: Individual and Community in the Construction of Rights to Traditional Designs', *Modern Law Review*, **64**, pp. 215–42.
Winter, T. (2007), *Post-Conflict Heritage, Postcolonial Tourism: Culture, Politics and Development at Angkor*, London: Routledge.
Xanthaki, A. (2007), *Indigenous Rights and United Nations Standards: Self-Determination, Culture and Land*, Cambridge: Cambridge University Press.
Young, I.M. (1990), *Justice and the Politics of Difference*, Princeton, NJ: Princeton University Press.
Young, J.O. (2000), 'The Ethics of Cultural Appropriation', *Dalhousie Review*, **80**, pp. 301–16.

Part I
Foundations

[1]

Cultural Property Internationalism

John Henry Merryman*

Abstract: Cultural property internationalism is shorthand for the proposition that everyone has an interest in the preservation and enjoyment of cultural property, wherever it is situated, from whatever cultural or geographic source it derives. This article describes its historical development and its expression in the international law of war, in the work of UNESCO, and in the international trade in cultural objects and assesses the ways in which cultural-property world actors support or resist the implications of cultural property internationalism.

"Cultural property internationalism" is shorthand for the proposition that everyone has an interest in the preservation and enjoyment of cultural property,[1] wherever it is situated, from whatever cultural or geographic source it derives. In the frequently quoted words of the 1954 Hague Convention, cultural property is "the cultural heritage of all mankind."[2] In an earlier article[3] I briefly described and contrasted "cultural internationalism" and "cultural nationalism," as they concern cultural property. Here I return to cultural property internationalism, describing its historical development and its expression in the international law of war, in the work of UNESCO, and in the international trade in cultural objects.

What is "cultural property?" It sometimes seems that any human artifact (matchbook covers? baseball cards? fruit box labels? perfume bottles?) can qualify.[4] Most people, however, will discriminate, reserving the "cultural property" title for a more limited range of objects that are distinguishable from the ordinary run of artifacts by their special cultural significance and/or rarity. Any attempt at a definition will reveal that the cultural property category is heterogeneous. The problems created by including Matisse paintings, archaic Chinese bronzes, and African masks in the same "cultural property" category are not pursued here, although such disparities clearly must, at some level, eventually require distinctive treatment. As cultural property law and

---

*Stanford Law School. Email: Merry@law.stanford.edu

ACKNOWLEDGMENTS. My thanks to Robert Hallman, Jody Maxmin, Nora Niedzelski-Eichner and Stephen Urice for their thoughtful criticisms and suggestions.

policy are currently structured, however, that process has barely begun. The UNESCO instruments described later in this article, for example, typically define "cultural property" to include anything and everything and treat the category as a collective unit. Much source nation legislation is similarly structured. Most recently, a practical distinction between antiquities and other cultural objects seems to have emerged.[5]

The cultural property category is also amorphous and boundless. Thus the 1995 *UNIDROIT Convention on Stolen or Illegally Exported Cultural Objects*[6] applies to objects "which, on religious or secular grounds, are of importance for archaeology, prehistory, history, literature, art or science [what else is there?] and belong to one of the categories listed in the Annex to this Convention."[7]

Empirically, cultural property centrally includes the sorts of things that dealers deal in, collectors collect, and museums acquire and display: principally works of art, antiquities, and ethnographic objects. These are the foci of a social subsystem we can call "the cultural property world," which is populated by artists, collectors, dealers and auction houses, museums and their professionals, art historians, archaeologists and ethnographers, and source nation cultural officials, among others. These people and institutions form a kind of ecology; whatever significantly affects one actor affects the others.

The cultural property world is international. Ethnographic museums in London and Berlin maintain extensive collections of African, Oceanic, and American objects. The Metropolitan Museum mounts a Vermeer exhibition from a variety of foreign and domestic lenders and its own collections. Japanese dealers attend New York and London auctions to bid on works by French impressionists and German expressionists. Swiss dealers offer Greek and Roman antiquities in widely distributed illustrated catalogs. American collectors build important art and antiquity collections of works from Europe, Africa, East and South Asia, the Middle East, and Latin America. The works of American artists are acquired by Dutch museums and German collectors. In this empirical sense, cultural property internationalism is not an argument or a hypothesis; it is an observable fact.[8]

No thinking person argues for free trade in cultural property. Regulation is necessary in order to preserve cultural property and to support its proper international circulation. Appropriate regulation serves the international interest of "all mankind" in the preservation and enjoyment of its "cultural heritage." Excessive regulation, however, thwarts that same international interest. Regrettably but predictably, the various cultural-property world actors do not always agree on whether a restriction is or is not "excessive." The international cultural property world is divided along this and other dimensions. I address these divisions, with particular emphasis on their implications for cultural internationalism, at a number of points in this article.

In my view, source nation regulations preserve the cultural heritage when and to the extent that they protect fragile objects that are likely to be damaged or destroyed by movement and when they prevent the dismemberment of complex objects, like the panels of an altarpiece or the components of a sculptural group. When antiquities are removed from their contexts in order to preserve, study, and enjoy them, archaeologists rightly urge and source nations rightly require that the removal be done with care and that it be accompanied by full documentation. It seems right that objects of ritual/religious importance to living cultures remain with or be returned to the representatives of those cultures, as were the Afo-a-Kom[9] and, under NAGPRA,[10] American Indian artifacts. And finally, it is internationally important that the inhabitants of every nation, including the poorest survivors of colonial exploitation, have access to a fully representative collection of objects that represent their history and culture.

We begin with the history of the idea that cultural property should be protected from destruction and plunder in war.

CULTURAL PROPERTY AND WAR

Classical international law placed few restraints on the destruction or plunder of enemy property, cultural or other. Our history of the topic begins with Polybius of Athens, writing before 146 B.C.:

> One may perhaps have some reason for amassing gold and silver; in fact, it would be impossible to attain universal dominion without appropriating these resources from other peoples, in order to weaken them. In the case of every other form of wealth, however, it is more glorious to leave it where it was, together with the envy it inspired, and to base our nation's glory, not on the abundance and beauty of its paintings and statues, but on its sober customs and noble sentiments. Moreover, I hope that future conquerors will learn from these thoughts not to plunder the cities subjugated by them, and not to make the misfortunes of other peoples the adornments of their own country.[11]

As a historian, Polybius is here making an argument ("it is more glorious") and expressing a wish ("I hope that") and does not suggest that his proposition is in any sense law. His wish was not soon fulfilled. In the reigning pattern of conquest established by the Romans, victors appropriated works of art and other cultural treasures from conquered peoples as trophies of war, to be displayed in triumphal marches and installed in the Roman Forum. The Forum became the world's first great outdoor museum, adorned with works whose presence affirmed Roman military power and illustrated its conquests. The Roman style was revived by the Venetians and other Italian powers during the Crusades and the Renaissance.

The legal status of cultural property in war began to change in the seventeenth century with Grotius, who summarized the weight of received legal opinion and international practice from antiquity up to his time in this way:

> That it is not contrary to nature to despoil him whom it is honorable to kill, was said by Cicero. Therefore it is not strange that the law of nations has permitted the destruction and plunder of the property of enemies, the slaughter of whom it has permitted.[12]

While accepting that this harsh rule was law, Grotius argued for its moderation. In a particularly pertinent passage, he proposed that sacred or artistic works should not be destroyed where there is no military advantage in doing so, citing Polybius, Marcellus and Cicero:

> Polybius says it is a sign of an infuriated mind to destroy those things which, if destroyed, do not weaken the enemy nor bring gain to the one who destroys them: such things are temples, colonnades, statues and the like. Marcellus, whom Cicero praises, spared all the buildings of Syracuse, public and private, sacred and profane, just as if he had come with his army to defend them, not to capture them.[13]

Grotius, a natural lawyer, is here employing general philosophical principles of moderation and proportion: destruction that neither weakens the enemy nor helps the destroyer is immoderate and disproportionate. Grotius appears to deplore the violation of these principles, rather than the resulting loss of cultural property.

Two centuries later Vattel provided a more robust argument for the protection of works of art and architecture in time of war:

> For whatever cause a country is ravaged, we ought to spare those edifices which do honor to human society, and do not contribute to the enemy's strength—such as temples, tombs, public buildings, and all works of remarkable beauty. What advantage is obtained by destroying them? It is declaring one's self an enemy to mankind, thus wantonly to deprive them of these monuments of art and models of taste; and in that light Belisarius represented the matter to Tittila, King of the Goths. We still detest those barbarians who destroyed so many wonders of art, when they overran the Roman Empire.[14]

Here we see what may have been the earliest expression of true cultural property internationalism: Vattel argues that cultural property should be spared in the interests of "mankind" and "human society," and he broadens the basis for protection to include aesthetics ("works of remarkable beauty"). Like Grotius, Vattel recognizes the primacy of military necessity but he also draws a distinction between necessity and mere convenience:

> Nobody presumes to blame a general who lays waste gardens, vineyards, or orchards, for the purpose of encamping on the ground, and throwing up an entrenchment. If any beautiful production of art be thereby destroyed, it is an accident, an unhappy consequence of the war; and the general will not be blamed, except in those cases when he might have pitched his camp elsewhere without the smallest inconvenience to himself.[15]

We will return to military necessity below.

A major development in the history of cultural property internationalism took form as a reaction against Napoléon's appropriation of works of art for the Musée Français (later to become the Louvre) during his first Italian Campaign in 1796–99. The planning for this extended plundering enterprise began in Paris, where "as early as October 16, 1794, the Commission temporaire des arts had appointed a subcommittee of four members to compile full information concerning works of art and science to be found in countries which the republican armies were expected to invade."[16] Accompanied by commissioners armed with these lists, Napoléon exacted huge concessions of works of art from the Italians, formalizing some of them as "reparations" in the terms of armistice treaties imposed on the losers. Thus the Duke of Modena surrendered forty-nine pictures; Parma another forty-seven; Milan twenty-five; Venice its famous bronze horses, the lion from St. Mark's, sixteen pictures and other treasures; and so it went. The list is long, and at one time Napoléon boasted that "We have stripped Italy of everything of artistic worth, with the exception of a few objects in Turin and Naples!"[17]

The French plunder of Italian art excited strong feelings. Poets declaimed and intellectuals argued. Some emphasized the benefit to a larger public of mounting and publicly displaying so great a concentration of important works of art that had formerly been widely dispersed, often among private holders, and visible only to the few. The French defended their behavior on a variety of grounds: compensation for the blood and toil of French soldiers; the cultural superiority of France, which made it only right that great art be brought and kept there; if France did not "give a home" to Italian cultural treasures they would be acquired by England or the Tsar through purchase; they had been ceded to France in treaties and they were now legally French; and so on. Others referred to the French actions as those of "a band of practiced robbers" and "hordes of thieves."[18]

Among the French intellectuals who opposed the plunder of Italy's art was Quatremère de Quincy, whose published protest in the form of letters addressed to one of Napoléon's generals, *Letters to Miranda*, contained the following passages (my translation):

> [I]n Europe the arts and sciences form a republic whose members, joined by the love of and quest for truth and beauty, tend less to isolate themselves in their respective nations than to pursue their interests from the point of view of a universal fraternity. . . . [T]he arts and sciences belong to all of Europe and are no longer the exclusive property of any nation. . . . [I]t is as a member of that general republic of arts and sciences, and not as an inhabitant of this or that nation, that I will discuss the interest that all parties have in the conservation of all. What is that interest? It is that of civilization, of perfection of the means of welfare and pleasure, of the advancement and progress of education and thought, of amelioration of the human condition. Everything that could contribute to this end belongs to all peoples; no one has the right to dispose arbitrarily of it.[19]

The cited volume also sets out two contemporary petitions addressed to the Directoire.[20] One, dated 16 August 1796, "supporting the theses of Quatremère de Quincy" and signed by fifty artists, requested that before removing works of art from Rome a commission composed of artists and men of letters be appointed by the National Institute to prepare a report on the topic. The other, dated 30 October of the same year and signed by thirty-nine artists "to support the seizure of works of art in Italy," spoke aggressively throughout of "the honor, the glory of the French name."

There is no evidence that Quatremère de Quincy's plea had any restraining effect on the French forces in Italy, but it may have influenced the decision of an English judge in an 1813 prize case, *The Marquis de Somerueles*.[21] The case is unusually interesting for two main reasons: it appears to be the earliest reported judicial decision to treat works of art as cultural property excepted from ordinary rules of the law of war, and the opinion provides a rare and eloquent judicial statement of cultural property internationalism.

The case arose during the War of 1812 between the United States and England. An American merchant vessel carrying a shipment of paintings and prints bound from Italy to the Pennsylvania Academy of the Fine Arts in Philadelphia was seized by a British ship and taken to the British Court of Vice-Admiralty in Halifax, Nova Scotia, for judgment as prize. A petition from the Academy, pleading that "even war does not leave science and art unprotected," asked that the paintings and prints be released, and the judge, Dr. Croke,[22] so ordered, stating that:

> The same law of nations, which prescribes that all property belonging to the enemy shall be liable to confiscation, has likewise its modifications and relaxations of that rule. The arts and sciences are admitted amongst all civilized nations, as forming an exception to the severe rights of warfare, and as entitled to favour and protection. They are considered not as the peculium of this or that nation, but as the property of mankind at large, and as belonging to the common interests of the whole species.

The similarities to Quatremère de Quincy's language are striking. His book would likely have been known to a cosmopolitan English civilian, and Dr. Croke would have found the book's argument to be congenial, if only because, in opposing Napoléon's actions, it supported the British side in the conflict with France. It seems probable that Quatremère de Quincy is Dr. Croke's immediate source for his statement of the law of nations.

There is, however, a more fundamental source for that statement in the humane component of later Enlightenment and natural law thought about the law of war,[23] of which Vattel and Quatremère de Quincy provide examples. The ideal of restraints on belligerent behavior in order to protect art and science for humanity was in the air breathed by cosmopolitan Europeans in the latter half of the eighteenth century. Dr. Croke's opinion contains substantial internal evidence of this kind of thinking,[24] to which he was attuned by his civilian education and outlook.[25] Passages in his opinion clearly reflect the conflict between the humane internationalist ideal to which he appealed and the nationalist glorification of military campaigns that the French under Bonaparte (that "foreign despot") had embraced. The conflict persists today in the international law of cultural property.[26]

American writers in the first half of the nineteenth century took a narrower and less internationalist view than the Europeans. Thus Wheaton, writing in 1836, neither refers to nor displays awareness of the *Letters to Miranda* or Dr. Croke's opinion in *The Marquis de Somerueles*. His discussion of the law concerning enemy cultural property is briefer and less nuanced than Vattel's:

> By the ancient law of nations, even what were called *res sacrae* were not exempt from capture and confiscation.... But by the modern usage of nations, which has now acquired the force of law, temples of religion, public edifices devoted to civil purposes only, monuments of art, and repositories of science, are exempted from the general operations of war.[27]

Wheaton's basis for this relaxation of the ancient rule was, like that of Grotius, the application of natural law principles of moderation and proportion: the "principle of international law, which authorizes us to use against an enemy such a degree of violence, and such only, as may be necessary to secure the object of hostilities."[28] Wheaton makes no reference to a general interest of mankind in the preservation and enjoyment of cultural property.

Halleck, writing on the eve of the American Civil War, also displayed no awareness of Quatremère de Quincy or Dr. Croke. Unlike Wheaton, however, he distinguished destruction from plunder and immovables from movables:

> No belligerent would be justifiable in destroying temples, tombs, statutes [*sic*], paintings, or other works of art (except so far as their destruction may be the accidental or necessary result of military operations.) But, may he not seize and appropriate to his own use such works of genius and taste as belong to the hostile state, and are of a moveable character? This was done by the French armies in the wars of conquest which followed the revolution of 1789.... The acquisitions of the Parisian galleries and museums from the conquest of Italy, were generally obtained by means of treaty stipulations, or forced contributions levied by Napoleon on the Italian princes.[29]

Halleck recognized that opinions differed on the legal effect of such forced treaty stipulations, but his discussion shows that he clearly favored the view that they were binding.

In July 1862, when the same Halleck became General-in-Chief of the Union Armies in the American Civil War, the stage was set for the next development. Francis Lieber, a German emigré who was a professor at Columbia College, had earlier collaborated with Halleck in an effort to define guerilla warfare. At Halleck's request, Lieber now prepared a proposed code of conduct for the Union forces. Issued as General Orders No. 100 on April 24, 1863, these *Instructions for the Governance of Armies of the United States in the Field*, later known as the *Lieber Code*,[30] contained 157 articles. The provisions on protection of cultural property appear in articles 34–36:

> 34. As a general rule, the property belonging to churches, to hospitals, or other establishments of an exclusively charitable character, to establishments of education, or foundations for the promotion of knowledge, whether public schools, universities, academies of learning or observatories, museums of the fine arts, or of a scientific character—such property is not to be considered public property in the sense of paragraph 31 [authorizing seizure of enemy public property]; but it may be taxed or used when the public service may require it.
>
> 35. Classical works of art, libraries, scientific collections, or precious instruments, such as astronomical telescopes, as well as hospitals, must be secured

> against all avoidable injury, even when they are contained in fortified places whilst besieged or bombarded.
>
> 36. If such works of art, libraries, collections, or instruments belonging to a hostile nation or government, can be removed without injury, the ruler of the conquering state or nation may order them to be seized and removed for the benefit of the said nation. The ultimate ownership is to be settled by the ensuing treaty of peace.

The *Lieber Code* was one of the earliest attempts to state a comprehensive body of principles to govern the conduct of belligerents in enemy territory. It was widely admired as an enlightened and humane document, was frequently copied in Europe, and provided the template for modern international conventions on the law of war. The influence of the *Lieber Code*'s treatment of cultural property can be traced through Article 8 of the *Declaration of Brussels* (1874)[31]; Article 56 of the Institute of International Law's *Manual of the Laws and Customs of War* (1880)[32]; Article 56 of the "*Regulations Respecting the Laws and customs of War on Land*" under Hague II (1907)[33]; article 56 of the corresponding Regulations under Hague IV (1907)[34]; Article 5 of the *Convention Concerning Bombardment by Naval Forces in Time of War* of October 8, 1907 (Hague IX)[35]; Articles XXV and XXVI of the *Hague Rules of Air Warfare* (1922)[36]; and other international instruments, culminating in the 1954 Hague Convention, which is discussed below.

As World War II approached, the *Roerich Pact*,[37] promulgated by the Organization of American States at its meeting in Washington, D.C. in 1935, was the first multinational convention entirely devoted to the protection of cultural property in war. Most American states, including the United States, became members. It stated:

> Article 1. The historic monuments, museums, scientific, artistic, educational and cultural institutions shall be considered as neutral and as such respected and protected by belligerents. The same respect and protection shall be due to the personnel of the institutions mentioned above. The same respect and protection shall be accorded to the historic monuments, museums, scientific, artistic, educational and cultural institutions in time of peace as well as in war.

The *Roerich Pact* was limited to the Western hemisphere, protected only immovable cultural properties and "institutions," lacked essential details and, although still in force, is in practice a dead letter.

Following the signature of the *Roerich Pact*, attempts were undertaken to draft a more comprehensive convention for the protection of monuments and works of art in time of war. In 1939, a *Preliminary Draft International Convention for the Protection of Monuments and Works of Art in Time of War*,[38] elaborated under the auspices of the League of Nations International Museums Office, was presented to governments by the Netherlands, but it was an early casualty of the outbreak of World War II.

During World War II the German Nazis engaged in a highly organized campaign of art plunder. The operation was placed in the hands of a "special unit" (*Ein-*

satzstab) directed by Alfred Rosenberg, a high Nazi official. The *Einsatzstab Reichsleiter Rosenberg* was separate from the German military and uninhibited by the military's traditional policy against looting. As the German armies invaded and occupied other nations, the *Einsatzstab* seized the property of Jews and great quantities of other works that Nazi party officials, principally Hitler and Goering, directed to be seized. The quantity of art taken and shipped to Germany was enormous. Rosenberg produced an illustrated catalog of 39 volumes, with about 2,500 photographs of works seized. If the entire body of loot had been photographed and catalogued it would have run to about 300 volumes. The similarities and contrasts with Napoléon's Italian campaign are a tempting topic that cannot be pursued here.[39]

On August 8, 1945 the victorious Allied Powers signed the agreement constituting the Allied Military Tribunal and ordering the Nuremberg trials of major Nazi officials. At Nuremberg, Rosenberg was charged with multiple crimes against peace, war crimes, and crimes against humanity. Among the war crimes charged was "looting and plundering of works of art." Rosenberg was found guilty of this and other charges and was hanged.[40]

A new proposal for an international convention was submitted to UNESCO by the Netherlands in 1948. UNESCO convened a committee of government experts to draft a convention in 1951, and an intergovernmental conference of 56 nations held at The Hague adopted the *Hague Convention for the Protection of Cultural Property in the Event of Armed Conflict*[41] on 14 May 1954. Although the United States has not become a party, Hague 1954 has been widely adopted by other nations (105 as of March, 2003) and represents the reigning international consensus about the protection of cultural property from destruction and plunder in war.

In addition to the powerful statement of cultural property internationalism in its Preamble that "damage to cultural property belonging to any people whatsoever means damage to the cultural heritage of all mankind, since each people makes its contribution to the culture of the world," the Convention contains the following interesting provision in Article 29:

> The High Contracting Parties undertake to take, within the framework of their ordinary criminal jurisdiction, all necessary steps to prosecute and impose penal or disciplinary sanctions upon those persons, of whatever nationality, who commit or order to be committed a breach of the present Convention.

This post-Nuremberg language is itself an extraordinary expression of cultural property internationalism. States by becoming Parties acquire jurisdiction to try as crimes breaches of the Convention committed by individuals anywhere whose States may or may not be Parties.

The widespread adoption of Hague 1954 assured a prominent place for cultural property internationalism in the law of war, but changes in weapons and modes of warfare since the 1940s and the resulting new threats to cultural property led to concern about its adequacy. This concern became more general during the early 1990s, particularly during the Gulf War and the wars in the former Yugoslavia. Largely stimulated (again) by the government of the Netherlands, a series of studies, meetings of experts, and meetings of governmental representatives that began in 1991 eventually led to the diplomatic conference in The Hague in March, 1999, that adopted the *Second Protocol to the Hague Convention of 1954 for the Protection of Cultural Property in the Event of Armed Conflict*.[42] The protocol increases cultural property protections and establishes a Secretariat to administer the Convention's terms.

All of the authorities and conventions so far mentioned, with the sole exception of the *Roerich Pact*, include a significant concession to nationalism: the doctrine of "military necessity." As stated in Articles 14-15 of the *Lieber Code*:

> Military necessity, as understood by modern civilized nations, consists in the necessity of those measures which are indispensable for securing the end of war, and which are lawful according to the modern law and usages of war. . . . Military necessity . . . allows of all destruction of property. . . .

Hague 1954 is not greatly different. Article 4(2) provides that the obligation to respect cultural property "may be waived . . . in cases where military necessity imperatively requires such a waiver." Article 6a of the Second Protocol to Hague 1954 retains but limits and clarifies the military necessity waiver.[43]

The exception for military necessity, whose origin has been attributed to Prussian militarism—"*La célèbre conception prussienne de la Kriegsraison*"[44]—was strongly debated at the diplomatic conference that produced Hague 1954 and was retained by a divided vote. Nahlik describes the debates and says that the United States, Great Britain, and Turkey insisted on including an exception for military necessity, while the USSR, Romania, Greece, Belgium, Ecuador, and Spain argued that such an exception was "incompatible with the spirit and essential principles of the Convention." It is ironic that the United States, which argued that it could not ratify the Convention if it did not contain the military necessity clause, thus compelling its inclusion, has never become a party to Hague 1954.[45]

It is not entirely clear when the international interest in protecting cultural property from the hazards of war began to expand into a more general cultural property internationalism. We do know that by 1945, when UNESCO was created, that evolution was well advanced and, in its expanded form, was expressly incorporated into UNESCO's cultural property competence, as the following discussion demonstrates.

UNESCO

A United Nations Conference for the establishment of an educational and cultural organization convened in London in November 1945, attended by the representatives of forty-four countries. Led by France and the United Kingdom, the delegates hoped to create an organization that would embody a genuine culture of peace. In their eyes, the new organization should establish the "intellectual and moral solidarity of mankind" and, in so doing, help to prevent the outbreak of another world war. The Constitution of UNESCO was signed on 16 November 1945. As of October 2003, UNESCO had 190 Member States and 6 Associate Members.

Cultural internationalism obviously is basic to UNESCO's existence and legitimacy. The preamble to its Constitution speaks of "the history of mankind," "peoples of the world," "the diffusion of culture" and "the education of mankind," and Article 1 states that:

> The purpose of the Organization is to contribute to peace and security by promoting collaboration among the nations through education, science and culture in order to further universal respect for justice, for the rule of law and for the human rights and fundamental freedoms which are affirmed for the peoples of the world, without distinction of race, sex, language or religion, by the Charter of the United Nations.

Achievement of these internationalist objectives, however, is limited by a domestic jurisdiction clause, which also appears in Article 1:

> With a view to preserving the independence, integrity and fruitful diversity of the cultures and educational systems of the States members of this Organization, the Organization is prohibited from intervening in matters which are essentially within their domestic jurisdiction.[46]

As a result, UNESCO's cultural sector activities display a familiar kind of interplay between group and member interests whose results are ultimately embodied in UNESCO conventions and recommendations.

Article 1(2)(c) of the UNESCO Constitution states the organization's cultural property competence: 1) conservation and protection; 2) recommending international conventions; and 3) encouraging international exchange. "Conservation and protection" is a simple but important logical expansion of the protection of cultural property during war: whether in war or at peace, cultural property should be preserved against damage or destruction. The third commitment, to encouragement of the international exchange of cultural property, has been variously interpreted, as will appear below. UNESCO's pursuance of the second activity is amply demonstrated in the legal instruments it has produced,[47] to the most important of which we will turn below.

Something important seems to be missing from the language of Article 1(2)(c). I have argued elsewhere[48] for a related triad of regulatory imperatives. The most basic is preservation: protecting the object and its context from impairment. Next comes the quest for knowledge, for valid information about the human past, for the historical, scientific, cultural, and aesthetic truth that the object and its context can provide. Finally we want the object to be optimally accessible to scholars for study and to the public for education and enjoyment. This triad may be summed up as "preservation, truth, and access." The addition of "truth" adds meaning and weight to "preservation" and "access."

As to "recommending international conventions," the 1954 Hague Convention, which we have already seen, is one such instrument. Like it, the others assume, and usually contain language invoking, the international interest in cultural property.

They significantly differ, however, in the ways in which they characterize and pursue that interest, as the following brief examination of some particularly relevant UNESCO instruments shows.

UNESCO 1970. We begin with the 1970 *UNESCO Convention on the Means of Prohibiting and Preventing the Illicit Import, Export and Transfer of Ownership of Cultural Property*,[49] under which, in Article 7(a), States Parties agree to enforce each others' cultural property export controls and related legislation. The Preamble, however, consistently with the UNESCO Constitution's commitment to encouraging the international "interchange" of cultural property, states that:

> the interchange of cultural property among nations for scientific, cultural and educational purposes increases the knowledge of the civilization of Man, enriches the cultural life of all peoples and inspires mutual respect and appreciation among nations

The answer to any apparent inconsistency between promoting international interchange and enforcing national export controls appears to be obvious: UNESCO 1970s provisions are aimed only at "illicit" exports; "licit" exports are not a problem. That distinction, however, requires us to look more closely at the Convention and the meaning of "licit."

The Convention defines "cultural property" in Articles 1 and 4 as, in effect, anything that the authorities of a State so designate, and it provides in Article 3 that "The import, export or transfer of ownership of cultural property" without a certificate, described in Article 6, "shall be illicit." Thus, for example, the export of van Gogh and Matisse paintings by their Italian owners without certificates (which were denied) would be "illicit." The same would be true of an Italian collector's export of Adolf Hitler water colors of Austrian scenes and exports by French owners of a Yuan vase, a collection of Italian drawings, and a painting by a Swiss artist of a Swiss scene painted in Switzerland, for all of which export certificates were denied.

Skeptics might conclude that this Convention, in the name of cultural property internationalism, actually supports a strong form of cultural property nationalism. It imposes no discipline on a State's definition of the cultural property that may not be exported without permission. It leaves States free to make their own self-interested decisions about whether or not to grant or deny export permission in specific cases. The only likely applicants for such permission are, in the words of Article 5(e), "curators, collectors, antique dealers, etc." who have little voice in such decision-making. In this way, the Convention condones and supports the widespread practice of over-retention or, less politely, hoarding of cultural property. To some skeptical eyes, this does not look much like encouragement of international exchange. The problems created by the notorious practice of overretention are explored elsewhere.[50]

The 1976 Recommendation. UNESCO's 1976 *Recommendation Concerning the International Exchange of Cultural Property*,[51] on the contrary, encourages cultural property exchanges and recommends measures for regularizing and securing such transactions. One might suppose that this support would extend to circulation through market transactions, which are the principal medium for the international circulation of goods of all kinds. The Recommendation, however, while supporting the international *exchange* of cultural property, opposes international *trade*, stating that:

> the international circulation of cultural property is still largely dependent on the activities of self-seeking parties and so tends to lead to speculation which causes the price of such property to rise, making it inaccessible to poorer countries and institutions while at the same time encouraging the spread of illicit trading.

This curious statement, exuding disapproval of the market, calls buyers and sellers of cultural objects "self-seeking parties" and the normal human tendency to base present action on assumptions about the future "speculation." It advances the economically naive supposition that speculation "causes" the prices of works of art and other cultural objects to rise, although it seems clear that "speculation," to the extent that it can "cause" price behavior at all, can just as easily "cause" prices to fall.

Constricting the licit supply of cultural objects would appear to most knowledgeable people to be a more effective way to cause prices to rise and to encourage the spread of illicit trading. That is of course what excessive source nation export controls and their enforcement under the 1970 UNESCO Convention combine to do. As to "poorer countries," many of which are source nations, the orderly marketing of surplus cultural objects could *pro tanto* displace the black market, while providing a significant source of income to the source nation and its citizens. That major source nations typically hoard stocks of marketable surplus objects is confirmed by another paragraph in the *Recommendation*'s Preamble:

> Many cultural institutions, whatever their financial resources, possess several identical or similar specimens of cultural objects of indisputable quality and origin which are amply documented, and ... some of these items, which are of only minor or secondary importance for these institutions because of their plurality, would be welcomed as valuable accessions by institutions in other countries.[52]

It hardly needs to be said that such objects would also be welcomed to the licit international market by museums, collectors and the art trade.

The *Recommendation*, however, does not say it. Instead, it rejects the market and relies exclusively on interinstitutional (government to government and museum to museum) exchanges as the medium through which to promote enrichment of cultures and mutual understanding and appreciation among nations. Such exchanges are a valuable tool of museum collections management. They are, however, a form of barter, with all of barter's considerable limitations. The market is a much more efficient and productive mechanism for the international circulation of cultural property, and to exclude it seems misguided. In its exclusion of market transactions this Recommendation appears to discourage, rather than encourage, the interchange of cultural property.

In its exclusive preference for interinstitutional and inter-governmental exchanges, the *Recommendation* contemplates a cultural property world that is populated solely by governments and "institutions":[53]

> "International exchange" shall be taken to mean any transfer of ownership, use or custody of cultural property between States or cultural institutions in different countries—whether it takes the form of the loan, deposit, sale or donation of such property—carried out under such conditions as may be agreed between the parties concerned.

Under this interpretation of "international exchange," there is no place for private collectors or an active art trade and no scope for a licit market. There is no recognition of the historic roles of collectors and dealers in supporting artists and promoting their work; in building private collections that ultimately enrich museums; and in pioneering the collection of objects that eventually are recognized for their cultural importance. Nor is there any recognition of the utility of the market as an efficient transactional arena and a provider of price indicators of value.

The 1978 Recommendation for the Protection of Movable Cultural Property.[54] This Recommendation is unusual in that it recognizes the existence of collectors, dealers, and other international market participants, but only to express concern about the safety of cultural objects in their hands. It warns States that growing public interest in cultural property has led to "an increase in all the dangers to which cultural property is exposed as a result of particularly easy access or inadequate protection, the risks inherent in transport, and the recrudescence, in some countries, of clandestine excavations, thefts, illicit traffic and acts of vandalism," and counsels that:

> The growing perils which threaten the movable cultural heritage should incite all those responsible for protecting it, in whatever capacity, to play their part: staff of national and local administrations in charge of safeguarding cultural property, administrators and curators of museums and similar institutions, private owners and those responsible for religious buildings, art and antique dealers, security experts, services responsible for the suppression of crime, customs officials and the other public authorities involved.

In Articles 11-24, in language sometimes reminiscent of Polonius, the Recommendation provides a set of admonitions about protective measures, including in Articles 14 and 15 those that should be taken to protect cultural objects in private hands. In no provision does this Recommendation indicate approval of dealers, collectors, or the market.

The 2001 UNESCO Convention on Protection of the Underwater Cultural Heritage.[55] This Convention provides that States Parties shall preserve underwater cultural heritage *in situ* "for the benefit of humanity in conformity with the provisions of this Convention." Underwater cultural heritage is defined as:

> all traces of human existence having a cultural, historical or archaeological character which have been partially or totally under water, periodically

or continuously, for at least 100 years such as: (i) sites, structures, buildings, artefacts and human remains, together with their archaeological and natural context; (ii) vessels, aircraft, other vehicles or any part thereof, their cargo or other contents, together with their archaeological and natural context; and (iii) objects of prehistoric character.

The Convention demonstrates that UNESCO's antimarket bias has grown stronger since promulgation of the 1976 Recommendation, discussed above. Article 2 (7) of the Convention states in its entirety:

> Underwater cultural heritage shall not be commercially exploited.

This breathtaking provision is elucidated in Rule 2 of the *Rules concerning the activities directed at underwater cultural heritage* annexed to the Convention:

> The commercial exploitation of underwater cultural heritage for trade or speculation or its irretrievable dispersal is fundamentally incompatible with the protection and proper management of underwater cultural heritage. Underwater cultural heritage shall not be traded, sold, bought or bartered as commercial goods.

The statement that market transactions are "fundamentally incompatible with the protection and proper management of underwater cultural heritage" expresses a position that, as we shall see below, is broadly embraced by the archaeological establishment in the United Kingdom and the United States.

As of September 2004, the Convention, which requires 20 adoptions to enter into force, had been ratified only by Panama (5/20/03) and Bulgaria (6/10/03). This apparently unenthusiastic reception may demonstrate a lack of consensus among the world's nations concerning the importance of protecting underwater sites, structures and objects. Or it may represent a reaction to the severity of the Convention's prohibition of commercial exploitation and its prohibition, in Article 38, of reservations. Or it may simply reflect national desires to retain unfettered control over their internal waters, archipelagic waters, territorial sea, and contiguous zones.

UNESCO Declaration Concerning the Intentional Destruction of Cultural Heritage of 17 October 2003.[56] In the wake of the Taliban's demolition of the Bamiyan Buddhas, the destruction of Kosovo churches and the Mostar bridge, and the United States military actions in Afghanistan and Iraq, the General Conference of UNESCO published this Declaration, which emphatically restates the international interest in cultural property and calls on all States to act to prevent its intentional destruction. Article VII also urges States to assert jurisdiction over and prosecute individuals who commit or order the commission of acts of destruction of cultural heritage. Your author is not aware that any such prosecutions have been instituted by any States.

UNESCO Convention For the Safeguarding of the Intangible Cultural Heritage of 17 October 2003.[57] According to Article 2 of this important instrument:

> The intangible cultural heritage ... is manifested inter alia in the following domains: (a) oral traditions and expressions, including language as a vehi-

cle of the intangible cultural heritage; (b) performing arts; (c) social practices, rituals and festive events; (d) knowledge and practices concerning nature and the universe; (e) traditional craftsmanship.

The preamble states the internationalist credentials of this Convention when it refers to "the universal will and the common concern to safeguard the intangible cultural heritage of humanity"; recognizes that "communities, in particular indigenous communities, groups and, in some cases, individuals, play an important role in the production, safeguarding, maintenance and re-creation of the intangible cultural heritage, thus helping to enrich cultural diversity and human creativity"; and asserts that "the international community should contribute, together with the States Parties to this Convention, to the safeguarding of such heritage in a spirit of cooperation and mutual assistance." States Parties are to draw up inventories of the intangible cultural heritage present in their territories, and an Intergovernmental Committee is to prepare and maintain a "Representative List of the Intangible Cultural Heritage of Humanity" and a "List of Intangible Cultural Heritage in Need of Urgent Safeguarding."

In fact, "safeguarding" the intangible cultural heritage is the primary concern of the Convention. Article 3 states that:

> "Safeguarding" means measures aimed at ensuring the viability of the intangible cultural heritage, including the identification, documentation, research, preservation, protection, promotion, enhancement, transmission, particularly through formal and non-formal education, as well as the revitalization of the various aspects of such heritage.

The Convention contains no reference to international traffic, whether by barter or market transaction, in intangible cultural heritage. Nor does it deal with retention. Indeed, it takes a stretch of the imagination to suggest ways in which a loss of intangible cultural heritage through export might occur. A Korean induces a Japanese "living national treasure" to emigrate? The few remaining members of an isolated tribe of First People in Canada join a thriving related group in Minnesota? The French Minister of Culture persuades the Dance Theater of Harlem to establish its seat in Paris? As of August 20, 1904, five nations had adopted this Convention. Thirty adoptions are necessary for it to come into force.

****

This brief survey of UNESCO instruments dealing with cultural property illustrates an interesting range of actions taken to meet UNESCO's three constitutional obligations to the "cultural heritage of all mankind": conservation and protection, recommending international conventions, and encouraging international exchange. Given the difficulties commonly encountered in reaching international consensus and the notorious inertia of large bureaucracies, UNESCO's record as an advocate for cultural property internationalism may seem to others, as it does to me, impressive.

That record, however, is flawed. The instruments we have examined reveal two major deviations from UNESCO's internationalist mission. One, implied in the contents of some of those instruments and openly expressed in the 1976 Recommendation, was pressed to a logical extreme in the 2001 Underwater Convention's provision that "Underwater cultural heritage shall not be commercially exploited." This drastic and potentially damaging (to underwater cultural heritage) provision was only made possible by narrowly interpreting the words "international exchange" in UNESCO's Constitution to exclude market transactions.

In this way, the international cultural property world's principal actors (all of the uncountable numbers of artists and artisans, the zillions of collectors, the thousands of dealers and auction houses, etc.) and the overwhelming majority of international cultural property transactions are made to disappear. What remains is a shriveled and stunted cultural property world, peopled only by governments and "institutions" that lend to, borrow from, and barter with each other. Where did such a diminished image of the cultural property world come from?

Collectors and the art trade generally respect legal restraints on international trade in cultural objects. They are encouraged to do so by the widespread adoption in the major market nations of statements of approved professional practices and codes of ethics for dealers. Members of the Art Dealers Association of America, for example, agree to observe the CINOA[58] *Guidelines*. The same or comparable principles have been adopted by national dealers' organizations in Britain (the British Art Market Association) and other nations and by a European federation of dealers' associations (Fédération Européenne des Associations de Galeries d'Art).

In 1999 UNESCO adopted a *Code of Ethics for Dealers in Cultural Property*[59] that was drafted with the assistance of dealers. This Code is remarkable in that, by offering principles to regulate the conduct of dealers, UNESCO recognized their existence and implied the legitimacy of collectors, dealers, and a market in cultural objects (but only in order to express concern about the safety of cultural objects in their hands). The Code states in its entirety that:

> Members of the trade in cultural property recognize the key role that trade has traditionally played in the dissemination of culture and in the distribution to museums and private collectors of foreign cultural property for the education and inspiration of all peoples.
>
> They acknowledge the world wide concern over the traffic in stolen, illegally alienated, clandestinely excavated and illegally exported cultural property and accept as binding the following principles of professional practice intended to distinguish cultural property being illicitly traded from that in licit trade and they will seek to eliminate the former from their professional activities.
>
> ARTICLE 1 Professional traders in cultural property will not import, export or transfer the ownership of this property when they have reasonable cause to believe it has been stolen, illegally alienated, clandestinely excavated or illegally exported.

ARTICLE 2 A trader who is acting as agent for the seller is not deemed to guarantee title to the property, provided that he makes known to the buyer the full name and address of the seller. A trader who is himself the seller is deemed to guarantee to the buyer the title to the goods.

ARTICLE 3 A trader who has reasonable cause to believe that an object has been the product of a clandestine excavation, or has been acquired illegally or dishonestly from an official excavation site or monument will not assist in any further transaction with that object, except with the agreement of the country where the site or monument exists. A trader who is in possession of the object, where that country seeks its return within a reasonable period of time, will take all legally permissible steps to co-operate in the return of that object to the country of origin.

ARTICLE 4 A trader who has reasonable cause to believe that an item of cultural property has been illegally exported will not assist in any further transaction with that item, except with the agreement of the country of export. A trader who is in possession of the item, where the country of export seeks its return within a reasonable period of time, will take all legally permissible steps to co-operate in the return of that object to the country of export.

ARTICLE 5 Traders in cultural property will not exhibit, describe, attribute, appraise or retain any item of cultural property with the intention of promoting or failing to prevent its illicit transfer or export. Traders will not refer the seller or other person offering the item to those who may perform such services.

ARTICLE 6 Traders in cultural property will not dismember or sell separately parts of one complete item of cultural property.

ARTICLE 7 Traders in cultural property undertake to the best of their ability to keep together items of cultural heritage that were originally meant to be kept together.

ARTICLE 8 Violations of this Code of Ethics will be rigorously investigated by (a body to be nominated by participating dealers). A person aggrieved by the failure of a trader to adhere to the principles of this Code of Ethics may lay a complaint before that body, which shall investigate that complaint. Results of the complaint and the principles applied will be made public.

This Code of Ethics seems to be reasonable and constructive. Unfortunately, however, the context in which it applies is permeated by source-nation trade restraints that, as we have seen, are excessive in concept and in practice. Those excesses are implicitly condoned by other UNESCO instruments, particularly the 1970 Convention.

As was said earlier, no thinking person argues for free trade in cultural property. Regulation is necessary in order to preserve cultural property and to support its proper international circulation. Such regulation serves the international interest of "all mankind" in preservation and enjoyment of its "cultural heritage." Excessive regulation, however, violates rather than serves the international interest, and a prohibition against trading clearly is excessive. The archaeologists' war against acquisitors (collectors, museums, and the art trade), to which we now turn, is another source of excess.

WAR AND PEACE

Archaeologists have a complex relationship with cultural property internationalism. The field of archaeology clearly is international; sites and objects of archaeological interest exist everywhere, and the profession is interested in all of them. Individual archaeologists, however, are not typically internationalists. An archaeologist's fieldwork usually requires commitment to the sites of a specific culture in a defined area to which the archaeologist typically returns over a period of years and often becomes deeply attached. When American archaeologists work outside the United States, they tend to identify more strongly with the host nation than with the international community or "all mankind." Archaeologists' dependence on host nations for excavation permits, support services, and access to sites further inclines them to identify with the host nation and support its cultural property policies.

Context is centrally important to archaeology. In conducting excavations, professional archaeologists carefully document sites, the excavation process, and the precise locations and postures of unearthed objects. Clandestine excavation and the undocumented removal of antiquities from archaeological sites, even if carefully done, destroy potentially important information about the past. The objects taken become "orphans" whose sources, contextual identities, and meaning are lost or diminished.

All source nations have laws criminalizing clandestine excavation and the unauthorized removal of antiquities from their sites. Often, such laws also declare that antiquities are property of the nation, with the intention of making their unauthorized removal theft. Archaeologists strongly support such laws and their enforcement by market nations, as provided in the 1970 *UNESCO Convention on the Means of Prohibiting and Preventing the Illicit Import, Export and Transfer of Ownership of Cultural Property*, previously mentioned; the U.S. Convention on Cultural Property Implementation Act of 1983, 19 U.S.C. §§2601ff; and the 1995 *Unidroit Convention on Stolen or Illegally Exported Cultural Objects*.[60]

The above considerations converge to lead archaeologists to support national policies and laws and international conventions that limit the international movement of cultural objects. We have seen that the UNESCO Constitution, in Article 1(2)(c), commits the Organization to three interrelated kinds of cultural property activities: 1) conservation and protection; 2) recommending international conventions; and 3) encouraging international exchange. The prevailing ideology among archaeologists supports the first two of these but not the third. Archaeologists do not actively oppose the barter or loan of antiquities by governments and museums. They do, however, oppose international trade.

Indeed, since the 1970s, archaeologists have effectively promoted the thesis that collectors and dealers are responsible for the illicit trade in antiquities and destruction of the archaeological record. Their logic is simple: if collectors did not collect and dealers did not deal there would be no antiquities market, and if there were no market, the illicit traffic in antiquities would disappear. Although some archaeologists take a more nuanced view,[61] the archaeological establishment as a whole has vigorously embraced and propagated this reductive argument, which I have criticized elsewhere, though with little apparent effect.[62] Consequently, to the archaeological establishment, every commercial antiquities transaction is suspect. If not proven to be blameless by archaeologists' standards it is blameworthy, illicit. Elaborate due diligence is not enough. An anecdote will illustrate the point.

In 1987 The Getty Museum adopted an elaborate new due diligence policy for the acquisition of antiquities. When an interesting object was offered to it, the Museum thoroughly researched the object and compiled a dossier which was sent to the antiquities authorities of all plausible nations of origin, asking whether they saw any reason why the Museum should not acquire the object. If any such objection were made, the Museum declined to acquire it. The Museum's curator of antiquities also actively assisted source nations in the recovery of offered objects that appeared to have been stolen. To many observers this policy appeared to be responsible and constructive.

In 1989 the Museum organized a private two-day conference of source nation officials, archaeologists, museum professionals, dealers, lawyers, and academics (including the author) to discuss this policy and to initiate a dialogue that might lead to a resolution of differences among the interested parties. Instead, the conference provided a dispiriting glimpse of a tendency toward archaeological fundamentalism when a number of the archaeologists present attacked the Museum's new acquisition policy as disingenuous and damaging. Such attacks continued after the conference.

In 1995 the Getty trustees felt compelled to bow to the archaeologists. They announced that the Museum would forego the acquisition of any antiquities that were not previously published or otherwise documented as parts of established collections. Every proposed acquisition or loan would now be treated as "illicit" unless proved to be "licit." Some other cultural property world actors have since adopted this "guilty unless proved innocent" presumption. Archaeologists now feel free to condemn, as "looters" and worse, collectors who acquire and museums that display antiquities that no nation claims and that no one has shown to have been improperly acquired.

Excessive source nation retention of cultural property is a potent instrument in the war against acquisitors. As we have seen, the 1970 UNESCO Convention leaves it to each State Party, within broad limits and subject to no review, to provide its own definition of "cultural property"; to establish its own limitations on the "import, export or transfer of ownership" of cultural property so self-defined; and provides that any transaction that violates these controls "shall be illicit." So encouraged, most source nations have adopted excessively retentive legislation that, in practice, prohibits the export of objects that bear no significant relation to the nation's culture, objects of slight cultural importance, and redundant objects—particularly antiquities—that it will never study or exhibit.

Consider a typical law prohibiting export of works of art over 100 years old. Such a law may protect works too fragile to travel, but it also immobilizes sturdier works that could circulate without significant risk of damage or destruction. The same law may keep at home works of outstanding importance to the nation's history and culture but, as we have seen, it also can be and has been used to prevent the export of works that have no such relationship or importance. Similarly, a law that prohibits trade in antiquities can help immobilize objects that ought to be retained in place, but it will also add to the hoarded stocks of redundant antiquities that languish unconserved, unstudied, unpublished, unseen, and unloved in the warehouses of major source nations. The considerable problems thus created are explored elsewhere.[63]

UNESCO instruments tell us that the international interchange of cultural property "increases the knowledge of the civilization of Man, enriches the cultural life of all peoples and insures mutual respect and appreciation among nations"[64] and leads to "a better use of the international community's cultural heritage."[65] Excessive restraints thwart these internationalist goals by improperly limiting the international interchange of cultural property. And by artificially expanding the meaning of "illicit" they reduce the possibilities for a licit cultural property trade.

The liberalization of international trade by the World Trade Organization (WTO)[66] and the European Communities (EC) provides a potentially strong counterforce to the archaeologists' crusade and source nation overretention. Both the WTO and EC treaties[67] prohibit export controls on "goods,"[68] which the European Court of Justice ruled, in *Commission v. Italy*, includes works of art."[69] Both treaties, however, WTO in Article 130 and EC in Article 30, permit national measures for "the protection of national treasures possessing artistic, historic or archaeological value."[70] This key phrase has until now received little judicial attention. Eminent commentators agree, however, that it should be treated as restrictive.[71] "The exception's purpose is not to preserve the totality of an artistic patrimony," but to safeguard its "essential and fundamental elements."[72]

Source nation export controls that prohibit the international exchange of works that are neither "national" nor "treasures" and do not "protect" them from anything but export clearly exceed permissible limits under these treaties. Cases involving the interpretation of WTO Article 130 and EC Article 30 have not yet arisen, but when they do, some inescapable questions will present themselves. Does the object in question fall within an appropriately restrictive interpretation of "national treasures?" If so, does application of the export control "protect" it? Can the treaty's application be evaded by legislation declaring that cultural objects are "national property"? Such questions will ultimately be answered by the European Court of Justice and the WTO dispute resolution panels. Will they disarm the source nation-archaeologists alliance of one of its major weapons and help bring peace to the cultural property world? We do not know.

WHITHER CULTURAL PROPERTY INTERNATIONALISM?

People everywhere, including all of the actors in the cultural property world, share an interest in the preservation, study, and enjoyment of cultural property. In addition, collectors, museums, dealers, and auction houses have their own particular self-interests in an active, licit international art and antiquities market. Source nations, UNESCO, and archaeologists have their own particular self-interests, which have led them to oppose or restrict an otherwise licit market and to limit the interchange of cultural objects to interinstitutional loans and exchanges.

All of these diverse interests are, in principle, legitimate. That they sometimes conflict simply reflects the reality that the cultural property world is complex. I am aware of no basis for supposing that any of the conflicting interests, even those of the archaeologists, dwell on a higher moral plane than any of the others. The reasonable course is for the interested parties to seek the optimal accommodation of their various interests, and that requires that the parties speak and listen to each other.

That dialogue, although frequently called for, has yet to begin. Source nations, supported by UNESCO and archaeologists, continue to hoard cultural objects, in apparent conflict with trade liberalization treaties, while calling on other nations to enforce their excessive restrictions on export and their blanket declarations of "ownership." Prominent archaeologists hold fast to the position that they are right; collectors, museums, and the art trade are iniquitously wrong; and the international interest in the circulation of cultural objects, if it is considered at all, is adequately served by rhetoric about interinstitutional loans and exchanges. UNESCO conventions support source nations and archaeologists, contemplate a cultural property world inhabited solely by governments and "institutions," and expressly oppose markets in cultural goods.

In short, the prospects look dark for those who favor a licit international trade in cultural objects. Under present conditions a large, growing demand confronts a sharply restricted licit supply. If one set out to design a system that would discourage a licit market and encourage a black market, it would be difficult to improve on the present one. As Quentin Byrne-Sutton put it: "*On arrive ainsi à la situation ridicule où une réglementation alimente ce qu'elle cherche à éliminer.*"[73] Right.

Finally, it should be obvious that such a system, dictated by the preferences of retentive source nations and zealous archaeologists, even if it is embodied in UNESCO instruments, does not provide optimal conditions for the preservation of the cultural heritage of all mankind or its optimal distribution for access, study, and enjoyment. Will the situation right itself? Do social systems automatically self-correct when things get too far out of line? Or, to use another figure, if the pendulum swings too far in one direction, will it eventually swing back? Will enforcement of the WTO and EC trade-liberalizing treaty provisions finally start a process that will eventually restore the balance? Can articles like this one help, or do they make things worse, or are they irrelevant? All good questions, to which no one knows the answers.

ENDNOTES

1. The terms cultural "property," "objects," "heritage," and "patrimony" variously appear in legislation and the scholarly and popular literatures, but there do not appear to be any agreed meanings or standard usage. In this article "cultural property" and "cultural objects" interchangeably serve the same purpose: to designate objects of cultural significance. "Cultural heritage" includes such objects and immaterial cultural expressions, such as folklore and traditional knowledge, which are not ordinarily considered to be cultural property and are not considered in this article. "Cultural patrimony" usually appears in contexts that assume or express cultural nationalism, i.e., the attribution of national character (the nation of origin or of the *situs*) to cultural objects.

2. The quoted words first appear in the Preamble of the 1954 *Hague Convention for the Protection of Cultural Property in the Event of Armed Conflict* (hereinafter Hague 1954), and are repeated or paraphrased in the subsequent UNESCO instruments collected in UNESCO, *Conventions and Recommendations of UNESCO Concerning the Protection of the Cultural Heritage*, cited herein as *UNESCO Conventions and Recommendations*.

3. Merryman, "Two Ways of Thinking About Cultural Property."

4. Most, perhaps all, value is attributed rather than intrinsic, and the value attributed to a given object is itself a cultural expression that often changes over time. The point is elegantly developed in Thompson, *Rubbish Theory*.

5. In the fourth edition of Merryman and Elsen, *Law, Ethics and the Visual Arts*, works of art are considered in Chapter 2 and antiquities are treated in a separate Chapter 3.

6. The *UNIDROIT Convention* can be viewed at <http://www.unidroit.org/english/conventions/c-cult.htm> (Last visited 8/17/04).

7. The Annex lists the following Categories of Cultural Objects:
(a) Rare collections and specimens of fauna, flora, minerals and anatomy, and objects of palaeontological interest; (b) property relating to history, including the history of science and technology and military and social history, to the lives of national leaders, thinkers, scientists and artists and to events of national importance; (c) products of archaeological excavations (including regular and clandestine) or of archaeological discoveries; (d) elements of artistic or historical monuments or archaeological sites which have been dismembered; (e) antiquities more than one hundred years old, such as inscriptions, coins or engraved seals; (f) articles of ethnological interest; (g) articles of artistic interest, such as: (i) pictures, paintings and drawings produced entirely by hand on any support and in any material (excluding industrial designs and manufactured articles decorated by hand); (ii) original works of statuary art and sculpture in any material; (iii) original engravings, prints and lithographs; (iv) original artistic assemblages and montages in any material; (h) rare manuscripts and incunabula, old books, documents and publications of special interest (historical, artistic, scientific, literary, etc.), singly or in collections; (i) postage, revenue and similar stamps, singly or in collections; (j) archives, including sound, photographic and cinematographic archives; (k) articles of furniture more than one hundred years old and old musical instruments.

8. Another observable fact is that nonwealthy nations do not have substantial private or museum collections of artifacts from wealthy nation cultures. The international traffic in cultural objects, like the traffic in other goods, thus reflects the wealth disparity between the first and third worlds. The significance of this phenomenon for cultural property internationalism is unclear. To date, most efforts have focused on aiding in the establishment and preservation of national collections of works of art and artifacts in third world nations. Chapters IV and V of the UNESCO *Convention Concerning the Protection of the World Cultural and National Heritage* of 16 November 1972, in UNESCO, *Conventions and Recommendations* 75 ff., set out an apparatus for assisting source nations through a "Fund for the Protection of the World Cultural and National Heritage," but a survey of the literature produces little evidence that the Fund has provided significant assistance to needy nations.

9. The case of the Afo-A-Kom, a statue that "embodies the spiritual, political and religious essence of the 35,000 people of the West African kingdom of Kom in Cameroon," is described in Merryman and Elsen, *Law, Ethics, and the Visual Arts*, 267.

10. NAGPRA is the acronym for the *Native American Graves Protection and Repatriation Act* of 1990, 25 U.S.C. §§3001 ff., under which American museums were required to inventory cultural objects and human remains and, on request, return them to recognized Indian nations.

11. Polybius, in *The Histories*, (before 146 B.C.). The English text of this quotation is taken from de Visscher, "International Protection of Works of Art and Historic Monuments," which itself is a translation (translator unidentified) of the passage in de Visscher's originally French article.

12. Grotius, *The Law of War* III, Chapter V, Section I.

13. Grotius, *The Law of War* III, Chapter VI, Section XII.

14. Vattel, *The Law of Nations* III, Chapter 9, Section 168.

15. Vattel, *The Law of Nations* III, Chapter 9, Section 168.

16. Gould, *Trophy of Conquest*, 41. For fuller accounts of the art confiscations of the Italian campaign see Gould, *Trophy of Conquest*, 13ff., and Treue, *Art Plunder*, 147ff.

17. Quoted in Treue, *Art Plunder*, 151.

18. For a discussion of the varying reactions, see Treue, *Art Plunder: The Fate of Works of Art in War and Unrest* (Basil Creighton trans. 1960), 175ff.

19. Quatremère de Quincy, *Lettres au général Miranda sur le déplacement des monuments de l'art de l'Italie*, 88–89. As the title indicates, the letters were an atypical French reaction against and condemnation of the appropriation of works of art by the French armies in Napoléon's Italian campaign.

20. Quatremère de Quincy, *Lettres au général Miranda sur le déplacement des monuments de l'art de l'Italie*, 141–146.

21. Stewart, *Reports of cases argued and determined in the Court of Vice-admiralty at Halifax, in Nova Scotia*. 482. See also Merryman, "Note on *The Marquis de Somerueles*."

22. That the Judge, Alexander (later Sir Alexander) Croke, is referred to as *Dr*. Croke signifies that, like other admiralty judges of the time, he was a civil lawyer. Typically, the English civilians held doctorates from Oxford or Cambridge and were qualified to appear as advocates before the ecclesiastical courts and the Court of Admiralty. The entry for Sir Alexander Croke in the *Dictionary of National Biography* states that he received BCL and DCL degrees from Oxford and was a member of the College of Advocates. In the competition between the civilians and the common lawyers, history was on the latter side, and the College of Advocates was doomed when the Court of Probate Act 1857 abolished the testamentary jurisdiction of the ecclesiastical courts and established the common law Court of Probate. The last surviving member of Doctors' Commons, *alter ego* of the College of Advocates, was Dr. Thomas Hutchinson Tristram, who died in 1912. For the full history see Squibb, *Doctors' Commons*.

23. These ideas are developed in chapters 1–3 of Best, *Humanity in Warfare*.

24. The language of the opinion is dominated by the humane ideal, both in the quoted passage and throughout its text, while French actions seen to be in conflict with that ideal are condemned: "[T]he present governor of *France*, under whose controul that country has fallen back whole centuries in barbarism. . . ." (p. 483). "The lawless government of *France*. . . ." (p. 484). There is, of course, a subtext. Britain was also at war with France, which supported the Americans, and much of the opinion can be read as an effort to separate the Americans, whose interests lay with "the land of their forefathers," from France, the "common enemy."

25. "In part due to their romantic search for the *ius gentium* of the Roman law texts, and in part to their very real international career system, later English civilians developed a commitment to cosmopolitanism and to the ideal of a rational, universal legal science. This civilian commitment was often in sharp contrast to the localized outlook of the common lawyers." Coquillette, *The Civilian Writers of Doctors' Commons*, 8.

26. See Merryman, "Two Ways of Thinking About Cultural Property."

27. Wheaton, *Elements of International Law*, Section 346, 341.

28. Wheaton, *Elements of International Law*, Section 347.

29. Halleck, *International Law*, Ch. XIX, Sections 10–11.

30. The Lieber Code is set out and discussed in Hartigan, *Lieber's Code and the Law of War*, and in Friedman, *The Law of War*, 158ff.

31. Friedman, *The Law of War*, 194.

32. Institute of International Law, *Resolutions of the Institute of International Law Dealing with the Law of Nations*, 36-37.

33. *Convention with Respect to the Law and Customs of War on Land of July 29, 1899*, in Friedman, *The Law of War*, 234.

34. *Convention on the Laws and Customs of War on Land of October 18, 1907*, in Friedman, *The Law of War*, 323.

35. 36 Stat. 2351, TS No. 542.

36. The Hague Rules of Air Warfare of December, 1922-February, 1923, in Friedman, *The Law of War*, 437.

37. League of Nations, *Interamerican Treaty on the Protection of Artistic and Scientific Institutions and Monuments* (hereinafter the *Roerich Pact*).

38. U.S. Department of State, *Draft Declaration and Draft International Convention for the Protection of Monuments and Works of Art in Time of War*.

39. The topic is discussed at <http://www.houseofice.com/history/napoleonandhitler.shtml> last consulted 8/11/04.

40. See materials in Merryman and Elsen, *Law, Ethics and the Visual Arts*, 26–33.

41. The texts of the Convention and its accompanying Protocol (the "First Protocol") are set out in UNESCO, *Conventions and Recommendations*, 13. For a history and commentary on the Convention see Toman, *The Protection of Cultural Property in the Event of Armed Conflict*.

42. The Second Protocol may be viewed at <http://www.unesco.org/culture/laws/hague/html_eng/protocol2.shtml> (Last viewed on 8/17/04) and is reproduced in Merryman and Elsen, *Law, Ethics and the Visual Arts*, 1174. For accounts of the genesis and content of the Second Protocol see Desch, "The Second Protocol to the 1954 Hague Convention for the Protection of Cultural Property in the Event of Armed Conflict," Henckaerts, "New Rules for the Protection of Cultural Property in Armed Conflict," 593. As of December 2003, 20 nations had become parties to the Second Protocol. The United States is not a party.

43. Article 6 (a) of the Second Protocol provides that: "a waiver on the basis of imperative military necessity pursuant to Article 4 paragraph 2 of the Convention may only be invoked to direct an act of hostility against cultural property when and for as long as: i. that cultural property has, by its function, been made into a military objective; and ii. there is no feasible alternative available to obtain a similar military advantage to that offered by directing an act of hostility against that objective; . . . the decision to invoke imperative military necessity shall only be taken by an officer commanding a force the equivalent of a battalion in size or larger, or a force smaller in size where circumstances do not permit otherwise; . . ."

44. Nahlik, *La Protection internationale des biens culturels en cas de conflit armé*, 87.

45. The military necessity doctrine is more fully considered in Merryman, "Two Ways of Thinking About Cultural Property."

46. Constitution of the United Nations Educational, Scientific and cultural Organization Adopted in London on 16 November 1945 and amended by the General Conference at its second, third, fourth, fifth, sixth, seventh, eighth, ninth, tenth, twelfth, fifteenth, seventeenth, nineteenth, twentieth, twenty-first, twenty-fourth, and twenty-fifth sessions.

47. There are 33 such UNESCO instruments. They are listed and reproduced at: <http://portal.unesco.org/en/ev.php-URL_ID=13649&URL_DO=DO_TOPIC&URL_SECTION=-471.html> (last consulted 5/25/04). Those promulgated up to 1980 are published in UNESCO, *Conventions and Recommendations*.

48. Merryman, "The Nation and the Object."

49. UNESCO, *Conventions and Recommendations*, 59ff. As of 5/28/04 there were 104 parties.

50. Merryman, "The Retention of Cultural Property," Merryman, "A Licit International Trade in Cultural Objects," Merryman, "Cultural Property, International Trade, and Human Rights."

51. UNESCO, *Conventions and Recommendations*, 183.

52. Gaskill makes the point more strongly in "They Smuggle History," 21: "Almost nobody has any idea what enormous, fantastic mountains of such 'duplicates' exist in the state-owned museums around the Mediterranean. Italian archaeologists laugh hollowly when newspapers report the theft of some 'unique, priceless' Etruscan vase. They know, but the public does not, how many thousands of these 'unique, priceless' vases they already have in storage and quite literally don't know what to do with."

53. The Convention defines "cultural institution" in Art. 1: " 'cultural institution' shall be taken to mean any permanent establishment administered in the general interest for the purpose of preserving, studying and enhancing cultural property and making it accessible to the public and which is licensed or approved by the competent public authorities of each State."

54. UNESCO, *Conventions and Recommendations*, 211.

55. Online at <http://portal.unesco.org/en/ev.php-URL_ID=13520&URL_DO=DO_TOPIC&URL_SECTION=201.html> Last visited on 8/31/04. As this is written there appear to be only two ratifications, by Panama and Bulgaria.

56. The Declaration is available at <http://portal.unesco.org/en/ev.php-URL_ID=17718&URL_DO=DO_TOPIC&URL_SECTION=201.html> Last viewed on 10/2/04.

57. The Convention may be viewed at <http://portal.unesco.org/en/ev.php-URL_ID=17716&URL_DO=DO_TOPIC&URL_SECTION=201.html> Last visited 9/7/04.

58. CINOA (Confédération des Négociants en Oeuvres d'Art) is an international confederation of art and antiquities dealer associations. Its full *Guidelines* can be found at <http://www.cinoa.org/index.cfm> (Last visited 11/10/04).

59. The Code is set out at, together with information about its origin, at www.unesco.org/culture/legalprotection/committee/html_eng/ethics3.shtml>, last viewed 14 October 2004.

60. The Convention can be viewed at <http://www.unidroit.org/english/conventions/c-cult.htm> last visited 9/17/04.

61. See for example Chippindale and Gill, "Material Consequences of Contemporary Classical Collecting," 505–506.

62. Merryman, "A Licit International Trade in Cultural Objects," 19; Merryman, "Archaeologists Are Not Helping," 26.

63. See for example, Merryman, "The Retention of Cultural Property," Merryman, "A Licit International Trade in Cultural Objects," Merryman, "Cultural Property, International Trade, and Human Rights."

64. The quoted words appear in the Preamble of the 1970 UNESCO *Convention on the Means of Prohibiting and Preventing the Illicit Import, Export, and Transfer of Ownership of Cultural Property*.

65. The quoted words appear in the Preamble of the 1976 UNESCO *Recommendation Concerning the International Exchange of Cultural Property*.

66. The World Trade Organization had 148 members as of 13 October 2004.

67. The North American Free Trade Agreement (NAFTA) and other international trade agreements incorporate the same provisions by reference.

68. Article 29 of the EC Treaty prohibits "Quantitative restrictions on exports, and all measures having equivalent effect" between Member States. The equivalent GATT provision appears in Article XI.

69. The European Court of Justice held, in *Commission of the European Communities v. Republic of Italy*, Judgment of 10 December 1968, Case 7-68, that works of art are "goods" within the meaning of the Treaty of Rome and thus, in principle, subject to the same trade liberalizing rules as other "goods."

70. The English version of the Treaty of Rome uses "national treasures," as does the French version. The German version is *nationales Kulturgut* and the Italian is *patrimonio nazionale*. Commenting on this difference in nomenclature, Biondi, "The Merchant, the Thief & the Citizen," states in footnote 27: "However, there is no doubt that the definition should be uniform, and considering the ECJ's case law on other exceptions, it might be argued that [for Italy] the expression 'national treasures' should be preferred as it is narrower."

71. This topic is explored in Pescatore, "Le Commerce de l'art et le Marché Commun," and Biondi, "The Merchant, the Thief & the Citizen."

72. Pescatore, "Le Commerce de l'art et le Marché Commun." Judge Pescatore wrote the decision of the European Court of Justice in *the Commission v. Italy* case, mentioned in note 69 above.

73. Byrne-Sutton, *Le trafic international des biens culturels sous l'angle de leur revendication par l'Etat d'origine*, 1.

BIBLIOGRAPHY

Best, Geoffrey Francis Andrew. *Humanity in Warfare*. New York: Columbia University Press, 1980.

Biondi, Andrea. "The Merchant, the Thief & the Citizen: The Circulation of Works of Art Within the European Union." *Common Market Law Review* 34 (1997): 1173–1195

Byrne-Sutton, Quentin. *Le Trafic International des Biens Culturels Sous l'Angle de Leur Revendication par l'Etat d'Origine: Aspects de Droit International Privé*. Zurich: Schulthess, 1988.

Chippindale, Christopher, and David W. J. Gill. "Material Consequences of Contemporary Classical Collecting," *American Journal of Archaeology* 104 (2000): 463–511.

Coquillette, Daniel R. *The Civilian Writers of Doctors' Commons, London: Three Centuries of Juristic Innovation in Comparative, Commercial and International Law*. Berlin: Duncker & Humblot, 1988.

Desch, Thomas. "The Second Protocol to the 1954 Hague Convention for the Protection of Cultural Property in the Event of Armed Conflict." *Yearbook of International Humanitarian Law* 2 (1999): 63–90.

de Vattel, Emer de. *The Law of Nations; or, Principles of the Law of Nature, Applied to the Conduct and Affairs of Nations and Sovereigns*, edited by Joseph Chitty. Philadelphia: T. & J. W. Johnson, 1852.

de Visscher, Charles. *International Protection of Works of Art and Historic Monuments*. International Information and Cultural Series 8. Washington: U.S. Department of State, 1949. (Reprinted from Documents and State Papers of June 1949).

Friedman, Leon. *The Law of War: A Documentary History*. New York: Random House, 1972.

Gould, Cecil Hilton Monk. *Trophy of Conquest; The Musée Napoléon and the Creation of the Louvre*. London: Faber and Faber, 1965.

Grotius, Hugo, 1583–1645. *The Rights of War and Peace; Together with the Law of Nature and of Nations*, translated by A. C. Campbell. New York: M. Walter Dunne, 1901.

Halleck, Henry Wager. *International Law: Or, Rules Regulating the Intercourse of States in Peace and War*. San Francisco: H.H. Bancroft, 1861; Holmes Beach, Fl.: Gaunt, 2000.

Hartigan, Richard Shelly, ed. *Lieber's Code and the Law of War*. Chicago: Precedent, 1983.

Henckaerts, Jean-Marie. "New Rules for the Protection of Cultural Property in Armed Conflict." *International Review of the Red Cross* 835 (1999): 593–620.

Institute of International Law, *Resolutions of the Institute of International Law Dealing with the Law of Nations*, edited by James Brown Scott. New York: Oxford University Press, 1916.

League of Nations. *Interamerican Treaty on the Protection of Artistic and Scientific Institutions and Monuments* [the Roerich Pact]. League of Nations Treaty Series 167 (1935): 279. <http://fletcher.tufts.edu/multi/www/roerich.html> (Last visited 8/13/04)

Merryman, John Henry, "Two Ways of Thinking About Cultural Property." *American Journal of International Law* 80 (1986): 831–53. Reprinted in Merryman, *Thinking About the Elgin Marbles*, 67–91.

———. "The Retention of Cultural Property." *University of California at Davis Law Review* 21 (1988): 477–513. Reprinted in *Critical Essays*, 122–156.

———. "The Nation and the Object." *International Journal of Cultural Property* 3 (1994): 61–76. Reprinted in *Critical Essays*, 158–73.

———. "Archaeologists Are Not Helping." *The Art Newspaper*, January 1996. Reprinted in *Critical Essays*, 28–83.

———. "A Licit International Trade in Cultural Objects." *International Journal of Cultural Property* 4 (1995): 13–60. Reprinted in *Critical Essays*, 176–226.

———. "Note on *The Marquie de Somerueles*." *International Journal of Cultural Property* 5 (1996): 321–29.

———. *Thinking About the Elgin Marbles: Critical Essays on Cultural Property, Art and Law*. London, Dordrecht & Cambridge, Mass.: Kluwer Law International, 2000.

———. "Cultural Property, International Trade, and Human Rights." *Cardozo Arts & Entertainment Law Journal* 19 (2001): 51–67. Republished as *Occasional Papers in Intellectual Property from Benjamin N. Cardozo School of Law*, No. 9.

——— and Elsen, Albert E. *Law, Ethics and the Visual Arts*. Fourth Edition. London, The Hague, New York: Kluwer Law International, 2002.

———. "A Licit International Trade in Cultural Objects." In TEFAF (The European Fine Arts Foundation), *Art Market Matters*, 13–36. Helvoirt, Netherlands: TEFAF, 2004.

Nahlik, Stanislaw E. "La Protection internationale des biens culturels en cas de conflit armé." *Recueil des Cours* 120, I (1967): 61–163.

Pescatore, Pierre. "Le Commerce de l'art et le Marché Commun." *Revue trimestrielle de droit Européenne* 21 (1985): 451–62.

Polybius. *The Histories*. Translated by W. R. Paton. Cambridge, Mass.: Harvard University Press; London: Heinemann, 1960.

Quatremère de Quincy, Antoine-Chrysostome. *Lettres au général Miranda sur le déplacement des monuments de l'art de l'Italie*, reproduced with an introduction and notes by Édouard Pommier. Paris: Macula, 1989.

Squibb, George Drewery. *Doctors' Commons: A History of the College of Advocates and Doctors of Law*. Oxford and New York: Clarendon Press, 1977.

Stewart, James. *Reports of cases argued and determined in the Court of Vice-admiralty at Halifax, in Nova Scotia*. London: J. Butterworth, 1813.

Thompson, Michael. *Rubbish Theory: The Creation and Destruction of Value*. Oxford and New York: Oxford University Press, 1979.

Toman, Jiri. *The Protection of Cultural Property in the Event of Armed Conflict*. Aldershot: Dartmouth Publishing Co.; Paris: UNESCO, 1996.

Treue, Wilhelm. *Art Plunder; the Fate of Works of Art in War, Revolution and Peace*, translated by Basil Creighton. London: Methuen, 1960.

UNIDROIT. *Convention on Stolen or Illegally Exported Cultural Objects* of 24 June 1995. http://www.unidroit.org/english/conventions/c-cult.htm (accessed 18 August 2004).

United Nations Educational, Scientific and Cultural Organization. *Convention Concerning the Protection of the World Cultural and National Heritage* of 16 November 1972. In UNESCO, *Conventions and Recommendations*, 75.

———. *Conventions and Recommendations of UNESCO Concerning the Protection of the Cultural Heritage*. Paris: UNESCO, 1983. Reprinted and updated in 1985.

U.S. Department of State. *Draft Declaration and Draft International Convention for the Protection of Monuments and Works of Art in Time of War*. Documents and State Papers 1 (1949 [1939]): 859.

Wheaton, Henry. *Elements of International Law*, edited by Richard Henry Dana, 8th ed. Boston: Little, Brown, 1866.

[2]

ON DEFINING THE CULTURAL HERITAGE

Janet Blake*

I. THE DEVELOPMENT OF INTERNATIONAL CULTURAL HERITAGE LAW

Examples can be found from ancient times of concern for the protection of cultural artefacts[1] and early legislation to protect monuments and works of art first appeared in Europe in the 15th century.[2] Cultural heritage was first addressed in international law in 1907[3] and a body of international treaties and texts for its protection has been developed by UNESCO and other intergovernmental organisations since the 1950's. The 1954 Convention for the Protection of Cultural Property in the Event of Armed Conflict[4] of UNESCO (henceforth the "Hague Convention") is the earliest of these modern international texts and was developed in great part in response to the destruction and looting of monuments and works of art during the Second World War. It grew out of a feeling that action to prevent their deterioration or destruction was one responsibility of the emerging international world order and an element in reconciliation and the prevention of future conflicts. International law relating to the protection of cultural heritage thus began with comparatively narrow objectives, the protection of cultural property in time of war.

In 1956 UNESCO adopted a Recommendation on the conduct of archaeological excavations[5] which, despite its limited subject-matter, contained principles fundamental to subsequent UNESCO instruments: that the protection of cultural heritage is incumbent on States owing to the importance which it holds for all of Mankind and as a means of encouraging international co-operation and thus prevention of international conflict, as well as "the feelings aroused by the ... study of works of the past do much to foster mutual understanding between nations, and that ... the international community as a whole is nevertheless the richer for such discoveries", (Preamble). Further UNESCO Recommendations followed on specific questions, including the accessibility of museums

---

* University of Glasgow.
 1. *Vide:* B. G. Trigger *A History of Archaeological Thought* (sixth edition, Cambridge University Press, 1994) at pp.29–30 and 36.
 2. L. V. Prott and P. J. O'Keefe *Law and the Cultural Heritage* volume I (Professional Books, 1984) at p.34.
 3. 1907 Hague Regulations concerning the Law and Customs of War on Land protect "historic monuments" from sieges and bombardments.
 4. 249 U.N.T.S. 24.
 5. Recommendation on International Principles Applicable to Archaeological Excavations, UNESCO 5 Dec. 1956.

(1960),[6] safeguarding the beauty of landscapes and sites (1962)[7] and preserving cultural property endangered by public or private works (1968).[8] Two UNESCO Conventions were adopted in the early 1970s, relating to the prohibition and prevention of trafficking in cultural property (1970)[9] and the protection of world cultural and natural heritage (1972),[10] while five further UNESCO Recommendations were adopted between 1972 and 1980. Thus the main body of international texts relating to the protection and preservation of cultural heritage is of relatively recent date. It is worth noting that the three Conventions so far adopted by UNESCO reflect the political and/or intellectual concerns of the time at which they were developed: the 1954 Convention expressed the powerful post-World War II desire to reduce potential sources of international conflict; the 1970 Convention embodied an approach to cultural property which might be characterised as "nationalist" or "statist" whereby the interest of the State of origin (often in the developing world) should be paramount, mirroring the strong feeling within UNESCO during the 1970's amongst developing nations that the power of the dominant developed States should be counteracted;[11] and the 1972 Convention reflected both the growing concern in environmentalist issues in its integration of the cultural with the natural heritage as well as the concept of a "common heritage of mankind" which had been developing at this time in relation to seabed mineral resources.

II. THE PROBLEM WITH "CULTURAL HERITAGE"

To some degree, therefore, the growing body of international instruments and other texts relating to cultural heritage was driven by contemporary concerns and intellectual fashions, further illustrating the lack of a single set of well-established principles underpinning this body of international law. There exists a difficulty of interpretation of the core concepts of "Cultural heritage" (or "cultural property") and "cultural heritage of mankind" and as yet no generally agreed definition of the

---

6. Recommendation concerning the most Effective Means of Rendering Museums Accessible to Everyone, UNESCO 14 Dec. 1960.
7. Recommendation concerning the Safeguarding of the Beauty and Character of Landscapes and Sites, UNESCO 11 Dec. 1962.
8. Recommendation concerning the Preservation of Cultural Property Endangered by Public or Private Works, UNESCO 19 Nov. 1968.
9. Convention on the Means of Prohibiting and Preventing the Illicit Import, Export and Transfer of Ownership of Cultural Property, 14 Nov. 1970 [823 U.N.T.S. 231].
10. Convention concerning the Protection of the World Cultural and Natural Heritage, 16 Nov. 1972 [11 I.L.M. 1358].
11. M'Bow, then Director-General of UNESCO, voiced such sentiments in *A plea for the Return of an Irreplaceable Cultural heritage to those who Created It* delivered in 1979: "The men and women of these [despoiled] countries have the right to recover these cultural assets which are part of their being... The return of a work of art to the country which created it enables a people to recover part of its memory and identity...", UNESCO Doc.SHC–76/CONF.615.5 (1979).

content of these terms appears to exist. The increasing global importance of cultural heritage instruments and the ever-expanding scope of the term and the areas in which it is used require a workable definition of the nature of the cultural heritage. Each such expansion introduces much more complex issues concerning the nature of cultural heritage and the construction of cultural identity than were apparent in earlier developments in this field. The danger therefore exists of creating future international instruments which extend the range of the term without having settled on a clear understanding of its meaning as employed in existing texts.

Writing in 1984, Prott and O'Keefe[12] noted that, "... for various reasons each Convention and Recommendation has a definition drafted for the purposes of that instrument alone; it may not, at this stage be possible to achieve a general definition suitable for use in a variety of contexts". Fifteen years on, it is time for lawyers and other specialists in the area of the cultural heritage to confront this and to consider the different meanings given to the above terms in various international legal texts as well as those implicit in their use but not explicitly stated. Although each instrument includes a definition which lists or otherwise describes the subject of that text, the lack of any generally agreed definition means that these must be interpreted internally without reference to any set of principles. This should not be seen as a criticism of the existing treaty texts and Recommendations themselves. The three UNESCO multilateral Conventions are similar to human rights instruments in setting standards worldwide and the Recommendations can have great influence on national practice despite not being binding on Parties. They have an important role in confronting specific problems and threats to the cultural heritage. However, there now exists a critical mass of treaty and other texts (including those from other intergovernmental organisations) which form a recognised body of international law and it is time to reassess its exact nature since cultural heritage as a concept has grown so far that it may well have become greater than the sum of its constituent parts.

Indeed, there appears to be the assumption of a common understanding of the content of the "cultural heritage" which fails to take into consideration its wider implications. This is compounded by the fact that the concept of "cultural heritage" has itself been imported from other academic disciplines such as anthropology and archaeology without incorporating the theoretical background which led to its development *viz.* the conceptual framework which gives it content and meaning. This difficulty was signalled by Prott writing in 1989,[13] "While cultural experts

---

12. Prott and O'Keefe, *op. cit. supra* n.2, at p.8.
13. L. V. Prott "Problems of Private International Law for the Protection of the Cultural Heritage", *Recueil des Cours* vol.V (1989) pp.224–317 at p.224.

of various disciplines have a fairly clear conception of the subject-matter of their study, the legal definition of the cultural heritage is one of the most difficult confronting scholars today." There may be no difficulty, for example, in understanding the intention of the 1970 UNESCO Convention as to the nature of the "cultural property" which it protects. There is, however, a difficulty with any attempt to identify exactly the range of meanings encompassed by the term cultural heritage as used now in international law and related areas since it has grown beyond the much narrower definitions included on a text-by-text basis. Recent work at UNESCO to develop strategies for the protection of intangible cultural heritage illustrates this problem.[14] First, there is a great difficulty in identifying the exact content and nature of intangible cultural heritage to be protected and, to some degree, this is a question which should have been addressed earlier in relation to the cultural heritage in general. Second, the characterisation of folklore as "part of the universal heritage of humanity"[15] while at the same time noting its power in asserting the cultural identity of the community which produced it contains an inherent contradiction since the very character which renders this heritage folklore—its intimate relationship to the identity of a specific community or people—is in opposition to the idea of it being a "heritage of mankind" in any but a very distant sense. This illustrates a wider problem of cultural heritage law articulated by Lowenthal:[16] "Too much is asked of heritage. In the same breath, we commend national patrimony, regional and ethnic legacies and a global heritage shared and sheltered in common. We forget that these aims are usually incompatible." As Prott notes, globalist concepts of the cultural heritage have now been adopted into legal discourse and UNESCO's universalist task in setting international standards is in parallel with such developments as well as globalisation of the economy.[17] An illustration of this is the UNESCO programme aimed at creating a world list of "masterpieces of the intangible and oral heritage" modelled on the 1972 World Heritage Convention.[18] Further elaboration of the core concepts of "cultural heritage of humankind"

---

14. Recommendation on the Safeguarding of Traditional Culture and Folklore, UNESCO 15 Nov. 1989. The Executive Council of UNESCO has also established a programme for the identification "masterpieces of the intangible and oral heritage of mankind" for their protection [UNESCO Doc.155/EX 15, Paris 25 Aug. 1998].
15. 1989 Recommendation, *op. cit. supra*.
16. D. Lowenthal *The Heritage Crusade and the Spoils of History* (Viking, 1997) at p.227.
17. L. V. Prott "International Standards for Cultural Heritage," in UNESCO *World Culture Report* (Unesco publishing, Paris, 1998) at pp.222–236.
18. *Vide supra* n.14 for details.

(and similar terms) is clearly needed since the current conflation of inconsistent categories is problematic in the long term.[19]

III. IDENTIFYING CULTURAL HERITAGE

A. *"Cultural heritage" or "cultural property"?*

Traditionally, "cultural property" has generally been the term of art employed in international law to denote the subject of protection. Examples of this would be UNESCO's 1954 Hague Convention protecting cultural property in the event of armed conflict and the 1970 Convention controlling the illicit movement of cultural items.[20] The items concerned require protection because they are being treated as property to be bought and sold in the market-place without primary regard given to their value as cultural heritage. The 1978 UNESCO Recommendation[21] gives the following definition: "movable cultural property shall be taken to mean all movable objects which are the expression and testimony of human creation or of the evolution of nature and which are of archaeological, historical, artistic, scientific or technical value and interest ..." (Article 1). This makes reference to the importance of other values, such as the informational one derived from context, but such qualifications do not answer the broader difficulties with the term "property" as applied to cultural artefacts.

As a broad category to describe elements of the cultural heritage in international law it remains problematic and an alternative usage which does not carry with it the ideological baggage of "cultural property" is preferable. Property is a fundamental legal concept around which important political and philosophical theories have developed.[22] It carries with it a range of ideological baggage which is difficult to shed when using the term in relation to the cultural heritage or environmental protection where one needs to modify these associated traditional values in order to achieve the social goals desired. It is problematic to apply a legal concept involving the rights of the possessor to the protection of cultural resources which may involve a severe curtailment of such rights and the separation

---

19. Prott, *op. cit. supra* n.17, at p.228 notes: "The precise legal implications of terms such as 'the common cultural heritage', 'world cultural heritage' and similar phrases are not yet clear, although their use in legal instruments makes it imperative to explore the subject."
20. Cited, *supra* n.4 and n.9.
21. Recommendation for the Protection of Movable Cultural Property, UNESCO 28 Nov. 1978.
22. L. V. Prott and P. J. O'Keefe " 'Cultural Heritage' or 'Cultural Property'?" 1:2 I.J.C.P. (1992) pp.307–320 at pp.309–312 consider traditional property law values in the context of cultural heritage law, making reference to points such as: the protection of the rights of the possessor; the important function of "property" and "ownership" in Western legal tradition; and the dangers of commoditisation of cultural heritage.

of access and control from ownership.[23] Implicit also in the use of the term "cultural property" is the idea of assigning to it a market value, in other words the "commodification" of cultural artefacts and related elements by treating them as commodities to be bought and sold. There has been much debate over the ethics of trading in cultural artefacts, in particular archaeological materials, and the value of different legal approaches.[24]

The strongest argument against the use of the term "cultural property" is that it is too limited to encompass the range of possible elements—both tangible and intangible—which can comprise the cultural elements being described. These might include monuments and complexes of buildings, sites of archaeological or historic significance, ancient works of art (including rock carvings and cave paintings), ethnographic items, places associated with the development of a technology or industry, landscapes and topographical features, grave sites, sacred places and ritual sites, natural features endowed with special cultural significance to a people, items of clothing or jewellery, weapons, daily utensils, ritual items, musical instruments, objects associated with certain historical characters, coins, carved obsidian or ivory, fossils, skeletal remains, pollen samples, ancient copper or tin mines—the potential list is extensive. These examples given above relate only to physical remains which have typically been the subject of laws for the protection of the cultural heritage. There exist also elements of intangible culture which would include, for example, the know-how related to a particular type of ship-building, oral poetry or musical traditions, ceremonial and ritual traditions, aspects of the way of life of certain societies and the special relationship between certain peoples and the land they inhabit. This category above all makes clear the extreme limitations of applying the term "cultural property" to such elements, some of which are expressed only in terms of knowledge or ideas. Prott[25] notes that it is a purely Western legal category which is far too narrow and that it has been global influences that have allowed the broadening of the concept of cultural heritage.

The relationship between "cultural property" or "cultural heritage" is unclear, appearing interchangeable in some cases, while in others, cultural property is a sub-group within "cultural heritage". The 1968 UNESCO Recommendation,[26] suggests that "cultural property" has a

---

23. Such as French Law No.89–874 of 1 Dec. 1989 on Maritime Cultural Property which allows the State to intervene for the preservation of archaeological wrecks if the identified owner fails to do so themself (Art. 11).

24. *Vide*: J. H. Merryman "A Licit International Trade in Cultural Objects", 4 I.J.C.P. (1995) pp.13–60; C. Coggins "A Licit International Trade in Ancient Art: Let There be Light!" 4 I.J.C.P. (1995) pp.61–80; and H. K. Wiehe "Licit International Traffic in Cultural Objects for Art's Sake" 4 I.J.C.P. (1995) pp.81–90.

25. Prott, *op. cit. supra* n.17.

26. Cited *supra* n.8.

meaning extending well beyond objects themselves: "... the product and witness of the different traditions and of the spiritual achievements of the past and thus is an essential element in the personality of the peoples of the world (preamble)". The definition of the term "cultural property" given in Article 1 of the Hague Convention (1954) as "movable or immovable property of great importance to the cultural heritage" clearly shows it to be one element within the cultural heritage. Only two UNESCO instruments refer to "cultural heritage" in their titles[27] and it is worth noting that both deal with "cultural and natural heritage". This is no doubt in part due to the fact that to talk of "natural property" would be a very strange construction but there is, however, a more significant point which suggests a common character between cultural and natural heritage as resources (one man-made, the other not) which should be preserved for future generations in view of their importance on a cultural and environmental level. There is an aspect of "natural heritage" which forms a part of the cultural heritage given the importance of certain landscapes and natural features to particular groups and cultures.[28] Cultural heritage as defined in these two instruments includes elements of an apparently mundane character such as topographical features and cultural landscapes and it is the relationship of humans to these elements (an intangible element) which gives them their importance and which renders them subject to protection. This leads one to the conclusion that "cultural heritage" has now become the term of art in international law[29] since it is capable of encompassing this much broader range of possible elements, including the intangibles mentioned above.

B. *The nature of "cultural heritage"*

Clearly, when seeking to understand the nature and content of the term "cultural heritage" it is necessary to consider the two constituent elements which make it up: "culture" and "heritage". A major difficulty lies with the identification of "culture" and what constitutes it and if we look at the following definition of "culture" given by an anthropologist,[30] the complexity of the question becomes clear:

> ... it is a totalizing concept because everything becomes, or is considered, culture. There are material culture, ritual culture, symbolic culture, social

---

27. 1972 Convention cited *supra* n.10; Recommendation concerning the Protection, at National Level, of the Cultural and Natural Heritage, UNESCO 16 Nov. 1972.
28. As the 1962 UNESCO Recommendation cited *supra* n.7 asserts, landscapes "represent a powerful physical, moral and spiritual regenerating influence, while at the same time contributing to the artistic and cultural life of peoples ...".
29. Prott and O'Keefe, *op. cit. supra* n.22.
30. G. M. Sider *Culture and Class in Anthropology and History* (Cambridge University Press, 1986) at p.6.

institutions, patterned behaviour, language-as-culture, values, beliefs, ideas ideologies, meanings and so forth. Second, not only is almost everything in a society culture, but the concept is also totalizing because everything in the society is supposed to have the same culture (as in the concept of culture as shared values) ...

This definition is far too extensive and inclusive to be of use as the basis for defining the "culture" at the root of cultural heritage legislation. It does, however, underline the existence of a strong intangible element to culture and it is clear that the material culture—the apparent subject of most existing cultural heritage legislation—makes up only a part of all that might be regarded as "culture". Cultural heritage is obviously a more limited category than that of "culture" with "heritage" acting as a qualifier which allows us to narrow it down to a more manageable set of elements. The concept of "heritage" also provides one of the central characteristics of the phrase which determine its legal significance. It would include such elements as the "material culture, ritual culture, symbolic culture" and even "language-as-culture, values, beliefs", while, in some circumstances, "ideas ideologies, [and] meanings" might also be included. Clearly a useful definition of cultural heritage for the purposes of this study cannot include "everything in society". Rather, our understanding of the term will be gained by understanding the relationship between cultural heritage and culture itself. It is the symbolic relationship of the cultural heritage to culture in its widest sense (culture-as-society) which is central to understanding the nature of cultural heritage.

One must recognise that the identification of cultural heritage is based on an active choice as to which elements of this broader "culture" are deemed worthy of preservation as an "inheritance" for the future. Through this, the significance of cultural heritage as symbolic of the culture and those aspects of it which a society (or group) views as valuable is recognised. It is this role of cultural heritage which lends it its powerful political dimension since the decision as to what is deemed worthy of protection and preservation is generally made by State authorities on national level and by intergovernmental organisations—comprising member States—on international level. The national legislation and international law relating to cultural heritage are the formal expression of these political decisions and, as with most political questions, there is always room for controversy and competing claims. Indeed, competing claims and conflicts of interest on national and international level are endemic to any discussion of cultural heritage. It is not simply that decisions concerning cultural heritage often have important political consequences which they clearly do, but also the more fundamental point that the identification of cultural heritage is in itself a political act given its symbolic relationship to culture and society in general.

The idea of inheritance is central to the force of the term cultural heritage and adds a further set of notions to its meaning. It appears relatively straightforward to view cultural heritage as a valuable resource which we as a society wish to preserve in order to pass it on to future generations as their inheritance. This view of cultural heritage lies behind much of the rhetoric of the international law on the subject and reflects a powerful emotional impulse as well as an intellectual position. The 1972 UNESCO Convention[31] makes this clear in the following duty placed on contracting States in Article 4: "... of ensuring the identification, protection, conservation, presentation and *transmission to future generations* of the cultural and natural heritage" (emphasis added). The 1968 UNESCO Recommendation[32] expresses a similar attitude in the preamble, stating that: "cultural property is the product and witness of the different traditions and of the spiritual achievements of the past ...". Relatively few UNESCO Conventions and Recommendations make such explicit statements of the character of cultural heritage as an inheritance from past generations (and the present) to be passed on to future ones. However, it is implicit in most (whether they refer to the term "heritage" or not in the text) and provides a basic principle which underpins this whole body of international law. Thus far, there seems little difficulty in accepting this approach since it resonates with an instinctive response which most of us feel towards what we view as our cultural heritage. However, one should not forget the political aspect of the decision as to what is to be preserved for future generations. A central idea which accompanies the view of cultural heritage as a form of inheritance is its characterisation as a non-renewable resource akin to the environment or even mineral resources. Lowenthal[33] draws out the connection between the cultural heritage and natural resources: "That the natural heritage is global is now beyond dispute. Fresh water and fossil fuels, rain forests and gene pools are legacies common to us all and need all care. Cultural resources likewise form part of the universal heritage."

This reference to "universal heritage" brings into the equation a further characterisation of cultural heritage as the "common heritage of mankind" (CHM), placing it alongside a broader category of non-renewable resources. Joyner identifies five elements of the CHM notion

---

31. Cited *supra* n.10.
32. Cited *supra* n.8.
33. Lowenthal, *op. cit. supra* n.16, at p.228.

as applied to common space areas,[34] and these should be borne in mind when considering its application to cultural heritage. The CHM doctrine was first developed in international law in relation to deep seabed mineral resources[35] and was subsequently applied to the moon and its natural resources.[36] The Preamble to the 1959 Antarctic Treaty makes reference to the notion,[37] although its failure to designate the area as non-appropriable as well as the exclusivity of the "Antarctic Club" of the 12 original signatory States (plus "consultative parties") mean that the notion has minimal influence in the area.[38]

The CHM notion has become an influential concept in our thinking about cultural heritage and is one that requires us to re-assess many of our assumptions about the nature of cultural heritage and rights to its enjoyment and control. There are, however, difficulties with applying the notion to cultural heritage.[39] For example, one of the first attempts was in the 1982 Law of the Sea Convention (and thus in the context of resource-related law). This illustrates the potential for contradiction inherent in applying the notion to elements of cultural heritage given the need also to respect the special interests of the State of origin.[40] In contrast, the Convention on Biological Diversity[41] uses the term "common concern of humankind" in order to avoid attributing the status of a

---

34. C. Joyner "Legal Implications of the Concept of the Common Heritage of Mankind", 35 I.C.L.Q. (1986) pp.190–199 at 192. The five elements listed are that: the areas are not subject to appropriation of any kind and sovereignty is absent; all people are expected to share in the management of the area and States act only as agents of "all mankind"; resources should only be exploited under the auspices of a common space regime mandate and any economic benefits should be shared internationally; uses of the area should be for exclusively peaceful purposes; and scientific research should be freely and openly permissible and for the benefit of all peoples. See also: A-C. Kiss "La notion du patrimoine commun de l'humanite," *Recueil des Cours* (1992 –II) pp.99–256.
35. UN Law of the Sea Convention (1982) [21 I.L.M. 1261]—Art.136 states: "The [deep seabed] Area and its resources are the common heritage of mankind" and Art.137 proceeds to set out the legal status of the Area and its resources.
36. Agreement Governing the Activities of States on the Moon and Other Celestial Bodies [UN Doc.A/AC.105/L.113/Add.4 (1979)] entered into force on 11 June 1984 [18 I.L.M. 1434], known as the "Moon Treaty". Art.11(1) reads: "The moon and its natural resources are the common heritage of mankind."
37. 402 U.N.T.S. 71, 1 Dec. 1959; Preamble notes that, "it is in the interests of all mankind that Antarctic shall continue forever to be used exclusively for peaceful purposes ...".
38. *Vide*: B. Larschan and B. Brennan "The Common Heritage of Mankind Principle in International Law", 21:2 *Columbia Journal of Transnational Law* (1983) pp.305–337 at p.334; and F. Francioni (ed.) *International Environmental Law for Antarctica* (Giuffre Editore, Milan, 1992).
39. *Vide supra* at n.16.
40. Art.149 reads: "All objects of an archaeological and historical nature found in the Area shall be preserved or disposed of for the benefit of mankind as a whole, particular regard being paid to the preferential rights of the State or country of origin, or the State of cultural origin, or the State of historical and archaeological origin."
41. UN Convention on Biodiversity, 22 June 1992 [31 I.L.M. 818].

"common heritage" to biological resources with its legal implications.[42] By using this formulation, international interest in the conservation and use of the resource is legitimised without challenging the territorial sovereignty of the State where it is located. The desire to avoid internationalising the ownership of biological resources[43] is also relevant to cultural heritage.[44] The 1979 UNESCO Convention,[45] which stresses the non-renewable character of cultural heritage, also respects State territorial sovereignty[46] although characterising it as CHM at the same time. Thus cultural heritage remains under the legislation and sovereignty of the territorial State while also representing a universal value towards whose protection the whole international community should co-operate. Kiss[47] sees this as a significant aspect of the Convention, although other commentators have criticised it for failing to go further and establishing an international agency to administer those elements of cultural heritage that form a "universal heritage".[48] Thus there remain unresolved questions over the application of the CHM notion to cultural heritage, how best to do this effectively and whether it should be applied to its full extent or in a more limited sense.

The common space areas to which the CHM notion is applied are also treated as an inheritance to be transmitted to future generations, a sort of international patrimony. This last echoes strongly the way in which cultural heritage characterised as "cultural heritage of mankind" is viewed. Regarding the cultural heritage as an inheritance is not new and dates at least from the birth of UNESCO: Article 1 of the UNESCO Constitution (1948)[49] requires the Organisation to "assure the conservation and protection of the world's inheritance of works of art and

---

42. M. Bowman and C. Redgwell *International Law and the Conservation of Biological Diversity* (Kluwer Law, London, 1996) at p.40.
43. As the 1982 LOSC (cited *supra* n.35) does for deep seabed mineral deposits, for example.
44. Cultural heritage shares many of the characteristics of biological resources, such as its non-renewable nature and the importance given to safeguarding cultural diversity.
45. Cited *supra* n.10.
46. Art.6(1). This has been criticised as a compromise that limits the effectiveness of the Convention although it is a necessary one to ensure a sufficient number of signatory States.
47. Kiss, *op. cit. supra* n.34, at p.171: "Elle consacre le principe que certains biens se trouvant sous la souverainte d'Etats ont un interet qui concerne tout l'humanite et que, de ce fait, ils doivent etre conserves par les soins de la communaute internationale tout entiere."
48. J. Simmonds "UNESCO World Heritage Convention", 2:3 *Art, Antiquity and Law* (1997) pp.251–281 at p.253 makes the point that: "[t]he Convention in no way 'internationalises' outstanding property, but rather emphasis that the primary responsibility for it lies with international co-operation and assistance in a supplementary role. The more radical approach would have established a distinct and novel international heritage, administered by an international agency."
49. Constitution of the United Nations Educational, Scientific and Cultural Organisation (1945) [4 U.N.T.S. 275].

monuments of history and science". What has changed over the years is the great broadening of the concept of what is to be regarded as comprising this inheritance, moving from a narrow definition of selected physical elements of "high culture" to often mundane cultural artefacts which express society more generally, and even to non-material elements of culture. The connection made between culture and nature (the environment) as expressed by the 1972 UNESCO Convention,[50] whereby cultural heritage is viewed as non-renewable resource in the same way as a wilderness area or rainforest, an extension of the concept from 1948 and one which also adds a further dimension to the idea of cultural heritage. This relates also to the rights of indigenes to their natural environment as a cultural as well as natural resource, underlining both the intricate relationship between environment and culture and between cultural heritage and cultural rights.[51] The submission from the Czech Republic to the Helsinki Conference of the Council of Europe in 1995[52] sums up this development of the concept:

> Enlargement of the concept of cultural heritage to cultural aspects or cultural resources of the environment and of society—listed and unlisted, known and unknown, material and immaterial. They are similarly non-renewable and for human life, health and safety as necessary as natural resources of the environment.

When searching for a satisfactory definition of "cultural heritage", a fundamental question is to the extent of the term. Is it limited only to those physical elements such as monuments, sites and artefacts already regarded as part of it or does it extend also to cover the non-material "intangibles" upon which people(s) pin their sense of identity? Since the mid-1980's, there has been an increasing appreciation that these intangibles which relate to sets of knowledge and know-how, patterns of behaviour and oral traditions, for example, have been ignored in international law relating to the cultural heritage. There have been moves to remedy this in the work by UNESCO on expressions of traditional culture and folklore[53] and in the area of the cultural rights of indigenous

---

50. For example, Bouchenaki, M. notes in "The world heritage" 3 *European Heritage* (1995) that: "This Convention, adopted in Paris in 1972, is a real breakthrough in that it reflects the international community's awakening of (*sic*) two crucial factors: firstly, the connection between culture and nature and, secondly, the need for a permanent protective framework covering both legal, administrative and financial aspects."

51. *Vide*: J. Sutherland *et al* "Emerging Legal Standards for Comprehensive Rights", 27/1 *Environmental Policy & Law* (1997) at pp.13–30.

52. *Enhancement of the Cultural Heritage of Central and Eastern Europe* (Strasbourg, 1996), Doc.MPC-4(96)5 at p.3.

53. *Vide supra* n.14. An international conference on *A Global Assessment of The 1989 Recommendation on the Safeguarding of Traditional Culture and Folklore: Local Empowerment and International Cooperation* was jointly held by the Smithsonian Institution and UNESCO in Washington D.C., 27–30 June 1999 in order to assess the 1989 Recommendation and UNESCO's other work in the area of intangible cultural heritage.

and tribal peoples.[54] It is appropriate also to mention recent developments in the Council of Europe in this area since there has been a growing acceptance in that Organisation of the importance of this aspect of the cultural heritage both in the cultural and human rights domains. The broadening of the concept of cultural heritage at the Council of Europe level is illustrated by work begun in the late-1980's[55] aimed at identifying the concept of cultural landscapes as a new component of cultural heritage policy. Although still a physical element of the cultural heritage, cultural landscapes bring us closer to the intangible elements since their study often relates to ethnographic information about the way of life of people as well as the close links existing between certain topographical and landscape features and cultural identity.

In 1993, a summit meeting of the Council of Europe Heads of State[56] made a direct connection between cultural heritage and the human rights dimension of the work of the Organisation, calling for it to "[give] expression in the legal field to the values that define our European identity" which also suggests a relationship between the political aims of pluralist democracy and human rights, cultural heritage and its role in the construction of identity. Following this, texts emanating from the Helsinki Conference of Ministers responsible for the Cultural Heritage (1995)[57] recognised that existing definitions of cultural heritage are too limited. The new elements to be included generally relate to the immaterial aspects of cultural heritage, as in the interface between material elements and a sense of cultural identity. The general text from the 1995 Helsinki Conference,[58] for example, states that present definitions of cultural heritage are still too narrow and that:

> "the relationship that must exist between the cultural heritage and the natural and social environment to which it belongs is underestimated. Lastly, being based on architectural and archaeological heritage, these definitions focus on the physical side, completely ignoring the question of its function in contemporary society." (at 5)

A further document from the Helsinki Conference produced by Finland[59] proposes a definition of cultural heritage which concentrates particularly on its intangible elements: "In a wide sense, the concept of the cultural heritage covers all the manifestations and messages of

---

54. *Vide supra* n.52.
55. Following adoption of the 1985 Convention on the Architectural Heritage of Europe [*ETS* no.121].
56. *Vienna Declaration* of the Council of Europe Summit, Vienna, 9 Oct. 1993.
57. IVth European Conference of Ministers responsible for the Cultural Heritage, Helsinki, 30–31 May 1995, Docs. MPC–4(96)1 rev. to MPC–4(96)15.
58. *The Cultural Heritage—an Economic and Social Challenge* (produced as a General text of the conference) at p.5.
59. *Cultural Heritage—a Key to the Future* (Strasbourg, 1996) Doc. MPC–4(96)7 p.1.

intellectual activity in our environment. These messages are passed on from generation to generation through learning, intellectual quest and insights." Such manifestations of cultural heritage (in all its various forms) are seen as "mediated through" the built environment and the landscape. Thus we have the idea that the physical elements of cultural heritage—that which has been traditionally viewed as comprising it—are in fact the vehicles by which cultural heritage (in its intangible sense) is mediated to us. This strongly suggests the importance of considering these intangibles when framing future instruments, even where the ostensible subject may be material cultural elements.[60] The intimate relationship between cultural heritage and the social and political dimension—its function in society—is made clear by the Swedish delegation's text[61] which states that:

> Clearly, the development of society can be interpreted through cultural heritage which sheds light on the problems and difficulties facing us. Similarly, it can be used to legitimise social and political ambitions, which is not necessarily a good thing. However, if properly used, the cultural heritage provides an identity and a measure of stability for multi-ethnic societies and in periods marked by mobility and rapid change.

The significance of this statement is the stress it places on the importance of understanding the political and social aspects of policies towards cultural heritage and the way in which this can work as a power for good or for bad. It is for this reason that a clear understanding and definition at international level of the concept of cultural heritage is vital since much can flow from this in terms both of public policy and of possible unintended outcomes. It is also imperative to understand the degree to which the notion of what is deemed to comprise cultural heritage is not an absolute but is in fact an act of deliberate selection, as shown by Williams:[62]

> For tradition ("our cultural heritage") is self-evidently a process of deliberate continuity, yet any tradition can be shown, by analysis, to be a selection and reselection of those significant received and recovered elements of the past which represent not a necessary but a desired continuity.

This act of selection is often a "political" decision undertaken by national authorities, and various UNESCO texts relating to cultural heritage and cultural property also stress the political context within

---

60. For example, current work by a diplomatic conference established by UNESCO to review the 1954 Hague Convention is illustrative of a recognition that the existing law does not take sufficient account of the motivation behind the destruction of cultural heritage in time of armed conflict which relates to its role in the construction of identity.
61. *Aspects of Heritage and Education* (Strasbourg, 1996), Doc.MPC–4(96)15 p.3.
62. R. Williams, *Culture* (Fontana, Glasgow, 1982) p.187.

which such protective measures operate.[63] For example, the 1972 Convention[64] states in its Preamble that the "deterioration or disappearance of any item of cultural or natural heritage constitutes a harmful impoverishment of all the nations in the world" while the 1970 Convention[65] notes that "the interchange of cultural property among nations for scientific, cultural and educational purposes ... inspires mutual respect and appreciation among nations" (Preamble). These international instruments should be placed in the context of their underlying politics which is more complex than these statements suggest. The 1970 Convention, for or example, reflected a contemporary struggle between developing and developed nations over control of art-works and archaeological remains set in the wider political context of post-colonialism.[66] The 1972 Convention can be seen as reflecting another ideological position gaining currency at the time, that of a globalist approach towards protection of natural (and cultural) resources as the "common heritage of mankind".[67] A further illustration of the way in which cultural heritage texts can be seen as reflecting the political interests of the organisation to which they belong is given in the Final Declaration from the Helsinki Conference: "... the values inherent in cultural heritage and the policies needed to conserve it can make an important contribution to the aims of democracy and balanced development pursued by the Council of Europe."[68] Recognising the importance of intangibles to the concept of cultural heritage, in particular, has some serious implications in political and social terms which extend well beyond the traditionally accepted boundaries of the term. These include, for example, complex areas such as the construction of cultural identity, the significance of the destruction of cultural (and religious) monuments as a weapon of war and the existence of cultural rights of minorities and indigenous and tribal peoples which introduce a completely different and at times subversive view of the cultural heritage.

C. *Cultural heritage, cultural identity and cultural rights*

One area in which this broadening of the concept of cultural heritage has taken place is that of cultural rights, which in the 1990's has involved

---

63. *Vide* A. D. Smith *Nations and Nationalism in a Global Era* (Polity Press, 1998) pp. 121–143 for a critique of attempts at creating a European "super-state" and European identity.
64. Cited *supra* n.10.
65. Cited *supra* n.9.
66. Universal Declaration of the Rights of Peoples (Algiers, 1976) cited in L. V. Prott "Cultural Rights and Peoples' Rights in International Law" in J. Crawford *The Rights of Peoples* (Clarendon Press, Oxford, 1988) at pp.93–106.
67. *Vide supra* n.34.
68. *Final Declaration* of the 1995 Helsinki Conference of the Council of Europe *vide supra* n.31, point I.C. at p.2.

direct consideration of the humanitarian and human rights aspects of the cultural heritage. This has been spurred on by recent conflict in former Yugoslavia, involving attempts by one party to the conflict to eradicate the cultural heritage of the other in order to destroy their ethnic/cultural identity as a weapon of war. The importance of this to the present discussion is the manner in which it illustrates that the material culture is understood to be symbolic of cultural identity on a deeper level. The deliberate destruction of cultural monuments and artefacts during periods of armed conflict, particularly between groups who define their opposition in ethnic terms, serves to illuminate the nature of the cultural heritage itself and its role in the construction of identity. Indeed, it could be seen that it is the intangible heritage—the relationship of a people to their cultural heritage—which is really under attack in such conditions. A Council of Europe report on the subject of minority rights placed this idea within the political context of Europe and the conflict in former Yugoslavia:[69] "... les conflits actuels que l'on constate dans une partie de l'Europe justifient une reflexion urgent sur le theme de l'identite culturelle dont le patrimoine, au sens plus large, est la manifestation la plus tangible". There have been moves at international level to consider the protection of cultures under threat and the material remains of these cultures through human rights mechanisms. This work illustrates the extreme complexity of the area of cultural rights and the associated concept of cultural identity. Preparatory work by the Council of Europe in 1992 relating to the possible preparation of an additional Protocol to the European Convention on Human Rights (the ECHR), recognised the need for a comprehensive definition of "cultural" for the purposes of any attempt at identifying "cultural rights". The problems inherent in this were clear:

> "Cultural" embraces all aspects of culture—not only arts, sciences, languages and values but all the traditions which determine lifestyles. The idea is to avoid the confusion created by numerous texts which simply append "cultural" to a list of other adjectives (e.g. artistic, scientific and cultural).[70]

Thus we see that, in the quest to define cultural rights, the same difficulties exist of identifying the nature of the "culture" to which these rights are to be related as when identifying the nature of the "culture" of which the "heritage" is to be protected and passed onto future generations. By seeking to identify "culture" in relation to cultural rights and cultural

---

69. *Democratie, droits de l'homme, minorites: les aspects educatifs at culturels* (Strasbourg, 1993) Doc.DECS/SE/DHDM(93)6.
70. *Preliminary Draft Protocol to the European Convention for the Protection of Human Rights and Freedoms Concerning the Recognition of Cultural Rights—Concise Summary*, prepared by Human Rights Directorate, Council of Europe (Strasbourg, 1992) at p.2.

identity, we can gain a better understanding of the nature of cultural heritage itself. This becomes clearer when one considers that cultural rights may include a set of rights of people (or a people) to the cultural heritage, a corollary to the rights of the cultural heritage to protection and preservation generally provided for by cultural heritage texts. In other words, the traditional approach towards protecting the physical elements that represent cultural heritage expresses the right of those elements (the cultural heritage) to protection. This new generation of (cultural) rights would relate rather to the rights of people (or a people) to their cultural heritage, a right which includes the protection of that heritage but much broader issues also. Thus the more recent right, by implication, includes the former—that of the cultural heritage to be protected—and elucidates the concept.

Any discussion of cultural rights inevitably involves issues relating to the cultural identity of the people or peoples to which such rights are ascribed. Indeed, it is its role in the construction of cultural identity which is the element being protected when cultural heritage is treated as an element within human rights. Kamenka sets out the relationship between the notions of cultural rights, cultural identity and cultural heritage in the following passage which refers to:[71]

> ... the importance to human beings of the sense of identity, given not so much by material improvement, but by customs and traditions, by historical identification, by religion ... [That sense of identity] is, for most people, essential to their dignity and self-confidence, values that underlie in part the concept of human rights itself.

Here the relationship between material and non-material cultural heritage and human rights is clear. Understanding the importance of a sense of cultural identity to us all as individuals, a group, or humankind and the role of cultural heritage in its construction helps us to understand the nature of cultural heritage itself. Generally speaking, the justification for protecting cultural heritage has always been assumed in cultural heritage law as a given which needs little further elaboration. However, consideration of the existence and nature of the cultural rights associated with cultural heritage involves complex issues of identity that can lead to widely conflicting interests.

Human rights theory has always accepted the existence of a range of cultural rights,[72] such as the freedoms of religion and of expression, but its

---

71. E. Kamenka "Human Rights and Peoples' Rights" in Crawford, *op. cit. supra* n.67, pp.127–139 at p.134.
72. The Preamble to the Universal Declaration of Human Rights (1948) [U.N.G.A. Res.127A (III); UN Doc.A/811] refers to "economic, social and cultural rights" and, in 1966, the UN adopted the International Covenant on Economic, Social and Cultural Rights [993 U.N.T.S. 3].

connection with cultural heritage is a relatively new idea. As Prott notes,[73] even if they were not designed for this purpose, the existence of cultural rights is a prerequisite for the protection of culture. UNESCO has a special role in relation to cultural rights.[74] Article 1 of its Constitution reads: "[The purpose of the Organisation] is to contribute to peace and security by promoting collaboration among nations through education, science and culture in order to further universal respect for justice, the rule of law and for the human rights and fundamental freedoms which are affirmed for the peoples of the world, without distinction of race, sex, language or religion, by the Charter of the United nations." In 1966, the International Covenant on Civil and Political Rights (ICCPR) and the International Covenant on Economic, Social and Cultural Rights (ICESCR) were adopted,[75] although economic, social and cultural rights have tended to be regarded as secondary to civil and political rights by governments and other bodies.[76] Even where cultural rights have been given a formal expression in the ICESCR they have not been given sufficient attention and have often been treated under relevant provisions of the ICCPR.[77] For example, UNESCO stated in 1977 that,[78] " '[c]ultural rights' is a relatively new concept ... The preoccupation with political rights was followed up by the recognition of 'economic rights'—the right to work, the right to leisure, the right to security. It is perhaps understandable that a formulation of the concept of 'cultural rights' should have followed these."

The difficulty in arriving at an exact definition of "culture" itself[79] and in talking about rights in relation to cultural matters may well have contributed to this, with moves to create a right to the cultural heritage as

---

73. Prott, *op. cit. supra* n.67, at p.95.

74. In recognition of this is the publication of UNESCO *Cultural Rights and Wrongs* (Unesco Publishing, Paris, 1998) which explores cultural rights, including their relationship with the cultural heritage, to mark the 50th anniversary of the 1948 Universal Declaration of Human Rights.

75. ICCPR [999 U.N.T.S. 171] and IESCR [993 U.N.T.S. 3]. *Vide*: L. Sohn *Guide to Interpretation of the International Covenant on Economic, Social and Cultural Rights* (Transnational Publishing, New York, 1993); and M. Craven *The International Covenant on Economic, Social and Cultural Rights* (Clarendon Press, Oxford, 1995).

76. Non-governmental human rights organisations, for example, work almost exclusively in the field of civil and political rights, although specialist agencies of the UN (such as the FAO and WHO) deal with economic and social rights while UNESCO deals with cultural rights.

77. Such as those dealing with non-discrimination, the rights of minorities, and the freedom of expression, religion and association. *Vide*: H. J. Steiner and P. Alston *International Human Rights in Context—Law, Politics and Morals* (Oxford University Press, 1996) at p.264.

78. Working Paper by the Secretariat in UNESCO *Cultural Rights as Human Rights* (Unesco, Paris, 1977) pp.9–14 at p.9.

79. *Vide*: R. Stavenhagen "Cultural Rights and Universal Human Rights", in A. Eide, C. Krause and A. Rosas (eds.) *Economic, Social and Cultural Rights: a Textbook* (Martinus Nijhoff, Dordrecht, 1995) pp.63–77 at p.65.

a response. Given the importance of cultural heritage to the creation and assertion of cultural identity, such moves reflect a shift away from talking about cultural rights as rights of the individual towards collective and group rights of people.[80] The idea that groups have rights and that these will be taken care of by protecting individuals' rights has always been an underlying assumption of human rights instruments.[81] There are, however, difficulties associated with ascribing collective rather than individual human rights in particular that what constitutes a "people" for the purposes of one right is not necessarily the same for another.[82] In the case of rights related to cultural identity, this is compounded by the fact that the concept of a "people" is difficult to define without reference to cultural criteria (including that of identity) while it is difficult to define "culture" (except some universal culture) without reference to the concept of a "people".[83]

Certain claims asserted by groups, such as maintaining the cultural and linguistic identity of communities, have not been adequately protected under traditional human rights approaches. This has led to calls for new concepts and principles despite the difficulties entailed. The right to the cultural heritage (including access to the cultural heritage of mankind) should be considered in the context of the new "third generation" human rights such as the right to development[84] or a decent environment[85] which have been the subject of much debate.[86] This has also been seen as a tactical move to bring within the scope of human rights certain

---

80. Prott, *op. cit. supra* n.74, at pp.96–97 lists eleven cultural rights identified in existing human rights instruments. Six of these are relevant to the cultural heritage and are peoples' rights.

81. I. Brownlie "The Rights of Peoples in Modern International Law", in Crawford, *op. cit. supra* n.54, pp.1–16 at p.4.

82. J. Crawford "Some Conclusions" in Crawford, *op. cit. supra* n.67, pp.159–175 at p.170 states that: "What constitutes a people may be different for the purposes of different rights. For example, the right to existence (incorporating the right not to be subjected to genocide and the right not to be deprived of one's subsistence) is plainly applicable to a very broad category of groups, considerably more so than the principle of self-determination, or any view of that principle."

83. Prott, *op. cit. supra* n.67, at p.97.

84. *Vide*: R. Rich "The Right to Development as an Emerging Human Right", 23 Va.J.I.L. (1982/1983) at p.287.

85. *Vide*: A. E. Boyle "The Role of Human Rights in the Protection of the Environment", in A. E. Boyle and M. R. Anderson *Human Rights Approaches to Environmental Protection* (Clarendon Press, Oxford, 1996) pp.43–65.

86. *Vide*: K. Vasak "Pour une troisieme generation des droits de l'homme", in C. Swinarski (ed.) *Studies and Essays in International Humanitarian Law and Red Cross Principles in Honour of Jean Pictet* (1984); and P. Alston "A third generation of solidarity rights: progressive development or obfustication of human rights law?" 29 N.I.L.R. (1982) pp.307–322.

international concerns in order to give them greater force and appeal,[87] at risk of an inflation of rights and a consequent distortion of existing human rights. A useful comparison can be drawn between the proposed new right to a decent environment and the right to the cultural heritage.[88] While noting that environmental rights could fit easily within the diverse categories of human rights and offer beneficial access and remedies, Boyle[89] concludes that there are strong arguments against such an approach. He makes the point that, in view of existing international law for the protection of the environment, such a new right would be redundant. If applied to cultural heritage, this suggests that the roots of the perceived problem may lie in the low importance accorded to existing cultural rights. Rather than creating a new right to the cultural heritage, better enforcement of existing cultural heritage instruments and the development of areas of cultural heritage law are needed.

An instrument which makes explicit reference to a right to the cultural heritage is the Banjul Charter (1981) of the Organisation of African Unity (OAU) which includes a reference in Article 22.1 to the right of all people to "their economic, social and cultural development with due regard to their freedom and identity and in the equal enjoyment of the cultural heritage of mankind".[90] It is not clear exactly what this equal enjoyment of the cultural heritage of humankind would actually entail. Does it refer to the outstanding examples of cultural heritage as defined by the 1972 World Heritage Convention?[91] Is it the right to cultural exchanges or a call for international assistance to developing States for the safeguarding of their cultural heritage? This uncertainty raises questions as to the appropriacy of seeking to create such rights to cultural heritage, in particular to the equal enjoyment of the cultural heritage of mankind. There exists, for example, the potential for clashes between the right to cultural heritage and another new "third generation" right, that of development. Assertion of a right to development in support of building a major dam or encouraging mass tourism may well run counter to the right to preserve a culture and its related heritage.

---

87. Crawford, *op. cit. supra* n.82, at p.163 notes that activists and NGO's in Western countries "had a range of concerns not met by the traditional and individual rights. These concerns extended to the environment, to peace ... to cultural rights, and to the rights of various oppressed groups which did not fall within the orthodox framework of self-determination. It was from this diverse combination—coalition would be the wrong word—that claims to a 'third generation' of peoples' rights emerged."

88. There are many obvious similarities between the protection of the environment and the cultural heritage, such as the idea that both are a finite and non-renewable resource to be preserved for future generations.

89. Boyle, *op. cit. supra* n.85.

90. African Charter on Human Rights and Peoples' Rights ("Banjul Charter"), adopted by the Organisation of African Unity (OAU) in 1981 [21 I.L.M. 58].

91. Cited *supra* n.10.

It has been in relation to the rights of indigenous and tribal peoples that recent interest in these new rights in relation to cultural identity and the cultural heritage has been most active.[92] This finds expression, for example, in Article 2.2(b) of the International Labour Organisation (ILO) Convention on Indigenous and Tribal Peoples (1989)[93] in which "... promoting the full realization of the social, economic and cultural rights of these peoples with respect for their social and cultural identity, their customs and traditions and their institutions" is made a government responsibility. More recently, the link between human rights and the cultural heritage has been made directly. For example, the European Round Table final document (Helsinki, 1993),[94] includes in Article 3 a reference to: "[the] right to protection and development of cultures in which to participate, including preservation of the national and international cultural heritage..." with a direct reference to the "Protection of Cultural Heritage" in Article 23. The protection of cultural heritage is also given importance in the Fribourg Draft Protocol (1994)[95] which states in article 2 that:

> Everyone, both individually and collectively, has a right to the protection of his cultural heritage in all its forms. This implies:
> — the right to respect of all cultural assets specific to the various communities to which the individual belongs;
> — the right not to be unduly separated from mankind's common heritage comprising the totality of cultures accompanied by respect for their specific characteristics.

Here the right to the protection of one's own cultural heritage accompanied by access to and enjoyment of the cultural heritage characterised as the "common heritage of mankind" is firmly placed within the body of human rights.

Where the debate over creating such new rights in relation to cultural heritage is of particular interest is the insight it can give into the nature of cultural heritage and those aspects that are insufficiently recognised and protected. The concept of cultural identity is intimately related to that of cultural rights and provides an important link between cultural rights and cultural heritage. The ILO Convention illustrates the linkage of these

---

92. Existing formulations of minority rights (such as Art.27 of the ICCPR) only protect the rights of individuals who are members of a minority group and not the collective rights of the group itself. There has thus been pressure for collective rights of ethnic minorities to ensure the future survival of the group, its culture and cultural identity.

93. International Labour Organisation Convention concerning Indigenous and Tribal Peoples (1989) [28 I.L.M. 1382].

94. *Human Rights and Cultural Policies in a Changing Europe: the Right to Participate in Cultural Life—Final Statement* (1993) of the European Round Table on Human Rights and Cultural Policies, Helsinki 30 Apr.–2 May 1993.

95. *Preliminary Draft Protocol [to the E.C.H.R.]* (Freibourg, 1994), the "Freibourg Protocol".

concepts in the phrase: "Promoting ... cultural rights of these peoples with respect for their social and cultural identity" (Article 2.2(b)). The existence of rights relating to cultural identity in the context of human rights (of minorities) is also expressed in Article 3 of Recommendation 1201 (1993) of the Parliamentary Assembly of the Council of Europe:[96] "Every person belonging to a national minority shall have the right to express, preserve and develop in complete freedom his/her ... cultural identity." This idea is extended further by Recommendation 3 of the European Round Table (Helsinki, 1993) which states that the right to participate in a cultural life should be interpreted as including: "... rights necessary to protect the cultural identity of the group ... [including the] preservation of the national and international cultural heritage". Thus cultural heritage is an integral part of cultural identity and it is the need to protect the cultural identity of individuals, groups and humankind which justifies the requirement to protect and preserve cultural heritage. This takes us beyond the general assumption that its protection and preservation "is a good thing" and is a central aspect of understanding the nature of cultural heritage. One should bear in mind, however, Prott's warning that cultural identity in terms of a "people" is a problematic concept from a legal viewpoint.[97] This proviso again underlines the fact that, when using terms such as cultural identity or cultural heritage, one must guard against assuming that the definition (in a legal sense) will be straightforward. It also suggests that an examination of the development of these ideas in their original, non-legal, contexts is important for informing and elucidating the legal texts.[98] As such literature makes clear, cultural identity and its construction is a very difficult concept *per se* and so the law is entering dangerous intellectual ground when treating such subject-matter. For these reasons, the identification of an exact legal definition which can account for these complexities is no simple matter.

The relationship between material remains and cultural identity is well illustrated by the case of grave sites and human remains of indigenous peoples. It is not surprising that the problems associated with excavating human remains have most often occurred in the context of burial sites of indigenous peoples such as the native Americans and the Australian aboriginals.[99] This has arisen because of the sacred and cultural signifi-

---

96. Recommendation 1201 on an additional protocol on the rights of national minorities to the European Convention on Human Rights, text adopted by the Parliamentary Assembly of the Council of Europe on 1 Feb. 1993 (22nd sitting).
97. *Vide supra* n.83.
98. *Vide inter alia*: S. Jones *The Archaeology of Ethnicity: constructing identities in the past and present* (Routledge, 1997); J. Friedman *Cultural Identity and Global Process* (Sage Publications, London, 1994); and S. Shennan (ed.) *Archaeological Approaches to Cultural Identity* (Routledge, London, 1994).
99. L. Pinkerton "The Native American Graves Protection and Repatriation Act: an introduction", 2 I.J.C.P. (1993) at pp.297–306.

cance which such peoples invest in the burial sites of their often distant ancestors, a view not always shared or understood by archaeologists from a "European" cultural tradition. This is an issue which has been subject to much debate amongst archaeologists and museum professionals over the last two decades[100] reflected in some high-profile cases resulting in the return by museums and universities of Aboriginal and Native American artefacts and skeletal remains.[101] As a result, many museums and other institutions with holdings of human (and other) remains of indigenous peoples have adopted policies favouring their return where their cultural and spiritual significance can be demonstrated. The ICOM Code of Ethics (1986)[102] and the Museums Association (UK) Code of Ethics for Museums Professionals,[103] for example, both refer to the sensitivities surrounding collections of human remains and other such material. The ICOM Code requires that governing bodies and museum professionals "consider all the ethical and legal implications before continuing the active or passive acquisition of human remains" and that requests for the return of human remains should "involve consideration of ownership, cultural significance, the scientific, educational and religious value of the interested individuals or groups, the strength of their relationship to the remains in question..." (s.6.7). The Museums Association Code requires professionals to be "aware that the curation of human remains... can be a sensitive issue. A number of interested parties may claim rights over such material. These include actual and cultural descendants, legal owners and the nationwide scientific community." Both these ethical codes make clear the complexity of the different interests where human remains are concerned and that the cultural heritage, both in its material and non-material forms, is one of the distinctive features of the identity of any group. This highlights not only the importance of cultural heritage in the construction of cultural identity, but also the related fact that, group identity being more often than not exclusive, it involves conflicts of interest and conflicting claims which require a sophisticated understanding of the cultural heritage to address.

IV. CONCLUSION

WHAT then are the common elements of cultural heritage as understood in international law? First, is the sense that it is a form of inheritance to be

---

100. *Vide*: R. Layton (ed.) *Who Needs the Past? Indigenous Values and Archaeology* (Unwin Hyman, London, 1989).
101. Recent cases include the decision by Edinburgh University to return a collection of shrunken heads to the Maori community in New Zealand and the return of the native American "ghost-dancing" shirt from Kelvingrove Museum, Glasgow.
102. Code of the International Council of Museums (ICOM) adopted at Buenos Aires in 1986.
103. Code of Conduct for Museum Professionals, Museums Association, adopted in 1977 and amended in 1987.

kept in safekeeping and handed down to future generations. Another important aspect of cultural heritage is its linkage with group identity and it is both a symbol of the cultural identity of a self-identified group, be it a nation or a people, and an essential element in the construction of that group's identity. This characteristic of cultural heritage is thus "less a substance than a quality"[104] and is some kind of added value which carries an emotional impact, such as the colonial architecture which may inspire a sense of familiarity and even pride in a British visitor to India while providing a source of offence to many Indians. In this way, cultural heritage is less of an objective, physical existence than the range of associations which accompany an object or monument and which provide the sense of being part of a group. The role of cultural heritage as a vehicle for the expression and even construction of a nation or group's cultural identity is a double-edged sword which can act both for the good and for the bad. It can lead to an aggressive assertion of identity, whether national or ethnic, which may cause and certainly foster armed conflict in which the destruction of cultural monuments—the symbols of the cultural identity of one of the parties to the conflict—often becomes a weapon of war. It also has great potential for creating cohesion within a group, be it a self-identified ethnic minority within a State, a nation State or even a supranational body.

Both the European Union and the Council of Europe have sought to recruit cultural heritage, in so far as it reflects pan-European characteristics, as a vehicle for the construction of a sense of European identity.[105] This enterprise, however, is by no means free of difficulty. For example, the formulation "a common cultural heritage enriched by its diversity" by the Council of Europe is an attempt to reconcile the idea of a common European heritage/identity with a recognition of the cultures of national minorities which results in a mutually contradictory position.[106] UNESCO instruments also illustrate the way in which the rhetoric relating to cultural heritage reflects a political view of the Organisation. For example, the 1970 UNESCO Convention states,[107] "Considering that the interchange of cultural property among nations for scientific, cultural and educational purposes increases the knowledge of the civilization of Man, enriches the cultural life of all peoples and inspires mutual respect

---

104. R. R. Knoop "The Role of the Cultural Heritage Organisations", 3 *European Heritage* (1995) pp.23–25 at p.23.
105. The choice of the Bronze Age in Europe as the subject for an awareness raising campaign on archaeology within the Council of Europe in 1993 illustrates the political character of such decisions—it was seen as one of the few periods in the history or prehistory of the "Greater Europe" when it was culturally inter-connected without the controversy of imperialism and conquest.
106. Vienna Declaration (1993) cited *supra* n.57.
107. Cited *supra* n.9.

and appreciation among nations" (Preamble). Such sentiments also serve to support the Organisation's view of its own political importance by setting out the advantages for international relations of the kind of international interchange on the cultural level which is one of UNESCO's main raisons d'etre. In this way, heritage is placed at the centre of a sense of collective international identity based on mutual self-respect.

Thus the concept of cultural heritage is one which serves many present purposes be they cultural, social or political and this is crucial to understanding the meaning of the term and, more importantly, the implications which flow from its employment in international law. There are undoubted benefits to be had for individual peoples, nations or the international community as a whole from developing the notion of cultural heritage and creating an international legal framework for its protection. There is no question of the value of, for example: attempting to prevent the destruction, deliberate or otherwise, of artefacts and other remains with a cultural significance during armed conflict; seeking to prevent the illicit excavation of archaeological sites and control the illicit trade in cultural artefacts; or creating a mechanism for the protection and preservation of sites and monuments judged to be of "universal" significance with the States where they are located acting as trustee on behalf of the world community. Where the difficulty lies is in the fact that these are all narrowly-targeted responses to specific problems which do not provide a single, generally agreed, definition of the cultural heritage and fail to recognise the deeper implications of the concepts applied. International cultural heritage law has developed with an uncertainty at its centre over the exact nature of its subject-matter and based on a set of principles which are not always coherent. Indeed, as this paper suggests, applying these principles may at times lead to contradictory positions and unintended outcomes.

[3]
The Expanding Purview of Cultural Properties and Their Politics

Rosemary J. Coombe

Canada Research Chair in Law, Communication and Culture, York University, Toronto, Ontario M3J 1P3, Canada; email: rcoombe@yorku.ca

INTRODUCTION: LEGAL, ECONOMIC, AND POLITICAL CONTEXT

The topics that might be addressed in a survey of law and social science literature pertaining to cultural property have multiplied exponentially in the past decade. In international law, it was once possible to consider cultural property and cultural heritage as two discrete categories, but even then, commentators bemoaned the fact that the terms in different languages they referred to were seldom translations of the same concepts. *Biens culturels, beni culturali, bienes culturales, Kulturgut*, and *bens culturais*, for example, do not have the same legal meanings (Frigo 2004, p. 370). Such interpretive difficulties now seem provincial. In any case, these promise only to proliferate as these categories expand, their distinction implodes, and their subject matter and fields of reference proliferate.

No longer an esoteric area of law devoted to the protection of antiquities and their proper provenance, the concept of cultural property today is used to refer to intangibles as well as tangibles from folklore to foodstuffs as well as the lifeways and landscapes from which they spring. From seeds to seascapes, the world of things bearing cultural significance and the struggle over ownership rights apportioned to and appropriate to their significance have increased dramatically in scope and complexity.

Understanding the causes and consequences of the proliferation of cultural properties and of the even greater range of cultural rights claims is a natural area of inquiry for law and social science scholars and the field of sociolegal studies. Arguably, however, very little of the available scholarship is as interdisciplinary in scope as the politics of this dynamic field ideally demands. Few scholars fully understand the international legal frameworks and transnational policy initiatives that are driving governments, nongovernmental organizations (NGOs), development agencies, multilateral institutions, indigenous peoples, and communities, at various scales, to treat "culture as a resource" (Yudice 2003). Slightly more work has been done to relate this movement to new patterns of capital accumulation in a global political economy in which informational capital (Castells 1996–1998) has achieved new prominence (Verdery & Humphrey 2004, Watts 2006), but scholars are only beginning to consider the empirical specificities of informational capitalism in the emergence of culture as a resource (Harvey 2001, Parry 2004, Whatmore 2002).

Culture considered as a resource encompasses a wider range of values than the purely economic emphasis that culture conceived of as an asset tends to project. These values include social cohesion, community autonomy, political recognition, and concerns about inappropriate forms of cultural appropriation, misrepresentation, and loss of languages and local knowledge. These latter anxieties are integrally related to the spread of new communications technologies that have enabled cultural forms to be reproduced and publicized at a speed and velocity never before experienced (Burri-Nenova 2008). If digitalization has accelerated processes of social decontextualization, however, it has also heightened awareness of the exploitation of cultural heritage resources and enhanced political consciousness about the injuries they may affect (Coleman & Coombe 2009) while spurring new initiatives for managing and sharing cultural heritage resources in a politically sensitive manner (Christen 2005, 2009; Kansa et al. 2005).

More scholarship is needed to link the assertion of cultural properties to the political climate in which indigenous people have secured unprecedented new rights (Filbo & DeSouza 2007; Gow 2008; Hirtz 2003; Sylvain 2002, 2005) and to relate the revitalization of indigenous rights and identities to neoliberalism (Clark 2005, Coffey 2003, Hale 2002, Hristov 2005, Jung 2003, Perreault 2005, Speed 2007) and the rights-based practices (Goodale 2007) increasingly engaged to resist neoliberal development agendas (Coombe 2007, Weismantel 2006). Cultural claims are central to the collective struggles of many marginalized people for whom culture is a concept used reflexively to engage with wider state or nongovernmental institutions for purposes of identity assertion, greater inclusion in political life, the defense of local autonomy, and new forms of engagement with global markets (as well as resistances thereto). Academic recognition of this new politics of cultural properties and cultural rights has renewed scholarly concern with the conditions of cultural consciousness and relations of objectification, reification, authenticity, and decontextualization (Clifford 2004, Handler 2003, Harrison 2000, Kaneff & King 2004, Kirsch 2004).

Cultural rights in international law include intellectual property rights (or more generally, rights pertaining to moral and material interests in the works of which one is an author), rights of minorities to maintain and to develop cultural heritage, rights to participate in cultural life, rights to benefit from the arts and scientific achievement, and rights to international cultural cooperation (Helfer 2007, Macmillan 2008, Symonides 1998, Yu 2007). These are augmented by the cultural heritage provisions of the 2007 UN Declaration on the Rights of Indigenous Peoples, which even in draft form was an important part of the international customary law used to interpret other rights (Ahmed et al. 2008). Regional human rights instruments also assert the cultural rights of collectivities (Jovanovic 2005). More recent UNESCO conventions have put new emphasis on intangible cultural heritage and cultural diversity, leading to greater state scrutiny of cultural assets and an enhanced reification of cultural traditions (Albro 2005a,b; 2007). Whether the objective is rural development, environmental sustainability, or rights-based development, an emphasis on maintaining (and in some cases profiting from) cultural distinction has assumed new significance in international arenas (Coombe 2005a; Ensor 2005; Radcliffe & Laurie 2006a,b). Certainly not all cultural rights struggles involve claims to cultural property. However, to the extent that assertions of cultural rights tend to assume a possessive rhetorical form and neoliberal ideological domination of government and institutional reform agendas tend to emphasize market-based solutions, cultural properties always figure on the policy horizons of these discourses, practices, and controversies.

New forms of cultural or ethnodevelopment, for instance, which may include ecotourism and the cultivation of culturally distinctive export goods, have been implemented as a means for realizing rural economic revitalization, social cohesion, human security, and political autonomy (Andolino et al. 2005; Aylwin & Coombe 2010; Laurie et al. 2005; Perreault 2003a,b; Radcliffe 2006b; Rhoades 2006). This is a distinctive area of neoliberal governmentality, involving both multilateral institutions and NGOs that seek to empower local communities, recognize traditions as sources of social capital (Bebbington 2004b, Dervyttere 2004, Perreault 2003c), and otherwise encourage people to adopt a possessive and entrepreneurial attitude toward their culture and the social relations of reproduction that have traditionally sustained them (Elyachar 2005, Greene 2004, Lowrey 2008). These representations have their sources in diverse international legal instruments and their interpretation, in the institutional policies (Kingsbury 1999) that respond to them, and in the discourse of human and indigenous rights that shape local, NGO, and transnational responses to these policies. The latter provide normative resources for alternative articulations of culture as a source of moral economy, social meaning, and dignified livelihood (Edelman 2005, Gow 2008, Perreault 2005b, Saugestad 2001, Stewart-Harawira 2005).

Implementation of several international agreements and new programs of legal negotiation illustrate a recent acceleration of global policymaking with respect to culture. The Trade-Related Aspects of Intellectual Property (TRIPs) Agreement; the Convention on Biological Diversity (CBD) Working Group on Article 8(j) activities; the World Intellectual Property Organization (WIPO) Inter-Governmental Committee on Traditional Knowledge, Traditional Cultural Expression, and Genetic Resources negotiation of draft provisions protecting traditional knowledge and traditional cultural expressions and state proposals for an international legal instrument to bind member states; the World Bank's Indigenous Knowledge for Development program; and the passage of UNESCO treaties on the Protection and Promotion of the Diversity of Cultural Expressions and the Protection of Intangible Cultural Heritage are all arguably reshaping local social relations while linking places into transnational networks of activity.

Although the role of NGOs and multilateral institutions in world policymaking and the political importance of indigenism as a global people's movement have received increased scholarly attention in the last decade, there is as yet little academic recognition of these institutions' significant role in the practices through which proprietary relationships to culture are evoked. They bring new notions of modernity and tradition to bear on local practices (Bebbington 2004a), reworking local understandings of relations between nature and culture, emphasizing the significance of social attachments to place, and encouraging local people to express territorial relationships in cultural and proprietary terms (Escobar 2001, 2003, 2008). Environmental and indigenous NGOs play an important role in the processes by which people come to understand themselves as indigenous, as constituting, in the words of the CBD, "local communities embodying traditional lifestyles" or as possessing traditional environmental knowledge (Li 2000a,b; Tsing 1999). NGOs may exercise new forms of governmentality under neoliberal regimes (Bebbington 2005; Bryant 2002a,b), such as those that attempt to protect biological and cultural diversity, locate traditional knowledge and traditional cultural expressions, create inventories of intangible cultural heritage, and bring culturally distinct goods to market (Coombe 2010a,b). This is an area that has received scant sociolegal attention.

It is impossible to canvass the scholarly literature in all these areas relevant to cultural property. Instead, I focus on areas of particularly strong concentrations of scholarship, arguing that the proliferation of claims to cultural property might be more significant as an indicator of and impetus toward transformations in political relationships than as an area requiring domestic or international property law reform, although such reforms seem imminent at different scales in various jurisdictions. The production, exchange, and consumption of cultural property involves the construction, recognition, and acceptance of social groups and group identities in global public spheres as much as it concerns control over objects per se. Changing practices, behaviors, attitudes, and protocols regarding cultural heritage both index and reflect transformations in social relationships that are indicative of larger patterns of late modernity and decolonization.

RETHINKING CULTURAL HERITAGE

As geographer David Harvey (2001) suggests, a concern with the past and with the proper treatment of material objects from that past has a long history reflective of a more general human concern with individual and group identities. Although the use of material culture to bolster national ideologies is well known, he argues that an undue emphasis on this modern phenomenon may work to preclude engagement with more central questions about the use of heritage in producing identities and legitimating power (Harvey 2001, pp. 320–33). Nonetheless, the particular discourse of heritage that emerged in nineteenth-century Europe continues to dominate theory and practice throughout the world by representing its values as universal ones. Its origins are linked to the development of nineteenth-century nationalism and liberal modernity, and although competing discourses do occur, "the dominant discourse is intrinsically embedded with a sense of the pastoral care of the material past" (Smith 2006, p. 17).

A concern with cultural heritage emerged from modern state anxieties around national social cohesion and identity and the need to inculcate national sentiment and civic responsibility.

A preoccupation with monuments as witnesses to history and as works of art, reflected in the French idea of *patrimoine* and the Romantically derived English conservation movement, became internationally naturalized in the twentieth century. Critical scholars show how it reinforces the power of national elites, upholds the stature of rarefied bodies of expertise, denies social diversities of experience, and ignores and obscures non-national community identities while constituting the public as passive and uncritical consumers of heritage, rather than as active creators and interpreters of it.

In the past two decades, heritage scholars have shifted attention from concrete sites, objects, and localities to consider the pervasive intangibility and contingency of heritage (Munjeri 2004). What makes things, monuments, and places "heritage" are not inherent cultural values or innate significance, but rather are "the present-day cultural processes and activities that are undertaken at and around them" (Smith 2006, p. 3) through which they are given value and meaning. Such processes as the management, conservation, and governance of places, sites, and objects are thus constitutive of their cultural valuation. In short, "heritage is a multi-layered performance—be this a performance of visiting, managing, interpretation or conservation—that embodies acts of remembrance and commemoration while negotiating and constructing a sense of place, belonging and understanding in the present" (Smith 2006, p. 3). The cultural process of identity formation that is basic to and constitutive of heritage, however, has been obscured by an ideological emphasis on things or objects and their provenance—linked and defined by concepts of monumentality and aesthetics (p. 4). This "authorized heritage discourse" serves to erase subaltern and popular practices through which received values are challenged, the meanings of the past are negotiated and reworked, and community and group identities are socially projected, perceived, and challenged. New understandings of heritage have emerged both from a backlash against the professionalization of the field of cultural heritage management

and from the challenges of minorities and indigenous peoples to monologic narratives of national history and identity that negatively affect their representation and self-understandings.

One instance of a practice through which archaeology and heritage studies have become engaged in identity politics involves cultural resource management (CRM), the policy and procedures used to protect, preserve, and/or conserve cultural heritage items, sites, places, and monuments, which is also the process through which the archaeological database is preserved and maintained (Smith 2004, p. 1). Those things that are managed by archaeologists as having universal cultural value (but often claimed by the state as national patrimony) are often crucial to the identities of others, as the proliferation of conflicts between archaeologists and indigenous peoples in the Americas and Australia clearly demonstrates. Through CRM, heritage scholar Laurajane Smith (2004, pp. 2–3) argues, archaeological knowledge and expertise are mobilized by public policy makers to help govern or regulate permissible expressions of social and cultural identity:

> The way in which any heritage item, site or place is managed, interpreted and understood has a direct impact on how those people who associated with, or who associate themselves with, that heritage, are themselves understood and perceived. The past, and the material culture that symbolizes that past, plays an important part in creating, recreating and underpinning a sense of identity.... Various groups or organizations and interests may use the past to give historical and cultural legitimacy to a range of claims about themselves and their experiences in the present (Smith 2004, p. 2).

As a form of expertise and an intellectual discipline that is privileged in Western societies in debates about the past, archaeology is a form of knowledge that functions as a technology of government. Its knowledge, techniques, and procedures become mobilized in the regulation of populations and the governance of social problems that interact with claims about the meaning of the past and its heritage. These are utilized by governments and policy makers who, through CRM, clarify and arbitrate competing demands and claims about the past from various interests. Moreover, archaeological knowledge is used to help define the interests and populations linked with social problems that intersect with particular understandings of the past. Thus, the discipline plays a role in legitimating or delegitimating interests, particularly in postcolonial contexts in which people seek to establish claims to land, sovereignty, and nationhood; "archaeological knowledge, and the discourse that frames that knowledge, can and does have a direct impact on people's sense of cultural identity, and thus becomes a legitimate target and point of contention for a range of interests" (Smith 2004, p. 3).

The subject of cultural heritage, scholars now widely recognize, is not a group of tangible things from the past—sites, places, and objects—with inherent historical values that can be properly owned, controlled, and managed. Rather, it is a set of values and meanings that are contested and negotiated in a wider field of social practices. Such things have value not because of their inherent significance, but because of their role in the transmission of identities and values (Smith 2006). A growing movement identifies and justifies desires to engage local communities more fully in heritage management, for example (Buggey & Mitchell 2008), and, as I discuss below, archaeological practice has slowly evolved to incorporate indigenous criticism into theory and research (Meskell 2002, Nicholas & Bannister 2004).

The valuation of cultural heritage is certainly a revitalized arena of cultural property politics. Cultural heritage is now understood by critical practitioners in the field as "culture and landscape cared for by communities" to be passed on to the future to serve people's need for a sense of identity and belonging, while at the same time serving as the basis for new industry (Loulanski 2006, p. 209). Heritage bridges the gaps between culture and the economy (and, increasingly, the environment). No longer focused primarily on the preservation of monuments, conservation is oriented toward future usages for social purposes. It embraces distinctive styles of living in unique areas and is no longer wholly encompassed by exhibits, archives, or tourist sites; there has been a shift in emphasis from preservation to sustainable use (Loulanski 2006, p. 211). State-led projects of institutionalized storage of objects are increasingly rejected in favor of community-based research and development focusing on improvements in local life and livelihoods (p. 211). Combining natural and cultural environments, cultural heritage protection is now linked to sustainable development, and cultural heritage politics is now oriented toward maintaining the unity between the tangible (objects) and the intangible (lived experience and practice).

As anthropologist Lisa Breglia (2006) explores, neoliberal policies have heightened controversies over the proper custodians of cultural heritage. The divestiture of state-owned enterprises and the decentralization of control over cultural institutions have simultaneously led to new forms of commodification and to new forms of identity politics. Heritage sites and objects are increasingly turned over to market forces and literally expected to earn their keep; their incorporation into new forms of tourist enterprise provokes intense responses from those who regard these as their own cultural patrimony. Breglia is particularly concerned with monuments, but similar politics can be discerned with respect to properties of cultural significance worldwide.

Although cultural property is often perceived either as the common heritage of humankind or as the inalienable property of a nation, the agencies involved in its protection, preservation, promotion, and development are actually far more diverse. In many parts of the world, for instance, particular families have assumed the role of caretakers for archaeological and religious sites for several generations, and other institutions that have supported their maintenance, excavation, and research may also have their own interests. To the extent that these sites are found on ancestral territories, descendant groups may have distinct claims.

Arguably, none of this diversity of interest is new. Numerous parties with competing and sometimes conflicting proprietary attachments to cultural patrimony and the proprieties of its treatment may, however, become more evident as the state either withdraws its protective agencies, delegates its authority, or, alternatively, becomes more aggressively involved in developing these resources for financial gain. Contemporary theoretical work on heritage has responded by moving away from studying heritage as material culture to understanding it as a political practice of social relationship (Breglia 2006, p. 14).

The international legal field of intangible cultural heritage has recently received an infusion of political energy, resulting in the 2007 Convention for the Safeguarding of Intangible Cultural Heritage, which has shifted emphasis from recognition of national masterpieces to preserving lived heritage at the borders between nature and culture, as maintained by the active participation of communities pursuant to human rights and sustainable development principles (Aikawa-Faure 2009). Another arena of cultural politics promises to be animated by the citations of cultural significance and celebrations of cultural difference that the legal and regulatory implementation of this convention promises to incite (Bendix 2009).

INDIGENOUS CULTURAL HERITAGE POLITICS

Perhaps the most remarkable transformation of social practices around the politics of cultural heritage involves rights to the material artifacts and intellectual property associated with sites of cultural significance to indigenous peoples. Intense debates about who controls the past, who regulates access to sites, material, and information, and whose interpretations of the past should have authority have characterized archaeological, anthropological, and museum research involving material of significance to aboriginal peoples in Australia, First Nations groups in Canada, and Native American groups in particular. Early debates focused upon repatriation, turning around charges of cultural appropriation and the propriety of possessing cultural goods, echoing older claims with respect to artistic artifacts (Glass 2004). However, responses to charges of appropriation have become progressively less exclusive and more inclusive in nature.

Archeologists conventionally treated their materials as empirical records of a universally defined cultural past that enriched scientific understanding of a common cultural heritage; no living group was accepted as having any justifiable right to restrict the research mandate of scientific experts (Nicholas & Wylie 2009, p. 15). Such beliefs have come under enhanced scrutiny; it is now acknowledged that very few archaeologists do purely disinterested scholarly work, and local and descendant communities have challenged these premises (Nicholas 2005). Archaeologists are increasingly accountable to a wider group of stakeholders who do not accept the privileging of their allegedly wholly scientific interests. The passage of the Native American Grave Protection and Repatriation Act in the United States in 1990 was but one of many acknowledgments of the rights of descendant communities that practitioners have come to recognize. Requests for the return of artifacts, historic photographs, and ethnographic information have become common. Ethical issues of accountability and professional responsibility now go beyond issues of stewardship of the archaeological record to encompass responsibilities for the welfare and empowerment of those descendant communities whose cultural properties (not only objects of cultural significance to them but those properties that are deemed representative of their culture) are involved in archaeological research.

Although some communities, including some nation-states, have adopted exclusive property models—refusing access to researchers interested in their cultural heritage, claiming all resulting intellectual property rights in any research, and/or insisting upon compensation and royalties—more innovative models of benefit sharing have also emerged. Some professional archaeologists and anthropologists still assume a proprietary interest in their discoveries and discount the necessity of considering descendant community interests, but others have become more sensitive to the colonial power dynamics that historically enabled the cultural records of some peoples to become the scientific records of others. Indigenous peoples may have significantly different attachments to what we consider history—ancient artifacts, human remains, and culturally significant places may retain a distinctive currency and/or spiritual properties in their unique moral economies. Acknowledging this respectfully has involved new processes of consultation, reciprocation, and collaborative practice:

> Some of the most creative of these initiatives are predicated on a commitment to involve Indigenous peoples directly in the process of archaeology, a process that often significantly reframes and enriches archaeological practice. Descendant Indigenous communities often raise questions that archaeologists had never addressed, and their traditional knowledge is vital for understanding the material traces of antecedent land-use patterns, resource-harvesting practices, and a range of other more social aspects of past lifeways (Nicholas & Wylie 2009, p. 18).

The archeological embrace of ideals of collaborative practice has resulted in a broadening of academic discourse and a disciplinary practice that is not only more ethically responsible, but also more theoretically robust (pp. 18–19). Indigenous communities may now assume direction of research projects that involve their territories, material history, or cultural heritage; develop elaborate protocols for consultation; restrict some forms of publication likely to cause social harm; and/or craft access and use guidelines designed to further community objectives (Nicholas 2008). Creative uses of intellectual property laws have enabled some indigenous peoples to limit inappropriate uses of cultural heritage. Potential laws promise to provide further proprietary forms of protection and redress, such as those proposed to protect indigenous cultural heritage, traditional knowledge, and traditional cultural expressions (Coombe 2008). Where researchers and local people achieve relations of goodwill, their joint interests may combine to address contemporary community needs for employment, resource management, language preservation, education, and sustainable forms of local development or to support territorial claims. Whether or not we consider these a result of the recognition of indigenous cultural property or simply a creative way to avoid proprietary solutions, there is little doubt that such benefit-sharing activities evince an increased ethical sensitivity to cultural rights.

These dynamic new forms of social relationship, moreover, also characterize other fields of contention more conventionally considered issues of cultural property, particularly in museum contexts. Contemporary source communities are recognized as having interests in properties of cultural significance that neither internationalist commitments to maintaining world heritage, state interests in controlling national cultural patrimony, nor commitments to market forces for distribution properly encompass (Busse 2008, Geismar 2008). Throughout the Pacific, for example, museums have played a significant role in negotiating among competing interests in cultural property to ensure that public interests are not ignored nor source communities alienated. For example, Te Papa Tongarewa, the Museum of New Zealand, was completely rebuilt and reorganized to recognize the bicultural nature of the state and the equality of its founding societies. Maori taonga, or cultural treasures, are held by the museum through an institution of guardianship. This may involve relinquishing items or exhibiting them in a culturally sensitive way but most significantly engages Maori representatives and leaders in decision-making processes. As anthropologist Heidi Geismar (2008, p. 115) explains:

> Rather than a condition of ownership, this notion of guardianship develops relationships of

consultation and collaboration. The acknowledgment that property is a relationship rather than an object (so evident to property theorists, yet so obfuscated [in cultural property debates]...) suggests an alternative view of cultural property, which acknowledges the political and social relations that objects are enmeshed within as vital to their identities.... Ownership does not only imply the right to freely do what one wants to with an object; it is far expanded beyond this commodity logic and also implies a state of responsibility. The two are not mutually incompatible. The notion of property (and cultural property) implies entitlement, use, placement, and circulation as well as commoditization.

The idea of museum guardianship has spread throughout the indigenous world and among diasporic communities. Although repatriation of objects is one course of action, recognizing guardianship may actually facilitate the keeping of cultural properties in public museums and enhance their use and display. The participation of artists, researchers, and elders from source communities in the work of the museum may be a productive source of new ideas, shifting emphasis from fixed objects owned by individuals, groups, or institutions "to a more relational understanding of the dynamic links between people and things" (Geismar 2008, p. 116). Indeed, recognition of the specificity of indigenous curatorial practices has emerged in concert with the understanding that museums play an active role in the preservation of intangible cultural heritage and require new partnerships with communities to do so. These efforts are shifting "museological thinking and practice from a focus on objects and material culture to a focus on people and the sociocultural practices, processes, and interactions associated with their cultural expressions" (Kreps 2009, p. 194).

In many instances involving indigenous peoples, new museum principles regarding access, use, and interpretation have reconnected communities with their cultural heritage and reinforced recognition of the role of the past in the present, thus revitalizing cultural pride. Such principles are based on relationships of respect and recognize that Western notions of private property do not necessarily do justice to the relationship between cultural properties and identity in indigenous communities (Bell et al. 2008). As anthropologist Brian Noble (2008, p. 465) suggests, "owning as property" emphasizes exclusivity with respect to possession and alienability for purposes of exchange and wealth maximization, whereas "owning as belonging" puts emphasis on transactions that strengthen relations of respect and responsibility among and between peoples. For example, strong attachments and obligations to items of significant cultural value to indigenous communities may be accompanied by distinctive forms of inalienability:

[T]ransfer and other forms of exchange of cultural property tend to strengthen, deepen and extend social and emotional connections among people, their histories, their material productions, their knowledge, their lands, their kin groups, and the Creator, rather than effect a separation, as would be expected of the predominantly Western understanding of property as a commodity.... [T]o reduce this connection to a simple relation between property and identity is to be too narrow. Modes of exchange, and relationships and obligations created through exchange, are also crucial to social and political formation (Noble (2008, p. 474).

To recognize other practices of ownership besides those of Western legality is to practice a form of mutual respect and recognition that arguably continues to elude most theorists of both property and culture. Effectively, it is to acknowledge that cultural property is just one dimension of cultural rights—a category of human rights that puts enhanced emphasis on moral rights, collective cultural identity, cultural integrity, cultural cooperation, cross cultural communications, and intercultural exchange.

CULTURE AND DEVELOPMENT

"[C]ulture has recently acquired a new visibility and salience in development thinking and practice" (Radcliffe 2006b, p. 1). Culture has been a core feature of development practice since the late 1990s; it indexes concerns about maintaining cultural diversity, respecting local value systems that ensure social cohesion, and ending discrimination against the socially marginalized (Radcliffe 2006b, pp. 1–8). Whether the objective is rural development or environmental sustainability, an emphasis on maintaining and in some cases profiting from cultural distinction has assumed new significance (Clarke 2008; Coombe 2005a; Coombe et al. 2007; Radcliffe & Laurie 2006a,b).

We have witnessed a growing possessiveness in relationship to cultural forms at exactly the same time that culture is being revalued, not only by indigenous peoples (Brown 2003, 2005) but also by communities, regions, and national governments. These latter stakeholders see cultural expressions, cultural distinctions, and cultural diversity as sources of meaning and value that promote social cohesion, prevent rural-to-urban migration, offer new livelihood opportunities, and, of course, have the potential to provide new sources of income. Intellectual property is central to these initiatives, and new forms of sui generis rights are being considered in a number of forums where traditions and cultural preservation have assumed new urgency. These deliberations involve a range of actors, including newly vocal indigenous peoples, diasporic religious communities, farmers, healers, artisans, and a growing array of NGOs.

Development's cultural turn has occurred in the context of both neoliberal policies and resistances thereto. Culture is embraced as a value that can be ascribed to a place, a group, an institution, a resource management strategy, or a site of material production (Radcliffe 2006c, pp. 229–31). If culture is increasingly seen as a new basis for capital accumulation, however, it may also be deployed in strategic interventions in the accumulation of mutual respect, recognition, and dignity. A recognition of cultural property, in other words, may engender consciousness of the need for cultural rights. As geographer Sarah Radcliffe (2006c) elaborates, development institutions' proclivity to address culture as a product treats culture as a set of material objects and distinctive behaviors, promoting the search for culturally distinct products and services for global markets. Alternatively, treating culture as an institution puts development emphasis on distinctive forms of organization, regulation, and governance (Radcliffe 2006c, pp. 235–36). Much more rarely, however, do development endeavors recognize cultural traditions as sources of innovation and political aspiration in which people attempt to express and forge a distinctive sense of who they are and the economic and political futures they desire (Appadurai 2004, Bebbington 2005).

To illustrate, appellations of origin and geographical indications—geographical names that designate the origin of a good where "the quality and characteristics exhibited by the product are essentially attributable to the geographical environment, including natural and human factors" (Höpperger 2007, p. 3)—are forms of intellectual property protection used to maintain local conditions of production and to recognize and value traditional methods and practices. Historically, they served to protect the rural traditions of European elites; in some areas, they have come to signify the very existence of local cultural distinction (Filippucci 2004). Increasingly, they are considered means to promote the development of others whose traditions may thereby assume new value. These market-based vehicles may be abused, particularly by states more anxious to secure new sources of export revenue than to support community traditions (Chan 2008). To the extent that such marks reify local culture, there is a risk that they may fix or freeze local practices rather than enable their ongoing generativity. Moreover, they are costly to administer and require technical expertise and major investments in marketing to provide benefits. Major public investments and/or international and NGO support will be necessary to prevent the most powerful private actors in a community from monopolizing these opportunities. These challenges are not insurmountable, however, and these vehicles have been embraced by many states, NGOs, and development agencies as holding potential for both environmental sustainability (Larson 2007) and economic development by creating markets for culturally distinctive goods (Bramley & Kirsten 2007, Aylwin & Coombe 2010, Coombe et al. 2007).

Minority and indigenous communities have also asserted affirmative intellectual property rights, insisting that their specific traditions are important sources of symbolic value. They seek to capitalize on the symbolic resource that authenticity holds in a global market, where some consumers value the heterogeneous in a field of homogeneity and seek out difference in a sea of sameness (e.g., Maori Trademarks in New Zealand and First Nations' certification marks in Canada). They are encouraged by international bodies such as UNESCO that stress the complementarity of cultural and economic aspects of development and encourage intercultural exchange as a political and social good. For better or worse, marks indicating conditions of origin (which also include collective and certification marks) have assumed a new popularity as vehicles to protect and project culturally distinctive forms of production and tradition-based goods while meeting sustainable development objectives (Aylwin & Coombe 2010). The possibility of their collective ownership and management makes them especially attractive vehicles for sustaining traditional relations of production and social relations of reproduction, rather than exacerbating local relations of inequality. The public nature of the rights that flow from their use raises hopes for the sustenance of localized production strategies that draw on historical memories while building local cultural pride.

These vehicles for protecting and projecting cultural properties may be attractive to so wide a range of social actors precisely because they combine development orientations toward treating culture as a product with recognitions of culture as an institution, while also holding out promise for communities seeking both recognition of their cultural rights and improvements in their livelihoods. The properties of culture are deployed for diverse ends. As legal scholar Madhavi Sunder (2007, p. 106) suggests, historically, indigenous peoples and so-called traditional communities were understood to be contributors to or guardians of the public domain; recognizing their traditional contributions as innovations has either been rejected as an oxymoron or demonized as a form of neoliberal false consciousness that extends intellectual property rights into forms of stewardship that go beyond the appropriate realm of cultivation. Nonetheless, the creative use of geographical indications is one example through which culture and commerce are conjoined and tradition potentially preserved through its commercialization: "[T]hird-world artisans recognize that '[e]xcept in a museum setting, no traditional craft skill can be sustained unless it has a viable market'" (Sunder 2007, p. 111). Sunder finds this consonant with the human capability approach to development that understands development as any action that expands the human capabilities that allow people to achieve central freedoms, including the freedom to participate and be remunerated in the market (p. 121). Recognition of indigenous and/or traditional peoples as authors and innovators enhances their access to essential goods, furthers development objectives, and improves intercultural relations (p. 121).

One might well argue that the enormous intensity of interest in traditional knowledge and its preservation in international policymaking circles has more to do with identifying and tapping into reservoirs of insight, technique, and systemic knowledge that hold promise for future developments in science and technology than it does with the maintenance of local people's livelihoods, the alleviation of their poverty, or the promotion of their political autonomy. Nonetheless, to the extent that the discourse provides grounds for recognition and valorization of cultural differences, it also thereby provides a means of making linkages to other human rights associated with cultural distinction and thus a covert ground for pressing more political claims.

Global efforts to respect, preserve, and value traditional knowledge arguably depoliticize positions of impoverishment by throwing the more acceptable mantle of culture over conditions of social marginalization. But to recognize the importance of cultural diversity in maintaining biological diversity, I have argued, is not to recognize cultural diversity in abstract, reified, or museological terms, but to recognize an emerging international human right that affirms the interrelationship of rights to food sovereignty, territorial security, and collective heritage (Coombe 2005b). At least part of the ideological work of culture in these new claims is related in a fundamental way to transformations in capital accumulation that create increasingly greater pressures to harness information so that it can be aggregated and transformed into works of intellectual property.

The drive to represent local people's knowledge and practices as innovative works—forms of intangible or intellectual property—integrally related to an indigenous identity or a traditional lifestyle emerges from within this political economy. It is in this context that we must situate efforts to culturalize or indigenize knowledge so that it might cease to be mere information and pass, instead, in the more valuable form of a work (Coombe 2003). Only then may claims be made to possess, control, preserve, and maintain it; only then will people be respected. Over the course of its interpretation during the last decade, the CBD has become the focus of many Third World governments', indigenous peoples', and nongovernmental or civil society organizations' energies because it appears to represent the only major international, legally binding treaty that has some potential to counter the neoliberal imperatives of the TRIPs Agreement (McAfee 1999). As indigenous peoples have become more active and sophisticated participants in this policymaking sphere and brought to it expertise honed in other United Nations venues, they have put issues of cultural integrity, democratic decision making, accountability, and self-determination squarely on the bargaining table. Their capacities to do so are greatly assisted by the rhetorical leverage provided by international human rights norms and the central, if ambiguous, place of culture within these.

Many indigenous peoples (and many of those who may be deemed to have traditional lifestyles) are resident in or enclosed by the jurisdictions of states with which they have long historical relationships of distrust, betrayal, and violence. Rather than trust state delegates to the CBD to represent their interests, they have used the CBD agenda, forums, funding, and publicity opportunities to further establish legitimacy and support for the Declaration on the Rights of Indigenous Peoples, the draft of which was negotiated almost simultaneously with debates about the implementation of the CBD. Negotiations over the draft, which in 2007 became a declaration to which most states are now signatories, created a distinctive vocabulary of representations and claims that have been reiterated in so many legal contexts that they may eventually be considered a form of international customary law.

According to international legal principles, only peoples may claim self-determination, and all peoples have cultures. Indigenous peoples' rights to their lands, territories, and resources are recognized as deriving from their cultures and spiritual traditions. Peoples are entitled to pursue their cultural development and to revitalize and protect cultural traditions. Indigenous peoples are also recognized as having the right to control their intellectual and cultural properties, and these include rights to special measures to control, develop, and protect their sciences, technologies, and cultural manifestations (including knowledge of local genetic resources). Principles for protection of indigenous heritage define it to include knowledge transmitted intergenerationally and pertaining to a particular people or its territory. Emphasis is placed on the dynamic and innovative nature of traditional knowledge. Moreover, the creation of the legal and political category of traditional knowledge has in turn created the political conditions through which traditional cultural expressions have also, for better or worse, become understood as cultural property to be managed.

TRADITIONAL CULTURAL EXPRESSIONS

Many of the practices referred to in this article presuppose that some level or kind of protection may or should be asserted with respect to traditional cultural goods. The protection of traditional cultural expressions from illicit appropriation, misrepresentation, and unauthorized commercialization, however, is an area fragmented by modern Western law into intellectual property, cultural human rights, common law tort liability, and, more recently, indigenous rights claims (Girsberger 2008, Graber 2008, Macmillan 2008). Despite years of international negotiations and transnational advocacy, no consensus has been reached on the advisability of either a global regime or the use of customary law as a viable means of protection (Wendland 2008). Protection itself is a concept with multiple and conflicting meanings that range from enabling commercialization to preventing it, depending on the subject matter and its social significance. Digital communications have amplified concerns in this area, increasing the risks of misappropriation and decontextualization while also offering new opportunities for communities to benefit from promoting new uses for traditional cultural expressions that promote sustainable development (Antons 2008a,b; Burri-Nenova 2008; Sahlfeld 2008).

The growing interest in protecting traditional cultural expression, however, is at least as indicative of state interests in locating and cultivating new investments, cultural export products, and tourism opportunities as it is evidence of concern with the livelihoods and well-being of those indigenous peoples and minority communities most likely to harbor distinctive cultural resources. Modern states have long histories of absorbing minority cultural traditions into nationalized cultural patrimony; indeed, even the concept of tradition has its origins in modernity and the constitution of an uncivilized, premodern, or non-Western other in need of redemption by civilizing processes.

In an excellent survey of the history of the category, historian Monika Dommann (2008) shows how folklore was defined as "knowledge of the people" untouched by modernity. It was also considered evidence of a human past that would inevitably disappear with the advent of progress unless it was salvaged for posterity by modern national science. Central to nineteenth-century European nation-building projects and colonial governance projects, the construction of distinctive cultural traditions in the making of national and colonial imagined communities often involved the reification of the distinctive customs of rural and/or tribal peoples. National archives were created to house cultural materials; property in these physical materials was usually held by the state, but the cultural content was deemed to be in the public domain, making the value in such material easy to exploit and sequester. With respect to traditional music, for example, any intellectual property rights were held only in original recordings and in new arrangements based on prior compositions.

This fragmentation of legal rights, enabled by the historical conditions under which these cultural materials were valued, collected, and exploited, has given rise to new cultural property controversies (Coleman & Coombe 2009). Postcolonial states have long disputed the universality of the nineteenth-century laws that enabled the dispossession of their cultural heritage as a continuation of injuries effected by colonialism that preclude their full social development. The one–member state, one-vote system at work in WIPO has enabled so-called developing countries to keep the issue on the table for global negotiations; some states, for example, have incorporated folklore into copyright legislation, creating lively national public domains under which new forms of creativity and cultural revitalization have thrived (Goodman 2002, 2005). UNESCO took up the issue in 1989, incorporating folklore into the "universal heritage of humanity," which attracted new forms of censure as both indigenous peoples and so-called traditional communities emerged as potential stakeholders. WIPO has reassumed leadership over international policy negotiations that recognize this new field of rights-holders. It has also added the denomination "traditional cultural expressions" to replace folklore for those who regard the latter term as an anachronistic reference to a frozen cultural archive that they consider, instead, to be a field of dynamic resources for continuing innovation.

Issues of jurisdiction and self-determination promise to further complicate this terrain of emerging rights and responsibilities, especially given the multiple meanings that attend to the concept of customary law, so often preferred as a means to recognize traditional systems of cultural management and further the political self-determination of indigenous and minority peoples. The so-called protection of traditional cultural expressions (like the protection of traditional knowledge) is arguably the questionable political work of centralized modern legal systems attempting to incorporate the cultural systems of peripheral societies, which they tend to do with peculiar cases of tunnel vision (Teubner & Fischer-Lescano 2008).

Aggressive global expansions of the Western intellectual property system driven by new strategies of capital accumulation and national policy objectives of preserving cultural and biological diversity often result in instrumental approaches to traditional cultural expression at odds with the needs, values, and rationalities of local communities. Anthropological studies of national efforts to protect traditional cultural resources ironically illustrate the vulnerability of minority social systems to state deployments of colonial regimes of customary law—ignoring the specificity of the social processes through which knowledge and cultural expressions are generated in the process of harnessing tradition for modern markets (e.g., Aragon 2008, Aragon & Leach 2008, Balliger 2007, Green 2007, Scher 2002).

As a consequence, those who seek to maintain the vitality of locally or regionally specific forms of knowledge and cultural expression must defend themselves against the incursions of modern global science, universalizing aesthetics, new forms of capital accumulation, and national elites hungry for new forms of exploitable resources. To do so, it appears that they often articulate their own specific aspirations through the rhetoric of human rights to culture, a term increasingly animated by community investments in maintaining and supporting identities, social systems, livelihoods, and alternative systems of value. As Fiona Macmillan (2008, p. 62) wonders:

> [P]erhaps, however, there is still enough vitality in the more specific concept of cultural rights to offer a political and legal counterbalance to the power of the WTO system. The UNESCO Conventions concluded this century might be thought to demonstrate this proposition. Nevertheless, the question of how we make cultural rights strong enough and specific enough to confer proper legal protection remains.

CONCLUSION

Many scholars remain skeptical about the value and consequences of marrying the anthropological idea of culture with the legal concept of property, particularly to the extent that critical theorists now understand culture as having its locus in symbolic processes that are continually recreated in social practices imbricated in relations of power. Such an understanding sits uneasily with a vision of culture "as a bounded entity, the properties of which can be 'inventoried'" (Handler 2003, p. 356). To the extent that heritage preservation and cultural property initiatives tend to assume an objectifying approach, they may fundamentally transform the symbolic processes they seek to protect by focusing too narrowly on objects, sites, and traditions to the detriment of the semiotic dimensions of culture (pp. 361–63).

To address the issue of cultural property is necessarily to consider the positing and positioning of social identities; collective identities are never objectively given, and groups have no objectively bounded existence: "Power is fundamentally engaged within claims of cultural appropriation and claims to 'culture'—both in attempts to address historical imbalances, such as past histories of dispossession and colonisation and also in the renegotiation of contemporary positions within societies" (Anderson 2009, p. 192). The rhetoric of cultural ownership may give rise to absurd claims (Comaroff & Comaroff 2009), particularly when contemporary social categories are deployed to make possessive assertions with respect to historical objects that long predate the identities of those claiming them (Appiah 2006). Still, we fundamentally misunderstand the very concept of property if we focus primarily upon a Western model of exclusive individual or corporate ownership, as so many critics of cultural and intellectual property implicitly do. As legal scholars Carpenter et al. (2009) suggest, critics of cultural property wrongly conflate it with a narrow and fundamentalist paradigm of property that emphasizes alienation, exclusivity, and commodification. It would seem prudent, however, to avoid fetishizing a particular concept of property simply in order to counter certain fetishizations of culture. Property plays many roles in societies; it makes itself manifest in ideologies, multiple legal systems, social relationships, social practices, and in the interrelationship between these (von Benda-Beckmann et al. 2006). The very topic of cultural property demands greater critical reflexivity with respect to property's diverse forms as well as enhanced scrutiny of Western proprietary prejudices.

The illustrative survey of interdisciplinary scholarly literature with respect to cultural property presented here suggests that proprietary and possessive claims based on cultural attachments to things—material and immaterial, tangible and intangible—are proliferating under conditions of neoliberalism, informational capitalism, and the establishment of new regimes of human rights. New subjects, institutions, laws, and fields of transnational politics are concurrently emergent. Nevertheless, attempts to construct new regimes of state-based property rights lag far behind traditional customs, contemporary mores, and, particularly, the new practices, protocols, ethics, and relationships of mutual respect and recognition that have been provoked by cultural property claims. Over the past two decades, then, we have witnessed a new and vital field of cultural rights norms and practices emerging in the shadows of cultural properties yet to be validated by formal systems of Western law. Arguably, this new field of negotiated *proprieties* holds as much if not greater promise for pluricultural ethics and intercultural futures than legislated cultural properties may afford. Interrelated concepts of property and culture are at work in the world in a diversity of ways that demand greater critical attention from social scientists of law.

DISCLOSURE STATEMENT

The author is not aware of any affiliations, memberships, funding, or financial holdings that might be perceived as affecting the objectivity of this review.

ACKNOWLEDGMENTS

The author thanks the Stellenbosch Institute for Advanced Study for its support for her research and providing peaceful environs for her scholarly work.

LITERATURE CITED

Ahmed MA, Aylwin N, Coombe RJ. 2008. Indigenous cultural heritage rights in international human rights law. See Bell & Paterson 2008, pp. 311–42

Aikawa-Faure N. 2009. From the proclamation of masterpieces to the Convention for the Safeguarding of Intangible Cultural Heritage. See Smith & Akagawa 2009, pp. 13–44

Albro R. 2005a. The challenges of asserting, promoting, and performing cultural heritage. *Theor. Cult. Herit.* 1:1–8

Albro R. 2005b. Managing culture at diversity's expense: thoughts on UNESCO's newest cultural policy. *J. Arts Manag. Law Soc.* 35(3):247–54

Albro R. 2007. The terms of participation in recent UNESCO cultural policy making. In *Safeguarding Intangible Cultural Heritage: Challenges and Approaches*, ed. J Blake, pp. 109–28. Builth Wells, Powys, UK: Inst. Art Law

Anderson J. 2009. *Law, Knowledge, Culture: The Production of Indigenous Knowledge in Intellectual Property Law.* Cheltenham, UK: Edward Elgar

Andolino R, Radcliffe S, Laurie N. 2005. Development and culture: transnational identity making in Bolivia. *Polit. Geogr.* 24:678–702

Antons C. 2008a. Traditional cultural expressions and their significance for development in a digital environment: examples from Australia and Southeast Asia. See Graber & Burri-Nenova 2008, pp. 287–302

Antons C, ed. 2008b. *Traditional Knowledge, Traditional Cultural Expressions and Intellectual Property Law in the Asia Pacific Region.* The Hague, Neth.: Kluwer Intl.

Appadurai A. 2004. The capacity to aspire: culture and the terms of recognition. In *Culture and Public Action: A Cross-Disciplinary Dialogue on Development Policy*, ed. V Rao, M Walton, pp. 59–84. Stanford, CA: Stanford Univ. Press

Appiah K. 2006. *Cosmopolitanism: Ethics in a World of Strangers.* New York: WW Norton

Aragon LV. 2008. *The local commons as a missing middle in debates over indigenous knowledge and intellectual property law.* Presented at Annu. Meet. Am. Anthropol. Assoc., 107th, San Francisco

Aragon L, Leach J. 2008. Arts and owners: intellectual property law and the politics of scale in Indonesian arts. *Am. Ethnol.* 35:607–31

Aylwin N, Coombe RJ. 2010. Marks indicating conditions of origin in rights-based and sustainable development. In *Human Rights, Development and Restorative Justice: An Osgoode Reader*, ed. P Zumbansen, R Buchanan. Oxford: Hart. In press

Balliger R. 2007. The politics of cultural value and the value of cultural politics: international intellectual property legislation in Trinidad. In *Trinidad Carnival: The Cultural Politics of a Transnational Festival*, ed. GL Green, PW Scher, pp. 198–215. Bloomington: Indiana Univ. Press

Bebbington A. 2004a. NGOs and uneven development: geographies of development intervention. *Prog. Hum. Geogr.* 28:725–45

Bebbington A. 2004b. Social capital and development studies 1: critique, debate, progress? *Prog. Dev. Stud.* 4:343–49

Bebbington A. 2005. Culture and public action: a cross-disciplinary dialogue on development policy. *Am. Anthropol.* 107:305–6

Bell C, Paterson R, eds. 2008. *Protection of First Nations Cultural Heritage: Laws, Policy, and Reform.* Vancouver: UBC

Bell C, Statt G, Solowan M, Jeffs A, Snyder E. 2008. First Nations cultural heritage: a selected survey of issues and initiatives. In *First Nations Cultural Heritage and Law: Case Studies, Voices and Perspectives*, ed. C Bell, V Napoleon, pp. 367–414. Vancouver: UBC Press

Bendix R. 2009. Heritage between economy and politics: an assessment from the perspective of cultural anthropology. See Smith & Akagawa, pp. 253–69

Bramley C, Kirsten JF. 2007. Exploring the economic rationale for protecting geographical indicators in agriculture. *Agrikon* 46:69–93

Breglia L. 2006. *Monumental Ambivalence: The Politics of Heritage.* Austin: Univ. Tex. Press

Brown M. 2003. *Who Owns Native Culture?* Cambridge, MA: Harvard Univ. Press

Brown M. 2005. Heritage trouble: recent work on the protection of intangible cultural property. *Int. J. Cult. Prop.* 12:40–61

Bryant RL. 2002a. False prophets? Mutant NGOs and Philippine environmentalism. *Soc. Nat. Resour.* 15:629–39

Bryant RL. 2002b. Non-governmental organizations and governmentality: consuming biodiversity and indigenous people in the Philippines. *Polit. Stud.* 50:268–92

Buggey S, Mitchell N. 2008. Cultural landscapes: venues for community-based conservation. In *Cultural Landscapes: Balancing Nature and Heritage in Preservation Practice*, ed. R Longstreth, pp. 164–79. Minneapolis: Univ. Minn. Press

Burri-Nenova M. 2008. The long tail of the rainbow serpent: new technologies and the protection and promotion of traditional cultural expressions. See Graber & Burri-Nenova 2008, pp. 205–36

Busse M. 2008. Museums and the things in them should be alive. *Int. J. Cult. Prop.* 15:189–200

Carpenter KA, Katyal SK, Riley AR. 2009. In defence of property. *Yale Law J.* 118:1022–125

Castells M. 1996-1998. *The Information Age: Economy, Society, and Culture*, Vols. 1–3. Oxford: Blackwell

Chan A. 2008. E-governance for artisans: intellectual property, networked culture, and the promiscuity of freedom in Peru. Presented at Annu. Meet. Am. Anthropol. Assoc., 107th, San Francisco

Christen K. 2005. Gone digital: Aboriginal remix and the cultural commons. *Int. J. Cult. Prop.* 12(5):315–45

Christen K. 2009. *Aboriginal Business: Alliances in a Remote Australian Town*. Santa Fe: Sch. Am. Res. Press

Clark AK. 2005. Ecuadorian indians, the nation, and class in historical perspective: rethinking a 'new social movement.' *Anthropologica* 47:53–65

Clarke G. 2008. From ethnocide to ethnodevelopment? Ethnic minorities and indigenous peoples in Southeast Asia. *Third World Q.* 22:413–36

Clifford J. 2004. Looking several ways: anthropology and native heritage in Alaska. *Curr. Anthropol.* 45:5–23

Coffey MK. 2003. From nation to community: museums and the reconfiguration of Mexican society under neoliberalism. In *Foucault, Cultural Studies and Governmentality*, ed. JZ Bratich, J Packer, C McCarthy, pp. 207–43. New York: SUNY Press

Coleman EB, Coombe RJ. 2009. A broken record: subjecting music to cultural rights. In *Ethics of Cultural Appropriation*, ed. JC Young, C Brunck, pp. 173–210. London: Blackwell

Comaroff J, Comaroff, J. 2009. *Ethnicity, Inc.* Chicago: Univ. Chicago Press.

Coombe RJ. 2003. Works in progress: indigenous knowledge, biological diversity and intellectual property in a neoliberal era. In *Globalization Under Construction: Governmentality, Law and Identity*, ed. RW Perry, W Maurer, pp. 273–314. Minneapolis: Univ. Minn. Press

Coombe RJ. 2005a. Legal claims to culture in and against the market: neoliberalism and the global proliferation of meaningful difference. *Law Cult. Hum.* 1:32–55

Coombe RJ. 2005b. Protecting traditional environmental knowledge and new social movements in the Americas: intellectual property, human right or claims to an alternative form of sustainable development? *Fla. J. Int. Law* 17:115–36

Coombe RJ. 2007. The work of rights at governmentality's limits. *Anthropologica* 49:284–99

Coombe RJ. 2008. First Nations' intangible cultural heritage concerns: prospects for protection of traditional knowledge and traditional cultural expressions in international law. See Bell & Paterson 2008, pp. 247–77

Coombe RJ. 2010a. Cultural agencies: the "construction" of community subjects and their traditions. In *The Making and Unmaking of Intellectual Property*, ed. M Biagioli, P Jaszi, M Woodmansee. Chicago: Univ. Chicago Press. In press

Coombe RJ. 2010b. Owning culture: locating communities and their properties. In *Ownership and Appropriation*, ed. M Busse, V Strang. London: Berg. In press

Coombe RJ, Schnoor S, Ahmed MA. 2007. Bearing cultural distinction: informational capital and new expectations for intellectual property. *Univ. Calif. Davis Law Rev.* 40:891–917

Dervyttere A. 2004. Indigenous peoples, development with identity and the Inter-American Development Bank: challenges and opportunities. In *Lessons of Indigenous Development in Latin America: The Proceedings of a World Bank Workshop on Indigenous Peoples Development*, ed. S Davis, JE Uquillas, MA Eltz, pp. 23–30. Washington, DC: World Bank Environ. Soc. Sustain. Dev. Dep.

Dommann M. 2008. Lost in tradition? Reconsidering the history of folklore and its legal protection since 1800. See Graber & Burri-Nenova 2008, pp. 3–16

Edelman M. 2005. Bringing the moral economy back in...to the study of 21st century transnational peasant movements. *Am. Anthropol.* 107:331–45

Elyachar J. 2005. *Markets of Dispossession: NGOs, Economic Development and the State in Cairo*. Durham, NC: Duke Univ. Press

Ensor J. 2005. Linking rights and culture. In *Reinventing Development: Translating Rights-Based Approaches from Theory into Practice*, ed. P Gready, J Ensor, pp. 254–77. London: Zed Books

Escobar A. 2001. Culture sits in places: reflections on globalism and subaltern strategies of localization. *Polit. Geogr.* 20:139–74

Escobar A. 2003. Place, nature, and culture in discourses of globalization. In *Localizing Knowledge in a Globalizing World: Recasting the Area Studies Debate*, ed. A Mirsepassi, A Basu, FS Weaver, pp. 37–59. Syracuse, NY: Syracuse Univ. Press

Escobar A. 2008. *Territories of Difference: Social Movements and Biodiversity Conservation in the Colombian Pacific.* Durham, NC: Duke Univ. Press

Filbo CF, de Souza M. 2007. Multiculturalism and collective rights [in Latin America]. In *Another Knowledge Is Possible: Beyond Northern Epistemologies*, ed. B Santos, pp. 74–114. London: Verso

Fillippucci P. 2004. A French place without a cheese: problems with heritage and identity in northeastern France. *Focaal: Eur. J. Anthropol.* 44:72–86

Frigo M. 2004. Cultural property *v.* cultural heritage: a "battle of concepts" in international law? *Int. Rev. Red Cross* 86:854–78

Geismar H. 2008. Cultural property, museums, and the Pacific: reframing the debates. *Int. J. Cult. Prop.* 15:109–22

Girsberger M. 2008. Legal protection of traditional cultural expressions: a policy perspective. See Graber & Burri-Nenova 2008, pp. 123–49

Glass A. 2004. Return to sender: on the politics of cultural property and the proper address of art. *J. Mater. Cult.* 9:115–139

Goodale M. 2007. Locating rights, envisioning law between the global and the local. In *The Practice of Human Rights: Tracking Law Between the Global and the Local*, ed. SE Merry, M Goodale, pp. 1–38. Cambridge, UK: Cambridge Univ. Press

Goodman J. 2002. Stealing our heritage? Women's folksongs, copyright law, and the public domain in Algeria. *Afr. Today* 49:85–97

Goodman J. 2005. *Berber Culture on the World Stage: From Village to Video.* Bloomington: Indiana Univ. Press

Gow D. 2008. *Countering Development: Indigenous Modernity and the Moral Imagination.* Durham, NC: Duke Univ. Press

Graber CB. 2008. Using human rights to tackle fragmentation in the field of traditional cultural expressions: an institutional approach. See Graber & Burri-Nenova 2008, pp. 96–122

Graber CB, Burri-Nenova M, eds. 2008. *Intellectual Property and Traditional Cultural Expressions: Legal Protection in a Digital Environment.* Cheltenham, UK: Edward Elgar

Green GL. 2007. "Come to life": authenticity, value, and the carnival as cultural commodity in Trinidad and Tobago. *Identities: Glob. Stud. Cult. Power* 14:203–24

Greene S. 2004. Indigenous people incorporated? Culture as politics, culture as property in pharmaceutical bioprospecting. *Curr. Anthropol.* 45:211–37

Hale CR. 2002. Does multiculturalism menace? Governance, cultural rights and the politics of identity in Guatemala. *J. Latin Am. Stud.* 34:485–524

Handler R. 2003. Cultural property and cultural theory. *J. Soc. Archaeol.* 3:353–65

Harrison S. 2000. From prestige goods to legacies: property and the objectification of culture in Melanesia. *Comp. Stud. Soc. Hist.* 42:662–79

Harvey D. 2001. Heritage pasts and heritage presents: temporality, meaning, and the scope of heritage studies. *Int. J. Herit. Stud.* 7:319–38

Helfer L. 2007. Toward a human rights framework for intellectual property. *Univ. Calif. Davis Law Rev.* 40:971–1020

Hirtz F. 2003. It takes modern means to be traditional: on recognizing indigenous cultural minorities in the Philippines. *Dev. Change* 34:887–917

Höpperger M. 2007. *Geographical indications in the international arena: the current situation.* Presented at WIPO/SAIC Int. Symp. Geogr. Indic., Beijing, China, June 26–28. **http://www.wipo.int/edocs/mdocs/geoind/en/wipo_geo_bei_07/wipo_geo_bei_07_www_81753.ppt**

Hristov J. 2005. Indigenous struggles for land and culture in Cauca, Columbia. *J. Peasant Stud.* 32:88–117

Jovanovic MA. 2005. Recognizing minority identities through collective rights. *Hum. Rights Q.* 27:625–51

Jung C. 2003. The politics of indigenous identity: neoliberalism, cultural rights and the Mexican Zapatistas. *Soc. Res.* 70:433–62

Kaneff D, King AD. 2004. Introduction: owning culture. *Focaal: Eur. J. Anthropol.* 44:3–19

Kansa EC, Schultz J, Bissell AN. 2005. Protecting traditional knowledge and expanding access to scientific data: juxtaposing intellectual property agendas via a "some rights reserved" model. *Int. J. Cult. Prop.* 12:285–314

Kingsbury BW. 1999. Operating policies of international institutions as part of the law making process: the World Bank and indigenous peoples. In *The Reality of International Law*, ed. GS Goodwin, S Talmon, pp. 323–47. Oxford: Clarendon

Kirsch S. 2004. Property limits: debates on the body, nature and culture. In *Translations and Creations: Property Debates and the Stimulus of Melanesia*, ed. M Strathern, E Hirsch, pp. 21–39. Oxford: Berghahn Books

Kreps C. 2009. Indigenous curation, museums, and intangible cultural heritage. See Smith & Akagawa 2009, pp. 193–208

Laurie N, Andolina R, Radcliffe S. 2005. Ethnodevelopment: social movements, creating experts and professionalising indigenous knowledge in Ecuador. *Antipode* 37:470–96

Larson J. 2007. *Relevance of geographical indications and designations of origin for the sustainable use of genetic resources*. Stud. Glob. Facil. Unit Underutil. Spec., Maccarese, Rome, Italy. **http://www.underutilized-species.org/Documents/PUBLICATIONS/gi_larson_lr.pdf**

Li T. 2000a. Articulating indigenous identity in Indonesia: resource politics and the tribal slot. *Comp. Stud. Soc. Hist.* 42:149–79

Li T. 2000b. Locating indigenous environmental knowledge in Indonesia. In *Indigenous Environmental Knowledge and Its Transformations: Critical Anthropological Perspectives*, ed. R Ellen, P Parkes, A Bicker, pp. 121–49. New York: Routledge

Loulanski T. 2006. Revising the concept for cultural heritage: an argument for a functional approach. *Int. J. Cult. Prop.* 13:207–33

Lowrey K. 2008. Incommensurability and new economic strategies among indigenous and traditional peoples. *J. Polit. Ecol.* 15:61–74

Macmillan F. 2008. Human rights, cultural property, and intellectual property: three concepts in search of a relationship. See Graber & Burri-Nenova 2008, pp. 50–63

McAfee K. 1999. Selling nature to save it? Biodiversity and green developmentalism. *Environ. Plan. D: Soc. Space* 17:133–54

Meskell L. 2002. The intersections of identity and politics in archaeology. *Annu. Rev. Anthropol.* 31:279–301

Munjeri D. 2004. Tangible and intangible heritage: from difference to convergence. *Museum Int.* 56:12–20

Nicholas GP. 2005. The persistence of memory; the politics of desire: archaeological impacts on Aboriginal peoples and their response. In *Indigenous Archaeologies: Decolonizing Theory and Practice*, ed. C Smith, HM Wobst, pp. 81–103. London: Routledge

Nicholas GP. 2008. Policies and protocols for archaeological sites and associated cultural and intellectual property. See Bell & Paterson 2008, pp. 203–22

Nicholas GP, Bannister KP. 2004. Copyrighting the past? *Curr. Anthropol.* 45:327–50

Nicholas GP, Wylie A. 2009. Archaeological finds: legacies of appropriation, modes of response. In *The Ethics of Cultural Appropriation*, ed. C Brunck, J Young, pp. 11–51. London: Blackwell

Noble B. 2008. Owning as belonging, owning as property: the crisis of power and respect in First Nations heritage transactions with Canada. In *First Nations Cultural Heritage and Law: Case Studies, Voices and Perspectives*, ed. C Bell, V Napoleon, pp. 465–88. Vancouver: UBC Press

Parry B. 2004. *Trading the Genome: Investigating the Commodification of Bio-Information*. New York: Columbia Univ. Press

Perreault T. 2003a. Changing places: transnational networks, ethnic politics, and community development in the Ecuadorian Amazon. *Polit. Geogr.* 22:61–88

Perreault T. 2003b. A people with our own identity: toward a cultural politics of development in Ecuadorian Amazonia. *Environ. Plan. D: Soc. Space* 21:583–606

Perreault T. 2003c. Social capital, development, and indigenous politics in Ecuadorian Amazonia. *Geogr. Rev.* 93:328–49

Perreault T. 2005. Geographies of neoliberalism in Latin America. *Environ. Plan. A* 37:191–201

Radcliffe S, ed. 2006a. *Culture and Development in a Globalizing World: Geographies, Actors, and Paradigms.* London/New York: Routledge

Radcliffe S. 2006b. Culture in development thinking: geographies, actors, and paradigms. See Radcliffe 2006a, pp. 1–29

Radcliffe S. 2006c. Conclusions: the future of culture and development. See Radcliffe 2006a, pp. 228–37

Radcliffe SA, Laurie N. 2006a. Culture and development: taking culture seriously in development for Andean indigenous people. *Environ. Plan. D: Soc. Space* 24:1–18

Radcliffe SA, Laurie N. 2006b. Indigenous groups, culturally appropriate development and the socio-spatial fix of Andean development. See Radcliffe 2006a, pp. 83–106

Rhoades RE, ed. 2006. *Development with Identity: Community, Culture and Sustainability in the Andes.* Cambridge, MA: CABI Publishing

Sahlfeld M. 2008. Commercializing cultural heritage? Criteria for a balanced instrumentalization of traditional cultural expressions for development in a globalized digital environment. See Graber & Burri-Nenova 2008, pp. 256–86

Saugestad S. 2001. *The Inconvenient Indigenous: Remote Area Development in Botswana, Donor Assistance, and the First Peoples of the Kalahari.* Boras: Nordic Afr. Inst.

Scher P. 2002. Copyright heritage: preservation, carnival and the state in Trinidad. *Anthropol. Q.* 75:453–84

Smith L. 2004. *Archaeological Theory and the Politics of Cultural Heritage.* London: Routledge

Smith L. 2006. *Uses of Heritage.* London: Routledge

Smith L, Akagawa N, eds. 2009. *Intangible Cultural Heritage.* London: Routledge

Speed S. 2007. *Rights in Rebellion: Indigenous Struggle and Human Rights.* Palo Alto, CA: Stanford Univ. Press

Stewart-Harawira M. 2005. *New Imperial Order: Indigenous Responses to Globalization.* London/New York: Zed Books

Sunder M. 2007. The invention of traditional knowledge. *Law Contemp. Soc. Probl.* 17:97–124

Sylvain R. 2002. Land, water and truth: San identity and global indigenism. *Am. Anthropol.* 104:1074–85

Sylvain R. 2005. Globalization and the idea of 'culture' in the Kalahari. *Am. Ethnol.* 32:354–70

Symonides J. 1998. The implementation of cultural rights by the international community. *Gazette* 60:7–25

Teubner G, Fischer-Lescano A. 2008. Cannibalizing epistemes: Will modern law protect traditional cultural expressions? See Graber & Burri-Nenova 2008, pp. 17–48

Tsing A. 1999. Becoming a tribal elder and other development fantasies. In *Transforming the Indonesian Uplands: Marginality, Power and Production*, ed. TM Li, pp. 159–202. London: Routledge

Verdery K, Humphrey C, eds. 2004. *Property in Question: Value Transformations in the Global Economy.* Oxford: Berg

von Benda-Beckmann F, von Benda-Beckmann K, Wiber MG. 2006. The properties of property. In *Changing Properties of Property*, ed. F von Benda-Beckmann, K von Benda-Beckmann, MG Wiber, pp. 1–36. London: Berghahn Books

Watts M. 2006. Culture, development and global neo-liberalism. See Radcliffe 2006a, pp. 30–57

Weismantel M. 2006. Ayllu: real and imagined communities in the Andes. In *The Seductions of Community: Emancipations, Oppressions, Quandaries*, ed. GW Creed, pp. 77–100. Santa Fe: Sch. Am. Res. Press

Wendland WB. 2008. 'It's a small world (after all)': some reflections on intellectual property and traditional cultural expressions. See Graber & Burri-Nenova 2008, pp. 150–81

Whatmore S. 2002. *Hybrid Geographies: Natures, Cultures, Spaces.* London: Sage

Yu P. 2007. Reconceptualizing intellectual property interests in a human rights framework. *Univ. Calif. Davis Law Rev.* 40:1039–149

Yudice G. 2003. *The Expediency of Culture.* Durham, NC: Duke Univ. Press

[4]
The Politics of Preservation: Privileging One Heritage over Another

Jonathan S. Bell*

Abstract: Heritage preservation is distinctly political, often presenting a privileged elitist interpretation of historic sites, while denigrating or even destroying later significant built environments. Structures that are the emanation of subsequent cultures, but similarly tied to the place, are often undervalued, underinterpreted, and even purposely obliterated from the landscape. This article considers the politics of heritage related to privileging one type of historic structure to the complete detriment of the other. The example of Gurna, in Egypt, serves as a powerful case study for the loss of a living historic built environment solely for the simplified or "flattened" interpretation of a place. In highlighting the preferential protection and presentation of the World Heritage Site of the Theban Necropolis and ultimate demise of the historic hamlets of Gurna, the article builds on previous work in the field on interpretation, the impact of tourism, and the conflicting identities of historic sites.

> [It] is not until a building has assumed this character, till it has been entrusted with the fame, and hallowed by the deeds of men, till its walls have been witnesses of suffering, and its pillars rise out of the shadows of death, that its existence, more lasting as it is than that of the natural objects of the world around it, can be gifted with even so much as these possess, of language and of life. —John Ruskin

INTRODUCTION

The preservation of heritage is inherently political. Archaeologists, cultural resource managers, conservators, and governments make particular decisions about the objects and places they preserve, the methods by which they interpret these relics of the past, and the histories they privilege in the process. Certain histories and

---

*Department of Urban Planning, UCLA Luskin School of Public Affairs, 3250 Public Affairs Building, Box 951656, Los Angeles, CA 90095-1656. Email: jsbell@ucla.edu.

physical remains are necessarily excluded, privileging one period, class, or category of heritage over the others in a given place. This act of marginalization is multiscalar and self-perpetuating in nature, attracting tourists and scholars alike from far and wide to partake in the consumption and reaffirmation of the showcased history, while ignoring or even denigrating the contiguous histories that are underinterpreted. As a singular, idealized association between history and place is established and reinforced, communities that value alternate meanings of a place are often disenfranchised and disempowered. This article presents a consideration of the politics of heritage as they relate to the sustainable coexistence of designated heritage sites and living historic communities. Considering the extreme example of the western hamlets of Gurna and their recent demise, the article questions whether the practice of preservation can be depoliticized to valorize a privileged heritage without denigrating an underprivileged one.

Although a decades-old corpus of sociological and anthropological literature considers power relationships in multiple contexts, it is only recently that scholars have focused this theoretical lens on the heritage disciplines, underscoring the intrinsic politics of heritage. In so doing, a number of imperial, colonial, and elitist rhetorics have come to light, questioning the legitimacy and appropriateness of preserving one heritage over another, or one spatial association over another. Indeed, there is a recent recognition of the profound conflict between the privileged and the marginalized over differing social values, lived traditions, and everyday practices that are collocated.

The village of Gurna, on Luxor's West Bank in Egypt, serves as a case study to represent the pinnacle of conflict between a local historic community established within and around a vast expanse of pharaonic remains. Efforts to uncover, study, and display the wonders of pharaonic Egypt intimately involved the local Gurnawis from the early days of European-led archaeological efforts. However, in more recent years, the privileged story of the pharaonic heritage and its related modern industries of archaeology, research, and tourism dramatically overwhelmed the Gurnawi presence and long intertwined existence in the area to allow forced relocation of the community and demolition of its own historic and striking vernacular. Only a few years later, the loss of Gurna symbolizes the failure of government officials and heritage professionals to preserve living communities amid the pharaonic tombs and structures that are the focus of economically important tourism and ongoing archaeological study.

In order to establish the historicity of the Gurnawi settlements and their close relationship to the European discovery of the pharaonic remains in the area during the 18th and 19th centuries, the article relies on content analysis of text, maps, and drawings from the period referring to the people of Gurna. Modern changes to the cultural landscape, particularly the demolition of the Gurnawi homes, are evident through before-and-after comparisons of satellite images, which further reveal the politically significant buildings that survived demolition. Recent literature on concepts of living heritage and approaches to preserve the multilayered value of cultural and historic sites provides a framework for considering Gurna and developing best practice models.

HERITAGE AS CONCEPT

The practice of heritage preservation has long been considered one of benevolence, safeguarding vestiges from the past for the benefit of the future. This concept, as understood by historic preservation professionals, derives principally from European architectural and art historians in the 19th century looking on the great ruins of the past with romanticism and developing theories about the sociocultural values of historic structures.[1] Social thinkers and architectural theorists of the time highlighted the significance with which monuments were imbued and argued over their legacy and preservation approaches.[2] From these theoretical writings and efforts to restore examples of the built heritage emerged a focus on preserving not only physical vestiges, but also understanding the technology and values imbued therein. James Marston Fitch notes that the "comprehensive protection of such monuments and artifacts, and the scholarly examination of the theories and techniques that produced them, is of central importance to our cultural future."[3] Focus, therefore, has typically been placed on the protection and examination of the physical in the first case, with more recent consideration of intangible values to ensure a holistic approach to preservation and interpretation of historic sites.[4]

Efforts to understand intangible values have highlighted the assignation of value as an intrinsic component of the "consumption" of historic sites, including not only use and admiration, but also protection and preservation. The 19th-century art historian Alois Reigl claimed "the term 'monument'... can only be meant subjectively, not objectively. We modern viewers, rather than the works themselves by virtue of their original purpose, assign meaning and significance to a monument."[5] Meaning is not intrinsic to a work of art or a monument, but is actively redefined by those who experience it, with each stakeholder group and, arguably, each individual adding a new layer of significance and meaning. Nearly a hundred years after Reigl was writing, David Lowenthal claimed that ongoing assignation of value is inherent to the use and care of things historic. "Heritage is ever revitalized; our legacy is not simply original but includes our forebears' alterations and additions. We treasure that heritage in our own protective *and* transformative fashion, handing it down in the faith that our heirs will also become creative as well as retentive stewards."[6] For Lowenthal, the admiration and protection of heritage are themselves acts of value assignment and, as such, create new associations with a place that are supplemental and cumulatively expand its significance. As the focus of cultural consumption, in one form or other, heritage becomes the object of "commodification" and takes on new meaning with each act of use, repair, study, or reuse.[7] Preservation aims to protect the most significant and documented of these layers of meaning, while respecting all physical and intangible accretions. However, it is a politically charged activity.

The selection of one assignation of meaning as the focus of preservation has political implications with socioeconomic and cultural manifestations. Laurajane Smith refers to this privileged rhetoric as the "authorized heritage discourse," which she contrasts with the existence of a "range of popular discourses and practices" that may counter the former.[8] Smith further highlights that the authorized heritage discourse is "self-referential," in that it establishes who has the capacity to inform it and, ultimately, who does not. In this way, a dominant interpretation of a heritage site can simply overwhelm other interpretations and discourses integral to its layered significance but not "authorized" as valid or valuable. The result is a disempowerment and disenfranchisement of the other "subaltern," to use Smith's language, viewpoints or associations. Casting aside of these layers of significance can lead to the ultimate loss of socioculturally and historically important information, including physical sites themselves.

It is necessary at this point to discuss the role of *place* in defining and empowering built heritage as a sociopolitical entity. Unlike an *objet d'art* that can be moved from locality to locality and is then recontextualized within each new environment, immovable heritage (e.g., constructed buildings, land art, grottoes, and natural sites) is inextricably intertwined with its physical, social, cultural, and economic context. As a backdrop to the creation, use, re-creation, modification, and decay of these sites, place is both *witness* and *participant* over time. It is much more than a geographical location pinpointed on a map and serves as the setting that creates, defines, and redefines over time the use and value of a cultural heritage site. The importance of place, as theorized by geographer Carl Sauer, is its identity as the "combination of natural and man-made elements."[9] This sense of identity is further elaborated by the concept of "place memory," defined by Dolores Hayden as the embodiment of "the human ability to connect with both the built and natural environments."[10] Place as a concept integrates both its physical components and the emotional associations with the setting. Arguably, the latter attachment may endure even though the former physical elements have changed or been removed. In other words, place embodies the varied assignments of values over time without temporal distinction and simultaneously recognizes endogenous and exogenous impacts on the creation, modification, and re-creation of these values. The preservation process, in its purest form, aims to identify, document, and safeguard all these superimposed layers of meaning and interpret their spatial associations.

SELECTING A PAST TO PROTECT

Nonetheless, the act of preservation often, if not always, requires some form of selection and identification of a privileged heritage discourse. Physical manifestations of the approved discourse are protected, while other physical accretions and evidence of later associations may be willfully destroyed. Preservation establishes a sanctioned perspective presented and interpreted for posterity that then serves to exclude and marginalize other layers of meaning. Such exclusion, in turn, can limit access to and use of a place, and disenfranchise entire communities with divergent associations to the heritage place, to the degree of affecting their lifestyle, livelihood, and even identity.

Much of the literature on the politics of preservation has focused on the very tangible processes of archaeology and related cultural tourism. On one hand, scholars identify archaeology as a tool for governments to promote specific agendas and control sociocultural conflict.[11] On the other, archaeologists and other heritage professionals take on the mantle of creating culture and defining heritage, often intricately interwoven with the process of establishing national identity and, more recently, legitimizing and coalescing subgroup identity.[12] Casting the preservation process as an application of moral relativism, whether promoted by government or by scholar, Meskell states in no uncertain terms that the "creation of heritage is a culturally generative act that is intrinsically political. Heritage consultants and archaeologists could be said to invent culture, and, in the process, constitute heritage."[13] Thus, the act of preservation, including herein the processes of discovery, study, and documentation, serves to establish a sanctioned, or authorized, discourse about a place. Those involved in this act, often an educated and/or governing elite, are then responsible for identifying and privileging one or more selected interpretations and uses of a heritage place.

The tourism industry represents another important stakeholder in the preservation process, itself creating accretions and new layers of meaning while often underscoring the authorized heritage discourse. As a mass act of cultural consumption,[14] tourism has enormous impact on the perceived significance and associations of a place. Hall identifies tourism as an inherently political power struggle that results in the domination of tourists over the indigenous population, and examples abound of the negative impact of tourism on the lives of residents.[15] This domination further accords tourists a simplified or "flattened" history that supersedes all others for the sake of presentation. The interpreted heritage site tends to tell the story of the local elite, often overlooking the underclasses intimately involved in the processes of creation, rediscovery, or present-day activity.[16] McKercher and du Cros note that tourism requires transformation of the cultural resource "to make it appealing and relevant to the tourist" and "simple and singular in its theme."[17] In this way, tourism often results in a singular interpretation of a site: one story with a simplistic message presented for the sake of outsiders. Tourists appear to occupy a Gramscian cultural hegemony that privileges their simplified understanding of the places they visit and reinforces a singular accepted discourse.[18] Although many cultural site managers strive to highlight multiple layers of historical significance and sociocultural values related to a place, loss of certain discourses through the selection process is inevitable. Nonetheless, heritage professionals should strive to preserve and interpret as many of the discourses as possible.

GURNA: A VILLAGE BUILT ON HISTORY

The village of Gurna that would become a north–south linear sprawl of sizable mudbrick houses on Luxor's West Bank was established at least as early as the 18th century on top of a vast field of pharaonic remains from Egypt's New Kingdom (roughly 1550–1069 BCE). Although the Gurnawis—those who live at the foot of the Theban Mount (*Al-Gurn*)—were themselves associated with the era of discovery and archaeology of the region, they and their communities have been marginalized by a history of contempt and a modern series of relocation efforts. The goal of these efforts, as expressed by the Egyptian authorities, was to remove the community from atop the ancient tombs that first brought it there. Events that began in 2006 resulted ultimately in the wholesale demolition of the community's historic buildings, forced relocation of residents, and refusal to interpret the community's historical associations to the World Heritage Site within which it resided.

The region in question, long known as Thebes and highlighted by Herodotus for the wonder of its pharaonic vestiges, regained interest among itinerant Europeans in the 18th century. An early drawing of the West Bank in 1743 (see Figure 1) depicts some of the larger pharaonic remains and two outlying villages within the Nile flood plains and near the edge of the desert, one of which is labeled Gurna.[19] Vivant Denon, a participant in the Napoleonic expeditions of Egypt and first director of the Louvre Museum, made multiple references to Gurna, which he called "Kurnu," and his interaction with the Gurnawis in his 1802 publication on Egypt.[20] He notes that hamlets of Gurna were already established amid the pharaonic tombs

FIGURE 1. Anonymous, *A View of Thebes, on the West of the Nile*, the village of Gurna is indicated by the letter "A," plate in Richard Pococke, *Description of the East and Some Other Countries, Vol. 1* (1743).

beyond the edge of the Nile flood plain and that some of the residents took shelter in them.[21] Despite the difficult and oft belligerent encounters between the Gurnawis and the French expedition, the former, which Denon interchangeably termed "incorrigible," "criminals," and "dogs," eventually agreed to guide him through some of the larger tombs of the pharaohs.[22] A later panoramic drawing of the Theban hillside by Robert Hay of Linplum[23] in the 1820s depicts the locals living and working amid the tombs (see Figure 2), presumably attracted more and more to the desert from the floodplains by the advent of Europeans involved in archaeological exploration and in need of paid labor.

As interest in Egypt grew from the early 19th century and beyond, more Europeans specializing in the discovery of pharaonic remains and eager for a "cultural" vacation came on the scene. Isabella Frances Romer published a work about her explorations of Egypt and Palestine and mentioned the village of Gurna and its people in the 1840s.[24] Alexander Henry Rhind commented on Romer's fanciful sketches of western Thebes dotted with villas as a potential vacation spot for British subjects.[25] A number of manor-like structures built as residences for Egyptologists and travelers spending time in the area became a part of the Theban landscape. It appears to be around this same period that the Gurnawis constructed similar manor-like homes in the area, presumably following the lead of their European neighbors, though adapting the construction to their own needs and expectations.

GURNAWI VERNACULAR

The three modern hamlets of Gurna that lay within the historic precinct were composed of multiple large, mudbrick family residences, sometimes of two or more

FIGURE 2. Robert Hay of Linplum, Detail from Panorama, 1820s (Hay Collection, British Library).

stories, and often brightly colored to contrast with the Theban desert landscape (see Figure 3). Irregular fenestration was common, with most windows on the east side of the structures, facing the flood plains and Nile beyond. Building interiors comprised organically organized spaces with undulating walls and earthen molded furnishings often built into the mudbrick walls or integrated into the clay floors. Of note were the towering pigeon roosts, integrated earthen ovens, and granaries and other storage areas protruding from the walls. As Hassan Fathy, famed architect and researcher of the Gurnawi vernacular, noted in his description of the residences, "the villagers allow themselves to mold the most individual and beautiful plastic forms ... the plan of a room or the line of a wall would not be a dull, square, measured thing but a sensitively molded shape, like a pot."[26] Often, a seamless integration of interior and exterior spaces composed the homes, integrating the unique plastic forms highlighted by Fathy (see Figure 4). The layout and program of these residences are representative of the Gurnawi response to their environment, using the only material readily available to them: mud from the Nile flood plains. Mud plasters usually covered both the interior and exterior of the walls, with shades of yellow, aquamarine, or pink often adorning the exterior. Some of these structures incorporated in their plan an underlying tomb, used as additional living space.

The location of the structures, grouped into three principal settlements that overlay an area dotted with thousands of New Kingdom pharaonic tombs, is testament to the strong physical relationship of Gurna and the Gurnawis to the discovery, reuse, and visitation of the tombs. Historic reference to and ongoing residence within some of the tombs, their documented involvement in the European archaeological endeavor, and Gurnawi interaction with modern tourists highlight the integral role of the pharaonic landscape and its consumption within Gurnawi culture and livelihood. Locals had not only lived with and among these ancient

FIGURE 3. Sheikh 'Abd el Gurna hamlet, view from southwest, February 2009 (author's photo).

FIGURE 4. Gurnawi house, Sheikh 'Abd el Gurna hamlet, view from northeast and above, with built-in earthen oven flue in foreground and mosque visible in distance, February 2009 (author's photo).

sites for at least two centuries, but they had also come to rely on their discovery, excavation, and visitation for their survival, often dedicating part of their homes to the manufacture and sale of tourist trinkets and, according to some officials, original artifacts.

The scenic architecture and lively participation of the Gurnawis in the life of the extensive archaeological site on the West Bank, which became a UNESCO World Heritage Site in 1979, has concerned Egyptian authorities since the 1940s and incited them to call for their relocation. The practical challenge proffered by the authorities is the policing of the thousands of tombs in the area that are overlaid and partially inhabited by the Gurnawis. Many Gurnawi houses have incorporated one or more pharaonic tombs as subterranean chambers used for storage, living quarters, barns, and countless other spaces for everyday use. Soon after Egyptian independence from Britain, the antiquities authorities began investigating ways to protect the tombs by relocating the Gurnawis who lived among them. As early as the 1940s, the authorities attempted to create a "New Gurna" far to the east and outside of the historic area, planning to relocate many of the inhabitants from the center of tourist activity, on which they relied for their livelihood. The unfinished village, designed by Hassan Fathy after extensive study of Gurnawi lifestyle and relationship to their built environment, failed as an endeavor, in part because Gurnawis vehemently resisted the move from their ancestral homes to a modern vernacular village dissimilar to their own aesthetic and lifestyle.[27] In the 70 years since, efforts to attract and forcibly relocate the villagers to new, climatically and culturally inappropriate concrete buildings have continued with mixed results. Most recently, the authorities addressed the question by demolishing nearly all the structures of Gurna's western hamlets and forcibly relocating the inhabitants. Although families resisted bulldozing of their earthen manors by continued

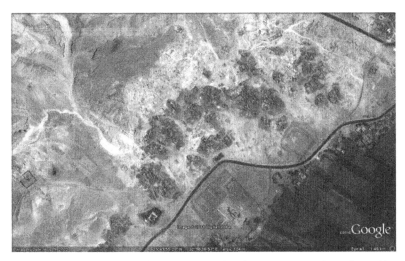

FIGURE 5. Satellite image of Sheikh 'Abd el Gurna hamlet, August 2002 (Google Earth).

occupancy, the majority of vernacular structures were destroyed between 2006 and 2009 (see Figures 5 and 6), affecting some 3500 families through forced relocation and dissolution of a once vibrant agglomeration of hamlets.[28]

PRESERVING THEM OUT OF HOUSE AND HOME

The loss of the Gurnawi homes represents the destruction of an historic vernacular architecture in favor of preserving the authorized, more highly valued

FIGURE 6. Satellite image of Sheikh 'Abd el Gurna hamlet, October 2009 (Google Earth).

heritage in the same place. Despite the expressed concern for the impact of the community on the prized subterranean heritage, the authorities simultaneously demolished a unique opportunity to interpret the story of Gurna and its residents: the first and only museum of Gurnawi history and culture housed within two restored historic structures. The Gurna Discovery Center, as it was called, had been established in April 2001 as a free museum of Gurna history and culture open to locals and tourists alike and authorized by the Supreme Council of Antiquities. Included in the exhibitions were copies of Robert Hay's panoramas, historic photos of Gurnawis and their residences, and reports and images of modern-day events relevant to the area. Although the protection of this center would have preserved some aspects of the Gurnawi story and a physical example of the built heritage, it was destroyed in 2010 during the last wave of demolitions, apparently approved by then-director of the Supreme Council of Antiquities, Zahi Hawass, as part of a plan to protect the nearby tomb of Nakht, an astronomer under the 18th Dynasty Pharaoh Thutmose IV (approximately 14th century BCE).[29] The website of the Discovery Center acknowledges its own demise with a banner stating "the information below is now history—yet another part of the vanished history of Gurna."[30] A sole building was preserved from within the destroyed Gurnawi hamlet of Sheikh 'Abd el Gurna. Metropolitan House, the 1912 field house built by the Metropolitan Museum of Art currently used by the Polish team working at the temple of Hatshepsut (see Figures 7 and 8), is linked to the elite history of Egyptology and ongoing archaeological discovery. Its continued presence amid the piles of rubble that once represented vibrantly colored, sizable Gurnawi residences underscores

FIGURE 7. Satellite image of Sheikh 'Abd el Gurna hamlet, August 2002; arrow indicates Metropolitan House (Google Earth).

FIGURE 8. Satellite image of Sheikh 'Abd el Gurna hamlet, October 2009; arrow indicates Metropolitan House (Google Earth).

the official preference for an archaeological past that is part of the authorized heritage discourse (see Figure 9). While targeting the local vernacular in the area for demolition, this building was protected as part of the site's archaeological heritage.

At the end of 2009, in the midst of one of the final campaigns of Gurna demolitions, the Egyptian cultural authorities, announced that Howard Carter's field house would be turned into a museum.[31] This announcement not only

FIGURE 9. Detail of built-in earthen oven amid the rubble of destroyed residence, February 2009 (author's photo).

underscored the undeniable significance of the ancient Egyptian heritage, but also formalized protection and interpretation of the history of its modern discovery. Previously, Hawass had often referred to inadvertent discoveries by villagers throughout Egypt as events precipitated by their pack animals or livestock rather than by the villagers themselves, reinforcing a common view that villagers had no active involvement in the archaeological endeavor.[32] Due in part to this official view, the Gurnawi contribution to the discoveries of Luxor's West Bank remains underrepresented and undervalued, and the relocation and demolition of the community undermine the association of Gurna with the pharaonic remains. The lack of physical vestiges of the Gurnawi community atop the pharaonic tombs removes the need for interpretation and allows for a privileged retelling or "cleansing" of the archaeological history that supports only the authorized discourse of the West Bank as a pharaonic city of the dead, omitting subsequent living communities.

A few scholars have considered the relationship between the politics of heritage and the previous efforts to relocate the Gurnawis. Mitchell highlights factors of identity construction and nation-making in Egypt as integral to the process of defining a pharaonic history that is separate from a more recent Islamic identity.[33] He further notes the changing polemic of the government from a focus on the protection of the pharaonic site in the 1940s to a concern for tourist experience and safety in the 1990s, in both cases denouncing the role of Gurnawis as participants in the archaeological discovery of the sites and in the tourism industry that now overruns them. Meskell in turn considers the relationship between violence and tourism, questioning the motivations behind the 1997 massacre of tourists that took place in the area, though not involving the Gurnawis, who were among the first to come to the aid of victims and overpower the terrorists. "It could be argued that the construct of 'global world heritage' is, in part, a remnant of colonialism."[34] She likens tourism and violence, respectively, to a form of imperialism and a backlash against foreign hegemony. Meskell further represents tourism in Egypt as a force for marginalization of modern local communities in light of the focus on pharaonic identity: tourists are not encouraged to discover the later periods of Egyptian history, and little or none of the revenue reaches the locals, remaining largely in the hands of foreign tourism companies and, once in Egypt, with national entities based in Cairo.[35] The heritage industry that caters largely to foreign tourists makes no effort to introduce a more informed history of the places they visit, causing both tourist and guide to overlook many rich and integral vestiges of local and regional history in favor of the authorized discourse. However, it is important to note that Gurnawis had, prior to the demolitions, integrated themselves somewhat effectively into the heritage industry on the West Bank, serving as unofficial guides, selling trinkets and wares, working with foreign missions, and even showcasing their own community and heritage to interested tourists.

The World Bank and USAID conducted studies in Luxor and throughout Egypt related to the protection of the pharaonic remains that privileged tourism while disenfranchising local communities. They lauded economic development efforts to increase high-end tourism by effectively separating tourists from local communities and preventing their interaction.[36] This reinforced an archaeological perspective on Egypt's history by extricating subsequent and even contemporary layers of habitation from the interpretation of these places. Quite surprisingly, USAID conducted studies of plans for Gurnawi relocation, including proposed designs of housing and research on their cultural values and lifestyle, all without questioning whether the relocation was indeed necessary or if there were viable options for mitigating concerns about the community's interaction with the pharaonic Necropolis.[37] The understanding that Gurnawis were "criminals" and "tomb robbers"[38] seems to rest on the judgments of 18th- and 19th-century European explorers without consideration for the modern socioeconomic context. Additionally, the significance of the thousands of adjacent pharaonic tombs, many of which are in deplorable condition and have been thoroughly documented, was never reconsidered in light of the living community sharing the land. Indeed, the value of the pharaonic landscape is uncontested, but authorities have refused to accept the significance of the community as an intrinsic component of this landscape. It is worth noting that many members of the Egyptology community were adamant that the Gurnawis or, at least, the physical evidence of their community should remain and become part of an overarching conservation and interpretation plan for the West Bank.[39] However, the concerns of the largely foreign archaeological community for the preservation of Gurna hamlets were met with simple government reiterations of the need to protect the pharaonic heritage.

CONCLUSION

Gurna is one of many examples of living communities disenfranchised by preservation efforts, but it provides a challenging and test-worthy case for considering alternatives to this approach of site protection inspired by eminent domain. Concerns for the pharaonic tombs that dot the landscape of the West Bank are justified; inappropriate use and introduction of waste water and animals have exacerbated their deterioration. In such cases, heritage professionals and government officials have the responsibility and, often, the mandate to take necessary action. Nonetheless, there appears to have been no attempt to educate the Gurnawis to work with site managers and mitigate these threats. The authorities instead focused on their forced relocation, conducting numerous trials and employing a diverse group of consultants to facilitate that process over a 70-year period that culminated in forced relocation and demolition. Although small numbers of residents did relocate in response to some earlier campaigns, the efforts were large failures overall and were even known to result in violence, as Mitchell notes occurred in 1998 when police opened fire on protesting villagers.[40] These failures, particularly with episodes of protest and violence, are clear evidence of the attachment of the villagers to their homes and land. As mentioned previously, this was not only an ancestral association or attachment to place, but for many this attachment was borne by economic necessity to earn from the tourism that engulfed them.

Reconciling a living community and its needs with the preservation of the heritage beneath was the principal question that unfortunately received no answer from the acts of demolition. There are multiple preservation options that better serve the interests of the Gurnawis, while still protecting the historic tombs and other pharaonic heritage in the vicinity. These approaches can be divided into two main categories: (1) community development models that aim to keep the Gurnawis living in their homes above the tombs and (2) preservation approaches that facilitate relocation of the residents while protecting and interpreting a corpus of their vernacular in situ. Each category has a broad spectrum of possibilities related to the size of the remaining community, the number of buildings preserved, amount of access locals and others have, and so forth. However, all these options must incorporate appropriate and adequate protection of the pharaonic tombs and relevant education about their significance.

In the first category of possible approaches, the government and site managers might have worked with the local community as partners and stakeholders in the preservation process, learning what activities threaten the pharaonic tombs and developing mitigation strategies, such as drainage for wastewater, systems of refuse removal, regulations about animals, and restrictions on tomb access and theft. In this way, the site managers could develop a working relationship with the villagers and involve them in strategies for protecting the heritage site on which they live, simultaneously increasing security and establishing a warning system for major problems of preservation. Concomitant with these efforts, they could underscore the importance of the living Gurnawi heritage, its physical manifestations, and the current lifestyle. The existence of the Gurna Discovery Center provided a unique opportunity to showcase the long history of the community and their significant association with the historic archaeological endeavor of the region. This approach requires long-term planning and intensive training, and carries with it heightened risk for continued damage to the tombs, but encourages a deepened respect for the heritage site by locals, allowing their continued habitation and establishing additional layers of desperately needed security and monitoring for the pharaonic sites. Involvement of the Gurnawis in the protection of the site could have been integrated into a preservation master plan for the West Bank, integrating their role in the process, while also interpreting the significance of the Gurnawi presence and their vernacular architecture to visitors.

The second category comprises options more readily implemented by preservation professionals and government officials, given that post-relocation protection and preservation are far more easily ensured by site managers. An initial education campaign would still be required to raise awareness about the significance and fragility of the pharaonic heritage among the Gurnawis, while encouraging their willingness to be relocated in cooperation with the government. However, a history of 70 years of largely unsuccessful relocation efforts underscores the improbability of unhindered, peaceful implementation. Nonetheless, over the years, some families did abandon their homes in favor of relocation. These abandoned buildings could have been preserved as part of the historic landscape of the West Bank, with one or more even open to tourism, as part of the interpretation of Gurnawi heritage presented by the Gurna Discovery Center. In the extreme scenario that occurred, with demolition of nearly all structures, the opportunity still remained to preserve a few select structures, including the Gurna Discovery Center, to serve as a signpost of the community and built heritage that was for centuries integral to the cultural landscape of the West Bank.

Although the above suggestions clearly have no opportunity for implementation in Gurna now, it is hoped that these approaches may be developed and tested in other cases where living communities of historic importance are threatened by calls for preservation of adjacent heritage sites. Preservation approaches that would have integrated the Gurnawi settlement would have been preferable to any other alternative, although they may have been difficult to implement without risking additional damage to the pharaonic tombs. In some cases, forced relocation may be necessary, but simply bulldozing homes as soon as inhabitants left for the day represents a barbaric and inhumane method of forcing compliance, since residents have no home to which to return. Other methods of relocation must be researched and considered. Even in the most dire of cases, where demolition may be determined necessary for most structures, the Gurna Discovery Center should have been preserved as the sole vestige of Gurna's past association to the pharaonic landscape. Ultimately, the loss of the Gurnawi houses represents a decision to privilege one authorized discourse over another. The active destruction of living cultural heritage embodied by historic settlements and the lives impacted together form undeniable testimony. Although the calls for relocation of the community and destruction of the homes arose from a perceived need to protect the pharaonic heritage, the drastic actions have resulted in an irreparable denigration of the cultural landscape and history that included the Gurna settlements.

ENDNOTES

1. This line of questioning and consideration of a matrix of human experiences and values is rooted in the classical historical tradition set forth by Herodotus. Although Herodotus' writings are undeniably concerned with temporal progression, earning him the moniker "The Father of History," his Homeric engagement with storytelling and the social context of events addresses physical spatialities. This, of course, should be understood in conjunction with his geographic breakdown of classical and preclassical events. The distinction here is that the interaction with history begins with the physical remains of times past as bearers of historic, present, and future social values, rather than the formless story.

2. Among these are John Ruskin and Eugène-Emmanuel Viollet-le-Duc, who agreed about the importance of certain examples of the built environment, but had contradicting views of the nature

of their value and the approach to preserve them. Indeed, Ruskin in his work *The Lamp of Memory* made clear that monuments were vestiges from the past that belonged to those who built them, but were shared by subsequent generations. Thus, according to his reasoning, it was not within the right of anyone to "obliterate" them and it was equally inconceivable to attempt restoration, which he saw as a form of destruction. Quite in contrast to this view, the French theorist and architect, Viollet-le-Duc, saw the care of historic buildings as an opportunity to improve on the original, re-creating and adding to a building to make it the best example of its type and period. Viollet-le-Duc was entrusted with the restoration of numerous medieval buildings in France, among them the cathedrals of Notre-Dame in Paris and Saint-Sernin in Toulouse. The latter has famously undergone a "derestoration" in recent years to remove his many additions and changes to the Romanesque basilica.

3. Fitch, *Historic Preservation*, 23.

4. Charters and guidelines for cultural heritage management and protection have reflected the development of the field, evolving from a simplistic focus on the physicality of monuments and built heritage, as highlighted within the 1964 Venice Charter, to more nuanced and multicultural concepts of intangible values and the significance of place and practice, in addition to physical remains, as developed by the 1979 Burra Charter and subsequent Nara Document in 1994.

5. Riegl, "The Modern Cult of Monuments," 72.

6. Lowenthal, "Stewarding the Past in a Perplexing Present," 22 (emphasis original).

7. See Appadurai, *The Social Life of Things*.

8. Smith, *Uses of Heritage*, 4.

9. Cited in Hayden, *The Power of Place*, 16.

10. Hayden, *Power of Place*, 46.

11. Smith, *Archaeological Theory*.

12. See Meskell, "Sites of Violence" and Meskell, "The Intersection of Identity and Politics in Archaeology," 279–301; Kohl, "Nationalism and Archaeology," 223–46.

13. Meskell, "Sites of Violence," 127.

14. A vast literature on cultural consumption exists, but the constraints of the current article do not allow for greater consideration of this. See Tally Katz-Gerro, "Cultural Consumption Research," 11–29 for a discussion of the field. A profound consideration of the implications and impacts of cultural tourism as a practice of consumption is Oakes, *Tourism and Modernity in China*.

15. Hall, "Politics and Place," 99–113. See also Wang, "From a Living City to a World Heritage City," 1–17 for a Chinese example of tourism and related preservation decisions disenfranchising and displacing the local community.

16. Hall, "Politics and Place," 108.

17. McKercher and Du Cros, *Cultural Tourism*, 127.

18. See Lears, "The Concept of Cultural Hegemony," 567–93 for an overview of Gramsci's concept.

19. The illustration appeared in Pococke, *Description of the East and Some Other Countries*.

20. Denon, *Travels in Upper and Lower Egypt*.

21. Denon, *Travels in Upper and Lower Egypt*, 112.

22. Denon, *Travels in Upper and Lower Egypt*, 238. See also Sonnini, *Travels in Upper and Lower Egypt*, for reference to Gurna and its inhabitants.

23. Robert Hay of Linplum (1799–?) arrived in Egypt in 1824 and assembled a team of artists and architects to record the many monuments and extensive art of ancient Egypt. His exquisite drawings, panoramic sketches, and notes remain a valuable resource to archaeologists and heritage professionals working in the region.

24. Romer, *A Pilgrimage to the Temples and Tombs of Egypt, Nubia, and Palestine*.

25. Rhind, *Egypt: Its Climate, Character, and Resources*, 55.

26. Fathy, *Architecture for the Poor*, 41.

27. The New Gurna project was under the charge of famed architect Hassan Fathy. See Fathy, *Architecture for the Poor* for a recount of the approach, trials, and failure of the project, as well as discussion of Gurnawi vernacular. One of the posited reasons for their original refusal is the fact that Gurnawis are Arab desert-dwellers and not *fellahin*, or peasant-farmers, and consider their place of

activity, livelihood, and social space to be on the desert sands rather than the fertile floodplains where New Gurna was located. Of course, the dissociation from the center of tourist activity and the related moneymaking opportunities, as well as their traditional homes, must also have been a factor.

  28. Jill Kamil, "Vindicating Gurna," *Al-Ahram*, 7 February 2008, http://weekly.ahram.org.eg/2008/883/feature.htm (accessed 20 February 2011).
  29. A number of communications between the founder and director of the Gurna Discovery Center, Caroline Simpson, and Egyptian officials are cited in a talk given by Simpson, "Theban Blindness."
  30. See http://www.Gurna.org/discovery.html (accessed 5 May 2011).
  31. "Tutankhamun finder's home on show."
  32. See Wynn, *Pyramids and Nightclubs*.
  33. Mitchell, "Making the Nation."
  34. Meskell, "Sites of Violence," 128.
  35. Meskell, "Sites of Violence," 130–31. Through personal communications with Egyptian site managers in Luxor, I have learned that revenue from ticket sales to enter the tombs and other sites are not available to the sites in question but held in Cairo and managed by the Supreme Council of Antiquities. This is evident when seeing the facilities and equipment of the antiquities offices in Luxor.
  36. Meskell, "Sites of Violence," 134.
  37. Mitchell, "Making the Nation," 224.
  38. Some of the monikers for Gurnawis in Denon, *Travels in Upper and Lower Egypt* and Fathy, *Architecture for the Poor*.
  39. The author had the privilege of attending three Luxor West Bank Conservation Planning meetings that involved government officials, members of a number of foreign archaeological missions, and the representatives of other organizations, such as the Getty Conservation Institute and USAID, working in the Necropolis. The fate of the Gurna hamlets was discussed during these meetings and in private conversations with government officials and foreign archaeologists.
  40. Mitchell, *Rule of Experts*.

BIBLIOGRAPHY

Anderson, Benedict R. *Imagined Communities: Reflections on the Origin and Spread of Nationalism*. London: Verso, 1983.

Appadurai, Arjun. *The Social Life of Things: Commodities in Cultural Perspective*. Cambridge: Cambridge University Press, 1986.

Denon, Vivant. *Travels in Upper and Lower Egypt, During the Campaigns of General Bonaparte in the Country*. Translated by Arthur Aikin. New York: Heard and Forman, 1803.

Fathy, Hassan. *Architecture for the Poor: An Experiment in Rural Egypt*. Chicago: University of Chicago Press, 1973.

Fitch, James Marston. *Historic Preservation: Curatorial Management of the Built World*. Charlottesville: University Press of Virginia, 1990.

Habermas, Jürgen, Sarah Lennox, and Frank Lennox. "The Public Sphere: An Encyclopedia Article." *New German Critique* 3 (Autumn 1974): 49–55.

Hall, C. Michael. "Politics and Place: An Analysis of Power in Tourism Communities." In *Tourism in Destination Communities*, edited by Shalini Singh, Dallen J. Timothy, and Ross Kingston Dowling, 99–113. Oxon, UK: Cabi, 2003.

Handler, Richard. *Nationalism and the Politics of Culture in Quebec*. Madison: University of Wisconsin Press, 1988.

Hayden, Dolores. *The Power of Place: Urban Landscapes as Public History*. Cambridge, MA: MIT Press, 1995.

"Howard Carter's Luxor Home Now a Museum," http://news.bbc.co.uk/2/hi/middle_east/8342428.stm (4 November 2009; accessed 10 January 2013).

Katz-Gerro, Tally. "Cultural Consumption Research: Review of Methodology, Theory, and Consequence." *International Review of Sociology* 4 (2004): 11–29.

Kohl, Philip. "Nationalism and Archaeology: On the Constructions of Nations and the Reconstructions of the Remote Past." *Annual Review of Anthropology* 27 (1998): 223–46.

Lears, T. J. Jackson. "The Concept of Cultural Hegemony: Problems and Possibilities." *The American Historical Review* 90 (1985): 567–93.

Lefebvre, Henri. *The Production of Space*. Translated by D. Nicholson Smith. Cambridge: Blackwell, 1991.

Logan, William. "Introduction: Voices from the Periphery: The Burra Charter in Context." *Historic Environment* 18, no. 1 (2004): 2–8.

Lowenthal, David. "Stewarding the Past in a Perplexing Present." In *Values and Heritage Conservation: Research Report*, edited by Erica Avrami, Randall C. Mason, and Marta de la Torre, 18–25. Los Angeles: Getty Conservation Institute, 2000.

McKercher, Bob, and Hilary Du Cros. *Cultural Tourism: The Partnership between Tourism and Cultural Heritage Management*. New York: Haworth Hospitality Press, 2002.

Meskell, Lynn. "The Intersection of Identity and Politics in Archaeology," *Annual Review of Anthropology* 31 (2002): 279–301.

———. "Sites of Violence: Terrorism, Tourism, and Heritage in the Archaeological Present." In *Embedding Ethics*, edited by Lynn Meskell and Peter Pels. Oxford: Berg, 2005.

Mitchell, Timothy. "Making the Nation: The Politics of Heritage in Egypt." In *Consuming Tradition, Manufacturing Heritage*, edited by Nezar Alsayyad. London: Routledge, 2001.

———. *Rule of Experts: Egypt, Techno-Politics, and Modernity*. Berkeley: University of California Press, 2002.

Oakes, Tim. *Tourism and Modernity in China*. London: Routledge, 1998.

Pococke, Richard. *Description of the East and Some Other Countries*, Vol. 1. London: W. Bowyer, 1743.

Rhind, Alexander Henry. *Egypt: Its Climate, Character, and Resources as a Winter Resort*. Edinburgh: Thomas Constable, 1856.

Riegl, Alois. "The Modern Cult of Monuments: Its Essence and Its Development." In *Historical and Philosophical Issues in the Conservation of Cultural Heritage*, edited by Nicholas Stanley Price, Mansfield Kirby Talley, and Alessandra Melucco Vaccaro, 69–83. Los Angeles: Getty Conservation Institute, 1996.

Romer, Isabella Frances. *A Pilgrimage to the Temples and Tombs of Egypt, Nubia, and Palestine, in 1845-6*. London: R. Bentley, 1846.

Ruskin, John. "The Lamp of Memory." In *Historical and Philosophical Issues in the Conservation of Cultural Heritage*, edited by Nicholas Stanley Price, Mansfield Kirby Talley, and Alessandra Melucco Vaccaro, 322–23. Los Angeles: Getty Conservation Institute, 1996.

Simpson, Caroline. "Theban Blindness: A Case History of Severe Archaeological Hypermetropia." Paper presented at the Disciplinary Measures: Histories of Egyptology in Multi-disciplinary Contexts conference, London, June 2010. http://www.qurna.org/links.html (accessed 10 June 2011).

Smith, Laurajane. *Archaeological Theory and the Politics of Cultural Heritage*. London; New York: Routledge, 2004.

———. *Uses of Heritage*. London: Routledge, 2006.

Sonnini, Charles Sigisbert. *Travels in Upper and Lower Egypt: Undertaken by Order of the Old Government of France*, Vol. III. London: J. Stockdale, 1807.

US/ICOMOS. "ICOMOS Charters & Other International Doctrinal Documents." *US/ICOMOS Scientific Journal* 1, no. 1 (1999).

Viollet-le-Duc, Eugène-Emmanuel. *The Architectural Theory of Viollet-le-Duc: Readings and Commentary*. Edited by M. F. Hearn. Cambridge, MA: MIT Press, 1990.

Wang, Shu-Yi. "From a Living City to a World Heritage City: Authorized Heritage Conservation and Development and Its Impact on the Local Community." *International Development Planning Review* 34 (2012): 1–17.

Wynn, L. L. *Pyramids and Nightclubs: A Travel Ethnography of Arab and Western Imaginations of Egypt, from King Tut and a Colony of Atlantis to Rumors of Sex Orgies, Urban Legends about a Marauding Prince, and Blonde Belly Dancers*. Austin: University of Texas Press, 2007.

Part II
Types of Cultural Heritage Rights

[5]
Nature and Culture: A New World Heritage Context

Shabnam Inanloo Dailoo* and Frits Pannekoek**

Abstract: The understanding of the relationship between culture and nature as manifested in the UNESCO declarations and practices has changed over the last few years. The World Heritage Convention is continuing to evolve its definitions to reflect the increasing complexities of world cultures as they grapple with the heritage conservation policies that reflect their multiple stakeholders. They are also integrating a greater cultural perspective in their recent resolutions to the convention. Although the links between nature and culture have been clarified through this new attention to cultural landscapes, many countries and their bureaucracies have not yet adopted these new perspectives. The article suggests that to achieve an integrated approach to conservation, national, regional, and international bodies and their professionals must be involved. Two examples are discussed to address the shortcomings of the application of the convention and to illustrate the complexities of defining and conserving cultural landscapes.

The relationship between nature and culture is unique and entirely dependent on each culture's perspective of nature, culture, and their interrelationship. The failure to recognize these differing cultural perspectives has resulted in inappropriate conservation decisions. In fact, the considerable debate over the interrelationship between culture and nature and also heritage conservation strategies has been largely driven by a Eurocentric view of how culture and nature interplay. These debates are reflected in the policies and activities of the World Heritage Convention (WHC), the international pioneer in conservation of cultural landscapes.

The concept of identifying and conserving the values of heritage places has been at the heart of the WHC (the UNESCO Convention Concerning the Protection of the World Cultural and Natural Heritage, 1972), and indeed, all international her-

---
*University of Calgary, Alberta, Canada. Email: dsinanlo@ucalgary.ca
**Athabasca University, Alberta, Canada. Email: fritsp@athabascau.ca

itage conservation policies. However, the application of the convention in different countries with diverse cultural roots has raised a key issue. How can both the cultural and natural values inherent in many heritage properties be conserved and valued in an integrated way? Around the world places exist where natural and cultural values are both significant and interdependent; none of the values would mean the same without the presence of the other. However, because one value may seem more prominent than the other, only that value is recognized; and in these cases, the application of the convention results in partial conservation. A failure to recognize the interrelationship of nature and culture has also resulted in a number of cultural landscapes being inappropriately identified. The long application of either natural or cultural criteria in isolation of the other within the framework of the convention has led to planning, conservation, and development policies and decisions that are incomplete and often at variance. Experience shows that only with the understanding of the influence of culture on an understanding of nature, with a complete assessment of the interrelationship of the two in theory and in practice, can world heritage be protected in a meaningful and holistic way.

Takht-e-Soleyman Archaeological Site in Iran and Head-Smashed-In Buffalo Jump in Canada are examples of the problem when sites are recognized based on a single dominant value. In both sites cultural values were initially identified and considered sufficient for their designation according to the criteria in the Operational Guidelines for the Implementation of the World Heritage Convention. Yet, the natural elements of both sites and their connection to the cultural aspects are critical to their understanding and conservation. They are practical examples that illustrate how lack of recognition of all values has resulted in a designation that is inappropriate and causes management and conservation challenges. They also illustrate how experiences at international level can influence national practices. Reviewing the current situation of the two with a focus on the reasons for the failure of an integrated natural and cultural conservation strategy assists the future nominations of similar heritage properties with multiple values. These cases are discussed in detail to illustrate the complexities of the application of the convention. Several possible solutions and their applicability such as renominations or amendments of new areas (the larger landscapes) are also examined. Analysis of these unsuccessful experiences should assist in improving future nominations.

NATURE AND CULTURE INTERPLAY

To understand how cultural and natural attributes of heritage sites have been applied in accordance to the World Heritage Operational Guidelines, it is important that the concept of nature and culture be understood. The varying perspectives on the relationship between nature and culture depend on the cultural origins of their holders. That nature and culture are interwoven[1] is accepted in many different cultures.

NATURE AND CULTURE

In a broad sense, *culture* refers to all human activities and their affects. Perhaps culture can be best understood as a process, a continuous combination of shared values, beliefs, behaviors, and practices that characterize a group of people. It is the social practices that produce and modify material culture. As well, the self-understanding of human beings in relationship to the wider world is evidenced by differing concepts of nature. *Nature* is a key part of humanized, culturally defined places. Even if nature is defined as a quality, a feature distinct from that of human civilization, the dualism that exists between culture and nature is still apparent, especially from a Western way of thinking.[2] Even though nature is not *made* by humans, it is a human intellectual construct. This relationship is wholly dependent on human intentions and thereby can be argued to be a cultural attribute.

Human activities have modified the environment, and their affects are evident in all aspects of nature. Many cultural and natural areas exist around the world that are evidences of such interplay and "are the meeting place of nature and people, of past and present, and of tangible and intangible values."[3] This integration of natural and cultural environments is the primary characteristic of cultural landscapes (Figure 1). At times, there is the debate that no such a thing as *purely cultural landscape* exists, because nature provides the basis for all human activities. There is also no such a thing as purely natural landscape because humans have always influenced the environment; nothing in the so-called natural environment can be found in its pristine form and devoid of human footprints; the pristine nature is "a mirage, receding as it is approached."[4] Natural scientists consider culture as a heritage of nature, whereas social scientists believe that nature is defined socioculturally[5]; and even the ways in which natural scientists attempt to approach nature conservancy are in fact cultural interventions, differing from one culture to another. It is impossible to consider nature and culture as two separate entities. This means that cultural landscapes are the places in which culture and nature inseparably come together.[6]

Sauer, a cultural geographer who introduced the term *cultural landscape* in 1925, believed that cultural landscape "is fashioned from a natural landscape by a cul-

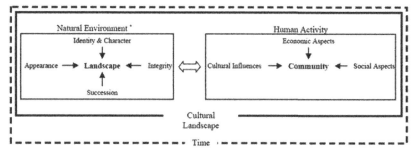

* Adopted From: Van Mansvelt & Pedroli (2003)

FIGURE 1. Integration of natural and cultural environments in cultural landscapes.

tural group. Culture is the agent, the natural area is the medium, and the cultural landscape is the result."[7] He acknowledged the fundamental importance of nature because it provides the basis for the cultural landscape, and of culture which shapes the landscape. In fact everything is culture and depends on or has been influenced by human "cultural values ... ascribed by different social groups, traditions, beliefs, or value systems ... fulfill humankind's need to understand, and connect in meaningful ways, to the environment of its origin and the rest of nature."[8] In other words, understanding a landscape is based on the way people experience and interpret the world.

Because peoples' activities and their cultural knowledge shape landscapes, it is never complete. Humans have shaped it in the past and always add to it.[9] This perspective disagrees with that of Sauer who believed that "under influence of a given culture, itself changing through time, the landscape undergoes development, passing through phases, and probably reaching ultimately the end of its cycle of development."[10] In fact landscape is subject to change both because of its very evolutionary nature and because of the changes that human beings have forced and continue to force on it to create a livable world.[11] Natural change is inevitable and an inherent characteristics of any given object. Cultural changes occur either because of the development of cultures or as a result of replacement of cultures; therefore, the current state of a landscape always differs from the original. Characteristics of a landscape can be analyzed and interpreted as a window on culture, because "cultural groups socially construct landscapes as reflections of themselves."[12] People use landscape to promote cultural continuity and to maintain these values into the future. A landscape is like a document that describes cultures that have been living there over time to create different layers of meaning.

FROM CULTURE *OR* NATURE TOWARD CULTURE *AND* NATURE

The dichotomy between culture and nature was evident early on in the UNESCO's WHC. The criteria set in the World Heritage Operational Guidelines for the purpose of the assessment of sites were divided into cultural criteria (six items) and natural criteria (four items). Even the two scientific advisory bodies of the World Heritage Committee, the International Council on Monuments and Sites (ICOMOS), and the World Conservation Union (IUCN), which are responsible for the assessment of the nominees, act separately. The argument by Philips on the nature and culture interaction clarifies that the long tradition of "the separation of nature and culture—of people from their surrounding environment—which has been a feature of western attitudes and education over the centuries, has blinded us to many of the interactive associations which exist between the world of nature and the world of culture."[13] The inscription of the first mixed cultural and natural heritage on the World Heritage List,[14] Tikal National Park in Guatemala, resulted in the acknowledgment that there might be sites that do not satisfy any of the criteria laid out in article 1 of the convention,[15] which outlines the types of cultural heritage that are a combination of both natural and cultural factors. The apparent limitations of the separate definitions of culture and nature in the WHC and lack of sufficient evaluation criteria were recognized when a rural landscape[16] failed to be inscribed as a cultural landscape on the list. Thereby, the Operational Guidelines were revised in 1992, and the new category of cultural landscape (under the category of cultural heritage) was added to the WHC.

The recognition of cultural landscape in the context of the convention was the first step toward bridging the gap between culture and nature. Prior to this recognition, such places as cultural landscapes (where nature had been culturally modified) were considered to have little value and were not recognized as a major area for conservation.[17] The recognition of cultural landscapes made them as valuable as previously recognized types of cultural and natural heritage. The definition of cultural landscape[18] emphasizes the interplay between nature and culture as well as between societies and environments through physical expression over time. It highlights the relationship between natural resource and cultural heritage values. Because natural resources are integral parts of the cultural landscape, they are considered "part of a site's historic fabric."[19] Nature conservation is also addressed in the definition of cultural landscape when it refers to the protection of cultural landscape as a contribution to sustainable land-use and the enhancement of natural values while maintaining biological diversity.[20] This approach toward cultural landscape tries to link the ICOMOS and IUCN activities vis-a-vis cultural landscapes.

The criteria for cultural properties set out in the Operational Guidelines were initially the basis of the evaluation of cultural landscapes. The issue of assessing the nomination of cultural and natural properties was addressed in the World Heritage Global Strategy Natural and Cultural Heritage Expert Meeting in Amsterdam in 1998. In spite of the conflicting opinions on the amalgamation of the natural and cultural criteria, the experts proposed establishing a new single set of criteria in place of the existing separate criteria for natural and cultural properties, hoping that this combination puts greater emphasis on the links between culture and nature.[21] The 2005 revision of the Operational Guidelines can be a considerable move to overcome the separation of culture and nature. Any or all of the new criteria will be considered in future nominations of properties as cultural landscapes or any other types of heritage.

The World Heritage Centre has noticed the dichotomy between nature and culture and has worked toward bridging the distances; however, it still needs to evolve and to develop further to become practical in different nations. The past dysfunctions have affected conservation activities. Many World Heritage Sites exist that are not designated as cultural landscapes and the resulting multidimensional values are neither identified nor addressed in planning decisions. Such sites are not fully protected because only traditional heritage elements or characteristics, not cultural landscapes are recognized.

CONSTRUCTION OF HERITAGE POLICY WITHIN THE WORLD HERITAGE CONVENTION

The primary aim of the WHC is to identify and safeguard cultural and natural sites that are considered to have outstanding universal value. The framework of the convention was originally driven by the separation of culture and nature long identified from Euro-American perspectives. In other words the selection of cultural properties for inscription on the World Heritage List is often criticized as Euro-American centric.[22] However, in recent years there are signs that this has changed. To correct both this perception and reality, there have been several conferences, thematic studies, and expert meetings in different regions (e.g., the first Global Strategy Meeting on African Cultural Heritage and the WHC in 1995, the 1997 meeting on the Identification of Potential Natural Heritage Sites in Arab Countries, or the 1998 Regional Thematic Meeting on Cultural Landscapes in the Andes).[23] They mainly focused on creating a more comprehensive and integrated approach to issues of the nature–culture interrelationship by considering under-represented cultures and both tangible and intangible types of heritage. The growing participation of other regions and cultures has challenged the application of criteria defined in the Operational Guidelines. The results have been to consider varied worldviews and to introduce different types of heritage values.

The knowledge of indigenous peoples offers another approach toward understanding the interaction of nature and culture. They view cultural, natural, and spiritual values in places as inseparable and in balance. Their history is embodied in the land. To them, culturally significant landscapes are not viewed as places of the past, but as places that are both alive and sacred today; these people often have a strong spiritual, rather than material, relationship with the land. As a result of their powerful association with the land, they tend to respect the land on which they dwell.[24] This perspective on nature–culture interaction is now regarded as a significant part of the application of the WHC.

Furthermore, attention given to the interaction of cultural and natural values at the World Heritage meetings led to the addition of the associative cultural landscape category to the World Heritage List. The primary concern was that an important aspect of cultural landscapes was not being addressed within the then-dominant Euro-American perspective. In determining associative cultural landscapes, the predominant character of the landscapes was to be derived from the natural environment and the meaning attached to the landscape from its cultural context.[25] This category now accommodates the inseparability of cultural, natural, and spiritual values in indigenous cultures and emphasizes the intangible aspects of a place and the cultural meanings to its people. The adoption of this category also confirmed that places could be nominated on the basis of outstanding universal value derived from cultural meaning attached to place, even though there were only intangible manifestations. In spite of that, limitations continue to exist in the inscription of associative cultural landscapes because criterion vi[26] of the Operational Guidelines for the assessment of outstanding universal value must still be accompanied by outstanding universal value in one of the other criteria. Head-Smashed-In Buffalo Jump is one of the few cases with associative values that have been ever enlisted on the World Heritage List only under criterion vi. Most associative cultural landscapes are now normally qualified for inscription on the list using other criteria such as criterion iii or criterion iv.[27]

CULTURAL LANDSCAPES WITHIN THE FRAMEWORK OF THE WORLD HERITAGE CONVENTION

According to the World Heritage Committee, there are three main categories for cultural landscapes[28]; all categories illustrate human relationship with the natural environment. The first property inscribed specifically as a cultural landscape on the list in 1993 was first nominated in 1990 as a natural heritage site.[29] It is a typical example of the WHC's shortcomings in ascribing integrated cultural and natural values to a place.

The first category, landscapes designed and created intentionally by man, is "easily identifiable" and usually under protection. This category is "often associated with religious and monumental buildings and ensembles" created for aesthetic reasons.[30] Historic gardens of different styles, such as Japanese, English, and Persian Garden, are the typical examples of this category.

The second category, the organically evolved landscape, is significant because of its "social, economic, administrative, and/or religious imperative," identified either as a relict or fossil landscape or a continuing landscape.[31] They can be identified without difficulty because they all have physical remains. However, a relict cultural landscape is more than an unstructured collection of monuments. For example, Takht-e-Soleyman Archaeological Site in Iran is an example of a relict cultural landscape. This landscape contains superimposed patterns of several periods, which provide evidence for changing or continuous patterns of landscape use and activity within a single area.[32] The adjacent village, farmlands, and orchards provide the opportunity for this World Heritage Site to be recognized as a continuing landscape as well.

Associative cultural landscape, the third category, is significant because of "the powerful religious, artistic or cultural associations of natural element"; the physical or material evidence "may be insignificant or even absent."[33] In other words, in associative landscapes, the link between the physical and religious aspects of landscape is highly significant, as evident in the Aboriginal landscapes in North America and Australia among other places, such as Head-Smashed-In Buffalo Jump in Canada. This site was used by First Nations peoples for thousands of years and its spirituality is as important as its natural features.

WORLD HERITAGE CONVENTION IN PRACTICE: TWO ILLUSTRATIVE EXAMPLES

What are the main obstacles to sites attempting to become designated as cultural landscapes? The Operational Guidelines for the Implementation of the WHC in its legal form could well be complete; however, its application in different cultures is more challenging. The different cultural backgrounds, varied heritage types at local levels, and most importantly heritage terms in different cultures are some of the challenging problems. The problem is that the concept of cultural landscape is still new to many cultures; there are countries that do not even have the terminology or the perfect translation for cultural landscape. The examples illustrate why the convention has not been effectively implemented even in the cases that are eligible for recognition as cultural landscapes. Obviously, if the notion of cultural landscape is not thoroughly understood by locals, chances are low that sites will be recognized and protected.

Head-Smashed-In Buffalo Jump, World Heritage Site of Canada
Natural and Cultural Values

Head-Smashed-In Buffalo Jump is located northwest of the town of Fort McLeod in southern part of the Province of Alberta where the Rocky Mountains meet the Great Plains. A specific form of cultural landscape is well represented by Head-Smashed-In Buffalo Jump. This fairly extensive site includes the gathering basin leading to the drive lanes (the lines of rocks that were laid out where natural elements were culturally modified to improve the utility); the sandstone cliff, a natural feature of the site (approximately 300 meters long and more than 9 meters high); the kill sites at the bottom of the cliff edge; and the nearby butchering camps (the campsite and processing area). There is also a connection down the various coulees[34] to the Old Man River Valley, the wintering grounds of the Blackfoot.

The key feature of Head-Smashed-In's natural landscape is the area that lies behind to the west of the buffalo jump, the gathering basin: a huge, natural, bowl-shaped depression. It acted as a natural trap, rich in grass and abundant water, to help contain the buffalo. The cultural and the natural elements coincide in this landscape. The great antiquity of the site, which has been used over 6000 years, is one of the key elements that define it as a cultural landscape. The other key factor is that it is extremely rich in terms of archeological material. There are deep layers of buried buffalo bones and stone tools that all tell the story of how Aboriginal people managed the hunt. There is also clearly a landscape component to that site. Its natural topography was vital to its successful use. It is a natural landscape that figures prominently in the cultural resources (Figure 2).

There are other associated cultural features, namely a vision quest site (a ceremonial location at the southern tip of the cliff side, which is thought to be a

FIGURE 2. Head-Smashed-In Buffalo Jump.

burial place), petroglyphs, and rock carvings. To the Aboriginal people, all these sites were a practical place of sustenance as well as a spiritual place created by Napi, the Old Man, a key folklore and spiritual figure to the Blackfoot; they are examples of physical and spiritual interfaces. There is also a strong visual connection between Head-Smashed-In and Chief Mountain, further south on the U.S.–Canadian border (another feature of religious and spiritual significance made by Napi) where the native people go for vision quests and prayers. The cultural values and spirits present at the site makes this landscape culturally significant. Even today some believe that the buffalo spirit dwells on the site. Collectively then, the site is characterized by natural, cultural, as well as spiritual attributes.

Head-Smashed-In is a unique site that represents the Blackfoot way of life. Everything was in perfect harmony, in terms of how Aboriginal peoples made the jump work, how the hunt was socially organized, and how it was run using their intimate knowledge of animal behavior to drive them to their death over the edge of a cliff. The native people's use of natural features and, in fact, the entire landscape was also significant; for example, they were familiar with the topography, climate, weather patterns, and prevailing winds. The whole story of the site, the Blackfoot people's way of thinking, and the archaeological findings by the Europeans are presented in the Interpretive Centre at the Head-Smashed-In Buffalo Jump, which is intentionally located underground in the cliff in a way that does not disturb the integrity of the site (Figure 3).

FIGURE 3. Interpretive centre at the Head-Smashed-In-Buffalo Jump.

Current Concerns

- Oil and gas developments: Recently, there has been strong pressure for oil and gas exploration. This might put the future of the site under threat.
- Subdivision: This area has a very low population density. There is tremendous pressure from Calgarians to build vacation houses. The economic pressures on the ranches in the surrounding Porcupine Hills might be so great that they will press to sell off their holdings in smaller parcels. The natural landscape that is so much a part of the traditions of Head-Smashed-In might be replaced with weekend housing estates.
- Windmills: If the region is rich in oil and gas, it is equally rich in environmentally friendly energy: wind. From the top of the Head-Smashed-In cliff, a long line of windmills marches into the horizon disturbing the view and the story and spirit of Head-Smashed-In. It might be argued that the windmills are not permanent in the landscape; their footprint would be virtually invisible should they be removed. The government does not own the lands that accommodate windmills, does not have any control on those lands, and has not developed a conservation plan for that area. There is not much control over what happens visually any distance from the site. This is linked to the issue of boundary of the site. There cannot be an indefinite boundary, but some regulations and designations are employed to avoid inappropriate interventions.

- World Heritage designation: The focus of Head-Smashed-In application was not cultural landscape; the notion of *cultural landscape* as a heritage type did not exist in the 1980s. The focus also was not Aboriginal people at all; there was little consultation with any Aboriginal group at the time of nomination, and the government prepared the nomination paper based on an archaeological draft. At the time of nominating the Head-Smashed-In Buffalo Jump to the World Heritage, the major focus of the application was on the archaeological part of the site that was more than 10 meters deep and at least 6000 years old. The application did describe the gathering basin back behind the cliff, the drive lanes, and so on; but it did not present it as a cultural landscape. The government would have a much better chance of conserving that site and its integrity if it had been designated a cultural landscape. It is the landscape that makes the story of Head-Smashed-In, not just the cliff and the bone bed at the base of the cliff.
- Conservation: The first protective tool at Head-Smashed-In is its Provincial Historic Resource status. Nothing physical and, in some cases, visual, can happen to the designated land that is owned by the government without the permission of the Minister of Tourism, Parks, Recreation and Culture. This area is under protection to prevent inappropriate development. Second is the *Special Places 2000* program's extension which provided a form of government review for any development. This program identified a broader range of naturally significant places in the Head-Smashed-In region, which were added to the original land designation. The original submission to UNESCO and the development plan that was produced became, in effect, the landscape management plan, because it identified the areas that required preservation and the need to maintain a grazing regime on those areas. There is no formal cultural landscape management plan for Head-Smashed-In, but the review of the earlier documents indicated that the existing management plans are acceptable as an alternate to a formal landscape management plan. There remains a need for a coherent cultural landscape management plan that reflects the need to conserve the rare and endangered species in the area, as well as heritage concerns, and addresses the concerns of key stakeholders including Aboriginal peoples, ranchers, and the different industries that give the community economic life.

Takht-e-Soleyman Archaeological Site, World Heritage Site of Iran

Natural and Cultural Values

In the West Azerbayejan Province of Iran, near the town of Takab and on southern border of Balkash Mountain, there is a highland famous for its geomorphological features as well as its historic sites; the most significant ones are Zendan-e-Soleyman and Takht-e-Soleyman. Beside the archaeological remains, the landscape of the area is characterized by other integral parts such as natural features (mountains, river, woodland, and thermal springs), agricultural areas (farmlands and orchards), and the small village of Takht-e-Soleyman located between Takht and Zendan (Figure 4 and Figure 5).

Around the opening of a great hollow sedimentary hill, known as Zendan-e-Soleyman (Solomon's Prison), there are remnants of a historic sacred place for worshiping Anahita, the Goddess of Water. Dateable potsherds found on these remnants show that they belong to the first millennium B.C. Zendan-e-Soleyman is a hollow hill approximately 110 meters high, which has a mouth approximately 60 meters wide and 100 meters deep. The region in west side of Zendan has many thermal water springs. Local people believe that these springs are of mysterious powers. Once a great thermal spring, Zendan-e-Soleyman dried up by its own sediments probably because of a seismic cataclysm. Taking it as the dissatisfaction of Anahita, the early residents left and settled around another thermal spring nearby, known as Takht-e-Soleyman (Throne of Solomon), to praise Anahita more respectfully.[35]

Takht-e-Soleyman is an elliptical platform (380 × 300 m) of calcareous sediments and surrounded by a masonry wall and buttresses that make it resemble a fort. In the middle of Takht, there is a lake that has a spring in the bottom with a mouth approximately 2 meters in diameter. The shape of the lake is also elliptical with a great diameter of 115 meters and is funnel-shaped in the vertical section

FIGURE 4. Takht-e-Soleyman archaeological site.

FIGURE 5. Zendan-e-Soleyman hill and Takht-e-Soleyman village.

(46–115 m deep). The lake has two streams going outside; therefore, the level of water is almost unchanged. There is evidence of a residential enclosure as a small hamlet from the Achaemenid period (six to fourth centuries B.C.) on the alluvial platform, called *Shiz* at that time. But the most important buildings on this site are those from the Sassanid period (third to seventh centuries A.D.). The Azargoshnasp fire temple was on Takht-e-Soleyman and with Anahita temple, water and fire were worshiped at the same place and at the same time. This fire was one of the three most respected fires in Sassanid period and as the symbol of unity of the nation. The ancient fire temple was destroyed in seventh century A.D., restored, and used again in 1270 as a hunting palace. It was neglected once again in the fourteenth century and abandoned with its ruined monuments until 1819.[36]

Takht-e-Soleyman is a testimony of the association of nature and history, revealing one of the great artistic achievements of Sassanid civilization and witnessing the organization of the landscape and the philosophical and religious activity in perfect harmony. The site has strong symbolic and spiritual significance and provides a valuable insight to Zoroastrianism, one of the oldest belief systems, as an official and royal religion and development of Persian art, architecture, and landscape planning. It is the only survival of the three important fire temples of the Sassanid Empire and the only representative of Zoroastrian sanctuary. Zoroastrians still perform annual religious ceremonies in this site. The symbolic relationship between Takht-e-Soleyman and the natural features (water and fire are among the fundamental elements respected by ancient Iranians) makes it culturally significant, as a testimony of the association of ancient beliefs.

Architectural style, design, and materials used for construction add a more physical value to the site. The ensemble of Takht-e-Soleyman is an outstanding example of the royal architecture of Sassanid period. The most significant characteristic of this site is that the principal architectural elements were joined together in a natural context and provided a harmonious composition of natural-architectural-cultural features. The ability of ancient people to use the lake as the center of the design represents their deep understanding of the relationship between their faith/philosophy and natural/geological feature.[37]

Although Takht was developed and modified over time with different architectural characteristics, it still occupies its original setting and foundations and retains its historic ruin area and therefore its integrity. Occasional lake flooding deposits calcareous sediments all over the platform. This has partially preserved different settlement periods in separated layers of sediments. The structures became ruined because of neglect and natural erosion.

Current Concerns

- Urban development: Presently, the site is protected from any urban encroachments simply because it is far from major cities. The only threat might be the development of the nearby village. There was a master plan in place for the village, and the primary works and infrastructures were implemented; but the project was later discontinued. The proposed plan was prepared based on major cities master planning and did not consider the historical context and the identity of the place. Topography and other environmental factors as well as ownership issues regarding the agricultural lands were all overlooked. Had the master plan been completely implemented, the historical identity of the area would have been lost. It is the historic, natural, cultural, and spiritual values of the site that are of high significance and demands specific attention. Currently, there is a will to prepare an improvement plan for the village instead of subdividing the agricultural lands for urban development.
- Land-use changes: The archaeological heritage of the site is enriched by the Sassanid town, which is now covered by surrounding agricultural fields and still needs to be excavated. Any land use changes in the area threaten the archaeological site and question the integrity of the landscape. The discontinuity of land use is a key factor in endangering the protection of the integrity of the site.

- New constructions: Takht-e-Soleyman has been historically used by people. Even though human activities have shaped and modified the landscape through interventions on the natural elements (vegetation) and the cultural features (buildings, structures, roads), they have always respected the landscape in its broader sense. New facilities are constructed both inside and outside the plateau with the purpose of enhancing the visiting experience. Because there has been no comprehensive planning for outside of Takht, the placement of the new facilities is inappropriate and problematic in terms of infrastructure and aesthetic.
- Mineral resources: Takht-e-Soleyman region has a high potential in terms of mineral resources. There exist numerous metallic and nonmetallic mines including historical gold and silver mines that might attract industrial activity. Nearby quarries also have historical significance. They were used for construction of Takht-e-Soleyman. There is a potential threat if these mines were to be heavily used. Not only would the landscape be changed by the mines themselves, but the refining processes could be an even greater intrusion.
- Conservation: The focus of conservation activities has been mainly within the plateau on excavations, restoration, and reconstruction of architectural structures. The Iranian Cultural Heritage, Handicraft and Tourism Organization is only responsible for the archaeological remains. Although the organization has identified the boundary of the site and categorized it in different zones with varied physical and visual development restrictions, they are not responsible for the conservation of natural elements and environment of the site. The ensemble of Takht-e-Soleyman falls within the boundaries of a protected area and a wildlife refuge recognized by the Department of Environment of Iran. These areas are important in terms of natural resources; strict regulations are in place for such areas, which control any type of developments. Lack of effective communication between organizations, difficulties in negotiations, and separation of the natural and cultural conservation are the main concerns at Takht-e-Soleyman. Both organizations are well informed about their specific areas of concern, one from the standpoint of protecting the environment and the other from a cultural resource perspective; but they do not collaborate as they should, because collaboration could be seen as interfering with each other's administrations, which leads to operational conflicts. Due attention should be paid to the full range of values represented in the landscape, both cultural and natural, so that the character and the spirit of place can be protected.

The Iranian Cultural Heritage, Handicrafts and Tourism Organization has defined a landscape buffer zone for the site. Takht-e-Soleyman is like a bowl in the middle, with some specific regulations. It would be an effective tool to control all activities in the area. Any kind of intervention or physical/functional modification should consider the conservation regulations according to the defined buffer zone.

TAKHT-E-SOLEYMAN ARCHAEOLOGICAL SITE AND HEAD-SMASHED-IN BUFFALO JUMP: CULTURAL HERITAGE OR CULTURAL LANDSCAPE?

At the time of Head-Smashed-In's designation in the early 1980s, cultural landscape was not even included in the World Heritage categories. The only option was designation as a cultural heritage site. Although in 2003 Takht-e-Soleyman could have been nominated as a cultural landscape rather than as a complex of scattered historic sites, the Iranian authority only emphasized the architectural, archaeological, and historic aspects of the site. The inscribed cultural heritage area is huge in size and includes 14 historic sites around Takht-e-Soleyman. The examples were inscribed on the list at different times: one prior to and the other after recognition of cultural landscape within the World Heritage context. However, the results remain the same, they are recognized as cultural landscapes neither internationally nor nationally. This ignores the fact that the sites are obviously cultural landscapes.

The result of such designations, where priority was given to the historical and cultural considerations, was a lack of effective management planning. Cultural landscapes demand a different type of conservation and management planning to manage the change because of their dynamic and evolutionary nature. They require a plan that considers the landscape in its whole and includes natural features that are crucial to the integrity of the site and important for the people living and working there. Such plans must address major challenges in conservation because cultural landscapes are complex, usually contested spaces with many stakeholders. The lessons learned in both cases suggest that the future of the world's cultural landscapes will be most appropriately met by appropriate inclusive designation criteria.

Many of the previously inscribed sites on the list are now in fact qualified to be identified as cultural landscapes.[38] The Operational Guidelines' limitation that each country can only nominate one cultural property per given year leaves no room for the renomination of previously inscribed sites. By nature, countries prefer to entitle a new site as a World Heritage Site instead of just changing the status. At Head-Smashed-In, for example, the efforts of the Historic Places Stewardship Branch within the Alberta Government has been to broaden the designation to include it as a cultural landscape. It is the one change that has come from the recommendations on the recent review of the state of the site (periodic reporting). There is a chance that Head-Smashed-In will be recognized at the UNESCO level as a cultural landscape, rather than simply the cultural resource. This is going to happen as an amendment, and not a renomination.

This is not the case for Takht-e-Soleyman. The Iranian government still considers the current designation appropriate; and unfortunately, there is no willingness to amend the designation in near future. Regardless of the existing management plan for Takht-e-Soleyman, a more recent report will clarify that this site would be incomplete without its environment and natural features, not to mention its other associated values. The areas around Takht-e-Soleyman must be included in the original designation to ensure full conservation of all aspects of the site.

Countries should take their periodic reporting to the World Heritage Committee more seriously and determine whether all the values of the site have been recognized and that all the values of the sites are protected and well managed. This would encourage state parties to evaluate their designation and to propose changes of status or to enforce new amendments. It can evolve as an effective tool that ensures a successful and all encompassing management plan.

To ensure appropriate designations, first there is a need to understand the notion of cultural landscape at local levels and develop conservation policies for such heritage sites at national levels and next take the nominations to the next stage: the World Heritage Committee. Presently, the nature–culture debate wages at international levels but has little relevance to national or local preservation agendas. For example, Iran does not identify any heritage property as a cultural landscape, and thus no national policies or guidelines are available at the moment. However, slow progress has been made toward introducing the concept to the professionals and preparing a definition for cultural landscape in accordance with its cultural background. It is impossible to have international designations without adopting any national definition and policies. In the Canadian situation, Parks Canada has defined the term *cultural landscape* at the national level[39]; however, the provinces have not used this category in their plans. Under the Canadian constitution the provincial governments have the power to protect heritage sites; in the case of provincial-owned heritage sites, the federal government has only commemoration power. That is, it only acknowledges the value of the heritage and has no legal jurisdiction to manage heritage sites. They only manage the sites that are federally owned, which are a minority of sites in Canada. The provinces must localize the definition of cultural landscape as defined by Parks Canada, but that will be difficult to achieve because provincial officials are rarely involved in international discussions.

Nominations still continue to be submitted without considering the cultural landscape option. Capacity building will be a highly effective tool to train experts in countries in different regions of the world. The 2006 International Expert Workshop on Enhanced Management and Planning of World Heritage Cultural Landscape was held in Persepolis, Iran. The workshop was co-organized by the Iranian Cultural Heritage and Tourism Organization and UNESCO as a part of capacity-building program during which experts were exposed to the recent developments on the concept of cultural landscape. Continuity of such programs is a key factor in the wider introduction of the concept of a cultural landscape; these capacity-building programs can contribute to a deeper understanding of values hidden in sites qualified as cultural landscapes.

Each country is responsible for preparing and submitting the nomination dossier to the World Heritage Committee. The advisory bodies to the Committee are responsible for reviewing the proposals and evaluating the values and criteria stated in the nomination application. In many cases they would not formally suggest changing the proposed category. If proposing countries could perform a thorough evaluation and a thorough comparative study before nominating the site and seek the advisory bodies' opinion prior to official nominations, it would likely make a noticeable difference toward avoiding disappointment. The limiting factors to achieving this importance are time frames and human and financial resources, which should be addressed within the World Heritage Committee.

CONCLUDING REMARKS

The international recognition of cultural landscapes has overcome the historic division of culture and nature in the WHC. The convention's new approach toward assessment of heritage sites and the recognition of the interaction between culture and nature can significantly influence conservation practices around the world. However, it has not been widely examined, and the implications of putting the two sets of criteria together are unclear. The situation will be clarified after a few years of experience and trial, and the outcome will be more apparent over time. Chances are high that new evaluation processes will result in possibly even more confusion in a number of countries. Many believe this new approach would not affect the existing inscriptions of cultural landscape, and the outcomes would remain the same; for example Canada could continue to nominate more natural heritage sites or Iran could continue with its all cultural heritage nominations. Others believe it will end the long-debated dichotomy between nature and culture and will present more appropriate nominations. Successful results can only be achieved if all aspects of a place are taken into consideration when identifying the appropriate criteria. And then these will only be effective if they are applied with knowledge.

Although UNESCO has recognized the links between nature and culture through attention to cultural landscapes, many nation states and their bureaucracies have not yet done so. Whether this new approach to evaluate heritage properties can be applied at national levels and whether the reassessment of national properties is achievable will largely depend on the local circumstances. They include not only local cultural beliefs, but also financial and operational opportunities, governments' willingness, and priorities.

Conservation of cultural landscapes can be included in a larger context, both in the field of historic preservation and the natural resource conservation. The primary obstacle in recognizing cultural landscapes within the preservation community and its practices has been the difficulty of identifying the landscape as a heritage resource. However, all three types of cultural landscapes (landscapes designed and created intentionally by man, organically evolved landscapes, and associative cultural landscapes) testify to the interaction of humankind and nature, as well as to how the passage of time adds to their values. In most cases of cultural heritage sites, the cultural values often overshadow their relationship with the natural environment. This issue is also evident in natural heritage sites where the natural influences are so significant that there is little room for cultural considerations. To be sure, the major problem in cultural landscapes designation is the identification of hidden heritage elements, finding their historic value and then preserving them in their context for future generations.

Conservation of cultural landscapes requires a framework that recognizes and evaluates the relationship between natural and cultural values. There is broad support both from academia and policymakers, but not in all countries, to link natural and cultural values. The Operational Guidelines' new set of criteria will hopefully influence local authorities and influence the system of identification, assessment, and inscription of heritage properties, as well as conservation practices. The convention's new approach may result in inscription of more cultural landscapes, which in turn will encourage the development of cultural landscape safeguarding practices. Indeed, it is crucial that countries reflect this integration into their heritage conservation policies considering their cultural circumstances. International bodies are critical to setting and championing standards; but in the end little will change without the engagement of the *owning* communities. National agencies must accept the responsibility for the dissemination of the latest information and policies to their local experts.

In addition, the close cooperation between cultural and natural institutions both at international and national levels must be encouraged to support the new amalgamated set of criteria. In fact, the new set includes 10 criteria, which are the same familiar ones that ICOMOS and IUCN have used for decades; ICOMOS used the six first criteria and IUCN applied the rest. It can be also suggested that instead of IUCN and ICOMOS each being responsible for the evaluation of cultural landscape, one new advisory body could be established within the World Heritage Centre and solely devote its work to cultural landscapes while collaborating with ICOMOS and IUCN. Conversely, establishing another body would add to the current financial and administrative complexities; nevertheless, it could be argued again that is reasonable when it results in better protection of the world's heritage. Many previously inscribed sites on the World Heritage List are eligible for recognition as cultural landscapes. It is not the intention of this article to suggest that all those sites must be renominated and their status changed. There is always the possibility that new categories of heritage could be identified in the near future, and it is impossible to review all inscribed sites each time there is a new addition to the already recognized categories. Rather, the hopes is to encourage the revision of the previous designations by each country to gain insights to support their future nominations and seriously consider cultural landscape as a heritage type. The World Heritage Committee's restriction that each country can only nominate one cultural property each year creates some reservations for renominating previously inscribed sites. Furthermore, this article recommends that countries consider amendments to the previous designations in cases that are undoubtedly cultural landscapes and when the futures of those landscapes are in danger.

To conclude, the UNESCO World Heritage Centre is exercising leadership in the identification of cultural landscapes; however, nation states are lagging behind in the application of the new criteria. This is resulting in planning and conservation problems. The first mandate in the World Heritage designation is to conserve the recognized values. Without appropriate designation, conservation and management practices will not focus on all values. There are, however, signs that in the next decade there might be a more holistic approach. This should result in better planning, management, and conservation practices that consider multiple values of all heritage properties.

ENDNOTES

1. Lowenthal, "Landscape as Heritage", "Cultural Landscapes", "Natural and Cultural Heritage"; Mitchell, "Cultural Landscapes." This issue is discussed in more details in the following literature: Amos, "The International Context for Heritage Conservation"; Buggey, "Associative Values"; Head, *Cultural Landscapes and Environmental Change*; Keisteri, "The Study of Changes in Cultural Landscapes"; Olwig, "Introduction"; Philips, "The Nature of Cultural Landscapes", "Why Lived-in Landscapes Matter"; Sauer, "The Morphology of Landscape"; von Droste, Plachter, and Rossler, "Cultural Landscapes: Reconnecting Culture and Nature."
2. Head, *Cultural Landscapes*.
3. Philips, "Why Lived-in Landscapes Matter," 10.
4. Head, *Cultural Landscapes and Environmental Change*, 4.
5. Olwig, "Introduction."
6. Lowenthal, "Natural and Cultural Heritage"; Buggey, "Associative Values."
7. Sauer, "The Morphology of Landscape," 343.
8. von Droste quoted in Williams, "The Four New 'Cultural Landscapes,'" 9. Founding Director of World Heritage Centre in 1992, von Droste has been involved in international programs for the conservation of the cultural and natural environments and has been involved in introducing the concept of cultural landscape in the WHC.
9. Ingold in Robertson and Richards, *Studying Cultural Landscapes*; Tilley, *A Phenomenology of Landscape*.
10. Sauer, "The Morphology of Landscape", 343.
11. Lewis, "The Challenge of the Ordinary."
12. Mitchell, "Cultural Landscapes"; Stoffle, Halmo, and Austin, "Cultural Landscapes and Traditional Cultural Properties," 229.
13. Philips, "The Nature of Cultural Landscapes," 36. Previous chair of the World Commission on Protected Areas, IUCN, he has more than 20 years of active involvement in IUCN, particularly landscape protection; and now he is involved in leading IUCN's work in the WHC.
14. Tikal National Park in Guatemala (an area of the tropical rainforest and one of the greatest Mayan city sites) was the first mixed site inscribed on the World Heritage List in 1979. By 1992 14 more mixed sites had been inscribed on the list.
15. According to article 1, *monuments, groups of buildings*, and *sites* are considered as cultural heritage.
16. The Lake District in the UK during 1980s.
17. von Droste, Platcher, and Rossler in Mitchell and Buggey, "Protected Landscapes and Cultural Landscapes."
18. Cultural landscapes are the "combined works of nature and of man. They are illustrative of the evolution of human society and settlement over time, under the influence of the physical constraints and/or opportunities presented by their natural environment and of successive social, eco-

nomic and cultural forces, both external and internal" (UNESCO World Heritage Centre, *Operational Guidelines*, 2005, clause 47).

19. Meier and Mitchell, in Buggey "Associative Values."
20. *Operational Guidelines*, 2005, Annex 3, Clause 9.
21. UNESCO World Heritage Committee, *Report of the World Heritage Global Strategy*.
22. Cleere, "The Concept of 'Outstanding Universal Value'"; Tunbridge and Ashworth, *Dissonant Heritage*.
23. UNESCO World Heritage Center, Global Strategy Website.
24. Buggey, "Associative Values."
25. Buggey, "Cultural Landscapes." Notes from e-mail to the author, September 7, 2005.
26. Criterion vi indicates that a nominee should be directly or tangibly associated with events or living traditions; ideas or beliefs; and artistic and literary works of outstanding universal significance.
27. UNESCO World Heritage Centre, *Operational Guidelines for the Implementation of the World Heritage Convention*, 2005, II.D. Criterion iii indicates that a nominee should be a unique or at least exceptional testimony to a cultural tradition or civilization. Criterion iv requires a nominee to be an outstanding example of a type of building, architectural or technological ensemble or landscape.
28. UNESCO World Heritage Centre, *Operational Guidelines for the Implementation of the World Heritage Convention*, 2005, Annex 3, Clause 10.
29. That is Tongariro (a mountain sacred to the Maori people in New Zealand). Uluru (Australia) was inscribed in 1994. Like Tongariro, this place is of extreme importance to the indigenous peoples of the area and had been inscribed on the World Heritage List initially only for its natural value.
30. UNESCO World Heritage Centre, *Operational Guidelines for the Implementation of the World Heritage Convention*, 2005, Annex 3, Clause 10(i).
31. UNESCO World Heritage Centre, *Operational Guidelines for the Implementation of the World Heritage Convention*, 2005, Annex 3, Clause 10(ii). In a relict landscape "an evolutionary process came to an end at some time in the past, either abruptly or over a period." In a continuing landscape "the evolutionary process is still in progress" and "retains an active social role in contemporary society closely associated with the traditional way of life."
32. Irani Behbahani, Sharifi, and Dailoo, "A Glance at the Conservation."
33. UNESCO World Heritage Centre, *Operational Guidelines for the Implementation of the World Heritage Convention*, 2005, Annex 3, Clause 10(iii); Cleere, "Cultural Landscapes as World Heritage."
34. A dry streambed (Merriam-Webster Online); a canyon that was once filled with water (University of Virginia. "A History of the Grand Coulle Dam").
35. Naumann, *Die Ruinen Von Tacht-E Suleiman*.
36. Naumann, *Die Ruinen Von Tacht-E Suleiman*.
37. Iranian Cultural Heritage Organization, "Takht-E Soleyman Fire Temple of Knights"; ICOMOS, *Evaluations of Cultural Properties*.
38. For example, Kakadu (Australia), Tikal (Guatemala), and Mount Athos (Greece) are all, in effect, cultural landscapes. Inclusion of cultural landscapes in the cultural properties category will result in a significant increase in the number of properties inscribed on the list that also manifest natural characteristics.
39. According to Parks Canada, cultural landscape is "any geographical area that has been modified, influenced, or given special cultural meaning by people." Parks Canada, "Guiding Principles."

BIBLIOGRAPHY

Amos, Bruce. "The International Context for Heritage Conservation in Canada." *Environments* 24 (1996): 13.

Australia ICOMOS. "Asia-Pacific Regional Workshop on Associative Landscapes: A Report by Australia ICOMOS to the World Heritage Committee. 27–29 April." New South Wales, April 27–29, 1995. http://whc.unesco.org/archive/cullan95.htm (accessed December 29, 2005).

Buggey, Susan. "Associative Values: Exploring Nonmaterial Qualities in Cultural Landscapes." *Association for Preservation Technology Bulletin* 31 (2000): 21–27.

———. "Cultural Landscapes." Notes from email to the author, September 7, 2005.

Cameron, Christina. "The Spirit of Place: The Physical Memory of Canada." *Journal of Canadian Studies* 35 (2000): 77.

Clarke, Ian. "Report on the State of Conservation of Head-Smashed-In Buffalo Jump." *Periodic Report on the Application of the World Heritage Convention*. Calgary: Province of Alberta, 2005.

Cleere, Henry. "Cultural Landscapes as World Heritage." *Conservation and Management of Archaeological Sites* 1 (1995): 63–68.

———. "The Concept of 'Outstanding Universal Value' in the World Heritage Convention." *Conservation and Management of Archaeological Sites* 1 (1996): 227–33.

———. "The World Heritage Convention in the Third World." In *Cultural Resource Management in Contemporary Society: Perspectives on Managing and Presenting the Past*, edited by Francis P. McManamon and Alf Hatton, 99–106. London and New York: Routledge, 2000.

Head, Lesley. *Cultural Landscapes and Environmental Change*. Edited by John A. Matthews, Raymond S. Bradley, Neil Roberts, and Martin A.J. Williams. Key Issues in Environmental Change Series. London: Arnold, 2000.

ICOMOS. *The Nara Document on Authenticity*. Nara, Japan, 1994. http://www.international.icomos.org/naradoc_eng.htm (accessed December 29, 2005).

———. "Evaluations of Cultural Properties: Takht-e-Suleiman (Iran)." *World Heritage Committee 27th Ordinary Session, Suzhou (China)*, 51–55. Paris: UNESCO World Heritage Centre, 2003. http://whc.unesco.org/archive/advisory_body_evaluation/1077.pdf (accessed August 10, 2007).

Irani Behbahani, Homa, Arta Sharifi, and Shabnam Inanloo Dailoo. "A Glance at the Conservation and Reclamation of Archeological Landscapes." *Iranian Architecture Quarterly* 3 (2003): 56–71.

Iranian Cultural Heritage Organization. "Takht-E Soleyman Fire Temple of Knights." UNESCO World Heritage Convention Nomination of Properties for Inclusion on the World Heritage List. Tehran: Iranian Cultural Heritage Organization, 2002. http://whc.unesco.org/archive/advisory_body_evaluation/1077.pdf (accessed January 15, 2006).

Jones, Michael. "The Concept of Cultural Landscape: Discourse and Narratives." In *Landscape Interfaces: Cultural Heritage in Changing Landscapes*, edited by Hannes Palang and Gary Fry, 2151. Dordrecht, Holland: Kluwer Academic Publishers, 2003.

Keisteri, Tarja Tuulikki. "The Study of Changes in Cultural Landscapes." PhD diss., Helsingin Yliopisto (Finland), 1990.

Lewis, Peirce. "The Challenge of the Ordinary: Preservation and the Cultural Landscape." *Historic Preservation Forum* 12 (1998): 18–28.

Lowenthal, David. "Landscape as Heritage: National Scenes and Global Changes." In *Heritage: Conservation, Interpretation, Enterprise*, edited by J. M. Fladmark, 3–15. London: Donhead Publishing, 1993.

———. "Cultural Landscapes." *UNESCO Courier* 50 (1997): 18–20.

———. "Natural and Cultural Heritage." *International Journal of Heritage Studies* 11 (2005): 81.

Merriam-Webster Online. "Coulee." http://merriamwebster.com/dictionary/coulee (accessed January 15, 2008).

Mitchell, Nora J. "Cultural Landscapes: Concepts of Culture and Nature as a Paradigm for Historic Preservation." PhD diss., Tufts University, 1996.

Mitchell, Nora J., and Susan Buggey. "Protected Landscapes and Cultural Landscapes: Taking Advantage of Diverse Approaches." *The George Wright Forum* 17 (2000): 35–46.

Naumann, Rudolf. *Die Ruinen Von Tacht-E Suleiman Und Zendan-E Suleiman*. Translated by Faramarz Nadjd Samii. Tehran: Iranian Cultural Heritage Organization, 1995.

Olwig, Kenneth R. "Introduction: The Nature of Cultural Heritage and the Culture of Natural Heritage-Northern Perspectives on a Contested Patrimony." *International Journal of Heritage Studies* 11 (2005): 3–7.

Parks Canada. "Guiding Principles and Operational Policies: Glossary." http://www.pc.gc.ca/docs/pc/poli/princip/gloss_E.asp (accessed January 27, 2008).

Philips, Adrian. "The Nature of Cultural Landscapes: A Nature Conservation Perspective." *Landscape Research* 23 (1998): 21–38.

———. "Why Lived-in Landscapes Matter to Nature Conservation." *Association for Preservation Technology Bulletin* 34 (2003): 5–10.

Robertson, Iain, and Penny Richards. *Studying Cultural Landscapes*. London: Hodder Arnold, 2003.

Sauer, Carl O. "The Morphology of Landscape." In *Land and Life: A Selection from the Writings of Carl Otwin Sauer*, edited by John Leighly, 315–50. Berkeley: University of California Press, 1963.

Stoffle, Richard W., David B. Halmo, and Diane E. Austin. "Cultural Landscapes and Traditional Cultural Properties: A Southern Paiute View of the Grand." *American Indian Quarterly* 21 (1997): 229–50.

Tilley, Christopher. *A Phenomenology of Landscape: Places, Paths and Monuments*. Providence and Oxford: Berg, 1994.

Tunbridge, J. E., and G. J. Ashworth. *Dissonant Heritage: The Management of the Past as a Resource in Conflict*. Chichester: John Wiley & Sons, 1996.

UNESCO World Heritage Centre. *Operational Guidelines for the Implementation of the World Heritage Convention*. Paris: World Heritage Centre, 1996.

———. *Report of the World Heritage Global Strategy Natural and Cultural Heritage Expert Meeting*. Paris: World Heritage Centre, 1998. http://whc.unesco.org/archive/amsterdam98.pdf (accessed January 22, 2006).

———. *Operational Guidelines for the Implementation of the World Heritage Convention*. Paris: World Heritage Centre 2005. http://whc.unesco.org/archive/opguide05-en.pdf (accessed January 15, 2006).

———. *Global Strategy*. Paris: World Heritage Centre. http://whc.unesco.org/pg.cfm?CID=136&l=EN (accessed January 17, 2006).

University of Virginia. "A History of the Grand Coulle Dam, 1801–2001." http://xroads.virginia.edu/~UG02/barnes/grandcoulee/daughter.html (accessed January 15, 2008).

Van Mansvelt, Jan Diek, and Bas Pedroli. "Landscape, A Matter of Identity and Integrity: Towards Sound Knowledge, Awareness and Involvement." In *Landscape Interfaces: Cultural Heritage in Changing Landscapes*. Landscape Series, edited by Palang Hannes, and Gary Fry, 375–94. Dordrecht, Holland: Kluwer Academic Publishers, 2003.

Von Droste, Bernd, Herald Plachter, and Mechtild Rossler. "Cultural Landscapes: Reconnecting Culture and Nature." In *Cultural Landscapes of Universal Value: Components of a Global Strategy*, edited by Herald Plachter and Mechtild Rossler, 15–18. Jena, Stuttgart, and New York: Gustav Fischer Verlag in cooperation with UNESCO, 1995.

Williams, Sue. "The Four New 'Cultural Landscapes'." *UNESCO Sources* 80 (1996): 9.

[6]

World Heritage and rights-based approaches to nature conservation

Gonzalo Oviedo* and Tatjana Puschkarsky

International Union for Conservation of Nature, 28 Rue Mauverney, 1196 Gland, Switzerland

(*Received 21 September 2011; final version received 19 December 2011*)

> The discourse and practice about protected areas and World Heritage sites has significantly evolved in the last decades. Efforts to empower local communities so that they can affirm their rights and act on their responsibilities, and to integrate natural and cultural values at sites overlapping with traditional lands, are increasingly seen as fundamental elements of conservation approaches. The fifth strategic objective of the World Heritage Committee encourages States Parties to pursue partnerships in the identification, nomination and protection of World Heritage sites, and to include communities as legitimate stakeholders in decision-making processes. However, there are weaknesses and challenges in achieving this objective. Rights-based approaches can help address such weaknesses, as they enable actors to understand the situation of marginalised communities in a systemic manner and to address the underlying factors of vulnerability, poverty and powerlessness. They can also help attain long-term conservation while supporting local people to live in dignity.
>
> **Keywords:** rights; conservation; heritage; indigenous communities; governance.

Introduction: the World Heritage Convention and the role of local communities

The UNESCO World Heritage Convention, created in 1972, is one of the most important global conservation instruments and has almost universal adoption among the nations of the world (UNESCO 1972). It is special among international conventions in the way it links conservation of natural and cultural properties. The convention is also unique in setting up advisory bodies of technical experts at the service of the treaty body. The existence of the expert organs for the World Heritage Convention – International Union for the Conservation of Nature (IUCN), International Council on Monuments and Sites (ICOMOS) and the International Centre for the Conservation and Restoration of Cultural Property (ICCROM) – makes it possible to institutionalise specific management practices.

As of July 2011, the World Heritage List (UNESCO 2011) unites 725 cultural, 183 natural and 28 mixed sites (making a total of 936 sites situated in 153 out of 187 States Parties), representing an international network of outstanding areas of conservation. The very existence of these places often means that they have been

---

*Corresponding author. Email: gonzalo.oviedo@iucn.org

valued and safeguarded by the local population for generations. In line with this recognition, States Parties to the World Heritage Convention have committed to support efforts that contribute towards this heritage having a continuing 'function in the life of the community'.

Together with credibility, conservation, capacity-building and communication, enhanced community participation is one of the five strategic objectives of the *Convention*. States Parties are encouraged to pursue a partnership approach in the identification, nomination and protection of World Heritage sites to include community actors as legitimate stakeholders in the decision-making process. The *Operational Guidelines* (UNESCO 2008) to the *Convention* acknowledge the fact that 'human activities, including those of traditional societies and local communities, often occur in natural areas' and that they can be compatible with conservation objectives if organised in a sustainable way. Community management is recognised as an adequate management form in the *Operational Guidelines*, and so is collective land tenure. However, partly due to its early adoption in 1972 when international and national protected area policy frameworks gave very little importance to the relationships with local communities, the *Convention* itself bears no reference to human rights or the rights of indigenous peoples and local communities.

IUCN has long been a promoter and supporter of effective community involvement in protected areas and of greater direct benefits to support local livelihoods. Key policy benchmarks in advancing this agenda were the IV and V World Congresses on Protected Areas (Caracas 1992, Durban 2003). More recently, and in line with the strategic objectives of the World Heritage Committee, particularly community participation, IUCN has actively made use of rights-based approaches (RBAs) in its conservation work, which brings the community focus to centre stage.

This article discusses the situation and role of local communities and Indigenous peoples in World Heritage sites, describes elements of the new conservation paradigm, in particular the introduction of RBAs in nature conservation, and explores the international framework that provides the background for these activities. The article argues that RBAs contribute to improving conservation regimes, are at the heart of the new conservation paradigm and should thus inform the work of international instruments such as the World Heritage Convention. We conclude this article by pointing to the possible ways to move forward considering the special role that IUCN, ICOMOS and ICCROM play as Advisory Bodies under the Convention and the potential they have to encourage and animate initiatives in this direction.

Background: the situation of local communities and indigenous peoples in protected areas and World Heritage sites

The idea of natural World Heritage sites as pristine areas of wilderness, undisturbed by human impact, has been prevalent in the thinking and practice of conservation agencies for a long time, and probably still persists in some places today. There is extensive literature showing that local and Indigenous communities who live in these areas or in their vicinity are often marginalised, impoverished and discriminated against by the majority population (e.g. Amend and Amend 1992, Oviedo and Sylva 1994 for Latin America, Lasgorceix and Kothari 2009 for India, Lele *et al.* 2010 for cases from Africa and elsewhere). Protected areas frequently overlap with traditional lands of Indigenous and other rural peoples, with their population traditionally practising stewardship of these sites. These areas often feature related tangible or intangible heritage and a richness of cultural expressions and cultural diversity associated with the natural environment and biological diversity (Kempf 1993). Unfortunately, the connection of local communities to their lands and their direct knowledge of natural processes are often underappreciated. Traditional subsistence activities such as hunting, fishing, fire practices and collecting of medicinal herbs have been an integral part of the dynamics and evolution of ecosystems, but are sometimes perceived as potentially detrimental to conservation efforts and, where allowed, have been subject to severe restrictions.

More evidently, human rights violations in protected areas including World Heritage sites in some countries have consisted of forced displacement, restrictions of access to culturally meaningful places or to resources critical for survival and oppressive enforcement measures including cases of cruel, inhuman or degrading treatment or punishment and arbitrary detention. As an example, as recently as in 2007 and 2009, the Special Rapporteur on the rights of Indigenous peoples of the Human Rights Council reported on human rights violations in the World Heritage site Chitwan National Park in Nepal, consisting of communities being:

> prevented from gathering food, medicinal herbs and firewood from the park area, which severely limits their livelihoods based on subsistence economies; [...] mistreatment, arbitrary detention and sexual abuse of Indigenous villagers, in particular Indigenous women, by Chitwan National Park rangers and military officials designated to patrol the park's premises. (UN Human Rights Council 2009, paragraphs 35–37)

Less evidently, through policies of avoiding or minimising the establishment and running of facilities, human rights violations have entailed the denial of services such as health or education for communities forced to remain isolated and without access to infrastructure. These facets of human rights violations have been aggravated by little or no tenure security for local communities and limited participation in decision-making processes, which affect their lives. Moreover, communities are sometimes not consulted on the establishment of a park or a World Heritage site within their traditional homeland and benefits resulting from World Heritage status are often not shared equitably.

The new conservation paradigm

Within a period of almost two decades, inaugurated by the IV World Protected Areas Congress in 1992 in Caracas, followed by the V Congress in 2003 in Durban and the adoption under the UN Convention on Biological Diversity (CBD) of the Programme of Work on Protected Areas (UN-SCBD 2004), the conventional model of insensitive protected areas which failed to consider the social and environmental context and respect fundamental rights has changed significantly. Four years after the 1992 Caracas Congress, WWF (formerly World Wide Fund For Nature / World Wildlife Fund) International developed and adopted a far-reaching policy on Indigenous peoples and conservation (WWF International 1996, reissued as WWF International 2008) – the first international environmental organisation to have adopted a policy of this kind. The same year, IUCN adopted at its Congress policy resolutions recognising the rights of Indigenous peoples in protected areas (IUCN 1997). Shortly after, IUCN and WWF issued a joint policy statement entitled *Indigenous and Traditional Peoples and Protected Areas: Principles, Guidelines and Case Studies* (Beltrán 2000). The 2003 Durban Congress's major outputs included key recommendations and commitments that took previous policies further on the basis of the recognition of fundamental rights (Larsen and Oviedo 2004).

The policy advances of this period are not only the result of a more socially sensitive position but also the consequence of learning from failed practices. Experience has shown that exclusionary 'fortress conservation' or a system of 'fences and fines' as it has been practised for many decades is often counterproductive to conservation objectives and can result in conflict, non-compliance and expensive protection mechanisms for the sites. Recognition has advanced on the need and importance of involving local communities in the management of protected areas and the development of World Heritage nominations and monitoring of the sites to provide substantial benefits for all those involved. More and more, procedural and participation rights are being considered as entry points for stronger collaboration between communities and the park management. Securing rights, including land rights and usufruct rights, is now seen as a fundamental condition for sustainability, giving the local population long-term security and promoting long-lasting stewardship of the land. Efforts to empower local communities so that they can affirm their rights and act on their responsibilities and integrating natural and cultural, tangible and intangible aspects at sites which often coalesce with traditional Indigenous homelands and bio-cultural diversity are no longer seen as alien to conservation objectives, but as preconditions for successful and lasting partnerships. Valuable local contributions such as traditional ecological knowledge or tracking skills can improve management techniques, and endogenous conservation by the people who have strong links to the land and deeply identify with it has become a way to gain widespread acceptance of conservation efforts. All these elements are indeed part of a substantial renovation of the thinking and practice of protected area establishment and management.

The international framework

International Indigenous rights instruments such as the International Labour Organization (ILO) Convention 169 adopted in 1989 and the 2007 UN Declaration on the Rights of Indigenous Peoples (UNDRIP) contain normative provisions that prohibit discrimination against Indigenous peoples and promote their full and effective participation in all matters of concern to them. Prior and informed consent was first developed as a concept in the medical sciences as a right of patients, and then applied to nation states as a defensive measure against dumping of toxic waste. Equally, in the CBD it is used as a defensive measure to protect sovereign rights of countries providing access to genetic resources. ILO Convention 169 used it for the first time related to Indigenous peoples when establishing in Article 16.2 that 'where the relocation of these peoples is considered necessary as an exceptional measure, such relocation shall take place only with their free and informed consent' (ILO 169 1989). In 2007, the concept of free, prior and informed consent (FPIC) was clearly articulated by the UNDRIP as a condition for the adoption of decisions that directly impact on the lands, territories and resources of Indigenous peoples (UNDRIP 2007). UNDRIP affirms in particular their right to development in accordance with their own aspirations and interests (see Articles 25, 26, 27 and 32). FPIC is increasingly being advocated and used as a standard for all interventions impacting on the traditional lands, resources and lives of Indigenous peoples – and is often also extended to other human communities.

The UN-CBD Programme of Work on Protected Areas (2004), in particular Programme Element 2 on 'Governance, Participation, Equity and Benefit Sharing', recognises the contributions by local and Indigenous communities in the protection of their lands and the associated *in situ* biodiversity conservation. It calls for their full and effective participation in the management of existing and the establishment of new protected areas in full respect of their rights and recognition of their responsibilities, including the need for their FPIC in cases where the establishment or management of protected areas requires resettlement of Indigenous communities. Article 8(j) of the CBD-Convention explicitly values the various contributions by local and Indigenous communities in the form of their knowledge, skills, resources, innovations and practices. Highly participatory processes, active stakeholder involvement and the fair and equitable sharing of costs and benefits arising from the establishment and management of protected areas are considered as an integral part of effective biodiversity conservation (cf CBD *Programme of Work on Protected Areas*; Article 10(c); *Nagoya Protocol on Access to Genetic Resources and the Fair and Equitable Sharing of Benefits Arising from their Utilisation to the CBD*) (UN-SCBD 2010).

Eight global nature conservation organisations including IUCN joined forces in 2009 to create a *Conservation Initiative on Human Rights* (CIHR) to support integration of rights in conservation policy and practice and ensure that conservation efforts do not undermine human rights but respect them. CIHR organisations have adopted a framework containing key human rights principles and measures to advance implementation (CIHR 2010). This is an encouraging development towards more inclusive and socially just conservation.

The topic of community participation, rights and obligations is a key debate in conservation today. The establishment of the category of *Cultural Landscapes* in 1992, which explicitly valued the interaction of human beings and nature as well as examples of good community relations at some World Heritage sites, shows that these issues also resonate within the World Heritage discourse (UNESCO, 2004).

RBAs and good governance

Conservation organisations, echoing claims from local communities and community rights advocates, and as a result of their own experience and practice, have been promoting changes in conservation practices on the ground and in reflection of the renewal of their policies, as described earlier, for more than a decade. National protected areas agencies in many countries have not been distant from this, although as a general rule their changes in policy and practice have followed those of the non-governmental movement. The shift from the previously dominant paradigm of 'fortress conservation' to one where local communities in or near conservation areas are seen as legitimate actors that need to be supported in the realisation of their rights seems to become gradually universal.

Much of the contemporary thinking about renewing conservation and especially protected area management is linked to the application of RBAs. These can be understood 'as integrating rights norms, standards and principles into policy, planning, implementations, and outcomes assessment to help ensure that conservation practice respects rights in all cases, and supports their further realisation where possible' (Campese 2009, p. 8).

In the UN Programme for Reform, which was launched in 1997, the UN Secretary-General called on all entities of the UN system to mainstream human rights into their various activities and programmes within the framework of their respective mandates. Following this instruction, in 2003 UN agencies adopted a 'Common Understanding' on applying RBAs to their work, under the principle that 'Human Rights are the mission of the entire UN system' (UN 2003). The 'Common Understanding' was based on three principles: (1) all development cooperation and assistance should further the realisation of human rights; (2) human rights standards and principles guide all development cooperation and programming in all sectors and in all phases of the programming process; and (3) development cooperation contributes to enhancing the capacities of 'duty-bearers' to meet their obligations and/or of 'rights-holders' to claim their rights.

As a result, most UN agencies adopted RBAs by taking human rights standards and principles as a yardstick for measuring the impact of their work and elaborating various schemes for RBAs to development according to their respective fields of action; thus, the FAO has included consideration of the right to food, the United Nations Development Programme (UNDP) of the right to development, the WHO of the right to health and the right to water, the UN Centre for Human Settlements (Habitat) of the right to housing and UNESCO of the right to education and cultural rights.

Within the nature conservation community, IUCN has been one of the first organisations to adopt and promote policies to apply RBAs in a systematic way. Under this concept, 'Conservation with justice means that all state and non-state actors planning or engaged in policies, projects, programmes and activities with potential impact on nature conservation shall secure to all potentially affected persons the substantive and procedural rights that are guaranteed by national and international law' (Greiber 2009, p. 6, Box 1). The emergence of this thinking is linked to a growing recognition that the situation of rural communities whose livelihoods and living conditions are closely dependent on decision-making related to protected areas and other conservation interventions, and that such situation needs to be framed in a clear understanding of their rights and entitlements as human beings and collectives. Decisions about ecosystems such communities depend on, if taken by other social and political groups without their involvement, creates a situation where these communities are systematically impacted upon in conservation as well as development, and ultimately on their capacity to enjoy their rights.

The fact however is that the entitlement of everybody to the realisation of economic, social and cultural rights indispensable to their dignity, as determined by Article 22 of the Human Rights Declaration – a concept most people from urban populations of developed societies rarely question – is often neglected for rural communities in developing countries, as well as in remote areas of some developed countries and economies in transition. The situation of social, economic and political marginalisation of rural communities linked to protected areas, including World Heritage sites, is part of a system based on structural inequities.

Ironically, at the same time, this occurs in a political context of countries that, at least at the highest levels, are committed to respect internationally proclaimed human rights, achieve the Millennium Development Goals, eradicate extreme poverty, democratise societies and provide food security for all. The obvious question is: what are the roots of the inconsistency between the political commitments of countries and the reality of social, economic and political marginalisation of communities within and around protected areas and World Heritage sites? Of course, protected areas and World Heritage sites cannot on their own change the inequities in a given country as such areas and sites are embedded in a complex historical legacy of political and legal frameworks, institutions and processes. However should such areas and sites not aim to make a contribution to those political commitments, by supporting the realisation of the economic, social and cultural rights of communities and help them achieve 'a standard of living adequate for the health and well being [of their members and families]', as called for by Article 25 of the Human Rights Declaration?

RBAs are an effort to look critically at the core matrix of social inequities that determines a reality of poverty and discrimination for rural people. Poverty and discrimination of rural communities usually do not happen by accident; they are the result of profound historical factors that systematically create and reproduce a web of inequities in access to economic assets, opportunities, voice, power and capacities. RBAs can help understand that the dependence of rural communities on and their connection to ecosystems and nature makes conservation inextricably linked to such a matrix of inequities. Deep down, inequities and social vulnerabilities have a dimension of differential access to the means and opportunities for the protection and realisation of rights, and conservation can influence, positively or negatively, the conditions that determine the differences in access.

For protected areas, this dimension of social inequities has a strong component of structural vulnerability of the communities, since protected areas are often established on marginal and remote lands, in places far away from development poles, in areas where human settlements have not developed or are still instable, and where land tenure is neither dominated by individual property nor actively managed by commercial and development actors. This often configures a situation of precarious and unclear legal frameworks, gaps in governance and institutional presence and lack of means for the rural communities to become visible and vocal players. It configures a situation of social vulnerability. In developing countries, protected areas have almost 'naturally' emerged in a social context characterised by the presence of vulnerable communities.

In a nutshell, RBAs applied to protected areas reply to the need to look at the situation of vulnerable communities in a careful and systematic manner, to make sure that conservation measures do not negatively affect them, supporting people to attain the rights that allow them to live in dignity. Vulnerabilities are a function of exposure, sensitivity and response capacity. In protected areas, the ones most vulnerable are usually local and Indigenous communities which are physically, culturally and spiritually dependent on these sites and their resources; they have therefore high exposure to decisions on natural resource management that can become destabilising factors for their livelihoods. Social inequities make them highly sensitive to external impacts and limit their response capacity, for example in terms of making their voice heard by decision makers on matters concerning their situation and interests. Addressing these problems requires building vulnerability assessments in social analyses, which form part of protected area planning and investigating the patterns of social inequities which create or aggravate vulnerabilities. Appropriate responses can be framed thereafter to support the communities to build up their resilience to change. A good example of such responses is helping communities to strengthen their position in negotiating decisions that affect them.

The substantive rights of communities begin with the ones established in the Universal Declaration of Human Rights, which protected areas and World Heritage sites should unconditionally respect; they are also the rights, or their applications, recognised by other complementary legal instruments. These include the right to tenure security as an application of the right to property and the so-called second-generation human rights to well-being, food, water, health and development. RBAs also include procedural rights, in particular the rights to participate in decision-making, to access relevant information, to be consulted on matters of their interest and to have access to justice systems.

Protected areas and World Heritage sites have to respect universally proclaimed human rights unconditionally: nobody in the world can be exempted from this obligation and protected area and World Heritage site managers should be able to demonstrate compliance with this fundamental principle if needed. Going beyond this norm, natural sites under protection regimes can positively contribute to the realisation of human rights of associated communities as they directly impact on the resources that these communities depend on for their livelihoods. World Heritage sites can contribute to rights realisation as they protect and enhance environmental services and natural and cultural resources. Well managed, they can reduce vulnerabilities and settle competing claims for land and resources. RBAs can help design better management regimes by securing land rights and providing clearer conflict resolution procedures, therefore easing tensions and supporting effective stewardship of these sites. Some of the challenges that protected area managers will have to face in this endeavour are legitimate but competing claims to land or scarce natural or cultural resources by different communities, conflicts between World Heritage boundaries and local communities' land claims, human–wildlife conflict in the context of endangered species conservation and limited resources for proactive rights fulfilment in general.

Rights-conservation links are shaped by the systems of governance in which they are embedded, and the cultural, historical, political, socio-economic and ecological contexts in which they occur. A focus on improving governance, which is exactly what a rights-based approach should pursue, can be an entry point for understanding and addressing rights issues over time through transparent, accountable and equitable processes. Many principles of good governance have been suggested – for IUCN, chief among them are the respect for human rights, fairness, accountability, access to information, access to justice, public participation and the rule of law (Dudley 2008). Protected areas and World Heritage sites should strive to set up and implement governance systems that follow these principles as part of the political commitments to the societies such protected areas are meant to contribute to and represent.

For the integration of rights considerations in World Heritage processes, it is important to assess the current legal situation of communities and their present status of rights, including tenure rights and governance involvement during the process of World Heritage site identification. There should also be an assessment of potential threats as a result of World Heritage site establishment. When appropriate, legitimate rights-holders to the respective lands and waters should have the right to FPIC for the protection measures to be established on their areas and with their resources, as well as the right to consultation, discussion of options for participation in management, design of mechanisms for the fair sharing of benefits and dispute-settlement procedures. Different institutional regimes for protected areas such as co-management and self-management by Indigenous peoples and local communities should be encouraged wherever appropriate and seen as a way to improve the involvement of local communities.

Challenges and possible ways forward

Reconciling the rights of everybody, individually and collectively, in relation to the environment and natural resources remains challenging. One of the facets of this is the fact that an articulation of the concept of environmental rights as part of human rights has yet to be completed at the international level, in spite of the fact that:

> close to 115 constitutions throughout the world [including nearly all adopted since 1992] guarantee a right to a clean and healthy environment, impose a duty on the State to prevent environmental harm, or mention the protection of the environment or natural resources. (Greiber 2009, p. 8)

Bringing the debate on the value and meaning of environmental rights into the discourse and practice of RBAs is needed, not only to enlighten practice but also to strengthen the doctrinal framework.

On the one hand, World Heritage sites are ideally placed to showcase new ideas in protected area management. They are highly visible models for demonstrating innovative approaches in conservation, receiving international attention and public scrutiny. In this sense, World Heritage sites have the opportunity to lead by example, by testing and applying approaches to governance, participatory management and equitable access to resources and benefits from which other protected areas and conservation measures can learn. Within its broader engagement with protected areas, the conservation community would see World Heritage sites as well suited to promote and test-case RBAs and community participation.

However, on the other hand, World Heritage sites are generally more difficult places to implement RBAs. Precisely their international visibility makes some countries more resistant to recognising and addressing situations of conflict or negative impacts on the population. At the same time, Outstanding Universal Values of World Heritage sites seem to intrinsically conflict with the rights of individuals and communities associated with them. This is because their significance, which is defined in the *Operational Guidelines* of the Convention as deriving from their 'common importance for present and future generations of all humanity', apparently overrides consideration of the specific situation of those individuals or communities for whom the sites' significance will never be at the same universal level.

However, looking at this dilemma from another angle, it could be argued that while Outstanding Universal Values of World Heritage sites embody the highest standards of human cultures and nature, the Universal Declaration on Human Rights represents the highest ethical standards about human beings living with each other – therefore they should be at the same level in terms of their universality and the ideals of humankind that they represent. Outstanding Universal Values of World Heritage sites are certainly of universal significance, but any single case of violation of human rights is also a matter of universal concern and obligation.

One particular problem that surrounds natural World Heritage sites especially is that before their nomination they would have normally become a protected area under national legislation and policies, and it is at that time when decisions would have been made regarding the associated communities and their rights of tenure, access and use of the lands and resources of the area. In Thailand, for example, the Wildlife Sanctuaries of Thung Yai Naresuan and Huai Kha Khaeng became a World Heritage Site in 1991; Thung Yai Naresuan had been declared Wildlife Sanctuary

17 years earlier, in 1974. It had been the traditional land of Karen ethnic communities for around 200 years. 'Since the 1970s', writes Buergin (2001, p. 2),

> after the demarcation of the Wildlife Sanctuaries, state authorities had started to evict [the Karen communities] in successive waves. In the beginning of 1990s, the removal of the remaining villages was announced in the nomination [as World Heritage site] for the near future.

There are still Karen communities living in the area, under constant pressure and harassment from the government which sees them as a threat to the Outstanding Universal Values – despite the Karen having a sophisticated knowledge of the forest and the ecological successions and having been the modellers of the ecosystem diversity that is at the origin of such values (Delang and Wong 2006).

The Kenya Lake System in the Great Rift Valley was inscribed as a serial World Heritage Site in 2011. The Endorois, a sub-tribe of the Tugen tribe of the Kalenjin family, had lived for centuries around Lake Bogoria – one of the lakes of the inscribed site. According to the claim of the Endorois Welfare Council to the African Commission on Human and Peoples' Rights, at the creation of the Lake Hannington Game Reserve in 1973, and the subsequent re-gazetting of the Lake Bogoria Game Reserve in 1978, the Endorois communities were forcibly removed and lost their rights to their ancestral lands and resources, as a result of which they were left in poverty. During the nomination process the issue of the dispossession of the Endorois was not raised, but it was still alive, and was again a subject brought before the African Commission on Human and Peoples' Rights which considered that the inscription of the site 'constitutes a violation of the Endorois' right to development under Article 22 of the African Charter' (ACHPR/Res.197 (L) 2011).

These two cases illustrate well the problem and the challenge. Clearly the World Heritage nomination process and related assessments are missing key facts and elements of the history and management of the areas where situations of negative impacts on communities, which could often be framed as violations of their rights, have occurred and which some governments consider normal or even necessary to guarantee the conservation of the sites. It does not seem to be difficult to improve the procedures and the standards of the evaluations of nominations to make sure that such problems are known and assessed. However, how much can a nomination process do to help solve the problems and bring justice to the communities? Doing so, in most cases, would require such fundamental changes in national law and policy frameworks that could make both objectives of protection of sites and justice for the communities unattainable in the short term. Are there shortcuts that can help move forward such objectives?

To be effective, new approaches based on the recognition of rights have to be systematically integrated into all aspects of World Heritage management since early phases of nomination. The Advisory Bodies to the Convention IUCN, ICOMOS and ICCROM have engaged in conversations on how best to meet the aim of the Committee to focus more on communities and inclusive conservation approaches. IUCN has suggested a multi-track process, comprising as a first step to improve the Advisory Body practice, in particular the support given to States Parties in the preparation of nominations (the so-called 'up-streaming process') and the role of its experts in evaluation and monitoring missions. As new complex issues with local rights-holders, intangible heritage and livelihoods have emerged as important aspects for the set-up and management of World Heritage sites, specific dispute resolution mechanisms and a different set of expert skills in both the design and assessment of World Heritage nominations and their status of conservation are required. To integrate human rights considerations at the early stages of World Heritage identification and nomination seems crucial as significant decisions about boundaries, zoning, management set-up, user rights and stakeholder involvement are taken during this stage.

A second element involves establishing partnerships with interested States Parties and international actors to implement and test tools and approaches to support them in these challenges, build further capacity of national agencies and stakeholders, and empower local communities. In the development of this initiative, it is indispensable to join forces with Indigenous and community organisations as well as with other conservation, development and humanitarian actors. A further element would consist in advising the Committee on the future of the *Convention* and the legal and policy frameworks and the developments of this initiative. The initiative should also aim to disseminate information on the best practices as many substantial efforts in the management of World Heritage sites have already taken place in regard to human rights considerations.

Notes on contributors

Gonzalo Oviedo is an anthropologist and environmentalist from Ecuador, South America. He is the senior adviser for Social Policy at IUCN Headquarters in Gland, Switzerland, where he facilitates the integration of social issues in IUCN's conservation work worldwide, with particular focus on livelihood security, Indigenous and traditional peoples, rights and governance.

Tatjana Puschkarsky studied English Literature and Political Sciences. She worked for the Global Footprint Network and IUCN's World Heritage Programme. She co-organised the International Youth Forum in 2010 with Germany's Gesellschaft für Internationale Zusammenarbeit (GIZ) and the UNESCO World Heritage Centre. She works on the links between protected areas and Indigenous peoples, communities, rights and biocultural diversity.

References

African Commission on Human and Peoples' Rights (ACHPR), 2011. *Resolution on the indigenous peoples' rights in the context of the World Heritage Convention and designation of lake bogoria as a world heritage site*. ACHPR/Res.197 (L) 2011: Banjul, The Gambia. Available from: http://www.achpr.org/english/resolutions/Resolution197_en.htm [Accessed 14 December 2011].
Amend, S. and Amend, T., eds., 1992. *National Parks without people? The South American experience*. Quito, Ecuador: IUCN.
Beltrán, J., ed., 2000. *Indigenous and traditional peoples and protected areas: principles*, Guidelines and Case Studies. Gland: IUCN and WWF.
Buergin, R., 2001. *Contested heritages: disputes on people, forests, and a world heritage site in globalizing thailand*. Freiburg: SEFUT Working Paper No. 9.
Campese, J., 2009. Rights-based approaches to conservation: an overview of concepts and questions. *In*: J. Campese, T. Sunderland, T. Greiber, and G. Oviedo, eds. *Rights-based approaches: exploring issues and opportunities for conservation*. Bogor: CIFOR and IUCN, 1–46.
CIHR, 2010. *Conservation and human rights framework* [online]. Available from: http://cms-data.iucn.org/downloads/cihr_framework_e_sept2010_1.pdf [Accessed 14 December 2011].
Delang, C.O. and Wong, T., 2006. The livelihood-based forest classification system of the Pwo karen in western Thailand. *Mountain Research and Development.*, 26 (2), 138–145.

Dudley, N., ed., 2008. *Guidelines for applying protected area management categories*. Gland: IUCN.
Greiber, T., ed., 2009. *Conservation with justice – a rights-based approach*. IUCN Environmental Law and Policy Paper No. 71. Gland: IUCN.
ILO, 169 1989. *Indigenous and tribal peoples convention*. Adopted at the 76th Session of the Conference, 27 June 1989 Geneva [online]. Available from: http://www.ilo.org/ilolex/cgi-lex/convde.pl?C169 [Accessed 14 December 2011].
IUCN, 1997. *World conservation congress: resolutions and recommendations*. Gland: IUCN.
Kempf, E., ed., 1993. *The law of the mother: protecting indigenous peoples in protected areas*. San Francisco, CA: Sierra Club Books.
Larsen, P.B. and Oviedo, G., 2004. *Protected areas and indigenous peoples: the Durban contributions to reconciliation and equity*. Gland: IUCN.
Lasgorceix, A. and Kothari, A., 2009. Displacement and relocation of protected areas: a synthesis and analysis of case studies. *EPW – Economic and Political Weekly*, Xliv (December), 38–49.
Lele, S., *et al.*, 2010. Beyond exclusion: alternative approaches to biodiversity conservation in the developing tropics. *Current Opinion in Environmental Sustainability*, 2 (1–2), 94–100.
Oviedo, G., 2004. Áreas Protegidas y Pueblos Indígenas [Protected areas and Indigenous peoples]. *In*: M.E. Arguedas, B.L. Castaño, and J.M. y Rodríguez, eds. *Lineamientos y Herramientas para Un Manejo Creativo de las Áreas Protegidas* [Guidelines and tools for creative management of protected areas]. Organización para Estudios Tropicales (OET). San José, Costa Rica: Programa de Política y Ciencias Ambientales, 188–299.
Oviedo, G. and Sylva, P. 1994. *Areas Silvestres Protegidas y Comunidades Locales en América Latina* [Protected Wilderness Areas and Local Communities in Latin America]. Santiago de Chile: FAO/PNUMA. RLAC/94/17 Documento Técnico N° 17.
UNDRIP, 2007. *United Nations declaration on the rights of indigenous peoples*. Adopted by the General Assembly Resolution 61/295, 13 September 2007.
UNESCO, 1972. *Convention concerning the protection of the world cultural and natural heritage*. Adopted by the General Conference at its seventeenth session in Paris, 16 November 1972.
UNESCO, 2004. *Linking universal and local values: managing a sustainable future for world heritage*. World Heritage Papers 13.
UNESCO, 2005. *World heritage at the Vth IUCN world parks congress. Durban (South Africa), 8–17 September 2003*. World Heritage Reports 16.
UNESCO, 2008. *Operational guidelines for the implementation of the world heritage convention*. WHC.08/01 [online]. Available from: http://whc.unesco.org/en/guidelines [Accessed 14 December 2011].
UNESCO, 2011. *World heritage list* [online]. Available from: http://whc.unesco.org/en/list [Accessed 14 December 2011].
UN Human Rights Council 2009: *Report by the special rapporteur on the situation of human rights and fundamental freedoms of indigenous people, James Anaya*. Addendum: report on the situation of indigenous peoples in Nepal. A/HRC/12/34/Add.3. 20 July 2009 [online]. Available from: http://www2.ohchr.org/english/bodies/hrcouncil/docs/12session/A-HRC-12-34-Add3_E.pdf [Accessed 14 December 2011].
United Nations (UN) 2003. *The human rights based approach to development cooperation: towards a common understanding among UN agencies* [online]. Available from: http://www.hreoc.gov.au/social_justice/conference/engaging_communities/un_common_understanding_rba.pdf [Accessed 14 December 2011].
United Nations Secretariat of the Convention on Biological Diversity (UN-SCBD), 2004. *Programme of work on protected areas*. Montreal [online]. Available from: http://www.cbd.int/protected/pow/learnmore/intro/.[Accessed 14 December 2011].
United Nations Secretariat of the Convention on Biological Diversity (UN-SCBD), 2010. *The nagoya protocol on access and benefit-sharing*. Adopted by the Conference of the Parties to the Convention on Biological Diversity, 29 October 2010 [online]. Available from: http://www.cbd.int/abs/ [Accessed 14 December 2011].
WWF International, 2008. *Indigenous peoples and conservation: WWF statement of principles*. Gland: WWF International.

[7]
Informal settlements and urban heritage landscapes in South Africa

Lindsay M. Weiss
Department of Anthropology, Stanford Archaeology Center,
Stanford University, USA

Abstract
Informal urban settlements and trade zones represent an increasingly pressing issue for urban heritage developers. In light of the recent revisitation of the UNESCO Recommendation on the Historic Urban Landscape, this article explores the current challenges faced at the intersection of heritage practice, urban planning, and informal communities. Heritage recommendations operate within the domain of soft law and their implementation relies on the voluntarism of public parties and the private sector. Such heritage recommendations are thus rarely taken up outside of city improvement districts with recognizable property-owning stakeholders, commercial infrastructures for security, maintenance, and investor marketing. In South Africa, the particular circumstances of the post-apartheid landscape render urban planning frameworks prone to reinforcing the marginalization of informal stakeholder engagement, ultimately perpetuating a socio-spatial inequality such programs set out to mitigate. The civic practices of new social movements and historical knowledge that emerges from the context of informal and neglected urban environments illustrate emergent answers to the exclusionary dynamics of urban heritage planning.

Keywords
urban heritage, slums, informal settlements, Historic Urban Landscape, South Africa, new social movements, labor

---

Corresponding author:
Lindsay M. Weiss, Department of Anthropology, Stanford Archaeology Center, Stanford University, Stanford, USA.
Email: linzyka@stanford.edu

Introduction: Post-colonial landscapes in South Africa

As of 2010, more people now live in cities than in rural areas. According to UN-Habitat, one in five people live in squats, slums, or on land that does not legally belong to them. In South Africa, this number is estimated as one in four and potentially one in three by 2050 (UN Human Settlements Programme, 2006). These numbers illustrate that the relationship between informal communities and urban heritage is one of increasing important to consider. By contrast, founding global protocols for urban heritage protection speak to an altogether different context. The 1964 Venice Charter broke new ground when historic preservation shifted "from museum object to architectural monument" (Ruggles, 2012). Yet despite the internationalist ethos of the charter, its emphasis on architectural conservatism and the prioritization of material authenticity restricted the category of the Historic Urban Landscape (HUL). The internationalist vision of the Nara document on authenticity, adopted 30 years later, addressed these issues with the Venice charter, stating that it was not possible to base judgment "of values and authenticity within fixed criteria" (International Council on Monuments and Sites, 1994). With this, the Intangible World Heritage Convention (2003) and the 2005 Convention on Cultural Diversity, UNESCO has, as its Assistant Director General Francesco Bandarin puts it, "cautiously opened the way to a culture-based appreciation of conservation values" (Bandarin and van Oers, 2012: xvi).

The concept of the HUL was proposed in a 2005 meeting convened by the World Heritage Committee. The purpose of the meeting was to revisit UNESCO recommendations for safeguarding of historic urban areas and the modern urban conservation paradigm more generally (Bandarin and van Oers, 2012: 62). The recent reconsideration of the concept of the HUL has recommended placing even greater emphasis upon integrating the concepts of HULs within the dynamic process of urban development. As a result, the phenomenon of increasingly stratified urban contexts may make the issue of the informal urban community in increasingly central one for urban heritage.

Central to the methodological implementation of new urban heritage policy is fostering increasingly intercultural and diverse contexts for civic engagement. Specifically, the 2011 recommendation on HUL states, "civic engagement tools should involve a diverse cross-section of stakeholders" (UNESCO, 2011). With an eye to posterity and austerity, the category of HUL takes on a very specific set of pressures and challenges in the post-colonial and post-Fordist context. In South Africa, growing areas of informal settlement and increasing numbers of unemployed or casual laborers constitute a vital and significant component of dynamic urban culture, increasingly recognized as an irreplaceable site of urban practices of "creativity and resourcefulness" (Bandarin and van Oers, 2012). Long recognized as critical sites whose residents provide key services upon which cities often survive (Scott, 1998), informal urban communities and their landscapes are vital for urban heritage specialists to consider outside of the terms of development. They provide the context for the recognition of alternative HULs as well as providing new arenas for forging best consultation practices. Recognizing the value of emergent techniques of civic engagement in these contexts could foster a more inclusionary vision of urban intangible heritage.

The challenges to understanding the wider urban cultural landscape are many. There is an unmistakable ambivalence with regard to the emergence of urban informal communities, often referred to as "slums", particularly in the mega-cities of the Global South. For some, "[t]he city appears under siege, imperiled by spatial mutations and occupation by the uncivil masses, a wasteland of broken modernist dreams..." (Prakash and Kruse, 2008: 6). For others, as Žižek (2004) quips, informal communities and landless people's movements have become abstractly valorized to the point where they are the Left's new proletariat, such as in the work of Davis (2006). This critical ambivalence stems from the neglect of the historical specificity of informal settlements, resulting in their abstraction. This problem stems from the context of heritage planning and development, where these mobile or informal communities are often presumed to be temporary sites with elusive membership, and consequently no historical application. Methodologically, these presumptions are reflected in a shallow form of consultation and stakeholder engagement, which, in turn, produces equally elusive and mobile forms of inclusion or transparency.

Citing examples from corporate-driven heritage development as well as urban revitalization schemes, this article charts the various methodological-institutional conjunctures at which community engagement stops short of its own rhetorical commitments. As heritage becomes increasingly wound up within urban development and revitalization projects, it is vital to reflect upon what sorts of stakeholders and constituencies emerge as ideal subjects for this vision of an increasingly self-reliant, sustainable, and disciplined project of civic remembrance. For many urban planners, developers, such informal communities ostensibly represent temporary, historyless, or unruly objects of mediation. Rather than succumbing to these views, engaged heritage consultation and research illustrates that many of informal communities practice rich modes of self-organizing and broader practices of liberal urban citizenship. These traditions epitomize the professed objectives of the HUL project: morally sensible, inclusive, and sustainable modes of curating the practices of dynamic urban culture. They mark the future of the HUL.

Historic Urban Landscapes in South Africa

In post-apartheid and unevenly developed/developing urban landscapes, the colonial legacy of systematic erasure continues to radiate a complex range of effects upon its inhabitants. The history of mechanical displacement and the subsequent process of economic restructuring presents a spatial landscape that implicitly challenges—almost at every angle—the desire for architectural authenticity to emerge from continuities of form, cultural practice, or endurance of original materials (Murray et al., 2007). It was precisely the dense urban conditions of 20th century South African "shantytowns", and their perceived threat to a minority racial rule that prompted the 1922 Transvaal Stallard Commission. The commission recommended that Africans be "confined to the construction of townships owned and administered by local authorities" (Stallard Commission, 1922). In this way, South African laborers were refigured as "temporary sojourners" in cities. Through a series of pass laws, they were restricted to limited residence periods at designated hostel and labor housing spaces, forced to live as "foreign visitors" in the urban context. Through a series of notorious slum clearances, those already living in cities were relocated in order to pursue their self-determination within bounded homelands appointed by the Verwoerd administration, in each of which the government established a pointedly rural "bantu investment corporation", to "set up and capitalise individual entrepreneurs" (Stallard Commission, 1922).

In grappling with the public meaning of this colonial legacy, the heritage of urban space in South Africa has been widely understood as being as much about erasure, memory, and sites of loss as being about the architectural landscape available to us in the present (Coombes, 2003). In part, this approach has been in order to prevent perpetuating the original cruelty of historical erasure by inordinately dwelling on those material forms and architectures that, for reasons of historical contingency or colonial policy, remain today. But it is also a rejection of the typical narrative of modernization by which the African city can only ever manifest as a (frequently tragic) residue or reflection of the broader modernity narrative (Cooper, 2002; Mbembe and Nuttall, 2004: 353).

There have been many important re-framings of the legacy of the African city that are relevant to consider in the context of pursuing a more holistic approach to the wider urban environment and the associated intangible cultural practices, values, and memorial dimensions. Because so much of urban historiography has been centered around the story of apartheid and displacement, there has been an almost compulsive emphasis on what Mbembe and Nuttall have termed, "the geographies of poverty, forced removals, and racially based slums" rather than alternative histories of sites of mobility, or affluence, spaces of idleness or play (2004: 353). In the last decade, particularly within the work of AbdouMaliq Simone, mobility and its associated urban practices (the rapid and often unpredictable interchange of contraband, images, music, remittances, and information via billboards, vehicles, wireless networks, tuck shops, etc.) have come to be identified as a key signature of the public cultural life of African cities. In recent work on Afropolitanism, this mobility has come to take on an almost emancipatory vein with respect to the geographies of poverty (Prakash and Kruse, 2008; Simone 2001a, 2001b, 2004, 2005). As Mbembe and Nuttall (2004: 30) state,

> Its boundaries have become so geographically and socially permeable and stretched that the city seems to have no fixed parts, no completeness, and almost no discrete center...Turning its back on the rigid rationalities of planning and racial separation, it has become, in spite of itself, a place of intermingling and improvisation. Its very porosity means that, released from the iron cage of apartheid, it can now continually fashion and refashion itself.

Both in the past and the present, the sheer aleatory force of urban circulation is a vital aspect of the experience of urban life in South Africa. Within the context of urban planning, however, this instability of movement comes to instigate a different sort of work. Urban planning, operating within a much more cadastral system of commercial districting and establishing bounded tourism zones, relies on a mesh of formal infrastructures and commercial transparency in order to produce financially viable and investment-friendly development. Increasingly, attempts to mitigate the associated perils of the impermanent stakeholder, such as lack of commercial transparency, eroding infrastructures, and ultimately unmarketable or unviable revitalization districts, have unleashed a "speculative arbitrage on the habits of the poor" (Roy, 2012: 213). Burgeoning urban mobility, then, while at one moment marking the aspirational horizon of the Afropolitan city-dweller, also marks out the frontier where new civic technologies of responsibilization map out the frontiers of entrepreneurial and civic dispositions amid the emergent urban precariat. UNESCO's renewed recommendation of accommodating the "dynamic nature of living cities" marks a policy directive that situates urban heritage practitioners squarely on both sides of the border between civic governmentality and its counter-publics. The question of informal urban areas, both as a category of analysis and as an actually occurring landscape in South Africa, is critical to understanding how urban heritage will emerge in the future.

Informal communities in urban theory

Informal communities, or what is often referred to in urban theory as "slums" have long marked a key "epistemological and ethical" anchoring point within urban studies (Rao, 2012). One side of the discussion identifies such urban landscapes as symptomatic of the extreme income inequality and poverty to be fixed. Particularly in the Global South, they are perceived as symptomatic of International Monetary Fund and World Bank Structural Adjustment Programs imposed upon debtor nations, with the ensuing privatization and stratification of housing markets (Davis, 2006: 63). The other major approach to this discussion sees these informal urban landscapes as providing emergent and even normative models for understanding how global cities are dynamically and flexibly renegotiating global flows of finance, manufacturing, and refiguring the technologies of capital and informational flows in the process. So, global cities of the south rather than cities of the Global South (Appadurai, 2002; Rao, 2012: 674).

In many ways, an urban heritage project taken up within the terms of revitalization and job-creation necessarily straddles both of these approaches. On the one hand, it valorizes and provides historical recognition for landscapes and practices of urban curation, circulation, and culture. On the other hand, it takes the enactment of this recognition as implicitly about identifying particular urban zones to be tackled through job-creation, revitalization, or restoration. This twinned goal imposes a subtle shifting of ethical registers on the part of heritage practitioners, asking that their work bridge what at one moment amounts to a primarily descriptive ethics, that which is entailed in the project of articulating, narrating, and curating widely diverse contexts of urban heritage for global recognition. At another moment, the designation of heritage landscapes as a technique of development, particularly in the processes of nominating, consulting, or evaluating, imposes a far narrower set of normative constraints on heritage practitioners (so for instance, calling upon a far less relativistic approach to the meaning of poverty, or ideal slum alleviation, or what constitutes an ideal stakeholder, or ideal modes of stakeholder engagement, etc.). Within such a system, informal urban areas or older/informal areas of townships can often emerge as "blind spots" in the grid of urban revitalization planning, even as they house critical heritage architectures, sites, and community practices that counteract current failures in the community consultation and development framework.

Post-industrial landscapes

Kimberley is far from an iconic world city such as Cape Town or Durban. With a population under 100,000, the city of Kimberley proper is far smaller than its adjoining townships of Galeshewe and Roodepan (Statistics South Africa, 2011). Yet, as the site of the De Beers Mine and the center of 20th century diamond mining in South Africa, Kimberley is iconic of the post-Fordist, post-extractive landscape increasingly faced by heritage planners, marked by high unemployment, neglected infrastructure, and a perennial faith in the economic promise of tourism (Conlin and Jolliffe, 2011). The city of Kimberley in the Northern Cape emerged as a seething colonial shantytown that rapidly flitted about the Karoo landscape with new diamond discoveries transforming its center practically overnight. By mid-1879, about 10 years after the start of the diamond rush, a colonial policy of locations was implemented and the largest of these, what was originally given the name of "location no. 2", was formally established.

Today, this historic district of the sprawling Galeshewe township represents one of the oldest townships in South Africa and it provides a stark contrast to the historical architecture found in the formerly colonial neighborhoods such as Belgravia and Ernestville. Inhabitants of Kimberley and neighboring Galeshewe regularly crisscross this divided urban landscape establishing the broader dynamic urban landscape of the former diamond fields. Galeshewe township's complex history includes many nationally important liberation heritage events. Most notably, it was the site of Pan African Congress founder Robert Sobukwe's house arrest and the site of the 1952 Mayibuye Uprising where 13 protestors were killed by police as they marched from Galeshewe township to Kimberley (Allen et al., 2012: 65; Swanepoel and Mngqolo, 2011). The example of Galeshewe's location no. 2 is iconic of historically important areas which risk getting overlooked in South Africa's post-industrial jumble of burgeoning Reconstruction and Development Program housing development emerging amidst shacks, dilapidated mud-brick houses, and improvizational combinations thereof. Local oral historians and heritage professionals working at the McGregor Museum have identified many "at risk" historic and conservation-worthy houses in this district, including those that were made from a local tradition of mud-brick construction, and many of which mirrored Victorian and Edwardian styles while using locally sourced materials, producing a distinct vernacular as well as an illustrating how these neighborhood architectures negotiated shifting periods of class differentiation and public style over the 20th century (Sephai Mngqolo, personal communication).

Viewed through the lens of urban planning, Galeshewe marks a challenging context for renewal. According to the Strengths, Weaknesses, Opportunities, and Threats analysis, Galeshewe represents an area with over 30% unemployment, exceptionally high rates of AIDS infection, as well as infrastructural challenges ranging from unpaved roads, lack of signage, to about 5000 households living in "informal dwellings". As land invasions increasingly evidence the public's impatience, rapidly implemented local urban renewal programs encounter tensions with local heritage preservation initiatives seeking to protect yet undeclared areas and sites, resulting in such distressing scenarios as a traffic congestion abatement project leveling a series of homes with historical value and the former offices of Pan Africanist Congress founder Robert Sobukwe threatened by private property owners and expansion of a local road (Figures 1 and 2).

Overshadowing these landscapes is the most prominent heritage draw of Kimberley, the De Beers' "Big Hole"—the 463-m wide and 240-m deep hollowed remains of the main De Beers diamond mine. This site emerged in the mid-20th century as an informal depot for historical memorabilia and De Beers somewhat unintentionally fell into custodianship of the first open air museum of the towns

Figure 1. Vernacular architecture in area no. 2., Galeshewe.

Figure 2. Law Office of Robert Sobukwe, Galeshewe.

mining heritage (Brown, 2005). Upon losing a bid to open a neighboring casino, De Beers decided to maintain the museum with low-cost pensioners acting as custodians (Brown, 2005). Yet coinciding with its final massive retrenchments and the selling of its exhausted underground mining operations, De Beers showcased the Big Hole museum as part of a broader social investment program attempting to reinvigorate flagging heritage tourism development in Kimberley (van der Merwe and Rogerson, 2013) (Figure 3).

This included a tourism route named the "Diamond Route", which connects a string of private nature reserves featuring gemsbok, blue wildebeest, red hartebeest, zebra, and kudu. These nature reserves circle the central mining landscapes of Kimberley, and they are presented as the natural culmination of the "full lifecycle of mines". The tourist who wishes to visit the landscape of the mines can also visit the Big Hole museum complex, which was renovated into a "world class" structure including what is today South Africa's largest full-scale open-air museum, drawing thousands of visitors a year. Kimberley mine (the Big Hole) and associated industries has even been put forward for South Africa's tentative World Heritage List with the justification that it marks the site where "the industrial revolution came to Africa", shaping what are somewhat euphemistically described as the subsequent urban labor systems in Johannesburg and the "origins of the migrant labor system" more generally. Ironically, the only tram which connected the visitor at the Big Hole's outdoor museum to any part of the actual city of Kimberley had to be

Figure 3. Big Hole Museum.

temporarily suspended due to the fact that the road risks collapse (along with several other businesses and buildings) into the eroding perimeter boundaries of the Big Hole (Figure 4). At the opening of the diamond route, former De Beers director David Noko stated, "we must preserve the areas where we operate so that people can see the legacy of what we leave behind when we finish mining" (van der Merwe, 2010). Yet the question remains, how does such corporate social responsibility heritage discourse circumvent the sprawling township-scapes populated by former casual laborers, impoverished pensioners and shack-dwellers who continue to live in the shadows of this industrial landscape?

This gap between how the landscape of industry is proposed and how it actually mediates daily life for remaining residents is a significant problematic for urban heritage in the wake of deindustrialization. The disavowal of De Beers' historical ties to the communities of former employees in the Galeshewe township illustrates the socio-economic stakes in the context of our rapidly shifting labor landscape. This intersects with a troubling historical glossing in the corporate-sponsored heritage revitalization endeavor more generally (CSR heritage). The Big Hole Project (BHP), coupled with the Diamond Route, speak to a landscape that circumvents its retrenched communities, illustrating a broader obscuring of the historical roots of labor insecurity within the urban development discourse. Within the sometimes muddled historical logics of planning and urban development, informal communities, "squatters", can swiftly become jumbled areas to be remediated—people to be capacitated or

Figure 4. Kimberley Big Hole viewed from the Big Hole Museum.

resituated—rather than marking sites of historically complex and politically rich practice with vital and meaningful connections to the recent past.

Actually existing participatory planning

Such disconnects raise broader anxieties about the role of heritage in the shadow of extractive industry (Esterhuysen, 2012). Kimberley's Big Hole Museum existing unbeknownst to former employees in Galeshewe's historic districts is significantly enabled by the rogue nature of concepts such as stakeholder engagement and community consultation. Despite the fact that the BHP had dutifully consulted with local archaeologists and historians, South African ICOMOS, South African Heritage Resources Agency, the Northern Cape Tourism experts, as well as MECs of arts and culture, and despite the local Non-Profit Organization formed between De Beers and local community stakeholders (the Big Hole Trust), in the end, the museum project came to be inexplicably led by a former car show manager (Brown, 2005), and the design and presentation of the visitors room was implemented by a consultancy known as Fuse Communications. Fuse Communications, a London- and Johannesburg-based group, was perhaps most notable for claiming insolvency after having been given a 12 million rand contract by De Beers and owing tens of thousands of dollars to local heritage subcontractors (Hoo, 2007). Many heritage professionals living in or affiliated with Galeshewe, working as Oral Historians or heritage experts at the local museum felt their involvement and input with the BHP was haphazard at best, and certain signaled a troubling autonomy on the part of corporate engagement actors.

The critiques of inadequate stakeholder consultation is rife in the heritage literature in Southern Africa, with consistent demands for better definitions of what is meant by "local communities" or "participation" (Chirikure et al., 2010) or for less Eurocentric categories for custodianship (Pereira de Jesus Jopela, 2011). Cumulatively, these critiques draw attention to the significant fact that even impeccable consultation protocols can fail to translate into the final product of heritage interpretation and regulation if these structures remain disconnected from the consultative process (Masuku van Damme and Meskell, 2009). Moreover, the national heritage resources act does not give an adequately precise definition of what social consultation should consist of, particularly in the context of South Africa's mass displacement of migrant laborers (Ndlovu, 2011).

Consultation and stakeholder engagement are decidedly central technologies by which urban governance negotiates diverse participants (stakeholders) and dynamic contexts (Cruikshank, 1999; Ellis, 2012). A recent piece by anthropologist Dina Rajak (2012) explores how consultation can unfold within the corporate-public context of "Platinum City", a conglomerate of mining concerns in Johannesburg's Rustenberg mining belt responsible for nearly half of the world's platinum. Rajak's (2012) ethnography explores the enactment of stakeholder engagement according to Rustenberg's integrated development plan (IDP). The IDP review process, a cornerstone of South Africa's municipal development forums, provides a setting for stakeholders to engage with the direction of sustainable initiatives and provide input on new directions for social development investments.

Yet, as Rajak (2012) illustrates through her account of the actual structure and language of IDP meetings, the distinction between "formal stakeholders" and "informal stakeholders" produced critical differences. The complaints of informal stakeholders, while nominally included, were invariably dismissed and treated as a temporary issue. Compounding this was the public perception that some form of clientelism with informal settlements was being capacitated through Anglo-Platinum's IDP meetings. As a result of this perception, alternative municipal welfare resources for informal settlements were actually attenuating. This ultimately brought about a scenario where, "informal settlements have become the subject of competing attempts to deny rather than assert social responsibility" (Rajak, 2012: 258). The role of stakeholder engagement extends beyond the purely corporate context as increasingly urban revitalization initiatives are undertaken through a contract bidding system requiring private consultants to liaise among diverse internal government departments as well as increasingly diverse public stakeholders.

City improvement districts and urban heritage

The role of cultural heritage in the urban context is increasingly centered around the speculative wager that historic districts carry the potential to promote economic growth and sustainable development. The African National Congress' shift from its initial (Keynsian) Reconstruction and Development Program to its Growth Employment and Reconstruction Program (GEAR) in 1998 meant that broader policies of trade liberalization were coupled with the effective restructuring of municipal government policy. Urban initiatives were devised according to the vision of cities as emergent financially independent private sector entities. Consequently, urban heritage initiatives were directed within typical private partnership policy charters for city improvement districts (CID) or business improvement district (BID) frameworks, which looked something like "Municipality Inc.'s" (Miraftab, 2007).

In South Africa, such urban planning frameworks are often not tailored to the specificities of the post-apartheid landscape, indeed Cape Town's CID having been modeled after Mayor Rudolph Giuliani's BID program for New York's revitalization in the 1980s (Miraftab, 2007). The attempt to generalize gentrification policy and import municipal planning policies into contexts with extremely incommensurate socio-political histories is redolent of what Peck (2010) terms "fast policy". The adjustment of such fast policy transfers to the local, "path-dependent" context sets the current challenge for urban heritage in a post-apartheid landscape. This fast-paced infusion of new constitutional legislation, ready-made policies made to fix societies in transition has given heritage practitioners the frustrating sense of negotiating a policy landscape in which there is a "lack of any meaningful integration of the heritage laws and the general urban and regional planning systems" (Ndoro and Pwiti, 2005: 160).

Of particular importance within the post-apartheid urban context is the influx of informal squatting communities and informal trade networks in the wake of the 1991 repeal of the apartheid Group Areas Act. Ironically, these informal landscapes, symptomatic of the diminished productive capacity of the post-Fordist urban economy, are set in friction with the prevailing entrepreneurial sentiment among developers. For developers, the best way to resolve the sustainability of the deindustrialized city and to progress toward orderly housing development is to expedite the upgrading and elimination of informal areas. This has ultimately produced such contentious legislative efforts as the Elimination and Prevention of Re-Emergence of Slums Bill in the KwaZulu-Natal in 2004 (subsequently overturned in the Constitutional Court) (Huchzermeyer, 2011). In the KwaZulu-Natal Province, Durban's tourism industry generates over three billion rand, supporting tens of thousands of jobs, yet Durban continues to rank only fourth in the nation for tourism, falling second to Cape Town. The impediments of crime, overcrowding, and informal settlements are perceived by planners to be the greatest contributing factors (Maharaj, 2006: 268)

For planners, and the heritage specialists who must work with them, these informal areas or gray economic zones of the post-industrial landscape challenge the goals of attracting private investment for readily identifiable tourism zones in which entrepreneurial forms of self-governance can be reliably elicited. Even when subjected to the deliberative context of robust civic debate and community consultation, sites that impede the prevailing culture of urgent development seem to ultimately concede the primacy of gentrification, with contested burial sites such as Cape Town's Prestwich Place Memorial producing a public ossuary as an unlikely appendage to the edgy yet cheerfully named Truth Coffee Shop (Shepherd, 2013).

The technologies by which participatory civic engagement and urban citizenship more generally have drifted into the paradigm of neoliberal governmentality are ascendant and bear critically upon the lived experience of urban life (Collier and Ong, 2008; Ong, 2006). These same technologies have very real ramifications for the project of public history and heritage. As consultative techniques and stakeholder engagement seem to move from the traditions of urban planning to heritage (rather than the reverse direction), these processes aggregate very particular sorts of historical landscapes and materially mediated pasts, rendering some historical narratives more sensible than others and inculcating certain temporalities over others (Herzfeld, 2009a, 2009b). Here, the potential exclusions of vulnerable spaces of urban informality, materially transient practices, and robust counter-publics become increasingly urgent for urban heritage practitioners to recognize.

The emphasis on vulnerable, historically marginalized, transient or impoverished counter-publics critically counterbalances the methodological calcifications that inhere within outdated academic epistemologies (Baird, 2012; Haber, 2013; Meskell and Scheermeyer, 2008; Shepherd, 2003). It also responds to the excesses of an unchecked deregulation of public history, where a certain speculative logic places value in the past unevenly, in a manner decidedly tilted against urban culture at its most dynamic. What Fabian (1983) initially explored as anthropological allochronism (the rhetorical distancing of the temporality of the Other) is very much at work "out there" too. For heritage, it has mutated into a geo-spatial distancing: a technology of producing partible landscapes and saleable historic urban districts—"boutique heritage". Such areas, "old towns" and other HULs proliferate and within them, new normativities surrounding cultural labor are cultivated, such as within Bahia's Pelourinho World Heritage Site (Collins, 2012).

Importantly, grassroots movements and informal settlements, even as they represent temporary sites which are not standardized or which exist across multiple districts (or which are enacted in opposition to municipal property regulations—such as land invasions) are of growing interest to world heritage specialists.[1] While the slippery techniques of consultation, stakeholder recognition, and development seem to elicit a predetermined set of civic dispositions rooted within the aspirational culture of urban elites (Ellis, 2012), it is of note that the South African National Heritage Council (NHC) is leading efforts to counteract what it perceives as a deepening of urban fragmentation and separation being perpetuated by a poorly integrated "boutique heritage approach" (National Heritage Council [NHC], 2010).

At the same moment, the NHC as well as its cognate organization, the South African Heritage Resources Agency, are institutionally enmeshed in broader governmental restructurings focused on optimizing legislative mandates within the terms of capacitation and service-delivery. Particularly in the context of rapid urban development, the heritage sector is under unprecedented pressure to streamline uncoordinated (at points non-existent) provincial heritage offices, site grading schemas, as well as out of date permit-granting systems into a so-called one stop shop system for developers. Heritage professionalism, according to a 2009 expert panel convened by the NHC, must increasingly target speedy delivery of access to permits and sites, aiming toward a "development-friendly heritage management" that "save[s] developers money" and above all, produces an "environment of certainty" for developers (NHC, 2010). Increasingly, comprehensive survey databases, integration within Spatial Development Frameworks, and Infrastructural Development Plans are pushed for heritage managers beleaguered by a crippling absence of public resources, administrative backlogs, and labyrinthine protocols as well as the challenge of maintaining the increasingly unsustainable budgets of failing remote sites. In this context of transitional heritage implementation, the integrity of stakeholder consultation, and the sorts of impact these outreach methods can have outside of credentialing the related site(s) comes in as a necessarily secondary set of priorities.

Yet seemingly at odds with this state of affairs is a growing optimism surrounding new modes of private sector involvement (Marschall, 2010) and the potential that populist mediation has for grassroots-driven institutional change (Appadurai, 2006; De Cesari, 2011; Roy, 2009). The question this raises in the context of South Africa is whether or not there is something "inherently and necessarily conservative" about neoliberal "arts of government", as Ferguson (2010) puts it, or whether such techniques as consultation and stakeholder engagement can "migrate across camps" and become taken up fully within the terms of alternative populist practices of urban citizenship.

The promised land: Urban informal communities and the evolution of stakeholder engagement

Its about you recognizing me as a human being, or my humanity.
You don't have backlog for that... its not a question of budget constraints.
S'bu Zikode

What is provocative about some of South Africa's informal land settlements is that their central role in a burgeoning urban rights movement would seem to counteract the received wisdom that informal settlements are dormant sites awaiting development. Like so many other informal settlements, despite its architecturally precarious quality, the Kennedy Road Settlement in Durban, KwaZulu Natal, represents a decidedly historical urban landscape (Figure 5). Many of its occupants have been living there since the 1970s, displaced by the mass evictions caused by the Inanda dam. When the area was zoned as Indian during apartheid, occupants were displaced or had to reside in secrecy. Yet when apartheid laws were relaxed in the

Figure 5. Kennedy Road Settlement, eThekwini, Durban.

1980s, former residents returned to find old friends and neighbors and return to jobs in the affluent neighboring Clare Estate, or to scavenge recyclables from the adjoining Bisasar landfill, the largest municipal dump in Africa (Pithouse, 2005). Today, Kennedy Road is best known for the *Abahlali baseMjondolo* movement that formed there in 2005. *Abahlali baseMjondolo* campaigns for shack dwellers' reasonable access to basic service delivery such as water, electricity, and toilets, and in the process *Abahlali* has emerged as a model of urban citizenship in informal settlements across South Africa (Gibson, 2011; Pithouse, 2006).

The story of the emergence of *Abahlali* is especially fascinating due to its unlikely origins in the context of a series of failed municipal consultation. Before there was *Abahlali*, there was the Kennedy Road Development Community, a comparably small-scale organization that held its first elections in 2000, culminating in a much-anticipated formal meeting with Durban municipal departments of waste, water, and health in 2004. There was much excitement about this meeting among members in the Kennedy Road settlement. The group had been given the impression from previous exchanges with municipal authorities that the sit-down consultation would both provide an opportunity for the city to collect vital information about their settlement, which, in turn, would result in an historic outcome favorable to the improvement of their quality of life.

The actual meeting unfolded less promisingly. On the day of the meeting, the senior most member of the organization had been specifically chosen to enter the municipal offices first. However, he was immediately inauspiciously shooed to the side of the waiting room, hailed with an expression of casual annoyance—"*eh baba!*"—as administrators noted his muddied boots. After what appeared to the uninitiated to have been an uneventful meeting, what followed for the community was a protracted waiting period. There was a promised report, which failed to materialize, and the community slowly became aware through alternate contacts in the municipal network that one of the central ministries had, in fact, been opposed to their attendance from the start. In a subsequent meeting with the housing municipality, during with a conciliatory patch of land close to easy bus transport was promised, results again failed to materialize concretely (after assiduously watching the land preparations over weeks, it came to be understood that the land was being granted to a private businessman for a bricklaying yard). At this point, the Kennedy Road Development Community mobilized and responded with civil protests. Their march blocked one of the main arterial roads to central Durban, and as a result, members were swiftly subjected to 14 arrests, exposed to police harassment and subsequently, the organization received prominent media coverage.

Within months, a cascade of attention from academics, lawyers, and innumerable neighboring informal communities produced *Abahlali* proper. In conversations with one of its key founding members, S'bu Zikode, the experience of the initial meeting played a critical if unexpected role. Zikode related how it was specifically his experiences attending meetings as a community representative which made him increasingly aware of the vulnerability of individual stakeholders or small-scale stakeholders, specifically their being susceptible to a form of dismissive or purely pro-forma consultation. In the municipal context of Durban, he recalled how disastrously inconsequential the presence of the Kennedy Road Development Community's senior-most member might have been without the presence of other members. He also felt very strongly that the emotional distress placed upon one individual to have to relay the experience of being received as insignificant or having to personally relay a failed engagement back to a group was not conducive to healthy or honest stakeholder engagement. The recalcitrant emphasis on profoundly communal formation, then, is not merely expedient or an accident of informal settlement life with *Abahlali*. It was a direct response to a keenly felt awareness of the power of bureaucratic indifference to marginalize individuals who cannot signal "proper" civic enthusiasm or the business professionalism of the ideal stakeholder for reasons of poverty, poor dress, continual health issues, or unfamiliarity with the proceduralist culture of municipal meetings and workshops more generally.

Equally concerning for *Abahlali* members was the experiences of engagement with cosmopolitan circuit of progressive movements. The subsequent flood of support from the international NGO community and academic community produced anxieties about the perils of being identified as stakeholders in the context of unregulated engagement with organizations that often were profoundly decontextualized from their experience of informal urban life. From some organizations, members recall with amusement being given guidebooks on "how to protest", and from the national government they were advised that their protests would not be heard unless they were appropriately channeled through the formalized structures of the Slum Dwellers International (a 70 million dollar Bill and Melinda Gates foundation initiative). As a result of these experiences, today, one cannot join *Abahlali* individually, but must form a collective of at least 50 individuals before they can become a "friend of *Abahlali*". For members, it is important that their organization, their culture and their priorities emerge from within each unique informal context, as one group joins another, they echo the sentiments expressed during the first united march of *Abahlali*, as each group hailed one another; "we are not here to support you but you are part of us, we are here because we feel we live in the same conditions as you".

Today Abahlali consists of 25 informal settlements in the KwaZulu Natal, and 35 across South Africa. In October 2009, *Abahlali* famously won the repeal of the slum clearance act of KZN in the Constitutional Court (Constitutional Court of South Africa, 2009) and continues to garner international recognition for their achievements. They unquestionably represent the living struggle for the Right to the City, the right of all urban inhabitants to experience their fullest inclusion in urban politics and life. When considering the vulnerability of informal communities in the consultative context, and the problem of "who" to consult in the context of urban displacement, *Abahlali* presents an urban constituency that has worked to legitimate the practice of stakeholder engagement in order to disable the excesses of corporate, municipal, and international attempts to relegate such encounters to footnotes in policy reports.

The organization of *Abahlali* is decidedly in response to the experience of failed consultation and its forms of stakeholder engagement by the municipality. It is a radically autonomous, horizontal, and decentralized collective, and the net result is that there is an entrenched set of organizational techniques employed with foreign non-government organizations, development organizations, and scholars which also means that any collaborative endeavor with *Abahlali* will necessarily foster a new bar for best practices and a legitimated quality of stakeholder engagement. Yet the vibrant urban practice of *Abahlali* is as much about the dynamic frontiers of urban development as it is radical urban citizenship.

The technologies and practices of *Abahlali* are a new benchmark of both participatory democracy as well as best practices by responsibilized citizens, and this is self-consciously articulated as such by the organization. Municipal indifference and shallow stakeholder engagement has produced a counter-governmentality emphasizing the centrality of pragmatic urban governance—one that is steeped in the daily culture of urban survival. As Zikode related from *Abahlali*'s downtown office headquarters, there is a strong sense that the techniques employed by government and municipal officials lack the dynamism, transparency, and awareness of the political stakes in neoliberal governance. With reference to municipal managers who seek to only consult with organizations such as *Abahlali* in the most nominalist terms, Zikode states, "maybe we have more solutions than you have. Don't pretend to be knowing everything, the

Figure 6. Birds in a Cornfield Exhibit (Masekeng), Museum Africa, Johannesburg.

very same beneficiaries could help you to deliver". This echoes an emergent sensibility among scholars who identify "poor peoples' practices as a public good, a commons and a public resource from which the indeterminate political future of urban spaces emerges" (Elyachar, 2012: 122).

Because informal social movements such as these represent a tremendously important aspect of urban cultural life in South Africa today, they are important to think about as a critical aspect of South Africa's urban liberation heritage. ABM is not the only such organization in informal settlements, there are many including the Landless People's Movement (Gauteng), the Rural Network (KwaZulu-Natal), and the Western Cape Anti-Eviction Campaign, which along with *Abahlali*, collectively constitute the Poor People's Alliance. The poor people's alliance, in many critical ways, marks the contemporary legacy of the urban practices of liberation heritage of South Africa, and the critical and historical intersection of the urban space and poverty with the rights struggle. Such a connection between the informal settlement and political organization has been thoughtfully engaged and memorialized within museum contexts, such as the "Birds in a Cornfield" installation in Johannesburg's Museum Africa, the Lwandle Migrant Labor Museum in the Helderberg Basin, and the Worker's museum in Newtown, Johannesburg (Figure 6)[1]. There have even been museums architecturally inspired by the materiality of the shack as redolent of struggle memories, particularly with the evocative

---

[1] For a fascinating discussion of the Birds in a Cornfield Exhibit, see Coombes (2003: 79–89).

"memory boxes" of the Red Location Museums situated in the eponymous township of Port Elizabeth (Baines, 2007).

Yet the tradition of political organizing within the township and the informal settlement has yet to be recognized as a living intangible heritage that is inextricable from the South African urban landscape and which houses the tradition of perhaps South Africa's most internationally recognized heritage, the modern struggle for effective redistribution of rights and participatory democracy. Because these new social movements necessarily unfold outside of formal housing, property ownership, and the formal demarcations of proper citizenship, because, with the casualization of labor they operate outside of the tradition of labor unions, these current struggles are often construed as separate from the historical rights struggle in South Africa, rather than existing as their continuation, merely inscribed with the conditions of the neoliberal urban precariat (Friedman, 2012).

Conclusion

In 1954, UNESCO sponsored a conference in Abidjan on the topic of the social impact of industrialization and urban conditions in Africa, centering around the pivotal role of wage labor and colonial/post-colonial development to cultural changes in the urban landscape (Cooper, 2002). As early as the 1950s, Georges Balandier's work in Brazzaville shifted the traditional anthropological categories of urban analysis in order to make sense of urban "makeshifts" and "unrest" that demonstrated informal urban networks as both symptomatic of "badly realized" development of late colonialism and "Africans struggling to build new communities in their own ways" (Cooper, 2002: 12). Within the context of development and governance, the persistent indeterminacy of informal spaces continually evoke the anxiety as to whether such sites mark the decline of the liberal development project, or whether they are about a certain ascendancy of the neoliberal laissez-faire citizen, in which urban migrants secure "makeshift" platforms for attaining expanded urban participation. This is the history of urban "flux and reflux", where urban mobility pitches between being only the residuum of the inadequacies of colonial mobilization or contemporary development, to what is actually constitutive of "citiness" (Nuttall and Mbembe, 2005).

Expanding urban heritage to explicitly address the central quality of informal communities and their practices marks several critical opportunities of relevance in the post-industrial urban context. It gives the opportunity to address the mistaken notion that informal communities (and by association, their inhabitants) have no architectural, material or cultural history that could be widely appreciated as either important or universally outstanding. In the context of the new economy and post-industrial globalization, addressing the heritage of dislocated or foreign enclaves in urban spaces is arguably a global and ascendant project. Slums or informal settlements mark the daily enactment of practices that materially and bodily assert the right to the city even in a profound state of socioeconomic disenfranchisement. These practices give meaning to the urban landscape as an agent of social change and political practice. Sensitizing a global audience to these sites as possessing formal histories, meriting considered engagement with regard to their histories, practices, and political life, presents a project which is necessitated in the context of urban revitalization, identifying social capital, or revitalization through tourism. It provides an exceptional opportunity to revisit practices of consultation and stakeholder engagement that are critically in need of challenging engagement and, in the process, it provides an opportunity to revitalize the very concept of dynamic urban heritage.

Acknowledgements

This paper was first presented at the Stanford Conference on *The Conservation of Historic Urban Landscapes and Sustainable Development* in May of 2013. Special thanks to Ron Jennings, Rosemary Coombe, Lynn Meskell, Thabo Manetsi, Carolyn Nakamura, Melissa Baird, Albino Pereira de Jesus Jopela, Sophia Labadi and David Morris for their assistance in discussing these ideas. I am particularly grateful to Sibusiso Innocent Zikode and Reverend Mavuso Mbhekiseni for their generosity and hospitality. *Imikhonzo evela yepulazi i kuya imijondolo.*

Note

1. The 2012 recognition of Rio de Janeiro as a World Heritage site raises the complex question of how the Santa Marta and Babilônia favelas will participate in this inscription.

References

Constitutional Court of South Africa (2009) Abahlali baseMjondolo Movement of South Africa and Sibusiso Zikode v. Premier of the Province of KwaZulu-Natal, Member of the Executive Council for Local Government, Housing and Traditional Affairs, KwaZulu-Natal, Minister of Human Settlements and Minister of Rural Development and Law Reform, CCT z2/ op. Decided on October 14, 2009. Available at: http://www.saflii.org/za/cases/ZACC.

Allen V, Mngqolo S and Swanepoel S (2012) *The Struggle for Liberation and Freedom in the Northern Cape: 1850–1994*. Kimberley: McGregor Museum.

Appadurai A (2002) Deep democracy: Urban governmentality and the horizon of politics. *Public Culture* 14: 21–47.

Appadurai A (2006) *Fear of Small Numbers : An Essay on the Geography of Anger*. Durham, NC: Duke University Press.

Baines G (2007) The politics of public history in post-apartheid South Africa. In: Hans ES (ed.) *History Making and Present Day Politics: The Meaning of Collective Memory in South Africa*. Uppsala: Nordica Africa Institute, pp. 167–182.

Baird MF (2012) The breath of the mountain is my heart: Indigenous cultural landscapes and the politics of heritage. *International Journal of Heritage Studies* 19: 327–340.

Bandarin F and van Oers R (2012) The historic urban landscape managing heritage in an urban century. Chichester: Wiley Blackwell.

Brown M (2005) Re-envisioning the Kimberley mine museum. Research Report, Master of Arts (Heritage Studies). University of the Witwatersrand.

Chirikure S, Munyaradzi M, Webber N, et al. (2010) Unfulfilled promises? Heritage management and community participation at some of Africa's cultural heritage sites. *International Journal of Heritage Studies* 16: 30–44.

Collier SJ and Ong A (2008) Global assemblages, anthropological problems. In: Ong A, Collier SJ and Malden (eds) *Global Assemblages: Technology, Politics, and Ethics as Anthropological Problems*. Malden, MA: Blackwell, pp. 3–21.

Collins J (2012) Reconstructing the "Cradle of Brazil": The detachability of morality and the nature of cultural labor in Salvador, Bahia's Pelourinho world heritage site. *International Journal of Cultural Property* 19: 423–452.

Conlin MV and Jolliffe L (2011) What happens when mining leaves? In: Conlin MV and Jolliffe L (eds) *Mining Heritage and Tourism*. New York: Routledge, pp. 1–10.

Coombes AE (2003) *History after apartheid: Visual culture and public memory in a democratic South Africa*. Durham, NC: Duke University Press.

Cooper F (2002) Decolonizing situations: The rise, fall, and rise of colonial studies, 1951–2001. *French Politics, Culture and Society* 20(2): 47–76.

Cruikshank B (1999) *The will to empower: Democratic citizens and other subjects*. Ithaca, NY/London: Cornell University Press.

Davis M (2006) *Planet of Slums*. London: Verso.

De Cesari C (2011) Creative heritage: Palestinian heritage NGOs and defiant arts of government. *American Anthropologist* 112: 625–637.

Ellis R (2012) "A world class city of your own!": Civic governmentality in Chennai, India. *Antipode* 44: 1143–1160.

Elyachar J (2012) Next practices: Knowledges, infrastructure, and public goods at the bottom of the pyramid. *Public Culture* 1: 109–129.

Esterhuysen A (2012) The Cinderella metaphor: South African archaeology (still) in the making. *Azania: Archaeological Research in Africa* 47: 5–13.

Fabian J (1983) *Time and the Other: How Anthropology Makes Its Object*. New York: Columbia University Press.

Ferguson J (2010) The uses of neoliberalism. *Antipode* 41: 166–184.

Friedman S (2012) Beyond the fringe? South African social movements and the politics of redistribution. *Review of African Political Economy* 39: 85–100.

Gibson NC (2011) *Fanonian Practices in South Africa : From Steve Biko to Abahlali Basemjondolo*, 1st edn. New York: Palgrave Macmillan.

Haber A (2013) Evestigation, nomethodology and deictics: Movements in un-disciplining archaeology. In: Gonzalez-Ruibal A (ed.) *Reclaiming Archaeology: Beyond the Tropes of Modernity*, pp. 79–89.

Herzfeld M (2009a) *Evicted from eternity : The restructuring of modern Rome*. Chicago: University of Chicago Press.

Herzfeld M (2009b) Rhythm, tempo, and historical time: Experiencing temporality in the Neoliberal Age. *Public Archaeology* 8: 108–123.

Hoo SK (2007) R52m Big Hole project in Shambles. Available at: http://www.iol.co.za/news/south-africa/r52m-big-hole-project-in-shambles-1.317118 (accessed 1 June 2008).

Huchzermeyer M (2011) *Cities with "Slums" : From Informal Settlement Eradication to a Right to the City in Africa*. Claremont: UCT Press.

ICOMOS (1994) The Nara document on authenticity. Paris: ICOMOS.

Maharaj B, Sucheran R and Pillay V (2006) Durban—A tourism Mecca? Challenges of the post-apartheid era. *Urban Forum* 17(3): 262–281.

Marschall S (2010) Private sector involvement in public history production in South Africa: The Sunday Times heritage project. *African Studies Review* 53: 35.

Masuku van Damme LS and Meskell L (2009) Producing conservation and community in South Africa. *Ethics, Place & Environment* 12: 69–89.

Mbembe A and Nuttall S (2004) Johannesburg-the elusive metropolis. *Public Culture* 16: 347–372.
Meskell L and Scheermeyer C (2008) Heritage as therapy: Set pieces from the New South Africa. *Journal of Material Culture* 13: 153–173.
Miraftab F (2007) Governing post apartheid spatiality: Implementing city improvement districts in Cape Town. *Antipode* 39: 602–626.
Murray N, Shepherd N and Hall M (2007) *Desire Lines: Space, Memory and Identity in the Post-Apartheid City*. London: Routledge.
National Heritage Council (NHC) (2010) *Mainstreaming Heritage in Development: Draft Discussion Framework*. Unpublished discussion document, Pretoria.
Ndlovu N (2011) Legislation as an instrument in South African heritage management: Is it effective? *Conservation and Management of Archaeological Sites* 13: 31–57.
Ndoro W and Pwiti G (2005) Heritage management in Southern Africa: Local, national and international discourse. In: Corsane G (ed.) *Heritage, Museums and Galleries: An Introductory Reader*. London: Routledge, pp. 154–168.
Nuttall S and Mbembe A (2005) A blase attitude? A response to Michael Watts. *Public Culture* 17: 193–201.
Ong A (2006) *Neoliberalism as exception : Mutations in citizenship and sovereignty*. Durham, NC: Duke University Press.
Peck J (2010) *Constructions of neoliberal reason*. Oxford/New York: Oxford University Press.
Pereira de Jesus Jopela A (2011) Traditional custodianship: A useful framework for heritage management in Southern Africa? *Conservation and Management of Archaeological Sites* 13: 103–122.
Pithouse R (2005) The left in the slum: The rise of a Shack Dwellers' movement in Durban, South Africa. Unpublished paper presented at the History & African Studies Seminar, 23 November 2005.
Pithouse R (2006) Thinking resistance in the shanty town. In: Mute (ed.) *Naked Cities – Struggle in the Global Slums*. London: Mute Publishing Ltd., pp. 16–31.
Prakash G and Kruse KM (2008) *The Spaces of the Modern City: Imaginaries, Politics, and Everyday Life*. Princeton: Princeton University Press.
Rajak D (2012) Platinum city and the new South African dream. *Africa: The Journal of the International African Institute* 82: 252–271.
Rao V (2012) *Slum as Theory: Mega-Cities and Urban Models* (The Sage Handbook of Architectural Theory). London: Sage.
Roy A (2009) Civic governmentality: The politics of inclusion in Beirut and Mumbai. *Antipode* 41: 159–179.
Roy A (2012) Ethical subjects: Market rule in an age of poverty. *Public Culture* 24: 105–108.
Ruggles DF (2012) Introduction: The social and urban scale of heritage. In: Ruggles DF (ed.) *On Location: Heritage Cities and Sites*. New York: Springer, pp. 1–15.
Scott JC (1998) *Seeing Like a State: How Certain Schemes to Improve the Human Condition Have Failed*. New Haven, CT: Yale University Press.
Shepherd N (2003) "When the hand that holds the trowel is black..."; disciplinary practices of self-representation and the issue of "Native" labour in archaeology. *Journal of Social Archaeology* 3: 334–352.
Shepherd N (2013) Ruin memory: A hauntology of Cape Town. In: González-Ruibal A (ed.) *Reclaiming Archaeology: Beyond the Tropes of Modernity*. London: Routledge.

Simone AM (2001a) On the worlding of African cities. *African Studies Review* 44: 15–41.
Simone AM (2001b) Straddling the divides: Remaking associational life in the informal African city. *International Journal of Urban and Regional Research* 25: 102–118.
Simone AM (2004) *For the City yet to Come: Changing African Life in Four Cities.* Durham, NC: Duke University Press.
Simone AM (2005) Urban circulation and the everyday politics of African urban youth: The case of Douala, Cameroon. *International Journal of Urban and Regional Research* 29: 516–532.
Stallard Commission (1922) Report of the local government comission. In: *Secondary Report of the Local Government Comission.* Reprint. Pretoria: Author.
Statistics South Africa (2011) *Census 2011.* Census in Brief. Pretoria: Statistics South Africa.
Swanepoel S and Mngqolo S (2011) *Galeshewe: Champion of the People.* Kimberley: Sol Plaatje Educational Trust.
UNESCO (2011) *Recommendation on the Historic Urban Landscape.* Paris: UNESCO.
UN Human Settlements Programme (2006) The state of the world's cities. London: Earthscan on behalf of UN-Habitat.
van der Merwe C (2010) De beers opens diamond route in South Africa. *Mining Weekly Online.* Available at: http://www.miningweekly.com/print-version/de-beers-opens-diamond-route-in-south-africa-2010-02-04 (accessed 11 February 2011).
van der Merwe C and Rogerson CM (2013) Industrial heritage tourism at the 'Big Hole', Kimberley, South Africa. *African Journal for Physical, Health Education, Recreation and Dance* 19: 155–171.
Žižek (2004) Knee-Deep; Review of: *Free World: Why a Crisis of the West Reveals the Opportunity of Our Time by Timothy Garton Ash.* London Review of Books, vol. 26, no. 17, pp. 12–13, September 2.

Author Biography

Lindsay M. Weiss is a postdoctoral scholar at Stanford University in the Department of Anthropology and the Stanford Archaeology Center. Her work examines the politics of public history and heritage in contemporary South Africa.

[8]

SIR, HOW MUCH IS THAT MING VASE IN THE WINDOW?: Protecting Cultural Relics in the People's Republic of China

MICHAEL L. DUTRA[*]

I. INTRODUCTION
II. CULTURAL PROPERTY IN A SHRINKING WORLD
    A. *What is Cultural Property?*
    B. *The Global Black Market for Antiquities*
    C. *Cultural Property in China*
    D. *The Challenge of Protecting Chinese Cultural Property*
III. THE INTERNATIONAL LEGAL REGIME TO PROTECT CULTURAL PROPERTY
    A. *1970 UNESCO Convention*
    B. *UNIDROIT Convention*
IV. CHINA'S LEGAL REGIME FOR CULTURAL PROPERTY: KEEPING THE DRAGON IN THE BOX
    A. *China's Regulation of Cultural Property*
    B. *The 2002 Law Protecting Cultural Relics*
    C. *The 1997 Criminal Law and Cultural Property*
V. MAKING THE FUTURE SAFE FOR CHINA'S CULTURAL TREASURES
    A. *Educational Programs*
    B. *Incentive Programs*
    C. *Reducing Government Regulation of the Legal Relics Market*
    D. *State-Sponsored Auctions*
VI. CONCLUSION

---

[*] Associate, White & Case LLP, New York; J.D., 2003, *cum laude*, Georgetown University Law Center; B.A. International Relations & Political Science, 2000, *summa cum laude*, University of Southern California. I would like to thank Professor James Feinerman for his suggestions and comments and Jacqueline Tully for her patience.

I. INTRODUCTION

An explosion rumbled through the hills of Hebei Province outside the village of Xiyanchuan in the summer of 1994. As the dust cleared, a dozen black-clad men emerged from behind boulders and used shovels and picks to clear a path through the rubble that was moments earlier the capstone covering the entrance to the tomb of Wang Chuzi, military governor for the region during the 10th century Fifth Dynasty. Climbing into the gaping hole, the men lowered themselves into the underground tunnel and entered Wang Chuzi's burial chamber adorned with intricately carved marble reliefs and vivid painted landscapes. The tomb robbers used chisels and crowbars to strip the walls of ten marble sculptures, causing irreparable damage to the remaining contents of Wang Chuzi's tomb and destroying invaluable archaeological objects in their haste to remove the priceless wall panels. The thieves then slipped out of the tomb carrying the wall friezes and disappeared into the shadows of the night, never to be apprehended.[1]

Five years later, in 1999, a prominent Hong Kong auction house listed a single marble wall relief for sale with Christie's in New York. Vigilant Chinese officials determined that the piece listed for sale was identical to one missing from Wang Chuzi's tomb. China sought the assistance of American officials to have the relief returned under the terms of the 1970 UNESCO Convention on the Means of Prohibiting and Preventing the Illicit Import, Export and Transfer of Ownership of Cultural Property ("1970 UNESCO Convention").[2] The United States, complying with its obligations under the 1970 UNESCO Convention, brought a successful forfeiture action against Christie's, and the auction house eventually surrendered the frieze. The artwork was then

---

[1] *See* Jane Levine, *Returning Stolen Cultural Property*, 25 CULTURAL RESOURCE MANAGEMENT 17 (2002), *available at* http://crm.cr.nps.gov/archive/25-02/25-2-7.pdf (last visited Jan. 29, 2003); *see also US Returns Seized Ancient Sculpture to China*, PEOPLE'S DAILY, May 24, 2001, *available at* http://fpeng.peoplesdaily.com.cn/200105/24/eng20010524_70878.html (last visited Oct. 21, 2003).

The recovered frieze from Wang Chuzi's tomb has not been the only instance of Sino-American cooperation on the repatriation of Chinese relics. In June 2003, the U.S. Department of Homeland Security recovered six terracotta warriors looted from a Han Dynasty tomb and smuggled out of China the previous year. American officials seized the figures after they were offered for sale in a Sotheby's auction catalog and returned them to China. *See* Hannah Beech, *Spirited Away*, TIME, Oct. 13, 2003 (Asia ed.), *available at* http://www.time.com/time/asia/covers/501031020/story.html (last visited Oct. 23, 2003); Xinhua News Agency, *US Returns Smuggled Terracotta Figures to China*, June 18, 2003, *available at* http://www.newsgd.com/culture/life/200306180012.htm (last visited Oct. 22, 2003).

[2] *See* UNESCO Convention on the Means of Prohibiting and Preventing the Illicit Import, Export, and Transfer of Ownership of Cultural Property, Nov. 14, 1970, 823 U.N.T.S. 232 [hereinafter "1970 UNESCO Convention"].

repatriated to the People's Republic of China in May 2001.[3] The looting of Wang Chuzi's tomb and the recovery of the marble relief embodies the great challenges that the Chinese government faces in dealing with the looting of cultural property and antiquities, and their subsequent sale in China and abroad. One of the lost sculptures from Wang Chuzi's tomb was recovered years after the theft, but at the price of knowing that the nine other missing reliefs may never resurface on the open market — they are likely gone forever.

Such examples illustrate that China's current legal regime for protecting the nation's cultural property is failing to preserve priceless antiquities and the archaeological heritage of the Chinese people. Without dramatic changes, China may risk losing a vast portion of its past. The purpose of this article is to probe two aspects of the problem. First, this article assesses international treaties and China's domestic laws that protect cultural property and their effectiveness in preventing the loss of Chinese antiquities and archaeological artifacts. Second, this article examines the weaknesses inherent in China's legal regime protecting cultural property and proposes modifications that will provide greater protection for China's cultural legacy.

Part II of this article describes the context surrounding the flow of cultural property out of China and into the hands of art and antiquities collectors around the world. This section focuses on the forces that drive the export of cultural property, the damage to ancient sites, and the losses to scholarship that occur as a result of the illicit removal of such property. Part III examines the implementation, compliance and effectiveness of various international agreements designed to stem the illegal cross-border flow of cultural property. Part IV addresses China's domestic legal regime in place for the preservation and protection of cultural property. This critical analysis reveals the inherent weaknesses of China's legal system, which, as a result, have failed to prevent the rise in the smuggling of antiquities and artifacts out of China. Part V proposes that China reduce the regulation of its domestic market for cultural relics and clarify the confusing and inconsistent elements of its legal regime protecting cultural property. Furthermore, China should institute educational and incentive programs, as well as state-sponsored

---

[3] The United States initiated the forfeiture proceeding against the possessors of the marble frieze under the Convention on Cultural Property Implementation Act ("CPIA"), 19 U.S.C.A. §§ 2601-2613, which implements the United States' treaty obligations under the 1970 UNESCO Convention. *See* Press Release, United States Customs Service, "US Customs Service Returns Rare 10th Century Burial Sculpture to China," (May 23, 2001) *available at* http://exchanges.state.gov/culprop/custpr3.html (last visited Jan. 29, 2003); *see also* Levine, *supra* note 1, at 17-18; *see generally* Marilyn Phelan, *Public International Law: Cultural Property*, 32 INT'L LAW. 447 (1998) (discussing Greece's successful campaign for the return of looted Bronze Age Mycenaean objects under the CPIA in 1996).

and managed relic auctions, to preserve at-risk archaeological sites and relics.

II. CULTURAL PROPERTY IN A SHRINKING WORLD

A. *What is Cultural Property?*

"Cultural property" is necessarily a broad term, as it covers almost every item that has some sort of significance or value to individual humans or societies at large. As with "art" there is no one single accepted definition of what constitutes "cultural property." However, for the purposes of this article, the term "cultural property" will be used to describe and apply to historical objects that have some scholarly value, historical meaning, or artistic merit. Synonyms for "cultural property" include "cultural patrimony," "antiquities," or "artifacts," and "cultural relics," the term the Chinese government favors. These terms can be used interchangeably.[4] In a seminal article on law and the international art trade, Professor Paul Bator succinctly defined cultural property as "all objects that are in fact prized and collected, whether they were originally designed to be useful, and whether or not they possess 'scientific' as well as aesthetic value."[5] This article adopts Professor Bator's definition of "cultural property." Thus, a Ming Dynasty vase, a fossilized dinosaur egg, and the Great Wall of China constitute "cultural property," although the latter is decidedly not portable.

The world's nations are divided into two major categories with regards to cultural property. The first is the group of source nations that possess a rich cultural history and where the majority of collectible artifacts are found. This is a varied group – including China, Egypt, Iraq, Sub-Saharan Africa, and several Latin American nations, as well as Italy and Greece, among others. Many source nations are poorer states with weak central governments that lack the resources or the will to protect and preserve archaeological sites and relics. The second group is the market nations, consisting of countries that import the cultural property of other states. Although these states may have considerable cultural property of their own, collectors domiciled in them seek to obtain collectable cultural property from the source nations. Market nations include rich industrialized states such as the United States,

---

[4] *See* n. 57 *infra* discussing the 1970 UNESCO Convention's definition of "cultural property."

[5] Paul M. Bator, *An Essay on the International Trade in Art*, 34 STAN. L. REV. 275, 285 (1982). This article was later reprinted as a monograph. *See* PAUL M. BATOR, THE INTERNATIONAL TRADE IN ART (1988). Further cites will refer to the 1988 text.

Canada, the United Kingdom, Germany, Japan, and Switzerland.[6] Collectors in those states have the resources to acquire cultural objects and antiquities from the source nations.

Collecting relics, according to Professor John Henry Merryman, "excite[s] a special emotion, give[s] perspective, awaken[s] the sleeping philosopher in us, [and] reduce[s] preoccupations of the busy present to a more appropriate scale."[7] Because of the rarity and demand for cultural objects in market nations, a brisk international market for their sale and resale has emerged. But as with any class of regulated objects, a thriving global black market for stolen or illicitly obtained cultural property exists in the shadow of the legal market as collectors seek ever more impressive or aesthetically desirable specimens — often through any means necessary.

B. *The Global Black Market for Antiquities*

The international black market for antiquities has burgeoned alongside economic globalization. In fact, the cross-border trade in illicitly obtained or stolen art and antiquities[8] follows only arms and narcotics in terms of dollar value.[9] Law enforcement agencies estimate that the global black market for illicit art and antiquities tops US$ 6 billion each year.[10] This number is likely to increase in the future as

---

[6] *See* Lisa J. Borodkin, Note, *The Economics of Antiquities Looting and a Proposed Legal Alternative*, 95 COLUM. L. REV. 377, 385-86 (1995). A state may, however, be both a source state, and a market state.

[7] John Henry Merryman, *The Public Interest in Cultural Property*, 77 CALIF. L. REV. 339, 349 (1989).

[8] The cultural objects included in the illegal art and antiquities trade can be divided into two groups: those that were stolen from bona fide owners and those that are looted or excavated from a site where the artifacts were resting. *See* Kathleen Anderson, Note, *The International Theft and Illegal Export of Cultural Property*, 8 NEW ENG. INT'L & COMP. L. ANN. 411, 413 (2002); Michele Kunitz, Comment, *Switzerland and the International Trade in Art and Antiquities*, 21 NW. J. INT'L L. & BUS. 519, 525 (2001); Monique Olivier, Comment, *The UNIDROIT Convention: Attempting to Regulate the International Trade and Traffic of Cultural Property*, 26 GOLDEN GATE U. L. REV. 627, 630-33 (1996); Robin Hardy Villanueva, Note, *Free Trade and the Protection of Cultural Property: The Need for an Economic Incentive to Report Newly Discovered Antiquities*, 29 GW J. INT'L L. & ECON. 548 (1995).

[9] *See* Ian M. Goldrich, Comment, *Balancing the Need for Repatriation of Illegally Removed Cultural Property with the Interests of Bona Fide Purchasers: Applying the UNIDROIT Convention to the Case of the Golden Phiale*, 23 FORDHAM INT'L L. J. 118, 118 (1999).

[10] *See* Kunitz, *supra* note 8, at 520. The international art market also provides an avenue for laundering money, particularly using "dirty" money to purchase illegally exported art in a nation, such as Switzerland, which has loose cultural property laws. *Id.*

more and more poor farmers and laborers in source nations recognize the market for such items and sell their cultural heritage to collectors in market nations. The looting of thousands of cultural objects and antiquities from the National Museum in Baghdad and other archaeological sites in Iraq during the recent United States-led occupation clearly illustrates the seductive allure of the black market for desperate populations or organized bands of thieves.[11] Professor Clemency Coggins describes the current situation in source states: "Archaeologically rich countries continue to be looted at an escalating rate. The 'new' ancient objects continue to be bought and sold in the antiquities market despite an array of international laws and agreements designed to stem the flow."[12]

Unfortunately, the illegal trade in antiquities often results in the destruction of archaeological information and material. Many tomb looters use crude methods such as homemade dynamite or pick-axes that damage sites. This often leads to the destruction of important evidence about the daily life of ancient cultures as well as their religious and political practices.[13] Furthermore, vandalism of non-collectible cultural property is rampant as treasure seekers often destroy or damage items without any obvious value. Such objects, however, are often of great use to archaeologists. Professor Coggins elaborates on the archaeological harms of looting:

> Once a site has been worked over by looters in order to remove a few saleable objects, the fragile fabric of its history is largely destroyed. Changes in soil color, the traces of ancient floors and fires, the imprint of vanished textiles and foodstuffs, the relation of one object to another, and the position of a skeleton – all of these sources of fugitive information are ignored and obliterated by archaeological looters.[14]

Additionally, the illegal looting and excavating of cultural property has caused great gaps in historical knowledge as falsified export papers often distort the provenance of cultural objects, making it easier for

---

[11] *See* Brooks Barnes & Karen Mazurkewich, *Racing the Black Market*, WALL ST. J., April 16, 2003, at B1; *see also* Andrew Lawler, *Beyond the Looting*, NAT. GEOGRAPHIC, Oct. 2003.

[12] Clemency Coggins, *Ownership and Protection of Heritage: Cultural Property Rights in the 21st Century: Cultural Property and Ownership: Antiquities*, 16 CONN. J. INT'L L. 183, 184-85 (2001).

[13] *See* Beech, *supra* note 1.

[14] Clemency Coggins, *Archaeology and the Art Market*, 175 SCIENCE 263 (1972).

forgeries to flood the market.[15] Professor Bator summarizes the tension between the art market and archaeological interest, noting that "the workings of the market . . . sets a higher price on art masterpieces than on the acquisition of archaeological knowledge."[16]

By imposing unrealistic and overly broad legal regimes to stem the flow of cultural property beyond their borders, source states are ultimately reinforcing the black market smuggling of relics. States that have attempted to nationalize all cultural property or impose unrealistic restrictions on ownership, sale, and export of antiquities have merely fostered the black market and encouraged smuggling of cultural property out of that state.[17]

C. Cultural Property in China

China's position in the world of cultural property is defined by its status as one of the most important source countries of historical artifacts.[18] Because Chinese civilization has existed for thousands of years and has a tradition rich in art, there are quite literally tens of millions of objects that qualify as cultural property in China. Professor Merryman states: "China, with its many centuries of high civilization and its vast area and large population, may be the richest source of cultural property of all."[19] As one of the world's last remaining repositories of large numbers of undiscovered cultural objects, China's antiquities have become increasingly popular with foreign collectors, particularly with overseas collectors in diverse places as Canada, Singapore, Malaysia, and the United States.[20]

In addition to the large overseas market for Chinese cultural objects, China's centuries-old domestic antiquities market has revived over the past two decades as China's market economy reforms have taken hold. This should be no surprise as the tradition of antiquarianism dates back hundreds of years in China, reflecting the Confucian

---

[15] Borodkin, *supra* note 6, at 383-84.

[16] Bator, *supra* note 5, at 26.

[17] *See id.* at 45.

[18] As China's economy continues to grow at a rapid pace, China may become both a source *and* market nation. *See* J. David Murphy, *Hong Kong, 1997, and the International Movement of Antiquities*, 4 INT'L J. CULTURAL PROP. 241, 241 (1995).

[19] John Henry Merryman, *Foreword to* J. DAVID MURPHY, PLUNDER AND PRESERVATION: CULTURAL PROPERTY LAW AND PRACTICE IN THE PEOPLE'S REPUBLIC OF CHINA, at xiii, xiv (1995).

[20] *See* J. DAVID MURPHY, PLUNDER AND PRESERVATION: CULTURAL PROPERTY LAW AND PRACTICE IN THE PEOPLE'S REPUBLIC OF CHINA 51-53 (1995); *see also* Beech, *supra* note 1.

veneration of and respect for the past. Historian J. Alsop illustrates this point:

> Antiques in astonishing variety were pursued as prizes by Chinese collectors during many centuries before Mao Zedong's revolution. Ancient bronzes had been taken from earliest times by tomb robbers for the value of their metal; but they began to be sought in another way – in fact, by antique collectors – in the Song Dynasty. . . . The Song Dynasty further produced a substantial body of antiquarian writing on the subject of ancient bronzes.[21]

Historian Rose Kerr also notes that "by the late 16th century when increased prosperity brought luxury goods and upper-class cultural tastes within the reach of a wider body of consumers, the possession and display of antiques and works of art was one of the indispensable pastimes of a gentleman."[22] Today, a similar situation is occurring as China's market economy and economic growth has allowed an expanding segment of China's population to dabble in antiquarianism.[23] The Chinese mindset towards antiquities is quite different from that in the West, as China has a long history of emulation, reproduction, and "improvement" of antiquities and historical relics, dating to the Song Dynasty.[24] In fact, some Chinese museums today display ancient replicas of even older pieces of art.[25] Additionally, China has a centuries-old tradition of fabrication and forgery of antiquities and valuable texts.[26]

Beijing has realized the importance and value of such cultural objects and has sought to prevent their export through a legal regime designed to keep the most valuable cultural objects in the hands of the Chinese government (discussed *infra* in Part III). Maintaining its cultural property is important to China for historical, cultural, and

---

[21] J. ALSOP, THE RARE ART TRADITIONS 249 (1982).

[22] ROSE KERR, CHINESE ART AND DESIGN 222 (1991).

[23] *See* MURPHY, *supra* note 20, at 28-30.

[24] *See id.* at 30-32. Archaeologists have discovered ancient workshops where even older artifacts were "improved" by encasing them in wax or removing the patinas on bronze objects so that they would appear "new." *Id.*

[25] *See id.*

[26] *See generally* WILLIAM P. ALFORD, TO STEAL A BOOK IS AN ELEGANT OFFENSE: INTELLECTUAL PROPERTY LAW IN CHINESE CIVILIZATION 9-29 (1995).

educational reasons, as well as economic ones.[27] Chinese officials have learned that well-preserved collections of artifacts and ancient art are lucrative tourist attractions that can provide revenue and jobs for their communities,[28] as China's State Council articulated in 2001.[29] The potential revenue from cultural tourism is so great that China has designated several politically sensitive locations as cultural heritage sites with the United Nations. For example, the Chinese government has listed the Potala, the Dalai Lama's former residence in Tibet, as a World Heritage Site with UNESCO, even though China considers the exiled Dalai Lama to be an enemy of the government.[30] Unfortunately, most tomb looters tend to have more individualistic goals and care little for the benefits that cultural property may bring their communities, particularly if they are from impoverished regions.

There is so much cultural property in China that it is an impossible task for the government to keep track of all of it, much less preserve the antiquities that have been turned over to the government. For instance, there are an estimated 400,000 archaeological sites in China, but only 70,000 of them have been recognized as such.[31] There are widespread reports of leaky, rodent-infested warehouses stuffed with ancient artifacts that are slowly being destroyed by the elements.[32] Local, county, and provincial governments, charged with administering certain sites and objects, lack the resources to provide guards to protect

---

[27] *See* MURPHY, *supra* note 20, at 107. The Chinese government has adopted a position that cultural resource management should be designed to increase revenue through tourism and sales. *See also* Bator, *supra* note 5, at 27.

[28] Some Chinese provinces have designed promotional campaigns around their cultural treasures to attract tourists. For instance, Henan Province held the International Dinosaur Festival in Nanyang, where a rich bed of fossilized dinosaur eggs was discovered. *See* Xinhua News Agency, *Henan To Offer Ten New Tourist Programs*, Nov. 7, 1995, *available at* 1995 WL 7715862.

[29] *See* People's Republic of China, Decisions of the State Council on Rectifying and Standardizing Order in the Market Economy, April 27, 2001, State Council of the People's Republic of China, *available at* LEXIS PRCLEG 1822. ("We should further rectify the cultural and tourism market. . . . . We will rectify the cultural relic market and standardize the operational order in the tourism industry.") *Id.* ch. 2(6).

[30] *See* Kanchana Wangkeo, *Monumental Challenges: The Lawfulness of Destroying Cultural Heritage During Peacetime*, 28 YALE J. INT'L L. 183, 191 (2003).

[31] Of the 70,000 officially designated archaeological sites in China, the central government has taken responsibility for 1,269 sites; approximately 7,000 sites are protected at the provincial level; and an astounding 60,000 sites are the responsibility of county and local governments. *See New Actions for Cultural Relics This Year*, People's Daily Overseas Edition, Oct. 7, 2003, *available at* http://www.chinacov.com/EN/displaynews.asp?id=99 (last visited Oct. 22, 2003).

[32] *See* MURPHY, *supra* note 20, at 64-65.

against grave robbers or to adequately preserve objects that have been turned over for safekeeping.[33]

D. *The Challenge of Protecting Chinese Cultural Property*

The task of preserving China's cultural heritage is one of massive magnitude considering the amount of culturally important objects and sites in China. The sheer number of objects and sites makes any sort of control or protection a daunting task. Tomb robbing is by far the most common source of illegal relics in China. Because of China's rich history, the landscape is littered with tombs from various eras—dating from 500 B.C. and earlier, up to the Qing dynasty. While tomb robbing and smuggling of cultural relics have been fixtures of China's past for centuries,[34] the Chinese Communist Party's rise to power in 1949 greatly curtailed the looting and smuggling of China's cultural patrimony, although many priceless relics were lost during the Cultural Revolution. As recently as 1983, Professor Bator noted that there was little or no cultural property leaving China, even illegally.[35]

Today, however, the situation has changed noticeably. Tomb robbing, particularly in the less economically developed inner provinces, provides many Chinese peasants with a way to supplement their meager incomes. These peasants often have no idea of the value of what they have excavated; they often consider the relics to be dusty junk.[36] These peasants, ignorant of the prices that such artifacts may bring at auctions in Hong Kong or New York, often sell relics to black market middlemen for a tiny fraction of the artifact's market value. But even receiving a relative pittance in comparison to an artifact's black market value can double or triple a subsistence farmer's annual income, all for a single night's labor.[37] This problem is only getting worse. China's State Bureau of Cultural Relics estimates that over 220,000 tombs have been robbed since 1998.[38] A troubling side effect of this looting is that the tomb robbers, like those that looted Wang Chuzi's tomb, often destroy invaluable archaeological data by plundering the tombs as quickly as possible and destroy priceless information in the process.[39]

---

[33] *See* MURPHY, *supra* note 20, at 65-67.

[34] *See id.* at 54.

[35] *See* Bator, *supra* note 5, at 43.

[36] *See* Beech, *supra* note 1.

[37] *See id.*

[38] *See id.*

[39] *See* MURPHY, *supra* note 20, at 52-53.

Tomb robbing is only part of the problem. The smuggling of illicitly obtained cultural property across China's borders has made Chinese relics available on the world market. In fact, antiquities are thought to be the most valuable single class of items smuggled out of China.[40] While Hong Kong is no longer the *entrepot* for smuggled antiquities that it was under British rule, both Hong Kong and Guangzhou remain the primary domestic destinations of contraband cultural property.[41] From there, the illegally removed antiquities and artifacts are smuggled on small aircraft, fishing boats, or other means to various other points, including Russia, the Philippines, Malaysia, and Singapore.[42]

Another emerging problem in protecting Chinese cultural property is the theft of relics and antiquities from state-owned museum collections.[43] The number of reported thefts has increased over 30 percent since the 1980s, and many more instances go unreported to authorities.[44] Thefts from institutions are up dramatically as security is often lax, inventories are incomplete, and museum workers are often poorly trained and underpaid, particularly in museums that local, county, or provincial governments fund.[45] Even if museum officials are not directly complicit in plots to steal artifacts or antiquities, they often turn a blind eye to the disappearance of less valuable cultural relics.

China's rapid economic growth in the mid-1990s has further imperiled Chinese cultural property. The most important factor is the rekindled interest in antiquarianism and collecting relics that sprang up with the economic liberalization of the last decade. This rise in demand has led to increased looting and smuggling, as well as the commodification of cultural property. In fact, "antique markets" appeared throughout China in the 1990s, particularly in the more prosperous coastal regions. One Chinese official has noted:

---

[40] *See*, Murphy, *supra* note 18, at 242.

[41] *See id.* at 246-47.

[42] *See id.* at 242-43; *see also* Claudia Caruthers, Comment, *International Cultural Property: Another Tragedy of the Commons*, 7 PAC. RIM L. & POL'Y 143, 160 (1998); *see also* Lee Siew Hua, *Saving Asia's Ancient Monuments*, STRAITS TIMES, Jan. 29, 1995, at 1. ("Singapore, which as a free port has no restrictions on the sale of stolen art pieces, is luring treasures from as far away as China...") *Id.*

[43] *See Security Chief Arrested for Cultural Relics Theft*, PEOPLE'S DAILY, June 19, 2003, available at http://english.peopledaily.com.cn/200306/19/eng20030619_118545.html (last visited Oct. 22, 2003) (reporting the museum security chief was arrested for stealing 158 relics, several of which were classified as Grade One); *see also* Beech, *supra* note 1.

[44] *See* MURPHY, *supra* note 20, at 62.

[45] *See id.* at 64-67.

> The appearance of markets in cities and villages and the appearance of . . . traders has provided a perfect opportunity for some people to make a fortune. They . . . trade in cultural relics under the guise of trading in crafts and become very rich. Hence, 'antique markets' of various scales have sprung up and are expanding in cities such as Beijing, Shanghai and Guangzhou.[46]

The increased prosperity brought by economic liberalization has revived the Chinese domestic market for artifacts and antiquities that had long been suppressed under Communist rule.[47] With the emergence of such a domestic market for relics in the prosperous coastal areas, subsistence farmers in the interior have started to supplement their meager incomes by searching for antiquities to sell to unscrupulous middlemen. As China's economy grows, the domestic demand for cultural objects will likely increase as collecting becomes more widespread.

Additionally, China's need for improved internal infrastructure—including transportation, housing, and power generation—has destroyed thousands of sites with cultural value and threatens many more. For instance, the massive Three Gorges Dam project alone has imperiled thousands of sites with archaeological importance. During construction of the dam, more than 2,500 tombs and five square kilometers of ruins were excavated; however, this is merely the tip of the iceberg as the Yangtze River valley has dozens of other unexcavated archaeological sites that will be submerged when the project is completed.[48]

In sum, the task of protecting cultural property in China is a herculean task of almost impossible magnitude. The sheer amount of cultural property in China is enormous. It is virtually impossible for the government to halt the illegal flow of cultural property out of – and within China. Because the international legal regime designed to protect cultural property is unlikely to be of much help, China must rely on its domestic laws to preserve its cultural heritage, as once objects have left Chinese territory, they are likely gone forever.[49] However, Chinese law is not yet capable of taking on this formidable task.[50]

---

[46] *See* MURPHY, *supra* note 20, at 51, citing FAZHI RIBAO, *Strengthen Management of the Circulation of Cultural Relics*, Feb. 7, 1992, at 3.

[47] There has always been a trend toward antiquarianism in China, dating to ancient times. Because Confucian thinking held the past in reverence, it is only logical that the imperial Chinese amassed large collections of cultural objects from prior periods. However, Mao Zedong attempted to stamp out such collecting during the Cultural Revolution. *See* Alsop, *supra* note 21, at 249.

[48] *See* MURPHY, *supra* note 20, at 51; *see also* Martin Fackler, *China Races to Save History*, Associated Press, Jan. 20, 2002, *available at* http://www.museum-security.org/02/016.html (last visited Apr. 24, 2003).

[49] Discussed in Parts III.A & B *infra*.

III. THE INTERNATIONAL LEGAL REGIME TO PROTECT CULTURAL PROPERTY

The international legal regime regulating the cross-border flow of cultural property remains weak, as a lack of consensus between source and market states has undermined efforts to create a single, enforceable regime. While the first international treaties on the treatment of cultural property dealt with the destruction and plundering of artwork and antiquities during times of war,[51] the modern international cultural property regime has attempted to stem the flow of cultural objects out of source nations. However, the two major international instruments designed to restrict the illegal flow of cultural property—the 1970 UNESCO Convention and the 1995 UNIDROIT Convention on Stolen or Illegally Exported Cultural Objects ("UNIDROIT Convention")[52]— have been less than successful in eliminating this illicit trade. Both treaties have provisions that are weak and difficult to enforce, and relatively few of the market nations, whose citizens are the major purchasers of illicitly obtained cultural property, are party to either convention, rendering them paper tigers without much actual effect.[53]

---

[50] Discussed in Part IV *infra*.

[51] The practice of protecting cultural property during times of conflict emerged in ancient times. The unregulated aspect of warfare, however, made such a goal unrealistic, as cultural property was often treated as spoils of war. One only has to walk through the halls of the Louvre and observe the masterpieces Napoleon seized during his conquests to understand this principle (or the Elgin Marbles from the Athenian acropolis on display in the United Kingdom). Only in the mid-nineteenth century did legal codes for the protection of cultural property, including the Lieber Code formulated during the United States' Civil War, first emerge. However, these codes were largely ineffective as the massive looting and plundering of cultural property during both World Wars underscored the need for a comprehensive code that would protect cultural property during time of conflict. The 1954 Hague Convention is the current international instrument, albeit a vague one, governing the destruction and plundering of cultural property during periods of armed conflict. *See* Goldrich, *supra* note 9, at 123-29, 133-34.

[52] *See* International Institute for the Unification of Private Law Convention on the International Return of Stolen or Illegally Exported Cultural Objects, June 24, 1995, 34 I.L.M. 1322 (1995) [hereinafter "UNIDROIT Convention"].

[53] *See, e.g., Attorney-General of New Zealand v. Ortiz*, 3 W.L.R. 571 (1982) *aff'd* 2 W.L.R. 809 (1983) (U.K.) (New Zealand sought repatriation of illegally exported Maori panels under its cultural property export law; British appeals court held that exporter maintained title to panels because title did not vest in government of New Zealand until panels were seized; New Zealand never seized the panels.). *Cf. Republic of Ecuador v. Danusso* (Court of Appeals of Turin 593/82) (1982) (Italy) (Ecuador sought repatriation of illegally exported artifacts under its cultural property law; Italian

Thus, the weakness of the international legal regime on cultural property places an even greater burden on the source nations' domestic laws to regulate the excavation and export of culturally significant articles and specimens. Once cultural property leaves the source nation, the odds are slim that it will ever be returned.[54] In economic terms, the ineffectiveness of the international legal regime for cultural property is a result of the market states' inability, or lack of will, to (1) regulate collectors' desire for cultural property (a failure to regulate the "demand-side" of the equation), and (2) place pressure on source nations to develop enforceable domestic laws (regulating the "supply-side" of the equation). While the international demand for cultural property continues to rise, suppliers will attempt to meet that demand (so long as there are tombs to loot and artifacts to be excavated). Thus, an increase in demand for cultural objects puts pressure on domestic cultural property legal regimes. China is the archetypal example of how the lack of international consensus on and regulation of cultural property erodes the effectiveness of the domestic legal system's response to the problem.[55] Should the international legal regime become more effective in regulating the demand for cultural objects (as it may if more market states sign the 1970 UNESCO and UNIDROIT Conventions), then pressure on the domestic legal regimes will ease, as the demand for illicit cultural property declines.

A. *1970 UNESCO Convention*

The 1970 UNESCO Convention was the world's first peacetime effort to regulate the illegal trafficking of cultural property, through the creation of a legalistic regime that puts obligations on market states to recover and repatriate illegally exported cultural property.[56] The Convention regulates the export of cultural property by allowing states to enter into reciprocal agreements to enforce each other's cultural property

---

appeals court awarded title to Ecuador under Italy's domestic legislation enacting the provisions of the 1970 UNESCO Convention). In these almost identical cases, the difference in outcome can be explained as a result of Italy's decision to sign the UNESCO Convention- largely because of the large amount of cultural property located in Italy- and the United Kingdom's decision, at the time, not to sign the Convention.

[54] One expert estimates that the recovery rate for stolen art is approximately 12 percent. *See* Constance Lowell, *Art for America's Sake*, WALL ST. J., July 26, 1989, at A10.

[55] Discussed in Part IV *infra*. *See* LYNDELL V. PROTT & P. J. O'KEEFE, 3 LAW AND THE CULTURAL HERITAGE – MOVEMENT 621-29.

[56] *See* UNESCO's website for a list of states party to the 1970 UNESCO Convention at http://www.unesco.org/culture/laws/1970/html_eng/page3.shtml (last visited Apr. 21 2003).

laws.[57] Although the Convention defines "cultural property" broadly,[58] its provisions apply only to items, articles, or sites that member states designate in advance as "cultural property." China, a signatory of the 1970 UNESCO Convention, has designated thousands of sites as "cultural property" under the Convention.[59] For instance, in the Beijing Municipality alone, there are more than 2,100 officially designated cultural property sites.[60] The 1970 UNESCO Convention has no enforcement mechanism, it merely requires party states to it to prevent illicit export or import when it is consistent with a given state's domestic law.[61] After a long period in which interest in the 1970 UNESCO Convention was essentially dormant, several of the major market nations, including both the United Kingdom and Japan, signed and ratified the Convention in 2002.[62]

While the 1970 UNESCO Convention resulted in an aspirational goal to protect states' cultural property, its implementation has been largely ineffective for several reasons. First, the Convention provides a relatively narrow scope of protection. If states do not specifically designate archaeological artifacts or sites as cultural property, they are left without protection under the Convention.[63] This means that cultural property from undesignated sites is not covered under the 1970

---

[57] *See* 1970 UNESCO Convention, *supra* note 2, art. 13, at 244.

[58] *See id.* art. 1, at 234-36. The 1970 UNESCO Convention sets forth seven categories and four sub-categories of cultural property protected by the Convention's provisions, so long as the property "is specifically designated by each State as being of importance for archaeology, prehistory, history, literature, art or science." *Id.* at 234. The seven enumerated categories include: (1) specimens and collections of fauna, flora, and paleontology; (2) property relating to history; (3) products of archaeological excavations; (4) elements of artistic or historical monuments; (5) antiquities over 100 years old; (6) objects of ethnological interest; (7) property of artistic interest including paintings, pictures, sculptures, statuary, engravings, manuscripts, compilations of artistic merit, furniture, and musical instruments. *See id.*

[59] China signed the 1970 UNESCO Convention, but has never specifically enacted any domestic implementing legislation. Some elements of the Convention, however, have been enacted as part of the 1982 Cultural Relics Protection Law and the 2002 Law Protecting Cultural Relics. *See generally* LPCR, *infra* note 78.

[60] *See* People's Republic of China, Plans for Protection of the Famous Historical Cultural Metropolis of Beijing, Being Municipality, art. 4.1.4, September 1, 2002, *available at* LEXIS PRCLEG 2460 [hereinafter "Beijing Plan"].

[61] *See* 1970 UNESCO Convention, *supra* note 2, arts. 4 & 13, at 240, 244.

[62] *See UNESCO Calls for Universal Ratification of the 1970 Convention, Following the Example Set By Key Art Market Countries*, September 9, 2002, *available at* http://www.museum-security.org/02/109.html (last visited Mar. 22 2003). The United Kingdom signed the 1970 UNESCO Convention in July 2002; Japan did so in October of the same year. Switzerland is considering signing the Convention. *See id.*

[63] *See* 1970 UNESCO Convention, *supra* note 2, art. 1, at 234-36.

UNESCO Convention and cannot be recovered under its provisions (states party to the Convention may designate an unexcavated site as cultural property).[64] Second, only a few of the major market nations—the United States, and recently, the United Kingdom and Japan—have joined the Convention, while most of the source states of cultural property have signed the Convention. Because other major market states including Germany and Switzerland are not party to the Convention, there is little chance for comprehensive enforcement.[65] Third, the 1970 UNESCO Convention places a remarkable burden on market nations, as it focuses exclusively on remedies, rather than preventative measures (a major reason why many of the major market nations never joined the Convention in the first place). The Convention's remedy-based focus puts the enforcement costs on the market nations, which are, not surprisingly, unenthusiastic about bearing such costs.[66] It is unclear what effect the United Kingdom's and Japan's recent ratifications will have on the effectiveness of the 1970 UNESCO Convention, but so long as other major market states decline to join the regime, a market for illicitly obtained art and antiquities will continue to thrive.

B.   *UNIDROIT Convention*

The drafters of the UNIDROIT Convention sought to rectify the shortcomings of the 1970 UNESCO Convention by applying the common law rule regarding stolen property to illegally obtained cultural property.[67] The UNIDROIT Convention addresses two areas not dealt with under the 1970 UNESCO Convention: disputes between original owners and good-faith purchasers, as well as the unauthorized cross-border removal of cultural property.[68] First, the UNIDROIT Convention treats *all* unlawfully excavated and lawfully excavated illegally obtained

---

[64] China had designated Wang Chuzi's tomb a "cultural property" site under the 1970 UNESCO Convention, even though it was unexcavated. Such designation allowed China to invoke the Convention when the missing marble frieze resurfaced in the United States (one of the few market states party to the 1970 UNSECO Convention).

[65] Illegally exported cultural property can be sold with impunity in nations that are not party to the 1970 UNESCO Convention. *See* Stephanie O. Forbes, *Securing the Future of Our Past: Current Efforts to Protect Cultural Property*, 9 TRANSNAT'L LAW. 235, 245 (1996) (criticizing market nations for not signing the 1970 UNESCO Convention).

[66] *See* Borodkin, *supra* note 6, at 388-89.

[67] *See* Phelan, *supra* note 3, at 448; Goldrich, *supra* note 9, at 140; Caruthers, *supra* note 42, at 149.

[68] *See* Goldrich, *supra* note 9, at 140-41.

artifacts, not just those registered or inventoried by a source nation,[69] as stolen property subject to return to the original owner.[70] The purchaser of the stolen property must return the property once the original owner files a successful claim in the courts of the nation in which the purchaser resides.[71] In essence, this imposes a diligence requirement on purchasers of cultural property in states that have ratified the UNIDROIT Convention to ensure the legal provenance of the objects they seek to acquire. As a further incentive for buyers to ensure that their purchases are legal, good-faith purchasers are eligible for compensation once the stolen property is returned to its original owner; those purchasers that do not make a good faith effort to prove the legality of their purchase, on the other hand, are not entitled to any recompense.[72] Second, the UNIDROIT Convention requires repatriation of stolen cultural property, no matter if the state of the possessor has domestic legislation to prevent the importation of illegally exported cultural property (a major weakness of the 1970 UNESCO Convention).[73] Additionally, the UNIDROIT Convention provides an arbitration option for the recovery of stolen or illegally exported cultural objects, in addition to the legal options provided under the Convention.[74]

While the UNIDROIT Convention is a marked improvement over the 1970 UNESCO Convention and has been more effective in providing for the repatriation of illegally obtained cultural property, it has not been ratified by enough market states to make it an effective means by which a source state, such as China (which has acceded to the UNIDROIT Convention), can reclaim illegally exported antiquities and cultural relics.[75] As long as the major market nations refuse to ratify the

---

[69] *See* Villanueva, *supra* note 8, at 574.

[70] The original owner is often the government of the state where the artifact was discovered as many source nations have legislatively nationalized all undiscovered cultural property. Such is the case with China, as the National People's Congress has passed several laws stating that all unexcavated cultural relics are the property of the national government. *See* Phelan, *supra* note 3, at 448.

[71] *See* UNIDROIT Convention, *supra* note 52, art. 6(1), 34 I.L.M. at 1332.

[72] *See id.* arts. 4 & 6, 34 I.L.M. at 1332-33.

[73] *See id.* art. 5, 34 I.L.M. at 1332-33.

[74] *See id.* art. 8(2), 34 I.L.M. 1333; Folarin Shyllon, *The Recovery of Cultural Objects by African States Through the UNESCO and UNIDROIT Conventions and the Role of Arbitration*, 5 REVUE DE DROIT UNIFORME 219, 225 (2000).

[75] The UNIDROIT Convention has been ratified by Lithuania, Paraguay, Romania, Hungary, Peru, Bolivia, Italy, Croatia, Finland, Cambodia, and Portugal. It has been acceded to by China, Ecuador, Brazil, El Salvador, Argentina, Norway, and Spain. None of the major cultural property market states have ratified or acceded to the UNIDROIT Convention, making the treaty largely ineffective. *See* Status Report:

UNIDROIT Convention, there is little hope that the Convention's provisions will significantly impact the cross-border flow of illegally obtained cultural objects.[76] If a critical mass of market states were to adopt the UNIDROIT Convention, it would serve as a strong foundation on which an effective international legal regime for cultural property could be built. Until that time, it merely represents a set of worthy aspirational legal norms with little practical value. Thus, the primary burden of protecting cultural property falls on the source states and their domestic legislation because the international conventions are of little consequence in preventing the cross-border cultural property trade.

IV. CHINA'S LEGAL REGIME FOR CULTURAL PROPERTY: KEEPING THE DRAGON IN THE BOX

The Chinese government has constructed a domestic legal regime that regulates the possession and ownership of archaeological artifacts or relics in order to protect its rich cultural heritage. Unfortunately, this cultural property regime, like the 1970 UNESCO and UNIDROIT Conventions,[77] has proven to be largely ineffective. This is evidenced by the steady flow of illegally exported or illicitly obtained Chinese artifacts appearing on the international art market. China's legal regime for cultural property is primarily based on two major laws, the 2002 Revised Law on the Protection of Cultural Relics ("2002 LPCR")[78] and the 1997 Criminal Law,[79] which mandate strict regulation of any discovered

---

UNIDROIT Convention on Stolen or Illegally Exported Cultural Objects, Opened to Signature on 24.VI.1995 *available at* http://www.unidroit.org/english/implement/i-95.htm (last visited Feb. 26, 2003); *see also* Phelan, *supra* note 3, at 448 (discussing the need for a critical mass of market states to ratify the UNIDROIT Convention in order for it to be effective).

[76] *See id.*

[77] There are reports that China has attempted to negotiate a bilateral agreement with the United States for the return of cultural property. However, as of this time, no agreement has been made public. *See* Meg Maggio, *China and US Drafting Anti-Smuggling Agreement*, THE ART NEWSPAPER, *available at* http://www.theartnewspaper.com/news/article.asp?idart=3715 (last visited Oct. 22 2003).

[78] *See* PEOPLE'S REPUBLIC OF CHINA, LAW ON THE PROTECTION OF CULTURAL RELICS (adopted at the 30th Meeting of the Standing Committee of the 9th National People's Congress, Oct. 28, 2002), *available at* LEXIS PRCLEG 2506 [hereinafter "2002 LPCR"].

[79] *See* PEOPLE'S REPUBLIC OF CHINA, CRIMINAL LAW (adopted at the 5th session of the 8th National People's Congress, Mar. 14, 1997) [hereinafter "1997 CRIMINAL LAW"].

cultural relics, as well as harsh punishments for failure to comply with such regulations. On one hand, these efforts to reform China's flawed system for regulating its cultural property are a step in the right direction; however, on the other hand, they perpetuate the extant system's already entrenched flaws and shortcomings.

A. *China's Regulation of Cultural Property*

China, like many other source nations, has taken steps to regulate the cultural property[80] existing within its borders through (1) the nationalization of all cultural artifacts, relics, and antiquities found within its borders and (2) the regulation of privately-held relics. The basis for China's cultural property legislation can be found in its 1982 Constitution. Article 22 of the Constitution provides that it is the state's responsibility to protect "important items of China's historical and cultural heritage."[81] Despite this grant of power to the central government for regulating cultural property, many provinces, autonomous regions, and local governments have taken it upon themselves to pass their own cultural property policies, which often conflict with those that the Ministry of Culture and the State Bureau of Cultural Relics promulgate.[82] For instance, when the Municipality of Beijing issued a plan for protecting cultural property and relics within the municipality's borders in September 2002, it included a provision for protection of "ancient and famous trees" as cultural relics per the 1982

---

[80] It is important to note that the Chinese government uses the term "cultural relic" to refer to all types of cultural property, not just certain antiquities.

[81] PEOPLE'S REPUBLIC OF CHINA, CONSTITUTION, ch. 1, art. 22 (1982). In addition, Article 119 of the Constitution grants the governments of autonomous regions the power to "independently administer their own cultural affairs."

[82] Article 8 of the 2002 LPCR sets forth the system of governmental accountability for various cultural relics:

> Local People's Governments at various levels shall be responsible for the work of protecting cultural relics in their respective administrative jurisdictions. The departments of local People's Governments at and above the county level that undertake the protection of cultural relics shall supervise and administer cultural relics protection within their respective administrative jurisdictions.

2002 LPCR, art. 8, *supra* note 78; *see also* PEOPLE'S REPUBLIC OF CHINA, RULES FOR THE IMPLEMENTATION OF THE CULTURAL RELICS PROTECTION LAW, art. 8, April 30, 1992 *available at* LEXIS PRCLEG 697 [hereinafter "1992 RULES"]. The vagueness of this language and the difficulty in ascertaining which level of government has administrative jurisdiction over any particular cultural relic and the level of protection required is readily apparent. *See* Anne Carlisle Schmidt, *The Confuciusornis Sanctus: An Examination of Chinese Cultural Property Law and Policy in Action*, 23 B.C. INT'L & COMP. L. REV. 185, 199-200 (2000).

Cultural Relics Protection Law ("1982 CRPL").[83] But neither the 1982 CRPL nor the 2002 LPCR provide for the protection of trees—living or dead.[84] This is but one example of the many inconsistencies in the administration of China's legal regime to protect cultural property. In addition, the recent promulgation of the 2002 LPCR does not clarify such ambiguities and fails to remedy the flaws in the regime.[85] Chinese legal commentator, Jin Zitong, has critiqued the multitude of conflicting Chinese cultural property laws. Jin notes that there exists "a large number of relevant laws and regulations, the ill-organized legal system, and the lack of coordination between the relevant legal provisions."[86] The 2002 LPCR addresses, but does not solve, these fundamental problems. For example, one issue that remains unresolved is which governmental level—local, county, provincial, or central—has primary jurisdiction over any particular cultural relic or archaeological site. Currently, jurisdiction is decided based on the rarity and value of the relic or site, which leaves a haze of uncertainty as to which authority shall be responsible for the initial protection prior to a final determination.

---

[83] *See* Beijing Plan, *supra* note 60, art. 16. It should be noted that the Beijing Municipality plan was announced in early-September 2002, before the passage of the 2002 LPCR in October. Thus, the 1982 CRPL was the governing law at the time the Beijing Municipality plan was promulgated. In any case, the 2002 LPCR does not provide for the protection of trees as cultural relics either. *See* PEOPLE'S REPUBLIC OF CHINA, CULTURAL RELICS PROTECTION LAW (adopted at the 25th Meeting of the Standing Committee of the 5th National People's Congress, Nov. 19, 1982) *in* THE LAWS OF THE PEOPLE'S REPUBLIC OF CHINA 1979-1982 313 (1982) [hereinafter "1982 CRPL"].

[84] The only category of protected cultural relic that trees might possibly fall into under the 2002 LPCR would be "important historical sites." However, the explanatory notes in the 2002 LPCR suggest that such sites should be buildings or be other physical objects related to major historical events. It is unlikely that a tree will qualify as such a site merely because it is several hundred years old. *See* 2002 LPCR, *supra* note 78, art. 2(2).

[85] *See* J. David Murphy, *An Annotated Chronological Index of People's Republic of China Statutory and Other Materials Relating to Cultural Property*, 3 INT'L J. CULTURAL PROP. 159 (1994). Murphy has compiled a comprehensive list of Chinese rules, regulations, laws, circulars, announcements, and administrative measures by various local, county, and provincial governments, as well as the national government dating from 1930 through 1993.

[86] MURPHY, *supra* note 20, at 110-11.

B. *The 2002 Law Protecting Cultural Relics*[87]

In late October 2002, after considerable debate, the Standing Committee of the National People's Congress passed the 2002 LPCR,[88] which replaced the 1982 CRPL.[89] Although the 2002 LPCR and the 1982 CRPL are similar in several ways, there are significant differences between the two, particularly with regards to the alienability of cultural relics and individual ownership of such relics. Because of the 2002 LPCR was passed less than two years ago, it is unclear what sort of impact, if any, it will have on China's domestic antiquities market and on stemming the flow of illegally obtained cultural objects out of China. Upon careful analysis, it appears that the 2002 LPCR will likely result in some increased preservation of cultural objects because it permits the private ownership and collection of cultural relics. However, the LPCR will not effectively reduce the illicit trade of Chinese antiquities because the law does create enough incentives for individuals to turn discovered

---

[87] For the sake of clarity, this article will discuss the 2002 LPCR as a different piece of legislation from the 1982 CRPL because there are substantive differences between them, although technically, the 2002 LPCR is a revision of the 1982 CRPL.

[88] Beginning in early 2002, the 27th session of the Standing Committee of the 9th National People's Congress reviewed draft legislation ending the 1982 CRPL's ban on cultural property transactions between private parties. Citing the fact that private collecting is an alternative for state protection cultural objects, Zhou Keyu, Vice-Director of the NPC's Law Committee, introduced the proposed legislation which would eventually become the 2002 LPCR. One of the primary justifications for the 2002 LPCR was articulated by legislator Xie Youqing. "Private transaction of cultural property will help collect those treasures that have been drained" and ease the burden on the state in preserving such objects. *See Chinese Lawmakers Fiercely Debated Whether the Country Should Open Its Cultural Property Market to Private Collectors*, May 8, 2002, *available at* http://www.museum-security.org/02/058.html#4 (last visited June 11, 2004).

[89] The 2002 LPCR is largely based upon the legal regime for protecting cultural property that the 1982 CRPL created. The 1982 CRPL, in essence, nationalized almost all cultural property in China, with the exception of relics already held by private individuals (although they were often pressured to sell or "donate" such relics to state-owned museums or institutions). *See* 1982 CRPL, *supra* note 83. The 1982 CRPL set forth a relatively broad definition of "cultural relics" including antiquities, fossils, art, and buildings of historical value, as well as "all cultural relics remaining underground." *Id.* arts. 1-6. Any relics owned by private individuals were protected by the central government. The owners of such objects are strictly regulated by the state and are not allowed to exploit the cultural property in their possession without prior permission from the government. Article 7 of the 1982 CRPL reads that "Cultural relics . . . shall be designated as sites to be protected for their historical and cultural value at different levels according to their historical, artistic, or scientific value." *Id.* art. 7. The CRPL delegated the authority to protect the most valuable relics to the central government while provincial and local governments were charged with protecting lower value relics. *See id.* A similar system, discussed *infra*, exists under the 2002 LPCR.

relics over to the state. The LPCR also continues the jurisdictional and definitional flaws of the 1982 CRPL, rather than remedy them. Finally, the 2002 LPCR fails to promote education or provide sufficient funding to preserve China's cultural legacy. Thus, rather than correct the errant policies for managing China's cultural resources embodied in the 1982 CRPL, the 2002 LPCR merely perpetuates those very policies.

The most significant difference between the 2002 LPCR and the 1982 CRPL is the legalization of private transactions involving cultural relics. Previously, such transactions had been prohibited.[90] Now, Article 50 of the 2002 LPCR permits "citizens, legal persons, and other organizations" to collect cultural relics obtained through any of the following methods: (1) legal inheritance or gift; (2) purchase from cultural relics shops; (3) purchase from cultural relics auction enterprises; (4) exchanges or transfers between individual citizens pursuant to law; and (5) other methods authorized by the central government.[91] The Chinese government, however, has prohibited private transactions involving state-owned relics (including newly discovered relics or artifacts excavated within China's borders), non-state-owned relics in institutional collections, and murals, sculptures and other structural components included in any state-owned immovable cultural relics.[92] A Chinese government official must examine and certify any cultural relics sold in cultural relic shops or through auction enterprises.[93] Per Article 56 of the 2002 LPCR, cultural relics sold through relic shops or up for auction must be examined by the provincial government and a report including the seller and purchaser be sent to the State Bureau of Cultural Relics.[94] If the provincial government cannot determine if a relic is eligible for sale, it must refer the matter to the State Bureau of Cultural Relics for inspection and certification.[95]

Another major change embodied in the 2002 LPCR, is the establishment of officially sanctioned cultural relics shops and auction

---

[90] *See* MURPHY, *supra* note 20, at 93-94.

[91] *See* 2002 LPCR, *supra* note 78, art. 50.

[92] *See id.* art. 51.

[93] *See id.* arts. 56 & 58.

[94] Auction houses that are involved in the sale of cultural relics are also subject to the requirements of the 1996 Auction Law which requires that "auction enterprise[s] engaged in the auction of cultural relics shall have a registered capital of RMB 10 million or more and employees equipped with the professional knowledge about the auction of cultural relics." PEOPLE'S REPUBLIC OF CHINA, AUCTION LAW (adopted at the 20th Meeting of the Standing Committee of the 8th National People's Congress, July 5, 1996) art. 13, *available at* LEXIS PRCLEG 525.

[95] *See* 2002 LPCR, *supra* note 78, art. 56.

enterprises, which merely authorizes the extant, formerly illicit, trade in cultural relics and antiquities that sprang up over the past 15 years.[96] Interestingly, the 2002 LPCR bans cultural relic shops from running auction enterprises and vice versa.[97] Most importantly, however, Article 58 of the 2002 LPCR permits the government to buy any cultural relic submitted for the mandatory inspection before sale pursuant to Article 56,[98] and "[t]he purchase price shall be determined by the representative of the cultural relics collection entity [government institution] and the trustor of the cultural relics through negotiation."[99] There are further provisions in the 2002 LPCR requiring the relic shops and auction enterprises to keep records on who purchases each cultural relic.[100]

While the 2002 LPCR is a significant departure from the earlier Chinese mindset that all cultural property belongs to the state, it recognizes the prevailing reality that China has a burgeoning market for cultural relics. Yet, even this revised system for tracking cultural property will not remedy the illicit trade in relics and antiquities. One reason is that the right of first refusal for purchase of any or all cultural relics sold by the relic shops or auction enterprises at a price negotiated between the government and the individual. It is unlikely that the government will offer the owner of the cultural property the full market value for the article. This is particularly true when government officials set the compensation. Furthermore, the recordation provision is problematic because many buyers and sellers seek anonymity in cultural property transactions. Thus, the black market trade for such objects will likely remain vibrant as an alternative to the state-sanctioned system for selling cultural relics.

To place the 2002 LPCR in context, one must also understand the Chinese government's long-standing practice to grade cultural relics. The indeterminacy of the grading system reveals the difficulties faced in fixing China's legal regime to protect cultural property.[101] The State Bureau of Cultural Relics has long adhered to a classification system that divides cultural relics into two categories—"precious" and "ordinary"— in conjunction with China's various laws protecting cultural relics. "Precious" relics are further subdivided into three different grades

---

[96] *See* MURPHY, *supra* note 20, at 51.

[97] *See* 2002 LPCR, *supra* note 78, arts. 53-54. The 2002 LPCR also prohibits Chinese-foreign joint venture entities from establishing cultural relic shops or auction enterprises. *See id.* art. 55.

[98] *See id.* art. 58.

[99] *Id.*

[100] *See id.* art. 57.

[101] *See* 2002 LPCR, *supra* note 78, art. 3.

(which are used mainly for determining penalties for illicit smuggling or theft of such cultural relics). Grade One "precious" relics are those that are "especially important for historical, artistic, and scientific values."[102] "Precious" relics that fall under Grade Two are those that have "important" cultural value.[103] Grade Three covers "relatively important" and "precious" relics.[104] Lastly, "ordinary" relics are those that have "certain historical, artistic and scientific value."[105] Prior to 2001, these vague categories were of little use because it was impossible to differentiate between relics that were "especially important," "important," or "relatively important," and whether the relic in question had "certain historical, artistic, or scientific value."[106] Curators and art dealers found it impossible to predict in which category any one relic may be classified. A Hong Kong museum curator tersely stated the problem and its consequences: "It is Grade One because the State Bureau of Cultural Relics says it is."[107]

However, in April 2001, the Ministry of Culture issued a new set of relic grading criteria. Although the basic criteria for categorizing the cultural relics are as vague as similar prior promulgations, this most recent articulation contained an appendix that sets out specific rules for what constitutes a Grade One "precious" relic for various categories including jade ware, stone artifacts, pottery, and chinaware, among others.[108] For instance, weapons that "represent the ordinance level of a historical phase in the history of weapon development; those used in important battles or important events; weapons used by famous persons through the ages" may qualify as Grade One cultural relics.[109]

---

[102] People's Republic of China, Rating Standards for Cultural Relics Collections, art. 1, Order of the Ministry of Culture of the People's Republic of China, Apr. 5, 2001, art. 1, *available at* LEXIS PRCLEG 1829 [hereinafter "2001 Rating Standards"]; *see also* 1992 RULES, *supra* note 82.

[103] *See* 2001 Rating Standards, *supra* note 102, art. 2.

[104] *Id.* art. 3.

[105] *Id.* art 4.

[106] *See* 1992 RULES, *supra* note 82, art. 2; *see also* Schmidt, *supra* note 82.

[107] *See* MURPHY, *supra* note 20, at 86.

[108] Other categories examined included bronze ware, ironware, gold and silver ware, lacquers, sculptures, carved stones and tiles, calligraphies and paintings, ink-slabs, bones and tortoise shells, seals and chops, coins, ivory and bone ware, woodcarvings, furniture, enamels, fabrics and embroideries, books, weapons, documents, and legacies of famous persons. *See* 2001 Rating Standards, *supra* note 102, art. 6.

[109] *Id.* art. 6(22).

Unfortunately, the 2001 regulations set forth criteria only for Grade One relics, which still leaves the grading of Grades Two and Three "precious" relics open to subjective interpretation.[110] Additionally, the 2001 regulations do not clearly define the differences between "ordinary" and "precious" relics. Even though these standards and examples are more specific and may aid in the categorization of some relics, it is difficult to effectively deal with non-fungible objects like antiquities by applying subjective criteria. It is likely that the vagaries of a system based on categorization of relics will continue to plague Chinese efforts to preserve its cultural heritage because of the inherent difficulties associated with classifying unique items. The 2002 LPCR does not further clarify the system of grading, but instead reaffirms the primacy of the extant relic classification system.

The 2002 LPCR also perpetuates the multi-tiered system of administration and care for cultural relics originally set forth in the 1982 CRPL. The classification of cultural relics under the grading system determines which level of government is responsible for the administration and preservation of those relics. The central government protects only the most valuable "precious" relics leaving the remaining relics for local, county, and provincial governments, which are required to preserve and ensure the safety of the lower grade relics in their possession.[111] The 2002 LPCR affords the lower level governmental entities wide latitude in balancing preservation of relics and economic development;[112] the responsibilities of preserving cultural relics placed upon local, county, and provincial governments, which often strain their already limited resources. An additional problem is which level of government has the responsibility of protecting cultural relics and archaeological sites before a determination is made as to categorization of the relics contained therein. Even if such governments had the inclination and the resources to protect cultural relics, the sheer magnitude of the task makes completion near impossible. Foreign researchers have gone to numerous local, county, and provincial museums throughout China and found plundered displays or leaky warehouses crammed with relics that the central government chose not to protect. Instead the local governmental bodies left such relics to the

---

[110] *See id.* art. 6(26) ("Examples of the rating standards for second-class [Grade Two] and third-class [Grade Three] cultural relics may be analogized according to the examples of the rating standards for first-class [Grade One] cultural relics.").

[111] *See* 1992 RULES, *supra* note 82, arts. 8-10.

[112] *See* 2002 LPCR, *supra* note 78, art. 9 ("The People's Governments at various levels shall stress the protection of cultural relics, properly handle the relationship between economic construction, social development, and cultural relics protection, and ensure the safety of cultural relics.").

local and provincial governments for safekeeping.[113] The 2002 LPCR perpetuates this burdensome system by leaving it in place.[114] Although provisions of the 2002 LPCR require that the income earned from publicly-owned cultural sites and museums be used solely for preserving cultural relics (and not misappropriated for other purposes), they include only vague language hinting at a future increase in budgetary allocations for cultural property protection, and only if the central government's revenue increases—an uncertain proposition.[115] The 2002 LPCR does nothing to ease the burden on local, county, and provincial governments for cultural relic preservation, and instead it imposes new requirements that all museums and other facilities for storing cultural relics be protected with fire prevention and anti-theft systems.[116]

The 2002 LPCR also perpetuates the 1982 CRPL failed ban on the export of "precious" cultural relics, with limited exceptions for exhibitions.[117] The ban on exporting "precious" Chinese antiquities is almost impossible to enforce as it suffers from the same definitional vagueness as to what is a "precious" relic. The 2002 LPCR's definitional ambiguity, however, does afford Chinese officials greater flexibility in deciding whether export permits should be issued for individual relics. "Ordinary" relics may, however, be exported with proper permits from the State Bureau of Cultural Relics.

Professor Bator argues that regulations broadly limiting the export of art or antiquities are easy to circumvent and promote the black market smuggling of antiquities:

> The attempt to embargo the flow of art to other countries suffers from . . . a vice. The broader and more inclusive the embargo, the more difficult it is, physically and economically and politically, to enforce effectively. The interdiction of smuggling is an expensive, cumbersome, and inefficient process. The more comprehensively it is attempted, the more expensive, cumbersome, and inefficient it becomes. It is highly vulnerable to corruption. . . . The basic difficulty of most existing export regulation

---

[113] See MURPHY, supra note 20, at 64-65.

[114] See 2002 LPCR, supra note 78, arts. 13-15.

[115] See id. art. 10 ("The State financial allocation used in cultural relics protection shall be increased with the increase of financial revenue.").

[116] See id. art. 47.

[117] See id. art. 60 ("State-owned cultural relics, valuable non-state owned cultural relics and other cultural relics prohibited from exiting the boundary by the state may not be taken out of China, except those taken out of China for exhibitions pursuant to this Law or upon the approval of the State Council for special needs.").

is, in sum, that it is overbroad and overinclusive. It is these characteristics that make it ineffective in most cases. Embargo itself perversely fuels the black market; total interdiction is usually financially, politically, and psychologically unfeasible.[118]

Thus, it is highly likely that the relics that would be classified as "precious" under the 2002 LPCR and 1982 CRPL will eventually find their way out of China because strict export regulations are almost impossible to enforce. Consequently, smuggling has been, and remains, a most serious problem. The flow of Chinese cultural antiquities will go unstaunched so long as there is an eager market for such items outside of China. The 2002 LPCR does little to rectify the situation and its vagueness does not solve the problem.

The 2002 LPCR also contains several miscellaneous provisions providing incentives and administrative punishments. First, the 2002 LPCR contains a provision for "moral encouragement or material awards" to be granted to individuals who assist in implementing the LPCR's policies and provides small monetary rewards for turning discovered cultural property over to the government, donating privately held relics to state institutions, and fighting the smuggling of relics.[119] This language mirrors an almost identical section in the 1982 CRPL.[120] An elaborate scheme of awards, up to a maximum of RMB 5,000, was set forth in 1991 for assistance in preserving relics.[121] However, realistically, these awards are insufficient in comparison to the potential profits that can be made from the illicit export of cultural property. For example, if a farmer finds a rare piece of pottery in his field and turns it over under the current incentive system, the government would only pay him a fraction of what a black market middle man would pay. Clearly, there is no real incentive for anyone to turn over discovered relics to the state, particularly, if all they can expect in return is "moral encouragement" or a nominal finder's fee.

Second, the 2002 LPCR's administrative penalty provisions do have more bite than those in the 1982 CRPL. Specifically, Article 64 of the 2002 LPCR refers to the Criminal Law and states that anyone illegally excavating tombs, damaging or destroying state-protected relics, or unlawfully trading or smuggling relics will be subject to criminal liabilities under the 1997 Criminal Law.[122] Additionally, the 2002 LPCR

---

[118] Bator, *supra* note 5, at 43.

[119] *See* 2002 LPCR, *supra* note 78, art. 12.

[120] *See* 1982 CRPL, *supra* note 83, art. 29.

[121] *See also* MURPHY, *supra* note 20, at 95.

[122] *See* 2002 LPCR, *supra* note 78, art. 64.

provides for various civil and administrative penalties including warnings, fines, restitution for damages, civil liability, seizure of any illicitly obtained cultural objects, and disgorgement of proceeds of any illegal sales.[123] Some of the most important administrative penalty provisions contained in the 2002 LPCR apply to government or museum officials who abuse their positions or do not perform their duties capably, a reflection of China's recent crackdown on public corruption. Officials who improperly transfer, embezzle or misappropriate cultural relics are subject to large fines (up to RMB 200,000), dismissal, and may be required to make restitution, in addition to any criminal penalties that may be applied.[124] Similar administrative penalties and fines are applied to individuals or entities that damage immovable cultural relics through pollution;[125] undertake construction projects that damage immovable cultural relics;[126] transfer or mortgage non-state owned immovable relics without permission;[127] transfer prohibited cultural objects to foreigners;[128] establish unauthorized relics shops or auction enterprises;[129] fail to turn discovered relics over to the state;[130] or fail to record the transfer of relics with the appropriate governmental entity.[131] Additionally, if relic shops operate auctions, auction enterprises buy and sell relics, or museums engage in buying and selling relics, they will be subject to administrative punishments under the 2002 LPCR.[132]

C.   *The 1997 Criminal Law and Cultural Property*

As smuggling of cultural property out of China became rampant in the late-1980s and early-1990s, China enacted a series of harsh criminal penalties for those involved in the illicit removal of cultural relics. Unfortunately, the 1997 Criminal Law's provisions are as vague

---

[123] *See* 2002 LPCR, *supra* note 78, arts. 65-77.

[124] *See id.* arts. 70 & 78.

[125] *See id.* art. 67.

[126] *See id.* art. 66.

[127] *See* 2002 LPCR, *supra* note 78, art. 68.

[128] *See id.* art. 71.

[129] *See id.* art. 75.

[130] *See id.* art. 74.

[131] *See* 2002 LPCR, *supra* note 78, art. 72.

[132] *See id.* art. 73.

and confusing as those found in the 2002 LPCR and 1982 CRPL. Articles 324 to 329 of the 1997 Criminal Law deal with "crimes of obstructing cultural and historical relics control." These sections address the criminal equivalents to the administrative penalties set forth in the 2002 LPCR, including damaging or destroying cultural property,[133] private selling,[134] selling for profit,[135] selling by a museum,[136] or illegal excavation of ancient tombs or remains.[137]

The 1997 Criminal Law also sets out a scheme for determining the appropriate penalties for violating these provisions. These sanctions include prison sentences, fines, criminal detention,[138] confiscation of property, and, in some cases, even death.[139] The degree of punishment depends on the grade of the relic in question and the "seriousness" of the offense. "Serious" offenses are punishable with long prison sentences or death, in particularly "heinous" cases. Article 328 is the only section that specifically delineates what sort of behavior can upgrade an ordinary offense into a "serious" one. Such behavior includes illegally excavating at state protected sites, being a ringleader of a criminal syndicate that engages in illegal excavation, repeated illegal excavation, and illegal excavation that causes serious damage to the cultural property.[140] Articles 324 and 326 have harsher penalties for "serious" offenses, but do not specify what constitutes a "serious" offense under those particular code sections.[141] Presumably, the same types of factors such as recidivist activity and heading a conspiracy to break the laws set forth in those code sections would upgrade a normal violation of these sections to a "serious" crime. Only particularly egregious "serious" violations would constitute "heinous" cases in which the death penalty would be applicable. Interestingly, Article 326 includes language specifying even harsher penalties for offenses that are "exceptionally serious."[142]

---

[133] *See* 1997 CRIMINAL LAW, *supra* note 79, art. 324.

[134] *See id.* art. 325.

[135] *See id.* art. 326.

[136] *See id.* art. 327.

[137] *See* 1997 CRIMINAL LAW, *supra* note 79, art. 328.

[138] Criminal detention is a period of incarceration of over a month, but less than six months, where the prisoner can go home one or two days each month, but must return to serve the rest of his sentence. *See id.* art. 43.

[139] *See id.* art. 264.

[140] *See id.* art. 328.

[141] *See* 1997 CRIMINAL LAW, *supra* note 79, arts. 324 & 326.

[142] *See id.* art. 326.

However, there is no mention of how an "exceptionally serious" offense differs from a "serious" one. There is also no mention of how an "extremely serious" offense differs from a "heinous" offense or if an "extremely serious" offense also subjects its perpetrator to application of the death penalty. The statute is not clear as to any of these issues. Furthermore, Articles 324, 325, and 328, include language that those sections apply only to "precious" relics, rather than "ordinary" relics.[143] Presumably, this means that the remaining code sections in this chapter of the 1997 Criminal Law are applicable to both "precious" and "ordinary" relics as determined by the State Bureau of Cultural Relics (which is a difficult proposition considering the inherent vagueness of the terms "precious" and "ordinary," as discussed *supra*).

There are further sections of the 1997 Criminal Law that are applicable to protecting cultural property. Article 264 of the 1997 Criminal Law provides for serious consequences for encroaching on state or private property to steal cultural relics. The section provides that "those committing serious thefts of precious cultural relics . . . are to be given life sentences or sentenced to death in addition to confiscation of property."[144] Article 264 suffers from the same problem as many of the aforementioned criminal code sections—vagueness. Both "serious" and "precious" are subjective. Furthermore, how the "theft" language of Article 264 operates in conjunction with Articles 324-329 is unclear. None of them use the "theft" language, but focus on more specific acts involving the excavation and sale of artifacts or antiquities. It is not clear if Article 264 was intended to complement Articles 324-329 or to serve as an alternative. It should be noted that Article 264's provisions only apply to "precious" cultural relics. The theft of "ordinary" cultural relics is covered under Article 263 of the 1997 Criminal Law, the general theft provision. Sentences are much shorter under Article 263, ranging from three to ten years.[145] Additionally, Articles 263 and 264 require only "theft," not intent to export the stolen relics. Some commentators have speculated that Article 264 was specifically aimed at discouraging the emerging Chinese domestic market for collectible cultural relics.[146]

The 1997 Criminal Law's general smuggling provision addresses the illicit transportation of the cultural property out of China. Article 151 explicitly forbids the cross-border transportation of "prohibited

---

[143] *See* 1997 CRIMINAL LAW, *supra* note 79, arts. 324-25 & 328.

[144] *Id.* art. 264.

[145] *See id.* art. 263. It is possible to receive a harsher sentence, including the death penalty under Article 263, but only for certain enumerated offenses. Theft of "ordinary" cultural relics does not qualify.

[146] *See* Schmidt, *supra* note 82, n.175 at 211.

cultural relics" with a minimum sentence of five years for violators.[147] Like the other sections of the 1997 Criminal Law, there are increased penalties for "serious" offenses with penalties including forfeiture of property, life imprisonment, and death.[148] Additionally, government personnel who cause the loss or damage of "precious" cultural relics through negligence can be imprisoned for up to three years or face criminal detention.[149]

The flexibility in sentencing provisions for crimes related to cultural property under the 1997 Criminal Law enables Chinese judges to tailor the punishment to the particular crime, as well as the capability to impose severe sentences to make an example of certain individuals. For instance, in 1994, two peasants were sentenced to six years in prison for illegally attempting to sell six Grade 2 and 148 Grade 3 dinosaur fossils in Henan Province.[150] The court justified such a harsh sentence based on the large numbers of fossils being sold.[151] In 1987, a thief was sentenced to death for breaking into the Emperor Qin Museum in Xi'an and stealing the head of one of the terracotta warriors, a Grade 1 relic according to the State Bureau of Cultural Relics.[152] One of the most celebrated prosecutions for tomb looting occurred in Shaanxi Province during 2001. Four men were sentenced to death and 16 others given lesser sentences for the armed looting of two archaeological sites.[153] The flexibility in the sentencing provisions strengthens the government's hand as those who violate the law will never know the severity of the punishment that they may receive for violating the law; thus, the indeterminacy of the punishment provides a certain level of deterrence. However, Chinese judges must impose a wide range of penalties for similar crimes in order for such a crime deterrence theory to be effective. On the other hand, Chinese judges may rarely impose the harsh, statutorily prescribed penalties for relatively minor violations relating to

---

[147] *See* 1997 Criminal Law, *supra* note 79, art. 151.

[148] *See id.*

[149] *See id.* art. 419.

[150] *Case of Zhang Biliang and Others Selling for Profit and Speculating in Fossilized Dinosaur Eggs*, Henan Province Xixia County People's Court (1994) *reprinted in* 3 RENMIN FAYUAN XUAN SELECTED CASES OF THE PEOPLE'S COURT 43-46 (China Practicing Law Institute, ed. 1996).

[151] *See id.*

[152] *See* People's Republic of China, Circular of the Supreme People's Court of the People's Republic of China, April 1987, at 25.

[153] *See Four Sentenced to Death for Robbing Cultural Relics*, PEOPLE'S DAILY, May 15, 2001, *available at* http://english.peopledaily.com.cn/200105/15/eng20010515_70022.html (last viewed Oct. 22 2003).

cultural property, thus hampering government enforcement of the China's legal regime for controlling cultural property.

In sum, China's domestic legal regime for regulating cultural property is a well-intentioned, but ultimately vague and confused effort, which fails to stem the flow of its cultural heritage to private collectors. The vagueness and lack of standards for the grading and classification of relics is a major problem, as well as the split jurisdictions as to which level of government is responsible for protecting differently graded cultural relics. While the 2002 LPCR represents a step in the right direction with regards to the alienability of relics, the new law does not solve many of the problems that emerged under the 1982 CRPL. Furthermore, the absence of a clear definition for what constitutes "serious," "extremely serious," or "heinous" offenses under the relevant section of the 1997 Criminal Law hinders enforcement. The continued illicit removal of artifacts and antiquities and the resultant black market underscores the ineffectiveness of the current Chinese legal regime to protect the nation's cultural patrimony.

V. Making the Future Safe for China's Cultural Treasures

The legacy of Chinese civilization, four thousand years in the making, is clearly at risk as looters and smugglers continue to sell China's heritage to the highest bidder. The Chinese legal system has proven ineffective at stopping the looting, plundering, and theft of important and irreplaceable cultural objects. The effectiveness of the 2002 LPCR remains to be seen, but it will unlikely be much more effective than the 1982 CRPL. In addition, the 1997 Criminal Law, with its vague and rarely enforced punishments, is widely flouted. In order to begin to remedy these issues, China must set forth more precise definitions for the grading and classification of relics as either "precious" or "ordinary," as well as the subclassifications of "precious" relics. Fixing the classification system will clarify the multitude of unnecessary and confusing ambiguities in the 1997 Criminal Law and make legal enforcement of the 2002 LPCR more effective. China must refine and define the provisions of the 1997 Criminal Law that apply to cultural relics. Defining what constitutes "heinous," "serious," and "extremely serious" offenses for each code section would be a good place to start. Centralization of all relic preservation under the auspices of the Ministry of Culture and the State Bureau of Cultural Relics would ensure uniform administration of relics, rather than delegating the administration to poorly funded, trained, and equipped local, county, and provincial governments to care for them. Although China customarily delegates power to local governments, this centralization is the only way to ensure uniform enforcement of the cultural property legal regime and preservation of China's cultural heritage.

In addition to governmental reorganization of the extant legal regime, several other steps could be taken to save China's cultural heritage. First, education is the key to preserving China's cultural property in the future. Only by educating the population at a grassroots level as to the value of cultural property and providing the populace with warnings about the consequences of looting tombs or selling illegally obtained cultural objects will the black market be curtailed. Second, providing adequate monetary incentives to bona fide finders of cultural property will keep some artifacts and antiquities off the black market. Third, the legalization of private ownership and trade of cultural relics under the 2002 LPCR is a step in the right direction, but excessive government regulation of cultural relics shops, auction enterprises, as well as the government's right of first refusal to purchase cultural relics should be eliminated in order to induce the sellers of cultural property not to turn to the black market. Fourth, state-sponsored auctions of redundant and lower-grade relics could result in better preservation of relics and provide funds for better museum facilities and further archaeological expeditions.

A. *Educational Programs*

Education is a tool that can be used to change attitudes toward cultural relics in several ways. First, education can be utilized by the government to inform the Chinese people, particularly those in rural areas most prone to tomb looting, about the value of cultural property and the need to preserve China's heritage for future generations. Education must focus on more than just the monetary value of the objects, which might inadvertently increase looting. Rather education must focus on increasing the awareness and appreciation of the non-economic value of cultural items to Chinese society.[154] Creating outreach programs between archeologists and local populations creates a link between the community and efforts to preserve relics. Explaining to local populations why cultural property should be preserved and not sold to black market traffickers is of the utmost importance.[155] A campaign of this sort would parallel recent Chinese programs that promote China's cultural identity and nationalism.[156] UNESCO is another resource that China can tap, if it chooses to do so. While Beijing has been reluctant to

---

[154] *See* Schmidt, *supra* note 82, at 219.

[155] *See* PATRICK J. O'KEEFE, TRADE IN ANTIQUITIES: REDUCING DESTRUCTION AND THEFT 91 (1997).

[156] *See id.* at 94 (discussing Greece's use of antiquities, particularly the Elgin Marbles, as tools for promoting national identity).

allow international organizations to operate in China, UNESCO has led successful educational efforts about cultural artifacts and relics in both Africa and South America.[157]

Second, although disseminating general legal information is an ongoing process, the central government should focus efforts on publicizing the penalty provisions of the 2002 LPCR and 1997 Criminal Law that deal with cultural property. By publicizing the law and the consequences for breaking it, the message that the central government will not tolerate tomb looting or smuggling of cultural objects will be clearly conveyed. For instance, the central government may also choose to publicize certain high profile prosecutions and resultant executions under the 1997 Criminal Law and 2002 LPCR as examples of the ramifications or penalties that result from violations of these statutes. While this is admittedly harsh, it parallels the deterrence approach that the Chinese government has taken with other sorts of illegal activity.

Third, standardized education and training of the professionals who are engaged in dealing with cultural relics on a daily basis will improve the preservation of cultural relics. Groups engaged in the enforcement of China's cultural property legal regime, police, customs officials, and prosecutors, should be specifically targeted in such educational programs, so that they have an idea of what to look for and how the 2002 LPCR and 1997 Criminal Law should be enforced.[158]

Although education does not offer a quick fix to the problem, it is part of the long-term solution to maintaining and preserving China's cultural heritage. Education alone will not work in every situation or community, particularly in those places where the local people feel that they have no other way to make a living or that they have a right to continue excavating antiquities. However, education is the first (and easiest) step that should be taken.

B. *Incentive Programs*

While the 2002 LPCR provides for monetary awards to Chinese citizens who turn over discovered artifacts and relics to the state, the nominal amount provided for in the statute creates little to no incentive to do so. The Chinese government should expand the incentive program to reward bona fide finders of cultural property with substantial cash payments or awards for turning over such objects to the government. Although these awards do not have to be anywhere near the fair market value of the discovered relic or artifact, many Chinese people would likely be willing to give the government such property if the offered incentive is close to the amount that they would obtain from black market traffickers. Of course, any incentive program would have to be

---

[157] *See* O'KEEFE, *supra* note 155, at 96.

[158] *See id.* at 89-90.

carefully designed so as not to promote tomb robbing or the plundering of other cultural sites. Any object for which the government pays an incentive must have been found on accident, rather than have been located specifically to collect such a bounty from the government.

As an alternative to monetary incentives, the government could also provide public recognition for the finders of cultural relics. Such recognition could include prominent mention in news reports and permanent plaques listing those who have contributed discovered cultural relics to museums. One famous example is when peasants discovered Emperor Qin Shi Huang's army of terracotta warriors at Xi'an in Shaanxi Province while digging a well in 1974; the three peasants—Yang Zhifa, Yang Buzhi, and Yang Pengyue—all received acclaim throughout China for finding and reporting their discovery to the local cultural center.[159]

C. Reducing Government Regulation of the Legal Relics Market

While the 2002 LPCR marks a significant step forward in the regulation of Chinese cultural relics as it permits private transactions for cultural relics, it will not result in the elimination of the black market. Further deregulation of the cultural relics market is the only way to curtail black market sales. As discussed in Section IV-B *supra*, Article 58 of the LPCR gives the government a right of first refusal to purchase any cultural relic sold through cultural relic shops or auction enterprises at a "negotiated price."[160] Additionally, the 2002 LPCR requires governmental authorities to record each and every sale of cultural property.[161] The combined effect of these provisions is to create incentives that promote the black market as sellers will be able to sell their relics anonymously at higher prices and not have to worry about possible government acquisition of the relics at a below market price or government recordation of the transaction. Thus, ironically, the 2002 LPCR does not eliminate the black market, but rather entrenches it as sellers will continue to have incentives to circumvent the governmentally regulated system for the sale of relics.

Elimination of the governmental right of first refusal to buy cultural relics and the recordation of transactions is the only way that the black market for Chinese antiquities will be curbed. The reasons for the black market's existence, anonymity and evasion of potential governmental expropriation at a "negotiated price," would be eliminated,

---

[159] *See* Sonja Larsen, *The Eighth Wonder of the World*, available at http://www.onid.orst.edu/~wielands/terracotta323.htm (last visited Apr. 21 2003).

[160] *See* 2002 LPCR, *supra* note 78, art. 58.

[161] *See id.* arts. 56-57.

creating greater transparency in the marketplace and permitting the Chinese government to assess the effectiveness of its legal and non-legal policies to protect cultural property. Furthermore, the creation of an open, licit domestic market for cultural relics will undercut the profits that motivate black market traffickers to deal in such relics. As the lucrative profits that drive the black market dry up, illicit trading will decline over time.[162]

Admittedly, deregulating the market for cultural relics would likely be unpopular with the leadership of the Chinese Communist Party and may possibly result in a temporary spike in the illegal exportation of cultural relics as long-time owners of such items dump them into the market; inevitably some of the relics in the market will be exported. But, over the long term, greater transparency through deregulation of China's domestic market for cultural relics will likely curtail the black market and reduce the administrative burden on local, county, and provincial governments, permitting them to devote their resources to preserving cultural resources and to educational programs aimed at preventing the removal of antiquities from their resting places. It should be noted, however, that this article does not initially advocate relaxation of the rules regulating the sale of cultural relics to foreigners or the export control regime for relics set forth in the 2002 LPCR. Easing these restrictions should only be done if the proposed domestic reforms have some degree of success.

D. *State-Sponsored Auctions*

The sale of state owned redundant or lower quality cultural relics to collectors could serve to further promote the preservation of cultural relics. Such would put millions of lower quality cultural relics that are currently locked away in deteriorating warehouses into the hands of private collectors. Professor Merryman states the rationale behind this proposal: "Source nations that already hold significant supplies of redundant objects in storage, as many are said to do, could begin to release them to a licit market."[163] China would seem to fit this description. As of 1994, the State Bureau of Cultural Relics had an estimated ten million relics in storage, only one percent of which are

---

[162] *See* J. David Murphy, *The People's Republic of China and the Illicit Trade in Cultural Property: Is the Embargo Approach the Answer?*, 3 INT'L J. CULTURAL PROP. 227, 235 (1994).

[163] John Henry Merryman, *A Licit Trade in Cultural Objects*, 4 INT'L J. CULTURAL PROP. 13, 37 (1995). Such auctions of already warehoused items would not result in the destruction of archaeological knowledge as such objects have already been removed from the context of their surroundings or they may have no archaeological record at all. *See* O'KEEFE, *supra* note 155, at 74-75.

believed to be classified as "precious."[164] Local, county, and provincial governments have millions more relics stored away, although they are of lower quality. If the central government took over administration of all cultural relics, innumerable lower quality pieces could be made available for sale.

State-sponsored auctions are not new to China.[165] As early as 1974, several government ministries proposed the sale of surplus relics overseas to raise foreign currency.[166] Although that proposal never came to fruition, the concept of state-sponsored sales of relics did not disappear. In October 1992, the central government sponsored an auction where 1,250 cultural relics including several Grade Two and Three "precious" relics were put on the block. Unfortunately, the sale was not a success and many of the buyers present were disappointed in the low quality of pieces offered for sale, as well as the unrealistically high reserve prices. Only 641 of the cultural relics offered for sale were sold, and none of the reserve prices for the "precious" relics offered were met.[167] There have also been several auctions of items confiscated from smugglers, some of which have included "ordinary" cultural relics.[168] Several state-owned enterprises have also created a state-owned auction house, China Guardian Auction Co., which has auctioned several lots of cultural relics consigned by government institutions.[169]

Thus, the Chinese government has the expertise and experience to conduct state-sponsored auctions of cultural relics. The relaxation on rules governing private ownership of cultural relics under the 2002 LPCR makes such state-sponsored auctions offering relics to private collectors in China's domestic and foreign markets feasible. Revenues from such auctions could be used to finance archaeological efforts such as the excavation of Emperor Qin Shi Huang's tomb in Xi'an, improve the security of Chinese museums, and train curators and other personnel

---

[164] *See* Murphy, *supra* note 162, at 233.

[165] *See id.*

[166] *See* People's Republic of China, Circular Concerning the Opinion on Strengthening Cultural Relics Commercial Administration and Implementing the Policy on the Protection of Cultural Relics, State Council of the People's Republic of China, Dec. 16, 1974.

[167] *See* MURPHY, *supra* note 20, at 167. The highest price realized at the October 1992 auction was $200,000 for a jadeite necklace which was consigned by an international seller—not the Chinese government. *See id.*

[168] *See id.* at 179 n.62.

[169] *See id.* at 168-69. It should be noted that China Guardian Auction Co. operates under heavy scrutiny from the State Bureau of Cultural Relics, and the auction house is only permitted to sell certain lots of cultural property to state-owned museums and institutions. Overseas collectors and government-owned institutions have listed many of the lots of cultural relics that China Guardian Auction Co. has sold. *See id.*

proper handling of cultural relics. Furthermore, putting lower-grade relics in the hands of collectors will result in greater preservation of those artifacts as they will be better able to preserve them than the overburdened local, county, and provincial governments because the collectors have every incentive to preserve their purchases. As Professor Bator has noted, "the best way to keep art is to let a lot of it go."[170]

Learning from the lessons of the October 1992 auction, realistic reserve prices must be set and there must be enough high-grade relics included in the sale to spark the interest of bidders. Otherwise, such auctions will be doomed to failure. Furthermore, it would inadvisable to allow local, county, or provincial authorities to conduct such auctions as there is great potential for collusion and abuse of the system. Centralization of such auctions with oversight from the State Bureau of Cultural Relics and the Ministry of Culture will serve to protect the sanctity of the auctions and regulate those orchestrating the auctions themselves.

VI. CONCLUSION

China's cultural heritage is at risk. China's present legal regime for protecting cultural property has proven incapable of preventing the widespread looting of artifacts, thefts from museums, and smuggling of antiquities that have accompanied China's transition to a market economy. As international efforts to stem the cross-border flow of cultural property, such as the 1970 UNESCO Convention and the 1995 UNIDROIT Convention, have been ineffective, a greater burden has been placed on China's domestic law to stop the flood of antiquities out of China. However, China's legal regime to protect cultural property has failed to meet this challenge. While the 2002 LPCR is a step in the right direction with its loosening of ownership restrictions, it does not solve all of the problems of the 1982 CRPL. In fact, the 2002 LPCR appears to perpetuate several of the 1982 CRPL most serious flaws. The imprecise terms for grading artifacts and overlapping jurisdictions for their preservation set forth in the 2002 LPCR add to the problem and make enforcement of the cultural property laws difficult, if not impossible. The definitional ambiguities in the 2002 LPCR also contribute to the difficulty of applying the 1997 Criminal Law in a consistent manner.

Yet, all is not lost. China can reform its legal regime for preserving cultural property, despite the confusing and often contradictory scheme for protecting artifacts and antiquities. If the central government fixes the ambiguities and contradictions in the 2002 LPCR and 1997 Criminal Law, makes a concerted effort to educate the populace as to the value of relics, sets up incentive programs to turn

---

[170] Bator, *supra* note 5, at 46.

relics over to the government, loosens the market regulations on the sale of cultural relics in the domestic market, and organizes state-sponsored relics auctions, there is hope that China will be able to preserve its cultural property. But each passing day with no action results in more looted tombs and more priceless artifacts lost to the Chinese people forever. Mao Zedong, who ordered the massive destruction of relics during the Cultural Revolution, once said, "Let the past serve the present." Ironically, now is the time to heed Mao's words before China's cultural heritage disappears just like the marble reliefs torn from the walls of Wang Chuzi's looted tomb.

[9]

2001 UNESCO Convention on the Protection of the Underwater Cultural Heritage

Sarah Dromgoole*
Senior Lecturer in Law, University of Leicester, UK

ABSTRACT

The UNESCO Convention on the Protection of the Underwater Cultural Heritage, adopted in November 2001, is designed to create a legal framework to regulate interference with underwater cultural heritage (UCH) in international waters. This article briefly considers the background to the Convention and discusses its main provisions. These relate to the scope of application of the Convention; its objectives and general principles; its approach to private rights; its treatment of state vessels and the question of sovereign immunity; and its relationship with the UN Convention on the Law of the Sea 1982. The article then goes on to examine in detail the control mechanisms that the Convention adopts in respect of each maritime zone and the sanctions that contracting states will be required to impose for violations. Finally, dispute settlement procedures are briefly considered, before the article concludes with comments on the Convention's likely impact and effectiveness.

Introduction

In 1985, the *Titanic* was discovered, 2.5 miles underwater; shortly afterwards, artefacts were recovered from the site.[1] These events, which were the subject of massive publicity, served to highlight advances in deep-sea technology and the increasing vulnerability of the underwater cultural heritage (UCH). They also acted as a catalyst for international action to control such activities.

---

* The author would like to acknowledge the support of the University of Leicester in awarding her study leave enabling her to complete this article. She would also like to thank Nicholas Gaskell, David Jackson Professor of Maritime and Commercial Law, Institute of Maritime Law, University of Southampton, for his helpful comments on the text and Gwenaelle Le Gurun, Legal Officer, International Seabed Authority, for information provided. Any views expressed are, of course, those of the author alone.

[1] In 1987 approximately 1,800 artefacts were recovered. Further artefacts were recovered in 1993. See *RMS Titanic, Inc.* v *The Wrecked and Abandoned Vessel believed to be the RMS Titanic*, USCA 4th Cir., 12 April 2002 (appeal to the Supreme Court declined, 7 October 2002).

In 1993, UNESCO began to consider the feasibility of drafting an international instrument for the protection of the UCH.[2] While the organisation recognised that the UN Convention on the Law of the Sea 1982 (LOSC) made some provision for UCH in international waters, it felt that a more detailed framework for legal protection was required. It also recognised that any instrument in this field would need to tackle a number of issues that were both controversial and complex. For example, there was a risk of interfering with the delicate compromise package achieved in the LOSC, especially on the question of the extent of coastal state jurisdiction. Difficult issues also arose concerning the relationship of any instrument with salvage law and the rights of owners; its treatment of warships and the question of sovereign immunity; and the balance that should be struck between archaeological and commercial interests.

Many believed that UNESCO's initiative would ultimately end in failure, as a similar initiative had done in 1985.[3] However, after three years of intense and at times febrile negotiations by government experts, a text was finally agreed upon. In November 2001 the UNESCO Convention on the Protection of the Underwater Cultural Heritage was adopted and the support shown for the Convention in the UNESCO forum suggests that it will not be long before it comes into force.[4]

The main aim of this article is to examine the mechanisms adopted by the Convention to control interference with UCH in international waters. Before doing so, the background to the Convention will be briefly explained, and its main provisions discussed. Among other things, consideration will be given to the ways in which the final text differs from the draft text produced in 1998 (and discussed in this journal in 1999).[5]

Background

As far back as 1978 there was international recognition of the need for a convention to protect the UCH.[6] Unfortunately, an attempt to draft a European convention on the matter had to be aborted in 1985, apparently as a result of an intractable dispute between Greece and Turkey over the territorial scope of

---

[2] At its 141st Session in 1993, the UNESCO Executive Board adopted Resolution 5.5.1., para. 15, requesting the Director-General to undertake a feasibility study. For the feasibility study itself, see UNESCO Secretariat, "Feasibility Study for the Drafting of a New Instrument for the Protection of the Underwater Cultural Heritage", presented to the 146th Session of the UNESCO Executive Board, Paris, 23 March 1995, Doc. 146 EX/27.
[3] See further below.
[4] Twenty instruments of ratification, acceptance or approval are required to bring the Convention into force: see Art. 27.
[5] See (1999) 14 IJMCL 171–192.
[6] See Council of Europe Recommendation 848 (1978) on the Underwater Cultural Heritage (Doc. 4200, Strasbourg). It is interesting to note that the Council of Europe has recently adopted Recommendation 1486 (2000) on the Maritime and Fluvial Cultural Heritage. The new Recommendation relates to maritime heritage of various kinds, not solely the UCH. However, it contains a number of recommendations in respect of the UCH that have been informed by the development of the UNESCO Convention, and that are aligned with its fundamental principles.

application of the Convention. The LOSC addressed the issue, but the two articles it includes relating to the UCH are short and vague.[7] In 1988 a new initiative commenced, when the International Law Association (ILA) established a Committee on Cultural Heritage Law, which decided that its first task should be the drafting of a convention on the protection of the UCH. The ILA eventually adopted a draft in 1994, which was submitted to UNESCO for consideration.[8] Using the ILA draft as a basis, a preliminary draft text was prepared by UNESCO in 1998.[9] This draft was discussed at two meetings of government experts, the first in June/July 1998 and the second in April 1999. A revised draft, adopted by the participants at the second meeting, formed the basis for work at a third meeting held in July 2000, but was not formally amended at that meeting.[10] A fourth meeting was scheduled in March/April 2001 and it was made clear by the Director-General of UNESCO that this was to be the last meeting before a text was finalised.[11] The pressure to reach agreement on all points meant that the meeting was extended into a second session held in July. At this fourth meeting, the focus of attention was a Single Negotiating Text produced by the Chairman, Mr Carsten Lund of Denmark. Despite strenuous efforts to do so, it was not possible to achieve a consensus on all issues given the time constraints. Lund's text, with amendments, was therefore adopted at the 31st Session of the UNESCO General Conference on 6 November 2001 by 87 votes in favour, four against, and 15 abstentions.[12] The UK was one of the states that abstained.[13]

---

[7] LOSC, Arts. 149 and 303. These provisions have been subjected to detailed examination and criticism over the years. See, e.g. L. Caflisch, "Submarine Antiquities and the International Law of the Sea", (1982) XIII *Netherlands Yearbook of International Law* 3; A. Arend, "Archaeological and Historical Objects: The International Legal Implications of LOSC III", (1982) 22 *Virginia Journal of International Law* 777; A. Strati, "Deep Seabed Cultural Property and the Common Heritage of Mankind", (1991) 40 *International and Comparative Law Quarterly* 859; P. O'Keefe and J. Nafziger, "The Draft Convention on the Protection of the Underwater Cultural Heritage", (1994) 25 *Ocean Development and International Law* 391.

[8] On the basis that UNESCO was felt to be the appropriate body to take action on the matter: see UNESCO Secretariat, "Feasibility Study for the Drafting of a New Instrument for the Protection of the Underwater Cultural Heritage", presented to the 146th Session of the UNESCO Executive Board, Paris, 23 March 1995, Doc. 146 EX/27, para. 19.

[9] Doc. CLT-96/Conf.202/5, April 1998. For a discussion of this draft, see S. Dromgoole and N. Gaskell, "Draft UNESCO Convention on the Protection of the Underwater Cultural Heritage 1998", (1999) 14 IJMCL 171–192. The text of the 1998 draft was included as an appendix to that article: see pp. 193–206.

[10] Doc. CLT-96/CONF.205/5 Rev. 2, July 1999. This draft was very much a working text and will not be considered here.

[11] The Director-General made this clear in invitations to the fourth meeting: see P. O'Keefe, *Shipwrecked Heritage: A Commentary on the UNESCO Convention on Underwater Cultural Heritage* (2002), p. 30.

[12] Under UNESCO's procedures for the adoption of conventions, there is no signature procedure, but rather conventions are adopted at the General Conference, preferably by consensus or alternatively by vote: see O'Keefe, note 11 above, p. 1.

[13] The others were Brazil, Czech Republic, Colombia, France, Germany, Greece, Iceland, Israel, Guinea-Bissau, Netherlands, Paraguay, Sweden, Switzerland and Uruguay. Those that voted

From early on in its initiative, the ILA recognised that a set of objective archaeological standards was required against which the appropriateness of activities affecting the UCH could be judged.[14] Therefore, at its request, the International Council for Monuments and Sites (ICOMOS) produced a Charter on the Protection and Management of Underwater Cultural Heritage,[15] which was attached to the ILA draft as an Annex. The scheme of the protective measures set out in the ILA draft sought to ensure that activities affecting the UCH were undertaken in accordance with the standards set out in the Annex. However, during the course of the UNESCO-led negotiations, questions arose in respect of both the status, and the content, of these standards. As far as their status was concerned, the question was whether they should form an integral part of the Convention, or simply be incorporated in a document referred to in the Convention but not part of it. Since the standards were intended to be a benchmark of archaeological good practice, ideally they should be amended from time to time to keep up with developments in that practice. The advantage of their being separate from the Convention was that the procedure for amendment could be made a great deal easier than if they were a formal part of the Convention. However, the complexities involved in working out a procedure for amendments that would be acceptable to contracting states were such that it was eventually concluded that the standards should be an integral part of the Convention.[16] As far as their content was concerned, while they are based on the ICOMOS Charter, amendments were made to the wording to put it into a form that was both suitable for inclusion in a convention, and politically acceptable.[17]

As we shall see, the final text of the Convention differs significantly from the initial draft produced by UNESCO in 1998. As is always the case, political pressures during the negotiating process did much to shape the final form of the Convention. In particular, the USA and the UK, together with other maritime powers,[18] exerted considerable influence and this influence is evidenced in many of the changes that have been made.[19] The complex issue of ownership has now

---

cont.
    against were the Russian Federation, Norway, Turkey and Venezuela. For some of the reasons for the abstentions and objections, see T. Scovazzi, "Convention on the Protection of Underwater Cultural Heritage", (2002) 32 *Environmental Policy and Law* 152–157.

[14] See O'Keefe, note 11 above, p. 152.
[15] Charter on the Protection and Management of Underwater Cultural Heritage (1996), ratified by the 11th ICOMOS General Assembly, held in Sofia, Bulgaria, 5–9 October 1996. This Charter should not be confused with the ICOMOS Charter for the Protection and Management of Archaeological Heritage 1990. The 1996 Charter supplements the 1990 Charter.
[16] Art. 33 provides: "The Rules annexed to this Convention form an integral part of it and, unless expressly provided otherwise, a reference to this Convention includes a reference to the Rules."
[17] The wording of a rule relating to commercial exploitation caused particular difficulty. On this rule, see p. 66 below.
[18] Notably France, Germany, Japan, Netherlands, Norway and Russia.
[19] Despite this, all of these states—with the exception of Japan and the USA—either voted against the Convention or abstained from voting. Japan voted in favour; the USA did not have a vote, as it is not a member of UNESCO.

been left well alone: in particular, the Convention no longer applies only to UCH, which has been abandoned, and the highly controversial "deemed abandonment" provision has been omitted. The interrelationship between the Convention and the law of salvage has been clarified, and warships and other state vessels are now covered by the Convention. In general, the Convention's provisions apply to a more limited range of activities than the 1998 draft, focusing on activities "directed at", rather than merely "affecting", the UCH. Finally, no attempt is now made, at least overtly, to extend coastal state jurisdiction beyond the confines of established international law and the LOSC. Instead, the drafters have resorted to some very complex mechanisms to try to control salvage activities on UCH sites beyond traditional territorial limits.

Outline of Main Provisions

The Convention comprises 35 articles, together with 36 rules in the Annex. The main provisions will be discussed here, before attention is focused on the control mechanisms.

Scope of Application

The Convention's provisions apply to UCH as defined in Article 1. This provides that "underwater cultural heritage" means "all traces of human existence having a cultural, historical or archaeological character which have been partially or totally underwater, periodically or continuously, for at least 100 years".[20] It then goes on to give some non-exclusive examples, including: "vessels, aircraft, other vehicles or any part thereof, their cargo or other contents, together with their archaeological and natural context".[21] Wrecks of ships are the main component of the UCH, and are the element on which this article focuses. The only types of remains that have been specifically *excluded* are pipelines and cables, whether or not in use, and other "installations" where still in use.[22]

One or two points about the definition are worthy of particular note. First of all, it only covers material that has been underwater for "at least 100 years". Therefore it will be some time before the Convention applies to wrecks such as the *Titanic* and remains from the two World Wars. The 1998 draft also used this 100-year cut-off point, but had a provision that a state could unilaterally decide to include remains *less than* 100 years old;[23] this has now been omitted. The flexibility afforded by this provision would have been useful in providing protection for more recent UCH, but the power it gave to states was so broad

---

[20] Art. 1(1)(a).
[21] Art. 1(1)(a)(ii).
[22] This provision should allay fears expressed by the cable industry about the possible impact of the Convention on its activities. It also reflects the special treatment afforded to cables, pipelines and certain other installations by the LOSC.
[23] 1998 UNESCO draft, Art. 1(b). For a discussion of this provision, see Dromgoole and Gaskell, note 9 above, p. 174.

that it could have seriously undermined the 100-year general rule. A further interesting development is that the definition now includes a "significance" criterion: it covers only traces of human existence having "a cultural, historical or archaeological character". The question of whether or not there should be a significance criterion had been hotly debated, the attitude of states to this point largely depending on whether or not their domestic legislation included such a criterion. Generally speaking, common law countries provide protection for certain UCH sites considered of particular significance.[24] Civil law countries, on the other hand, tend to adopt a much more protectionist approach, providing "blanket" protection for all sites over a certain age, or otherwise classified as "antiquities" or "cultural heritage". The fact that a significance criterion has been included suggests that proponents of such a criterion won the debate. However, the wording of the criterion really does little to restrict the scope of the Convention since arguably *anything* over 100 years of age has a "cultural, historical or archaeological character". The fact that it has such character does not mean that it has any cultural or archaeological *value* or *importance*. The inclusion of this criterion is therefore a fudge, which is unlikely to satisfy those who argued for greater limitation of the scope of the Convention. Indeed, the UK has expressed serious reservations on this particular point.[25] However, the reality is that on this issue there was really no room for a compromise solution. Either one approach or the other had to be taken. The fact that it would usually be necessary to undertake extensive archaeological work on a site in order to determine its cultural value or importance meant that the adoption of a significance criterion based on such qualities would conflict with one of the fundamental principles of the Convention: that wherever possible sites should be left undisturbed and protected *in situ*.[26]

Objectives and General Principles

The objectives and general principles of the Convention are referred to in the Preamble, set out more specifically in Article 2, and given effect to in other provisions, including the Rules in the Annex. The overall objective is clearly to "protect" the UCH.[27] It is also clear for whose benefit it is to be protected: for

---

[24] For example, in the UK, the Protection of Wrecks Act 1973 provides for the designation of wrecks of "historical, archaeological or artistic importance", and under the Ancient Monuments and Archaeological Areas Act 1979 wrecks and other UCH sites can be scheduled if they are of "national importance".

[25] See further pp. 77–78 below. See also the discussion on commercial participation in the underwater cultural resource at pp. 66–67 below.

[26] See further p. 65 below. For further arguments in favour of blanket protection, see G. Henderson, "Significance Assessment or Blanket Protection" in L. Prott, E. Planche, R. Roca-Hachem (eds.), *Background Materials on the Protection of the Underwater Cultural Heritage* (UNESCO, 2000), vol. 2, pp. 350–352.

[27] See, e.g., Art. 2(1) and Art. 2(2). The Convention therefore adds flesh to the duty upon states imposed by Art. 303(1) of the LOSC to protect objects of an archaeological and historical nature found at sea.

"humanity".[28] But from *what* is it to be protected? From the very beginning of the initiative, the primary threat to the UCH was recognised to come from salvage activities, particularly by treasure hunters. Such activities have been posing an increasingly serious problem because technological advances in recent years have made 98 per cent of the sea-bed accessible.[29] During the course of negotiations, a matter of some debate was the extent to which the threat posed to the UCH by other human activities, such as fishing, pipeline and cable laying, and drilling for oil and gas, should be dealt with by the Convention. Such activities certainly have the potential to cause serious damage to wrecks or other material lying on or in the sea-bed. However, dealing with this threat comprehensively proved to raise too many sensitive political and economic issues to be practicable. Therefore, rather than relating to "activities affecting" the UCH, as the 1998 draft had done, the final text distinguishes between activities "directed at" the UCH and those "incidentally affecting" it, and focuses on controlling the former.[30] Nonetheless, there is quite a broad general provision that a "State Party shall use the best practicable means at its disposal to prevent or mitigate any adverse effects that might arise from activities under its jurisdiction incidentally affecting underwater cultural heritage".[31]

What exactly does the Convention envisage when it refers to the "protection" of the UCH? Article 2(5) makes clear that protection *in situ* "shall be considered as the first option".[32] This is in accordance with established archaeological principles, under which excavation should take place in two circumstances only: where a site is under threat, or for legitimate research purposes. The Convention clearly anticipates excavation and recovery in some circumstances, and spells out what those circumstances should be. Rule 1 of the Annex provides that activities "may be authorised for the purpose of making a significant contribution to protection or knowledge or enhancement" of UCH and Rule 4 refers to circumstances where excavation or recovery is "necessary for the purpose of

---

[28] Art. 2(3). LOSC, Art. 149 provides that archaeological objects found in the Area shall be preserved or disposed of "for the benefit of mankind as a whole". Under the new Convention, the notion of general human benefit is extended to all maritime zones.

[29] E. O'Hara, "Maritime and Fluvial Cultural Heritage", Report of the Committee on Culture and Education, Parliamentary Assembly of the Council of Europe, Doc. 8867, 12 October 2000, para. 3.4.3. Remotely operated vehicles (ROVs) can operate at depths of 6,000m. Manned submersibles can operate at depths of 3,600m: *ibid.*

[30] "Activities directed at underwater cultural heritage" are defined as "activities having underwater cultural heritage as their primary object and which may, directly or indirectly, physically disturb or otherwise damage underwater cultural heritage": Art. 1(6). "Activities incidentally affecting underwater cultural heritage" are defined as "activities which, despite not having underwater cultural heritage as their primary object or one of their objects, may physically disturb or otherwise damage underwater cultural heritage": Art. 1(7).

[31] Art. 5. The breadth of Art. 5 is significant. It relates to activities *under the jurisdiction* of a state party and could therefore apply to certain activities in the EEZ or on the continental shelf of a state party, as well as to activities engaged in by flag states and nationals of states parties. For a particular example of its potential impact, see p. 86 below.

[32] See also the Preamble, and Rule 1 of the Annex.

scientific studies or for the ultimate protection" of UCH.[33] Within these guidelines arguably there is a considerable degree of latitude and different states parties may interpret them very differently. However, where activities are authorised, the Convention tries to ensure that they are undertaken in accordance with the benchmark rules set out in the Annex. These make provision for, *inter alia*, project funding and design, project team competence, recording of information, conservation, site management, the reporting and dissemination of finds, and curation of project archives. The standards imposed are high, although they are in accordance with standards set internationally for land sites.[34]

What the Convention makes absolutely clear is that the sale or irretrievable dispersal of UCH is incompatible with its protection. Article 2(7) provides that "[u]nderwater cultural heritage shall not be commercially exploited" and this provision is elucidated in Rule 2 of the Annex, which provides:

> "The commercial exploitation of underwater cultural heritage for trade or speculation or its irretrievable dispersal is fundamentally incompatible with the protection and proper management of underwater cultural heritage. Underwater cultural heritage shall not be traded, sold, bought or bartered as commercial goods."

From Rule 2, it appears that commercial exploitation through, for example, the sale of films or photographs of the site, public tours and public exhibition of material will not be an infringement of the Convention, but any sale of material will be. Furthermore, any action that will lead to the irretrievable dispersal of material from a site will also be an infringement. These restrictions are clear-cut and without exception.[35] Their effect is to provide little room within the framework of the Convention for commercial salvors to share in the underwater cultural resource, or to co-operate with archaeologists in work on UCH sites, as

---

[33] See also the Preamble, which refers to the "careful recovery" of UCH "if necessary for scientific or protective purposes".

[34] See, e.g., the ICOMOS Charter for the Protection and Management of the Archaeological Heritage 1990. See also the Council of Europe's European Convention on the Protection of the Archaeological Heritage (Revised) 1992, sometimes referred to as the Valletta Convention, which entered into force in 1995. The Valletta Convention is particular relevant because it applies to UCH "located in any area within the jurisdiction of the Parties": Art. 1(2)(iii). As the Explanatory Report makes clear, this includes parts of the marine zone, although exactly which parts is not so clear. It states that "the actual area of State jurisdiction depends on the individual States and in respect of this there are many possibilities. Territorially, the area can be coextensive with the territorial sea, the contiguous zone, the continental shelf, the exclusive economic zone or a cultural protection zone." (The UK ratified the Valletta Convention in 2000.)

[35] Having said that, it should be noted that a second clause to Rule 2 makes it clear that Rule 2: (i) does not preclude the buying in of the services of archaeological consultants, and (ii) probably would not preclude sale of an assemblage to a museum or similar institution, provided it was available for professional and public access, and was not irretrievably dispersed. See further, note 43 below.

some shipwreck salvors have advocated.[36] Recent litigation involving RMS Titanic Inc., the company that has been exploiting the wreck of the *Titanic*, suggests that commercial exploitation through public exhibition, public tours, etc., *without* the sale of artefacts may well be financially unviable.[37] In the author's opinion, the restrictions on sale and dispersal of UCH sway the balance of interests between archaeologists and commercial salvors too far in the archaeologists' favour, particularly given the ineffectiveness of the significance criterion in limiting the scope of the Convention. As well as placing restrictions on the recovery of material that may be of commercial interest but of little or no cultural importance, the drafters have also missed a valuable opportunity to develop a regime that allows for some participation by commercial operators. Managed properly, this could have been of benefit to the archaeological community and humanity as a whole, by utilising the considerable financial and technological resources of commercial organisations for work on sites under threat or where research is desirable.[38]

Exactly how it is envisaged that "humanity" will benefit from the protection afforded by the Convention to the UCH is not entirely clear. As we shall see, there is provision for the seizure of UCH, and material that is so seized must then be disposed of "for the public benefit".[39] Provision is also made for public access,[40] for the raising of public awareness,[41] and for the establishment or reinforcement of "competent authorities".[42] However, this provision is in very general terms and does little more than reiterate the archaeological principle that the public should have access to the cultural heritage except where such access is

---

[36] ProSEA, the Professional Shipwreck Explorers Association, argues that it is possible for shipwreck exploration to be done ethically and has developed a "Code of Ethics" for its members: see further, http://www.prosea.org.

[37] *RMS Titanic, Inc. v The Wrecked and Abandoned Vessel believed to be the RMS Titanic*, USCA 4th Cir., 12 April 2002. Appeal to the Supreme Court declined, 7 October 2002.

[38] It is interesting to note that on 27 September 2002 the UK government signed a "partnering agreement" with Odyssey Marine Exploration, a US company, concerning the wreck of HMS *Sussex*, a British warship that sank off Gibraltar in 1694. A Ministry of Defence press release dated 7 October 2002 states that the agreement "is an important step in the development of a 'partnering' approach to deep-sea archaeology whereby any recoveries from the wreck will be conducted under recognised and accepted archaeological methodologies, and professional official observers will be engaged in the detailed processes of any future survey and recovery activities from the site". According to the Odyssey Marine Exploration website, "[a]t approximately 3,000 feet below the surface, it will be the deepest extensive archaeological excavation of a shipwreck ever undertaken exclusively by robotic intervention". The *Sussex* was believed to have been carrying up to ten tons of gold coins and, under the terms of the agreement, Odyssey and the government will share in the financial proceeds. A memorandum of the partnering agreement has been published (see http://www.shipwreck.net/pam/), but the exact terms of the agreement remain confidential.

[39] Art. 18(4). See further, pp. 87–88 below.

[40] See the Preamble, Art. 2(10), Art. 18(4), Rules 7 and 33.

[41] See, in particular, Art. 20.

[42] Art. 22. Effective presentation of the UCH, and education, are two of the matters listed in Art. 22 as falling within the remit of such authorities.

incompatible with its protection. The Convention makes no specific provision for public funding, or for the creation or enhancement of museums, and the mechanisms whereby museums might acquire material are far from clear.[43] Furthermore, there is no intention to interfere with ownership rights, which presumably continue to exist,[44] and there is recognition that certain states may have a special interest in particular wrecks (referred to in the Convention as a "verifiable link").[45] However, the Convention provides no guidance on how the interests of humanity will interact with these other rights and interests.

At the very heart of the Convention lies the principle of co-operation. The Preamble makes it clear that co-operation among states, other organisations and parties "is essential" for the protection of the UCH[46] and, as we shall see, co-operation and information sharing between states is a fundamental plank in the protective regime created by the Convention. Indeed, without such co-operation the regime simply will not work. Consequently states parties are placed under a positive duty to co-operate in the protection of UCH.[47] As well as co-operating in respect of the notification and protection regimes, the enforcement of sanctions, and other matters under the Convention, states parties are also expressly encouraged to enter into inter-state agreements to protect the UCH, provided such agreements are "in full conformity" with the Convention and do not "dilute its universal character".[48] It is envisaged that such agreements may be successful in achieving greater, or better, protection for the UCH than the terms of the Convention.[49] Interestingly, the Convention makes provision for a

---

[43] In particular, it is unclear whether or not material that has been recovered through an authorised excavation in full conformity with the Convention could be sold to museums. This depends on the meaning of Rule 2(b) of the Annex: see C. Forrest, "A New International Regime for the Protection of Underwater Cultural Heritage", (2002) 51 *International and Comparative Law Quarterly* 511, 540.

[44] See further below pp. 69–70.

[45] In Arts. 6(2), 7(3), 9(5) and 18(4), the Convention refers to states with a verifiable link, "especially a cultural, historical or archaeological link". In Arts. 11(4) and 12(6), which relate to the Area, reference is made "to the preferential rights of States of cultural, historical or archaeological origin", wording which derives from Art. 149 of the LOSC. The Convention makes provision for states with a verifiable link to UCH in certain circumstances to be consulted on what protective measures should be taken.

[46] Interestingly, the reference to "salvors" in those listed in the 1998 draft as needing to co-operate has been omitted from the final text.

[47] Art. 2(2). This provision reflects Art. 303(1) of the LOSC, which provides that: "States have the duty to protect objects of an archaeological and historical nature found at sea and shall co-operate for this purpose."

[48] Art. 6.

[49] See the last sentence of Art. 6(1). Such agreements could be entered into in respect of enclosed or semi-enclosed seas, e.g. the Mediterranean or the Baltic, or in respect of particular wrecks. It is perhaps worth noting here that the text of an agreement between the UK, USA, Canada and France in respect of the *Titanic* was finalised in 2000, although the agreement has not yet been signed. However, the *Titanic* does not fall within the definition of UCH in the Convention and therefore this agreement would not need to conform to the Convention.

"Meeting of States Parties" once every two years,[50] and leaves it for that Meeting to decide on its functions and responsibilities, which potentially could be quite considerable.[51]

Treatment of Private Rights

At present, broadly speaking, anyone is free to recover sunken property on the high seas[52] and to then claim a salvage reward from the owner.[53] Until the reward is paid, the salvor will have a maritime lien on the recovered property. In cases where there is no known owner, or the owner has abandoned title, a finder may be awarded title to the property under the law of finds.[54] Where an owner can be traced, and there has been no abandonment of title, the ownership rights may be recognised even after the passage of many years. One of the most difficult issues facing the drafters of the Convention was how to deal with these private rights.[55]

As far as ownership rights are concerned, any attempt in the Convention to deprive owners of their rights might lead to conflict with the domestic constitutional laws of states parties and to the possibility that compensation might need to be paid under these laws. The 1998 draft tried to avoid interfering with ownership rights by applying only to abandoned UCH. However, its definition of abandonment, which set out the circumstances in which abandonment would be "deemed", proved highly controversial and unacceptable to many states.[56] As a consequence the deemed abandonment provision was dropped and the Convention now applies to UCH whether abandoned or not. Indeed, the final text of the Convention makes no reference to ownership at all.

---

[50] Art. 23. Extraordinary Meetings may also be called at the request of a majority of states parties: Art. 23(1).
[51] Among other things, the Meeting of States Parties may establish a Scientific and Technical Advisory Body to assist "in questions of a scientific or technical nature regarding the implementation of the Rules": Art. 23 paras. (4) and (5). Assistance "in implementing the decisions of the Meetings of States Parties" shall be provided by a secretariat, for which the Director-General of UNESCO will be responsible: Art. 24.
[52] While there is some academic debate on the point, the weight of opinion seems to be that this is the position even in the case of sunken warships: see Dromgoole and Gaskell, note 9 above, p. 184.
[53] Whether they will be entitled to a salvage reward depends on the law that is applied by the court hearing the case. Under the Salvage Convention 1989, for example, a salvage reward can be claimed where a salvor voluntarily succeeds in saving a vessel or other property that is in danger in navigable waters. However, the Convention does not define "danger" and therefore the question of whether property that has been lying on the sea-bed, possibly for centuries, is in danger is left for determination under the applicable law.
[54] Alternatively, the state may claim ownership. For example, under the UK's Merchant Shipping Act 1995, s.241, the Crown is entitled to unclaimed wreck found in UK territorial waters. Unclaimed wreck found outside territorial waters will be returned to the finder (*Pierce v Bemis (The Lusitania)* [1986] QB 384).
[55] For a detailed discussion of these rights, see S. Dromgoole and N. Gaskell, "Interests in Wreck" in N. Palmer and E. McKendrick (eds.), *Interests in Goods* (2nd ed., 1998).
[56] See the discussion of the deemed abandonment provision in Dromgoole and Gaskell, note 9 above, pp. 179–183.

While this was undoubtedly the easiest solution, in a sense all that it has done is to hide an issue that really needs to be addressed. There is, after all, an inevitable tension between rights of ownership and several of the Convention's fundamental principles and objectives, for example, that humanity is to benefit from the UCH, that UCH should not be sold or dispersed, that it should be preserved *in situ* wherever possible, that any activities directed at it should be undertaken in conformity with the Annex. This tension gives rise to many questions. For example, can an owner be prohibited from recovering its property in circumstances where *in situ* protection is considered a preferable option? Can an owner be made to conform to the Rules in the Annex in undertaking recovery operations? In either case if the answer is yes, then the owner's rights are being interfered with. Indeed, many of the Convention's provisions have a potential impact on ownership rights, and there is no evidence that this impact has been thought through at all.[57]

Right from the start of the initiative in 1988, a question that engaged particular interest was whether or not the law of salvage should be excluded from applying to UCH as defined by the Convention. For years, many commentators have argued that salvage law is completely inappropriate to be applied to UCH since it encourages excavation and recovery, and is therefore in direct conflict with the archaeological principle of protection *in situ*.[58] Indeed, some acknowledgement that UCH may warrant special treatment was made in the 1989 Salvage Convention, which permits reservations in respect of its applicability to "maritime cultural property of prehistoric, archaeological or historical interest ... situated on the seabed".[59]

In the 1994 ILA draft, salvage law was excluded from applying to the UCH.[60] However, in the 1998 UNESCO draft, the exclusion was omitted and replaced with Article 12(2), which provided for the "non-application of any internal law or regulation having the effect of providing commercial incentives for the excavation and removal of underwater cultural heritage". Since salvage law is an obvious example of a law having the effect of providing commercial incentives for removal, it was difficult to see how a state party could avoid disengaging salvage law from the UCH.[61] The effect of Article 12(2) would therefore probably have been much the same as an outright exclusion. However, one problem with an outright exclusion, and probably also with Article 12(2), was

---

[57] See further, the discussion of Art. 4 (relating to salvage and finding) and Art. 18 (relating to seizure), below.
[58] See, e.g. L. Prott and P. O'Keefe, "Law and the Underwater Heritage" in UNESCO, *Protection of the Underwater Heritage* (1981), p. 193; A. Strati, *The Protection of the Underwater Cultural Heritage: An Emerging Objective of the Contemporary Law of the Sea* (1995), pp. 45–49. On the other hand, there are those that have strongly argued for the retention of salvage law: see, e.g. G. Brice, "Salvage and the underwater cultural heritage", (1996) 20 *Marine Policy* 337; D. Bederman, "The UNESCO Draft Convention on Underwater Cultural Heritage: A Critique and Counter-Proposal", (1999) 30 *Journal of Maritime Law and Commerce* 331, 341–345.
[59] 1989 Salvage Convention, Art. 30(1)(d).

that they could lead to a possible conflict with the 1989 Salvage Convention, unless a state that was party to both Conventions had made the reservation to the Salvage Convention mentioned above.[62]

In the final text of the Convention, the law of salvage and the law of finds are specifically addressed in Article 4. This provides:

> "Any activity relating to underwater cultural heritage to which this Convention applies shall not be subject to the law of salvage or law of finds, unless it:
> (a) is authorized by the competent authorities, and
> (b) is in full conformity with this Convention, and
> (c) ensures that any recovery of the underwater cultural heritage achieves its maximum protection."

This is a major retreat from an outright exclusion of salvage law. Provided the conditions in (a), (b) and (c) are met, the finder can claim a salvage reward from the owner and, where there is no owner, may be awarded the property recovered under the law of finds.[63] If salvage law applies, then presumably any artefacts will be returned to the owner after the payment of salvage, unless the owner agrees to sell its rights in the artefacts to the salvor. If the law of finds applies, then the finder will acquire title against all but the true owner. In either case, private individuals appear to have, or to acquire, rights of ownership and possession. But if this is the case, how will the sale and "irretrievable dispersal" of those artefacts be prevented? How will they be made available "for the benefit of humanity" if they are in a private collection?

There is less conceptual difficulty in circumstances where the conditions in (a), (b) and (c) are not met. In such circumstances, salvage and finds laws must not be applied. It is logical that a salvor who undertakes unauthorised activities or activities that are not in accordance with the Convention should not have the benefit of salvage or finds laws. Indeed, it is at least arguable that the salvor's misconduct under the UNESCO Convention would be construed as misconduct

---

[60] ILA draft, Art. 4.
[61] The same can also be said of the law of finds, and in this respect Art. 12(2) went further than the ILA draft.
[62] Under Art. 30(1)(d). See text attached to note 59 above. Eleven of the 25 parties to the Salvage Convention have made this reservation: O'Hara, note 29 above, para. 5.1.2. Reservations need to be made at the time of ratification, otherwise a state would have to denounce the Convention and then re-ratify: Dromgoole and Gaskell, note 9 above, p. 190, fn. 60. The argument that is sometimes raised that an exclusion of salvage law would create a conflict with Art. 303(3) of the LOSC is probably incorrect: see *ibid.*, p. 178.
[63] Carducci suggests that a fourth condition should be implied in respect of the law of finds and that is that there must be clear evidence of abandonment and that it cannot be presumed: see G. Carducci, "The Expanding Protection of the Underwater Cultural Heritage: The New UNESCO Convention versus Existing International Law" in G. Camarda, T. Scovazzi (eds.), *The Protection of the Underwater Cultural Heritage: Legal Aspects* (2002).

under the 1989 Salvage Convention,[64] thereby avoiding conflict with that Convention. However, any deterrent effect this provision might have will be effective only where a salvor does not have a great deal of choice but to land the material recovered in a state party to the Convention. If he is able to land it in a non-state party, then he may still be able to make a claim under the laws of salvage or finds, depending on the law that is eventually applied to the claim.

It is interesting to note that what the Convention has done is to retain the laws of salvage and finds, while excluding commercial exploitation. This is directly contrary to the policy of the US Abandoned Shipwrecks Act of 1987, which excludes the laws of salvage and finds from applying to UCH to which the Act applies, but allows for "private sector recovery" so long as it is consistent with the protection of "historical values". It has been argued quite convincingly that this approach, which recognises multiple interests in the UCH and seeks to foster a "partnership" with these interests, should have been followed by the Convention.[65]

Treatment of Sunken State Vessels and Sovereign Immunity Issues[66]

The 1998 UNESCO draft excluded warships and other state-owned or operated vessels and aircraft used for non-commercial purposes from the scope of application of the Convention.[67] There were understandable reasons for the exclusion: international law in relation to warships is complex and uncertain, and the issue is politically highly sensitive. Nonetheless, it meant that a very significant proportion of the UCH would not be covered by the protective regime of the Convention and for this reason the exclusion was much criticised.[68]

One of the barriers to removing the exclusion was the provision in the 1998 draft for abandonment "to be deemed" in certain cases. The application of this provision to state vessels was unacceptable to many states, who strongly argue that their ownership rights can be lost only through an express abandonment.[69] Once the decision was made to delete the deemed abandonment provision, this opened the way for the inclusion of state vessels.[70] The fact that such vessels are

---

[64] Salvage Convention 1989, Art. 18.
[65] O. Varmer, "The Case Against the 'Salvage' of the Cultural Heritage", (1999) 30 *Journal of Maritime Law and Commerce* 279.
[66] The issue of sovereign immunity in respect of sunken warships needs to be distinguished from that relating to warships and other government ships in service. Art. 13 is headed "Sovereign immunity" and is designed to relieve warships of the obligation to report since this might interfere with the need for secrecy in their operations. However, states must ensure that "as far as is reasonable and practicable" reporting requirements are met.
[67] 1998 UNESCO draft, Art. 2(2).
[68] See, e.g. Dromgoole and Gaskell, note 9 above, pp. 186–187.
[69] See *ibid.*, p. 184.
[70] Article 2(8) of the final text provides that "... nothing in this Convention shall be interpreted as modifying the rules of international law and State practice pertaining to sovereign immunities, *nor any State's rights with respect to its State vessels and aircraft*" (emphasis added). As O'Keefe points out, this reference to a state's rights apart from its sovereign immunities must refer to its rights of ownership: O'Keefe, note 11 above, p. 53.

included within the Convention's protective regime is a major achievement, since the purpose of the Convention would otherwise have been seriously undermined. The inclusion should also be viewed positively by states for the following reason: the Convention may well afford protection to various interests they may have in their sunken vessels besides any interest in their cultural significance.[71] The clearest example of this is that specific provision is made in the Convention in regard to preserving the sanctity of human remains,[72] an issue that can raise particular concerns for states where a vessel was lost in military action.

Whether or not a warship, once sunk, is subject to sovereign immunity is a matter of some debate,[73] but many states argue that it is, and that consequently sunken warships are subject to the exclusive sovereignty of the flag state and may only be interfered with if the express permission of that state is given. Understandably, therefore, there were concerns about the extent to which any new convention would afford coastal state jurisdiction in respect of state vessels. The final text of the Convention tries to take into account the political sensitivities in this regard and to draw a compromise between the interests of flag states and coastal states. In Article 2(8), it is made clear that "... nothing in this Convention shall be interpreted as modifying the rules of international law and State practice pertaining to sovereign immunities ...". The Convention then goes on to make specific provision for state wrecks[74] depending on the maritime zone in which they lie. Where a state vessel is discovered in the territorial waters of another state, a jurisdictional conflict may clearly arise. Indeed, such conflicts have arisen in the past and have eventually been settled by means of an inter-state agreement.[75] Under Article 7(3) of the Convention, where a state vessel is discovered in the territorial or archipelagic waters of a state party,[76] that state should inform the flag state (if party to the Convention) of the discovery, with a view to co-operating on the best methods of protecting the wreck. At first sight, this appears a useful provision from the point of view of flag states (provided, of course, that they are party to the Convention). However, use of the word "should" rather than "shall" has proved highly contentious. Furthermore, Article 2(8) provides room for a flag state to argue that it has the exclusive right to prohibit or regulate interference with the wreck on the grounds of its sovereign

---

[71] For a discussion of these interests, see Dromgoole and Gaskell, note 9 above, pp. 185–186.
[72] See Art. 2(9) and Rule 5 of the Annex.
[73] See Dromgoole and Gaskell, note 9 above, pp. 183–184.
[74] All the provisions apply to state aircraft as well as vessels. A definition of "state vessels and aircraft" is provided in Art. 1(8).
[75] For example, a formal agreement was signed in the dispute between France and the USA over the wreck of the Confederate raider, CSS *Alabama*, which was discovered in 1984 in French waters: see further, O'Keefe, note 11 above, pp. 76–77; see also Dromgoole and Gaskell, note 9 above, p. 186. The UK and South Africa also reached an agreement in the form of an Exchange of Notes in respect of HMS *Birkenhead*, a UK warship which sank in South African waters in 1852: see *ibid.*, p. 185.
[76] Unlike the rest of Art. 7, Art. 7(3) refers only to territorial and archipelagic waters, and not to internal waters.

immunity. The position in respect of the EEZ and continental shelf is no more satisfactory. While in this case Article 10(7) provides that no activity shall be conducted without the agreement of the flag state, this is made subject to two provisos. One is in respect of situations where emergency measures are required to prevent "immediate danger" to UCH from "human activities or any other cause, including looting",[77] in which case the agreement of the flag state does not have to be obtained first. The second proviso relates to situations where the sovereign rights or jurisdiction of a state party in its EEZ or on its continental shelf may be interfered with unless it takes action to prohibit or authorise activities directed at UCH located in that zone. In such cases, that state party may prohibit or authorise those activities without first consulting the flag state. Clearly, flag states are bound to see the possibility of a coastal state acting under one of these provisos as an infringement of their sovereign rights, and therefore—again using Article 2(8)—they may challenge the coastal state's right to act. Finally, in respect of state vessels located in the Area, Article 12(7) prohibits states parties from undertaking or authorising activities without the consent of the flag state. As O'Keefe points out, what is notable here is that this provision refers to the activities of *states parties*. What it does not do is to oblige states parties to prohibit their nationals or ships flying their flag from undertaking activities on the state vessels of other states.[78]

Unfortunately, on the sovereign immunity issue, the Convention has failed to provide a satisfactory and workable compromise between the interests of flag states and coastal states. This is a great pity as it is likely to prove a major obstacle to the adoption of the Convention by a number of states. For example, in a note explaining the UK's abstention from voting on the final text of the Convention, one of the two reasons[79] given for its position was the unacceptability of the text on the sovereign immunity issue:

> "The United Kingdom considers that the current text erodes the fundamental principles of customary international law, codified in [the LOSC], of Sovereign Immunity which is retained by a State's warships and vessels and aircraft used for non commercial service until expressly abandoned by that State. The text purports to alter the fine balance between the equal, but conflicting rights of Coastal and Flag States, carefully negotiated in [the LOSC], in a way that is unacceptable to the United Kingdom."[80]

---

[77] Art. 10(4).
[78] O'Keefe, note 11 above, p. 100.
[79] For the second reason, see pp. 77–78 below.
[80] "UK Explanation of Vote", circulated by the Foreign and Commonwealth Office to interested parties on 31 October 2001. The warships issue was also cited by the US delegation as one of several reasons why it could not accept the Convention: see Scovazzi, note 13 above, fn. 2.

Relationship Between the Convention and the LOSC

It was of course inevitable that one of the most contentious issues concerning the Convention would be its interrelationship with the LOSC. Article 303(4) of the LOSC seemed to anticipate a subsequent international agreement in respect of the UCH, which might build on the very limited provisions in Article 303 and Article 149. However, the question was whether a new convention could extend coastal state jurisdiction to control activities affecting the UCH beyond the limits established by the LOSC. Predictably, different states held very different views about this. Flag states had the usual concerns about "creeping jurisdiction" and used the well-worn argument that the LOSC was a delicately balanced "package" that could not be disturbed.[81] Other states saw little point in a new convention *unless* it went further than the LOSC.

The compromise solution that has been adopted is set out in Article 3:

"Nothing in this Convention shall prejudice the rights, jurisdiction and duties of States under international law, including the United Nations Convention on the Law of the Sea. This Convention shall be interpreted and applied in the context of and in a manner consistent with international law, including the United Nations Convention on the Law of the Sea."

The compromise comes in the form of the references to "international law, including" the LOSC. As O'Keefe points out, this wording "allows for future developments in the interpretation of [the LOSC] and in international law through custom or other international instruments".[82] The interpretation of the new Convention is therefore a movable feast: it may develop and change as international law develops and changes. The nature of this compromise is clever and it also assists the overall aim of the Convention by allowing for an increasing level of protection for the UCH over time. However, the wording of Article 3 will be subject to very different interpretations and may well simply be unacceptable to some states.[83]

The original 1994 ILA draft had proposed a "cultural heritage zone", a new type of jurisdictional zone in addition to those already defined by international law.[84] Under the draft, a cultural heritage zone could be established by a state party over an area extending beyond its territorial sea up to the outer limit of its continental shelf. Within that area the state would have jurisdiction over

---

[81] The UN General Assembly also made its view clear that the Convention should be in full conformity with the LOSC through a number of resolutions to this effect: see O'Keefe, note 11 above, p. 59, fn. 9.

[82] *Ibid.*, p. 58. See also the wording of the final paragraph of the Preamble, which refers to the need to "codify and progressively develop" rules on the protection of the UCH.

[83] The relationship of the new Convention to the LOSC was apparently one of the objections to the final text raised by the USA: see Scovazzi, note 13 above, fn. 2.

[84] The notion of a cultural heritage zone was not new. It had originally been proposed in Council of Europe Recommendation 848 (1978).

activities affecting the UCH. However, the creation of a new zone proved particularly controversial and, in the 1998 UNESCO draft, the notion was dropped. In its place was a provision using existing maritime zones, namely the continental shelf and the exclusive economic zone (EEZ), as a basis for state control over activities affecting the UCH.[85] However, while use of the EEZ may just possibly have been justifiable under the LOSC,[86] use of the continental shelf certainly was not.[87] The maritime powers fiercely opposed any suggestion that there was evidence of developing state practice in this regard,[88] and in the end this provision too was dropped.[89]

Rather than an extension of coastal state jurisdiction, what the drafters eventually opted to do was to create a series of control mechanisms that make full use of existing coastal state jurisdiction, and the flag state, nationality and territorial jurisdictional principles, but that have a built-in degree of flexibility to allow for developments in international law. Inevitably, the protective framework that results is highly complex.

Control Mechanisms

As will be seen below, Articles 7 to 12 of the Convention make specific provision for the protection of UCH in each maritime zone. The overall aim is to ensure that *in situ* protection is considered as the first option but, where it is concluded that recovery is appropriate, to ensure that it is undertaken in accordance with the terms of the Annex. Curiously, nowhere does the Convention expressly state that activities must be *authorised* before they are capable of complying with the Annex.[90] However, the whole structure of the protective framework is such that this must be a necessary implication.[91] Articles 7 to 12 are supplemented with three significant general provisions. First of all, Article 14 requires states to take measures to prevent the entry into their territory of material that has been

---

[85] 1998 UNESCO draft, Art. 5.
[86] Art. 56 of the LOSC gives coastal states rights in respect of activities for the "economic exploitation and exploration" of the EEZ. Certainly the activities of treasure salvors can be said to be "economic".
[87] Art. 77 of the LOSC, relating to the continental shelf, refers to coastal states' rights in respect of "natural resources". UCH cannot be said to be a natural resource: see the *Report of the International Law Commission to the General Assembly*, 11th Session, GAOR Supp. No. 9, UN Doc. A/3159 (1956), reprinted in (1956) 2 *Yearbook of the International Law Commission* 298.
[88] See further p. 82 below.
[89] The acutely difficult nature of this issue is illustrated by the fact that the working text produced in 1999 (see above p. 61, note 10) set out three alternative options in respect of jurisdiction.
[90] If this was not the case, a salvor could undertake activities without authorisation, but argue that they were being conducted in accordance with the Annex and were therefore not in breach of the Convention. This would undermine the principle that protection *in situ* should always be considered as the first option, since it would be left to the salvor (rather than the competent authority of a state party) to determine whether or not excavation and recovery were justifiable.
[91] See, e.g. Rule 1 of the Annex, and Art. 4 (which provides that the laws of salvage and finds will not apply unless, *inter alia*, interference has been authorised).

recovered contrary to the Convention.[92] Secondly, Article 15 requires states to take measures to prohibit the use of territory under their exclusive jurisdiction or control, including their maritime ports, in support of any activity that is not in conformity with the Convention. Thirdly, Article 16 requires states parties to take all practicable measures to ensure that their nationals and vessels flying their flag do not engage in activities that do not conform to the Convention. These three articles need to be borne in mind when one assesses the potential effectiveness of the provisions in Articles 7 to 12 and the range of control measures available to states parties in each maritime zone. Finally, in order to deter the violation of measures taken under the Convention, each state party is required to impose sanctions, including the seizure of UCH that has been recovered contrary to the terms of the Convention.

Provisions in Respect of Existing Maritime Zones

Territorial waters, archipelagic and internal waters
Article 7(1) of the Convention reiterates the already well-established position that coastal states have an exclusive right to regulate and authorise activities in their territorial, archipelagic and internal waters.[93] Indeed, many states already have domestic legislation protecting UCH in these waters. However, Article 7(2) goes further by requiring states parties to apply the Rules in the Annex to activities directed at the UCH. States minded to ratify the Convention will therefore need to scrutinise their domestic legislation to ensure that it accords with these Rules. They will also need to ensure that their legislation applies to UCH *as defined by* the Convention. Indeed, for some states compliance with the definition will cause more problems than compliance with the Rules. This is certainly the case for the UK, where the two relevant statutes employ significance criteria which are much more restrictive than the "character" criterion in the Convention.[94] Indeed, the UK has cited this as a second reason[95] for its abstention from voting on the final text of the Convention:

---

[92] Specifically, Art. 14 provides: "States Parties shall take measures to prevent the entry into their territory, the dealing in, or the possession of, underwater cultural heritage illicitly exported and/or recovered, where recovery was contrary to this Convention." This article has wide ramifications and is fully discussed by O'Keefe, note 11 above, pp. 103–106. As Carducci points out, Art. 14 contributes to the "wider fight" already taking place to control the theft and illicit export of cultural material, in particular by making "a fundamental link between preventing the entry into the territory (of the receiving state) and the illicit character of the export of UCH (from the export state): see Carducci, note 63 above, p. 177. The UNESCO Convention on the Means of Prohibiting and Preventing the Illicit Import, Export and Transfer of Ownership of Cultural Property 1970 and the UNIDROIT Convention on Stolen or Illegally Exported Cultural Objects 1995 are specific examples of other international measures on this front.
[93] Although note the special rule in Art. 7(3) in respect of identifiable state vessels and aircraft. See above, p. 73.
[94] See note 24 above.
[95] The first relates to the sovereign immunity issue: see further, p. 74 above.

"The procedures for the protection of underwater archaeology adopted in the Annex are those which are already followed by the United Kingdom with regard to the designation of wreck sites within its territorial sea and internal waters. However, the text obliges signatory States to extend the same very high standards of protection to all underwater archaeology over 100 years old. It is estimated that there are probably about 10,000 wreck sites on the seabed under the United Kingdom's territorial sea and it would neither be possible nor desirable to extend legal protection to all of them. The United Kingdom believes that it is better to focus its efforts and resources on protecting the most important and unique examples of underwater cultural heritage. It would simply be impossible to enforce the application of the rules in the Annex to every one of the thousands of wreck sites."[96]

Contiguous zone
Article 8 provides that states parties may regulate and authorise activities directed at the UCH in their contiguous zone[97] "in accordance with" Article 303(2) of the LOSC. Article 8 also makes clear that it is "without prejudice to and in addition to Articles 9 and 10", which relate to the continental shelf and EEZ.[98] Where a state does take up its right under Article 8 to regulate and authorise activities directed at UCH, it must require that the Rules in the Annex be applied.

Article 303(2) of the LOSC provided states with an international legal basis for action to control traffic in objects of an archaeological and historical nature found within the contiguous zone. A coastal state is allowed to presume that the removal of objects from its contiguous zone without its approval would amount to an infringement within its territory or territorial sea of customs, fiscal, immigration or sanitary regulations. This legal fiction allows the state to exercise the control necessary to prevent such infringement, as permitted by Article 33 of the LOSC. However, the question has been *how* states can exercise that control, as there has been some debate about whether Article 303(2) creates only enforcement competence or legislative competence.[99] Despite this, some states have asserted legislative competence in respect of the UCH in the contiguous

---

[96] "UK Explanation of Vote", circulated by the Foreign and Commonwealth Office to interested parties on 31 October 2001.
[97] The contiguous zone extends 24nm from the baseline from which the breadth of the territorial sea is measured: see LOSC, Art. 33(2). A state does not have to claim a contiguous zone, although about one-third of coastal states do: R. Churchill and A. Lowe, *The Law of the Sea* (3rd ed., 1999), p. 136.
[98] The reason for this is that the contiguous zone falls within the EEZ, which extends from the outer limit of the territorial sea: LOSC, Art. 55.
[99] See B. Oxman "The Third United Nations Conference on the Law of the Sea: The Ninth Session (1980)", (1981) 75 *American Journal of International Law* 211, 240; Caflisch, note 7 above, pp. 19–20. See also Churchill and Lowe, note 97 above, pp. 137–139.

zone.¹⁰⁰ It should be noted, however, that Article 303(2) relates only to the *removal* of objects, and therefore does not legitimate the regulation of activities on a site that do not involve removal. Nonetheless, it is unlikely that states have, or will, make that distinction.

The power given to states parties in Article 8 is said to be "in accordance with" Article 303(2). There was no intention, therefore, that Article 8 should go beyond Article 303(2), and it cannot be interpreted as so doing. However, it does make it easier to defend the exercise of legislative rather than merely enforcement jurisdiction, and this in itself will help to contribute to the aim of protecting the UCH. Article 8 is also useful in that it reaffirms the basis for action in Article 303(2) and may therefore encourage more states to assert competence of one sort or another over this area.[101] However, it is a pity that it is only permissive in form and therefore states parties will not be obliged to make use of it. Nonetheless, it must be borne in mind that the contiguous zone is merely a 12-mile wide strip adjacent to the territorial sea. While this zone was once believed by some to be of particular significance for the protection of the UCH because of its shallowness and proximity to the shore,[102] technological advances mean that measures to protect UCH in the vast expanses of water further offshore are now of much greater consequence.

EEZ and continental shelf
The difficulty of creating control mechanisms for the EEZ and continental shelf is evidenced by the fact that the final text of the Convention has had to resort to two long and complex articles to deal with these zones. Instead of relying upon an extension of coastal state jurisdiction, as earlier drafts had done, Articles 9 and 10 of the final text make use of existing coastal state rights, and of the nationality and flag state principles of jurisdiction.

Article 9 makes it clear that states have a duty to protect the UCH in these zones, reiterating the general duty set out in Art. 303(1) of the LOSC.[103] However, it then goes on to elaborate on the LOSC by specifying the means by which this duty must be put into effect. Essentially, a state party is obliged to require its national,[104] or the master of a vessel flying its flag, to report any discovery of UCH or any intention to engage in activities directed at the UCH, either in its own EEZ or on its continental shelf, or in the EEZ or on the

---

[100] For example, France and Denmark.
[101] The question arose in respect of Art. 303(2) of the LOSC, and arises again in respect of Art. 8, whether a state must formally declare a contiguous zone before it can exercise rights under these articles: on this, see Carducci, note 63 above, pp. 193–195.
[102] Oxman, note 99 above, p. 240.
[103] Since Art. 303 is located in the "General Provisions" section of the LOSC, it appears that the duty set out in paragraph 1 applies to all areas of the sea.
[104] See O'Keefe, note 11 above, p. 84 for an interesting discussion of how the reference to a state's "national" should be interpreted. Presumably "national" includes companies incorporated, or having their seat, in the relevant state, but *quaere*: would it include companies having their principal place of business there, but no other association?

continental shelf of another state party.[105] Provision is made for reports to be transmitted to interested states, including the relevant coastal state and any state with a verifiable link. All reports must also be notified to the Director-General of UNESCO, who shall promptly make the information available to all states parties.[106]

Knowledge that UCH has been discovered, or that someone is planning to undertake activities in respect of it, is of course useful, but the crucial question is what mechanisms does the Convention afford to enable activities in the EEZ or on the continental shelf to be prohibited or regulated? Here we need to look at Article 10.

The key provision is in fact Article 10(2). This provides that:

> "A State Party in whose exclusive economic zone or on whose continental shelf underwater cultural heritage is located has the right to prohibit or authorise any activity directed at such heritage to prevent interference with its sovereign rights or jurisdiction as provided for by international law including the United Nations Convention on the Law of the Sea."

This provision gives states parties a basis for acting to prohibit or authorise activities directed at the UCH in their EEZ or on their continental shelf. States are able to so act, provided that their "sovereign rights or jurisdiction" under international law, including the LOSC, are threatened. A simple reading of Articles 56 and 77 of the LOSC makes it clear that it should not be too difficult for a coastal state to claim that this is the case.[107] In both zones, the coastal state has rights over natural resources, both living and non-living; in the EEZ it also has rights or jurisdiction in respect of economic exploration and exploitation, installations and structures, marine scientific research, and preservation of the marine environment. With the exercise of a little imagination, the potential power of Article 10(2) quickly becomes evident. In particular, it is the coastal state's rights over its natural resources that are likely to be most useful in providing grounds for action. Fish and other marine life tend to congregate on and in wrecks and other objects on the sea-bed, which provide them with a protective environment. In the frequent situations where this is the case, it is inevitable that activities in respect of the UCH will interfere with these natural resources. While in principle there should be some degree of proportionality between the extent of the threat to sovereign rights and the action taken in

---

[105] See Art. 9(1)(a) and (b). Note that there is a "constructive", i.e. deliberate, ambiguity in Art. 9(1)(b) which means that it is (just about) possible to argue that the coastal state, provided that it is a party to the Convention, can require the nationals, or flag vessels, of another state (probably only if a state party) to report directly to it: see O'Keefe, note 11 above, pp. 82–83; Carducci, note 63 above, p. 198.

[106] See Art. 9(3) and (4). Note that provision is made for confidentiality to be maintained in cases where UCH might be put at risk by disclosure of information: see Art. 19(3).

[107] Art. 10(2) assumes that there may also be other rules of international law besides the provisions in the LOSC that afford sovereign rights and jurisdiction in these zones to coastal states.

response, in practice it is unlikely that any action taken by a state to protect its sovereign rights or jurisdiction would be called into question by another state.[108]

The fact that the provision gives a coastal state the right to "prohibit", as well as to "authorise", activities in its EEZ or on its continental shelf is also highly significant. It means that states will now have a concrete method of preventing interference with the UCH and of implementing the principle of *in situ* protection enshrined in the Convention. If a state is alerted to the possibility of interference, either under the notification procedures in Article 9 or in any other way, it will have a basis to prevent it. Also, in circumstances where interference is considered justified, the coastal state will have a means of ensuring that any work carried out is undertaken in accordance with the Rules in the Annex.[109]

Even where Article 10(2) cannot be used, Article 10, paragraphs (3) to (6) go on to provide for a system of consultation between states with a verifiable link and the coastal state on the best means of protecting UCH which has been discovered in the EEZ or on the continental shelf, or where it is known that someone has the intention of interfering with UCH in these zones. Provision is made for the appointment of a "co-ordinating state", which may well be the coastal state,[110] and, among other things, this state may be required to implement any agreed protective measures.[111] Where UCH is threatened by an "immediate danger", including looting, the co-ordinating state may even take measures *prior* to consultation.[112] However, while reference is made to the taking of measures and also to the issuing of authorisations, any measures taken must be consistent with international law, including the LOSC.[113] In view of this, the measures the co-ordinating state could take in practice to prohibit interference, or even to ensure that interference is conducted in accordance with the Rules in the Annex, are likely to be fairly limited. It could certainly take action in accordance with Article 16 to control the activities of its own nationals or vessels flying its flag. It could also try to ensure that other states parties take similar action. Furthermore, it could make it clear to any transgressor that measures will be taken by the co-ordinating state and other states parties under Articles 14 and 15 to prevent entry into their territory of recovered material, and to prohibit the use of their ports by the transgressor's vessels. Over the course of time, state practice will obviously develop in this regard and it will be interesting to see how it does.

The interrelationship between Article 10(2) and Article 10, paragraphs (3) to

---

[108] See O'Keefe, note 11, p. 90.
[109] Strangely perhaps, Art. 10(2) does not specifically require that authorisations be in accordance with the Rules in the Annex, but this must surely be the implication.
[110] The coastal state will be the co-ordinating state unless it declares a wish not to be. It may do this if it has concerns about the expenditure the role might involve, especially if the UCH has no direct connection with it.
[111] Unless it is agreed that another state party shall implement those measures.
[112] In all its actions under Art. 10, however, the co-ordinating state must act on behalf of the "States Parties as a whole and not in its own interest": Art. 10(6).
[113] In accordance with Art. 3.

(6) is extremely curious, and the article provides no guidance on this. In particular, does a coastal state acting under Article 10(2) to prohibit or authorise activities have to consult any states parties who have declared an interest in the UCH and follow the other procedures laid out in paragraphs (3) to (6)? Certainly paragraphs (3) to (6) do not expressly state that they only apply in cases where Article 10(2) is not applicable. However, the consultative procedures set out in paragraphs (3) to (6) could clearly conflict with the coastal state's "right" under Article 10(2) to act to prevent interference with its sovereign rights. Surely it cannot have been envisaged that the coastal state should have to consult with other interested states before so acting? The question also arises of what the position would be if the coastal state decides to authorise activities on a wreck site and the flag state declares an interest. In such circumstances, it would still seem to fetter the "right" of the coastal state to act, if it was *required* to consult and implement only *agreed* measures of protection. Therefore presumably the provisions of paragraphs (3) to (6) are not intended to apply in these circumstances. However, the whole scheme of the Convention is based on cooperation and therefore coastal states may feel under at least a moral obligation to consult with other interested states, and in some cases may even follow the procedures laid out in paragraphs (3) to (6).

A further interesting question arises. A number of states have acted unilaterally to assert control over UCH on the continental shelf and in the EEZ, despite the fact that there is little or no basis in treaty law for such action.[114] What is their position if they decide to ratify the Convention? Not surprisingly, given their evident concern to protect the UCH, at least three of these states voted in favour of the Convention: Australia, Ireland and Spain.[115] Would ratification of the Convention affect the exercise of their extended jurisdiction? O'Keefe suggests not, noting that Article 3 provides that nothing in the Convention "shall prejudice the rights, jurisdiction and duties of States under international law ...".[116] However, this argument seems to be based on the premise that these unilateral extensions of jurisdiction are evidence of a customary rule of law in this regard, when in fact many would argue that all they evidence is creeping jurisdiction.[117] In any event, if these states decide to ratify the Convention, it will be interesting to see to what extent—if at all—they amend their domestic legislation in order to comply particularly with the provisions of Article 10. Article 10(1) provides that:

---

[114] See p. 76 above. On customary law, see note 117 below.
[115] All of these states have asserted jurisdiction in respect of the UCH over their continental shelf. Some states, such as Morocco, have asserted such jurisdiction over the EEZ, but this is less common.
[116] O'Keefe, note 11 above, p. 59.
[117] Strati argues that the number of states that have expanded their jurisdiction is too limited to provide the basis for a customary rule: Strati, note 58 above, p. 269. The practice has also been inconsistent, with states expanding their jurisdiction over different areas of the sea. However, it could be argued that there is a developing international practice in this regard.

"No authorisation shall be granted for an activity directed at underwater cultural heritage located in the exclusive economic zone or on the continental shelf *except in conformity with the provisions of this Article.*"[118]

Therefore, the consultation procedures in Article 10, paragraphs (3) to (6) will need to be complied with, unless it can be argued that existing legislation is justifiable under Article 10(2). The wording of Article 10(2) might allow for this, depending on one's view of the legitimacy of the unilateral extensions of jurisdiction:

"A State Party in whose exclusive economic zone or on whose continental shelf underwater cultural heritage is located has the right to prohibit or authorise any activity directed at such heritage to prevent interference with its sovereign rights *or jurisdiction as provided for by international law* including the United Nations Convention on the Law of the Sea."[119]

Apparently no objections have been made to date to the unilateral extensions, but states may find it easier to object in the future by arguing that a state party to the Convention is acting contrary to its terms.[120]

The Area

Finding an effective means of controlling activities in the Area, in other words the deep sea-bed beyond other zones,[121] is of crucial importance because it is in the Area that the most well-preserved and undisturbed wrecks of all may be found.[122] However, it also represented a challenge to the drafters of the Convention because of the special status of this zone under the LOSC. Articles 11 and 12 of the new Convention make provision in respect of the Area, and reflect the form (if not the entire substance) of the provisions in Articles 9 and 10 in respect of the EEZ and continental shelf.

Article 11(1) provides that states parties have a responsibility to protect UCH in the Area, in conformity both with the terms of the Convention and Article 149 of the LOSC. However, the duty in Article 11(1) is set out in broader and clearer terms than Article 149. The latter imposes a duty to "preserve" or "dispose" of "objects", suggesting that objects have to be found, and possibly even recovered,

---

[118] Emphasis added.
[119] Emphasis added.
[120] Forrest makes a similar suggestion: note 43 above, p. 518.
[121] This maritime zone was created by the LOSC, which defines the Area as "the seabed and ocean floor and subsoil thereof, beyond the limits of national jurisdiction", in other words beyond the EEZ and continental shelf of states (see LOSC, Art. 1(1)). The LOSC requires that activities in the Area be carried out for the benefit of mankind as a whole (see LOSC, Art. 140). The new Convention defines the Area in identical terms (see Art. 1(5)).
[122] P. O'Keefe and J. Nafziger, note 7 above, p. 393. The importance of this zone was also acknowledged by UNESCO in its original feasibility study for the drafting of a new instrument: see UNESCO Secretariat, "Feasibility Study for the Drafting of a New Instrument for the Protection of the Underwater Cultural Heritage", presented to the 146th Session of the UNESCO Executive Board, Paris, 23 March 1995, Doc. 146 EX/27, para. 10.

before the duty takes effect. The reference in Article 149 to disposing of objects also seems to conflict with the notion of preservation, which is a core feature of the new Convention. By contrast, the duty in Article 11(1) is reflective of the general aim of the new Convention to protect UCH sites *in situ* wherever possible.[123]

As was the case with Article 9, Article 11 utilises the nationality and flag state principles of jurisdiction to establish a system for the reporting of discoveries or plans to engage in activities in the Area. States parties are obliged to require their nationals, or the master of a vessel flying their flag, to report any discovery of UCH or any intention to engage in activities directed at UCH located in the Area. States are then required to pass on reports to the Director-General of UNESCO and the Secretary-General of the International Sea-bed Authority (ISA),[124] and the Director-General of UNESCO is required to make such reports available "promptly" to all states parties.[125] States with a verifiable link to UCH may declare to the Director-General their interest in being consulted on how effective protection can be ensured.[126] Article 12 then goes on to establish a similar consultation system to that set out in Article 10, paragraphs (3) to (6). In this case, the Director-General of UNESCO must invite states that have declared an interest in the UCH to consult together on the best means of protection, and to appoint a co-ordinating state to implement agreed protective measures.[127] An invitation must also be extended to the ISA to participate in the consultations. Under Article 12(3), all states parties (rather than only the co-ordinating state) may take measures *prior* to consultation, where UCH is threatened by immediate danger.[128]

In respect of the Area, considerable reliance is placed upon the office of the

---

[123] What is perhaps curious is that Art. 11 does not refer to Art. 303(1) of the LOSC, which applies to all areas of the sea including the Area, and which imposes a general duty upon states to "protect" objects of an archaeological and historical nature. However, again there is emphasis on objects rather than sites. For an interesting discussion of the duties set out in Arts. 149 and 303 and their relationship with the concept of *in situ* protection, see L. Migliorino, "*In Situ* Protection of the Underwater Cultural Heritage under International Treaties and National legislation", (1995) 10 IJMCL 483, 485–487.

[124] Art. 11(2).

[125] Art. 11(3).

[126] Art. 11(4). In establishing a verifiable link in this case, Art. 11(4) provides that "particular regard [shall be] paid to the preferential rights of States of cultural, historical or archaeological origin", thereby at least to some extent echoing the wording of Art. 149 of the LOSC. However, in practice qualifying as a state with a verifiable link is unlikely to be any different here from any other case under the Convention.

[127] Art. 12(2)–(5). Obviously there is no coastal state in this case to act as co-ordinating state so presumably the co-ordinating state will be one of the states with a verifiable link, although there is no requirement that this be so. The co-ordinating state must act "for the benefit of humanity as a whole, on behalf of all States Parties" and "[p]articular regard" must be paid "to the preferential rights of States of cultural, historical or archaeological origin": Art. 12(6). Cf. Art. 10(6): see note 112 above. While the wording of Art. 12(6) is designed to reflect the content of Arts. 140 and 149 of the LOSC, it is unlikely to make any practical difference.

[128] Art. 12(3).

Director-General of UNESCO since it must act as a conduit for all reports, and must also co-ordinate declarations of interest by states with a verifiable interest. The Director-General will therefore need to set in place an organisational framework to handle these matters and UNESCO will need to devote resources for this. There will also need to be liaison between UNESCO and the ISA. The ISA was set up under the LOSC as "the organisation through which States Parties shall ... organise and control activities in the Area, particularly with a view to administering the resources of the Area."[129] According to Hayashi, the ISA's role under the LOSC is limited to controlling activities connected with the exploration and exploitation of mineral resources and no role was intended for it in respect of the UCH.[130] However, the new Convention does not envisage that the ISA should have responsibility for controlling activities affecting UCH in the Area, but simply that it should be notified of finds and involved in consultations concerning how best to protect them. This involvement seems entirely appropriate. After all, it is not possible to completely separate issues relating to different activities in the Area, any more than it is in any other part of the sea. Mineral exploration and exploitation activities clearly have the potential to endanger the UCH, and measures to protect the UCH may clearly impact on such activities. Indeed, it is interesting to note that in July 2000 the ISA adopted regulations in respect of mineral exploration in the Area that require that contractors immediately notify the Secretary-General of any finds of archaeological objects, and also require that this information be transmitted to the Director-General of UNESCO.[131] Furthermore, contractors must take all reasonable measures to avoid disturbing such objects.[132]

Some idea of the potential extent of the interrelationship between the mineral exploration regime and the UNESCO Convention's UCH regime can be gleaned from the following statement of the Secretary-General of the ISA to the ISA's Assembly:

"In the event that the UNESCO Convention enters into force, it would appear that there are two main implications for the Authority. On the one hand, in approving an application for a plan of work for exploration in an area where a finding of underwater cultural heritage has been notified in accordance with the UNESCO Convention, the Legal and Technical Commission and the Council [of the ISA] would need to take into account

---

[129] LOSC, Art. 157(1). See also Art. 157(2), which provides that "[t]he powers and functions of the Authority shall be those expressly conferred upon it by this Convention. The Authority shall have such incidental powers, consistent with this Convention, as are implicit in and necessary for the exercise of those powers and functions with respect to activities in the Area."
[130] M. Hayashi, "Archaeological and Historical Objects under the UN Convention on the Law of the Sea", (1996) 20 *Marine Policy* 291, 293.
[131] See Regulations 8 and 34 of the *Regulations on Prospecting and Exploration for Polymetallic Nodules in the Area* (ISBA/6/A/18/Annex, 4 October 2000).
[132] Regulation 34.

the existence of such finding or activity, although there is no suggestion that the mere existence of an item of underwater cultural heritage in a proposed exploration area would prevent the approval of a plan of work for exploration. On the other hand, in the event that the Authority is notified by a contractor of the finding in its exploration area of an object of an archaeological or historical nature, a State party to the UNESCO Convention may wish to invoke the provisions of articles 11 and 12 of that Convention where such object is also part of the underwater cultural heritage. It must be noted, in any event, that the rights and obligations of the contractor arise from the terms of its contract with the Authority."[133]

The relationship between the two regimes clearly gives rise to all sorts of interesting questions. For example, while the Secretary-General stated that "the rights and obligations of the contractor arise from the terms of its contract with the Authority", its rights and obligations are not solely governed by that contract. In particular, a contractor may be subject to the jurisdiction of a state party to the UNESCO Convention under flag state or nationality principles of jurisdiction. It may then find itself under a duty to report a discovery of UCH to two different authorities: the Secretary-General under the mineral exploration regulations, and the state party under Article 11(1) of the Convention.[134] While the Secretary-General's statement that "there is no suggestion that the mere existence of an item of underwater cultural heritage in a proposed exploration area would prevent the approval of a plan of work for exploration" may provide a contractor with some reassurance that reporting a find will not unduly interfere with its planned activities, the spectre of a state party to the Convention "invok[ing] the provisions of Articles 11 and 12" may cause some concern. In practice, the measures a state party could take against the contractor under Articles 11 and 12 are fairly limited, although it is interesting to note that the contractor will not be exempt from such action by reason of the fact that it will be engaged in activities "incidentally affecting", rather than "directed at", UCH. In particular, the contractor's activities could justify a state party in taking emergency action under Article 12(3) to prevent "immediate danger" to UCH, since such danger may arise from any "human activity", not just looting. While the Secretary-General did not refer to it, a state party would also be able to act under Article 5[135] if the contractor is subject to its jurisdiction under flag state or nationality principles of jurisdiction. Even the simple fact that a number of states could legitimately take an interest in the fate of the UCH under Articles 11 and

---

[133] *Report of the Secretary-General of the International Seabed Authority under article 166, paragraph 4, of the United Nations Convention on the Law of the Sea*, ISBA/8/A/5, 7 June 2002, para. 58.
[134] Although the contractor would not have an intention to engage in activities "directed at" the UCH, such intention is not necessary for the reporting requirement under Art. 11(1) to be triggered: a discovery of UCH is enough.
[135] See further p. 65, especially note 31 above.

12, may mean that the situation will look quite politically discomforting. As a result of all this, contractors may think twice about reporting any finds.[136]

The drafters of the Convention have probably made the most of the opportunities open to them to create a protective regime for the Area while working within the tight constraints of the LOSC. However, the range of measures available to either the co-ordinating state or states parties in general to prevent threats to the UCH, or at least to make sure that any interference is undertaken in accordance with the Rules in the Annex, is limited in much the same way as the provisions in Article 10, paragraphs (3) to (6) in respect of the EEZ and continental shelf. Furthermore, in respect of the Area, the Convention is unfortunately unable to make available a powerful provision like Article 10(2).

Sanctions

Under Article 17 states parties are required to impose sanctions for violation of measures they have taken to implement the Convention.[137] The sanctions taken shall be:

> "adequate in severity to be effective in securing compliance with [the] Convention and to discourage violations wherever they occur *and shall deprive offenders of the benefit deriving from their illegal activities*".[138]

Traditional criminal sanctions, such as fines and prison sentences, will not have the effect of depriving offenders of the benefit they derive from their activities and therefore clearly sanctions of other sorts are envisaged (presumably to be used alongside, rather than instead of, the more traditional penalties). In fact, Article 18 goes on to make provision for a specific sanction of an administrative nature that will have the effect of depriving offenders of the benefit of their activities: that is, the seizure of UCH that has been recovered contrary to the terms of the Convention. This sanction could prove a highly effective deterrent if widely implemented and properly enforced.

Article 18 imposes surprisingly onerous duties upon states parties. They must take measures providing for the seizure of UCH in their territory that has been recovered in a manner not in conformity with the Convention. These measures relate not only to UCH that is *recovered* in their territory, but to any UCH *brought into* their territory at *any* time. Furthermore, the seizure may be from anyone, not only the party who undertook the recovery. Once such seizures have been made, states parties are then required to "record, protect and take all reasonable measures to stabilise" the UCH seized, and to "ensure that its

---

[136] It needs to be borne in mind that only a handful of contractors are currently undertaking exploration activities on the deep sea-bed and the commercial exploitation of mineral resources seems a distant prospect. Therefore, these issues are likely to remain fairly theoretical.

[137] They are also specifically required to co-operate to ensure enforcement of sanctions that are imposed: Art. 17(3).

[138] Art. 17(2). Emphasis added.

disposition be for the public benefit".[139] Notification of seizures must be given to the Director-General of UNESCO and any state with a verifiable link, and the interests of such states must be taken into account in making decisions about the disposition of material. The implementation of these obligations will require the establishment of administrative structures[140] and potentially very significant expenditure on conservation, exhibition, etc. Furthermore, the co-operation and assistance of other states parties, and the provision of information about the provenance of material, will be essential if the system envisaged by the article is to work. Oddly perhaps, Article 18 does not refer specifically to co-operation and information-sharing by states parties. However, Article 19 makes specific provision in this respect. While this article relates to the protection and management of UCH under the Convention generally, it has particular import in relation to Article 18.

The seizure provisions give rise to difficult questions about the deprivation of property rights and possible entitlements to compensation. By virtue of Article 4, there will be no salvage rights or finders' rights to consider, but what about circumstances where the property has not been abandoned and the owner is known? Even where the property is seized from someone other than the owner, the provisions in Article 18(4) regarding disposition suggest that the property is not to be returned to the owner. If this is the case, will the owner be entitled to compensation?[141] Does the material become the property of the seizing state, of a state with a verifiable link, of humankind as a whole, or does it in fact become ownerless? None of these questions are answered by the Convention, and therefore states parties will need to give some thought to how they are going to deal with these issues.[142] While consistency is clearly desirable, different states may take rather different approaches, depending at least to some extent on their domestic legal backgrounds and attitudes to the concept of property.

---

[139] In making provision for its disposition, account must be taken of, *inter alia*, the need for conservation and research; re-assembly of a collection; and public access, exhibition and education.

[140] Art. 22 provides for the establishment of competent authorities or the reinforcement of existing ones to provide for the effective protection and management of the UCH including, presumably, seized UCH.

[141] States party to the First Protocol of the European Convention on Human Rights will also need to consider the implications of Art. 1 of that Protocol. This provides that "no one shall be deprived of his possessions except in the public interest". For a discussion of the article, see P. Fletcher-Tomenius and M. Williams, "The Protection of Wrecks Act 1973: A Breach of Human Rights?", (1998) 13 IJMCL 623.

[142] Questions also arise in relation to the property rights of *bona fide* purchasers. In this respect, note the interrelationship between the seizure provision in Art. 18, and Art. 14, which requires states parties to take measures to prevent "the dealing in, or the possession of, underwater cultural heritage illicitly exported and/or recovered, where recovery was contrary" to the Convention (see above, pp. 76–77, especially note 92).

Dispute Settlement Procedures

The whole framework of the Convention is based on the principle of co-operation between states parties and the preceding discussion of the Convention's control mechanisms shows how reliant these are on states being able to reach agreement on the best means of protecting the UCH. When one examines the detail of these mechanisms, it becomes clear that there is huge potential for disputes to arise. As we have seen, the systems set up by the Convention to deal with UCH discovered in the EEZ or on the continental shelf of a state party, or in the Area, all rely to a large extent upon co-operation and agreement by two or more states. Agreement may also need to be reached between a flag state and a coastal state over measures to be taken in respect of a wrecked state vessel. Where UCH has been the subject of seizure, the seizing state will need to seek the agreement of any state with a verifiable link about the ultimate disposition of the UCH. There is clearly a danger in all these cases that consultations may reach a stalemate, resulting in delays in action and consequent risks to the UCH.

The Convention anticipates that disputes may arise by making provision for settlement procedures in Article 25. States parties in dispute may choose any means of settlement, provided it is peaceful.[143] If the dispute is not settled by those means within a reasonable time, it may be submitted to UNESCO for mediation, provided that the parties agree that this should occur.[144] If no settlement is reached by these means, provision is made for resort to the complex dispute settlement machinery set out in Part XV of the LOSC. A controversial question is whether or not non-state parties to the LOSC will be bound to use these procedures. This question arises because of the wording of Article 25(3):

> "If mediation is not undertaken or if there is no settlement by mediation, the provisions relating to the settlement of disputes set out in Part XV of the United Nations Convention on the Law of the Sea apply *mutatis mutandis* to any dispute between States Parties to this Convention concerning the interpretation or application of this Convention, *whether or not they are also Parties to the United Nations Convention on the Law of the Sea.*"[145]

Non-state parties to the LOSC have already expressed concern about this provision,[146] but O'Keefe suggests that Article 291(2) of the LOSC overrides it. This provides that the dispute settlement procedures in Part XV shall be open to non-states parties and other entities only as specifically provided for by the LOSC. Whether or not this is the case, the complexity of the LOSC machinery is likely to ensure that it will rarely if ever be resorted to. Where states parties fail to

---

[143] Art. 25(1).
[144] Art. 25(2).
[145] Emphasis added.
[146] O'Keefe, note 11 above, p. 137.

resolve a dispute themselves, the mediation services of UNESCO or, indeed, the Meeting of States Parties[147] should be able to negotiate a settlement.

Conclusions

Twenty-five years after the Council of Europe accorded the first international recognition of the need for a convention to protect the UCH, such a convention now exists, and there is a serious prospect of it coming into force. This, in itself, is a major achievement. The fact that it adds considerable flesh to Articles 149 and 303 of the LOSC, and creates a bold and ambitious framework for the protection of the UCH, is even more remarkable. However, the price for this may have been the failure to achieve a consensus on the final text. Nonetheless, on balance it is probably better to have a strong convention acceptable to many, than a watered-down convention acceptable to all, especially when some states—notably the USA—are unlikely to sign in any event.

The fact that the Convention relies heavily upon flag state, nationality and territorial principles of jurisdiction means that—unless it is widely adopted by both flag states and coastal states—treasure hunters will be able to evade its control mechanisms by using "flags of convenience" and "ports of convenience". The strength of the vote in favour of the Convention in 2001 suggests that the Convention may be quite widely adopted by coastal states, but it seems unlikely that significant flag states, including the USA and UK, will sign. The holes that this will create in the protective system, together with the inevitable difficulties of enforcement (especially in the wide expanses of the open oceans), mean that the effectiveness of the Convention will probably be patchy at best.

Nonetheless, the Convention is still likely to have considerable influence. Its very existence may encourage courts and legislatures in non-contracting states to continue a process that has already begun of modifying traditional principles of salvage law to take into account archaeological considerations.[148] The standards set out in the Annex to the Convention may well become the benchmark for the treatment of UCH even in non-contracting states.[149] The fact that the Convention encourages co-operation between states and the adoption of inter-state agreements means that such agreements may become increasingly common, adopted by both states parties to the Convention and non-contracting states.[150]

---

[147] See p. 69 above.
[148] For details, see P. Fletcher-Tomenius, *et al.*, "Salvor in Possession: Friend or Foe to Marine Archaeology?", (2000) 9 *International Journal of Cultural Property* 263–314.
[149] The UK government, for example, has made it clear that it supports most, if not all, of the provisions in the Annex: "UK Explanation of Vote", circulated by the Foreign and Commonwealth Office to interested parties on 31 October 2001. See also P. Roberts and S. Trow, *Taking to the Water: English Heritage's Initial Policy for the Management of Maritime Archaeology in England* (English Heritage, 2002), para. 7.3.
[150] The fact that both the USA and the UK have been engaged in negotiating such an agreement in respect of the *Titanic* shows that these states are not adverse to this sort of international co-operation to protect culturally significant wreck sites. See further, note 49 above.

Furthermore, if those states that become party to the Convention assert their rights over the contiguous zone (under Article 8), and over the continental shelf and EEZ (especially under Article 10(2)), this may encourage non-contracting states to extend their jurisdictions, especially if there is seen to be a developing customary rule of law in this respect.[151] Most significantly of all perhaps, now that the legitimacy of commercially motivated recovery of UCH has been called into question at an international level, there is likely to be a gradual hardening of attitudes towards the treasure salvage industry.[152] While it presently operates openly and, indeed, courts a great deal of publicity for its exploits, within the foreseeable future there is a very real likelihood that its activities will be forced underground. If this is the case, the impact of the Convention will have been profound.

---

[151] Indeed, the USA has already shown itself willing to exercise jurisdiction beyond traditional territorial limits. For example, it asserts jurisdiction in respect of submerged cultural resources in the EEZ under the National Marine Sanctuaries Act of 1972 (NMSA) (as amended in 1992): see further R. Elia, "US Protection of Underwater Cultural Heritage Beyond the Territorial Sea: Problems and Prospects", (2000) 29 *International Journal of Nautical Archaeology* 43–56. Also, under Presidential Proclamation 7219 of 2 September 1999, the USA declared a contiguous zone 24nm from baselines, and this will aid the enforcement of the NMSA and several other archaeologically-related statutes: see *ibid*. See also the *Craft* litigation outlined in O. Varmer, "United States of America" in S. Dromgoole (ed.), *Legal Protection of the Underwater Cultural Heritage: National and International Perspectives* (1999), pp. 216–217.

[152] Much furore has been caused by the UK government's decision to enter into an agreement with a US marine exploration company for the recovery of material from the seventeenth century warship, HMS *Sussex* (see further note 38 above). Among the arguments being used by those with serious concerns about the agreement is the fact that it appears to be in breach of the spirit, if not the letter, of the UNESCO Convention: see, e.g. the speech of Lord Renfrew of Kaimsthorn in a debate on heritage assets in the House of Lords, asking a government Treasury spokesperson to explain the "apparent disparity" between the government's action in entering into a commercial agreement in respect of HMS Sussex and its recorded support for the principles, if not the detail, of the UNESCO Convention: see Hansard, H.L. Col. 92, 28 October 2002.

[10]

Heritage Trouble: Recent Work on the Protection of Intangible Cultural Property

Michael F. Brown*

Abstract: A major factor driving contemporary concerns about the fate of intangible cultural property is the rise of the Information Society, which has proven adept at stripping information from the cultural contexts that give it meaning. Efforts to preserve intangible heritage have tended to follow Information Society models by proposing that heritage be inventoried, then removed from the public domain and returned to the exclusive control of its putative creators. This essay reviews recent scholarly work and policy initiatives related to intangible cultural property, with an eye toward identifying their merits and flaws. It argues for a more ecological perspective, one that takes account of the unpredictable quality of information flows as well as the costs of attempting to manage them. Also explored are some of the difficult, unanswered questions about whether all intangible cultural heritage is equally worthy of protection.

When comparing today's discussions of cultural property with those taking place only two decades ago, one is immediately struck by the radical broadening of the field's scope. Prior to the early 1980s, "cultural property" was invoked largely to denote portable works of art and architectural monuments that embodied the history and identity of particular peoples or nation-states. Today the expression is applied to things as disparate in their scale and characteristics as human remains, art genres, and regional landscapes. Indigenous-rights advocates have gone so far as to identify biological species (as distinct from plant or animal *populations*) as items of cultural or intellectual property.[1] Even though the most sweeping of these cultural-property claims stand little chance of garnering support from policy-makers and the general

---

*Department of Anthropology and Sociology, Williams College. Email: mbrown@williams.edu

ACKNOWLEDGMENTS. This article benefited greatly from the thoughtful criticism of Alexander Bauer, Stuart Kirsch, John H. Merryman, Daniel Shapiro, and Madhavi Sunder, for which I am grateful. Any errors of fact or interpretation are my own.

public, the mere fact that they are made speaks eloquently about the spirit of our times.

The force that John Henry Merryman refers to as "cultural internationalism" emerged in the late nineteenth and early twentieth centuries in response to concerns about the destruction of cultural treasures in wartime. What drove efforts to protect cultural property was an emerging conviction that, as the Hague Convention of 1954 put it, "damage to cultural property belonging to any people whatsoever means damage to the cultural heritage of all mankind, since each people makes its contribution to the culture of the world."[2] By the 1970s, however, growing interest in folkloric traditions, especially those of the world's indigenous peoples, prompted discussion about whether a focus on monuments and portable art was too narrow and, by implication, ethnocentric. Many of the cultural treasures of indigenous and peasant societies are found in oral traditions and public events of one sort or another, and the significance of these intangible, performative resources often outweighs that of material culture. Surely, it was argued, these merit the same consideration as cathedrals and archaeological sites.

In tandem with a marked expansion of scope there has arisen a tendency to substitute the expression "cultural heritage" for cultural property. This shift, by no means consistent or complete, signals growing doubt about the universality of Western notions of property and widespread recognition that culture cannot be reduced to an inventory of objects without marginalizing its most important features.[3] The dematerialization of heritage–the rising salience of stories, designs, musical forms, and information in discussions of heritage protection–offers the prospect of more comprehensive management of traditional cultural productions, yet it also creates daunting complexities for policy-makers.

This article reviews recent work in the area of heritage protection, with particular emphasis on books, essays, and policy documents published since 2000 that focus on intangible cultural property. I write as an anthropologist who only recently has begun to grapple with the sophisticated debates on cultural property offered by art historians, museum professionals, and legal scholars, many of whom have been thinking about these questions for decades. I have experienced a newcomer's thrill when encountering the dazzling erudition of the field's leading figures as well as a newcomer's perplexity at the narrowness with which certain influential arguments are formulated. It is impossible to survey the emerging literature without noticing that some of the assumptions which undergird debates on cultural property fail to serve the field's expanding ambitions. What made perfect sense when debate focused primarily on the fate of paintings, churches, and archaeological sites becomes questionable when applied to other kinds of cultural productions.

Much as early work in cultural property led scholars to rethink the meaning of property, so work on intangible cultural heritage must remain attentive to the broader significance of *information*, including the practical, political, and moral impact of its proposed regulation. Information answers to its own rules. Most conspicuously, it can reside in an infinite number of places simultaneously. The homelessness of information undermines the distinction between real and counterfeit, just as it weakens the bonds that tie units of information together in meaningful systems.[4]

My goal in the present essay is to identify the roots of what can be defined loosely as "heritage trouble"—that is, diffuse global anxiety about the movement of information among different cultures—and to assess proposed strategies for responding to it. I shall underscore the virtues of thinking about information ecologically, as a total system of mutually influencing relationships and forces.[5] Ecological thinking is characterized by holism and awareness of interconnections. It recognizes that the management of complex systems demands attention not to one variable but to many, and that there will always be uncertainty about how changes in individual variables affect the whole.[6] An ecological approach to intangible cultural property resists the siren call of monolithic solutions, exhorting instead that we consider all components of the information ecosystem when contemplating reforms in any of its subsystems. Unfortunately, the nature of modern advocacy work leads many of those involved in heritage protection to keep their sights fixed narrowly on the goal of defending intangible culture, however defined. The resulting proposals may ignore how that laudable objective amplifies, conflicts with, or otherwise reshapes information policies elsewhere in society.[7]

BACKGROUND: THE RISE OF THE INFORMATION SOCIETY

Public discussions of intangible cultural heritage that began in the 1990s were shaped by a cluster of interrelated social forces. Arguably the most important was the rise of what has been variously labeled the "Information Society," the "Information Age," the "Knowledge Economy," or, most recently, the "Network Society." The latter appellation is associated with the work of Manuel Castells, who in a series of influential books and articles has argued that new information technologies have transformed global society just as radically as the Industrial Revolution changed the nineteenth-century world. In a summary assessment of his theory of the Network Society, Castells identifies its three major effects: (1) the creation of new economies based on information rather than on the manufacture of material goods; (2) the globalization of corporations and public institutions, with a corresponding shift in power away from the traditional nation-state; and (3) the forging of new networks that, among other things, reconfigure labor relations, politics, and economic activity.[8]

There are reasons to be skeptical of Castells' sweeping claims, not the least of which is that the United States, presumably the apotheosis of the Network Society, continues to spend more on old-fashioned durable goods and energy resources, now largely imported from other countries, than it generates in information exports, suggesting that this new economy may not be as sustainable as its prophets believe.[9] Nevertheless, the work of Castells and like-minded social theorists brings into focus trends whose importance is beyond dispute. These include the phenomenon of globalization in its multiple manifestations and the meteoric rise of intellectual property rights (IPR) as a matter of global contention.

Globalization has become a convenient scapegoat for anything that seems unjust or disorienting about contemporary life. Yet all but the most intransigent globophobes admit that its effects are not entirely negative. The salience of intangible cultural property as a matter of worldwide concern, as well as the ability of advocacy groups to muster international support for heritage protection, are both examples of globalization's positive effects. There is little question, however, that the intrusion of cosmopolitan news and entertainment media into even the most isolated outposts of humanity has evoked anxiety in many quarters. Citizens fear that their languages, traditional practices, and values are being subverted by cultural influences originating elsewhere, mostly in the developed West. Time itself is thus transformed from a local phenomenon to a global one, pushed by 24-hour news reporting and nonstop trading in world financial markets. These factors have led to demands that the movement of alien images and information be regulated in the interests of local cultural integrity. In Europe and the United States, a juggernaut of media consolidation has given rise to fears that artistic creativity and the expression of diverse viewpoints are seriously imperiled.[10]

Academic opinion in the past decade has steadily shifted from an indulgent view of cultural mixing, characterized by appreciation for its charming ironies and postmodern playfulness, to a more critical stance emphasizing the extent to which the global flows of culture may threaten a community's sense of its own authenticity. A rare dissent is registered by the economist Tyler Cowen, whose book *Creative Destruction* reviews the evidence and concludes that global monopolies and imported technologies often promote local creativity by creating lucrative markets for innovative, high-quality artistic productions. Examples include Tuvan throat singing from Mongolia, local interest in which has been stimulated by sales of recordings abroad and a recent American feature film, and the colorful cotton *molas* produced by the Kuna people of Panama, a synthetic art form that combined a tradition of bark painting with sewing techniques and materials acquired from Europeans.[11] Neither a simpleminded defense of free trade nor an antiglobalization screed, Cowen's book offers a nuanced assessment of the positive and negative impacts of cultural flows, including their power to generate new forms of local authenticity.

More is at stake than authenticity in the contemporary crisis of cultural heritage. By its nature, the Information Society undermines social norms and institutions, thus magnifying the importance of culture, defined narrowly as a set of values and moral commitments. Cultural identity itself may become, as the anthropologist Simon Harrison has observed, a scarce resource to be defended as another form of property, either personal or collective. Heritage, the retrospective expression of culture, is likewise transformed into a highly politicized commodity.[12]

Meanwhile, the rising economic importance of information has served to magnify the value of IPR. Copyrights, patents, trademarks, and trade secrets have become keys to prosperity in an era when controlling prototypes is at least as profitable as actually replicating them.[13] Global markets require global regimes of control to protect IPR, hence the TRIPs (*Trade-Related Aspects of Intellectual Property*) agreement and similar legal instruments that have become a target of globalization's many critics. More significant than efforts to expand the reach of IPR in space (through agreements such as TRIPs) and in time (through industry's never-ending campaign to lengthen the terms of copyrights and patents) is the dramatic broadening of what is held to be intellectual property in the first instance. Software engineering and biotechnology have opened new panoramas for the assertion of IPR, including gene sequences, life-forms, and the manipulation of information in databases. These social forces have converged to incite a moral panic about intellectual property and its impact on the political, cultural, and economic life of societies everywhere.

CULTURAL APPROPRIATION IN THE CONTEXT OF INFORMATION SOCIETIES

An unsettling characteristic of the Information Society is its power to strip the smallest bits of performative content (i.e., information, in the Batesonian sense of "a difference that makes a difference") from their value-context and then use technology to put these bits to work, typically with the goal of realizing a profit. This ability to pluck images, sounds, and practices from their original setting and relocate them elsewhere has received various labels, the broadest being "cultural appropriation." Questions of cultural appropriation have given rise to a wave of work assessing the movement of cultural elements from the politically weak to the politically strong. The reverse process, appropriation of cultural products by the weak (e.g., the flamboyant violation of copyrights on popular music and film common in the developing world) is either ignored entirely or celebrated as an act of cultural resistance.[14]

Cultural appropriation is held to be wrong for two main reasons. First, it is disrespectful of the cultural values of the source community, which rarely has sanctioned the imitation of its creations by outsiders. Second, it subjects that community to material harm, either by denying it legitimate economic benefits or by undermining shared understandings essential to its social health.

Respect is notoriously difficult to guarantee by legislative means, even if minority communities can be afforded legal safeguards to protect them from overt discrimination. For this reason, critiques of cultural appropriation gravitate to the question of material damages, with an eye toward the promotion of legal reforms that would compensate communities for such harms and, better still, prevent them from happening in the first place. The goal of rectifying civil wrongs thrusts heritage protection into the provinces of intellectual property and tort law. It is therefore hardly surprising that legal scholars have done much of the heavy lifting in debates about cultural ownership.[15]

A typical article on law and intangible heritage goes something like this. The author notes the injustices arising from the ability of outsiders to alienate elements of traditional knowledge or expressive culture at will, largely because folklore is legally defined as residing in the public domain, where it is accessible to all. There is then a review of ways that existing intellectual property law might be modified to encompass folklore and traditional knowledge—say, by making it subject to trade-secrets statutes, broadening the definition of trademark, or by inventing marks of authenticity for folkloric products. This is followed by a systematic survey of other areas of law that might offer additional protections: land titling, antidefamation statutes and notions of group libel, historic-preservation law, civil-rights law, legislation mandating the repatriation of human remains and sacred objects, and international human-rights protocols. The prototype article closes by observing that none of these legal strategies fit the circumstances of intangible heritage particularly well and that it probably makes sense to create new *sui generis* regulatory regimes to meet the specific needs of traditional communities, especially indigenous ones.[16]

Anthropologists, who have also been prominent contributors to cultural-property debates, share the progressive sentiments that motivate legal scholarship on cultural protection, but they often express uneasiness about law's received categories. Most social anthropologists, in fact, have never met a category they weren't prepared to deconstruct—or, as the expression goes, to "problematize." From this habit of mind arises the impulse to reject the commodification inherent in the very notion of cultural property and to express doubts about the way the culture concept in general is represented in international forums such as UNESCO. Objections to granting culture transcendent legal status stress the concept's tendency to freeze social life in time, to imagine stable boundaries where none exist, and to attribute to social groups (especially indigenous ones) a vague, even mystical otherness. These familiar arguments reflect an underlying resentment that anthropology's concept of culture was hijacked by global policymakers just as many anthropologists were preparing to abandon it.[17]

In the most recent work, however, scholars are moving beyond the critique of culture to a more pragmatic appreciation of the concept's utility. Bruce Robbins and Elsa Stamatopoulou urge anthropologists to get past their fear of "theoretical incorrectness" and recognize that pursuit of cultural rights offers the advantage of helping indigenous peoples achieve a degree of self-determination without directly challenging the territorial integrity of the nation-state. They view the culture concept's vagueness as an asset rather than as a liability.[18]

Anthropologists may be making peace with culture, but they are also beginning to question the validity and political implications of "the indigenous" as a category of people. In North and South America, indigenousness is easy to define, at least in principle: it refers to the descendants of the New World's original inhabitants. (Because of generations of intermarriage and cultural blending, however, the question of which individuals qualify as indigenous remains irksome.) In regions such as South Asia and Africa, in contrast, claims of prior occupation may be extremely divisive in political arenas already plagued by violence and instability. The rise of indigenism and the special rights that it typically advances—to say nothing of the romance and primal authenticity with which native culture is imbued in the popular imagination—have made it increasingly attractive to claim, or reclaim, an indigenous identity. Debates about indigenous identities seem destined to intensify in the coming years.[19]

In legal scholarship, initial enthusiasm about prospects for modifying intellectual property laws to protect intangible heritage seems to be cooling. The most recent work is characterized by greater skepticism about the utility of IPR law, recognition of the value of legal flexibility, and an openness to alternative formulations. One of the most persistent alternatives, dating back to the path-breaking work of Darrell Posey and Graham Dutfield in the mid-1990s, insists that indigenous cultures must be seen as total social systems in which land, the natural environment, social practices, and traditional knowledge form a seamless whole. Expressing sentiments similar to Posey and Dutfield's, Russel L. Barsh declares that for indigenous peoples "knowledge is indistinguishable from land and culture," an observation that Barsh uses to argue against piecemeal, reductionist legal strategies of cultural protection.[20]

At a high level of abstraction, Barsh's observation is surely correct. Still, I've yet to meet an indigenous person incapable of telling the difference between, say, a mountain and a ritual, even if the two are linked symbolically. What Barsh means by knowledge is really closer to wisdom, understanding permeated by moral meaning. The gap between "data" on the one hand and "wisdom" on the other is the crux of the conflict between Information Societies and folkloric ones. As the anthropologist Marilyn Strathern observes, "The market thus disembeds what is usable, whereas the thrust of the indigenous IPR movement is to re-embed, re-contextualize, indigenous ownership in indigenous traditional culture. Tradition, we may remark, is an embedding concept."[21]

Although the speed and pervasiveness of this disembedding are surely new, the reduction of sacred wholes to their component parts has been with us since the Enlightenment. And since the Enlightenment, antireductionists have come forward to oppose the analytical dismantling of whatever has arrested the attention of scientists and humanist intellectuals: sacred texts, the human body, works of art, or the speciation of the planet's flora and fauna. When President George W. Bush implements a policy that limits research involving embryonic stem cells, he is taking a similarly antireductive stance—in this case, by refusing to allow unrestricted access to cells that may have originated in a human fetus, which Bush and others insist must be seen as a sacred whole rather than as a morally neutral aggregation of tissues.

This observation should not be interpreted as a defense of current information practices or criticism of efforts to restrict exploitation of indigenous knowledge. It is simply to note that the rejection of categorical distinctions is a time-honored tactic for setting one group apart from others. It may serve a useful purpose—for instance, by challenging the views of policymakers who gravitate too readily toward conventional categories ("art," "biological knowledge," "monument," "property") that may mean something quite different, or be meaningless altogether, for particular communities. But in a world organized around the parsing of differences, insistence that no distinctions are legitimate presents a formidable obstacle to legal reform. It makes a compelling sound bite but contributes little to the cause of intercultural dialogue. In the case of indigenous-rights policies, the claim that land and culture are indistinguishable also casts a shadow over the aspirations of those indigenous peoples who lack a traditional land base but maintain commitments to native values.

Less sweeping in their claims, but more subtly subversive in their implications, are emerging ethnographic studies of views of cultural ownership in specific places, as distinct from the abstract and often romanticized depictions of traditional ownership practices that typically dominate policy discussions in multilateral organizations such as UNESCO. Many of these studies come from Papua New Guinea, a region that has turned exchange relations into an art form. In one such study, James Leach shows that for the people of Papua New Guinea's Rai Coast, elements of culture are seen as more useful and productive in circulation than when returned to their source. These customary practices and beliefs challenge UNESCO's view that the default setting for human communities is an overwhelming desire to possess and control cultural property. For Leach's Rai Coast interlocutors, repatriation severs relationships instead of strengthening them. The case illustrates how matters that seem relatively simple from afar reveal surprising complexities on the ground.[22]

INFORMATION SOCIETY SOLUTIONS TO INFORMATION SOCIETY PROBLEMS?

A significant landmark in global efforts to protect traditional knowledge and cultural productions is UNESCO's adoption of the Convention for the Safeguarding of the Intangible Cultural Heritage (CSICH) at the organization's 32nd General Conference in 2003. The convention calls for a range of measures "aimed at ensuring the viability of the intangible cultural heritage, including the identification, documentation, research, preservation, protection, promotion, enhancement, transmission, particularly through formal and non-formal education, as well as the revitalization of the various aspects of such heritage."[23]

The CSICH should be seen in the context of UNESCO's broader efforts to promote global information democracy while at the same time validating the right of nations to defend their cultures against unwanted external influence. The most controversial measure under consideration is a draft treaty, usually referred to as the Convention on Cultural Diversity, that proposes to defend local cultures by validating the right of member states to control the importation of alien cultural products, including books, films, and recorded music. Such a policy is vigorously opposed by the world's largest media corporations, disproportionately based in the United States, who denounce it as a threat to free expression and an unwelcome restraint of trade.[24] If implemented, UNESCO's cultural diversity convention would register its most immediate impact on national media industries. In contrast, the CSICH is directed primarily to preindustrial, folkloric traditions.

One of the ironies of the CSICH is that its language and administrative strategies are patterned on the very Information Society practices they are ostensibly trying to counter. The convention portrays intangible heritage as an objectified resource amenable to modern management techniques. In such a legalistic vision, heritage cannot be protected until it is thoroughly documented. Hence the CSICH's call for preparation of "one or more inventories of the intangible cultural heritage present in [each nation's] territory." The scale of the required list-making beggars the imagination, especially for large or conspicuously multiethnic states such as Russia, China, India, and Canada, to say nothing of Papua New Guinea, and Peru. The policy is oddly reminiscent of early anthropology, which was driven by the conviction that primitive cultures should be documented in their entirety—from basketry techniques and healing arts to kinship systems and religious beliefs—because their extinction was inevitable. The discipline long ago concluded that documentation has only a modest role in the preservation of culture. To think otherwise is to make the classic error of mistaking a map for the territory it represents. So although there is nothing obviously harmful about the CSICH's ambitious program of cultural documentation, one struggles to imagine how it will protect cultures as living, dynamic systems. Perhaps it is enough that the convention ratifies the importance of folkloric cultures by putting the status of local knowledge on the world's agenda as an issue worthy of attention.[25]

The CSICH has inspired a handful of national campaigns to use electronic resources to combat the loss of local traditions. India, for example, has announced plans to "carry out extensive documentation of intangible heritage to provide the preservation of each expression of heritage by making exhaustive inventories and storing them electronically for the future." Unfortunately, there is reason to doubt that such technocratic and top-down approaches to heritage protection have much to offer. First, experts in library science and data management are beginning to confront the startling fragility of electronic records. Digital media degrade far faster than was once recognized. Worse still, the technologies required to read them change so rapidly that within a decade or two many records are orphaned, made unreadable because no one possesses the obsolete equipment required to access them. Second, the Internet and other intrusions of the Information Society have pushed many native peoples toward greater secrecy. The notion that knowledge must be recorded by outsiders in order to save it from loss is impossible to reconcile with the inward-looking, protective turn now observed in many indigenous communities. This shift in the direction of secrecy drives indigenous demands for the "repatriation of information"—that is, the return (and, in rare cases, the destruction) of ethnographic texts and images that communities wish to see removed from the public domain on the grounds that the knowledge documented in these materials should never have been public in the first place. Even when specific indigenous communities do not actively endorse greater secrecy, they are increasingly fearful that documentation of their intangible heritage will not protect it but simply facilitate its exploitation, thus giving the notion of "heritage protection" an

Orwellian connotation. Their preferred strategy is, as one anthropologist has put it, "security through obscurity."²⁶

A more promising Information Society tactic has been adopted by the World Intellectual Property Organization (WIPO) and the American Association for the Advancement of Science, both of which now sponsor online "prior art databases," to which India and China are prominent contributors. The idea behind the databases is to publish traditional pharmacopoeias and thereby prevent patent applicants who draw on them from claiming they have discovered something novel. Whether the prior-art approach can prevail over the indigenous move toward greater secrecy remains to be seen.²⁷

LESSONS, QUESTIONS, PROSPECTS

Weighty questions remain unresolved in global discussions about intangible cultural heritage. One concerns the balance between heritage as a resource for all of humanity and as something that properly belongs to, and remains controlled by, its communities of origin. Most major policy documents on this subject begin by declaring that folklore and traditional knowledge are the common heritage of all humankind. They then outline schemes that would effectively remove much of this knowledge from the global commons and privatize it in the communities where it is thought to have arisen, and where it may be considered communal property. In a discussion of similar tensions in the world of tangible cultural property, John Merryman distinguishes between cultural internationalists and cultural nationalists, the latter holding that items of cultural heritage properly reside in their communities or nations of origin. The internationalist side of the debate has been most recently voiced in the controversial *Declaration on the Importance and Value of Universal Museums* issued by directors of some of the world's most important art museums. There is little doubt, however, that cultural nationalists are in the ascendancy today.²⁸

The contradiction between rhetorical appeals to notions of common human heritage and policies designed to slow the movement of traditional knowledge into the public domain is addressed in a recent essay by the legal scholar and anthropologist Rosemary Coombe, long an incisive commentator on issues of intellectual property and the global ecology of information. Coombe observes that the lively public domain sought by cultural internationalists can only prosper if minority cultures survive the current process of globalization. A cultural public domain, she asserts, depends on responsibilities as well as rights. Such responsibilities would include repudiation of "takings of cultural goods" that "create cultural, social and political harms to peoples for whom cultural forms are more tightly interwoven with specific forms of subsistence in local lifeworlds of meaning." Without a better balance of openness and discretion, in other words, the cultural public domain could be reduced to an ideal devoid of content. This illustrates an aspect of what Tyler Cowen calls the "paradox of diversity." "[T]he world as a whole may be more diverse," he writes, "if some societies refuse to accept diversity as a value. Those cultures will continue to generate highly unique creations, given their status as cultural outliers." Conversely, generalized diversity may produce greater uniformity because of the cultural blending that it inevitably produces.[29]

Coombe's powerful argument for more aggressive sequestration of traditional knowledge leads inevitably to another unresolved question in these debates: Is this best accomplished through modifications of existing law, or should the global community craft *sui generis* regimes to do the job? The case-study material presented in Coombe's essay suggests that the creative use of legal mechanisms already in place can accomplish a great deal. Despite more than a decade of calls for *sui generis* alternatives, relatively few proposals have been laid out in a detailed way, I suspect because when committed to formal language their many flaws are readily apparent. An example is offered by the legal scholar Susan Scafidi, who has proposed a new category of copyright-like protections for "cultural products" such as ethnic festivals.[30] Scafidi's novel proposal is convincing until one begins to imagine the administrative apparatus that would be necessary to implement it on a national or global scale. In common with many such ideas floated in international forums, it seems sublimely detached from the practical circumstances of tribal and peasant communities in much of the developing world, who find themselves at the margins of modern communications and, more to the point, the rule of law. Given the zero-sum nature of budgets at the national and international levels, we must ask whether funds spent on the creation of complex schemes of cultural protection, which are typically administered by nonindigenous elites, might be more responsibly invested in programs that directly benefit target communities. At any rate, considerations of practicality and administrative overhead need to be brought into discussions of novel regimes of cultural protection, just as "transaction costs" must be assessed by governments considering the increasingly expansive forms of intellectual property proposed by industry.

Also rarely discussed is how the world community should respond to intangible heritage that is inconsistent with emerging global moral and ethical norms. What are we to make of the complaint that, for instance, the global ban on commercial whaling is ethnocentric and destructive of traditional Japanese cuisine and Japanese heritage in general? Similar questions have long taken center stage in debates about multiculturalism and democracy, but they are increasingly framed in terms of "rights to heritage," thus piggybacking on public enthusiasm for heritage in its multiple forms.[31] At present, debates about how one reconciles divergent values in pluralist societies intersect only rarely with proposals for the preservation of intangible heritage. Nevertheless, collisions of discrepant values are inevitable. The Orange Order's annual marching rituals in Northern Ireland come immediately to mind. Advocates for these customs deploy the same rhetoric used by defenders of heritage elsewhere. The parades, for instance, are described as the "culture, tradition, and heritage of Ulster Protestants" and "a powerful symbol of their freedom to express their culture."[32] Yet given their harmful impact in a volatile political situation, to say nothing of their glorification of centuries of colonial oppression, do they merit formal recognition and protection? Readers can doubtless think of similarly troubling examples from their own region or cultural community.

Equally challenging is the question of who controls the representation of a community's heritage, especially if de facto ownership of heritage, intangible or otherwise, becomes enshrined in formal law.[33] To a considerable extent this debate turns on what one defines as the optimal balance of individual and cultural rights, a complex philosophical issue beyond the scope of this essay. Suffice to say that an overly broad interpretation of group rights to heritage can lead to situations in which marginalized members of cultural communities (women, gays and lesbians, religious apostates, political dissidents) find themselves silenced by the power of a majority to represent its values and practices to the world at large. The authoritarian potential of cultural rights is easily overstated, of course, and it should not be seen as nullifying their potential value. But any move in the direction of cultural rights requires constant attention to the relationship of the few to the many, of the core values of a cultural community to the internal resistances that give all societies a dynamic political life and ensure their ability to respond successfully to change.[34]

INFORMATION ECOLOGY REVISITED

If we look at the information ecosystem in its totality (see Figure 1), it is obvious that heritage-protection efforts have largely been focused on the IP Domain–specifically, the possible extension of the rights of the IP Domain to traditional communities, which ideally would be complemented by more restricted access for private industry. This is justified but by no means unproblematic. It is easy to *declare* that intangible cultural property now enjoys protections analogous to copyright or patent. It is another matter to determine what qualifies as intangible culture in the first place and then to devise cost-effective mechanisms to protect it. The contemporary heritage crisis invites sweeping claims of cultural ownership that have little basis in fact. In an ethnographic study of American Neo-pagans, for example, Sabina Magliocco mentions that in 1993 neo-pagan groups were denounced by Lakota Indian elders: "Members of the Lakota delegation [to an international gathering of religious leaders] assumed that certain Pagan practices such as worshipping in a circle, invoking the four directions, and purifying with burning herbs were imitations of Native American practice, whereas in fact these particular practices developed independently in Europe, an example of polygenesis [independent invention]."[35]

Efforts to regulate "traditional" expressive culture are bound to have a chilling effect on fair use and artistic expression, especially given the constantly changing, entirely negotiable content of heritage. Free expression is not a social good that trumps every other, of course. Neither is it a right that we should jettison casually. An ecological approach to the IP Domain requires that we maintain a legal high-wire act: balancing the sometimes opposed goals of heritage preservation and the values of an open society.

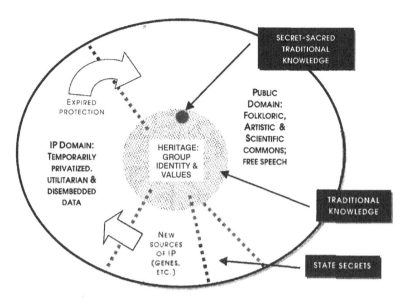

FIGURE 1. Intangible cultural heritage and the information ecosystem (after Graham Dutfield, "The Public and Private Domains," 286)

Subject to more limited consideration, at least thus far, is the public domain and the ways it might be reinvented to promote cultural diversity at the global level. A handful of innovative approaches are worthy of note. The California-based organization Creative Commons, a pioneer in the creation of voluntaristic alternatives to copyright, is working on plans to create a framework for the sharing of scientific databases that will also respect indigenous canons of confidentiality. The Creative Commons is explicitly advancing a vision of a broadened rather than a more restrictive public domain, which admittedly is difficult to square with indigenous concerns about the preservation of knowledge in its original context. But the organization's inventiveness may inspire other groups actively seeking alternatives to existing IPR practices. At the opposite end of the public domain spectrum, but equally intriguing, are efforts to bolster protections for the "Secret-Sacred" zone of the information ecosystem by creating indigenous archives or "keeping places" to secure intangible heritage under conditions of confidentiality consistent with local norms. Because such norms may be illiberal from the perspective of democratic values, however, they raise formidable questions that will be resolved only after vigorous debate and a fair amount of compromise.[36]

An important strategy for survival in situations of ecological stress is crossbreeding or hybridity. New circumstances may require new regulatory approaches. Yet perhaps because hybridity has come to be seen as part of the problem rather than part of the solution, much discussion has focused on whether customary law offers a viable alternative to western IPR concepts. This is appealing because of its consonance with a politics of ethnic sovereignty. One must ask, though, whether the world will be a better place if we replace one expansive, flawed, ethnocentric system by a thicket of small-scale, flawed, ethnocentric systems whose sole virtue is that local communities are familiar with them. Even sympathetic observers acknowledge that wholesale acceptance of customary law would force large multicultural states to deal with dozens or even hundreds of legal systems on a daily basis. Such an explosion of legal diversity would impose an immense administrative burden and conflict with the liberal democratic principle (admittedly, more often declared than realized in fact) that all citizens should be subject to the same laws.[37]

An alternative to formal recognition of customary law is the development of hybrid approaches that interweave elements of western law and local, traditional rules for the circulation of knowledge. Drawing on ideas originating in Papua New Guinea, Marilyn Strathern provides examples of what such hybrid approaches might look like, and we have reason to hope that similarly imaginative thinking will arise elsewhere. The much-cited *Bulun Bulun* decision in Australia (*Bulun Bulun and Milpurrurru v. R & T Textiles*, 1998) may be a harbinger of change because it acknowledges that Aboriginal clan communities have specific fiduciary rights in religious art that must be reckoned with outside their communities, although these rights do not legally qualify as joint authorship.[38] The preponderance of evidence strongly suggests that the best prospects for legal hybridity are at the local rather than the global level, although schemes that work well in one local context are likely to spread to others in an organic way as new approaches to authorship, ownership, and the circulation of cultural resources become familiar to wider publics.

In keeping with a holistic perspective, I close with a final question that expands the analytical frame beyond the information ecosystem. My query is inspired by a provocative essay on human rights by the political philosopher Wendy Brown. Human rights are important, Brown says, but are they "the most that can be hoped for at this point in history?" Might not an unrelenting focus on human rights stand in the way of more far-reaching possibilities for making the world a better place? Human rights advocacy, Brown avers, "is a politics and it organizes political space, often with the aim of monopolizing it."[39]

Similarly unsparing questions must be asked about our current enthusiasm for the management of intangible cultural property. Heritage preservation is, or should be, a means to the end of fostering societies in which minority communities have a voice in decisions about their future and where they can attain the same prosperity available to everyone else, should they choose to do so. Cultural heritage is important to their well-being, but it is not the only issue that merits attention. What about public health, education, and self-government? As the legal scholar Michael H. Davis asks, can massive cultural appropriation of the intangible cultural heritage of indigenous peoples be treated as an autonomous issue, or does it follow more or less inevitably from the power difference between small-scale societies and the world's industrial giants? If the latter, then will new laws regarding folklore and traditional knowledge make much of a difference?[40]

54   MICHAEL F. BROWN

When confronted by the ambitious schemes now emerging on the heritage-protection front—proposals that illuminate with remarkable fidelity Max Weber's vision of a world driven by bureaucratic logic and a compulsion to rationalize—one sometimes wonders whether all the legal creativity risks missing the point. For if global cultural diversity is preserved on digital recording devices while the people who gave rise to this artistry and knowledge have disappeared, then efforts to preserve intangible heritage will be judged a failure. That unhappy prospect should always be kept in mind as we consider comprehensive plans that presume to manage the intellectual and artistic achievements of the world's most vulnerable societies.

ENDNOTES

1. On the insistence that Australia's native species are the intellectual property of Aboriginal Australians, see "Aboriginals up in Arms over Symbols, *The Australian*, 29 January 2002, 2, accessed via Lexis-Nexis. On landscape as indigenous intellectual and cultural property, see Ross Barnett, "Sacred Sights," *The Australian*, 5 March 2004, 14, accessed via Lexis-Nexis; on the heritage status of places construed more broadly, an indispensable recent work is Thomas F. King, *Places That Count*. The status of history and prehistory as intellectual or cultural properties is taken up in George P. Nicholas and Kelly P. Bannister, "Copyrighting the Past?"

2. Quoted in John Henry Merryman, "Two Ways of Thinking About Cultural Property," 836. Useful sources for historical and theoretical background on international efforts to protect indigenous heritage include S. James Anaya, *Indigenous Peoples in International Law*, and Lawrence Rosen, "The Right to Be Different." On the question of whether privately held art should be seen as public cultural property, an important work is Joseph L. Sax, *Playing Darts with a Rembrandt*.

3. See especially Lyndel V. Prott and Patrick J. O'Keefe, "'Cultural Heritage' or 'Cultural Property?'" Although Prott and O'Keefe's arguments for using "cultural heritage" in preference to "cultural property" are persuasive, the latter's inscription in law and international treaties makes it an unavoidable element of contemporary debate. A concise comparison of definitions of cultural property has been posted on the Internet by the Department of Arts Policy and Management, City University of London, at <www.city.ac.uk/artspol/cult-def.html> accessed 24 June 2004. Two recent essays that explore the implications of the now-conventional juxtaposition of culture and property are Michael Rowlands, "Cultural Rights and Wrongs," and Michael F. Brown, "Heritage as Property." For an explanation of the many difficulties that attend the concept of "cultural heritage," see Janet Blake, "On Defining the Cultural Heritage."

4. An engaging survey of the effects of our ability to reproduce images, texts, and sounds at will is Hillel Schwartz, *The Culture of the Copy*.

5. To the best of my knowledge, the concept of "information ecology" has remained underdeveloped, although it is increasingly used in library science and among knowledge-management consultants in business contexts. See, for example, Thomas H. Davenport, *Information Ecology*.

6. These issues are explored, with particular reference the management of business information, in Davenport, *Information Ecology*, 28–45.

7. Stuart Kirsch and others have argued that a second major factor promoting anxiety about cultural heritage is the global diffusion of western property models. For details, see Kirsch, "Property Limits."

8. Castells offers a concise summary of these themes in the essay "Materials for an Exploratory Theory of the Network Society."

9. For a vigorous critique of the work of Castells and like-minded social theorists, see Christopher May, *The Information Society*.

10. On information's transformation of time and space, see Paul Virilio, *The Information Bomb*, 113. Works that consider the impact of monopoly control of global media include Peter Drahos and John Braithwaite, *Information Feudalism*; Lawrence Lessig, *Free Culture*; Kembrew McLeod, *Owning Culture*; and Siva Vaidhyanathan, *Copyrights and Copywrongs*.

11. Tyler Cowen, *Creative Destruction*, 24–33.

12. Simon Harrison, "Identity as a Scarce Resource." On the impact of the Information Society on culture, see especially Scott Lash, *Critique of Information*, 26–27.

13. Lash, op. cit., 81–82.

14. My allusion to the work of Gregory Bateson draws on his essay, "Form, Substance, and Difference," in *Steps to an Ecology of Mind*, 453. The literature on cultural appropriation is too vast to inventory here. Two influential works that bring together a range of perspectives and case-study material are Rosemary J. Coombe, *The Cultural Life of Intellectual Properties*, and Bruce Ziff and Pratima V. Rao, eds., *Borrowed Power*. More recent essay-length works that explore different aspects of appropriation include S. Michelle Erasmus, "Repatriating Words"; Thomas Heyd, "Rock Art Aesthetics and Cultural Appropriation"; Peter Shand, "Scenes from the Colonial Catwalk"; Rebecca Tsosie, "Reclaiming Native Stories"; and James O. Young, "The Ethics of Cultural Appropriation."

15. Studies of heritage protection and IPR published since 2000 by legal scholars include Rachael Grad, "Indigenous Rights and Intellectual Property Law"; William J. Hapiuk, Jr., "Of Kitsch and Kachinas"; Sarah Harding, "Defining Traditional Knowledge"; Terri Janke, "Minding Culture"; Amina Para Matlon, "Safeguarding Native American Sacred Art by Partnering Tribal Law and Equity"; Owen Morgan, "Protecting Indigenous Signs and Trade Marks"; James D. Nason, "Traditional Property and Modern Laws"; Gelvina Rodriguez Stevenson, "Trade Secrets"; Coenraad J. Visser, "Making Intellectual Property Laws Work for Traditional Knowledge"; and Daniel Wüger, "Prevention of Misappropriation of Intangible Cultural Heritage Through Intellectual Property Laws." For sheer comprehensiveness of legal research, Silke von Lewinski, ed., *Indigenous Heritage and Intellectual Property* has few peers.

16. Recent contributions from fields other than law include Michael F. Brown, *Who Owns Native Culture?*; Elizabeth Coleman, "Aboriginal Art and Identity"; Stuart Kirsch, "Lost Worlds"; Mary Riley, ed., *Indigenous Intellectual Property Rights*; and Peter Seitel, ed., *Safeguarding Traditional Cultures*.

17. Among many recent forays into the debate about culture are Jane K. Cowan, Marie-Bénédicte Dembour, and Richard A. Wilson, "Introduction," in *Culture and Rights*; Thomas Hylland Eriksen, "Between Universalism and Relativism"; Clifford Geertz, *Available Light*, 68–88; and Peter J. M. Nas, "Masterpieces of Oral and Intangible Heritage." For a study of how notions of indigenous culture play out in a bioprospecting controversy, see Shane Greene, "Indigenous People Incorporated?"

18. Bruce Robbins and Elsa Stamatopoulou, "Reflections on Culture and Cultural Rights," especially 422 and 426. Various anthropologists have come to similar conclusions, although by different analytical routes. See, for example, James Clifford, "Indigenous Articulations," and the essays in Erich Kasten, ed., *Properties of Culture–Culture as Property*.

19. For an assessment of the global indigenous-rights movement, see Ronald Niezen, *The Origins of Indigenism*. Recent critiques of the notion of indigenousness include John R. Bowen, "Should We Have a Universal Concept of 'Indigenous Peoples' Rights?'" and Adam Kuper, "The Return of the Native."

20. Work raising doubts about IPR approaches includes Sarah Harding, "Cultural Property and the Limitations of Preservation," and Stephen D. Osborne, "Protecting Tribal Stories." My allusion to the work of Darrell A. Posey and Graham Dutfield refers to *Beyond Intellectual Property*. The passage by Russel Barsh is from "How Do You Patent a Landscape?" 40.

21. Marilyn Strathern, *Property, Substance, and Effect*, 167.

22. James Leach, "Owning Creativity"; see also Jacob L. Simet, "Copyrighting Traditional Tolai Knowledge?"; Marilyn Strathern, "Multiple Perspectives on Intellectual Property"; and the essays in Lawrence Kalinoe and James Leach, eds., *Rationales of Ownership*.

23. Article 2, section 3.

24. On the proposed cultural diversity convention, see Peter Ford, "Global Pushback Against 'Titanic' Culture," *Christian Science Monitor*, 20 October 2003, 1. Ironically, at least some media critics in the United States are beginning to complain that globalizing media have undermined the quality of Amer-

ican arts and culture as well. See David Kipen, "Offshoring the Audience," for an assessment of how pressures to make movies that sell as well abroad as in the U.S. now militate against screenplays that address uniquely American experiences and dilemmas.

25. The passage quoted from the CSICH is from Article 12, section 1. I express my reservations about the CSICH in greater detail in "Safeguarding the Intangible." My essay prompted a thoughtful rejoinder from Richard Kurin, director of the Smithsonian Center for Folklife and Cultural Heritage, who participated actively in UNESCO debates about the specific language of the CSICH. Although acknowledging the convention's flaws, Kurin argues that the CSICH will have a constructive effect because it asserts that "the practice of one's culture is a human right" and confirms that "all cultures give purpose and meaning to lives and thus deserve to be safeguarded." See Kurin, "Tangible Progress."

26. Information on India's heritage protection plan is from Akshaya Mukul, "Government's Intangible Heritage Plan," *Times of India*, 2 October 2003, <www.timesofindia.com>, accessed 26 October 2003. On the fragility of digital records, see Alexander Stille, "Are we losing our memory?" The practical, legal, and ethical issues surrounding group secrecy, are discussed in Brown, *Who Owns Native Culture?* 27–42, and Harding, "Cultural Secrecy and the Protection of Cultural Property." The expression "security through obscurity" comes from Eric C. Kansa, personal communication.

27. World Intellectual Property Organization (WIPO), "Portal of Online Databases and Registries of Traditional Knowledge and Genetic Resources" <www.wipo.int/tk/en/databases/tkportal/index.html Geneva>, accessed 28 July 2004; American Association for the Advancement of Science (AAAS), "Traditional Ecological Knowledge Prior Art Database" <ip.aaas.org/tekindex.nsf Washington, DC>, accessed 28 July 2004.

28. John Henry Merryman, "Two Ways of Thinking About Cultural Property," especially 846. The difficulty of reconciling the universal and local ownership of cultural heritage is explored in Blake, "On Defining the Cultural Heritage." The *Declaration on the Importance and Value of Universal Museums* was issued in 2002, and copies are available in multiple sources on the Internet.

29. Rosemary J. Coombe, "Fear, Hope, and Longing for the Future of Authorship and a Revitalized Public Domain in Global Regimes of Intellectual Property," 1185; Cowen, *Creative Destruction*, 146.

30. Susan Scafidi, "Intellectual Property and Cultural Products."

31. Calvin Sims, "Japan, Feasting on Whale, Sniffs at 'Culinary Imperialism' of U.S," *New York Times*, 10 August 2000, A1. A Japanese dentist quoted in the article remarks, "As a child, we ate miso soup with whale meat every New Year's Eve. It was a centuries-old tradition in my village. You can't imagine how precious this soup is to me right now." In comments on an earlier draft of this paper, Stuart Kirsch pointed out that the renewal of traditional whaling among the Makah Indians of Washington State is justified in language similar to that of advocates for Japanese whaling. He wondered why I do not mention the Makah case in the same paragraph. He makes a valid point, although I would insist that the scale of whaling in the two cases is so different that the Makah merit different treatment.

32. See, for instance, the website entitled "Protestant Parades in Northern Ireland," <www.ulsterloyal.freeservers.com/parades_culture_tradtion.html>, accessed 26 July 2004. One of the few works that addresses awkward conflicts about the nature and value of "heritage" is Robert Shannan Peckham, ed., *Rethinking Heritage*. For observations on the politics of remembering and forgetting, see David Lowenthal, *The Heritage Crusade and the Spoils of History*.

33. An essay that sounds a cautionary note in this regard is Madhavi Sunder, "Intellectual Property and Identity Politics." See also her "Cultural Dissent."

34. For a vigorous defense of cultural rights, see Bruce Robbins and Elsa Stamatopoulou, "Reflections on Culture and Cultural Rights." In contrast, the political scientist Brian Barry, in *Culture and Equality*, argues that most important collective rights are adequately encompassed, and with fewer risks to individual freedom, by a broad interpretation of liberal theories about individuals' right of free association. A centrist position not unsympathetic to cultural rights but sensitive to their potential problems is argued in Lawrence G. Sager, "The Free Exercise of Culture."

35. Two key works that come closest to following an ecological approach to information rights are James Boyle, *Shamans, Software, and Spleens*, and Rosemary J. Coombe, *The Cultural Life of Intellectual*

Properties. Also notable for its holism is Graham Dutfield, "The Public and Private Domains." On Lakota claims of ownership of religious practices, see Sabina Magliocco, *Witching Culture*, 234.

36. Creative Commons provides background information on its history and goals in its website, <www.creativecommons.org>. A statement by the College of Indigenous Aboriginal Peoples of New South Wales, Australia, explains that part of its mission is to serve as a "keeping place for the safe protection of Indigenous Intellectual and Cultural Property and the advancement of shared scholarship with Bundjalung Elders" <www.dev.scu.edu.au/schools/ciap>, accessed 28 July 2004.

37. Silke von Lewinski, "Final Considerations," in S. von Lewinski, ed., *Indigenous Heritage and Intellectual Property*, 386–387, regarding the difficulties of recognizing customary law in pluralist states.

38. See especially Strathern's *Property, Substance, and Effect*, 179–203, as well as Dutfield, "The Public and Private Domains," 289, and Kirsch, "Property Limits." The *Bulun Bulun* case is formally known as *Bulun Bulun and Milpurrurru v. R & T Textiles Pty Ltd* [1998] 1082 FCA (3 Sept. 1998).

39. Wendy Brown, "'The Most We Can Hope for . . .'."

40. Michael H. Davis, "Some Realism About Indigenism."

BIBLIOGRAPHY

American Association for the Advancement of Science (AAAS). *Traditional Ecological Knowledge Prior Art Database*. 28 July 2004 <ip.aaas.org/tekindex.nsf>.

Anaya, S. James. *Indigenous Peoples in International Law*. New York: Oxford University Press, 1996.

Barry, Brian. *Culture and Equality*. Cambridge, Mass.: Harvard University Press, 2001.

Barsh, Russel L. "How Do You Patent a Landscape? The Perils of Dichotomizing Cultural and Intellectual Property." *International Journal of Cultural Property* 8, no. 1 (1999): 14–47.

Bateson, Gregory. *Steps to an Ecology of Mind*. New York: Ballantine, 1972.

Blake, Janet. "On Defining the Cultural Heritage." *International and Comparative Law Quarterly* 49 (2000): 61–85.

Bowen, John R. "Should We Have a Universal Concept of 'Indigenous Peoples' Rights?' Ethnicity and Essentialism in the Twenty-First Century." *Anthropology Today* 16, no. 4 (August 2000): 12–16.

Boyle, James. *Shamans, Software, and Spleens: Law and the Construction of the Information Society*. Cambridge, Mass.: Harvard University Press, 1996.

Brown, Michael F. *Who Owns Native Culture?* Cambridge, Mass.: Harvard University Press, 2003.

———. "Safeguarding the Intangible." Center for Arts and Culture, Washington, D.C. <http://www.culturalcommons.org/comment-print.cfm?ID=12>, accessed 27 August 2004.

———. "Heritage as Property." In *Property in Question: Value Transformation in the Global Economy*, edited by Katherine Verdery and Caroline Humphrey. Oxford: Berg, 2004., 49–68.

Brown, Wendy. "'The Most We Can Hope for . . .': Human Rights and the Politics of Fatalism." *South Atlantic Quarterly* 103, no. 2-3 (2004): 451–463.

Castells, Manuel. "Materials for an Exploratory Theory of the Network Society." *British Journal of Sociology* 51, no. 1 (2000): 5–24.

Clifford, James. "Indigenous Articulations." *The Contemporary Pacific* 13, no. 2 (2001): 468–490.

Coleman, Elizabeth. "Aboriginal Art and Identity: Crossing the Border of Law's Imagination." *Journal of Political Philosophy* 12, no. 1 (2004): 20–40.

Coombe, Rosemary J. *The Cultural Life of Intellectual Properties: Authorship, Appropriation, and the Law.* Durham, N.C.: Duke University Press, 1998.

———. "Fear, Hope, and Longing for the Future of Authorship and a Revitalized Public Domain in Global Regimes of Intellectual Property." *DePaul Law Revew* 53 (2003): 1171–1191.

Cowen, Tyler. *Creative Destruction: How Globalization is Changing the World's Cultures.* Princeton, N.J.: Princeton University Press, 2002.

Davenport, Thomas H. *Information Ecology: Mastering the Information and Knowledge Environment.* New York: Oxford University Press, 1997.

Davis, Michael H. "Some Realism About Indigenism." *Cardozo Journal of International and Comparative Law* 11, no. 3 (2003): 815–830.

Drahos, Peter, with John Braithwaite. *Information Feudalism: Who Owns the Knowledge Economy?* New York: The New Press, 2003.

Dutfield, Graham. "The Public and Private Domains: Intellectual Property Rights in Traditional Knowledge." *Science Communication* 21 (2000): 274–295.

Erasmus, S. Michelle. "Repatriating Words: Local Knowledge in a Global Context." *American Indian Quarterly* 26, no. 2 (2002): 286–307.

Eriksen, Thomas Hylland. "Between Universalism and Relativism: A Critique of the UNESCO Concept of Culture." In *Culture and Rights: Anthropological Perspectives*, edited by Jane K. Cowan, Marie-Bénédicte Dembour, and Richard A. Wilson, 127–148. Cambridge: Cambridge University Press, 2001.

Geertz, Clifford. *Available Light: Anthropological Reflections on Philosophical Topics.* Princeton, N.J.: Princeton University Press, 2000.

Grad, Rachael. "Indigenous Rights and Intellectual Property Law: A Comparison of the United States and Australia." *Duke Journal of Comparative and International Law* 13, no. 1 (2003): 203–231.

Greene, Shane. "Indigenous People Incorporated? Culture as Politics, Culture as Property in Pharmaceutical Bioprospecting." *Current Anthropology* 45, no. 2 (2004): 211–237.

Hapiuk, William J., Jr. "Of Kitsch and Kachinas: A Critical Analysis of the *Indian Arts and Crafts Act of 1990.*" *Stanford Law Review* 53 (2001): 1009–1075.

Harding, Sarah. "Cultural Secrecy and the Protection of Cultural Property." In *Topics in Cultural Resource Law*, 69–78. Washington, DC: Society for American Archaeology, 2000.

———. "Cultural Property and the Limitations of Preservation." *Law and Policy* 25, no. 1 (2003): 17–36.

———. "Defining Traditional Knowledge–Lessons from Cultural Property." *Cardozo Journal of International and Comparative Law* 11, no. 2 (2003): 511–518.

Harrison, Simon. "Identity as a Scarce Resource." *Social Anthropology* 7, no. 3 (1999): 239–251.

Heyd, Thomas. "Rock Art Aesthetics and Cultural Appropriation." *The Journal of Aesthetics and Art Criticism* 61, no. 1 (2003): 37–46.

Janke, Terri. "Minding Culture: Case Studies in Intellectual Property and Traditional Cultural Expression," <www.wipo.int/tk/en/studies/cultural/minding-culture/studies/finalstudy.pdf> (2003). Accessed 20 July 2004

Kalinoe, Lawrence, and James Leach, eds. *Rationales of Ownership: Ethnographic Studies of Transactions and Claims to Ownership in Contemporary Papua New Guinea.* New Delhi: UBS Publishers' Distributors Ltd., 2001.

Kasten, Erich, ed. *Properties of Culture–Culture as Property: Pathways to Reform in Post-Soviet Siberia.* Berlin: Dietrich Reimer Verlag, 2004.

King, Thomas F. *Places That Count: Traditional Cultural Properties in Cultural Resource Management.* Walnut Creek, Cal.: AltaMira Press, 2003.

Kipen, David. "Offshoring the Audience." *Atlantic Monthly* (Boston), June 2004, 115–120.

Kirsch, Stuart. "Lost Worlds: Environmental Disaster, 'Cultural Loss,' and the Law." *Current Anthropology* 42, no. 2 (2001): 167–198.

———. "Property Limits: Debates on the Body, Nature and Culture." In *Transactions and Creations: Property Debates and the Stimulus of Melanesia,* edited by Eric Hirsch and Marilyn Stathern, 21–39. New York: Berghahn Books, 2004.

Kuper, Adam. "The Return of the Native." *Current Anthropology* 44, no. 3 (2003): 389–402.

Kurin, Richard. "Tangible Progress." Center for Arts and Culture, Washington, D.C. <http://www.culturalcommons.org/kurin.htm>, accessed 27 August 2004.

Lash, Scott. *Critique of Information.* London: Sage Publications, 2002.

Leach, James. "Owning Creativity: Cultural Property and the Efficacy of Custom on the Rai Coast of Papua New Guinea." *Journal of Material Culture* 8, no. 2 (2003): 123–144.

Lessig, Lawrence. *Free Culture: How Big Media Uses Technology and the Law to Lock Down Culture and Control Creativity.* New York: Penguin, 2004.

Lowenthal, David. *The Heritage Crusade and the Spoils of History.* Cambridge: Cambridge University Press, 1998.

Magliocco, Sabina. *Witching Culture: Folklore and Neo-Paganism in America.* Philadelphia: University of Pennsylvania Press, 2004.

Matlon, Amina Para. "Safeguarding Native American Sacred Art by Partnering Tribal Law and Equity: An Exploratory Case Study Applying the *Bulun Bulun* Equity to Navajo Sandpainting." *Columbia Journal of Law and the Arts* 27 (2004): 211–247.

May, Christopher. *The Information Society: A Sceptical View.* Cambridge, U.K.: Polity Press/Blackwell, 2002.

McLeod, Kembrew. *Owning Culture: Authorship, Ownership, and Intellectual Property Law.* New York: Peter Lang, 2001.

Merryman, John Henry. "Two Ways of Thinking About Cultural Property." *American Journal of International Law* 80 (1986): 831–853.

Morgan, Owen. "Protecting Indigenous Signs and Trade Marks: The New Zealand Experience." *Intellectual Property Quarterly* 1, no. Winter (2004): 58–84.

Nas, Peter J. M. "Masterpieces of Oral and Intangible Heritage." *Current Anthropology* 43, no. 1 (2003): 139–148.

Nason, James D. "Traditional Property and Modern Laws: The Need for Native American Community Intellectual Property Rights Legislation." *Stanford Law and Policy Review* 12, no. 2 (2001): 255–266.

Nicholas, George P., and Kelly P. Bannister. "Copyrighting the Past? Emerging Intellectual Property Rights Issues in Archaeology." *Current Anthropology* 45, no. 3 (2004): 327–350.

Niezen, Ronald. *The Origins of Indigenism: Human Rights and the Politics of Identity*. Berkeley, Cal.: University of California Press, 2003.

Osborne, Stephen D. "Protecting Tribal Stories: The Perils of Propertization." *American Indian Law Review* 28 (2003): 203–236.

Peckham, Robert Shannan, ed. *Rethinking Heritage: Cultures and Politics in Europe*. London: I.B. Taurus, 2003.

Posey, Darrell A., and Graham Dutfield. *Beyond Intellectual Property: Toward Traditional Resource Rights for Indigenous Peoples and Local Communities*. Ottawa: International Development Research Centre, 1996.

Prott, Lyndel V., and Patrick J. O'Keefe. "'Cultural Heritage' or 'Cultural Property?'" *International Journal of Cultural Property* 1 (1992): 307–320.

Riley, Mary, ed. *Indigenous Intellectual Property Rights: Legal Obstacles and Innovative Solutions*. Lanham, Md.: AltaMira Press, 2004.

Robbins, Bruce, and Elsa Stamatopoulou. "Reflections on Culture and Cultural Rights." *South Atlantic Quarterly* 103, no. 2/3 (2004): 419–434.

Rosen, Lawrence. "The Right to be Different: Indigenous Peoples and the Quest for a Unified Theory." *Yale Law Journal* 107, no. 1 (October 1997): 227–259.

Rowlands, Michael. "Cultural Rights and Wrongs: Uses of the Concept of Property." In *Property in Question: Value Transformation in the Global Economy*, edited by Katherine Verdery and Caroline Humphrey, 207–226. Oxford: Berg, 2004.

Sager, Lawrence G. "The Free Exercise of Culture: Some Doubts and Distinctions." In *Engaging Cultural Differences: The Multicultural Challenge in Liberal Democracies*, edited by Richard Shweder, Martha Minow, and Hazel Rose Markus, 165–176. New York: Russell Sage Foundation, 2002.

Sax, Joseph L. *Playing Darts with a Rembrandt: Public and Private Rights in Cultural Treasures*. Ann Arbor, Mich.: University of Michigan Press, 1999.

Scafidi, Susan. "Intellectual Property and Cultural Products." *Boston University Law Review* 81 (2001): 793–842.

Schwartz, Hillel. *The Culture of the Copy: Striking Likenesses, Unreasonable Facsimiles*. New York: Zone Books, 1996.

Seitel, Peter, ed. *Safeguarding Traditional Cultures: A Global Assessment*. Washington, D.C.: Center for Folklife and Cultural Heritage, Smithsonian Institution, 2001.

Shand, Peter. "Scenes from the Colonial Catwalk: Cultural Appropriation, Intellectual Property Rights, and Fashion." *Cultural Analysis* 3 (2002): 47–88.

Simet, Jacob L. "Copyrighting Traditional Tolai Knowledge?" In *Protection of Intellectual, Biological, and Cultural Property in Papua New Guinea*, edited by Kathy Whimp and Mark Busse, 62–80. Canberra: Asia Pacific Press/Conservation Melanesia, 2000.

Stevenson, Gelvina Rodriguez. "Trade Secrets: The Secret to Protecting Indigenous Ethnobiological (Medicinal) Knowledge." *New York University Journal of International Law and Politics* 32 (2000): 1119–1174.

Stille, Alexander. "Are We Losing Our Memory? or the Museum of Obsolete Technology." In *The Future of the Past*, 299–310. New York: Farrar, Straus and Giroux, 2002.

Strathern, Marilyn. "Multiple Perspectives on Intellectual Property." In *Protection of Intellectual, Biological, and Cultural Property in Papua New Guinea*, edited by Kathy Whimp and Mark Busse, 47–61. Canberra, 2000.

———. *Property, Substance and Effect: Anthropological Essays on Persons and Things*. London: Athlone Press, 1999.

Sunder, Madhavi. "Intellectual Property and Identity Politics: Playing with Fire." *Journal of Gender, Race, and Justice* 4, no. No. 1 (2000): 69–98.

———. "Cultural Dissent." *Stanford Law Review* 54, no. 3 (2001): 495–567.

Tsosie, Rebecca. "Reclaiming Native Stories: An Essay on Cultural Appropriation and Cultural Rights." *Arizona State Law Journal* 34 (2002): 299–358.

Vaidhyanathan, Siva. *Copyrights and Copywrongs: The Rise of Intellectual Property and How It Threatens Creativity*. New York: New York University Press, 2001.

Virilio, Paul. *The Information Bomb*. London: Verso, 2000.

Visser, Coenraad J. "Making Intellectual Property Laws Work for Traditional Knowledge." In *Poor People's Knowledge: Promoting Intellectual Property in Developing Countries*, edited by J. Michael Finger and Philip Schuler, 207–240. Washington, D.C.: World Bank/Oxford University Press, 2004.

von Lewinski, Silke, ed. *Indigenous Heritage and Intellectual Property: Genetic Resources, Traditional Knowledge and Folklore*. The Hague: Kluwer, 2004.

Wüger, Daniel. "Prevention of Misappropriation of Intangible Cultural Heritage Through Intellectual Property Laws." In *Poor People's Knowledge: Promoting Intellectual Property in Developing Countries*, edited by J. Michael Finger and Philip Schuler, 183–206. Washington, D.C.: World Bank/Oxford University Press, 2004.

Young, James O. "The Ethics of Cultural Appropriation." *Dalhousie Review* 80 (2000): 301–316.

Ziff, Bruce, and Pratima V. Rao, eds. *Borrowed Power: Essays on Cultural Appropriation*. New Brunswick, N.J.: Rutgers University Press, 1997.

[11]
The UNESCO Concept of Safeguarding Intangible Cultural Heritage: Its Background and *Marrakchi* Roots

Thomas M. Schmitt

In 1998 UNESCO started a programme for the proclamation of 'Masterpieces of the oral and intangible heritage of humanity', a pre-project for the new UNESCO Convention for the Safeguarding of the Intangible Cultural Heritage. Jemaa el Fna Square in Marrakech was one of the first Masterpieces proclaimed by UNESCO in 2001. This paper examines the genesis and history of this new UNESCO concept of safeguarding intangible heritage. The Spanish writer Juan Goytisolo gave the decisive impulse for the new UNESCO concept in 1996 in order to safeguard Jemaa el Fna Square in Marrakech. Worrying that contemporary plans of local authorities would definitely change the character of the square and destroy its cultural traditions, Goytisolo asked UNESCO to proclaim the square as 'oral heritage of humanity'. The wish to protect Jemaa el Fna Square on the one hand, and the existing Convention for the Protection of the World Cultural and Natural Heritage on the other, can be seen as two reference points for the new UNESCO concept.

Keywords: UNESCO; Intangible Heritage; Jemaa el Fna; Marrakech; International Organisation; Juan Goytisolo

Introduction

In 2003 a new Convention for the Safeguarding of the Intangible Cultural Heritage of Humanity was adopted by UNESCO's General Assembly. In 1998 UNESCO had already started a programme for the Proclamation of Masterpieces of the Oral and Intangible Heritage of Humanity, and a total of 90 objects were proclaimed as such Masterpieces in three proclamation rounds between 2001 and 2005. The proclamation programme and the new Convention based on it are intended as a means of protecting

---

Thomas M. Schmitt, University of Bonn. Correspondence to: t.schmitt@giub.uni-bonn.de

local cultural traditions in times of social change or in the face of certain modernisation processes. Examples of the new UNESCO category of intangible heritage are the Kutiyattam Sanskrit Theatre in the southern Indian province of Kerala, the Andean Cosmovision of the Kallawaya in Bolivia, or—one of the comparatively few European examples—the *Mystery Play of Elche*, Spain, which has been staged largely unchanged every year on the Feast of the Assumption of the Blessed Virgin Mary since the late Middle Ages.[1] With the entry into force of the new UNESCO Convention in April 2006, the Masterpieces programme was discontinued; under the terms of the Convention, all existing Masterpieces should be entered automatically in the new Representative List of the Intangible Cultural Heritage of Humanity,[2] which is modelled on the well-known UNESCO World Heritage List.

UNESCO's new efforts to protect the intangible heritage are receiving increasing attention from the media and in discussions among experts.[3] This paper[4] examines the genesis of these UNESCO activities. It is an attempt to reconstruct some of the important stages in the development of the new UNESCO concept for the protection of intangible heritage, with the aim of increasing our understanding of the ideas which shaped this new concept. The main impulse for the development of UNESCO's new protection concept did not come from isolated expert think tanks, as some clichés on the development of ideas in international organisations would suggest. Rather, this impulse reflects the acute threat in the 1990s to a cultural space, namely Jemaa el Fna Square in Marrakech. This paper should therefore be seen as shedding light on a detail of recent history. It reveals some facts concerning the development of the new UNESCO concept, and it attempts to show to what extent the special role played by Jemaa el Fna in the genesis of the UNESCO concept is reflected in the Convention. A knowledge of these facts is of great potential interest for any future research in the cultural sciences relating to the new UNESCO concept.

Early Measures Taken by UNESCO for the Preservation of Intangible Cultural Heritage

The full background of the development of this new programme for the proclamation of Masterpieces is obviously not familiar even to authors who have discussed the concept.[5] In some publications, a number of events are (correctly) listed which prompted treatment of the question of intangible heritage at an international level, for instance an initiative by the government of Bolivia to protect the intellectual property rights of popular culture (1973), or the UNESCO *Recommendation on the Safeguarding of Traditional Culture and Folklore* of 1989. However, this recommendation was hardly implemented by the member states, and internal UNESCO analyses declared it to be ineffective just a few years after it was adopted. This list of UNESCO activities in the area of intangible heritage could be continued. For instance, in the 1990s the UNESCO Section for Intangible Cultural Heritage, which had already been set up, created a collection on CD of traditional music from all over the world. In a way, at least in retrospect, the development of the new UNESCO Convention for the Safeguarding of the Intangible Cultural Heritage could be construed as an almost unavoidable consequence of UNESCO's previous successes and failures in this field. However, it took a decisive external impulse (and many authors who discuss the programme and the Convention which grew out of it are obviously not aware of this fact) to get the development of a convention placed on the agenda at UNESCO. With the development of the Proclamation programme and the Convention, UNESCO was giving birth to a new conceptual and institutional entity, and it was Jemaa el Fna Square in Marrakech which acted as the midwife.

Towards the Development of a New Convention

The Impulse from Marrakech

For many travellers to Morocco, Jemaa el Fna Square in the old city of Marrakech is the stuff of myth; it would be difficult to find an account of the country's tourist attractions that fails to describe it. The square is known for its musicians, storytellers, acrobats, snake charmers and seers, and the many other actors who perform daily in front of a local (and increasingly also tourist) audience and thereby—to use the language of social sciences—reproduce and modify cultural traditions (see Figure 1). As expressed by UNESCO in its tribute,[6] Jemaa el Fna Square brings together popular oral and intangible Moroccan traditions in a unique way. We find evidence of the existence of intangible traditions on Jemaa el Fna Square in historical sources dating from the 17th century.[7] However, the square is located in the middle of an aspiring Moroccan city

Figure 1 The storyteller Ahmed Bouchama with his audience on Jemaa el Fna Square (2004).

and has thus been exposed to increasing pressures in the interest of commercial and urban development.⁸

In the mid-1990s, the Spanish writer Juan Goytisolo, who occasionally lives in the Medina of Marrakech, took an initiative which finally—and in a form not intended by him at the time—led to the new Convention for the Safeguarding of the Intangible Cultural Heritage. As perhaps the most intimate European connoisseur of Jemaa el Fna Square and its oral traditions, both of which figure in his novels and short stories, he saw the cultural versatility of the square threatened by local authority plans to build right beside it a new tower block with a glass façade and an underground car park. As Juan Goytisolo remembered in an interview:

> At the beginning [of the debate] were some plans on the part of the city authorities; a meeting of the *municipalité* took place, at which three projects were approved [...] Two of them were intended as a valorisation of the square [Jemaa el Fna]: an underground carpark and a building that would be fifteen metres high [...] I spoke briefly and said that all this would endanger the square, and that one should think twice before doing anything. How do you say it in French? Don't put the cart before the horse. And I must add that my objection was listened to in icy silence by those present. (Interview with Goytisolo, May 2005)⁹

Apart from the fact that these plans were scarcely compatible with the status of the Medina of Marrakech as a World Heritage Site, they would—in the opinion of Goytisolo—irrevocably destroy the traditions of the square. Goytisolo urged in drastic terms the importance of saving the art of storytelling as found in Jemaa el Fna: 'It is important to understand that the loss of a single *halaiqui* (here: performer, especially storyteller) is much more serious for humanity than the death of 200 best-selling authors.'¹⁰

Goytisolo obviously saw no way he could definitively stop these plans within a local framework at that time. In January 1996, through his publisher, Hans Meinke, Goytisolo informed the General Director of UNESCO, Federico Mayor, of the threats to Jemaa el Fna Square and proposed that the square be placed under the protection of UNESCO as *patrimonio oral de humanidad* (oral heritage of humanity). A report in *El País* on a reading held in Madrid by Goytisolo from the closing chapter (on Jemaa el Fna) of his novel *Makbara* (cf. Goytisolo, 1993, orig. 1980), and essays published later on in the international press,¹¹ brought to the attention of a wider international public the idea of asking UNESCO to safeguard Jemaa el Fna. The fundamental significance of Goytisolo's proposal for the new UNESCO programme and thus also the new Convention is sufficiently substantiated by letters and other written sources. As a typical example we can quote from a letter from Hans Meinke to the General Director of UNESCO, which to my knowledge is the first written formulation of the proposal:

> Dear Federico,
>
> [...] yesterday your ears must have been burning, for Juan Goytisolo came to talk [to me] about taking action on behalf of the famous Jemaa el Fna Square in Marrakech, and about the possibility of persuading UNESCO to declare it as 'oral heritage of humanity'. According to Goytisolo, this square, with its storytellers and reciters, is the only place in the Arab world where the tradition of oral literature is still cultivated.

Apparently it is advisable to propose its protection by UNESCO in order to avoid it being destroyed by speculation.[12]

In early internal memoranda at UNESCO we also find references to Goytisolo's proposal, the 'Proposition de Juan Goytisolo', which reveal how the idea of a programme for the safeguarding of intangible traditions increasingly began to take shape. Similarly, as proposer and joint founder of a civil society—the Association Place Jemaa el Fna Patrimoine oral de l'humanité—Goytisolo created the prerequisites for the protection of Jemaa el Fna Square at a local level in Marrakech. Thus this cosmopolitan intellectual succeeded in getting a local problem placed on the agenda of an international organisation. Below I will explain the factors that led to the success of Juan Goytisolo's intervention.

From Jemaa el Fna to a Globally Valid Concept

The concept of globally regulated protection of local cultural traditions was mainly developed between 1996 and 1998 in close cooperation between UNESCO's Paris headquarters and experts from Africa, Asia, Europe and the Americas, including a group of Moroccan intellectuals and Juan Goytisolo. During this process, what started as a vague idea of proclaiming objects as oral and intangible heritage of humanity was gradually transformed into a set of conceptual instruments, and suitable institutions, structures and procedures for this purpose were designed.

UNESCO staff immediately recognised the generalisability of Goytisolo's 'new idea' for the protection of Jemaa el Fna, and they also first formulated it as a *problem*: the proclamation of Jemaa el Fna alone as oral heritage of humanity might cause offence to other countries with great oral and intangible traditions:

> The request submitted by the writer Juan Goytisolo is indeed a new and very interesting idea, but to implement it would be rather complicated. The concept of 'oral heritage' is not included among UNESCO's different categories of heritage. UNESCO will therefore need to define this new category, and then to propose its adoption by the States Parties.
>
> [...] The act of declaring this square in Marrakech as 'oral heritage of humanity' might also cause offence to other countries where a rich oral tradition has been kept alive. This applies in particular to the countries of black Africa.[13]

Expanding a concrete cultural instance, both in content and in geographical terms, to create a worldwide programme happened to coincide with the interests of various UNESCO departments which saw that Goytisolo's idea could be used as an effective lever for the protection of intangible traditions, since previous attempts—in particular UNESCO's *Recommendation on the Safeguarding of Traditional Culture and Folklore* of 1989—had largely failed due to their lack of commitment, as well as incentives and possible sanctions. At the same time, this expansion from a place in need of protection to a global scheme can be interpreted as an expression of the inherent logic behind the practice of a global institution. In the face of a request to protect Jemaa el Fna, it was obviously necessary to treat this unique problem in a generalising way, and to find a new concept for the purpose—modelled on the well-known World Heritage List. In cultural studies, the idea of local appropriation of global goods is found frequently.[14] But the history of the development of the programme for the Proclamation of Masterpieces of the Oral and Intangible Heritage can be interpreted the other way around, in other words as the *appropriation of a locality*—Jemaa el Fna Square in Marrakech—by a global organisation.

At least during the period from 1996 to 1998, discussions relating to the development of the new UNESCO concept reflect the situation of Jemaa el Fna; in particular, this is shown by the fact that during this phase special emphasis was laid firstly on oral traditions, and secondly on the protection of *cultural spaces*. It is clear that the main idea initially was that most of the Masterpieces to be proclaimed should also be clearly defined places. However, subsequent expert meetings—in particular a colloquium held in Marrakech in 1997—led to the conclusion that Jemaa el Fna as a clearly defined place (in this case no bigger than a square) where certain cultural traditions are practised is a very rare phenomenon in global terms. Intangible traditions comparable to those of Jemaa el Fna and judged to be equally in need of urgent protection can, as a rule, be ascribed only to ill-defined and much larger areas. Thus, the spatial components in UNESCO's conceptions for the safeguarding of intangible traditions become less important as time goes on. In the decisive texts relating to the programme for the Proclamation of Masterpieces, the 'space' that represents a 'strong concentration of the intangible cultural heritage of outstanding value' appears beside the 'forms of cultural expression [...] of outstanding value from a historical, artistic, ethnological, sociological, anthropological, linguistic or literary point of view' as one of two basic forms of Masterpiece.[15]

The text of the 2003 Convention on *intangible heritage* attaches less importance attaches less importance to the spatial component, as shown by the following definition:

> The 'intangible cultural heritage' means the practices, representations, expressions, knowledge, skills—as well as the instruments, objects, artefacts and cultural spaces [!] associated therewith—that communities, groups and, in some cases, individuals recognize as part of their cultural heritage.[16]

A significant intermediate step in the development of the UNESCO concept was the International Consultation on the Preservation of Popular Cultural Spaces held in June 1997 in Marrakech. Both the choice of venue and the preparation of the conference by the Moroccan National Commission for UNESCO with the collaboration of Goytisolo and Moroccan intellectuals clearly show that the conference had a double orientation: a local reference to the safeguarding of Jemaa el Fna, and at the same time a global interest in the development of a generally valid concept for the safeguarding of intangible heritage.

The head (at that time) of the UNESCO department for intangible heritage summed up this conference in a letter to the Moroccan government as follows:

> I was particularly aware of the fact that all the international experts at this gathering in Marrakech recognised the exceptional artistic and historical value of the popular cultural performances presented in Jemaa El Fna Square, and that the study carried out by the group of Moroccan specialists and the writer Juan Goytisolo has given the concept of 'oral heritage of humanity' a universal relevance. (Letter from N. Aïkawa, 25 July 1997. Translated from the French by Ruth Schubert)

As a courtesy letter to the Moroccan government, it may be that this letter overemphasises the importance of the role played by Moroccan specialists in the development of the UNESCO programme, especially since UNESCO had commissioned other important papers from international, non-Moroccan experts when preparing this conference (cf., for instance, Denhez, *Working Paper*). But it is indisputable that this conference marks a decisive stage in the subsequent development of the concept, especially since the preparation for the conference involved many activities, which were used in the subsequent development of the programme.

As I have shown, Juan Goytisolo and some Moroccan intellectuals played a special role in the development of the UNESCO concept for the safeguarding of intangible heritage. However, the performers in Jemaa el Fna Square who were directly affected, the 'carriers' of the intangible traditions, were not involved; in the Proclamation process they were objects of reflection rather than acting subjects.

Borrowing from the World Heritage Convention

In 1996/1997 UNESCO staff considered the possibility of extending the existing 1972 World Heritage Convention to include the safeguarding of intangible heritage. This would have had the advantage of responding to certain criticisms of the existing World Heritage List, in particular the objection that some countries, especially in Africa, Asia and Latin America, are under-represented on the list, with the result that it is geographically unbalanced. This idea of extending the existing Convention, as well as the idea of *directly* creating a new Convention for the protection of intangible heritage, was not followed up in 1997/1998. The main reasons for this, according to the sources consulted, lay in the relatively long process required before the adoption of a new Convention would be possible, and the uncertain issue of any attempt to create a new Convention or to make corresponding changes to the existing Convention of 1972.[17] The UNESCO administration thus chose the less complicated solution of setting up a *programme* to safeguard intangible traditions.

But even the new programme for the Proclamation of Masterpieces (which ceased to be valid with the entry into force of the 2003 Convention) was to be modelled on the well-established procedures for the inclusion of sites in the World Heritage List, '[i]n a way roughly similar to the World Heritage List',[18] but deliberately simplified for the purposes of the Proclamation programme. For example, while the members of the World Heritage Committee are elected by the States Parties to the Convention during the UNESCO General Assembly,[19] the jury for the Proclamation of intangible masterpieces was merely appointed by the General Director of UNESCO. The Convention of 2003, however, unlike the 1998 Masterpieces programme, is largely modelled on the standards of the World Heritage Convention of 1972. This gives greater legitimacy to the selection of objects for inclusion in the list. At the same time, this might be seen as a regrettable step from a professional point of view: each future committee, which will largely be composed of diplomats and representatives of the national ministries of culture, will find it difficult to stand their ground in comparison to the creative, cosmopolitan personalities in the first jury for the Masterpieces Proclamation programme (of which Juan Goytisolo was the chairman).[20]

In some key terms, the 2003 Convention clearly departs both from the Masterpieces programme and from the 1972 World Heritage Convention. The 2003 Convention deliberately avoids the term Masterpiece (French: *chef d'œuvre*) as used in the Proclamation programme, since it is normally used to refer to the work of an individual artist or architect rather than to traditions that have grown up over many decades or centuries, and that have frequently become marginalised. The 2003 Convention also contains no requirement that the objects to be included in the list must be of *outstanding universal value*, which is still a key concept of the 1972 World Heritage Convention. The 2003 Convention was thus deliberately more modest in its key wording than both the 1972 World Heritage Convention and the 1998 Masterpiece Proclamation Programme. The list *as a whole* must be representative, but each individual cultural tradition does not need to be of outstanding universal value.

Conclusion I: A Local–Global Story and its Factors of Success

The development of the new UNESCO Convention has been narrated here essentially as the history of interactions between actors from Marrakech and the headquarters of UNESCO in Paris, and as that of the global appropriation of a locality. As mentioned above, other authors have told a completely different story of the origins of the UNESCO Convention by referring, for instance, to the role of protecting the intellectual property rights of Indigenous peoples. These accounts are not 'wrong', but they are incomplete. They explain some important factors that contributed to the development of the new Convention. On the other hand, it was Jemaa el Fna Square, as I have tried to show in this paper, which initially sparked off the development of the Proclamation programme, and only this can explain certain particularities in this programme and in the Convention. With its deliberate emphasis on the role played by Jemaa el Fna and Juan Goytisolo's idea, this paper, not least for reasons of space, cannot describe other events which led to the development of the new UNESCO Convention. Thus it is also not a complete account of the background to the development of the new Convention.

From the point of view of political geography, it is interesting to see how a local idea, the safeguarding of a square, was able to change the agenda of an international organisation, and how this led to expansion of the idea both in content and in geographical terms.

But why was Goytisolo's request to UNESCO so successful that it became the decisive impulse for the new UNESCO activities in the field of intangible heritage? Let us look at the essential factors:

(1) A vital element in the process seems to have been the double localisation of Juan Goytisolo, who not only lives in the Medina of Marrakech but is also an internationally renowned writer and intellectual with access to the world of global cultural politics. Thus he was able to take what started as a local concern in Marrakech and

lift it straight onto an international agenda, bypassing national authorities in the first instance. In generalised terms, Goytisolo can be referred to in this case study as a scale hybrid social actor, a doubly localised social actor, able to act on different socio-spatial levels of a local–global interaction process.

Here, I refer to actors as scale hybrid in a given context if they are able to act effectively on several socio-spatial levels at the same time, especially on the local and the global level of a specific process (such as a complex interaction process, a conflict, etc.). In such cases, access to resources and integration in formal or informal structures or networks are important conditions for effective action. Scale hybridity is a key term referring to the double localisation of an actor in global–local interaction contexts.[21]

(2) At the same time, the global organisation UNESCO was open from the beginning to Goytisolo's suggestion, the generalisability of which was quickly recognised. It was obviously seen as an opportunity to try a new form of international protection for intangible traditions, following several largely unsuccessful attempts, linked discursively to existing UNESCO concepts for the safeguarding of the intangible heritage.

(3) The fact that the General Director of UNESCO at the time happened to be from Spain, like Goytisolo, and that they were acquainted with each other, was certainly a help for Goytisolo in getting his request heard.

(4) Finally, the authorities at the national level in Morocco, which have scarcely been discussed in this paper, also contributed to what, at least in the short term, was a success story, by not blocking the UNESCO initiative for the protection of Jemaa el Fna, and even encouraging it. As an intergovernmental organisation, UNESCO could not have taken any action in respect of safeguarding Jemaa el Fna Square in Morocco without the agreement of the Moroccan government.

As I have shown, the city administration in Marrakech wanted to transform the square in line with models of 'contemporary' urbanism, while national authorities accepted the UNESCO proposal. Not only the relevant Moroccan ministries, but also King Hassan II, when asked for his opinion by the minister responsible, indicated his support for the Proclamation and safeguarding of Jemaa el Fna. This declaration of support by the king provided a positive impetus for the project, as Juan Goytisolo, looking back, also admits,[22] and probably had consequences beyond Marrakech: it is quite possible that if the royal court had said 'no' at an early stage, all further UNESCO activities in this respect would have been stopped, putting an end to the development of this globally relevant concept.

Conclusion II: The Square in the Convention

In the above list of factors which probably contributed to the successful development of the new UNESCO concept on the basis of Goytisolo's suggestion, one factor has not been mentioned which, in the author's opinion, was also significant. At least in retrospect, it appears that Jemaa el Fna Square was a particularly suitable reference example for the development of a global concept for the protection of local intangible traditions. The following points support this idea:

(1) At the time in question, Jemaa el Fna Square was already relatively *well known*, a fact which is reflected not least by its appearance in literary works, such as Juan Goytisolo's novel *Makbara* (1993; orig. 1980) or the earlier *Voices of Marrakesh* by Elias Canetti (2003; written in 1954). It can be assumed that the stereotype of Jemaa el Fna as a place where the visitor is offered 'oriental life in a thousand variations [...] as if from a cornucopia'[23] was relatively widespread in the 1990s.

(2) In the mid-1990s, the square was acutely *endangered*. The local government's plans to construct a high-rise building at the side of the square constituted a concrete threat which would have radically altered the square both as a physical place and as a cultural space. But this concrete danger was easily warded off by urging that the plans be abandoned. The example of Jemaa el Fna thus clearly revealed that a set of instruments for the protection of local cultural traditions can be useful and effective. At the same time Jemaa el Fna served as a reference point for further reflection on possible threats to local cultural traditions, or, to put it more neutrally, influences which might affect them, such as international tourism, urban expansion and social modernisation.

(3) A central factor which, in the opinion of the author, makes Jemaa el Fna a particularly suitable reference example is the great *diversity of performances and intangible traditions* that are concentrated here in a small space and which have probably always mutually influenced each other to some extent. They include the sacred and the profane, oral literature, drama, comedy, dancing and music (see Figure 2), rhythm and song, codified and spontaneous performances, old traditions and recent new forms, and traditionally urban and originally rural cultural elements. These last elements stem from various geographical cultural backgrounds, ranging from the Haouz of Marrakech to the mountainous regions of the High Atlas, and, especially in the case of the Gnauwa,[24] sub-Saharan Africa (see Figure 3). Jemaa el Fna is thus a kind of panopticon (in the literal, not the pejorative sense), representing a large number of possible forms of local intangible heritage worthy of protection, as defined by UNESCO. If I claim here retrospectively that Jemaa el Fna is particularly suitable for the development of the UNESCO concept, this is strictly speaking a circular argument. It is naturally to be expected that an object which served as a reference point during the development of a concept should fit this concept particularly well. However, scarcely any other cultural tradition proclaimed by UNESCO as a Masterpiece has such a great variety of performing traditions as Jemaa el Fna.

It would be only a slight exaggeration to say that the 2003 UNESCO Convention for the Safeguarding of the Intangible Cultural Heritage can be interpreted as an adaptation of the 1972 World Heritage Convention in respect of places and traditions such as Jemaa el Fna. On the other hand, it is clear that in the course of its development, from the initial considerations to the adopting of the new Convention, the new UNESCO

Figure 2 Berber musicians on Jemaa el Fna Square (2006).

concept gradually came to be based less and less on Jemaa el Fna as its (only) reference point.

The mediatisation of the new UNESCO concept in brochures or magazines has produced a new kind of global cultural geography which sometimes conforms to and is sometimes in opposition to usual global cultural geographies. Unlike in the classical World Heritage List, states or sub-continental spaces are represented not by their built monuments, which are generally associated with advanced civilisation, but by local and regional cultural traditions and practices which are being or have been marginalised, at least in some respects, within the local, regional and national context. By proclaiming objects as intangible heritage, UNESCO was at the same time expanding the concept of (World) Heritage in a way that was perceivable to a broader public and not only in professional circles. The concept has also been expanded in other ways, for instance by subsuming former industrial plants under the umbrella of cultural heritage or the preservation of historic monuments; such expansions have always given rise to objections. If the term heritage—which always relates to the past—is expanded or restricted, this involves a shifting of the social boundaries of inclusion and exclusion in the present.[25] This is obviously true on the worldwide scale of the UNESCO concept, but it is also true within the local and national context of Marrakech and Morocco, where forms of popular culture that once were marginalised have now been declared as heritage (Arabic: *turath*; French: *patrimoine*).

Figure 3 *Gnauwa* dancers and drummers on Jemaa el Fna Square (2006).

Mechanisms: The Generation of Concepts in International Organisations

This reconstruction of a vital stage in the genesis of the UNESCO concept for the safeguarding of intangible traditions can be linked to a debate in the social sciences on the creation of new concepts in international organisations. In the course of the so-called *cultural turn*, authors from the fields of social and political science have for some years approached international institutions and organisations from the perspective of cultural studies, and in particular from a constructivist perspective. One question here is that of the *genesis* and the *discursive power* of ideas that are propagated by international institutions and organisations.[26] Existing studies are concerned mainly with the big economic institutions, such as the World Trade Organisation and the World Bank.[27] UNESCO is certainly not one of the 'most powerful multilateral institutions' in the eyes of the general public.[28] But precisely for this reason it can be illuminating to contrast central theses such as those proposed by Bøås and McNeill for the genesis of ideas in international institutions, with the history of the development of the new UNESCO concept concerning the intangible heritage of humanity. Not only can this be enriching for the broader debate on the genesis of ideas in international organisations but it can also lead to deeper reflection concerning this particular case history.

If we take, for instance, all the papers in the volume edited by Bøås and McNeill that deal with the genesis of ideas in international organisations, the central theses can be summed up as followed:

(1) As a rule, international institutions try to choose key terms for their own programmes that will help to ensure consensual and hegemonic implementation of the concept by local and national actors, and which hardly anyone can seriously contest. An example of this is the concept of good governance ('Being against good governance is rather like being against motherhood and apple-pie').[29]
(2) New ideas developed by international organisations correspond to the interests of important global actors, especially to the interests of the most important donor countries of the international organisation; in the economic institutions there is a high degree of donor control.
(3) Once they have made their appearance, new ideas undergo operationalisation and technocratic modification within the international institution. They are rendered compatible with the existing ideas of the organisation.
(4) The concepts are ostensibly and externally depoliticised. They are also charged economically, in the sense of being endowed with a neoliberal agenda.

How far do these conceptions apply to the case history studied here concerning the genesis of the concept for safeguarding the intangible heritage? The case history of the genesis of the UNESCO concept is located on the periphery rather than at the centre of international regulation and the whole framework of international institutions. If Bøås and McNeill's theses are accepted in principle, it can plausibly be assumed that some but not all of the elements postulated by both authors for the genesis and development of ideas in international institutions will apply to the UNESCO concept for safeguarding the intangible heritage.

Ad (1): if UNESCO proclaims local cultural traditions as 'heritage of humanity', then it is using familiar terminology that everyone associates with the World Heritage of the 1972 Convention. This terminology is highly appropriate for creating a worldwide consensus on the necessity of safeguarding intangible traditions. However, it must not be overlooked that this choice of terms is not based on UNESCO's explicit strategic intentions but is the result of Juan Goytisolo's intuition.

Ad (2): at the time of implementation of the Masterpiece programme, UNESCO's most important donor countries were Japan and Germany or the countries of the EU in general. Indeed, Japan had a strong politico-cultural interest in the development of the Masterpiece programme and in the new Convention; they had many points in common with projects that Japan had been supporting for years in an attempt to safeguard its national intangible heritage. While many countries in the South were highly interested in the new UNESCO concept, this cannot be said of all European countries. Germany, for instance, has not ratified the new Convention even today. The thesis that the donor countries have a strong influence on UNESCO can be neither confirmed nor refuted on the basis of this case history.

Ad (3): in the history of the development of the UNESCO concept for safeguarding the intangible heritage, it is possible to discern processes of operationalisation and concomitant technocratic modification of the original idea. When UNESCO is asked to do something like safeguarding Jemaa el Fna, the matter has to be put in a 'normal form' that can be handled by UNESCO; this was achieved by a process of generalisation and by the setting up of regulations based on those of the successful 1972 World Heritage Convention.

Ad (4): there is no explicit depoliticisation of the idea of safeguarding intangible heritage in the measures taken by UNESCO; rather, certain cultural practices have gained a previously unknown political importance. There can be no question of a comprehensive 'economisation' of the idea as a result of its appropriation by the politico-cultural organisation UNESCO. The institutionalisation of a concept for the safeguarding of the intangible heritage can be interpreted as meaning that the politico-cultural organisation UNESCO undertakes a kind of cultural upgrading of objects, instead of economisation as in the case of economic organisations; in the example studied here, a cultural upgrading of traditional practices has taken place as a result of the Proclamation. This is indicated by the term Masterpiece that was used by UNESCO up to 2005, a term which is commonly associated with the creation of works of art showing extraordinary skill, normally by an individual artist, writer, builder, etc. Even if UNESCO deliberately avoided using this term in the new Convention, it will hardly be possible to avoid a 'cultural upgrading' effect when intangible traditions are inscribed on the new Representative List of the Intangible Cultural Heritage of Humanity.

The exceptional story told here of the genesis of international protection concepts on the basis of concern over a potential threat to a single locality, Jemaa el Fna Square, scarcely matches the cliché of global institutions that obtain their concepts from isolated think tanks in accordance with the interests of the most powerful member countries and from deductive ideological considerations.[30] This does not mean that the cliché can be refuted as inappropriate in every case. But the exceptional story at least shows that other forms of production of global concepts are possible, in this case along a local–global axis between the Medina of Marrakesh and the UNESCO headquarters in Paris. It cannot be a coincidence that this exceptional story concerning the genesis of a new form of international governance was possible with an organisation having the self-image of UNESCO.

Notes

[1] Cf. UNESCO, *Première Proclamation des chefs-d'œuvre du patrimoine oral et immatériel de l'humanité*; UNESCO, *Second Proclamation of Masterpieces of the Oral and Intangible Heritage of Humanity*.

[2] UNESCO, *International Convention for the Safeguarding of the Intangible Cultural Heritage*, Art. 31.

[3] Cf., among others: Nas, 'Masterpieces of Oral and Intangible Culture'; Kirshenblatt-Gimblett, 'Intangible Heritage as Metacultural Production'.

[4] Some of the ideas developed here and parts of the empirical data can be found (in German) in Schmitt, 'Die UNESCO und der Platz Jemaa el Fna in Marrakech'. I am grateful to the 'Local Action in Africa in the Context of Global Influences' collaborative research centre at the University of Bayreuth, Germany, and the German Research Foundation for their financial support. My thanks go to Herbert Popp for his suggestion that I should make a study of Jemaa el Fna Square, and to my former colleagues in Bayreuth for their critical discussions. Finally, I would like to thank all my interview partners in Marrakech, Rabat and Paris, and especially the performers in Jemaa el Fna Square.

[5] See, for instance, Blake, *Developing a New Standard-setting Instrument for the Safeguarding of Intangible Cultural Heritage*; Kirshenblatt-Gimblett, 'Intangible Heritage as Metacultural Production'.
[6] Cf. UNESCO, *Première Proclamation des chefs-d'œuvre du patrimoine oral et immatériel de l'humanité*, 5.
[7] Cf. the historical travel report by Hassan Al Youssi, dating from the 17th century; quoted in, among others, Tebbaa and El Faïz, *Jemâa el Fna*, 98.
[8] For a more extensive ethnographic approach to Jemaa el Fna Square and a discussion of the question as to how far proclamation as a Masterpiece changed the square, see Schmitt, 'Jemaa el Fna Square in Marrakech'; *idem*, 'Interkultureller Begegnungsraum Place Jemaa el Fna'.
[9] Original: 'Au début, il y avait des projets de [...] la municipalité, il y a eu une réunion de la municipalité où on a approuvé [...] trois projets dont deux signifiaient la valorisation de la place. Un parking souterrain et un bâtiment de 15 mètres de haut [...] J'ai fait une petite intervention pour dire que tout ça mettait en danger vraiment la place et qu'il fallait réfléchir avant de faire des choses. Comment dire en français? Il faut pas mettre la charrette avant le bœuf. C'est-à-dire que mon intervention était accueillie avec un silence glacial par l'ensemble des gens qui étaient là-bas' (interview with J. Goytisolo, May 2005).
[10] Quoted according to N.N., 'UNESCO to the Rescue of the *Halaiquis*', *UNESCO-Courier* 12, December 2000 [accessed 20 September 2004], available from www.unesco.org/Courier/2000_12/uk/doss7.htm
[11] Goytisolo, 'Jemaa-el-Fna: patrimoine oral de l'humanité'.
[12] Letter from Hans Meinke to Federico Mayor, 26 January 1996—original: 'Querido Federico, [...] Ayer te debieron sonar los oídos, porque me visitó Juan Goytisolo para hablar de una acción en favor de la famosa plaza de Xemáa-El-Fná de Marrakech y de la posibilidad de conseguir que sea declarada por Unesco 'patrimonio oral de la humanidad'. Según Juan Goytisolo, esta plaza de cuentistas y narradores es el único lugar del mundo árabe en el que todavía se cultiva la tradición oral de la literatura. Al parecer, es aconsejable proponer su protección por Unesco para evitar que la especulación la destruya.'
[13] Note made by a UNESCO staff member, February 1996, translation: Thomas Schmitt and Ruth Schubert—original: 'La demande de l'écrivain Juan Goytisolo est, en effet, une idée nouvelle très intéressante, mais dont la mise en œuvre s'avère compliqué. Le concept de 'patrimoine oral' n'est pas prévu parmi les différentes catégories de patrimoine retenues par l'UNESCO. Il faudra donc que l'UNESCO définisse cette nouvelle catégorie, puis propose aux Etats membres de l'adopter [...] Le fait de déclarer cette place de Marrakech 'patrimoine oral de l'humanité' pourrait par ailleurs éveiller des susceptibilités dans d'autres pays où la tradition orale, d'une grande richesse, reste très vivante. C'est le cas notamment des pays de l'Afrique noire.'
[14] Cf., for instance, Hahn, 'Global Goods and the Process of Appropriation'.
[15] Regulations relating to the Proclamation by UNESCO of Masterpieces of the oral and intangible heritage of humanity, Section 6 ('Criteria'), Paris, November 1998.
[16] UNESCO, *International Convention for the Safeguarding of the Intangible Cultural Heritage*, Art. 2, para. 1.
[17] Cf. Sasson, *Intervention du Représentant du Directeur Général*, 4.
[18] Denhez, *Working Paper on a Proposed System to Honour 'Cultural Spaces' with Remarkable Intangible Heritage*, 1.
[19] Cf. UNESCO, *Convention for the Protection of the World Cultural and Natural Heritage*, Art. 8.1.
[20] This should not be understood as a critique of the staff of the ministries of culture, etc., but rather as a tribute to the majority of the members of the first jury.
[21] Scale hybridity is distinguished in this sense from other kinds of hybridity, in particular from cultural hybridity, as introduced in cultural studies in connection with interculturality (see, for instance, Papastergiadis, 'Tracing Hybridity in Theory'). Both terms, scalar hybridity as introduced here and cultural hybridity, refer either explicitly or implicitly to globalisation

phenomena, and they are both of relevance for theories of globalisation. We could now ask whether the concept of scalar hybrid actors would be useful apart from this particular case history and the person of Goytisolo. For Geertz ('Thick Description'), the close linking of a term from social or cultural studies to a particular episode, to a particular study and its interpretation, is not a negative criterion, but he sees this as a typical feature of ethnographic research and the basis on which social and cultural theories are formed. My use of the term does not necessarily define a new 'class' of actors relevant to globalisation processes, but shows possible ways in which single social actors can play a role in them.

[22] Interview with Juan Goytisolo, May 2005.
[23] Bonn, *Marokko. Blick hinter den Schleier*, 153; published 1950.
[24] The *Gnauwa* were originally members of an Islamic brotherhood in Morocco which was almost exclusively composed of black Africans. They developed their own particular style of music, which is influenced by sub-Saharan musical traditions. Today the term *Gnauwa* also refers to *musicians* whose music follows the tradition of this brotherhood.
[25] Graham et al., *A Geography of Heritage*; see also Soyez, 'Kulturlandschaftspflege', 34.
[26] Cf. Bøås and McNeill, *Global Institutions and Development*, 2004.
[27] Cf. ibid.
[28] Cf. *idem*, 'Ideas and Institutions', 212.
[29] George and Sabelli, *Faith and Credit*, 150, quoted in Bøås and McNeill, 'Introduction', 2.
[30] Bøås and McNeill, 'Ideas and Institutions', 206.

References

Blake, J. *Developing a New Standard-setting Instrument for the Safeguarding of Intangible Cultural Heritage: Elements for Consideration*, edited by UNESCO. Paris: UNESCO, 2001.
Bøås, M. and D. McNeill. eds. *Global Institutions and Development*. London: Routledge, 2004.
———. 'Ideas and Institutions: Who is Framing What?' In *Global Institutions and Development*, edited by M. Bøås and D. McNeill. London: Routledge, 2004: 206–24.
———. 'Introduction. Power and Ideas in Multilateral Institutions: Towards an Interpretative Framework'. In *Global Institutions and Development*, edited by M. Bøås and D. McNeill. London: Routledge, 2004: 1–13.
Bonn, G. *Marokko. Blick hinter den Schleier*. Stuttgart: Deutsche Hausbücherei.
Canetti, E. *The Voices of Marrakesh*. Written 1954; original 1967. London: Marion Boyars, 2003.
Denhez, M. *Working Paper on a Proposed System to Honour 'Cultural Spaces' with Remarkable Intangible Heritage*. Unpublished document, edited by Moroccan National Commission for UNESCO, Rabat and Paris, 1997.
Geertz, C. 'Thick Description: Toward an Interpretative Theory of Culture'. In *The Interpretation of Cultures: Selected Essays*, by C. Geertz. New York: Basic Books, 1973: 3–30.
George, S. and F. Sabelli. *Faith and Credit: The World Bank's Secular Empire*. Harmondsworth: Penguin, 1994.
Goytisolo, J. *Makbara*. London: Serpent's Tail, 1993. Originally Barcelona, 1980.
———. 'Jemaa-el-Fna, patrimoine oral de l'humanité'. *Le Monde diplomatique* (French ed.) 6 (1997): 9.
Graham, B., G. J. Ashworth and J. E. Tunbridge. *A Geography of Heritage: Power, Culture and Economy*. London: Arnold, 2000.
Hahn, H. 'Global Goods and the Process of Appropriation'. In *Between Resistance and Expansion*, edited by P. Probst and G. Spittler. Münster: Lit, 2004: 211–29.
Kirshenblatt-Gimblett, B. 'Intangible Heritage as Metacultural Production'. *Museum International*, no. 1–2 (2004): 52–65.
Nas, P. J. M. 'Masterpieces of Oral and Intangible Culture: Reflections on the UNESCO World Heritage List'. *Current Anthropology* 43 (2002): 139–48.

Papastergiadis, N. 'Tracing Hybridity in Theory'. In *Debating Cultural Hybridity: Multi-cultural Identities and the Politics of Anti-Racism*, edited by P. Werbner and T. Modood. London: Zed Books, 1997: 257–81.

Sasson, A. *Intervention du Représentant du Directeur Général* (Consultation internationale de l'UNESCO sur la préservation des espaces culturelles populaires, Marrakech, June 1997; unpublished document). Rabat and Paris, 1997.

Schmitt, T. M. 'Die UNESCO und der Platz Jemaa el Fna in Marrakech: Zur Genese und Regulierung eines Konzepts zum globalen Schutz immateriellen Erbes der Menschheit'. *Geographische Zeitschrift* 93, no. 4 (2005): 237–53.

———. 'Interkultureller Begegnungsraum Place Jemaa el Fna—nichtmaterielles Weltkulturerbe in Marrakech (Marokko)'. In *Stadtgeographie für die Schule* (= Bayreuther Kontaktstudium Geographie vol. 3), edited by H. Popp and F. Meyer. Bayreuth: University of Bayreuth, 2005: 179–202.

———. 'Jemaa el Fna Square in Marrakech—Changes to a Social Space and to a UNESCO Masterpiece of the Oral and Intangible Heritage of Humanity as a Result of Global influences'. *The Arab World Geographer* 8, no. 4 (2005): 173–95.

Soyez, D. 'Kulturlandschaftspflege: Wessen Kultur? Welche Landschaft? Was für eine Pflege?' *Petermanns Geographische Mitteilungen* 147 (2003): 30–39.

Tebbaa, Ou. and M. El Faïz. *Jemâa el Fna*. Casablanca and Paris: Éditions Paris Méditerranée, 2003.

UNESCO. *Convention for the Protection of the World Cultural and Natural Heritage*. Paris: UNESCO, 1972.

———. *Recommendation on the Safeguarding of Traditional Culture and Folklore*. Paris: UNESCO, 1989.

———. *Première Proclamation des chefs-d'œuvre du patrimoine oral et immatériel de l'humanité* (brochure). Paris: UNESCO, 2001.

———. *International Convention for the Safeguarding of the Intangible Cultural Heritage*. Paris: UNESCO, 2003.

———. *Second Proclamation of Masterpieces of the Oral and Intangible Heritage of Humanity* (brochure). Paris: UNESCO, 2004.

[12]

Indigenous Cultural Heritage in Development and Trade: Perspectives from the Dynamics of Cultural Heritage Law and Policy

Rosemary J. Coombe* with Joseph F. Turcotte**

1. Introduction

The protection of cultural heritage has become a matter of great concern in the past two decades and been the subject of intense policy negotiations. An emerging awareness of the complexity of issues pertaining to indigenous cultural heritage (ICH) has been one consequence of this process and has arguably shaped it, enabling scholars, activists and international policy makers to more clearly understand cultural heritage as both a source of identity and a resource for sustainable development. In these global processes of deliberation, conventional international cultural policy principles that privilege the interests and agency of long-established European nation states and their definitions of cultural heritage are increasingly challenged.[1] New states and states assuming greater international prominence have put new issues on the cultural policy table, as have historically colonised peoples, minority groups and globally organised indigenous peoples' movements and their advocates. The latter, in particular, have contested the propriety of state dominance in protecting, maintaining and safeguarding heritage properties, while insisting upon the distinctive role that cultural heritage plays in the constitution of their identities and their futures as distinct peoples.[2] Linking issues of cultural heritage to the human rights principle of self-determination makes the issue of indigenous political participation in heritage management a central one. Any approach to issues of trade involving ICH, must take this political context as its starting point.

Considering the obligations with respect to the trade of ICH goods under international laws and policy frameworks pertaining to cultural heritage is a far more difficult task than it first appears, for reasons which relate precisely to the ways in which indigenous peoples and their cultural traditions have been historically marginalised, subjugated, appropriated and targeted for erasure

---

*   Canada Research Chair in Law, Culture and Communication, York University.
** PhD Candidate, Communication and Culture Program, York University.
[1] See Laurajane Smith, *Archaeological Theory and the Politics of Cultural Heritage*, London: Routledge, 2004.
[2] See Rosemary J. Coombe, 'The Expanding Purview of Cultural Properties and their Politics' (2009) *Annual Review of Law and Social Sciences*, 5, pp. 393-412.

and assimilation by the modern state. As a consequence of this history of dispossession, ICH is internationally governed by a variety of distinctive legal instruments, none of which has superior jurisdiction in all contexts. The very nature of the 'goods' that concern us – those cultural forms and their material manifestations that express meaning and significance constitutive of indigenous identity – advises us to adopt legal pluralism as a starting point for governance inquiries.

Indigenous cultural forms and their manifestations have histories that pre-exist those of modern nation states and their legal hegemony and indeed – at least in those instances where the settler state was founded upon treaty relationships with indigenous nations – underwrite those states' legitimacy.[3] Consequentially, we must acknowledge indigenous customary law as a legitimate source of relevant and authoritative juridical norms for governing heritage of such significance that it implicates the identities of indigenous collectives and polities. Although international cultural heritage law continues to privilege the nation state as holding and managing all heritage goods within its borders as part of its jurisdiction, this privilege may be politically challenged as a denial of basic human rights that undermines indigenous self-determination. Moreover, to the extent that it leaves indigenous peoples dependent upon states to recognise them as deserving 'communities' who bear the appropriate form of 'culture' deserving protection, state-centred and state-dominated regimes of governance for trade in ICH are unlikely to command respect or legitimacy amongst indigenous peoples.

We have approached our topic as far as possible so that we do not overlap with the work of other contributors to the volume. Thus, for example, we deal only with intangible heritage, assuming issues specific to tangible heritage to be capably covered by Rebecca Tsosie's consideration of cultural property,[4] and we deal with TCEs and TK only incidentally, as these are categories more properly within the remit of Christoph Antons',[5] as well as Martin Girsberger and Benny Müller's coverage of World Intellectual Property Office's (WIPO) activities,[6] and Brigitte Vézina's chapter on the public domain.[7] Finally, we deal with the area of intangible cultural heritage primarily as it has evolved historically through UNESCO Conventions, recognising that UNESCO is part of the UN system and fundamentally committed to human rights norms as these are expressed internationally. While there may be some dispute as to whether indigenous rights are human rights or distinctive rights (even amongst indigenous peoples),[8] we will follow the UNESCO practice, which we

---

[3] See for example the able legal argument elegantly expressed by James Sákéj Henderson, 'Sui Generis and Treaty Citizenship' (2002) *Citizenship Studies*, 6 (4), pp. 415-440.

[4] Rebecca Tsosie, 'International Trade in Indigenous Cultural Heritage: An Argument for Indigenous Governance of Cultural Property', in this volume.

[5] Christoph Antons, 'International Trade in Indigenous Cultural Heritage: A Perspective on the Intellectual Property Side of the Debate', in this volume.

[6] Martin Girsberger and Benny Müller, 'International Trade in Indigenous Cultural Heritage – An IP Perspective', in this volume.

[7] Brigitte Vézina, 'Are They In or Are They Out? Traditional Cultural Expressions and the Public Domain — Implications for Trade', in this volume.

[8] This is discussed in John Scott and Federico Lenzerini, 'International Indigenous and Human Rights Law in the Context of International Trade in Indigenous Cultural Heritage ', in this volume.

read as deferential to indigenous rights as part of recognised international human rights norms and practice, which is part of international customary – if not yet positive – law in most jurisdictions.[9] We have found it necessary to move beyond the positive doctrinal field encompassed by the international law of cultural heritage as conventionally understood to explore cultural heritage as a field of evolving postcolonial politics in which new understandings of culture are emergent and contested. Considering the issues potentially posed by trade in indigenous intangible cultural heritage, we encountered many gaps and aporias that remain unaddressed in both the law and secondary scholarship, requiring both speculation and further questions on our part.

We begin, then, by sizing the terrain within which questions of intangible cultural heritage law and policy have emerged as international issues through a succession of UNESCO Conventions and their implementation. We explore the development of these instruments and their interpretation and operation over time to consider the growing international acknowledgement of the significance of intangible cultural heritage as fundamental to human rights and to sustainable development based on the development of human capacities. We consider the specificity of indigenous concerns in this process, before addressing the difficulties of reconciling practices of international trade with those of safeguarding and revitalising intangible cultural heritage. Finally, we consider the trade-based implications of this history, making some modest proposals for the creative deployment of certain intellectual property vehicles that might encompass and advance indigenous development and self-determination in trade contexts.

2. Sizing the Political Terrain: International Cultural Heritage Protection and Policy as it Implicates Indigenous Peoples

Before moving into the history of UNESCO instruments that frame the international law addressing the protection of intangible cultural heritage, we need to understand the history of the concept of cultural heritage and the objectives that underlie its protection. The term 'cultural heritage' has no single definition internationally and definitions have substantially shifted and evolved even during the latter part of the twentieth century.[10] From the 1954 Hague Definition of 'the world's inheritance of works of art and monuments of history and science'[11] through 'manifestations of human life which represent a particular view of life and witness the history and validity of that view'[12] and, more recently, 'culture and landscape that are cared for by the community and passed on to the future to serve people's needs for a sense of identity and

---

[9] For the argument that indigenous rights are part of international customary law see James S. Anaya, *Indigenous Peoples in International Law*, 2nd edn, Oxford: Oxford University Press, 2004.

[10] There are five, or arguably, six, UNESCO Conventions on cultural heritage that span almost fifty years, beginning with the 1956 Hague Convention, and culminating with the Convention on Cultural Diversity in 2005. Because of the ad hoc approach of the Conventions, each of which was devised to deal with an emerging issue or recognised problem, no single definition captures the meaning of the term 'cultural heritage' for all purposes.

[11] Laurajane Smith, *Uses of Heritage*, New York: Routledge, 2006, at p. 74.

[12] Lyndell Prott and Patrick J. O' Keefe, 'Cultural Heritage or Cultural Property?' (1992) *International Journal of Cultural Property*, 1 (2), pp. 307-320, at p. 201.

belonging',[13] the concept has transformed to meet changing needs and interests. The value of cultural heritage lies in its significance to human communities and these values fundamentally relate to the kinds of significance it has. Since cultural heritage may be embodied in intangible forms as well as tangible ones, we are always dealing with terrains of cultural meaning and thus of potential social contestation. The notion of heritage presupposes a focus on inherited forms that may be passed on to future generations in the reproduction of social identities.

The protection of cultural heritage may involve a number of different activities depending upon the values the heritage in question is recognised to possess. When we wish to protect cultural heritage as heritage, we seek to protect not the object or the expression or particular expressive practice per se, but the significance that the object, expression or practice has to those for whom it is cultural heritage, according to legal scholar Craig Forrest in his superb overview of the field.[14] While intangible cultural heritage may be embodied in any number of expressive forms, it is not the expression itself that laws of intangible cultural heritage regimes seek to protect (unlike intellectual property regimes that do precisely that, so as to protect an author's moral or material interests). Rather, it is the significance of the expression in the social life of a community that is, or should be, the policy focus of heritage protection, according to contemporary wisdom. Moreover, just as processes of attributing value are dynamic and evolving, so too must relevant forms of legal protection be capable of evolution and change.

Nonetheless, certain values have assumed dominance in UNESCO regimes in particular time periods, dictating the form that protection has historically assumed. Cultural heritage may have expressive value that is aesthetic, religious or moral in nature, it may have historical and scientific value, and it may have economic value, to consider three forms of value that have received particular emphasis.[15]. Groups, communities, national 'publics', nation states, and in some instances, humankind as a whole may be interested in appropriate forms of valuation. The term 'culture' as a qualifier to the concept of heritage acknowledges a social collective to whom the forms have significance. The relative political power of a given community may determine whether and how heritage goods are valued. Minority groups and indigenous peoples with little formal authority in an international system dominated by nation states as sole sources of legitimate political authority, have limited capacities to define the scope of their relevant heritage or to object to heritage claims made by others. Social collectives have restricted capacities to act in national and international political arenas, although minorities, indigenous peoples and local communities increasingly challenge these restrictions on human rights grounds.[16] Group rights, although evolving, have yet to gain full normative recognition in international law, but these are increasingly recognised as an

---

[13] Toulani Loulanski, 'Revising the Concept of Cultural Heritage: The Argument for a Functional Approach' (2006) *International Journal of Cultural Property*, 13 (2), pp. 207-233, at p. 209.
[14] Craig Forrest, *International Law and the Protection of Cultural Heritage*, London and New York: Routledge, 2010, at pp. 3-4.
[15] Ibid., at pp. 3-5.
[16] Ibid., at pp. 8-9.

important dimension of sustainable development and environmental protection. The right of communities, minorities and indigenous peoples to participate in the process of determining how cultural heritage of significance to them will be protected is arguably the most important issue of cultural heritage law and policy today.[17]

European state governments historically valued cultural heritage as patrimony to be used in nation building exercises; all cultural forms located or created within state territory were considered public goods or public domain material. Still, nationalist sentiments have long co-existed with 'universalist' perspectives in which the state is considered primarily a steward or guardian for the 'common heritage of humankind'. The latter term, however, also has a long history of ideological deployment to legitimate diverse forms of plunder.[18] If cultural heritage is a public good – and the relevant 'public' may be contentious – it may still be ascribed economic value and subject to market exchange. Various combinations of public and private ventures may be deemed appropriate to realise economic value provided that cultural heritage significance is maintained. Intangible cultural heritage, for instance, is often the basis for tourism industries, which may include commodified performances, experiences of landscapes, handicraft sales and types of hospitality offered as new heritage products. It may also be the basis for new industries such as traditional medicine, ecological tourism, sustainable agriculture and environmental impact assessment.

According to a universalist position, cultural heritage is best appreciated and protected when it is visible and accessible to the largest numbers of persons.[19] Arguably, however, this privileges culturally specific presuppositions about meanings and values that may not accord with those of the group for whom such heritage is significant, whose own values must be given priority if it is to be protected *as* cultural heritage. Amongst developing countries, retaining cultural heritage has become an important means of protection because the economic benefits of tourism and the licensing of intellectual property rights promise more sustainable forms of development than the sale and export of cultural goods characteristic of their colonial past.[20] Heritage forms have scholarly value and convey information about human history and cultural development, but the conditions under which they do so are evolving to serve a broader range of interests than their historical capture as relics and antiquities to grace metropolitan museums. Those means of protection which serve general educational and scholarly needs, for example, no longer take precedence over activities that enable host communities to realise economic benefits from local patrimony. These objectives should not be

---

[17] For a process-based model of regulation where the participation of the most relevant stakeholders, including indigenous peoples, is a central element, see Christoph B. Graber, 'Stimulating Trade and Development of Indigenous Cultural Heritage by Means of International Law: Issues of Legitimacy and Method', in this volume.
[18] Forrest, supra note 14, at p. 12. See also Ugo Mattei and Laura Nadar, *Plunder: When the Rule of Law is Illegal*, San Francisco, CA: Wiley Publishers, 2008.
[19] Forrest, supra note 14, at p. 14.
[20] Ibid., at p. 17.

presumed to be antithetical, however, as community-based archaeological research on ICH increasingly illustrates.[21]

With respect to intangible cultural heritage, states have recently obliged themselves to 'safeguard' heritage values, a term that legal expert Janet Blake argues is broader than the concept of protection and requires states to engage in positive actions to promote intangible cultural heritage by creating environments conducive to its flourishing and future production.[22] This requires parties to take a participatory approach in relation to 'measures aimed at ensuring the viability of the intangible cultural heritage, including ... [its] identification, documentation, research, preservation, protection, promotion, enhancement, transmission ... revitalization'.[23] Finally, legal recognition itself provides a means of 'protecting' cultural heritage by reinforcing and legitimating heritage values.[24]

The term cultural heritage has special relevance for indigenous peoples in international law precisely because one of its earliest uses as a category emerges from the realisation that international legal recognition of world heritage and cultural property had historically ill-served them. In her influential report Protection of the Heritage of Indigenous Peoples (1995) – hereinafter the Daes Report – Erica Daes, as Special Rapporteur, stressed that in the UNESCO Declaration of the Principles of International Cultural Cooperation (1966), the free exchange of cultural knowledge was expressly linked with 'respect' and 'reciprocity' among cultures. Her study documented the extent to which respect and reciprocity have been lacking in the widespread practice of appropriation of indigenous peoples' cultural heritage by other societies. She expressed reservations about the term cultural property in international law, and suggested that the apparent division between tangible and intangible cultural heritage in international law was inappropriate as it pertained to indigenous peoples. The term cultural heritage, Daes suggested, more precisely signified the interrelationship between the tangible and intangible qualities of goods in a matrix of relationships that imply responsibilities by members of a collective that are more characteristic of indigenous values.[25] Since both cultural properties and intangible cultural

---

[21] See, for examples, the essays collected in Thomas Killian (ed.), *Opening Archaeology: Repatriation's Impact on Contemporary Research and Practice*, Santa Fe: School of American Research, 2008, at pp. 79-90; George Nicholas and Kelly Bannister, 'Copyrighting the Past? Emerging Intellectual Property Rights Issues in Archaeology' (2004) *Current Anthropology*, 45 (3), pp. 327-350; and more recently, Shelly Greer, 'Heritage and Empowerment: Community-based Indigenous Cultural Heritage in Northern Australia' (2010) *International Journal of Heritage Management*, 16 (1-2), pp. 45–58 and Jonathan Pragnall, Anne Ross and Brian Coghill, 'Power Relations and Community Involvement in Landscape-Based Cultural Heritage Management Practice: An Australian Case Study' (2010) *International Journal of Heritage Studies*, 16 (1), pp. 140-155.

[22] Janet E. Blake, *Commentary on the UNESCO 2003 Safeguarding of the Intangible Cultural Heritage*, Leicester: Institute of Art and Law, 2006, at p. 23.

[23] Janet E. Blake, 'UNESCO's 2003 Convention on Intangible Cultural Heritage: the Implications of Community Involvement in "Safeguarding"', in Laurajane Smith and Natsuko Akagawa (eds), *Intangible Heritage*, New York and London: Routledge, 2009, pp. 45-73, at p. 50.

[24] Forrest, supra note 14, at p. 19.

[25] See discussion in Mohsen al Attar, Nicole Aylwin and Rosemary J. Coombe, 'Indigenous Cultural Rights in International Human Rights Law', in Catherine Bell and Robert K. Paterson (eds),

goods are alienable as commodities – the latter through intellectual property laws – cultural heritage was proffered as a better concept for appreciating the complex forms of inalienability through which tangible and intangible goods together sustain indigenous collectivities. The concept of cultural heritage reflects the fact that goods of cultural significance, unlike properties per se, are not separate from the social processes that sustain their values. Understanding cultural heritage as a dynamic, expressive and productive practice of dialogue, rather than a passive appreciation for a field of static cultural works is consonant with an international movement to revalue cultural diversity and reconceptualise heritage values that clearly situates such cultural activities in the normative field of human rights.

The human rights orientation of cultural heritage protection is found in the very first Article of the Constitution of UNESCO, which establishes that its purpose is to:

> contribute to peace and security by promoting collaboration among the nations through education, science, and culture in order to further universal respect for justice, for the rule of law, and for the human rights and fundamental freedoms which are affirmed for the peoples of the world. ... by the Charter of the United Nations.[26]

Human rights principles expressly frame and limit intangible cultural heritage protections[27] and claims are politically articulated as human rights issues, especially when they involve indigenous peoples. This emphasis upon human rights as the overarching normative framework for interpreting cultural heritage law is especially important for indigenous peoples because intangible cultural heritage claims are central means by which the political, economic and social project of achieving self-determination[28] is facilitated.[29]

Principles for the protection of ICH emerged internationally in a human rights context, framed by the concerns of the Sub-Commission on the Human Rights and made their way into the United Nations Declaration on the Rights of Indigenous Peoples (UNDRIP), in which heritage rights clearly relate to territorial rights from which they are deemed inseparable and indivisible.[30] Indeed, international recognition of indigenous land rights is tied to its cultural value to indigenous peoples. It is suggested that 'the protection of Indigenous peoples' land rights fits more into the category of cultural rights rather than the right to property, and human rights law has provided indigenous peoples with legal avenues for the recognition of their specific cultural attachment to their

---

Protection of First Nations Cultural Heritage: Laws, Policy and Reform, Vancouver, BC: UBC Press, 2009, pp. 311-342, at p. 319.

[26] UNESCO, 'Constitution of the United Nations Educational, Scientific and Cultural Organization' (adopted 16 November 1945, amended at 31st session), Article 1.

[27] The Convention on Intangible Cultural Heritage's extensive preamble includes a prominent citation of the 1948 Universal Declaration on Human Rights and the two 1966 human rights Covenants in its second recital. Article 2 (1) provides that consideration shall only be given to such intangible cultural heritage as is compatible with existing international rights instruments.

[28] Forrest, supra note 14, at p. 363.

[29] Val Napoleon, 'Looking beyond the Law: Questions about Indigenous Peoples' Tangible and Intangible Property', in Catherine Bell and Robert K. Paterson (eds), *Protection of First Nations Cultural Heritage: Laws, Policy and Reform*, Vancouver, BC: UBC Press, 2009, pp. 370-393, at p. 371.

[30] Al Attar et al., supra note 25, at p. 317, note 28.

traditional territories.'[31] Indigenous communities' representatives and the non-governmental organisations that support them have been successful in compelling the international community to address issues of cultural protection, recognition and valuation of traditional knowledge and the integral relation of these to aboriginal territories.[32] Moreover, ICH protection is often linked to a broader project of decolonisation that stresses the inextricable link between cultural heritage and the maintenance, strengthening, transmission and renewal of indigenous peoples' identity, knowledge, laws and practices.[33]

UNDRIP has also provided a strong normative vocabulary with which to make these claims, providing as it does:

> an authoritative common understanding, at the global level, of the minimum content of the rights of indigenous peoples, upon a foundation of various sources of international human rights law ... The principles and rights affirmed in the Declaration constitute or add to the normative frameworks for the activities of United Nations human rights institutions, mechanisms and specialized agencies as they relate to indigenous peoples.[34]

Thus, human rights standards seem to be fundamental in framing most if not all principles of international ICH protection. With co-authors, Coombe has canvassed the field of international human rights law pertaining to ICH elsewhere to conclude that the rights of indigenous peoples to a measure of control over the use of their cultural heritage is widely recognised and arguably constitutes a principle of international customary law.[35]

UNESCO is the primary UN body responsible for preparing and interpreting international normative principles and instruments with regard to cultural rights as a special category of human rights in international law. International human rights norms generally demand a special sensitivity to the rights of the disadvantaged. Minorities and indigenous peoples are precisely those whose cultural rights have historically been violated, often through state sanctioned initiatives to forcibly assimilate them, prohibit their cultural practices, penalise the use of their languages and the practice of their spiritual life, seize their cultural goods and relegate their culture to a form of historical information.[36] Over the last two decades international policy has recognised

---

[31] Jeremie Gilbert, 'Custodians of the Land: Indigenous Peoples, Human Rights and Cultural Integrity', in Michele Langfield, William Logan and Mairead Nic Craith (eds), *Cultural Diversity, Heritage and Human Rights*, Abingdon: Routledge, 2010, pp. 31-44, at p. 35.

[32] Al Attar et al., supra note 25, at p. 323.

[33] George Nicholas et al., 'Intellectual Property Issues in Heritage Management Part 2: Legal Dimension, Ethical Considerations, and Collaborative Research Practices' (2010) *Heritage Management*, 3 (1), pp. 117-147, at p. 121.

[34] S. James Anaya (Special Rapporteur on the Situation of Human Rights and Fundamental Freedoms of Indigenous People), 'Promotion and Protection of all Human Rights, Civil, Political, Economic, Social and Cultural Rights, Including the Right to Development', UN, General Assembly, Human Rights Council, Ninth Session (UN Doc. A/HRC/9/9/Add-1, 2008).

[35] Al Attar et al., supra note 25.

[36] George Nicholas, 'Indigenous Cultural Heritage in the Age of Technological Reproducibility: Towards a Postcolonial Ethic of the Public Domain', in Rosemary J. Coombe, Darren Wershler and Martin Zeilinger (eds), *Dynamic Fair Dealing: Creating Canadian Culture Online*, Toronto: University of Toronto Press, in press. See also, Elizabeth Coleman and Rosemary J. Coombe, 'A Broken

that ICH is not a residual remainder of a lost past, but an evolving repertoire of knowledge, practices, innovations and expressions that are significant for maintaining the interlinked goods of cultural and biological diversity while providing the basis for sustainable development.[37] A number of international and national legal instruments promoting the ethnic, cultural, linguistic and religious identities of national minorities affirm community rights to participate in decisions that involve the use of their cultural heritage and recognize cultural diversity as grounds for sustainable development.

Our focus therefore, is primarily upon the protection, preservation, safeguarding and development of ICH as a cultural right, rather than as an economic right, which is more properly the purview of WIPO. Nonetheless, to the extent that UNESCO is committed to maintaining both cultural identity and furthering sustainable development, it becomes necessary to consider the extent to which economic rights may need to be shaped or limited to serve these objectives.

International instruments addressing the rights of indigenous peoples, it might be argued, have fundamentally altered the international consensus on the scope and meaning of cultural rights.[38] Prior to the negotiation of the UNDRIP (a twenty-year process), international law largely objectified culture. Cultural rights protected heritage practices and cultural identifications with heritage goods primarily as static monuments, icons, and symbols subject to state cultural recognition[39] not as material domains with respect to which communities other than nations might have legitimate authority and a political voice.[40] Regarded as an activity and as a resource, however, the political and economic dimensions of culture have come to the fore, putting new emphasis on community security, economic stability and sustainable development; cultural rights claims have increasingly enabled groups to achieve control over significant material resources[41] and heightened their stakes in fields of cultural representation.

Within the wider field of cultural rights (which includes the moral and material interests of authors more properly covered by a discussion of intellectual property) we focus on obligations to protect, safeguard, maintain and develop intangible cultural heritage of particular concern to indigenous peoples.[42] Although the term 'intangible cultural heritage' formally emerges

---

Record: Subjecting "Music" to Cultural Rights', in James C. Young and Conrad Brunck (eds), *Ethics of Cultural Appropriation*, London: Blackwell, 2008, pp. 179-210.

[37] Rosemary J. Coombe and Nicole Aylwin, 'Repositioning Cultural Heritage Ethics Using Human Rights Norms', in Rosemary J. Coombe, Darren Wershler and Martin Zeilinger (eds), *Dynamic Fair Dealing: Creating Canadian Culture Online*, Toronto: University of Toronto Press, in press.

[38] Cindy Holder, 'Culture as an Activity and Human Right: An Important Advance for Indigenous Peoples and International Law' (2008) *Alternatives*, 33, pp. 7-28.

[39] Ibid., at p. 17.

[40] Ibid., at p. 12.

[41] Bruce Robbins and Elsa Stamatapolou, 'Reflections on Culture and Cultural Rights' (2004) *South Atlantic Quarterly*, 103 (2/3), pp. 419-434.

[42] Reference will be made to other UNESCO Conventions and Instruments, as well as WIPO activities, only when these help to clarify issues that remain obscure when focusing primarily upon the major Conventions.

only with the 2003 Convention on the Intangible Cultural Heritage,[43] it would be a mistake to consider this the only UNESCO Convention concerned with the intangible dimensions of cultural heritage. Properties are only of interest to UNESCO to the extent that a property has the kind of value embraced by the term cultural heritage. Historically, the term 'cultural property' served as an expedient referent; nonetheless, 'it is essentially the value attributed to the objects that is to be protected'[44] and thus the intangible aspects that warranted policy attention. Nonetheless, critics point to the dominant meanings that property has as a concept in common law, particularly to commercial significations that privilege exclusive private rights of exclusion, alienation, exploitation, and even absolute rights of destruction that do not denote protective considerations. Although the term cultural heritage emerges in the 1972 World Heritage Convention (WHC)[45] as the target of protection, the Convention's limited application to immoveables, such as monuments, archaeological sites, relics and landscapes is perceived to have detracted attention from the values themselves.

In some cases, state and international focus upon the fixed property unfortunately damaged the cultural values that the form was designated as heritage to protect. For example, the physical protection of world heritage sites like Angkor (and their development for more widespread appreciation) is widely acknowledged to have damaged the cultural connection between the Cambodian people and this manifestation of their heritage. By 1995 experts recognized that the concept of cultural heritage, having become too based on architectural and archaeological heritage, unduly focuses on the physical side, 'completely ignoring the question of the function in contemporary society.'[46]

Other forms of cultural heritage that lacked tangible manifestation, such as ritual, behaviour, oral histories, knowledge, skills and practices were also slighted by this emphasis upon materiality. These intangible forms had not historically received protection arguably because they were possessed by less powerful peoples with denigrated cultural value systems[47] whose cultural forms were often deemed primitive and backward – destined to disappear under policies of modernity, assimilation and development. To the extent that these were legally recognized it was as folklore that was properly part of the public domain.[48] Ultimately, then, cultural heritage as a concept had become so associated with its tangible manifestations rather than the values therein embodied that policymakers deemed it necessary to add the qualifier 'intangible' to the primary term cultural heritage. This provided a clear means of referring to aspects of cultural heritage with no material fixity capable of rendering these properties (or authorship attributes capable of rendering them intellectual properties).

---

[43] UNESCO, Convention for the Safeguarding of the Intangible Cultural Heritage, 2368 UNTS 1 (adopted on 17 October 2003, entered into force 20 April 2006).
[44] Forrest, supra note 14, at p. 23.
[45] UNESCO, Convention Concerning the Protection of the World Cultural and Natural Heritage, 1037 UNTS 151 (adopted on 16 November 1972, entered into force 17 December 1975).
[46] As cited in Forrest, supra note 14, at p. 28.
[47] Jessica Myers Moran, 'Legal Means for Protecting the Intangible Cultural Heritage of Indigenous Peoples in a Post-Colonial World' (2008) Holy Cross Journal of Law and Public Policy, 12 (71), at p. 71.
[48] Coombe and Aylwin, supra note 37. See also Vézina, supra note 7.

During the 1980s, debates about the meaning and value of cultural heritage took place in relationship to larger international deliberations about the relationship between culture and development. In 1987, the UN launched its World Decade for Cultural Development (1987-1997), in which a more anthropological view of culture as a way of life and form of social organisation was adopted. This served to reinforce the idea that cultural heritage could not be restricted to historical sites and monuments but needed to include oral tradition and a wider field of expressive culture.[49] In 1995, at the UNESCO General Conference, The World Commission on Culture and Development solidified this new perspective in its report, *Our Creative Diversity*, by highlighting that heritage is made up of more than monuments and historical sites, and that both tangible and intangible cultural heritage are key to 'ensuring the flourishing of human existence.' [50]

In the collective struggles of many marginalised people, culture is a concept used reflexively to engage with state and non-governmental institutions for purposes of asserting identity, demanding greater inclusion in political life, local autonomy, and control over resources, while seeking new forms of engagement with global markets (as well as resistances thereto).[51] Cultural distinction has gained new international purchase as a valuable social, political and economic resource.[52] Cultural rights have become legal vehicles through which political claims are pursued; cultural rights claims now figure in struggles for political autonomy, legal entitlements to territory and other resources and designs for alternative forms of development.[53] Issues of safeguarding, managing, and developing ICH are integrally embedded in this larger field of politics.

---

[49] Blake, supra note 23, at p. 48.

[50] Lourdes Arizpe, 'The Cultural Politics of Intangible Cultural Heritage', in Janet Blake (ed.), *Safeguarding Intangible Cultural Heritage: Challenges and Approaches*, Builth Wells, Great Britain: Institute of Art and Law, 2007, pp. 25-41, at p. 32.

[51] See Rosemary J. Coombe, 'First Nations Intangible Cultural Heritage Concerns: Prospects for Protection of Traditional Knowledge and Traditional Cultural Expressions in International Law', in Catherine Bell and Robert K. Paterson (eds), *Protection of First Nations Cultural Heritage: Laws, Policy and Reform*, Vancouver, BC: UBC Press, 2009, pp. 247-277.

[52] As elaborated in John Comaroff and Jean Comaroff, *Ethnicity, Inc.*, Chicago: University of Chicago Press, 2009. See also, Rosemary J. Coombe, 'Legal Claims to Culture in and Against the Market: Neoliberalism and the Global Proliferation of Meaningful Difference' (2005) *Law, Culture and Humanities*, 1 (1), pp. 32-55; George Yudice, *The Expediency of Culture*, Durham: Duke University Press, 2003; and Vijayendra Rao and Michael Walton (eds), *Culture and Public Action*, Palo Alto, CA: Stanford University Press, 2004.

[53] See Rosemary J. Coombe, '"Possessing Culture": Political Economies of Community Subjects and their Properties', in Mark Busse and Veronica Strang (eds), *Ownership and Appropriation*, London: Berg Publishers, 2011, pp. 105-127 [hereinafter Coombe, 'Possessing Culture']; Rosemary J. Coombe, 'Cultural Agencies: "Constructing" Community Subjects and their Rights', in Mario Biagioli, Peter Jaszi, and Martha Woodmansee (eds), *Making and Unmaking Intellectual Property*, Chicago: University of Chicago Press, 2011, pp. 79-98 [hereinafter Coombe, 'Cultural Agencies']; Henrietta Marrie, 'The UNESCO Convention for the Safeguarding of the Intangible Cultural Heritage and the Protection and Maintenance of the Intangible Cultural Heritage of Indigenous Peoples', in Laurajane Smith and Natsuko Akagawa (eds), *Intangible Heritage*, New York and London: Routledge, 2009, pp. 169-192; and Bruce Robbins and Elsa Stamatapolou, 'Reflections on Culture and Cultural Rights' (2004) *South Atlantic Quarterly*, 103 (2/3), pp. 419-434.

3. The Development of Intangible Cultural Heritage Law and Policy

To explore the development of intangible cultural heritage law and policy within the international framework, we examine the UNESCO instruments most likely to impact upon indigenous intangible cultural heritage, avoiding those that pertain primarily to material cultural property except when these include sites of cultural significance to indigenous peoples from which significant forms of intangible cultural heritage might arise and require protection, preservation, or development. As the following summary description of the main features of the relevant legal instruments illustrates, UNESCO's interest in and commitment to the protection of intangible ICH has become stronger as institutional concerns have focused increasingly upon maintaining cultural identities and cultural diversity.

3.1. World Heritage Convention (WHC) 1972

The WHC reflects the convergence of three international initiatives, one for protecting monuments and sites of universal value, another for conservation of natural heritage, and a declaration on the value of human environments. Coming into force in 1975, it had been adopted by virtually all states by 2009. The Convention was based upon the universalist premise that heritage is the world heritage of global humankind and to qualify for the regime's inscription and protection, it must be of 'outstanding universal value'. This concept has been amended through Operational Guidelines that have had six distinct variations since 1977, reflecting a shift from iconic and historic sites to those more representative of the world's diversity and living traditions. Contemporary Guidelines evaluate a site's integrity and authenticity within the cultural context in which the site has significance.[54] Ultimately, however, it is the state party that must identify and nominate potential sites and pledge to conserve these. State sovereignty over heritage within its territory is fundamental to the regime but state duties have little discernible positive content. While states are encouraged to adopt policies that give the cultural and natural heritage a function in the life of the community, set-up services for protection, work out operating methods to counteract dangers to the heritage, and establish training centres for heritage protection, they are only asked to endeavour to do so. States are required to maintain inventories of sites suitable for inclusion in a Tentative List of possible nominations and for many years have been encouraged to prepare these lists 'with the participation of a wide variety of stakeholders, including site managers, local and regional governments, local communities, NGOs, and other interested parties and partners'.[55]

The International Council on Monuments and Sites (ICOMOS) was established in 1965 and played an important role in the conceptualisation of

---

[54] This first becomes apparent in 2005 (see, UNESCO, 'World Heritage Committee Operational Guidelines for the Implementation of the World Heritage Convention', (UNESCO Doc. WHC. 05/02, 2005), at paras 87-95, available online at http://whc.unesco.org/archive/opguide05-en.pdf) (all online sources were accessed 30 November 2011).

[55] Forrest, supra note 14, at p. 251.

cultural heritage. Its mandate was restricted to monuments (real property) and sites (a group of elements, whether natural or man-made or combinations of the two, which it is in the public interest to preserve) but did not extend to moveable property.[56] This reflected a growing interest in environmental and anthropological aspects of historical preservation[57] and an acknowledgment that the setting for archaeological works may be significant to their cultural value.[58] Sites may have heritage value because of their association with events, living traditions, ideas, beliefs or artistic and literary works of outstanding universal significance, for instance.

Still, the WHC definition of monuments 'which are of outstanding universal value from the point of view of history, art, or science' clearly privileges some kinds of intangible values over others. Similarly the definition of sites as 'works of man or combined works of man and nature' undervalues the cultural values that many indigenous communities hold with respect to natural sites.[59] Laurajane Smith provides an extensive critical discussion of how the politics of cultural resource management with respect to ICH in Australia has worked to empower archaeologists at the political expense of indigenous peoples themselves, devaluing their knowledge, denying their authority, defining their identity and in some cases even denying their contemporary existence as aboriginal peoples.[60] Despite the establishment of codes of ethics requiring archaeologists to consult with indigenous communities, some indigenous people have experienced these consultation processes as disrespectful, patronising and tokenistic – in short, monologic rather than dialogic. Significantly, Smith illustrates that many professional experts in this field remain ignorant of the political consequences of their work for indigenous peoples and the ways in which their historical pronouncements may impact upon aboriginal rights to land, resources and livelihoods. Her work helps to explain the distrust with which indigenous peoples may still greet legal processes of protecting cultural heritage and associated activities of state initiated cultural resource management.[61]

3.2. Instrument on Cultural Landscapes 1992

The recognition of cultural landscapes as an explicit category of heritage in 1992 was one response to allegations that the World Heritage Committee's selection criteria were unbalanced and Eurocentric and failed to appreciate the significance of ICH in many parts of the world. At about the same period, following the Rio Earth Summit, global policymakers were considering issues of biological diversity, which posited indigenous knowledge and its vulnerability as significant issues to be addressed. The WHC's definition of

---

[56] International Charter for the Conservation and Restoration of Monuments and Sites (The Venice Charter 1964) available online at http://www.international.icomos.org/charters/venice_e.htm.
[57] Forrest, supra note 14, at p. 226.
[58] Forrest, supra note 14, at p. 230.
[59] Laurajane Smith, *Uses of Heritage*, London: Routledge, 2006, at p. 96.
[60] Smith, supra note 11, at p. 96.
[61] See also Jane Lydon 'Contested Landscapes: Rights to History, Rights to Place: who controls archaeological places?', in Bruno David and Julian Thomas (eds), *Handbook of Landscape Archaeology*, Walnut Creek, CA: Left Coast Press, 2008, pp. 654-659.

heritage provided an innovative and powerful opportunity for the protection of cultural landscapes as 'combined works of nature and man'.[62] In 1992, the World Heritage Committee adopted three categories of cultural landscapes as qualifying for listing.[63] The most easily identifiable was the clearly defined landscape designed and created intentionally by man, which embraces garden and parkland landscapes constructed for aesthetic reasons that may be associated with religious or other monumental buildings. The second category is the organically evolved landscape that 'results from an initial social, economic, administrative, and/or religious imperative and has developed its present form by association with and in response to its natural environment' falling into two sub-categories, the first pertaining to relic landscapes that are no longer evolving, and the second, a continuing landscape which retains an active social role in contemporary society.[64] The final category of 'associative cultural landscapes' was deemed 'justifiable by virtue of the powerful religious, artistic or cultural associations of the natural element rather than material cultural evidence'. Thus the 'associated intangible values' of natural places of cultural significance could provide the basis for inscription on the World Heritage List.[65]

According to UNESCO insiders, the category of cultural landscape has been crucial for legitimating the heritage of local communities and indigenous people:

> The primary difference was the acceptance of communities and their relationship with the environment. There are many places with associative cultural values, or sacred sites, which may be physical entities or mental images embedded in a people's spirituality, cultural tradition, and practice. The category of sacred sites has an immense potential, as many protected areas have been basically protected because they are sacred places. Well before the categorization of protected areas into national parks, nature reserves, and landscapes, indigenous peoples have protected their sacred sites and groves. Through these mechanisms they have contributed to preserving unique sites, biological diversity and cultural spaces transmitted to future generations.[66]

---

[62] UNESCO, Convention Concerning the Protection of the World Cultural and Natural Heritage, 1037 UNTS 151 (adopted on 16 November 1972, entered into force 17 December 1975), Article 1 [hereinafter 'Heritage Convention'].

[63] UNESCO, 'World Heritage Committee Operational Guidelines for the Implementation of the World Heritage Convention', (UNESCO Doc. WHC. 2, 1992), at para. 23, available online at http://whc.unesco.org/archive/opguide92-en.pdf.

[64] 'Guidelines on the Inscription of Certain Types of Properties on the World Heritage List', Annex 3 to UNESCO, 'World Heritage Committee Operational Guidelines for the Implementation of the World Heritage Convention', (UNESCO Doc. WHC. 08/01, 2008), at para. 10(ii), available online at http://whc.unesco.org/archive/opguide08-en.pdf.

[65] See discussion in Jean-Louis Luxen, 'The Intangible Dimension of Monuments and Sites' (2000) ICOMOS Newsletter, March-July, available at http://www.international.icomos.org/ga2002.htm; and in Harriet J. Deacon and O. Beazley, 'The Safeguarding of Intangible Heritage Values under the World Heritage Convention: Auschwitz, Hiroshima and Robben Island', in Janet E. Blake (ed.), Safeguarding Intangible Cultural Heritage - Challenges and Approaches, Bulith Wells, UK: Institute of Art and Law, 2007, pp. 93-107.

[66] Mechtild Rössler, 'World Heritage Cultural Landscapes: A UNESCO Flagship Programme' (2006) Landscape Research, 31 (4), pp. 333-353, at p. 336.

It was only in 1998, however, that the Operational Guidelines were changed to allow for the inclusion of a traditionally managed natural site – East Rennell (Solomon Islands) – to be inscribed on the World Heritage List.[67] Consequentially, the involvement of local people in nomination processes was considered desirable; in 2005 the Operational Guidelines formally encouraged community involvement. Ideally, the Convention will evolve to recognise traditional management systems, customary law and traditional environmental knowledge as legitimate forms of protection and thereby 'contribute to sustainable local and regional development'.[68] New governance structures might combine community-managed systems and traditional national park management in a vision of shared responsibilities amongst stakeholders where local capacity building and employment for community members are linked to national institutional support and indigenous peoples are considered primary beneficiaries.[69]

As Janet Blake notes, this type of landscape is exemplified by Uluru Kata Tjuta National Park in Australia and Tongariro National Park in New Zealand, where indigenous peoples assume management roles.[70] Inscribed on the World Heritage List in 1994 as a cultural landscape manifesting the interaction of humanity and its natural environment as both a 'continuing' and 'associative' cultural landscape, the management of indigenous intangible cultural heritage has been structured so as to provide economic benefits for indigenous communities that may well be relevant for considerations of trade.

In Uluru Kata Tjuta National Park, Anangu Aboriginal peoples' cosmologies are central to the site's perceived significance and are reflected in traditional management practices that provide a code of behaviour governing both interpersonal relationships and environmental management. These include ceremonies performed according to *Tjukurpa*, an indigenous philosophy often referred to in English as the Dreaming – a term that Anangu reject because it implies that the relationships between humans, animals, plants, and their descendants are in some sense unreal or imaginary.[71] This philosophy is arguably local customary law in the region and is sometimes translated as 'time of the law'.[72] Moreover:

> ... the material forms of Uluru and Kata Tjuta incorporate the actions, artefacts and bodies of the ancestral beings celebrated in Anangu religion and culture through narratives, elaborate song cycles, visual arts and dance. The numerous paintings in the rock shelters at the foot of Uluru express the ideas (*kulini*, or

---

[67] UNESCO, 'World Heritage Committee Operational Guidelines for the Implementation of the World Heritage Convention', (UNESCO Doc. WHC. 99/02, 1999), at para. 24(ii), available online at http://whc.unesco.org/archive/opguide99-en.pdf.
[68] Rössler, supra note 66, at p. 334.
[69] Ibid., at p. 348.
[70] Blake, supra note 23, at p. 51. See also Julia Simmonds, 'UNESCO World Heritage Convention' (1997) *Art, Antiquity and Law*, 2 (3), pp. 251-281.
[71] Graeme Calma and Lynette Liddle, 'Uluru-Kata Tjuta National Park: Sustainable Management and Development', in UNESCO, *Cultural Landscapes: the Challenges of Conservation, World Heritage Papers No. 7*, Paris: World Heritage Centre, 2003, pp. 104-119, at p. 105.
[72] Robert Layton, 'Relating to the Country in the Western Desert', in Eric Hirsch and Michael O'Hanlon (eds), *The Anthropology of Landscape: Perspectives on Space and Place*, Oxford: Clarendon Press, 1997, pp. 210-231.

physical thinking) of *Tjukurpa*. They were made as a teaching tool . . . one of the park's Anangu rangers, describes the painted shelters as an 'Anangu blackboard'. It is incumbent on modern Anangu to follow *Tjukurpa*, both in their management of the environment and in their social relationships.[73]

It is precisely these spiritual 'associations' with 'country' that are protected through the Uluru-Kata Tjuta National Park Board of Management, the Central Land Council and the Office for Joint Management. The landscape is actively managed by Aboriginal communities 'using traditional practices and knowledge ... and management techniques to conserve biodiversity such as the use of fire and the creation and maintenance of water sources such as wells and rock waterholes' [74] as well as through maintenance of traditional ceremonial activities within Anangu communities. Management of the park, access to the sites, and the information conveyed to visitors all embody respect for Anangu ritual values and incorporate activities Anangu deem necessary for the maintenance of *Tjukurpa*, including transmission of traditional knowledge to youth to enable them to find water, food, and bush medicine, ritualised visiting of sacred sites, keeping visitors safe by respecting traditional forms of power vested in sites, caretaking through rockhole cleaning and traditional burning, and keeping the country alive through ceremony and song.[75] Anangu peoples are employed in all natural resource management activities and Anangu traditional ecological knowledge of flora, fauna, habitat, seasons, places and their history is valued in park management.[76]

Protecting *Nguraritja* 'intellectual and cultural property rights' is necessary to protect traditional knowledge and Anangu cultural work. *Nguraritja* refers to traditional custodians of sites, who acquire responsibilities through birth and ancestral connections. Although all Anangu peoples are recognised as having rights to control their cultural heritage, Anangu management plans vest such rights of control as responsibilities to be exercised by *Nguraritja*.[77] The Park features a Cultural Centre, opened ten years after the park was returned to its traditional Anangu owners; the documentation and storage of traditional knowledge as well as the transmission of *Tjurkurpa* values to future generations and to the public is one of its central missions.[78] New media such as film, video and digital sound recording store and transmit oral histories while recording relationships between songs and landscape features in the presentation of 'soundscapes' enables visitors to virtually explore the cultural landscape. Paintings on the rock faces reflect aspects of religion and ceremony and serve pedagogical purposes for both community members and visitors; Anangu use the same symbols today in sand drawings, body painting and acrylic paintings.

---

[73] Calma and Liddle, supra note 71, at p. 105.
[74] Ibid., at p. 107.
[75] Ibid., at p. 109.
[76] Ibid., at p. 108.
[77] Australian House of Representatives, Standing Committee on Environment, Recreation and the Arts, 'Managing Australia's World Heritage', *Committee Report* (4 November 1996), available online at http://www.aph.gov.au/house/committee/environ/whainq/whirpt/contents.htm, last updated 7 February 2011.
[78] Calma and Liddle, supra note 71, at p. 108.

Indigenous participation in the management of cultural landscapes is not restricted to World Heritage sites, however. UNESCO values may be translated into the domestic policies of state parties even where sites are not nominated for inscription. For example, Canada began to recognise cultural landscapes in the 1990s and added aboriginal cultural landscapes to its national parks system in 1999, [79] incorporating principles of community involvement and management that have put emphasis upon the significance of such sites to aboriginal peoples and privilege their management.[80] Certainly the evolution of world heritage to include cultural landscapes seems to better accord with indigenous values. Nonetheless, there is a long legacy of managing heritage sites in a way that privileges aesthetic values and displacing indigenous values with respect to natural sites that will need to be overcome.

Social geographer Jennifer Carter provides an extensive case study from Fraser Island in Australia that demonstrates the continuing tendency of professional experts to rhetorically 'depopulate' significant heritage sites, while misunderstanding the complex connections between nature and culture characteristic of indigenous values.[81] Despite official federal acknowledgment of the hybridity of nature and culture in heritage discourse, state planning and site management continues to maintain 'separate environmental impact and cultural heritage assessments, relying on documented evidence within a structured inventory and a material-centred approach to the categorising of "natural" or "cultural" values', [82] ignoring the indigenous imprint upon the landscape and the landscape's significance to aboriginal identity. Nonetheless, she acknowledges that the contemporary recognition of cultural landscapes 'might allow Indigenous people to more fully receive the benefits they desire through tourism, park management, fishing, education, planning, and the provision of roads and local services, and so forth. Whether or not re-nomination occurs, world heritage inscription needs to be realised as people's connection with place.' [83]

3.3. Convention for the Safeguarding of the Intangible Cultural Heritage 2003

If 'intangible cultural heritage is not an object, not a performance, not a site; … may be embodied or given material form in any of these, but basically … it is

---

[79] Meryl Olivier, 'Cultural Landscape Conservation Experiences in Canada', in UNESCO, *Cultural Landscapes: the Challenges of Conservation, World Heritage Papers No. 7*, Paris: World Heritage Centre, 2003, pp. 101-103.

[80] Susan Buggey and Nora Mitchell, 'Cultural Landscape Management Challenges and Promising New Directions in the United States and Canada', in UNESCO, *Cultural Landscapes: the Challenges of Conservation, World Heritage Papers No. 7*, Paris: World Heritage Centre, 2003, pp. 92-100, at p. 92.

[81] Jennifer Carter, 'Displacing Indigenous Cultural Landscapes: the Naturalistic Gaze at Fraser Island World Heritage Area' (2010) *Geographical Research*, 48 (4), pp. 398-410.

[82] Ibid., at p. 399, citing Germán I. Andrade, 'The Non-Material Values of the Machu Picchu World Heritage Site from Acknowledgement to Action' (2000) *Parks*, 10, pp. 49-62; and Sue Jackson, 'Compartmentalising Culture: the Articulation and Consideration of Values in Water Resource Management' (2006) *Australian Geographer*, 37, pp. 19–31.

[83] Ibid., at p. 408 (internal citations omitted).

an enactment of meanings embodied in collective memory',[84] it is not surprising that attempts to safeguard such an amorphous corpus for regulation have involved decades of struggle. Many societies value intangible heritage passed down over generations more than the physical manifestations of this heritage and view such manifestations as meaningless outside of the social context of their transmission, yet these values were effectively marginalised in global policy circles for decades. International attention was focused upon intangible cultural heritage by a remarkable confluence of concerns and energies that conjoined multiple international agencies.

The negotiation of the Convention for the Safeguarding of the Intangible Cultural Heritage (ICHC)[85] at the end of the twentieth century was influenced by a widely held concern that the dominance of commercial cultural forces had the potential to undermine the diversity of the world's cultural heritage and that the decline of languages, traditional practices and traditional knowledges posed grave consequences for the preservation of biological diversity and for sustainable development.[86] The preservation of intangible cultural heritage had thus become a matter of concern to international organisations that would not normally focus their energies on cultural matters per se. These include the United Nations Environment Programme, the Food and Agricultural Organisation (FAO), the International Labour Organization (ILO), the World Bank and the World Trade Organization, which has ensured that intangible cultural heritage is now addressed by multiple and overlapping regimes.

The intangible dimensions of culture have been long recognised by UNESCO, but no normative regime of protection emerged, despite years of attempts to facilitate law-making in this area, beginning in the early 1970s when UNESCO collaborated with WIPO to include folklore in model laws for copyright protection. It was not until 1989, however, that UNESCO adopted the Recommendation of the Safeguarding of Traditional Culture and Folklore,[87] which sought to encourage international co-operation between states and national measures for identification, conservation, protection and dissemination. Whether due to a lack of incentives and support, or to ideological opposition, few states gave effect to these proposed 'soft law' measures. The perceived overlap between intangible cultural heritage and intellectual property protections has continued to characterise international efforts, which indigenous peoples have regarded as putting too much emphasis upon proprietary models for protection.[88] Indeed, although it is beyond the scope of this chapter to argue, indigenous rejection of proprietary models arguably helped to shape the norms and values reflected in the ICHC

---

[84] Lourdes Arizpe, 'The Cultural Politics of Intangible Cultural Heritage' (2007) *Art, Antiquity and Law*, 12 (4), pp. 361-388, at p. 362.

[85] Supra note 43.

[86] Toshiyuki Kono, 'UNESCO and Intangible Cultural Heritage from the Viewpoint of Sustainable Development', in Abdulqawi A. Yusef (ed.), *Standard Setting in UNESCO: Normative Action in Education, Science and Culture*, Leiden: Martinus Nijhoff and UNESCO Publishing, 2007, pp. 237-265, at p. 237.

[87] 'Recommendation on Safeguarding Traditional Culture and Folklore', in UNESCO, 'Records of the General Conference. Twenty-fifth Session. Resolutions', 1989, annex I.B, available online at http://unesdoc.unesco.org/images/0008/000846/084696e.pdf#page=242.

[88] Marrie, supra note 53, at p. 181.

and its Operational Guidelines. Adopted in 2003 and entered into force in 2006, the ICHC had over one hundred state parties by 2008.

The full impact of the Convention is yet to be realised because guidelines for implementation have only recently been established.[89] The prehistory of its adoption is, however, of special significance to indigenous peoples. The ICHC is the product of negotiations marked by considerable political tension both between state parties and between states and those advocating for more local interests. Impetus for early developments such as the 'Living Human Treasures' program to celebrate 'exponents of traditional culture' came from Japan and Korea, who felt that criteria for recognition in the WHC disregarded the qualities of their cultural traditions. Moreover, frustration in the Global South with the criteria used to populate the World Heritage List and a perceived lack of global interest in the living form of cultural heritage in practical activities are amongst the reasons UNESCO was urged to amend the WHC to incorporate intangible cultural heritage.[90]

The failure of global efforts to protect folklore, the marginalisation of community interests in heritage, and the incorporation of folklore under WIPO's intellectual property mandate and its perceived tendencies to commercialisation were also factors in building the political will to develop an independent normative regime.[91] The Masterpieces of Oral and Intangible Heritage of Humanity programme in 1997 was thus launched as an awareness raising and educational tool to alert states to the importance of safeguarding oral heritage in danger of disappearing. Critics, however, assert that the programme privileges 'colourful and exotic examples of intangible heritage, that represent nationally valued cultural events or performances, and which coincide with romanticised Western perceptions, while Indigenous works remain underrepresented.'[92] Moreover, historical records suggest that the programme perturbed states with large indigenous populations.[93] Nonetheless, the ensuing debates about the propriety of the term 'masterpiece', the notion of 'universal value' and the importance of involving practitioner communities worked to clear the political ground for the ICHC.

The scope of UNESCO's interest in ICH is quite limited. Avoiding overlap with other UN agencies such as WIPO, ILO, World Health Organisation (WHO), Convention on Biological Diversity (CBD) and United Nations

---

[89] Nonetheless, because it is relatively recent and because the scholars and activists involved in its negotiation are still with us and deliberately documented its negotiation and are actively studying its implementation, we have a remarkable body of scholarship exploring its key concepts, against which its implementation can be assessed.

[90] Noriko Aikawa-Faure, 'From the Proclamation of Masterpieces to the Convention for the Safeguarding of Intangible Cultural Heritage', in Laurajane Smith and Natsuko Akagawa (eds), *Intangible Heritage*, New York and London: Routledge, 2009, pp. 13-44, at p. 15.

[91] Harriet J. Deacon et al., *The Subtle Power of Intangible Heritage: Legal and Financial Instruments for Safeguarding Intangible Heritage*, Cape Town: HSRC Press, 2004, at p. 17.

[92] Laurajane Smith and Natsuko Akagawa, 'Introduction', in Laurajane Smith and Natsuko Akagawa (eds), *Intangible Heritage*, New York and London: Routledge, 2009, pp. 1-12, at p. 4, citing Richard Kurin, 'Comments' (2002) *Current Anthropology*, 43 (1), pp. 144-145; Richard Kurin, 'Safeguarding Intangible Cultural Heritage in the 2003 UNESCO Convention: a Critical Appraisal' (2004) *Museum International*, 56 (1-2), pp. 66-76; and Barbara Kirshenblatt-Gimblett, 'Intangible Heritage as Metacultural Production' (2004) *Museum International*, 56 (1-2), pp. 52-64.

[93] Ibid., at p. 3.

Conference on Trade and Development (UNCTAD), it seeks primarily to further its priority policies in the field of culture, which at this point in time were the promotion of cultural diversity and cultural identity – hence the emphasis on the processes *within communities* that generate such diversity and identity.[94] Influenced, if only negatively, by prior collaborations between UNESCO and WIPO, many deliberators rejected the term folklore as being too oriented to products, rather than symbols, values and processes; they saw it as neglecting the practitioners and communities whose stake in creating, performing, enacting, preserving and disseminating traditional cultural forms was primary.[95] They favoured more holistic anthropological understandings of culture that put indigenous and traditional knowledge into an ecological context that emphasised ways of life or livelihood. Indeed, some participants felt that the Daes Report definition of intangible cultural heritage more clearly captured the spirit and meaning of the range of forms that a new instrument or Convention should attempt to protect.[96] The eventual definition of intangible cultural heritage adopted in the Convention is widely acknowledged to be vague but perhaps this is a strength given the unpredictability of those forms it may be asked to protect. Article 2.1 defines the intangible cultural heritage as:

> ... the practices, representations, expressions, knowledge, skills – as well as the instruments, objects, artefacts and cultural spaces associated therewith – that communities, groups and, in some cases, individuals recognize as part of their cultural heritage. This intangible cultural heritage, transmitted from generation to generation, is constantly recreated by communities and groups in response to their environment, their interaction with nature and their history, and provides them with a sense of identity and continuity, thus promoting respect for cultural diversity and human creativity.

Noriko Aikawa-Faure, responsible for the programme of intangible cultural heritage in UNESCO Headquarters from 1993 and witness to numerous and various deliberations leading to the Convention shows how criticisms of the earlier folklore deliberations triggered the creation of the ICHC and that perceptions of indigenous peoples' interests informed many of the expert reports relied upon to define intangible cultural heritage while shaping the principle of safeguarding that evolved to replace the concept of protection.[97] Nonetheless, according to indigenous critics, 'the general tone of

---

[94] Ibid.
[95] Aikawa-Faure, supra note 90, at p. 21. During the Convention's negotiation, experts routinely reaffirmed that UNESCO 'should not duplicate the activities of other organisations, particularly in the field of economic rights for which specialised agencies such as WIPO and World Trade Organization (WTO) have specific expertise' and that its emphasis should be upon 'the cultural dimension of ICH covering the domains not yet covered by other organizations' (ibid. at p. 34). Francesco Francioni, in particular, emphasised the limits of the intellectual property right approach, especially its failure to respect, acknowledge, or ensure the viability of the societal structures and processes through which cultural products are derived, or recognise innovations that are the collective expressions of social necessities transmitted from generation to generation, as discussed in Federico Lenzerini, 'Indigenous Peoples' Cultural Rights and the Controversy Over the Commercial Use of Their Traditional Knowledge', in Francesco Francioni and Martin Scheinin (eds), *Cultural Human Rights*, Leiden and Boston: Nijhoff, 2008, pp. 119-150, at p. 144.
[96] Blake, supra note 23, at pp. 49-51.
[97] Aikawa-Faure, supra note 90.

this Convention and its provisions fall way below that of the two bench-mark instruments by which it can be evaluated, namely, the UNDRIP and ILO Convention (No. 169) Concerning Indigenous and Tribal Peoples in Independent Countries (ILO Convention 169).'[98] Critical scholars have pointed to the divergence between the Convention Preamble, which provides the only mention of indigenous peoples (recognised for their important role in producing and safeguarding ICH), and the substantive provisions of the Convention, which require that state parties engage in activities with respect to intangible cultural heritage that may not be welcomed by indigenous communities themselves.[99] For example, the global demand that states create inventories and attempt to publicise intangible cultural heritage may be met with great distrust by indigenous peoples who are only too familiar with state attempts to locate, catalogue and 'salvage' their cultural goods and traditions. Long subject to state surveillance activities on cultural grounds, they are unlikely to welcome such initiatives.

The Convention does, however, require that states respect 'customary practices governing access', thereby acknowledging that indigenous peoples may have traditional strictures against the recording and transmission of some cultural forms, but this does not necessarily empower indigenous peoples with agency because indigenous peoples are historically quite familiar with having their 'customs' determined by state powers for ends that are not their own. There is very little in the Convention itself, save for exhortations to involve communities that would seem to provide independent *political* agency to those indigenous peoples whose heritage is endangered. The most ready explanation for the limits of the Convention 'is that Indigenous peoples were not included in the negotiation processes, either by having direct representation (for example, through the Working Group on Indigenous Populations or the UN Permanent Forum on Indigenous Issues), or by having Indigenous representation in the national delegations sent to negotiate the Convention.'[100]

It is worth noting that not only did many western countries not see any necessity for the Convention, those countries with significant indigenous populations expressed the most grave reservations, [101] indicating that international political support for indigenous community control over intangible cultural heritage remains limited. While there were no votes against the Convention, a number of countries, notably Australia, Canada, the UK, Switzerland and the USA, abstained.[102] This might suggest that these states are unlikely to use the Convention on behalf of indigenous peoples' interests. There is certainly no guarantee that inventories established and maintained by states will reflect the perils of cultural survival facing indigenous peoples as they themselves perceive these.

The capacities of the Convention to meet indigenous peoples' needs for the safeguarding, maintenance and development of their ICH lie in implementing and giving effect to the principles of community involvement that are unique

---

[98] Marrie, supra note 53, at p. 174.
[99] See, for example, Moran, supra note 47.
[100] Marrie, supra note 53, at p. 174.
[101] Smith and Akagawa, supra note 92, at p. 3.
[102] As noted in Kurin, supra note 92, at p. 66.

to it, and arguably unprecedented in international law. The specific character of ICH itself is necessarily dependent upon its continuing enactment by its practitioners; only by securing their involvement and participation in the maintenance and development of their heritage will it be safeguarded.[103] In this sense, the safeguarding of ICH is an exercise of cultural rights. If, as a matter of international law, states have primary agencies and duties, the Convention is structured so as to encourage state safeguarding activities to raise awareness of ICH in communities and to actively encourage community involvement in implementation. Recognising that global economic and cultural forces may be one of the threats to distinctive ICH held at the local level, communities and groups are to be empowered and capacitated to maintain ICH as the source of their own identities.[104]

Nonetheless, there is evidence that the nature of community participation was a matter of great controversy during the Convention's negotiation by the Intergovernmental Committee. Certainly both experts and state parties were divided between those inclined to give practitioner communities responsibilities and rights they could exercise and those who continued to prioritise state control and favoured only weak exhortations to encourage states to engage communities.[105] Although the ultimate priority given to the involvement of communities and civil society is evident, the appropriate mechanisms to achieve this without state initiative are still unclear. Indeed, the principle of community participation was difficult to implement even in the negotiations themselves. In more than ten governmental and non-governmental meetings, only two appear to have benefited from anything that might remotely be called the 'active participation' of 'representatives of communities and practitioners.'[106] Considerable work remains to be done to engage indigenous peoples and their representatives in UNESCO ICH decision-making processes; Henrietta Marrie suggests numerous procedural possibilities for so doing.[107] At the very least, we might expect that the UN Permanent Forum on Indigenous Issues will be more prominently represented in the implementation and operationalisation of UNESCO Conventions going forward, but a more formal intersessional process of consultation with indigenous groups on indigenous issues would be preferable from a rights-based perspective.

3.4. Convention on the Protection and Promotion of the Diversity of Cultural Expressions 2005

It might be argued that the Convention on the Protection and Promotion of the Diversity of Cultural Expressions (Diversity Convention)[108] does not concern itself with issues of cultural heritage and thus is not within our remit. Nonetheless, as the most recent international legal instrument to attend to

---

[103] Blake, supra note 23, at pp. 45-46.
[104] Ibid., at p. 47.
[105] Aikawa-Faure, supra note 90, at p. 28.
[106] Ibid., at p. 39.
[107] Marrie, supra note 53.
[108] UNESCO, Convention on the Protection and Promotion of the Diversity of Cultural Expressions, 2440 UNTS 311 (adopted on 20 October 2005, entered into force 18 March 2007).

issues of cultural protection and as the ultimate legal expression of UNESCO's 2001 Declaration on Cultural Diversity, it expresses values and commitments that are likely to influence approaches to cultural heritage issues. Certainly the preservation and safeguarding of diversity has been a core value in cultural heritage protections generally and ICH especially, because indigenous peoples are regarded as members of distinct societies whose distinction is manifested culturally. Moreover, as the first international instrument to express cultural rights principles in relationship to trade, the Diversity Convention speaks perhaps most squarely to this volume's themes. Nonetheless, we give it short shrift here for several reasons.

The Diversity Convention has two guiding rationales that are not always complementary. The first, grounded in human rights promotes cultural development and intercultural dialogue, whereas the second is premised on the desire to protect state autonomy with respect to the governance of the products of creative industries from production through distribution and consumption.[109] The Convention acknowledges 'that cultural goods and services have dual nature and constitute on the one hand, commodities that can be traded and are, on the other hand, "vehicles of identity, values and meaning".'[110] But the assertion that, therefore, 'the relationship between the two is somehow natural'[111] begs the question of when cultural goods and services become tradeable commodities and under what circumstances commodified exchange supports cultural identity and when it undermines it. The Convention does little to provide any guidance and largely focuses on the diversity of media as means to convey a diversity of expression. Sovereign parties are encouraged to undertake measures with respect to cultural policy that may include support for civil society initiatives and promotional and preservation initiatives, but since the Convention does not require that states even recognise diversity within their territories, and there are no monitoring bodies, measurement of the impact of the Convention is difficult

As a recent treaty there is understandably little commentary on the Diversity Convention's operation. However, even as a text, critics find it lacking in clarity, particularly as it confuses the larger issue of cultural diversity with the narrower question of diversity in cultural expressions and largely focuses on expressions that circulate primarily as market goods.[112] Although there are references in the Preamble to the cultures of minorities and indigenous peoples, manifested in their freedom to create, disseminate and

---

[109] Nina Obuljen, 'From Our Creative Diversity to the Convention on Cultural Diversity: Introduction to the Debate', in Nina Obuljen and Joost Smiers (eds), *UNESCO's Convention on the Protection and Promotion of the Diversity of Cultural Expression: Making it Work*, Zagreb: Institute for International Relations, 2006, pp. 17-38, at pp. 16-20.

[110] Mira Burri-Nenova, 'Trade and Culture: Making the WTO Legal Framework Conducive to Cultural Considerations' (2008) *Manchester Journal of International Economic Law*, 5 (3), pp. 2-38. See also Christoph B. Graber, 'The New UNESCO Convention on Cultural Diversity: A Counterbalance to the WTO?' (2006) *Journal of International Economic Law*, 9 (3), pp. 553-574, at pp. 566-567.

[111] Ibid., at p. 4.

[112] Karen Donders, 'The History of the UNESCO Convention on the Protection and Promotion of the Diversity of Cultural Expression', in Hildegard Schneider and Peter van den Bossche (eds), *Protection of Cultural Diversity from a European and International Perspective*, Antwerpen and Oxford: Intersentia, 2008, pp. 1-30.

distribute their traditional cultural expressions so as to benefit from them for their own development, the Diversity Convention puts overarching emphasis upon state sovereignty. It provides no rights to minorities, to communities, or to individuals, although civil society is acknowledged to play a fundamental role in creating, producing, disseminating and distributing diverse forms of cultural expression.[113] It contains few if any enforceable state obligations and the lack of any effective dispute settlement mechanism or the capacity to develop authoritative interpretations of the Convention's key provisions renders it of little legal consequence.[114]

Nonetheless civil society initiatives pursuant to the Convention such as those of the International Network for Cultural Diversity (INCD) emphasise a wider range of diversity and indicate a desire to assist indigenous peoples in protecting, promoting, and disseminating their distinctive cultural expressions. As director Garry Neil asserts:

> A key priority for the INCD in its organising activities is to continue to work to ensure that the concerns of traditionally marginalised communities are fully integrated into the global movement ... While the Convention does not provide a formal role for civil society groups to raise concerns about forms of cultural expressions that are 'at risk of extinction, under serious threat, or in urgent need of safeguarding,' this will be on INCD's agenda in the coming years. There are several priorities for building the movement. The first is to respond to the needs of the indigenous communities to create a forum, initially in the Americas, in which representatives from these communities can work together to address the particular challenges which globalisation presents to their arts and culture, including their languages. Preliminary work has been undertaken with a range of representatives from Indigenous Peoples in a number of countries.[115]

However, the momentum of this civil society network appears to have been slowed since the ratification of the Convention and there is insufficient evidence available to us to ascertain what if any impact this activity has had upon trade in intangible ICH. Due to the extent of the uncertainties that surround the international legitimacy and legality of this Convention's provisions and fact that any such uncertainties would be resolved by state action without provision for indigenous involvement, we will not cover it in any further detail here.

---

[113] Hélène Ruiz Fabri, 'Reflections on Possible Future Legal Implications of the Convention', in Nina Obuljen and Joost Smiers (eds), *UNESCO's Convention on the Protection and Promotion of the Diversity of Cultural Expression: Making it Work*, Zagreb: Institute for International Relations, 2006, pp. 71-88, at p. 81.

[114] Christoph B. Graber, 'Substantive Rights and Obligations under the UNESCO Convention on Cultural Diversity', in Hildegard Schneider and Peter van den Bossche (eds), *Protection of Cultural Diversity from a European and International Perspective*, Antwerpen and Oxford: Intersentia, 2008, pp. 141-162.

[115] Garry Neil, 'After the Convention: What's Next for INCD and the Cultural Diversity Movement?', in Nina Obuljen and Joost Smiers (eds), *UNESCO's Convention on the Protection and Promotion of the Diversity of Cultural Expression: Making it Work*, Zagreb: Institute for International Relations, 2006, pp. 255-266; and in Thomas MacPhail, *Global Communication and Technologies: Theories, Stakeholders and Trends*, 3rd edn, London: Wiley-Blackwell Publishers, 2010, at p. 22.

4. Considering Intangible Cultural Heritage and International Trade

Any reading of UNESCO documents and critical research on cultural heritage generally clearly illustrates that heritage is now expected to 'pay its keep'. As a central component of sustainable development agendas, new means are being found to ensure that ICH delivers economic benefits to communities. As Blake notes, as a topic of international policy, cultural heritage indexes combined concerns with identity and development. During the UN World Decade for Cultural Development (1987-1997), UNESCO officially noted the need to highlight the function of the intangible cultural heritage for the community as a living culture of the people, and asserted that it 'should be regarded as one of the major assets of a multidimensional type of development.'[116] Thus we have the strange policy phenomenon of states being asked to 'apply' 'bottom-up approaches' that are community-driven.[117]

Tourism and associated industries in souvenirs, the development of new placed-based marketing for traditional foodstuffs and services, and capitalising upon local handicrafts are popular means to ensure revenues from heritage industries.[118] As sociologist Antonio Arantes notes, UNESCO activities have encouraged emphasis upon 'traditional know-how and forms of expression. ... as effective cornerstones for the implementation and promotion of humanitarian as well as social and economic development programs in the poorer regions of the globe' and 'it is becoming part of the common sense among policy makers that the protection and enhancement of heritage can contribute to social and economic development.'[119]

Once distinctive cultural heritage is identified with specific social groups as a target of preservation or safeguarding efforts, it tends to become a resource for the production of consumer goods and services that circulate in wider economic circuits that may impose upon local communities demands that are in conflict with or put pressures upon local social organisation. Crafts production, for instance, when oriented to a tourist market tends to demand increased volumes, standardisation, and adaptation to tastes and values that are not necessarily the community's own. New demands tend to be brokered by outside agents, and there is always a danger of local communities losing control of the process and having their work processes transformed in ways that are alienating and break down community social bonds. The desire to maximise returns has inevitably led to questions of collective intellectual property,[120] an issue that continues to vex WIPO and is elsewhere addressed in this volume.

---

[116] UNESCO, 1990, at para. 209, cited in Noriko Aikawa-Faure, 'The Conceptual Development of UNESCO's Programme on Intangible Cultural Heritage', in James Blake (ed.), *Safeguarding Intangible Heritage: Challenges and Approaches*, Builth Wells, Great Britain: Institute or Art Law, 2007, pp. 43-72.
[117] Blake, supra note 23, at p. 49.
[118] Colin Long and Sophia Labadi, 'Introduction', in Sophia Labadi and Colin Long (eds), *Heritage and Globalisation*, London and New York: Routledge, 2010, pp. 1-16.
[119] Antonio Arantes, 'Diversity, Heritage and Cultural Politics' (2007) *Theory Culture Society*, 24, pp. 290-296, at p. 294.
[120] Ibid.

If we return to the management of cultural landscapes as world heritage, we witness a growing interest in finding ways to use these protected sites to support communities. In addition to employment in site management, tourism is recognised as adding value to the economic activities that have given rise to the distinctive cultural landscape,[121] particularly rural and associative cultural landscapes. Tourism is understood as potentially having a low impact on the cultural landscape, but helping to assist communities seeking transition to a more complex and diversified economic base, particularly when they are remote from metropolitan areas or in regions where more urban migration is undesirable. Seeking means to ensure that tourism benefits are reinvested in local communities, promoting local products that reflect local values, and seeking new governance structures for provision of transport, accommodation and touring that provide income and build capacity are all areas of ongoing research. As Lennon notes, 'generating income in ways that do not conflict with heritage conservation and are culturally sensitive is a management challenge'.[122]

Where the associative values that make cultural landscapes 'outstanding' are derived from the social life of resident communities, issues of sustainability become especially significant, which is one of the reasons why communities are now recognised as central agents in the process of maintaining heritage and finding ways to capitalise upon it. As the new Operational Directive under the ICHC stresses:

> Commercial activities that can emerge from certain forms of intangible cultural heritage and trade in cultural goods and services related to intangible cultural heritage can raise awareness about the importance of such heritage and generate income for its practitioners. They can contribute to improving the living standards of the communities that bear and practice the heritage, enhance the local economy, and contribute to social cohesion. These activities and trade should not, however, threaten the viability of the intangible cultural heritage, and all appropriate measures should be taken to ensure that the communities concerned are their primary beneficiaries. Particular attention should be given to the way such activities might affect the nature and viability of the intangible cultural heritage, in particular the intangible cultural heritage manifested in the domains of rituals, social practices or knowledge about nature and the universe.[123]

For example, farming communities may be encouraged to designate traditional foods that might be marketed without negatively affecting agricultural practice. Communities may need to find ways for traditional custodians to transmit landscape values to youth while providing viable employment for them in activities, such as cultural mapping, while using such

---

[121] Jane Lennon, 'Values as the Basis for Management of World Heritage Cultural Landscapes', in UNESCO, *Cultural Landscapes: the Challenges of Conservation, World Heritage Papers No. 7*, Paris: World Heritage Centre, 2003, pp. 120-126, at p. 123.
[122] Ibid.
[123] 'Operational Directives for the Implementation of the Convention For the Safeguarding of the Intangible Cultural Heritage', Annex to UNESCO, General Assembly of the States Parties to the Convention For the Safeguarding of the Intangible Cultural Heritage, 'Resolutions', Third Session (UNESCO Doc. ITH/10/3.GA/CONF.201/Resolutions Rev, 2010), Article 116.

maps to design activities for visitors. Sustainable development of ICH may also involve deciding how and if tourists will be welcome at festival and ritual events and what souvenirs they should take home with them. Although marketing is encouraged to increase revenues, promotional materials now focus more on the values of ICH for the communities themselves rather than educational or entertainment value for visitors.[124]

Janet Blake explains in great detail how communities are empowered under the ICHC (and its Operational Directives), and why their own free, prior, and informed consent is necessary for identification, nomination, inscription and for the preparation, recognition and implementation of any safeguarding programmes.[125] Since the community is the essential social context for maintaining the vitality and viability of ICH, the economic, social and cultural rights of communities in heritage management (and in some circumstances, groups and individuals) must assume priority. The new national policies envisioned under the ICHC are designed to give local communities far more power in determining what will be regarded as heritage, undermining state authority to designate official culture for a monolithic public, democratising the process of managing heritage, and providing better benefits to local communities in the process of giving them political voice.[126] Trade policy proposals must pay heed to these priorities, promoting trade in intangible heritage goods only where this further reinforces culture as a source of identity and furthers community sustainable development. Issues of representation, misrepresentation, and sustainability of economic practices to enhance community security need to be given emphasis. Rethinking unfair competition laws to meet community values in maintaining the integrity of indigenous identity, projecting community values through heritage goods that bear marks indicating conditions of origin, securing marketing assistance and building community capacities for communicating indigenous values in markets are all pressing needs.

We might also consider whether a single solution to managing indigenous ICH in a global trade regime is desirable, given the very different attitudes of states with respect to the recognition of indigenous peoples within their territories. Many indigenous peoples live within states that refuse to recognise them as such. Other groups have arbitrarily been declared 'extinct' by states that are not likely to negotiate on their behalf. Moreover, in some countries with colonial legacies there are many different layers of indigenous governance in place representing different moments in histories of decolonisation. Indigenous political representatives with whom states wish to negotiate are

---

[124] Ibid., Article 120.
[125] Blake, supra note 23, at pp. 48-52.
[126] To support the vision of community involvement with respect to managing intangible cultural heritage embodied here, Blake (ibid. at pp. 56-57) points to the Mataatua Declaration (1993) on the Intellectual and Cultural Property (ICP) Rights of Indigenous Peoples, which indicated that Indigenous communities should define their own intellectual and cultural property, define the principles under which it is recorded, establish educational, research, and training centres, develop and maintain customary practices for its protection, preservation and revitalisation, while creating local and representative bodies for this purpose.

not necessarily those whom communities recognise as legitimate.[127] Moreover, we need to recognise that indigenous identities and governance structures are evolving; not all indigenous peoples are in the same position in terms of the level and scale of their political organisation. Histories of cultural dispossession by the modern state have made it extremely difficult for indigenous peoples to fully reassemble and assert their customary laws; claims to control ICH are in fact integral to their struggle to reassert political autonomy.[128]

There is plenty of evidence to suggest that indigenous peoples, particularly those in Australia, Canada and New Zealand, have been independently engaged in this process over the past two decades. Hence a great deal of the local institutional work to enable indigenous peoples to connect to national heritage bodies and to seek UNESCO benefits may already have been done. Whether they will choose to do so, however, is another question. As Amanda Kearney suggests, indigenous peoples have their own impetus for developing autonomous, localised projects that reflect and reinforce indigenous knowledge systems and governance principles so as to document these in furtherance of their self-determination:

> internationally, Indigenous people are lobbying for the right to determine what constitutes their ICH, to administer the mechanisms for safeguarding, developing and promoting ICH and to control any research methodologies and investigations that purport to protect this heritage.[129]

The Yanyuwa, indigenous peoples in northern Australia, for example, engage in documentation of their intangible cultural heritage – 'expressions, knowledges, and intimacies associated with spiritually powerful places across their homelands'.[130] Such material is governed by customary law and mediated through community heritage management programs that involve scholars, filmmakers and lawyers in collaborative research projects with host communities that deploy this documentation to further indigenous land claims.[131]

Proponents of enhanced roles for communities point to precisely such activities as models for what Convention activities in member states might and should aspire to. Politically, however, this may be rather unrealistic. Where indigenous peoples have some political power and many outstanding legal complaints, the states in whose jurisdictions they are resident are unlikely to want to use an international instrument and the scrutiny it brings to bear to support activities that might further indigenous rights claims. On the other hand, the new normative obligations upon states that the ICHC imposes may provide new leverage and opportunities for indigenous peoples resident in

---

[127] See Kathy Bowrey, 'International Trade in Indigenous Cultural Heritage: An Australian Perspective', in this volume.

[128] See Rebecca Tsosie, 'International Trade in Indigenous Cultural Heritage in Development and Trade: Perspectives from the Dynamics of Cultural Heritage Law and Policy', in this volume.

[129] Amanda Kearney, 'Intangible cultural heritage: Global Awareness and Local Interest', in Laurajane Smith and Natsuko Akagawa (eds), *Intangible Heritage*, New York and London: Routledge, 2009, pp. 209-226, at p. 218.

[130] Ibid., at p. 219.

[131] Ibid.

state jurisdictions where relations are not so tense. Whether states will be prepared to assume a secondary and supportive role in relation to communities in new partnerships involving ICH is uncertain.

As anthropologist Regina Bendix suggests, the process of 'heritagisation' involves the strategic invocation of tradition and authenticity, the projection of identity and the cultivation of symbolic capital, the contestation of heritage values, and the symbolic work that goes into their marketing.[132] Inevitably, the intangibility of that which is ennobled as ICH will require new mechanisms to make it tangible in some way in order to ensure profit from this new status.[133] Although tourists may be entreated to come and imbibe pure values, they are likely to desire and to demand a more tangible takeaway, by way of photographs, videos, CDs, or souvenirs. Once the goods and experiences they consume are marked for marketing purposes, new forms of rivalry and competition may ensue. A community that successfully develops and builds its ICH into marketable goods will inevitably face competitors as well as counterfeiters.

As communities seek to maintain profits from heritage goods against competition, they may well consider forms of intellectual property as means to do so.[134] This is not an area over which UNESCO has any jurisdiction. WIPO will be the international body responsible, either for developing new forms of intellectual property, or new guidelines for its governance with respect to community and indigenous intangible cultural heritage. This has already been a prolonged process that has produced much in the way of principle, but little in the way of state requirements or implemented legislation.[135] Nonetheless, we would argue that certain kinds of intellectual property lend themselves to the goals of safeguarding ICH better than others.

Marks indicating conditions of origin, such as certification and collective marks as well as geographical indications, appear to be especially suitable for the marketing of goods based upon traditional knowledge and ICH.[136] Because they can be collectively held and managed, mark places of origin and the reputation of particular localities, may be used to reflect local cultural values and are in significant ways inalienable, they are amenable for use to advance the community development and empowerment envisioned by UNESCO and desired by indigenous peoples. For instance, we can imagine that in cultural landscapes protected as World Heritage sites as well as those recognised as such under national law, resident communities rightly seek employment

---

[132] Regina Bendix, 'Heritage Between Economy and Politics: An Assessment from the Perspective of Cultural Anthropology', in Laurajane Smith and Natsuko Akagawa (eds), *Intangible Heritage*, New York and London: Routledge, 2009, pp. 253-269, at p. 256.
[133] Ibid., at p. 263.
[134] For example see Markus Tauschek, 'Cultural Property as Strategy. The Carnival of Binche, the Creation of Cultural Heritage and Cultural Property' (2009) *Ethnologia Europaea*, 39 (2), pp. 67-80.
[135] See Girsberger and Müller, supra note 6.
[136] Rosemary J. Coombe and Nicole Aylwin, 'Bordering Diversity and Desire: Desire: Intellectual Property and Marking Place based Products in Commerce' (2011) *Environment and Planning A: Society and Space New Borders of Consumption*, 43 (9), pp. 2027-2042; and Nicole Aylwin and Rosemary J. Coombe, 'Marks Indicating Conditions of Origin in Rights-based and Sustainable Development', in Per Zumbansen and Ruth Buchanan (eds), *Human Rights, Development and Restorative Justice: An Osgoode Reader*, Oxford: Hart Publishing, forthcoming.

opportunities and economic benefits; they must decide whether or not to encourage tourism and under what conditions. If they do so and local cultural values do not otherwise discourage commercial use, indexical features such as petroglyphs or rock art significant to the community and characteristic of the site might be used to mark goods coming from this place of origin.

The use of a legally protected mark – a collective or certification mark or even a geographical indication – might provide communities with means to educate consumers, protect them against unauthentic goods, and protect themselves against the production and distribution of counterfeit goods that do not embody community values in their creation. This is one means by which indicia iconic of a particular cultural landscape might become the intellectual property of resident communities without resorting to inappropriate forms of privatisation or commodification. There is a growing emphasis upon the use of such marks to designate community heritage values. For example, Chiara Bortolotto shows how the Board of the Chamber of Commerce of Matera, a town in Southern Italy possessing inhabitable caves carved into limestone, encouraged use of a denomination of origin to promote and market traditional products based on traditional knowledge and traditional values associated with the site.[137] The community marked the interrelationship between the natural and cultural dimensions of their territorially based intangible cultural heritage using a collective mark that indicated the local origin and guaranteed the authenticity of products from the region.[138]

Such a strategy might well accord with and help to project indigenous values in a trade context while supporting arts and craftsmanship and protecting customary intellectual properties. To the extent that this strategy might also be integrated in the development of indigenous cultural tourism, further benefits are possible. Finally, the strategy has the benefit of being in compliance with the TRIPs Agreement,[139] avoiding the kinds of conflict of interest allegations that emerged with respect to the UNESCO Cultural Diversity Convention of 2005 and limited the perceived capacities of that instrument to achieve its mandate of internationally protecting cultural goods against trade-based pressures.[140] Indeed, we would go so far as to suggest that

---

[137] Chia Bortolotto, 'Globalising Intangible Cultural Heritage? Between International Arenas and Local Appropriations', in Sophia Lavbadi and Colin Long (eds), *Heritage and Globalisation*, London and New York: Routledge, 2010, pp. 97-114, at p. 108-109.

[138] Ibid., at p. 110.

[139] WTO, Agreement on Trade Related Aspects of Intellectual Property Rights, Marrakesh Agreement Establishing the World Trade Organization, Annex 1C, 1869 UNTS 299; 33 ILM 1197 (adopted on 15 April 1994, entered into force 1 January 1995).

[140] See Mira Burri-Nenova, 'Trade and Culture in International Law: Paths to (Re)conciliation' (2010) *Journal of World Trade*, 44 (1), pp. 49-80, at p. 49; Anke Dahrendorf 'Free Trade Meets Cultural Diversity: The Legal Relationship Between WTO Rules and the UNESCO Convention on the Protection of the Diversity of Cultural Expressions', in Hildegard Schneider and Peter van der Bossche (eds), *Protection of Cultural Diversity from a European and International Perspective*, Antwerpen and Oxford: Intersentia, 2008, pp. 31-84; Shin-Yi Peng, 'International Trade in "Cultural Products": UNESCO's Commitment to Promoting Cultural Diversity and its Relations with the WTO' (2008) *International Trade and Business Law Review*, 11, pp. 218-235; and Jan Wouters and Bart De Meester, 'Cultural Diversity and the WTO: David versus Goliath?', in Hildegard

marks indicating conditions of origin are rare among legal vehicles that might ensure that cultural goods and services retain their capacities to act as instruments of identity, projecting local meanings and values while being traded in commodity markets.

Other trade issues will inevitably emerge as indigenous communities become more involved in managing cultural heritage sites. What recourse do communities have against the state should the state seek to license others to manufacture goods bearing such indicia without their permission? To what extent do UNESCO principles of community safeguarding ICH give indigenous peoples any greater power than they would have if such materials were treated as being in the public domain? In what circumstances could or would UNESCO support community collective properties? If an indigenous community chooses *not* to commercialise indicia of their cultural landscapes, what recourse would they have against those who seek to capitalise upon the site's notoriety by marketing goods bearing these signs as souvenirs? Ironically, they might find themselves in a position of having to seek trademark, collective mark or certification mark protection to *prevent* unauthorised commercial usages of such symbolism. Some jurisdictions have allowed indigenous peoples to act as guardians of such symbols pursuant to legislation giving rights to public authorities to hold exclusive rights to the use of symbols in the public interest,[141] but such legislation is contentious and not widely available. Could UNESCO assume a proactive stance here, using its considerable powers as an international public authority to protect indigenous communities from unfair and misleading competition that would siphon profits away from community safeguarding efforts?

Such questions raise the issue of property in a new way. Although the understanding of cultural heritage *as* property is one that has been undermined, it is nonetheless the case that properties, intellectual or otherwise, may embody ICH.[142] Although the WHC clearly indicates that recognition of a site as world heritage is 'without prejudice to property rights as provided in national legislation',[143] this would not make such sites national property in situations where property rights are contested or under negotiation, as they are with respect to many of the territories and resources held or claimed by the world's indigenous peoples. With respect to ICH, property issues promise to be particularly problematic. As Kearney argues, if acknowledging cultural rights to be specific to particular groups and communities is the key theme of the ICHC, state parties maintain ultimate control over the processes involved

---

Schneider and Peter van der Bossche (eds), *Protection of Cultural Diversity from a European and International Perspective*, Antwerpen and Oxford: Intersentia, 2008, pp. 85-140.

[141] For example, indigenous communities in Canada have registered images from petroglyphs found in their ancestral territories as marks held by them as a public authority so as to prevent their reproduction by others in commercial contexts they found objectionable. See George P. Nicholas and Kelly P. Bannister, 'Intellectual Property Rights and Indigenous Cultural Heritage in Archaeology', in Mary Riley, (ed.), *Indigenous Intellectual Property Rights: Legal Obstacles and Innovative Solutions*, Walnut Creek, CA: Alta Mira Press, pp. 309-340, at p. 327.

[142] Manlio Frigo, 'Cultural Property v. Cultural Heritage: A "Battle of Concepts" in International law?', in Laurajane Smith and Natsuko Akagawa (eds), *Intangible Heritage*, New York and London: Routledge, 2009, pp. 45-73.

[143] Convention Concerning The Protection of the World Cultural and Natural Heritage, Article 6.1.

and are not called upon to formally recognise indigenous rights to ownership and control over their ICH.[144] No indigenous rights independent of those of states are acknowledged, which ultimately positions indigenous peoples as mere stakeholders with respect to the ICH that is acknowledged to provide them with a primary source of identity.

Although the WHC stressed the concept of 'the shared heritage' of humanity through its central focus on the concept of the 'universal value' of heritage, it was routinely criticised for legitimising a particular western – if not Western European – perception of heritage both in policy and in practice.[145] As we have shown, the World Heritage List was exposed as being not only Eurocentric in its vision and its composition, but as dominated by monumental and aesthetic valuations.[146] The ICHC is posited as a counterpoint to the WHC, and represents an honest attempt to acknowledge and privilege non-western manifestations and practices of heritage. Proponents stressed its greater relevance to Asian, African and South American countries and to indigenous heritage practices. [147] Arguably, ICHC embodies some fundamental contradictions; while it was deemed advisable to make reference to ICH as 'a universal heritage of humanity' in the Preamble as a justification for international activity, the term is not used in the definition itself, so as to safeguard the specific value that this heritage has for the community while underlining the need for its international protection.[148]

As we have seen, however, indigenous peoples themselves remain unconvinced that an international treaty produced without their input reflects their values, and to the extent that local cultural values are determinative in evaluating the significance of ICH, and such significance is the criteria for international recognition, UNESCO may find itself at an impasse with respect to indigenous intangible cultural heritage. This impasse may only be overcome if indigenous peoples are politically recognised as the primary actors with whom UNESCO must negotiate to incorporate intangible ICH into the intangible cultural heritage internationally recognised as in need of safeguarding, which seems unlikely except in those rare instances where indigenous peoples have considerable power *vis-à-vis* state governments (as, for example, they increasingly do in South America). Whether or not indigenous peoples wish to have their ICH so acknowledged is another discrete and distinct question, the answer to which will lie in the particular circumstances in which any given indigenous people or community finds itself in relationship to the state in which they are resident, their need for NGO and

---

[144] Kearney, supra note 129, at p. 209.
[145] See Smith and Akagawa, supra note 92, at p. 1; and Forrest, supra note 14, citing numerous scholars.
[146] Lourdes Arizpe with Alonso Guiomar, 'Culture, Trade and Globalization' (2000) *UN Development Programme, New York*, Human Development Report Working Papers, at p. 36; Henry Cleere, 'The Uneasy Bedfellows: Universality and Cultural Heritage', in Robert Layton, Peter G. Stone and Julian Thomas (eds), *Destruction and Conservation of Cultural Property*, London: Routledge, 2001, pp. 82-104; and Kenji Yoshida 'The Museum and the Intangible Cultural Heritage' (2004) *Museum International*, 56 (1-2), pp. 108-112, at p. 109.
[147] Smith and Akagawa, supra note 92; and Arizpe, supra note 50.
[148] Blake, supra note 23, at p. 12.

UNESCO assistance, and the political value of the international publicity that recognition of their ICH might afford.

State-based systems of assistance for trade in indigenous heritage goods pose particular dilemmas because of the likelihood that they will be based upon historical forms of governance over indigenous peoples and perpetuate state based identifications of indigenous peoples and their cultures that have been experienced as colonial forms of discipline and power. For example, New Zealand attempted to create a system whereby the designation of 'traditional Māori weaver' could be applied for to certify a craftsperson's goods and to prevent imitations of non-Māori origin from circulating as Māori goods.[149] In conversations with indigenous students, Coombe was told that the endeavour was resisted by Māori who were not willing to have themselves designated either as Māori or as traditional by a state government body that they themselves did not control. Indigenous peoples routinely reject state projects that identify them, ascertain their traditions, decide what is authentic, customary, or traditional to them, and otherwise recognise them according to criteria which are not their own. Any state-based system should avoid violating the human rights principle of indigenous self-identification.[150]

We must also consider the possibility that states party to the ICHC have interests in safeguarding ICH that are less exalted than serving the interests of humankind and that indigenous resistance to the incorporation of their ICH into such regimes of recognition is less a particular rejection of state involvement in a regime of benign cosmopolitanism, and rather a resistance to the state's desire to incorporate them into new regimes of neoliberal market governmentality. Anthropologist Philip Scher reminds us that new forms of state discipline and surveillance accompany a renewed global emphasis upon heritage and cultural patrimony and that the desire to capitalise upon these values under 'neoliberal nationalism' is accompanied by new forms of cultural privatisation.[151] The recent emphasis upon inventorising ICH, reifying it, assigning appropriate caretakers for it, and investing in 'capacity-building' to develop local expertise, arguably constitutes a new regime of power which poses both promise and peril for the local communities and indigenous peoples deemed to bear the distinctive culture that these new regimes seek to value.[152] To the extent that those who hold ICH are recognised as such because new markets in informational capital seek to locate those who can contractually negotiate with respect to its use, indigenous peoples have reason to be wary that the esteem in which their culture is suddenly held reflects the fact that it is being targeted in new regimes of capital accumulation that do not necessarily accord with their own values and aspirations.

---

[149] For a longer discussion of the state's designation of this initiative as a failure and its abandonment by the New Zealand government see Haidy Geismar, *Treasured Possessions: Property Relations and Indigenous Rights in the Face of the Free Market*, Durham: Duke University Press, forthcoming.

[150] The principle of self-identification can be gleaned from combining many rights held in the UN International Covenant on Civil and Political Rights, 999 UNTS 171 and 1057 UNTS 407; 6 ILM 368 (adopted on 16 December 1966, entered into force 23 March 1976), Articles 18-22 and 27.

[151] Philip Scher, 'UNESCO Conventions and Culture as a Resource' (2010) *Journal of Folklore Research*, 47 (1-2), pp. 197-202.

[152] Coombe, 'Possessing Culture', supra note 53.

Similarly, we need to remain wary of responsibilities being vested in 'communities' who are not provided with resources with which to meet these new demands, considering that 'communities' are often constituted as such by states, who have particular ways of making communities visible and legible that may not necessarily accord with local values or social histories of identification and belonging. The devolution of responsibilities to lower levels of governance may entail greater democratisation, but it is also a way of extending neoliberal systems of government that encumber local peoples without necessarily empowering them[153] and may subject them to new forms of moral opprobrium and blame[154] for situations not of their own making. Conflicts over the appropriate scales for managing both cultural properties and cultural commons are endemic under new conditions of informational capital.[155] We have little sense of whether UNESCO has any independent means or inclination to intervene on behalf of communities if a state party refuses to fully respect the principles of community participation and involvement in safeguarding activities, or does so in ways that indigenous communities find inappropriate. The ICHC may nonetheless achieve greater legitimacy amongst indigenous communities if the concepts and norms of property it validates are those recognised in indigenous customary law;[156] as will any trade-based measures.

5. Conclusion

International intangible cultural heritage protection has evolved over the last sixty years in a fashion that has brought it progressively more in line with human rights principles and indigenous interests in self-determination. Indeed, indigenous struggles to control cultural heritage to facilitate community development have helped to shape the direction of international law in this field. Although a history of preoccupation with issues of property, economic valuations, commercial considerations and the hegemony of market exchange is arguably rejected by recent policy developments pertaining to intangible cultural heritage, the desire to harness intangible cultural heritage for the purposes of community sustainable development are likely to ensure that issues of trade be reconsidered.

While rejecting state-based regimes as politically inappropriate, we have suggested that protection against misrepresentation coupled with the creative use of intellectual property vehicles such as pre-emptive trademarks, geographical indications and marks indicating conditions of origin more generally are potential means through which indigenous peoples may seek to benefit from intangible cultural heritage in trade contexts. Ultimately, however,

---

[153] Mary Coffee, 'From Nation to Community: Museums and the Reconfiguration of Mexican Society Under Neoliberalism', in Jack Z. Bratich, Jeremy Parker and Cameron McCarthy (eds), *Foucault, Cultural Studies and Governmentality*, Albany: Suny University Press, 2003, pp. 207-242.

[154] Kathryn Lafrenz Samuels, 'Material Heritage and Poverty Reduction', in Sophia Labadi and Colin Long (eds), *Heritage and Globalisation*, London and New York: Routledge, 2010, pp. 202-218.

[155] Lorraine V. Aragon and James Leach, 'Arts and Owners: Intellectual Property Law and the Politics of Scale in Indonesian Arts' (2008) *American Ethnologist*, 35 (4), pp. 607-631; and Coombe, 'Cultural Agencies', supra note 53.

[156] Kearney, supra note 129.

indigenous peoples are unlikely to accept principles and practices of international intangible cultural heritage law until they are recognised as political agents capable of representing their own interests in UNESCO policy-making fora. Only then will we be able to begin the difficult work of recognising the viability of indigenous customary law as a necessary and possibly superior juridical resource for addressing issues pertaining to trade in intangible cultural heritage.

[13]

Indigenous cultural landscapes and the politics of heritage

Melissa F. Baird*

Stanford Archaeology Center, Stanford University, Stanford, CA, USA

(*Received 21 September 2011; final version received 31 January 2012*)

> This paper examines the socio-political implications and consequences of heritage practices related to indigenous cultural landscapes in post-settler nations. Although cultural landscapes are natural and material, they are also, more importantly, inscribed with meaning by those for whom they are heritage. Using a critical heritage studies framework, this paper examines the historical, cultural and legal contexts of Tongariro National Park and its nomination to the World Heritage list. I argue that narratives surrounding the Gift of Tongariro silence the colonial histories of the Park. I show how the ecological integrity and scientific, aesthetic, and conservation values of the Park are promoted, and in the process, Maori people's complex and multifaceted relationships to the land are reframed as a relationship to the 'natural' world. I argue that to truly decolonise heritage, we must locate and acknowledge how our models, theories and practices of heritage work through systems of power and exclusion.
>
> **Keywords:** critical heritage studies; Tongariro National Park; cultural landscapes; UNESCO World Heritage; expert knowledge

Introduction: why heritage matters

Tongariro National Park is located in the central North Island, Aotearoa/New Zealand. The Ngati Tuwharetoa and Ngati Rangi are *tangata whenua*, glossed here as 'people of the land' (Taiepa *et al.* 1997), and have spiritual and custodial responsibilities to this region. In 1887, then Paramount Chief of Ngati Tuwharetoa, Horonuku Te Heuheu Tukino IV, 'gifted' the lands of Tongariro to the Crown, and in 1894 the Crown established New Zealand's first national park. In 1990, Tongariro National Park was listed as a natural World Heritage property, and in 1993 the Park became the first World Heritage cultural landscape.

In the following case study, I examine the socio-political implications and consequences of heritage practices related to indigenous cultural landscapes in post-settler nations. Are cultural landscape designations neutral or instead do they mask political dissent? Do heritage policies address critiques from indigenous groups and other stakeholders? Using a critical heritage framework, I present the historical, cultural and legal contexts of the Park's nomination to the World Heritage list, and show how narratives surrounding the Gift of Tongariro efface the complicated and colonial histories. I also suggest that the ecological integrity and scientific, aesthetic

---

*Email: mbaird@stanford.edu

and conservation values of the Park are promoted in such a way that they reframe Maori's complex and multifaceted relationships to landscapes as a relationship to the 'natural' world.

The practice and management of cultural heritage by anthropologists, archaeologists, geographers, landscape architects, museum practitioners and other 'experts' have implications for indigenous groups and local communities who may challenge how their heritage is classified and represented (e.g. Rose 1996, Bender and Winer 2001, Memmott and Long 2002, Strang 2006). Cultural heritage, as used here, refers to both the tangible and intangible culture as well as the meanings, values and practices by which people engage with, communicate and 'make meaning in and for the present' (Smith 2006, p. 1). For this reason, heritage is inherently political, engaging stakeholders and practitioners in sometimes adversarial debate and struggle. If, as Laurajane Smith (2006, p. 99) asserts, nomination to the United Nations Educational, Scientific and Cultural Organization (UNESCO) World Heritage list 'is a process of meaning making ... that ... defines which heritage places are globally important', then what are the implications for descendant communities? Growing evidence suggests that heritage practices privilege outsider experts and their knowledge (e.g. Long 2000, Carman 2002, 2005, Rose 2002, Smith 2004, 2006, Waterton 2005, Baird 2009, Kawharu 2009). Because such practices eclipse indigenous systems of knowledge, and more importantly, create obstacles for stakeholders to assert their social and political authority, there is a clear need for examining critically the practice and management of heritage.

Critical heritage studies

Critical heritage studies (CHS) investigate the political and social implications of the practices of heritage and seek to understand how knowledge is produced and interwoven with relations of power (Baird 2009). CHS question the neutrality of heritage practices and is informed by Smith's (2006, p. 4) concept of 'authorised heritage discourse', the idea that a larger hegemonic discourse mediates heritage laws and practices. CHS include insights from studies that encompass new directions in anthropology, environmental studies, history, public policy, indigenous studies, philosophy and law. This cross-disciplinary framework examines how different scholars and stakeholders engage with similar questions, and how these diverse responses add to or complicate what we know or think we know about heritage. Although the term 'critical heritage studies' has been used before and is the subject of an upcoming conference, at the time of this research, it had not been fully articulated (see Baird 2009).[1] That is not to say that these types of studies were not undertaken. For example, Kirshenblatt-Gimblett's (1995, 1998, see also McCarthy 2011) critique of museums' complicity in the production and 'possession' of heritage, and more recent work by Meskell (2012) on the 'the nature of heritage' in post-apartheid South Africa are excellent examples of how heritage is meditated within political struggles. Placed in dialogue, these studies bring into sharp relief how heritage is mobilised in knowledge claims, nation building and identity creation. In indigenous contexts, a CHS approach questions common assumptions and 'truths' about the history of indigenous peoples to understand how interactions are not one-sided, but instead involve resistance, appropriation, reinterpretation and adaptation. In this way, a CHS approach lends room to understand, for example, how indigenous peoples are engaged in negotiating and renegotiating heritage and using it in ways that reposition asymmetrical structural relations (see, e.g. Sissons 2005, McCarthy 2011).

This paper is based on interviews, institutional archives and historiographies. Archives offer unguarded insights into how experts view heritage, and combined with interviews with professional heritage managers (e.g. archaeologists, museum personnel and heritage practitioners), helped to identify how they understood and operationalised concepts of indigenous ancestral cultural landscapes. I do not include interviews with local Maori stakeholders here. Future work includes weaving together these data with new interviews together these data with new interviews.

I locate myself within this discussion as a western academic, that is North American, trained as an anthropological archaeologist, and until 2011, I was an international heritage expert for the International Council on Monuments and Sites (ICOMOS). I do not speak for the Maori or the Ngati Tuwharetoa, nor do I present the entire political history of the Park. It is important to note that each heritage site has its own contexts and histories, and as Sissons (2005, p. 8) reminds us, 'the concerns of most indigenous people remain deeply local and rooted in particular colonial struggles'. Nevertheless, I believe that this example sheds light on how colonial structures remain as hidden dimensions embedded in laws, policies and practices, and are largely unacknowledged. To understand how this may be playing out in the first indigenous World Heritage cultural landscape, Tongariro National Park, I begin my discussion with the cultural context of the Park.

'Tongariro is the mountain': the cultural context

'Te ha o taku maunga ko taku manawa' – the breath of the mountain is my heart – is how Ngati Tuwharetoa express their reverence for Tongariro. As ancestors, the mountains provide guidance to their *iwi* or tribe. Ngati Tuwharetoa recite their genealogy (Forbes 1993, p. 8) as:

> Ko Tongariro te Maunga
> Ko Taupo te Moana
> Ko Tuwharetoa te Iwi
> Ko Te Heuheu te tangata
> Tongariro is the mountain
> Taupo is the lake
> Ngati Tuwharetoa are the people
> Te Heuheu is the man (paramount chief)

Note how Tongariro is central and mediates relationships to place and between people. The cultural and natural qualities are closely bound; Tongariro offers a sense of place and acts as a spiritual guidepost for Ngati Tuwharetoa (see Forbes 1993, p. 7, 2003).

Prior to European colonisation, Maori 'were the *kaitaiki* (guardians) over all natural resources, *whenua* (lands) and *taonga* (treasured possessions)', including *wahi tapu* (sacred sites), described later (Matunga 1994, p. 217). In its broadest outlines, *taonga* contains a tribe's historical memories, and '[ties] people to land ... If *taonga* are separated from either their people or associated lands, they lose the context in which their knowledge was rehearsed and performed' (Tapsell 1997, p. 332, see also Henare 2007). In fact, Kawharu (2000, p. 365) cautions that *taonga* is not used by all tribal groups in the same way. Early settlers failed to fully grasp *taonga* or Maori systems of knowledge about and responsibilities to the land, and instead viewed New Zealand as a wilderness – 'a landscape devoid of geographical meaning inhabited by people without history' (Marr et al. 2001, p. 4, see also Ruru 2004). Ironically, historian Gentry (2009, p. 34) showed how settlers would later '[draw from] elements of Maori culture and history into their own conception of self'. In the process of renaming and appropriation, Maori scholar Paul Tapsell (1997, p. 332) noted that settlers transposed a 'European value system' onto the lands, which violated Maori peoples' customary land rights and laws. More importantly, in the process of colonisation, *taonga* 'became decontextualised as kin groups permanently lost control over their lands and peoples' (Tapsell 1997, p. 332).

When representatives of the British Crown and Maori chiefs signed the Treaty of Waitangi in 1840, *taonga* would most surely have been 'of great importance to Maori people' (Tapsell 1997, p. 326). The Treaty was viewed by the Crown as a way to secure control over land and regulate trade. Maori chiefs saw it as an alliance and as anthropologist Henare (2005, p. 121, see also 2007, p. 47) showed, it was a 'chiefly gift exchange, ensuring the retention of Maori authority'. The Treaty guaranteed Maori 'rights over all their lands, settlements, and ... their taonga' (Henare 2005, p. 121). In this sense, the Treaty established a set of protocols and responsibilities that would have most certainly bound the signers to protect *taonga*. Yet, as Tapsell (1997) noted, the Treaty worked in ways that reframed and decontextualised *taonga* and converted Maori land into Crown holdings, in violation of the original intent.

Maori are concerned when *taonga* and *wahi tapu*, glossed here as treasured possessions and sacred places of memory, respectively (Matunga 1994, pp. 219–220), are mismanaged. Article II of the Treaty guaranteed Maori rights over their lands, fisheries and *taonga*. *Taonga* and *wahi tapu* include many of the site types included in cultural landscape inventories. Maori are reluctant to reveal these: they cannot be cared for or managed by outsiders or by members of clans that do not own them. Problems have occurred, for example, when heritage experts classified sacred sites as archaeological sites under the Historic Places Act (Matunga 1994, p. 222, see also McCully and Mutu 2003). It would not be too bold to claim that *taonga* are at the heart of many contemporary land and restitution claims. In 1991, for example, members representing six Maori *iwi* filed the Wai 262 claim against the Crown seeking protection for their cultural knowledge and property. The claimants argued, in part, that the Crown violated their rights and failed to protect *toanga* (Solomon 2005). Much of what was learned in this claim can be useful in understanding challenges in viewing indigenous cultural landscapes as heritage (see, e.g. Kawharu 2009). Although Belgrave (2005) and McCarthy (2011, p. 215) have shown how Maori have actively used Waitangi Tribunal claims to reclaim and renegotiate heritage 'alienated in the colonial period', I suggest that in some ways, the cultural landscape designation – as imagined by western experts – repositioned indigenous peoples outside of their systems of authority and positioned heritage experts as mediators of their heritage.

The Gift of Tongariro

As popular accounts describe, by the late 1880s, Horonuku feared that his people's lands would be taken and divided. He told his son-in-law Lawrence Grace, a member of the House of Representatives:

> If our mountains of Tongariro are included in the blocks passed through the Court in the ordinary way, what will become of them? They will be cut up and perhaps sold, a piece going to one *pakeha* and a piece to another. They will become of no account, for the *tapu* will be gone. Tongariro is my ancestor, my *tupuna*; it is my head; my *mana* centres around Tongariro. (Cowan 1927, p. 33)

In an effort to protect and ensure Ngati Tuwharetoa's connection, Horonuku ceded an area of 2640 ha surrounding the mountains (but not the mountaintops) of Tongariro, Ngauruhoe and Ruapehu to the Crown.

Tongariro, 'as a remote, mysterious, and wild landscape ... conformed to Western Romantic international ideals' became central to preservationist strategies (Marr *et al.* 2001, p. 266). In 1893 Minister of Lands, John McKenzie, advised that Tongariro could not be productive as land but instead 'foresaw its thermal wonders and fine scenery' as its most impressive assets (Marr *et al.* 2001, p. 267). McKenzie was influenced by preservationist movements and campaigns aimed at preserving New Zealand's natural and historic heritage. In promoting tourism, and legitimising evolving national identities, the rights of Maori to control their cultural heritage were subverted and suppressed (Gentry 2009). Tongariro, with its vast volcanic landscapes and rugged terrains, fits within the canon of what was natural and wild, and in 1894, became New Zealand's first national park, under the Tongariro National Park Act. Although Horonuku supported the idea of Tongariro as a national park, the Act was a breach of the original intention of the Gift: the management of the Park would now follow ideas of what was natural, or wilderness, or aesthetically important.

The narrative of the Gift of Tongariro reveals a suite of contradictions. The way the history of the Gift is narrated, the Gift was uncontested and Horonuku and the Crown shared similar goals and motivations. New Zealand legal scholar Boast (2008) paints a different picture and shows how negotiations surrounding the Gift include numerous stakeholders, each with different motivations and strategies. Boast (2008, p. 343) presented a detailed legal and historical account of the complex and multi-year negotiations for the land and more importantly, showed how the idea of the Gift was seen by the Crown as a deed of conveyance that transferred ownership. In fact, the original area of the Gift was always intended to be expanded (Boast 2008). Yet, today, the Gift of Tongariro is promoted throughout Park management literatures, national histories and understandings as an example of good will and good governance and has 'entered into national folklore and ... acquired a kind of iconic significance' (Boast 2008, p. 343). We know that the Gift is understood differently by Maori (see Ruru 2004, p. 122, 126, see also Anderson 2005). Like the Treaty of Waitangi, the Gift was seen as a chiefly gift exchange that would require reciprocity and protection of the *taonga* and *wahi tapu* of the peaks. In fact, violations of this trust have forced Tuwharetoa Paramount Chief Tumu te Heuheu to speak publicly for the first time about his concerns about tourism and pollution, amongst other concerns (Stokes 2006).

Maori throughout Aotearoa are actively renegotiating and defending claims to lands, resources and rights. The 2009 'Treelords' deal, for example, represents the largest Waitangi Tribunal settlement to date and awarded North Island iwi a $500 million settlement which includes transferring Kaingaroa Forest. The settlement is not without conflict, but represents enormous economic opportunities for Maori as well as redefines structural asymmetries. In 2005, 40 claimants submitted claims to the Waitangi Tribunal and sought clarification on the context of the Gift and operations of the Native Land Court, amongst other issues. As of the writing of this paper, the claim, collectively named the National Park inquiry, had been completed but the final decision not yet reported.[2] The Tribunal commissioned historian Anderson (2005, p. 24) to write a report on the history of Tongariro, and her detailed account illustrated a number of competing claims and contestations. Anderson (2005, p. 29) calls attention to the challenges in determining ownership – particularly in matching Crown surveys with 'ancestral boundaries'. The Whanganui *iwi*, for example, dispute the Gift and argue that the Crown failed to acknowledge their rights to the region.

What the claimants and reports bring to light is the challenges and complexity of the Gift, the motivations of the Crown and relations between neighboring groups. It is not my purpose here to offer an opinion on the claim, but instead to ask how narratives of the Gift intersect with contemporary heritage practices. Does the 'Gift', as presented in Park and World Heritage narratives, interfere with ongoing political and social negotiations? Questions of consultation, chiefly authority, land claims, ownership, *hapu/iwi* boundaries, jurisdictional evidence, and so on, are central to the Gift and largely absent in heritage literatures of the Park.

Contemporary management of Tongariro National Park

Tongariro National Park is directed by the New Zealand Department of Conservation (DOC) and managed by the Tongariro/Taupō Conservancy DOC. The Conservancy includes the Tongariro/Taupō Conservation Board, which has 12 members, including five Ngati Tuwharetoa representatives and a permanent position for the Paramount Chief of the Ngati Tuwharetoa. The General Policy for National Parks and the Minister of Conservation has ultimate authority over Park decisions. In 2003, Chief Tumu te Heuheu was elected to the World Heritage Committee, and in 2005 was elected chair, a position that represents a move toward addressing unequal representation in World Heritage contexts. I have argued elsewhere (Baird 2009) that in World Heritage contexts, the lack of indigenous representation as experts, advisors, or members of advisory bodies, or as voting members of scientific committees and heritage managers, thwarts relations.

The Conservation Act requires that the DOC recognise the principles of the Treaty of Waitangi in the management of natural and historic resources. The Treaty gives the Crown the right to make laws and govern; guarantees Maori the right to control their resources and *taonga*; and provides avenues to address grievances. In the way the Park is managed today, the most prominent goal is to protect natural heritage. This is because Park managers must follow the provisions of the National Parks Act. This Act tends to naturalise the ecological and natural values of the Park, and privilege the needs of the public. As Maori legal scholar Ruru (2008, p. 108) argued the National Parks and Conservation acts 'render it near impossible to respect Maori ... when the managers have a mindset to preserve and protect the environment'. Although Maori interests are included in the Park's management philosophies, they are not a priority. For example, the Park includes the largest privately owned commercial ski areas on the North Island. As discussed, the peaks of Tongariro are part of Ngati Tuwharetoa's sacred landscapes and figure prominently in their oral histories and traditions. Yet, the ski field encroaches on these lands and intrudes on the original area of the Gift. The Park's stated values do not fully address how people accessing sacred areas violate *taonga*, and yet the Park expanded the ski areas, and added chair lifts and snowmaking operations in 2005 (DOC 2006, p. 208). In this way, the Park privileges the needs of the Crown, Park managers, concessionaires, ski area owners and recreational visitors.

Negotiating World Heritage values

Tongariro National Park's status as a World Heritage property in 1990 was seen by some as 'the highest privilege on New Zealanders as guardians to manage this unique site for all of humanity' (DOC 2006, p. 27). In the process of negotiating heritage, alliances between local and national and government departments worked to promote the Park and its 'universal' heritage values. World Heritage sites are used by nation-states and local and national governments for economic, development and identity and nation-building purposes. These appropriative and essentialised meanings of heritage are often not shared by all (see Baird 2009).

A review of how the Park became a World Heritage property is revealing. In 1986, New Zealand nominated Tongariro as a joint natural and cultural site, citing the Park's volcanism, scenic landscapes, range of ecological communities, traditional importance to the Maori people and its value as a 'significant tourist destination' (Department of Lands Survey [DLS] 1986, p. 14). That year, a World Conservation Union (IUCN) representative visited and recommended the park as a natural heritage property. IUCN requested that the ICOMOS – the lead advisory body to the World Heritage Committee for cultural landscape nominations – assess the cultural criteria, but for reasons that are not stated in the final nomination, ICOMOS did not.

DLS representatives prepared the joint natural and cultural nomination of Tongariro. They inventoried and described the natural resources and the management of these resources, with much discussion relating to the volcanoes, and flora and fauna of the Park, and stated that the Park is used 'principally for nature conservation and resource-base recreation ... and as a major tourist attraction' (DLS 1986, p. 11). In this way, representatives glossed over the cultural values of the Park, and stated that the Park was given as a gift so that the 'outstanding natural and scenic values' of the area would be protected. This is not the true nature of the Gift, and I will return to this later. The World Heritage Committee denied the cultural criterion and deferred the natural criteria until the impacts of the proposed ski area development and the role of the Maori were made clear.

In 1987, representatives of New Zealand provided additional information to 'support the cultural aspect of the nomination' and discussed the importance of the Park and the Centennial celebration (Titchen 1995, p. 36). To ground the cultural heritage values, the report discussed the material heritage within the Park: the *pou* (structural support) and Maori *whare* (ceremonial house) built for the Whakapapa Visitor Centre (Titchen 1995, p. 36). The Bureau of World Heritage Committee deferred their decision (UNESCO 1987, p. 7), as did the World Heritage Committee (UNESCO 1988, p. 10), based on the recommendation by IUCN in its technical evaluation and report (Titchen 1995, p. 360).

In 1990, the Committee reviewed the renomination, and listed the site as a natural heritage property. Although the rationale for the Committee's denial of the cultural heritage was not provided, I concluded that the Committee was influenced by IUCN representatives who lobbied against the cultural heritage designation (see

Baird 2009 for discussion). The report was based on research and three site visits by then president of IUCN, and devoted much attention to placing Tongariro in context with other volcanic landscapes throughout New Zealand and along the Pacific Rim. IUCN representatives consulted many public officials, but it appears spent little time consulting with Ngati Tuwharetoa members. This is surprising considering the implicit concern that the 'cultural values of the park [be] given prominence in the new management plan and the level of involvement by the local Maori people' (IUCN 1990, p. 3). Just how these values could be incorporated is not discussed, but what is discussed is how the natural values of the Park must be protected, to enhance the 'cultural and spiritual values associated with the Maori people' (IUCN 1990, p. 4). The separation of natural and cultural heritage values is prominent in most IUCN documents.

In 1993, New Zealand was keen to place Tongariro on the newly minted World Heritage cultural landscape designation to mark the Park's 100 year anniversary. Archaeologist Susan Forbes was commissioned to write the report and based most of her report on discussions with tribal elders. She highlighted the cultural importance of the Park, and included stories, songs and interviews. Forbes (personal communication, 2009) noted that it was

> vital for the report to emphasize oral traditions because when the tribe had put in a proposal for cultural and physical World Heritage status they were knocked back on the cultural aspects. This caused offence and also sadness because, for Maori, the mountains are of immense cultural importance.[3]

I believe that Forbes, like Sarah Titchen, described next, was addressing the lack of indigenous representation in nominations and the emphasis on 'natural' values.

That same year, ICOMOS commissioned archaeologist Sarah Titchen to report on the cultural heritage of the Park. Whereas earlier IUCN reports focused on the volcanic landscape as a natural resource, Titchen (1993, p. 2) interpreted these landscapes as central to the Ngati Tuwharetoa's cultural heritage. Not only did she make the cultural connection explicit, but she also expanded what constituted the heritage inventory to include intangible heritage, reframed the focus away from natural heritage values, and included the sacred and spiritual values of the mountains. The fundamentally different foci of these reports intimate how heritage experts direct outcomes and what is deemed significant within heritage inventories. Whereas earlier reports focused on natural heritage values, Forbes and Titchen focused on Maori's connection to place and oral histories to support the cultural heritage values. Still, the Committee was largely unconvinced of the cultural heritage values until a tangible and material connection was provided: the *pou* (structural support) and the *whare* (ceremonial house).

'We will do our utmost to sweeten this bitter pill'

Internal documents located at the World Heritage Centre include correspondence from members of IUCN, ICOMOS and the World Heritage Centre Secretariat, as well as letters and materials submitted by non-governmental and local and indigenous groups and provide a rich source of information.[4] In 1988, for example, Conservation Director wrote to the IUCN president and offered support for the removal of the cultural heritage criteria (although not explaining why), and wondered how to address the 'dual issues of recreational expansion and giving the Maori people a meaningful role in the park they gifted to the nation 100 years ago'.[5] The Director replied that this 'decision will probably not be well received in New Zealand but we will do our utmost to sweeten this bitter pill'.[6]

Here we can see the internal negotiations that are not evident in the final nominations. The Director's letter refers to a series of discussions between the World Heritage Centre and IUCN in which IUCN stressed the need to remove the cultural heritage values from World Heritage natural criteria. In a series of letters, IUCN representatives and Park managers discussed reducing the burden of IUCN in matters related to cultural heritage. The IUCN's position was that natural heritage and cultural heritage values were largely incompatible, and coordinated activities were not necessary. Although ICOMOS and IUCN representatives share common interests, including promoting and improving heritage resources, reducing impacts on resources, and serving the needs of the World Heritage Committee, IUCN representatives felt that the advisory bodies duplicated efforts and did not exchange information. These discussions led to the restructuring and rewording of the World Heritage natural criteria in the *Operational Guidelines* and resulted in the denial of the cultural heritage values in the 1986 nomination. IUCN stressed the need for cooperation with ICOMOS and the desire to avoid duplicate efforts while pursuing common objectives. I suspect that IUCN representatives downplayed the relevance of cultural heritage because their mission is to promote natural heritage values. The dynamic tension between the advisory bodies is likely related to the very different and somewhat incompatible visions of what constitutes the cultural landscapes inventory, and may have consequences for indigenous groups. Rather than harmonious relations and the pursuit of common goals, the internal debates strained already tenuous relations.

The view that World Heritage sites are economic engines for the larger community and nation-state is evident in the internal discussions between IUCN and the World Heritage Centre. In 1990, the Park was the part of New Zealand's sesquicentennial celebrations of the signing of the Treaty of Waitangi and national and local representatives organised events to commemorate the signing. The irony is that none of the Ngati Tuwharetoa chiefs signed the Treaty, and many Maori protested these celebrations and the events leading to the anniversary (Ivison *et al.* 2000, p. 103). The promotion of the Park as a tourist destination and economic resource is largely absent from the World Heritage public materials or final nominations, but does matter in internal discussions. For example, a DLS representative was encouraged because World Heritage sites 'open the door to tourism ... and that other areas in NZ' may be worthy of nomination.[7] The Park's status as a World Heritage site increases international status and translates into big money for the park and the tourism industry.

Other letters relate to concerns over stakeholder involvement. Maori voiced concern because they were not consulted, or they did not have access to data, that is, studies, reports and other documents related to the Committees' decisions. Some feared changes in Park policies and complained about the lack of transparency in World Heritage nominations. One IUCN official noted that he had to work closely with communities to overcome distrust and antipathy over the concept of World Heritage. What the letter writer references is the growing unease from stakeholders: Maori, guides, foresters and Park concessioners, to name a few. Many feared the Committee and its advisory bodies would have control of the Park. This is not actually what happens when a site is listed, because decision-making power would still rest with the New Zealand Commonwealth government and the DOC. Nevertheless, the idea of Tongariro as a World Heritage site made many members of the community uncomfortable, something that does not come through in Park or World Heritage public literature or documents.

The letters tell us what Park documents do not: that Maori were marginalised from the nomination process and were frustrated by their lack of representation. A few letter writers argued that the Committee had not shown sensitivity to their laws, customs and beliefs. They argued that UNESCO representatives had not consulted them about access to their sacred sites, and they were concerned about the increased access and international attention that a World Heritage listing would bring. In 1987, a direct descendent of Horonuku addressed the World Heritage Committee and stated that IUCN did not consult with Maori, who 'would certainly not sanction this nomination'.

These data direct our attention to the existing inequities in the control of heritage to show how certain voices were excluded. Overall, letters of protest appeared to have no impact on reports, summaries, and advisory body evaluations, nor were they considered in the nomination process. Further, until Forbes and Titchen reported on the cultural heritage in 1993, advisory bodies largely defined the heritage value or significance of the park without fully consulting local and indigenous stakeholders. The consequences are significant: Maori were not given a way to control or protect their sacred sites, nor were they able to interpret those sites for the public who would enter the Park.

Conclusion: heritage and identity in Tongariro National Park

The narrative of the 'Gift of Tongariro' continues today in Park management policies, popular accounts of Tongariro, and World Heritage nomination reports, surveys and documents. In these literatures and in my interviews, the Gift is often cited as evidence of the good will between Maori and the Crown. I believe that this narrative erases the historical and social conditions from the true contexts of the transaction. In the way the acquisition of the Park is narrated, evidence of dissent is suppressed about the transfer of lands to the Crown. This material is buried in reports and proceedings related to the Tongariro National Park Bill, but what it tells us is that the transfer was effected to ensure that Horonuku or other Maori who opposed the land transfer could not intervene.

The authority of Horonuku was repeatedly undermined by efforts to transfer ownership to the Crown. The loss of the lands, even as a gift, nullified Ngati Tuwharetoa's rights to resources on their ancestral lands and had a long-lasting impact; the Gift prevents Ngati Tuwharetoa or other *iwi* from claiming authority over their resources. Their access to resources was redefined and reinterpreted through legal texts and policies and by local authorities, and later by groups concerned with protecting the natural resources within the Park. Moreover, the original Gift has been expanded to include nearly 80,000 hectares.

An unintended consequence of the Gift was that the Crown acquired authority to manage the lands. As shown, national parks emphasise protecting and conserving the natural and heritage resources and values and park managers, the DOC, and the Tongariro/Taupō Conservancy are positioned as the spokespersons with few avenues for Ngati Tuwharetoa to provide direction. Although the Paramount Chief has a position on the Conservancy, this is not the same as joint management. The narrative of the Gift positions land managers as equal partners with similar goals, when clearly these relationships are asymmetrical with power vested, in some ways, outside of Maori. The promotion of shared goals masks the true nature of these relationships.

Cultural heritage is presented in such a way that it is subordinate to the natural values of the Park. The reasons behind the deferral of the cultural criteria can be gathered from the internal documentation, which indicates that IUCN representatives strongly felt cultural heritage criteria had little relevance in the determination of what sites merited inclusion to the World Heritage list. What is lost in the demotion of cultural heritage values are the long-term insights that Ngati Tuwharetoa and neighbouring *iwi* could offer in their knowledge of the Park. IUCN is not a single entity, but instead a 'green web' of networks of members, non-governmental bodies, national conservation agencies and individuals who work together to establish mandates, policies and protections for natural resources globally (Holdgate 1999). How are the natural heritage resources also part of a 'web' of meaning to Ngati Tuwharetoa? By ignoring this part of the heritage of the Park, IUCN effectively ignored the long-term relationship and custodial responsibilities of Ngati Tuwharetoa and other *iwi* to Tongariro.

Park managers and World Heritage representatives misguidedly rename *taonga* and *wahi tapu* as heritage resources. The World Heritage cultural landscape inventory includes songs, oral traditions, ecosystems, flora and fauna, memories, dreaming tracks, languages, knowledge systems, archaeological sites, historic buildings, rock art, geological formations, wetlands and karsts, amongst others. I have argued elsewhere (see Baird 2009) that this expanded inventory positions heritage managers as experts in many cases outside of their expertise, training, or qualifications. We must consider how cultural landscape heritage designations intervene and affect identities and indigenous claims to traditional homelands, resources and practices. What is the impact of this designation on indigenous groups and their knowledge systems? At the same time, heritage managers are constrained by the bureaucracies and institutions that rely on an overwhelming array of policies, procedures and guidelines. Ideas and practices of heritage are often subsumed within a rigid and complex framework that rewards compliance. Entrenched institutional interests represent a challenge for reform. Collective decision-making power primarily rests in the hands of a few, which masks struggles for power among stakeholders. Changing the bureaucracy would involve addressing the structures that prevent oversight and insulate the process of heritage from outside review (see Baird in preparation).

In many contexts, World Heritage works to erase the social, cultural, intellectual and political environments in which it operates. A CHS framework helps to tease out how in the process of nation building, national, state and local governments redefined indigenous' heritage and decoupled the history of their struggles. Why does this matter? The colonial histories of the Park are presented for an international audience, devoid of the larger political issues related to sovereignty, autonomy, and control of identity. A CHS framework brings in the historical, legal and political contexts that were largely absent in the heritage documents but were clearly intersecting with heritage practices. It calls attention to the silences and omissions in the stories of the Park to suggest that legacies of colonial policies are embedded in contemporary land management practices. Indigenous groups are challenged to make their claims within systems that are largely incompatible with their custodial responsibilities, knowledge practices and customary laws. In the process, outsiders construct and reinterpret histories that naturalise constructs of heritage, appropriate meanings of land, and silence the historical struggles. To truly decolonise heritage practices, we must locate and acknowledge how our models, theories and practices of heritage work through systems of power and exclusion.

Acknowledgement

I would like to thank Laurajane Smith and two anonymous reviewers for their thoughtful and valuable feedback. This research was supported by a Dissertation Fieldwork Grant from the Wenner-Gren Foundation for Anthropological Research and a Graduate Research Fellowship from the Oregon Humanities Center.

Notes on contributor

Melissa F. Baird is a postdoctoral scholar at the Stanford Archaeology Center and Woods Institute for the Environment at Stanford University. Her field, ethnographic and archival research on cultural landscapes and heritage politics seeks to understand how knowledge about non-western groups is produced and evaluated in heritage contexts. Her work at Stanford involves examining the intersections between natural and cultural heritages as a way to expand the context for indigenous knowledge in environmental management practices.

Notes

1. Cultural anthropologist Breglia (2006) used the term in her ethnographic study of the social contexts of archaeological heritage sites in Latin America.
2. More on claim can be found at, http://www.waitangi-tribunal.govt.nz/claims/claims_process.asp [Accessed 8 December 2011]. See also Stokes (2006).
3. This quote from and email dated January 2009 is confusing because Ngati Tuwharetoa members did not submit a nomination to the World Heritage Committee. I suspect that Forbes is referring to the nomination submitted by IUCN in 1986, which did not report on the cultural heritage values.
4. Because of the sensitive nature of these materials and given that these files are not meant to be viewed by the public, I do not include identifying data.
5. Name suppressed, 6 June 1988, World Heritage Centre Archives, Paris.
6. Name suppressed, 8 January 1988, World Heritage Centre Archives, Paris.
7. Name suppressed, 10 August 1987, World Heritage Centre Archives, Paris.

References

Anderson, R., 2005. *Tongariro National Park: an overview report on the relationship between Maori and the Crown in the establishment of the Tongariro National Park*. Waitangi Tribunal.

Baird, M.F., 2009. *The politics of place: heritage, identity, and the epistemologies of cultural landscapes*. Thesis (PhD). University of Oregon.

Baird, M.F., in prep. Institutional protection and gatekeeping in heritage: an ethnographic approach.

Belgrave, M., 2005. *Historical frictions: Māori claims and reinvented histories*. Auckland: Auckland University Press.

Bender, B. and Winer, M., eds., 2001. *Contested landscapes: movement, exile and place*. Oxford: Berg.

Boast, R., 2008. *Buying the land, selling the land: governments and Maori land in the North Island 1865–1921*. Wellington: Victoria University Press.

Breglia, L., 2006. *Monumental ambivalence: the politics of heritage*. Austin, TX: University of Texas Press.

Carman, J., 2002. *Archaeology and heritage: an introduction*. London: Continuum.

Carman, J., 2005. *Against cultural property: archaeology, heritage and ownership*. London: Duckworth.
Cowan, J., 1927. *The Tongariro National Park, New Zealand: its topography, geology, alpine and volcanic features, history and Maori folk-lore*. Wellington: Ferguson and Osbourne.
Department of Lands Survey (DLS), 1986. *Nomination of Tongariro National Park New Zealand for inclusion in the World Heritage list*. Wellington: National Parks and Reserves.
Department of Conservation (DOC), 2006. *Tongariro National Park management plan: te kaupapa whakahaere mo te papa rehia o Tongariro, 2006–2016*. Turangi: Department of Conservation.
Forbes, S., 1993. *Nomination of Tongariro National Park for inclusion in the World Heritage cultural list*. Consultant's Report, Kotuku Consultancy Limited. Manuscript on file at the ICOMOS Documentation Centre, Paris, and the Department of Conservation, Turangi.
Forbes, S., 2003. *Tongariro National Park World Heritage cultural list 'He koha tapu–a sacred gift'*. Auckland: Government of New Zealand.
Gentry, K., 2009. *Associations make identities: the origins and evolution of historic preservation in New Zealand*. Thesis (PhD). University of Melbourne.
Henare, A., 2005. *Museums, anthropology and imperial exchange*. New York, NY: Cambridge University Press.
Henare, A., 2007. Taonga Maori: encompassing rights and property in New Zealand. *In*: A. Henare, M. Holbraad, and S. Wastell, eds. *Thinking through things: theorising artefacts ethnographically*. London: Routledge, 47–67.
Holdgate, Martin W., 1999. *The green web: a union for World Conservation*. London: The World Conservation Union and Earthscan Publications.
International Union for Conservation of Nature and Natural Resources (IUCN), 1990. *World heritage nomination for tongariro national Park, IUCN Summary*. Paris: World Heritage Centre Archives.
Ivison, D., Patton, P., and Sanders, W., eds., 2000. *Political theory and the rights of indigenous peoples*. London: Cambridge University Press.
Kawharu, M., 2000. Kaitiakitanga: a Maori anthropological perspective of the Maori socio-environmental ethic of resource management. *The Journal of Polynesian Society*, 109 (4), 349–370.
Kawharu, M., 2009. Ancestral landscapes and World Heritage: a Maori viewpoint. *Journal of Polynesian Society*, 118 (4), 317–338.
Kirshenblatt-Gimblett, B., 1995. Theorizing heritage. *Ethnomusicology*, 39 (3), 367–380.
Kirshenblatt-Gimblett, B., ed., 1998. *Destination culture: tourism, museums, and heritage*. Berkeley: University of California Press.
Long, D.L., 2000. Cultural heritage management in post-colonial polities: not the heritage of the other. *International Journal of Heritage Studies*, 6 (4), 317–322.
Marr, C., Hodge, R., and White, B., 2001. *Crown laws, policies, and practices in relation to flora and fauna, 1840–1912*. Wellington: Waitangi Tribunal.
Matunga, H., 1994. Waahi tapu: Māori sacred sites. *In*: J. Carmichael, *et al.*, eds. *Sacred sites, sacred places*. London: Routledge, 217–226.
McCarthy, C., 2011. *Museums and Māori: heritage professionals, indigenous collections, current practice*. Walnut Creek: Left Coast Press.
McCully, M. and Mutu, M., 2003. *Te whānau moana: Ngā kaupapa me ngā tikanga (customs and protocols)*. Auckland: Reed Books.
Memmott, P. and Long, S., 2002. Place theory and place maintenance in indigenous Australia. *Urban Policy and Research*, 1, 39–56.
Meskell, L., 2012. *The nature of heritage: the new South Africa*. Oxford: Blackwell.
Rose, D.B., 1996. *Nourishing terrains: Australian aboriginal views of landscape and wilderness*. Canberra: Australian Heritage Commission.
Rose, D.B., 2002. *Country of the heart: an indigenous Australian homeland*. Canberra: Aboriginal Studies Press.
Ruru, J., 2004. Indigenous peoples' ownership and management of mountains: the Aotearoa/New Zealand experience. *Indigenous Law Journal*, 3, 111–137.

Ruru, J., 2008. A Māori right to own and manage national parks? *Journal of South Pacific Law*, 12 (1), 105–110.

Sissons, J., 2005. *First peoples: indigenous cultures and their futures*. London: Reaktion.

Smith, L., 2004. *Archaeological theory and the politics of cultural heritage*. London: Routledge.

Smith, L., 2006. *Uses of heritage*. London: Routledge.

Solomon, M., 2005. The Wai 262 claim: a claim by Maori to indigenous flora and fauna: me o ratou taonga katoa. *In*: M. Belgrave, M. Kawharu, and D. Williams, eds. *Waitangi revisited: perspectives on the Treaty of Waitangi*. Melbourne: Oxford University Press, 213–232.

Stokes, J., 21 October 2006. 'Tribe Want Mountains and Park Back,' New Zealand Herald. Available from: http://www.nzherald.co.nz/nz/news/article.cfm?c_id=1&objectid=10406966 [Accessed 8 December 2011].

Strang, V., 2006. A happy coincidence? Symbiosis and synthesis in anthropological and indigenous knowledges. *Current Anthropology*, 47 (6), 981–1008.

Taiepa, T., et al., 1997. Co-management of New Zealand's conservation estate by Māori and Pākehā: a review. *Environmental Conservation*, 24 (3), 236–250.

Tapsell, P., 1997. The flight of Parerautūtu: an investigation of taonga from a tribal perspective. *Journal of Polynesian Society*, 106, 323–374.

Titchen, Sarah, 1993. Evaluation of Tongariro national park, New Zealand as an associative cultural landscape of outstanding Universal value. A report to the international council on monuments and sites (ICOMOS). Manuscript on file at the ICOMOS Documentation Centre, Paris.

Titchen, Sarah, 1995. On the Construction of 'outstanding universal value': some comments on the implementation of the 1972 UNESCO world heritage convention. *Conservation and Management of Archaeological Sites*, 1 (4), 232–242.

UNESCO 1987. *Report of the World Heritage committee* [online]. Available from: http://whc.unesco.org/en/sessions/11COM [Accessed October 2011].

UNESCO 1988. *Report of the World Heritage committee* [online]. Available from: http://whc.unesco.org/en/sessions/12BUR/documents/ [Accessed October 2011].

Waterton, E., 2005. Whose sense of place? Reconciling archaeological perspectives with community values: cultural landscapes in England. *International Journal of Heritage Studies*, 11 (4), 309–325.

Part III
Contemporary Issues in Cultural Heritage Rights Law

[14]

RESOLVING MATERIAL CULTURE DISPUTES: HUMAN RIGHTS, PROPERTY RIGHTS AND CRIMES AGAINST HUMANITY

ROBERT K. PATERSON*

I. Introduction 155
II. The American Cases on Recovery of Nazi-Era Art 156
III. Nazi-Era Art as the Proceeds of a Crime Against Humanity 158
IV. Sacred Indigenous Material Culture as a Human Right 161
V. Alternative Dispute Resolution in Material Culture Disputes 165
VI. Institutional Means to Resolve Material Culture Disputes 168
   A. The United Kingdom Spoliation Advisory Panel 169
   B. The Native American Graves Protection and Repatriation Review Committee 172
VII. The Future of Dispute Resolution Involving Nazi-Era and Indigenous Restitution Claims 174
VIII. Conclusion 174

I. INTRODUCTION

Artworks stolen from victims of the Nazis, along with the material cultural heritage of many indigenous peoples removed during colonialism, have both been the subject of a significant literature in recent years.[1] Few writers, however, seem to have attempted to compare these two categories with each other. This may partly be explained by the scarcity of reported judicial decisions concerning claims for the

---

* Professor, Faculty of Law, University of British Columbia. His degrees include LL.B. (New Zealand) and J.S.M. (Stanford).
1. In the case of the 1933 to 1945 period in Europe, see, e.g. L.H. NICHOLAS, THE RAPE OF EUROPA (Knopf 1994); HECTOR FELICIANO, THE LOST MUSEUM: THE NAZI CONSPIRACY TO STEAL THE WORLD'S GREATEST WORKS OF ART (Basic Books 1997); JONATHAN PETROPOULOS, ART AS POLITICS IN THE THIRD REICH (1996); ELIZABETH SIMPSON, THE SPOILS OF WAR: WORLD WAR II AND ITS AFTERMATH (1997). In respect of indigenous material culture during colonialism, see, e.g. TIM BARRINGER & TOM FLYNN, COLONIALISM AND THE OBJECT: EMPIRE, MATERIAL CULTURE AND THE MUSEUM (Routledge 1998); CRESSIDA FFORDE ET AL., THE DEAD AND THEIR POSSESSIONS: REPATRIATION IN PRINCIPLE, POLICY AND PRACTICE (Routledge 2001); NICHOLAS THOMAS, ENTANGLED OBJECTS: EXCHANGE, MATERIAL CULTURE AND COLONIALISM IN THE PACIFIC (Harvard 1991).

return of indigenous material, in comparison to the relatively large number of cases brought to recover artworks stolen by the Nazi regime. This article will first endeavor to explore whether these two types of claims should be treated according to similar principles or whether they present differences that warrant contrasting approaches. It will then discuss appropriate strategies, besides litigation, for resolving disputes involving both types of claims.

II. THE AMERICAN CASES ON RECOVERY OF NAZI-ERA ART

Though claims by owners or their heirs seeking to recover Nazi-seized art have been brought before courts in several countries, American judges have decided by far the largest number of such cases.[2] The earliest example of these was *Menzel v. List,* where the Belgian owners of a Marc Chagall painting that had been seized by the German authorities in 1941 sued its subsequent purchaser in a replevin action.[3] The original owners had inadvertently discovered the whereabouts of their painting in 1962 when they saw a reproduction of it in an art book along with the name of its current possessor. Litigation ensued. Significantly, the trial court dismissed arguments that the Menzels had abandoned the painting, that its seizure by the Nazis be seen as war booty and that the Act of State doctrine precluded the court investigating the acts of the German government.[4] The dismissal of the latter argument was based on a finding that the seizure was not by a foreign sovereign government but by an organ of the Nazi party.[5] The seizure of the painting was, therefore, treated as being equivalent to outright theft and the court dismissed a statue of limitations argument by the good-faith purchaser based on what is now known as the "Demand and Refusal" rule. Under this rule, the statute of limitations does not start to run until the true owner discovers the whereabouts of his or her stolen property and the person in possession refuses the owner's demand for its return.[6]

---

2. *See* MICHAEL J. BAZYLER, HOLOCAUST JUSTICE: THE BATTLE FOR RESTITUTION IN AMERICA'S COURTS (N.Y.U. Press 2003); MICHAEL J. BAZYLER & ROGER P. ALFORD, HOLOCAUST RESTITUTION: PERSPECTIVES ON THE LITIGATION AND ITS LEGACY (N.Y.U. Press 2006).

3. 253 N.Y.S.2d 43 (1st Dep't. 1964) and 267 N.Y.S.2d 804 (Sup. Ct. N.Y. 1966), *modified on other grounds*, 279 N.Y.S.2d 608 (1st Dep't. 1967), *modification rev'd*, 298 N.Y.S.2d 976 (1969).

4. 267 N.Y.S.2d 804, 810-16.

5. *Id.* at 815.

6. For an outline of the rule, see PATTY GERSTENBLITH, ART, CULTURAL HERITAGE AND THE LAW: CASES AND MATERIALS 394-401(Carolina Academic Press 2004).

It is the issue of whether Nazi looted art claims, like the one in *Menzel*, are statute-barred that has been the pre-occupation of American courts asked to resolve such cases. As Lawrence Kaye, who has been actively involved in bringing claims on behalf of victims of the Holocaust, points out, the "Demand and Refusal" rule favors protection of the true owners of stolen property over that of honest purchasers.[7] The rule has been followed in New York state – not just in respect of Holocaust looted art but for stolen property in general. Given the stature of New York City as a world art market capital, the rule has significant scope for application in stolen art cases.

In most American jurisdictions, however, another approach to the application of limitation periods has developed. The so-called "Discovery Rule" replaces the owner-favoring "Demand and Refusal" rule with an approach that seeks to assess the relative equities of the parties.[8] In *Autocephalous Greek-Orthodox Church of Cypress et al. v. Goldberg, etc.*, a well-known case involving Byzantine antiquities looted from Cyprus, the U.S. Court of Appeals for the Seventh Circuit opined "[c]entral to ... the discovery rule .... is the determination of the plaintiff's diligence in investigating the potential cause of action ... if [the] plaintiff was not reasonably diligent in discovering fraud the statute will run from the time discovery ought to have been made."[9]

This test assesses the potential loss to each party if the stolen property is awarded to the other. It resembles another basis for denying a right to recover the possession of stolen property – the equitable doctrine of laches. *Guggenheim v. Lubell* involved an artwork stolen from the Guggenheim Museum in New York and purchased two years later.[10] When the Museum located its painting in 1985 it brought an action against the purchasers. The court said that if the defendants could show a lack of diligence, on the owner's part, in seeking to discover the whereabouts of its lost work, the balance of equities might justify the art being awarded to the purchasers. The case illustrates that laches could be an important defense in New York State where the operation of the "Demand and Refusal" rule will often exclude a statute of limitations defense.

---

7. Lawrence Kaye, *The Statute of Limitations in Art Recovery Cases: An Overview* 1 IFAR J. 22 (1998).
8. *See* GERSTENBLITH, *supra* note 6, at 401-13.
9. Autocephalous Greek-Orthodox Church of Cyprus v. Goldberg & Feldman Fine Arts, Inc., 917 F.2d 278, 288 (7th Cir. 1990) *cert. denied*, 112 U.S. 377 (1991).
10. Solomon R. Guggenheim Found. v. Lubell, 550 N.Y.S.2d 618 (App. Div. 1990), *aff'd*, 569 N.E.2d 426 (N.Y. 1991) (finding the defendant was prejudiced by the plaintiff's delay).

Despite some success in the courts, many of those concerned with the recovery and return of Holocaust artworks have pursued other venues besides courts to resolve their claims. At conferences and meetings around the world a movement gained momentum that urged museums and other institutions to open their archives so that the provenance of objects could be examined and requests for restitution made in appropriate cases. These initiatives include the Vilnius Forum Declaration on Holocaust Era Looted Cultural Assets, issued at a conference of European states and non-governmental organizations in October 2000,[11] and the Principles on Nazi-Confiscated Art of the Washington Conference on Holocaust-Era Assets in 1998.[12]

III. NAZI-ERA ART AS THE PROCEEDS OF A CRIME AGAINST HUMANITY

Despite general agreement that artwork stolen by the Nazi regime was wrongfully taken from its owners, there has been relatively little support for the argument that once an object is proven as having been taken in that context it must be returned regardless of the merits of a claim to its possession by a subsequent purchaser. This arose because all litigated claims have been dealt according to conventional legal remedies for the recovery of stolen property, remedies which do not allow for differentiation between various forms of theft. Another way of looking at such claims would be to regard the artworks involved as the proceeds of crimes against humanity, and thus not properly amenable to defenses based on the merits of its retention by others.

A change in the legal principles governing claims for the recovery of property by victims of a crime against humanity would be consistent with ongoing dissatisfaction with the legal regimes applicable to such claims.[13] While this dissatisfaction sometimes applies to the relationship of buyers of stolen art to the victims of its theft in general, it is even more compelling in the instance of takings that are not instances of mere theft but a crime of much greater magnitude. Although there have been many efforts and suggestions concerning title claims by Holocaust victims, progress in securing the recovery of artworks has been relatively

---

11. International Forum on Holocaust-Era Looted Cultural Assets, Vilnius, Lithuania, Oct. 3-5, 2000.

12. *Washington Conference Principles on Nazi-Confiscated Art* (Washington, D.C., Dec. 3, 1998) (released in connection with the Washington Conference on Holocaust-Era Assets); *see also* Looted Cultural Property, Parliamentary Assembly of the Council of Europe, Resolution 1205, Nov. 4, 1999.

13. *See* Steven A. Bibas, *The Case Against Statutes of Limitations for Stolen Art*, 103 YALE L.J. 2437 (1994).

modest.[14] This suggests that a principle-based solution is not only appropriate, but also necessary.

Clearly the Holocaust represented a crime against humanity.[15] The Charter of the International Military Tribunal, which sat at Nuremberg, represented the first time such crimes were articulated in international law.[16] The Nuremberg Tribunal, however, made clear that it was describing acts that had long been seen as contrary to international law and its findings merely represented a restatement of the law.[17] Crimes against humanity are included in the Statues of the International Criminal Tribunal for the former Yugoslavia[18] and the International Criminal Court.[19] While the specific crimes included within the category of crimes against humanity refer to acts against persons (such as torture and deportation), any resultant loss of property to the victims of such crimes must be seen as a direct outcome associated with such crimes against the person. Seen in this way, the proceeds of crimes against humanity should not be (along with the crimes themselves) subject to such defenses as statutes of limitation, whose underlying policy goals (closure and stale evidence) are not properly applicable, given the gravity of the criminal acts committed in connection with the property stolen.[20]

Recognition of an exception to a statute of limitations defense in the case of theft associated with crimes against humanity articulates

---

14. *See, e.g.*, Robert Schwartz, *The Limits of the Law: A Call for a New Attitude Toward Artwork Stolen During World War II*, 32 COLUM. J.L. & SOC. PROBS. 1 (1998); Kelly Diane Walton, *Leave No Stone Unturned: The Search for Art Stolen by the Nazis and the Legal Rules Governing Restitution of Stolen Art*, 9 FORDHAM INTELL. PROP. MEDIA & ENT. L.J. 549 (1999).

15. *See* M. CHERIF BASSIOUNI, CRIMES AGAINST HUMANITY IN INTERNATIONAL CRIMINAL LAW (1999); BENJAMIN RICCI, CRIMES AGAINST HUMANITY: A HISTORICAL PERSPECTIVE (2004).

16. Charter of the International Military Tribunal (1945).

17. *See* Judgment of the International Military Tribunal for the Trial of German Major War Criminals.

18. *See* Statute of the International Criminal Tribunal for the Former Yugoslavia, art. 5 (1993).

19. *See* Rome Statute of the International Criminal Court, art. 5(1)(b) (2002), *available at* http://www.icc-cpi.int/library/about/officialjournal/Rome_Statute_120704-EN.pdf; *see also* Statute of the International Tribunal for Rwanda, art. 3 (1994). The United States informed the U.N. Secretary-General on May 6, 2002 that it did not regard itself as having any legal obligations arising from its signature to the Rome Treaty on December 31, 2000. The United Nations has not removed the United States from the list of official signatories.

20. *See* Convention of the Non-Applicability of Statutory Limitations to War Crimes and Crimes Against Humanity, G.A. Res. 2391, U.N. GAOR, 23d Sess., U.N. Doc. A/7218 (1968); *see also* Rome Statute, *supra* note 19, art. 29; European Convention on the Non-Applicability of Statutory Limitations to Crimes Against Humanity and War Crimes, E 7582, 13 I.L.M. 540, Jan. 25, 1974.

concerns regarding the morally compelling nature of Holocaust art claims. It also represents a meaningful interpretation of national law that takes into account the current state of international law. The recognition of such a legal principle by national courts would depend on the law seen as applicable to a particular case. In Canada for instance, customary international law is already seen as part of domestic law, so there is scope for such an approach.[21]

Canada was a major force in the establishment of the International Criminal Court. The provisions of the Rome Statute of the International Criminal Court have been enacted into Canadian law in the form of the Crimes Against Humanity and War Crimes Act (the Act).[22] Under the Act it is an indictable offense to commit a crime against humanity outside Canada.[23] Furthermore, there are no limitation periods applicable to indictable offenses in Canada.[24] Canadian law also provides for the seizure of any property obtained outside Canada through the commission of what, according to Canadian law, is a crime against humanity. Returns are to be made to persons lawfully entitled to the property concerned.[25] Enforcement is still a major problem in connection with offenses of this nature. So far, Canada has focused on bringing individuals accused of war crimes to justice, but the legal framework is in place for the return of seized Nazi-era artworks that were earlier acquired in the context of crimes against humanity.[26]

---

21. *See* HUGH M. KINDRED ET AL., INTERNATIONAL LAW CHIEFLY AS INTERPRETED AND APPLIED IN CANADA 165-68 (Emond Montgomery Publications 6th ed. 2000).

22. S.C. 2000, c.24.

23. *Id.* at s.6. Section 4(3) of the Act defines a "crime against humanity" as meaning:
   murder, extermination, enslavement, deportation, imprisonment, torture, sexual violence, persecution or any other inhumane act or omission that is committed against any civilian population or any identifiable group and that, at the time and in the place of its commission, constitutes a crime against humanity according to customary international law or conventional international law or by virtue of its being criminal according to the general principles of law recognized by the community of nations, whether or not it constitutes a contravention of the law in force at the time and in the place of its commission.

24. *See* Sanjeev S. Anand, *Should Parliament Enact Statutory Limitation Periods for Criminal Offences?*, 44 CRIM. L.Q. 8 (2000). The only exception is for treason using force or violence.

25. Criminal Code, R.S.C. 1985, c. C-46, § 462.32(4.1)

26. *See* Fifth Annual Report; Canada's Crimes Against Humanity and War Crimes Program, 2001-2002, http://www.cic.gc.ca/english/pub/war2002/section 04.html#d. In 2005, Canada acceded to the two Protocols to the 1954 UNESCO *Convention for the Protection of Cultural Property in the Event of Armed Conflict*. Canada had ratified the Convention itself in 1998. Section 36.1 of the Canadian *Cultural Property Export and Import Act*, R.S.C. 1985, c. C-51, now makes it an offense for a Canadian citizen or resident to unlawfully remove cultural property (as that term is defined in Article 9(a) of the Convention) from an occupied

IV. SACRED INDIGENOUS MATERIAL CULTURE AS A HUMAN RIGHT

Like Holocaust claims involving cultural property, claims by indigenous peoples respecting material removed in colonial times presents challenging issues for conventional legal analysis.[27] Unlike Nazi-era claims, few indigenous claims have even been heard by domestic courts.[28] The principal reason, apart from a lack of financial resources, is probably the inability to uncover the actual circumstances surrounding the original acquisition of the cultural material involved. While the facts of certain removals are well known, such as the Benin bronzes taken from the territory of what is now Nigeria by the 1897 British Punitive Expedition, the vast majority are not.[29] The scope of such acquisitions was vast, in geographical, ethnic and numerical scope. Many items were traded or gifted, while others were stolen, obtained by force, misunderstanding or removed as part of the actions of early missionaries and others.[30] While some argue that the whole process of colonization by European powers represented a kind of genocide analogous to the Holocaust, the events involved are probably too varied and complex to really permit such a generalized evaluation.[31] It is the variety of situations through which indigenous cultural property was obtained that factually most distinguishes such cases from those that occurred as part of the Holocaust. That said, if the circumstances of any acquisition of indigenous cultural material can be shown to constitute a crime against humanity, then the victims of such takings or their descendants should have an unqualified right to the return of any cultural material involved.

Professor James Nafziger has said of the Native American Graves Protection and Repatriation Act (NAGPRA) in the United States that

---

territory of a State Party to the Second Protocol contrary to its laws (there are currently 42 parties to the Second Protocol, including Austria and Hungary). In these circumstances the government of a State Party can ask the Attorney-General of Canada to bring proceedings in Canada to obtain recovery and an order for the return of the property in question. No statutes of limitation apply to proceedings under s.36.1 (see s. 36.1(10)). *See also* Criminal Code, R.S.C., 1985, c. C-46, § 7(2.01).

27. *See* Catherine E. Bell, *Limitations, Legislation and Domestic Repatriation*, Special Issue UBC L. REV. 149 (1995).

28. *See, e.g.*, Mohawk Bands v. Glenbow Alberta Institute, 3 C.N. L.R. 70 (Alta. Q.B. 1988).

29. *See* JEANETTE GREENFIELD, THE RETURN OF CULTURAL TREASURES 141-48 (Cambridge U. Press 1989).

30. *See* DOUGLAS COLE, CAPTURED HERITAGE: THE SCRAMBLE FOR NORTHWEST COAST ARTIFACTS (Douglas P. McIntyre 1985).

31. This is the conclusion of David B. Macdonald, *Daring to Compare: The Debate About a Maori "Holocaust" in New Zealand*, 5 J. GENOCIDAL RES. 383 (2003).

NAGPRA is, first and foremost, human rights legislation. It is *not* property rights legislation. Nor is it a legislative framework for balancing interests although it was intended to operate within a collaborative framework that included such instruments as the Vermillion Accord. Congress clearly intended the legislation to repair past wrongs and ensure present and future rights. As such, it must be seen and interpreted against the backdrop of modern human rights legislation at both domestic and international levels. NAGPRA also conforms with a general theory for repatriation. Accordingly, it can be fairly described as an instrument of decolonization, self-determination and reparation; as a vindication of Native American religious and other cultural freedoms; as a means of enhancing cultural revival and transmission of cultural knowledge among tribes and Native Hawaiian groups; as a contributor to self-identity and community solidarity; and as a means for restoring Native American control over pertinent culture.[32]

The enormous advantage of a NAGPRA-like approach to claims by indigenous peoples is that the entitlement of claimants turns less on the provenance of particular material and more on the nature of the objects themselves.[33] While Anglo-American common law has never recognized different categories of personal property based on their cultural significance, some legal systems recognize a separate category of *res sacrae* that because of its sacred or religious character is not subject to the ordinary rules affecting personality.[34] Thus the Quebec Court of Appeal set aside sales of Roman Catholic 18th-century silver liturgical objects by a parish priest on the basis of their being sacred in character and not alienable without compliance with canon law.[35]

Many indigenous claims involve objects lost before the 1930s. Litigation may therefore raise the same issues concerning the application of statutes of limitation as arise with Nazi-era claims. This issue has been partly addressed in Canada and the United States where courts have suggested that it may be inappropriate to apply statutes of limitation to certain indigenous claims in view of factors such as the fiduciary obligation of the government or the equivocality of limitation statutes

---

32. James A.R. Nafziger, The Protection and Repatriation of Indigenous Cultural Heritage in the United States, 425 (2006) (unpublished paper to be included in CATHERINE BELL & ROBERT K. PATERSON, PROTECTING FIRST NATIONS CULTURAL HERITAGE: LAW, POLICY AND REFORM UBC PRESS).

33. 25 U.S.C. §§ 3001-3013 (2000).

34. *See* Kurt Siehr, *International Art Trade and the Law*, 243 RECUEIL DES COURS 64, 64-66 (1993).

35. *See* Benoit Pelletier, *The Case of the Treasures of L'Ange Gardien: An Overview*, 2 INT'L J. CULTURAL PROP. 371 (1993).

themselves.³⁶ NAGPRA overrides limitations' problems but it does not address indigenous cultural material outside the United States or that found in private collections. Neither the 1970 UNESCO Convention on the Means of Prohibiting and Preventing the Illicit Import, Export and Transfer of Ownership of Cultural Property nor the UNIDROIT Convention on Stolen or Illegally Exported Cultural Objects apply retroactively to require the return of objects illegally removed before these treaties were in effect.³⁷ This means most indigenous claims will either be statute-barred or unprovable due to the passage of time, the death of witnesses and other factual impediments.

Institutionalized and ad-hoc modes to resolve indigenous material culture claims show a similar pattern respecting which objects are seen as most susceptible to repatriation. Both NAGPRA and the Canadian Task Force Report on Museums and First Peoples present a hierarchical approach that places ancestral remains and sacred objects as the most qualified for return and, conversely, places utilitarian and domestic objects as less qualified.³⁸ This suggests that there may be an emerging standard that supports the right of indigenous peoples to the return of, at least, certain important religious or sacred material. These developments can also be seen as receiving some level of international support in the form of the new United Nations Declaration on the Rights of Indigenous Peoples. Article 12 of the UN Declaration states:

> 1. Indigenous peoples have the right to manifest, practice, develop and teach their spiritual and religious traditions, customs and ceremonies; the right to maintain, protect, and have access in privacy to their religious and cultural sites; the right to the use and control of their ceremonial objects; and the right to the repatriation of their human remains.
>
> 2. States shall seek to enable the access and/or repatriation of ceremonial objects and human remains in their possession through fair, transparent and effective mechanisms developed in conjunction with indigenous peoples concerned.³⁹

---

36. *See* Oneida, County of v. Oneida Indian Nation, 470 U.S. 226 (1985); Bell, *supra* note 27.

37. UNESCO Convention on the Means of Prohibiting and Preventing the Illicit Import, Export and Transfer of Ownership of Cultural Property, 10 INT'L LEGAL MATS. 189 (1971); 1995 UNIDROIT Convention on Stolen and Illegally Exported Cultural Objects, Rome, June 24, 1995.

38. *See* 25 U.S.C. §§ 3001-3013 (1988); TASK FORCE ON MUSEUMS AND FIRST PEOPLES, TURNING THE PAGE: FORGING NEW PARTNERSHIPS BETWEEN MUSEUMS AND FIRST PEOPLES 8-9 (Ottawa 2d ed. 1992).

39. Declaration on the Rights of Indigenous Peoples, GA Res.61/295, U.N. Doc. A/61/PV.107 (Sept. 13, 2007) (Canada and the United States dissented in the vote adopting the

The UN Declaration is still only evidence of the present state of international law on this subject but it continues to receive support from the practice of museums in several countries. Recently, the Association of Art Museum Directors (AAMD), in the United States issued a report of its Task Force on the Acquisition and Stewardship of Sacred Objects.[40] The report notes that the most commonly recognized works of art considered to be sacred are those deriving from indigenous cultures. It makes specific reference to First Nation cultures in Canada but notes that very few national or international laws dictate special consideration for such works. The report does not address the question of repatriation directly, but mainly concerns itself with raising the consciousness amongst its membership of the special character of sacred cultural material and the complexity of the issues such material presents for museums in terms of acquisition, handling and display.

Another informing aspect of the distinction between Nazi-era and indigenous claims is that the latter involves material that is culturally affiliated with indigenous peoples themselves, whereas the art appropriated by the Nazis and their agents comprised a variety of property, most of which had no specific cultural connection to its owners. In view of this distinction, it seems appropriate that recovery of the latter be based, not on the character of the property stolen but on the actions of the Nazis in taking it. Entitlement to indigenous cultural property, on the other hand, should not depend on the vagaries of the various levels of egregiousness surrounding its acquisition (unless crimes against humanity can be established) but on a human right to claim it based on the religious or cultural significance of the material to the indigenous claimant.

A further difference between Nazi-era and indigenous claims is that while the former are often brought against both institutions and private individuals, the latter almost always concern claims against museums or other public institutions. This is both a result of differences in the character of the objects whose return is sought and the different laws applicable to these two categories. As already mentioned, NAGPRA does not apply to private collectors, and the state of indigenous title law makes claims against them unpredictable at best. Even if one bases repatriation of indigenous cultural material on a human rights argument,

---

resolution); *see* Dean B. Suagee, *Human Rights and the Cultural Heritage of Indian Tribes in the United States*, 8 INT'L J. CULTURAL PROP. 48, 67 (1999).

40. *See* Report on the Stewardship and Acquisition of Sacred Objects of the Association of Art Museum Directors (June 1, 2006); Hugh Eakin, *Museums Set Guidelines for Use of Sacred Objects*, N.Y. TIMES, Aug. 10, 2006, at B3.

it may be harder to make that argument against private parties who, at least in the first instance, are not subject to the same international human rights norms as are states and state instrumentalities.[41] This is not to suggest, however, that the existence of indigenous cultural rights against governments might not have a "chilling effect" on the private collecting of sacred and religious indigenous objects, much as gaps in provenance have affected the private collecting of antiquities.[42]

V. ALTERNATIVE DISPUTE RESOLUTION IN MATERIAL CULTURE DISPUTES

The legal challenges involving the principles that should govern Nazi-era and indigenous claims carry forward into a consideration of the most effective means for resolving such disputes. Both types of claims challenge the ingenuity of courts in adequately responding to the problems of evidence, ethics and morality that typify these sorts of disputes. Many reported decisions display the awkwardness of applying generic legal rules about property to the unique and serious ethical, moral and cultural dimensions typically involved. This perception has led many to propose alternatives to litigation in these cases, such as mediation or arbitration.[43]

Although strategies such as treaties and litigation in domestic courts have achieved some success in addressing certain cultural property issues, many experts advocate the need for other innovative types of approaches.[44] To an extent, this anxiety arises from the unique nature of cultural objects and the special feelings they evoke because of their symbolic, religious, historical, and aesthetic qualities. Few laws seem to respond to these sorts of considerations because they often appear to be too elusive to permit of the precise definition lawyers usually seek.

Since 2004, the Committee on Cultural Heritage Law of the

---

41. *See* LYAL S. SUNGA, INDIVIDUAL RESPONSIBILITY IN INTERNATIONAL LAW FOR SERIOUS HUMAN RIGHTS VIOLATIONS (Nijhoff 1992).
42. *See* FRED R. MYERS, THE EMPIRE OF THINGS: REGIMES OF VALUE AND MATERIAL CULTURE (2001). This has achieved a degree of formal legal recognition in the United Kingdom under the provisions of the Dealing in Cultural Objects (Offences) Act, 2003 which criminalizes dealing in "tainted" objects (which includes objects illegally excavated in the United Kingdom or abroad).
43. *See, e.g.*, RESOLUTION OF CULTURAL PROPERTY DISPUTES: PAPERS EMANATING FROM THE SEVENTH PERMANENT COURT OF ARBITRATION INTERNATIONAL LAW SEMINAR, May 23, 2003 (Permanent Court of Arbitration/Peace Palace Papers, V. 7 2004); BARBARA T. HOFFMAN, ART AND CULTURAL HERITAGE: LAW, POLICY AND PRACTICE 463-87 (Cambridge 2006).
44. *See* RESOLUTION OF CULTURAL PROPERTY DISPUTES, *supra* note 43, at 265, 302.

International Law Association (ILA) has been working to prepare a set of Principles for Cooperation in the Mutual Protection and Transfer of Cultural Material (the ILA Principles), which were adopted at the June 2006 meeting of the International Law Association in Toronto, Canada.[45] The development of the ILA Principles was based on a desire to lessen the level of acrimony that can often surround disputes concerning cultural material. For example, the ILA Principles promote the exploration of alternatives to the outright return of objects, such as long-term loans, exchanges of objects, and the making of copies.

A 2001 agreement between the United States and Italy, which was renewed in January 2006, imposes import restrictions on certain categories of Italian archaeological material.[46] Like other similar agreements to which the United States is a party, the 2001 Agreement obliges the United States to return material improperly exported from Italy in certain specified circumstances.[47] The Italian agreement, however, in a break with precedent, also explores additional options to the outright return of cultural material. The agreement commits both sides to use their best efforts to facilitate contact between their respective museums and institutions and, in particular, increase loans of Italian cultural material to American museums.[48] Italy also agrees to continue to devote more funding to guard its archaeological sites and museums and develop tax incentives for the private support of legitimate archaeological excavation.[49]

This expanded version for a type of agreement more usually concerned solely with the recognition and enforcement of foreign cultural property export controls was followed in 2006 by another high-profile agreement between Italy and the Metropolitan Museum of Art in

---

45. Principles for Cooperation in the Mutual Protection and Transfer of Cultural Material, June 8, 2006, Res. 4/2006 International Law Association; see Robert K. Paterson, *The "Caring and Sharing" Alternative: Recent Progress in the International Law Association to Develop Draft Cultural Material Principles*, 12 INT'L J. CULTURAL PROP. 62 (2005).

46. Agreement Between the Government of the United States of America and the Government of the Republic of Italy Concerning the Imposition of Import Restrictions on Categories of Archaeological Material Representing the Pre-Classical, Classical and Imperial Roman Periods of Italy, Jan. 19, 2001, 40 I.L.M. 1031 (2001) [hereinafter Agreement]. The 2001 agreement has been extended until January 19, 2011 and article II replaced by the Extension and Amendment to the Agreement between the Government of the Untied States of America and the Government of the Republic of Italy concerning the Imposition of Import Restrictions on Categories of Archaeological Material Representing the Pre-Classical, Classical and Imperial Roman Periods of Italy (2006).

47. *Id.* at art. 1. For the status of import restrictions under the Convention on Cultural Property Implementation Act, see http://exchanges.state.gov/culprop/chart.html.

48. Agreement, *supra* note 46, at art. II: E(1).

49. *Id.* at art. II: B.

New York.[50] The Metropolitan agreement focused on the return of several archaeological objects from the museum's collection, including an esteemed fifth-century krater painted by Euphronios. Notably, however, the krater is to remain on loan at the museum until 2008, and other loans to the United States are to be arranged from Italy, including items discovered during excavations financed by the Metropolitan Museum or restored by its conservation personnel.

Many recent agreements to return objects acquired under questionable circumstances have required recipients to fund the making of copies of disputed artifacts. When the Stockholm Ethnographic Museum agreed to return a totem pole originally from British Columbia, Canada, the requesting Haisla First Nation agreed to make a replica for the Swedish museum to exhibit in place of the original. Such a solution means that a historical loss is not repeated.[51]

The ILA Principles are designed to be a voluntary basis for parties exploring ways to resolve requests for the return of cultural material in a broad range of situations. Thus, they suggest a sort of minimum standard to which parties can agree in advance. For instance, requests should be in writing, with a detailed description of any cultural material whose return is requested, together with reasons substantiating the request.[52] Recipients of such requests are required to respond in writing with reasons for agreeing or disagreeing to the request, along with a proposed timetable for implementation or further negotiations.[53]

Given the controversy surrounding the suitability of litigation in cases involving the return of cultural material, the ILA Principles contain a separate provision on dispute settlement that advocates the use of some form of alternate dispute mechanism (such as mediation or arbitration) over recourse to national courts.[54] Many museums and other institutions have already established internal repatriation committees to deal with requests for the return of cultural material.[55] These may offer cost savings, privacy, and more flexibility than the alternative of litigation.

---

50. *See* Elisabetta Provoledo, *Italy and U.S. Sign Antiquities Accord*, N.Y. TIMES, Feb. 22, 2006.

51. *See* Derah Hansen, *An Emotional Homecoming*, VANCOUVER SUN, Apr. 27, 2006, at B3.

52. Principles for Cooperation in the Mutual Protection and Transfer of Cultural Material, *supra* note 45, at Principle 2: Requests and Responses to Requests for the Transfer of Cultural Material.

53. *Id.*

54. *Id.* at Principle 9: Dispute Settlement.

55. *See, e.g.*, The Repatriation Guidelines of the Museum of Anthropology at the University of British Columbia, http://www.moa.ubc.ca/pdf/Repatriation_guidelines.pdf.

For instance, agreed-upon ethical and moral standards can be applied to cases where conventional legal principles may be seen to fall short of the parties' needs and expectations.

The ILA Principles do not, however, go so far as to eliminate litigation as an option because it can still sometimes expeditiously and imaginatively resolve difficult cases. One such instance is when a New Zealand court granted probate in respect of the estate of a long-deceased Maori warrior whose preserved tattooed head (toi moko) had been consigned for auction in London.[56] The issuance of letters of administration to an executor facilitated the withdrawal of the head from sale and its return to New Zealand for burial in accordance with indigenous Maori custom.[57]

There now seems to be an increased readiness among parties to disputes involving cultural material to experiment with new solutions. The ILA Principles, therefore, seem timely insofar as they confirm established practice and build upon it to develop standards that seek to facilitate non-confrontational outcomes. In a sense, the ILA Principles may even represent evidence of emerging international minimum standards concerning the treatment of certain cultural material and supplement the work of other international institutions such as UNESCO, UNIDROIT, and nongovernmental bodies including the International Council of Museums and the World Archaeological Congress. It now seems appropriate to many in the field of international cultural heritage law to move beyond choices that involve either appeasement or intransigence and to attempt enlightened and innovative solutions to these difficult issues.

VI. INSTITUTIONAL MEANS TO RESOLVE MATERIAL CULTURAL DISPUTES

Two contemporary examples of institutionalized alternatives to litigation in seeking resolution of repatriation disputes, involving Nazi-era property thefts and indigenous cultural material respectively, are the Spoliation Advisory Panel in the United Kingdom and the Native American Graves Protection and Repatriation Review Committee in the United States. The following is a brief outline of how these two procedures operate.

---

56. Re Estate of Tupuna Maori, No. P580/88 (High Court of New Zealand) (unreported case 1988).
57. Patrick J. O'Keefe, *Maoris Claim Head*, 1 INT'L J. CULTURAL PROP. 393 (1992).

A. The United Kingdom Spoliation Advisory Panel[58]

In February of 2000, the United Kingdom established a Spoliation Advisory Panel (the Panel) to assist both claimants and institutions respecting property lost during the Nazi-era and now held in national institutions. The Panel is chaired by a retired Lord Justice of Appeal, the Right Honourable Sir David Hirst and is intended to provide an alternative to litigation that is not a judicial body. So far the Panel has issued reports on five claims.

The most recent of these claims involved four drawings now in the possession of the British Museum.[59] It was brought on behalf of the heirs of Dr. Arthur Feldmann who had lost the drawings in March 1939 when the Gestapo seized his collection from his villa in Brno, Czechoslovakia. The British Museum subsequently acquired the drawings at an auction in England in 1946, as well as through bequest. Initially the Commission for Looted Art in Europe presented the claim in 2002 on behalf of the claimants. The U.K. Attorney-General then sought, with the Commission intervening with leave of the English court, a decision from the courts on whether the British Museum could lawfully return an object in its collection if it considered itself to be morally obliged to make such a return. The court answered in the negative, based on the language of the British Museum Act, which prohibits the museum disposing of objects in its collections, as being too unequivocal to permit an implied exception.[60]

The claimants then revoked the authority of the Commission and proceeded to make a joint submission, along with the British Museum, to the Panel. The submission proposed a "preferred solution" that the drawings remain at the British Museum and the claimants receive the full value of the drawings by way of compensation. The Panel's Terms of Reference oblige it to, *inter alia*:

> (c) examine and determine the circumstances in which the claimant was deprived of the object, whether by theft, forced sale, sale at an undervalue, or otherwise;

---

58. *See* DEPARTMENT FOR CULTURE MEDIA AND SPORT: SPOLIATION ADVISORY PANEL, http://www.culture.gov.uk/what_w_do/Cultural_property/sap.htm.

59. *See* REPORT OF THE SPOLIATION ADVISORY PANEL IN RESPECT OF FOUR DRAWINGS NOW IN THE POSSESSION OF THE BRITISH MUSEUM (The Stationery Office 2006), http://www.culture.gov.uk/Reference_library/Publications/archive_2006/sapreport_hc1052.htm.

60. British Museum Act 1963 (U.K.), 1963, c. 24, as amended by Museum and Galleries Act 1992 (U.K.) 1992, c. 44, s. 11(2), S ch. 8, pt. 1, s. 5(9); *see* Attorney-General v. Trustees of the British Museum [2005] 3 W.L.R. 396 (Ch.).

...

(e) give due weight to the moral strength of the claimant's case;

...

(g) consider whether any moral obligation rests on the institution, taking into account in particular the circumstances of its acquisition of the object, and its knowledge at that juncture of the object's provenance;

(h) take account of any relevant statutory provisions, including stipulations as to the institution's powers and duties, including any restrictions on its powers of disposal.[61]

The Panel stated that its duty to give weight to moral considerations was founded on the terms of two international instruments: the 1943 Inter-Allied Declaration Against Acts of Dispossession Committed in Territories Under Enemy Occupation or Control and the 1998 Principles with Respect to Nazi-Confiscated Art Issued by the Washington Conference on Holocaust-Era Assets. It went on to find that, since the parties had not sought a return of the drawings by the British Museum, the only two possible remedies the Panel could recommend were compensation or an *ex gratia* payment. The former was seen as inappropriate given the lack of clear legal entitlement to the drawings on the part of the claimants but that on the strength of their moral claim an *ex gratia* payment of £175,0000 was considered to be appropriate.

Other Panel decisions have shown a consistent and compatible approach to spoliation cases. In respect of a painting by Jan Griffier the Elder, that the claimant contended had been lost by his mother during the war, compensation was sought instead of physical possession of the painting.[62] The Panel examined issues of title and limitation periods and concluded that any claim against the Tate Gallery was now statute-barred under English law. Considering the level of diligence on the part of the Tate Gallery surrounding its acquisition of the painting, the Panel recommended an *ex gratia* payment to the claimant of £125,000, together with a recommendation that the Tate Gallery display alongside the picture an account of its history and provenance during and since the Nazi-era, with special reference to the interest of the claimant and his family.

---

61. *See* SPOLIATION ADVISORY PANEL CONSTITUTION AND TERMS OF REFERENCE, Paragraph 7, http://www.culture.gov.uk/NR/rdonlyres/9F0B7A06-16C4-4CBD-B52C-DCDC6805098B/0/SAPConstitutionandTermsofReferenceApril07.pdf.

62. *See* REPORT OF THE SPOLIATION ADVISORY PANEL IN RESPECT OF A PAINTING NOW IN THE POSSESSION OF THE TATE GALLERY (The Stationery Office 2001), http://www.culture.gov.uk/Reference_library/Publications/archive_2001/sapreport_hc111.htm.

In a claim involving a Chardin still-life in the possession of the Glasgow City Council as part of the Burrell Collection, the claimants contended that they had lost possession of the picture in 1936 as a result of a forced sale.[63] The Council argued the Panel should recommend an *ex gratia* payment. The Panel was informed, however, that the authenticity of the painting was seriously in question and since its owners had earlier received what, in retrospect, seemed a fair price when it was sold at auction, the Panel recommended restitution of the painting to the claimants.

Another Panel report dealt with a 12th-century manuscript in the possession of the British Library.[64] Conflicting evidence was presented to the Panel about the provenance of the manuscript, but the Panel concluded it had been looted in Italy between 1943 and the time of its acquisition by a British citizen from a Naples bookseller in 1944. The British Museum acquired the object in 1947 and it was transferred to the British Library in 1973. Since the Panel concluded the manuscript had been spoliated during the 1933-1945 period it found the claim was within its jurisdiction. The Panel then concluded the manuscript should be returned to Benevento Cathedral in Italy. Unfortunately for the Panel, English law prohibited the British Library from making such a return. It recommended that legislation be introduced to allow the de-accessioning of Nazi-spoliated objects. This would still not necessarily permit the Benevento manuscript to be returned as it may have been taken by a British soldier during the occupation of Benevento by the Allies after October 1943. In view of the Panel's recommendations, however, it has been suggested that an exception be legislated to allow the return of this particular item. In the meantime, based on the Panel's recommendations, negotiations are under way to allow the transfer of the manuscript by way of a loan to the Biblioteca Nazionale in Naples.

The UK Spoliation Panel's reports illustrate a level of flexibility surrounding the resolution of Nazi-era claims that cannot be achieved through litigation. Through its ability to take into account the moral aspects of claims brought before it, the Panel is able to temper the unequivocality of strictly legal options. The Panel is also not bound by

---

63. *See* REPORT OF THE SPOLIATION ADVISORY PANEL IN RESPECT OF A PAINTING NOW IN THE POSSESSION OF GLASGOW CITY COUNCIL (The Stationery Office 2004), http://www.culture.gov.uk/Reference_library/Publications/archive_2004/report_spa.htm.

64. *See* REPORT OF THE SPOLIATION ADVISORY PANEL IN RESPECT OF A 12TH CENTURY MANUSCRIPT NOW IN THE POSSESSION OF THE BRITISH LIBRARY (The Stationery Office 2005), http://www.culture.gov.uk/Reference_library/Publications/archive_2005/rpt_ spoliation _advisory_panel.htm.

the ordinary rules of the law of evidence so that it can consider facts that a court might not be able to access. In the claim concerning a painting in the possession of the Glasgow City Council, the Panel supported the claimants wish to remain anonymous (basing this decision on Article 8 of the European Convention on Human Rights). The Panel has also been ready to consider various instruments and codes even though they may not be legally binding in the United Kingdom, such as when the British Library Panel considered principles developed by the National Museum Directors' Conference. The terms of reference for the Panel also explicitly suggest several forms of recommended relief for resolving claims besides outright restitution. These include the ability to recommend *ex gratia* payments and the enactment of legislation to alter the legal powers and duties of institutions.

B. The Native American Graves Protection and Repatriation Review Committee

Any party to a dispute over a request for the return of certain American Indian or Native Hawaiian cultural material or human remains from an American museum or U.S. federal agency can request the Native American Graves Protection and Repatriation Review Committee (the Committee) to facilitate the resolution of the dispute.[65] Apart from dispute resolution, the Committee also assists in defining ambiguities surrounding the Native American Graves Protection and Repatriation Act (NAGPRA) itself and facilitating draft repatriation strategies to avoid disputes arising in the first place. The Committee is comprised of seven members; three nominees from indigenous communities themselves, three nominees of museums and scientific organizations, and one person chosen by the other six. If the Committee agrees to hear a request, it will peruse written documentation and may also hear from the parties. Committee recommendations are non-binding and made to the Secretary of the Interior.

During its approximately 16-year lifespan the Committee has met over 25 times and wrestled with many complex issues, including culturally unidentifiable remains and their reburial, the protection of sacred tribal information and repatriations to federally-unrecognized tribes. The recent work of the Committee has focused on dispute avoidance through the development of clearer definitions and principles.

---

65. 25 U.S.C. § 3006(c)(4) (2000); *see* C. Timothy McKeown & Sherry Hutt, *In the Smaller Scope of Conscience: The Native American Graves Protection & Repatriation Act Twelve Years After*, 21 UCLA J. ENVTL. L. & POL'Y 153, 202-05 (2002-2003).

This flexible approach has meant that the Committee has been able to effectively respond to the sorts of problems that are unique to indigenous repatriation—such as the contamination of remains and the nature of sacred objects—as well as increase the overall effectiveness of NAGPRA itself and relieve the perception that it presents a rigid and overly-legalistic approach to repatriation issues affecting American indigenous peoples.[66]

Determining whether an object is a "sacred object" is a perennial difficulty under NAGPRA. Often the answer is reached after consultation and collaboration between native groups and museums and federal agencies. "Sacred objects" are defined in NAGPRA as "specific ceremonial objects which are needed by traditional Native American religious leaders for the practice of traditional Native American religions by their present day adherents."[67] Who is a traditional religious leader is determined according to a person's recognition by members of an Indian tribe or Native Hawaiian organization as being responsible for cultural duties relating to the ceremonial or religious traditions of the tribe or organization.[68] Thus, in one case, the Committee found that a Hawaiian carved wooden figure was a "sacred object" and recommended its repatriation to Native Hawaiian organizations.[69] The museum responded to this recommendation by filing court proceedings. Subsequently the parties settled their dispute by agreement that the Office of Hawaiian Affairs pay $125,000 to the Providence Museum.[70]

The role and functioning of the Committee continues to provoke controversy and debate. This probably indicates it is doing its job. Many see NAGPRA as involving the repatriation process in radically different ways of understanding culture, history and ownership.[71] These challenges may be novel and confusing to some but they also reveal that the role of the Committee is central to the resolution of indigenous American claims for the return of their cultural heritage and it continues to exhibit an ability to develop more flexible solutions than those likely to emerge from litigation.

---

66. *See* Nafziger, *supra* note 32.
67. 25 U.S.C. § 3001 (3)(c) (2000).
68. *See* 43 C.F.R. § 10.2(d)(3).
69. *See* NAGPRA Review Committee Advisory Findings and Recommendations Regarding a Carved Wooden Figure from the Hawaiian Islands, 62 Fed. Reg. 23, 794-95 (May 1, 1997).
70. *See* Susan Kreifels, *Hawaiian Spear-Rest Expected Home: An OHA Representative Says a Compromise Will be Worked Out*, HONOLULU STAR-BULL., Mar. 19, 1998.
71. *See* Robert H. McLaughlin, *The American Archaeological Record: Authority to Dig, Power to Interpret*, 7 INT'L J. CULTURAL PROP. 342 (1998).

VII. THE FUTURE OF DISPUTE RESOLUTION INVOLVING NAZI-ERA AND INDIGENOUS RESTITUTION CLAIMS

Even as the state of international and national law relating to these sorts of cultural material claims continues to develop greater certainty, there seems to be a consensus that the courtroom is usually not the best place for them to be resolved. Alternative forms of dispute resolution, including institutional (as in the case of NAGPRA and the UK Spoliation Advisory Panel) or *ad hoc* procedures agreed to between the parties themselves, are increasingly producing realistic and meaningful solutions to what often at first seem to be intractable problems.

The ILA Principles represent the latest attempt at comprehensive guidelines for parties to disputes concerning cultural material. They are not intended to be definitive since the nuances of such cases defy uniform approaches. Not all indigenous communities want or can afford to even initiate claims. It is very unlikely the process of restitution will ever reach its conclusion. The practicalities are that museum collections of indigenous objects will likely continue to exist and long-lost Holocaust-era art objects will continue to be discovered. What is important about the ILA Principles is that they nurture the process of negotiating returns by focusing attention on what needs to accompany it – such as the making of inventories, the existence of protocols for the making and receipt of requests, and the notification of newly found material.

VIII. CONCLUSION

Alongside the evolution of new dispute resolution mechanisms, the norms applicable to the resolution of particularly challenging claims will continue to be refined. In this article, I suggest that in at least two instances (indigenous cultural material of a sacred or religious character and property stolen by the Nazi regime as part of the Holocaust) a consensus is emerging about the principles of entitlement. The ordinary rules pertaining to the right to personal property sometimes appear as compromised. In the case of indigenous sacred cultural material this compromise forms part of the human rights of the peoples themselves. In the case of the property of Jews and others, appropriated by the Nazi regime, a right to restitution should now be seen as premised on the commission of a crime against humanity.

[15]

Controlling the International Market in Antiquities: Reducing the Harm, Preserving the Past

Patty Gerstenblith[*]

The recent restitution of antiquities from several major American museums and the trial in Italy of former Getty antiquities curator Marion True and art dealer Robert Hecht have focused public attention on the illegal trade in looted antiquities to an extent rarely seen in the past.[1] The looting of the Iraq Museum in Baghdad in April 2003 and the even more disastrous large-scale looting of archaeological sites in southern Iraq since the beginning of the current Gulf War have brought the devastating effects of the international market in looted antiquities into even starker relief.[2] The looting of archaeological sites and the dismemberment of ancient monuments are problems that afflict countries as wealthy as the United States and the United Kingdom and as poor as Mali and Bolivia. Recent revelations concerning the functioning of the art market and the acquisition of antiquities with unknown origins now demonstrate that the looting of archaeological sites is a well-organized big business motivated primarily by profit.

The looting of archaeological sites creates negative externalities that harm society. Because the legal regime aims to eliminate societal harms, the law should force the actor to internalize the costs[3] and thereby discourage the negative

---

[*] Professor, DePaul University College of Law. I want to thank Megan Kossiakoff for her research assistance.

[1] For general discussions, see Tracy Wilkinson, *Ex-Getty Antiquities Curator Appears at Italian Court Session*, LA Times A9 (Nov 17, 2005) (discussing the trial of Getty curator Marion True); Jason Felch and Ralph Frammolino, *Several Museums May Possess Looted Art*, LA Times A16 (Nov 8, 2005) (discussing the trial of dealer Robert Hecht).

[2] For general discussion, see Micah Garen, *The War within the War*, 57 Archaeology 28, 31 (July–Aug 2004) (discussing site looting in Iraq); Neela Banerjee and Micah Garen, *Saving Iraq's Archaeological Past from Thieves Remains an Uphill Battle*, NY Times A16 (Apr 4, 2004) (discussing antiquities looting in Iraq); Joanne Farchakh, *Le Massacre du Patrimoine Irakienne*, Archaeologia 14, 25–29 (July–Aug 2003).

[3] Howard Demsetz, *Toward a Theory of Property Rights*, 57 Am Econ Rev 347 (1967) (presenting the classic statement of the effects of negative externalities, focusing on costs only in the monetary

activity. In this Article, the term "cost" indicates any harmful effect imposed on an individual or on society as a whole. The loss of cultural value is a cost paid by society. In the field of cultural heritage law, "value" usually indicates the intangible worth and significance of original contexts and rarely connotes monetary value.[4] This Article addresses the unique aspects of the trade in antiquities, that is, archaeological objects that have, over time, been buried in the ground with an associated assemblage of other artifacts, architectural remains, and natural features. Because of its link to the looting of sites, the trade in undocumented antiquities raises legal, ethical, and societal concerns distinguishing it from the trade in other forms of artwork.

In this Article, I will discuss three components. First, I will examine the harms that the looting of archaeological sites imposes on society. Second, I will discuss the responses to the problem, particularly in terms of the law that attempts to regulate this conduct, and some of the characteristics of the current legal regime and of the market in antiquities that prevent the law from achieving its full potential for deterrence. Third, this Article will examine and propose solutions to discourage site looting and encourage preservation of the remains of the past for the benefit of the future.

I. UNDERSTANDING THE PAST

There are several detrimental consequences of looting. First, the looting of archaeological sites imposes negative externalities on society by destroying our ability to fully understand and reconstruct the past. Humans have long been interested in the material remains of past cultures, and they have often collected artifacts as political symbols of domination[5] or as a means of enjoying past artistic accomplishments. The manner in which artifacts are recovered from the

---

sense). Demsetz uses these concepts to justify the development of a system of private property rights, reducing transaction costs and thereby eliminating economic inefficiencies. Id at 349.

[4] The translation of this type of value into economic terms is difficult. One attempt is codified in the Cultural Heritage Resource Crimes Sentencing Guideline in which "archaeological value" must be included in the valuation of a cultural heritage resource for sentencing purposes, 18 USC Appx § 2B1.5 Application Note 2(A)(i), and is defined as the cost of retrieving the scientific information from the archaeological resource, from research design to final publication, that was harmed through commission of the cultural heritage resource crime. See 18 USC Appx § 2B1.5 Application Note 2(C)(i).

[5] The Romans took cultural and religious symbols from the people and nations they conquered as a way of displaying their victories. One example is the depiction on the Arch of Titus in Rome of the triumphal parade including the Menorah removed from the Second Temple in Jerusalem, later destroyed by the Romans in 70 CE. Napoleon brought to Paris artistic and other cultural works from Europe, particularly Italy, both to flaunt his conquests and to establish Paris as an artistic center. John Henry Merryman and Albert E. Elsen, *Law, Ethics and the Visual Arts* 1–8 (Kluwer 3d ed 1998).

ground only became important after the development of archaeology as a science, with examples of stratigraphic excavation and recording known as early as the seventeenth century. Borrowing in large measure from the emerging fields of Darwinian evolutionary biology and paleontology that rely on the stratigraphic placement of fossils to reconstruct the chronological evolution of life forms, a modern understanding of the role of stratigraphic excavation as key to understanding human cultural evolution developed by the late eighteenth century.[6] Archaeology became a truly interdisciplinary field in the middle and late twentieth century with the adoption of scientific techniques, such as radiocarbon and thermoluminescence dating[7] and more sophisticated methods, in conjunction with the use of linguistic, philological, art historical, and anthropological analyses to understand the past.

Controlled scientific excavation of archaeological sites relies on an understanding of stratigraphy; remains of past cultures are deposited in layers (or strata), and each stratum represents a particular time period. Stratigraphic excavation requires that each layer be removed in reverse chronological order and that the remains be recovered separately by each stratum, with all the remains of the same period in association with each other. In this way, the archaeologist can determine the spatial and chronological relationship of all the remains, and many aspects of past life can be reconstructed including economics, trade, health, diet, religious ritual and function, burial methods, family structure, political organization, technology, and literature. Artistic and utilitarian objects, faunal and floral remains, architectural features, human remains, and their original contextual relationship to each other are all equally

---

[6] Excavations carried out by such diverse individuals as Thomas Jefferson in the late eighteenth century and William Pitt Rivers in the nineteenth century laid the groundwork for an understanding of the importance of stratigraphic excavation. Mortimer Wheeler, *Archaeology from the Earth* 25–29, 57–59 (Penguin 1956). In the mid-twentieth century, Sir Mortimer Wheeler and Dame Kathleen Kenyon, working in India and the Levant, respectively, further demonstrated the importance of scientific, controlled excavation and the recovery of contemporary material cultural remains in association with each other in order to reconstruct the past. Id at 20–37; Kathleen M. Kenyon, *Beginning in Archaeology* 68–114 (Praeger 1957).

[7] Radiocarbon (C-14) dating is a method of measuring the decay of the radioactive isotope of carbon in once living materials (such as trees or other organic materials). Living organisms absorb radiocarbon from the atmosphere; when they die they stop taking in C-14. The C-14 decays at a known rate; radiocarbon dating measures the amount of C-14 remaining in the sample. Thermoluminescence dating determines when ceramic materials were last fired and is useful for dating pottery and other fired materials. Thermoluminescence dating has an advantage over radiocarbon because it can date inorganic materials such as pottery and flint, and it can do so beyond the 50,000 year limit of C-14 dating. Yorke Rowan and Morag Kersel, *Glossary*, in Colin Renfrew and Paul Bahn, *Archaeology: Theories, Methods and Practice* (Thames & Hudson 4th ed 2004), available online at <http://www.thamesandhudsonusa.com/web/archaeology/glossary.html> (visited Apr 21, 2007).

essential in achieving an optimal understanding of the past. This full body of contextualized information is a destructible, nonrenewable cultural resource. Once it is destroyed, it cannot be regained. The looting of archaeological sites destroys this knowledge and forever impairs our ability to understand our past and ourselves.

A second detrimental consequence of looting is the corruption of the historical record through the introduction of artifacts that may be forgeries. The willingness of buyers to accept undocumented antiquities permits the proliferation of forged artifacts on the market. Looted, decontextualized artifacts provide no information beyond what is intrinsic in their shape and decoration. Little is known about their find-spot, their age, their original context, and even their authenticity. Entire categories of ancient artifacts, such as Cycladic figurines, are represented almost completely by looted examples.[8] Because of the large-scale looting of Cycladic figurines, it is impossible to determine what they were used for, whether they were primarily grave goods, what their date is, and from which of the islands in the Aegean they originate.[9] It is also impossible to tell which Cycladic figurines are authentic and which are fake.[10] Because authenticity is determined by comparing newly discovered objects with previously known exemplars, looted artifacts do not expand our knowledge. When a new type of archaeological artifact is excavated, it adds to our corpus of knowledge; when a new type is known only from examples sold on the market, it is generally rejected as fake. Therefore, while the market is often considered a source of fake objects that corrupt the historical record, it can do a further disservice to the historical record by leading to rejection of authentic artifacts. These points are explained by Chippindale and Gill:

> [T]he central *intellectual* consequence of the contemporary classical collections ... [is] an unwitting and unthinking conservatism. The new objects and the way they are treated contribute to our consolidated knowledge insofar as they confirm, reinforce, and strengthen the existing

---

[8] Christopher Chippindale and David W.J. Gill, *Cycladic Figures: Art versus Archaeology?* in Kathryn W. Tubb, ed, *Antiquities Trade or Betrayed: Legal, Ethical & Conservation Issues* 131, 132 (Archetype 1995) (noting that many Cycladic figures "surface" on the market with no recorded history); David W.J. Gill and Christopher Chippindale, *Material and Intellectual Consequences of Esteem for Cycladic Figures*, 97 Am J Archaeology 601 (1993). Cycladic figurines are small stone sculptures found on the Cycladic islands located in the Aegean Sea and are generally dated to the mid-third millennium BCE. New excavations being conducted by Colin Renfrew may help to explain many of the mysteries surrounding these figurines.

[9] Chippindale and Gill, *Cycladic Figures* at 133–34 (cited in note 8).

[10] Many rely on connoisseurship, the study of objects based on form, decoration, and other aesthetic criteria, to determine authenticity. However, connoisseurship cannot reliably determine authenticity as is demonstrated by the history of several Rembrandt paintings that were originally accepted as authentic, then considered inauthentic, and recently returned to authentic status. Kristine Wilton, *Deauthenticated Rembrandts Real after All*, ARTnews 84 (Mar 2006).

patterns of knowledge. Surfacing without secure information beyond what is immanent in themselves, the objects are unable to broaden our basis of knowledge. Interpreted and restored in light of prior expectations, they are reconciled with what we presently know, but they cannot amend and improve our present knowledge much, if at all. Where they do in themselves offer an anomaly or contradiction to established understanding, the ever-present dangers of overrestoration and falsity kick in; the truly unusual items that surface remain incomprehensible until their oddity is matched by a find for which there is a real security of knowledge. At that point, they can take up their accustomed role of confirming the correctness of that knowledge.[11]

The development of interdisciplinary methodologies for the study of the past coincided with the growth of the international art market in the years following World War II. The controlled excavation of archaeological sites, which is an inherently slow and painstaking process, inevitably conflicts with the desire of public and private collectors to have the maximum number of objects available on the market immediately and with minimal regulation. The proliferation of interdisciplinary methodologies for studying human history have reduced the relative importance of art historical analyses and connoisseurship, as they are now but one among many disciplines that are used in understanding the past. Furthermore, unlike other commodities, new antiquities cannot be manufactured to satisfy market demand (unless they are fakes). Therefore, as the wealth of Western nations increased and the art market grew to keep pace with the demand from collectors, the looting of archaeological sites to satisfy this demand became a significant detriment to the study of the past.

Ethnographic studies of looting in many countries demonstrate that looters loot for the money they earn. Looting activities respond to market demand for particular types of artifacts, and looting has moved from an occasional, opportunistic activity to a sophisticated, well-funded, well-organized business, including the hiring of looters on retainer so that they work full-time for particular middlemen.[12] While it is obviously important that looting at sites be

---

[11] Christopher Chippindale and David W.J. Gill, *Material Consequences of Contemporary Classical Collecting*, 104 Am J Archaeology 463, 504–05 (2000) (emphasis in original); see also Neil Brodie and Christina Luke, *Conclusion: The Social and Cultural Contexts of Collecting*, in Neil Brodie, et al, eds, *Archaeology, Cultural Heritage, and the Antiquities Trade* 303, 309–10 (Florida 2006).

[12] The contemporary nature of site looting is now documented in such disparate countries as Iraq, Italy, Israel and the West Bank, Peru, Turkey, and Thailand. See Morag K. Kersel, *License to Sell: The Legal Trade of Antiquities in Israel* (2006) (unpublished PhD Dissertation, University of Cambridge) (on file with author) (discussing Israel and the West Bank); Peter Watson and Cecilia Todeschini, *The Medici Conspiracy: The Illicit Journey of Looted Antiquities, From Italy's Tomb Raiders to the World's Greatest Museums* (Public Affairs 2006) (discussing Italy); Joanne Farchakh, *Mesopotamia Endangered: Witnessing the Loss of History*, Lecture at University of California, Berkeley (Feb 7, 2005), transcript available online at <http://webcast.berkeley.edu/events/details.php?webcastid=10048> (visited Apr 21, 2007) (discussing Iraq); Roger Atwood, *Stealing History: Tomb Robbers, Smugglers, and the Looting of the Ancient World* (St Martin's 2004) (discussing looting in Peru); C.H.

interdicted, the law in market countries should also impose detrimental consequences on sellers and purchasers in order to reduce demand and the incentive to loot archaeological sites.

II. THE MARKET AND THE LAW

A. LEGAL CONTROL OF THE MARKET

Looting imposes costs on society by destroying the original contexts of archaeological artifacts and impairing our ability to reconstruct and understand the past. Because looting is motivated by profit, the rate of looting should respond to the basic economic law of supply and demand. If collectors in the market nations refuse to buy undocumented artifacts, then incentives for the looting of artifacts will decrease. The law should therefore impose a cost on those who contribute directly or indirectly to the looting of sites by punishing the handling, selling, and buying of looted antiquities. The law in the US, which is generally regarded as the single largest market for antiquities in the world, may be examined as an example of a market nation's attempt to control the market in antiquities.[13]

In the nineteenth and twentieth centuries, many nations with a rich archaeological heritage enacted laws vesting ownership of undiscovered artifacts in themselves. While a free market proponent would view these laws only as inhibitions on the market,[14] others see these laws as a means of discouraging looting of sites by denying the finder and subsequent purchasers title to the artifacts. Despite these debates, US courts have recognized the efficacy of national ownership laws. In *United States v McClain*, the Fifth Circuit held that Mexico's law vested ownership of not-yet-discovered artifacts in Mexico, and

---

Roosevelt and C. Luke, *Looting Lydia: The Destruction of an Archaeological Landscape in Western Turkey*, in Brodie, et al, eds, *Archaeology, Cultural Heritage, and the Antiquities Trade* 173 (cited in note 11) (discussing Turkey); Rachanie Thosarat, *The Destruction of the Cultural Heritage of Thailand and Cambodia*, in Neil Brodie, Jennifer Doole, and Colin Renfrew, eds, *Trade in Illicit Antiquities: The Destruction of the World's Archaeological Heritage* 7 (McDonald Inst 2001) (discussing Thailand).

[13] The first federal law in the US to address the domestic archaeological heritage was the Antiquities Act of 1906, 16 USC §§ 431–433n (2000), which vested ownership and control of artifacts found on federally owned or controlled land in the federal government.

[14] While everyone involved in the debates surrounding antiquities decries the looting of archaeological sites, those who favor a free market in antiquities view national ownership laws as a particularly problematic form of restraint on the international market. See, for example, John Henry Merryman, *The Free International Movement of Cultural Property*, 31 NYU J Intl L & Pol 1, 4–12 (1998). Both national ownership laws and export controls are a restraint on the free circulation of antiquities through the market, but national ownership laws constitute a more severe restraint because antiquities taken in violation of national ownership laws are stolen property in market nations, as well as in the country of origin.

that any artifacts removed from Mexico without permission constituted stolen property.[15] The defendants were convicted of violating the National Stolen Property Act[16] by conspiring to deal in pre-Columbian artifacts owned by Mexico.[17] In *United States v Schultz*,[18] the Second Circuit adopted the *McClain* holding with the conviction of Frederick Schultz, a prominent New York antiquities dealer and former president of the National Association of Dealers in Ancient, Oriental, and Primitive Art ("NADAOPA"),[19] for conspiring to deal in antiquities removed from Egypt in violation of its 1983 national ownership law.[20] In addition to the National Stolen Property Act, the trafficking provisions of the Archaeological Resources Protection Act can be utilized to prosecute individuals involved in the interstate or international transport of stolen archaeological resources, including those taken in violation of a national

---

[15] The defendants' conviction on the substantive counts was reversed because the Fifth Circuit held that only Mexico's 1972 law was truly a vesting statute. Nonetheless, the defendants' conviction on the conspiracy count was affirmed. *United States v McClain*, 593 F2d 658, 671–72 (5th Cir 1979).

[16] See National Stolen Property Act, 18 USC §§ 2314–2315 (2000) (prohibiting the interstate or international movement of stolen property and the receipt, transfer, and possession of stolen property that has been transported across state or international boundaries, is worth $5,000 or more, and is known to have been stolen).

[17] See *United States v McClain*, 545 F2d 988, 1004 (5th Cir 1977). *McClain* was preceded by *United States v Hollinshead*, 495 F2d 1154, 1155 (9th Cir 1974), which recognized Guatemala's ownership of its pre-Columbian artifacts.

[18] *United States v Schultz*, 333 F3d 393 (2d Cir 2003).

[19] NADAOPA has filed amicus briefs in most of the major cultural property cases over the past thirty years. It also opposed implementation of the UNESCO Convention on the Means of Prohibiting and Preventing the Illicit Import, Export, and Transfer of Ownership of Cultural Property (1970), 823 UN Treaty Ser 231 ("1970 UNESCO Convention"), the form of the 1995 Unidroit Convention on Stolen and Illegally Exported Cultural Objects (1995), 34 ILM 1322 (1995), and most, if not all, of the bilateral agreements that the US has entered into pursuant to the Cultural Property Implementation Act, 19 USC §§ 2601–13 (2000). For examples of these objections, see Celestine Bohlen, *Old Rarities, New Respect: U.S. Works with Italy*, NY Times E5 (Feb 28, 2001); *Statement of Position of Concerned Members of the American Cultural Community regarding the Unidroit Convention on the International Return of Stolen or Illegally Exported Cultural Objects* (May 31, 1995) (copy on file with author); Unidroit Convention on Stolen and Illegally Exported Cultural Objects (1995), 34 ILM 1322 (1995), available online at <http://www.unidroit.org/english/conventions/1995culturalproperty/1995culturalproperty-e.htm> (visited Apr 21, 2007).

[20] Egyptian Law 117, art 6, quoted in *Schultz*, 333 F3d at 399–400.

ownership law.²¹ The status of foreign national ownership laws is now clearly established in those circuits with the most robust art markets.²²

Other legal restraints under US law include the requirement of proper declaration of value and country of origin for archaeological artifacts, as with all imported commercial goods.²³ Improper declaration can lead to the forfeiture of the goods and criminal prosecution of the importer if the misstatements were made knowingly or intentionally.²⁴ The requirement to declare the proper country of origin is crucial in determining what laws apply to the importation of the artifact.

The 1970 UNESCO Convention on the Means of Prohibiting and Preventing the Illicit Import, Export, and Transfer of Ownership of Cultural Property ("UNESCO Convention")²⁵ was the first international attempt to control the market in artworks and cultural objects. It was promulgated in response to the growth of the market in the 1960s and, in particular, the dismemberment of ancient monuments and sites to satisfy market demand.²⁶ There are currently 112 State Parties.²⁷ While the US was the first major market nation to ratify it,²⁸ most of the other major market nations, including Switzerland, the UK, France, and Japan, are now also parties.²⁹

---

[21] Archaeological Resources Protection Act, 16 USC § 470ee(c) (2000). Criminal prosecution would also be available under state statutes prohibiting possession and dealing in stolen property. See Ricardo A. St. Hilaire, *International Antiquities Trafficking: Theft by Another Name*, paper presented at the Feb 26, 2007 meeting of ICOM-CC, Issues in the Conservation of Cultural Heritage, 4–5.

[22] Those circuits include the Second Circuit (*Schultz*, 333 F3d 393), the Fifth and Eleventh Circuits (*McClain*, 593 F2d 658), and the Ninth Circuit (*United States v Hollinshead*, 495 F2d 1154 (9th Cir 1974)).

[23] 18 USC §§ 542, 545 (2000).

[24] See *United States v An Antique Platter of Gold*, 184 F3d 131, 136–37 (2d Cir 1999) (holding that the country of origin of an ancient gold *phiale* was Sicily, where it was excavated, rather than Switzerland, as declared by the importer, through which it was transported en route to the US); US Immigration and Customs Enforcement Press Release, *Department of Homeland Security Returns Rare Artifacts to the Pakistani Government* (Jan 23, 2007), available at <http://www.ice.gov/pi/news/newsreleases/articles/070123newark.htm> (visited Apr 21, 2007) (announcing the restitution of several Buddha statues and other antiquities to Pakistan because their country of origin was incorrectly stated to be Dubai).

[25] 1970 UNESCO Convention (cited in note 19).

[26] Clemency Chase Coggins, *United States Cultural Property Legislation: Observations of a Combatant*, 7 Intl J Cultural Prop 52, 52–54 (1998).

[27] For a list of State Parties, see <http://portal.unesco.org/la/convention.asp?KO=13039&language=E&order=alpha> (visited Apr 21, 2007).

[28] The Senate voted unanimously to accept the UNESCO Convention in 1972, but implementing legislation was delayed for eleven years due largely to the objections of the art market community and of Senator Daniel Patrick Moynihan. At the time of acceptance, the US stated one understanding and six reservations. Patrick J. O'Keefe, *Commentary on the UNESCO 1970 Convention on Illicit Traffic* 106–12 (Inst of Art and Law 2000); see generally Barbara B. Rosecrance,

In 1983, the US enacted the Convention on Cultural Property Implementation Act ("CPIA"),[30] implementing two sections, article 7(b) and article 9, of the UNESCO Convention. The CPIA prohibits the importation into the US of stolen cultural property that had been documented in the inventory of a museum, religious or secular public institution in another State Party.[31] The CPIA also grants the President the authority, pursuant to a request from a State Party, to impose import restrictions on designated categories of archaeological and ethnological materials that are subject to pillage in that State Party.[32] The CPIA provides only for civil forfeiture of the cultural materials at stake and has no criminal penalties.[33]

In addition to criminal prosecution and forfeiture actions that the government can take, the original owner (typically a foreign government) can bring a replevin claim in US court to recover its stolen property. Basing its right to ownership on the national vesting laws recognized in the *McClain* and *Schultz* decisions, a foreign nation can recover antiquities looted and removed without permission after the effective date of its national ownership law. Many such successful claims have been brought, including Turkey's recovery of the 360 objects in the Lydian hoard from the Metropolitan Museum of Art[34] and its recovery of the Elmali coin hoard from private collectors.[35] The recent successes of Italy and Greece in recovering artifacts from the Metropolitan Museum, the Boston Museum of Fine Arts, and the Getty Museum were also based on these nations' ability to recover stolen artifacts in actions for replevin.[36]

Harmonious Meeting: The McClain *Decision and the Cultural Property Implementation Act*, 19 Cornell Intl L J 311 (1986).

[29] Id. For a more detailed discussion of the British and Swiss implementing legislation, see Patty Gerstenblith, *From Bamiyan to Baghdad: Warfare and the Protection of Cultural Heritage at the Beginning of the 21st Century*, 37 Geo J Intl L 245, 332–34 (2006).

[30] 19 USC §§ 2601–13 (2000).

[31] 19 USC § 2607 (2000). The definition of "cultural property" tracks that given in Article 1 of the UNESCO Convention and is very broad. 19 USC § 2601(6) (2000).

[32] 19 USC §§ 2602–03 (2000). For a more detailed discussion of the CPIA process, see Gerstenblith, 37 Geo J Intl L at 319–24 (cited in note 29).

[33] 19 USC § 2609 (2000).

[34] Lawrence M. Kaye and Carla T. Main, *The Saga of the Lydian Hoard: Uşak to New York and Back Again*, in Tubb, ed, *Antiquities Trade or Betrayed* 150 (cited in note 8).

[35] *Republic of Turkey v OKS Partners*, 797 F Supp 64 (D Mass 1992).

[36] The agreements between Italy and the Metropolitan Museum of Art and between Italy and the Boston Museum of Fine Arts implicitly recognize Italy's proper title to the antiquities that were returned. For the Metropolitan Museum agreement, see *Agreement between The Ministry for Cultural Heritage and Activities of the Italian Republic and the Metropolitan Museum of Art, New York* (copy on file with author); for the Boston Museum of Fine Arts agreement, see *An Agreement with the Italian Ministry of Culture*, available at <http://www.mfa.org/collections/index.asp?key=2656> (visited

B. THE PROBLEM PERSISTS

A recent study of the international antiquities market by S.M.R. Mackenzie identifies reasons that existing legal restraints are less effective in this area than in other criminal markets.[37] White-collar criminals are heavily influenced by the risk of detection and the likelihood and severity of punishment. It is estimated that approximately 80 to 90 percent of the antiquities on the market lack sufficient provenience[38] to establish that they were discovered long enough ago that their acquisition would not raise legal problems. With such a large proportion of the antiquities on the international market lacking an adequate documented history, two conclusions can be drawn. First, market participants convince themselves that many of the market's undocumented antiquities are chance finds and that this excuses sales that may be illegal.[39] This rationalization

---

Apr 21, 2007). The fact that these museums agreed to return these artifacts suggests a recognition by the parties that Italy could likely have recovered these artifacts in a legal action.

[37] S.M.R. Mackenzie, *Going, Going, Gone: Regulating the Market in Illicit Antiquities* (Inst of Art and Law 2005). In contrast to the limited remedies available under the US laws described in the preceding section, Endangered Species Act, Pub L No 93-205, 81 Stat 884 (1972), codified at 16 USC §§ 1531–44 (2000 & supp 2004), authorizes civil penalties (fines and forfeiture of all equipment, including vessels, used in the violation of the statute), criminal penalties, and citizen suits to ensure enforcement. 16 USC § 1540 (2000). This legal regime regulating trade in endangered species is more stringent than that which addresses the trade in antiquities because of the wider availability of criminal sanctions and because of stricter enforcement; it is therefore also regarded as more effective. Mackenzie, *Going, Going, Gone* at 122–27 (cited in note 37). It is also more stringent because it prohibits trade in artifacts that incorporate body parts of endangered species, even though the artifacts were legally acquired before enactment of the legislation and is, in that sense, retroactive in nature. *Andrus v Allard*, 444 US 51 (1979) (holding that the retroactive application of the Eagle Protection Act and the Migratory Bird Treaty Act does not violate the Fifth Amendment's Takings Clause).

[38] Mackenzie, *Going, Going, Gone* at 32–50 (cited in note 37). One dealer interviewed by Mackenzie put the number of artifacts that come to him with information of their archaeological origins at 1 percent. Id at 32. Stephen Dyson estimates that in 1990, 80 percent of the antiquities available for sale on the market were illegally excavated and exported. Stephen L. Dyson, *In Pursuit of Ancient Pasts: A History of Classical Archaeology in the Nineteenth and Twentieth Centuries* 225 (Yale 2006). The term "provenience" is often used to indicate the history of an antiquity back to its archaeological origin. The term "provenance" indicates the history of ownership of a work of art. If a provenance for an antiquity is complete, then it satisfies the criteria of provenience. However, most antiquities on the market have only a very incomplete ownership history. Coggins, 7 Intl J Cultural Prop at 57 (cited in note 26); Mackenzie, *Going, Going, Gone* at 5–6 (cited in note 37).

[39] Mackenzie, *Going, Going, Gone* at 32–38, 163–65 (cited in note 37). One collector went so far as to classify any objects found by digging not carried out by an archaeologist as chance finds! Id at 56–57. This rationalization—that unprovenanced antiquities are chance finds—ignores the fact that chance finds are generally not in sufficiently good condition to make it into the international antiquities market. True chance finds are found near the surface and will be fragmentary, scattered, and weathered; objects that are of sufficiently high quality and condition to be collectible by a high-end collector or museum are most likely found in tombs. Tubb and Brodie commented that "true chance finds are difficult to come by . . . . Very few, if any, intact antiquities have been found [in twenty years

permits market participants to deny the causal connection between the funds they put into the market and site looting. Second, because the government, in a forfeiture or criminal prosecution, or the claimant in a civil suit bears the burden of proving that a particular artifact is stolen, even those who trade in antiquities that are the likely product of recent site looting often escape the reach of the law.

Mackenzie's study demonstrates that market participants indulge in a significant amount of denial about what they do. Many recognize that there are looted and stolen artifacts and unethical dealers, but they all claim that they themselves do not engage in any shady practices and that they conduct their business in an ethical manner. Some buyers delude themselves into thinking that they are legally protected by dealing only with those they know and trust and by engaging in transparently ridiculous ruses.[40] Market participants excuse their failure to research the backgrounds of the antiquities they acquire by saying they want to protect the seller by not asking too many questions, they want to maintain a competitive edge against other dealers, and they believe that lack of complete provenience information does not necessarily mean that an artifact is looted.[41]

While the potential for punishment may serve as a disincentive to the trade in undocumented antiquities, certain aspects of the structure of the legal regime restrain the full efficacy of the law. The most important restraint is that the government or claimant bears the burden of proof to establish the required elements. By definition, looted antiquities are undocumented before they appear on the international market. As a result, the claimant or the government can meet the legally required standard[42] only in the unusual circumstance that the

---

of archaeological surface surveys]. The published material consists largely of pieces of broken pottery and small architectural fragments. The idea that there are large quantities of antiquities lying about waiting to be found is a myth." Kathryn Walker Tubb and Neil Brodie, *From Museum to Mantelpiece: The Antiquities Trade in the United Kingdom*, in Robert Layton, Peter G. Stone & Julian Thomas, eds, *Destruction and Conservation of Cultural Property* 102, 106 (Routledge 2001). In the UK, where the Portable Antiquities Scheme requires the reporting of finds, only 9 percent of the finds reported in 2004–05 were found during construction, agricultural, and gardening activities and are therefore true chance finds. See *The Portable Antiquities Scheme Annual Report 2004–05*, 88 and Table 8, available at <http://www.finds.org.uk/documents/PAS_2004_05.pdf> (visited Apr 21, 2007).

[40] Mackenzie, *Going, Going, Gone* at 25–32 (cited in note 37).

[41] Id at 47–60.

[42] In a criminal prosecution, the government must establish beyond a reasonable doubt that the artifact is stolen and that the current possessor knew or consciously avoided learning that the artifact was stolen. See *Schultz*, 333 F3d at 413–14 (discussing the government's burden in proving a defendant's conscious avoidance). The plaintiff who seeks to recover stolen property must establish by a preponderance of the evidence his or her right to own the property and that it was stolen. See *Autocephalous Greek-Orthodox Church of Cyprus v Goldberg and Feldman Fine Arts*, 917 F2d 278, 290–92 (7th Cir 1990). The standard of proof in a civil forfeiture action brought under Title

artifact's time and place of discovery can be determined. The fact that so many of the artifacts on the market are undocumented poses an additional challenge for a prosecutor to establish that the possessor knew that this particular artifact was looted.

Because of the difficulty in establishing the required elements for a criminal prosecution, cases involving looted antiquities are more likely to be civil forfeitures and private replevin claims.[43] However, civil actions do not carry sufficiently meaningful punishment because possessors of looted artifacts face the possibility of losing only the artifacts' monetary value, and the amount of money that market participants have at stake is relatively small.[44] A few examples of the prices paid for antiquities at the source compared to their value in transit and destination markets[45] illustrate the point that sellers of antiquities have little financial investment in the antiquities they sell. While it is difficult to obtain first-hand information as to the price of looted antiquities paid at the source, the journalist Joanne Farchakh reported in May 2004 that at archaeological sites in southern Iraq a cuneiform tablet would sell for four dollars, a decorated vase would sell for between twenty and fifty dollars, and a sculpture would sell for about one hundred dollars.[46] In Baghdad, the journalist Joseph Braude paid two hundred dollars for each of three cylinder seals looted from the Iraq Museum.[47] In comparison, cylinder seals sold on the market in London or New York have

---

19 (the Customs statute) is one of probable cause, Civil Asset Forfeiture Reform Act, 18 USC § 983 (2000). However, in civil forfeiture actions brought under other statutory provisions, the government must prove its case to the usual civil standard of the preponderance of the evidence. Stefan D. Cassella, *Using the Forfeiture Laws to Protect Archaeological Resources*, in Sherry Hutt, Marion P. Forsyth, and David Tarler, eds, *Presenting Archaeology in Court: Legal Strategies for Protecting Cultural Resources* 169, 183 (AltaMira 2006).

[43] Mackenzie, *Going, Going, Gone* at 243–44 (cited in note 37).

[44] Auction houses traditionally have none of their own funds at stake in an art market transaction because they do not own the objects they sell; they merely act as agent for the owner. If a purchaser is required to return an antiquity to its proper owner, then the purchaser or the auction house recovers the purchase price from the seller. The auction house loses only its commission. Dealers, on the other hand, typically own the works they sell and therefore have more of their own funds at stake in a transaction, but because the mark-up on antiquities is so high, even dealers lose relatively little if they must give up an antiquity.

[45] For an explanation of transit and destination markets, see Morag M. Kersel, *From the Ground to the Buyer: A Market Analysis of the Trade in Illegal Antiquities*, in Brodie, et al, eds, *Archaeology, Cultural Heritage, and the Antiquities Trade* 188, 189–94 (cited in note 11).

[46] Joanne Farchakh, *Témoignages d'une Archéologie Héroïque*, Archeologia 14, 25 (May 2004).

[47] US Immigration and Customs Enforcement, *Press Release, Cultural Antiquity Returned to Iraqi Government after ICE Investigation* (Jan 18, 2005), available online at <http://www.ice.gov/pi/news/newsreleases/articles/iraqiartifact_011805.htm> (visited Apr 21, 2007). The seals stolen from the Iraq Museum were of good but not top quality.

an average value of one thousand dollars.[48] A recent cursory survey of comparable objects being offered on eBay showed that cylinder seals were priced at $350 to $2,000; cuneiform tablets were offered at a range of $350 up to £550 (approximately equivalent to $1027).[49] A recent Christie's catalogue gave high and low estimates of $1200 and $1800 for a cuneiform envelope and tablet, but it sold for $10,800.[50]

These price differentials demonstrate that from the source at a looted archaeological site (in southern Iraq), to the transit points (such as Baghdad), to the ultimate market in locations such as New York and London, mark-ups for antiquities can be a hundredfold or more. If a collector or dealer in London or New York must relinquish an artifact, he or she loses relatively little out-of-pocket. As Mackenzie points out,[51] so long as the risks of detection and meaningful punishment remain low, the conduct of those market participants who violate the law will not be deterred. It is difficult, however, to craft a legal system in which these impediments to meaningful punishment are eliminated.

III. SOLUTIONS

The problem that has been identified is the looting of archaeological sites and the harm that this imposes through the loss of context and knowledge of the past. Many mechanisms have been suggested for reducing the looting of sites.[52] However, within the scope of this Article, the only proposals that will be

---

[48] Cylinder seals sold at an auction in London in May 2003 ranged from $400 to $4,000 with an average of $1,000, while a seal auctioned by Christie's in 2001 sold for $424,000. See Neil Brodie, *The Plunder of Iraq's Archaeological Heritage 1991–2005 and the London Antiquities Trade*, in Brodie, et al, eds, *Archaeology, Cultural Heritage, and the Antiquities Trade* 206, 212 (cited in note 11); see Suzanne Charle, *Tiny Treasures Leave Big Void in Looted Iraq*, NY Times E3 (July 18, 2003).

[49] See, for example, <http://www.sandsoftimeantiquities.com> (visited Apr 21, 2007); <http://www.arsantiqua-online.com> (visited Apr 21, 2007); <http://www.artemission.com> (visited Apr 21, 2007). This is not intended to indicate that these particular artifacts are recently looted from Iraq; however, it demonstrates one market value that may be placed on artifacts.

[50] See Christie's, *New York Antiquities, Friday 16 June 2006* 25 (2006); Christie's, *Auction Result*, available online at <http://www.christies.com/auction/results/results_lotlist.asp?saleno=NYC1679&page=1> (visited Apr 21, 2007). The provenance given in the catalogue for the tablet and envelope went back to 1989. Iraq's antiquities law declaring national ownership dates to 1936; any artifact removed after this date without consent of the Iraqi government is stolen property. Article 3, Antiquities Law No 59 of 1936 and the two amendments, No 120 of 1974 and No 164 of 1975, available online at <http://developmentgateway.org/download/181160/Iraq-Antiquities-Law.rtf> (visited Apr 21, 2007). The sale price includes the buyer's premium. See <http://www.christies.com/auction/results/results_lotlist.asp?saleno=NYC1679&page=> (visited Apr 21, 2007).

[51] Mackenzie, *Going, Going, Gone* at 243 (cited at note 37).

[52] See, for example, Patrick J. O'Keefe, *Trade in Antiquities: Reducing Destruction and Theft* (Archetype 1997) (discussing increased education of the public in both archaeologically rich nations and

examined are those that are premised on manipulation of market demand for undocumented antiquities. Virtually all proposals involving the market focus on the question of the extent to which the market in undocumented antiquities should or should not be regulated. One approach focuses on decreasing regulation of the market; other approaches focus on increasing regulation of the market, through either direct or indirect means. Some of these representative proposals will be analyzed.

A. Decreasing Regulation of the Market in Antiquities

One group of proposals advocates for less regulation of the market in antiquities. Some of the proposals advocating for less regulation do not seem to regard the deterrence of all looting as a priority.[53] These proposals suggest that the increased movement of ancient art works through the world that can be achieved through a less regulated market is of greater value than what is learned through controlled excavation[54] or they reject the connection between site

---

market nations, greater publicity, and greater financial assistance to nations to aid them in guarding their sites).

[53] There is admittedly a certain amount of contradiction in that everyone decries intentional looting or looting of identified or official archaeological sites, but some distinguish this from other forms of looting, although the basis for doing so is unclear. See, for example, John Boardman, *Archaeologists, Collectors, and Museums*, in Eleanor Robson, Luke Treadwell, and Chris Gosden, eds, *Who Owns Objects? The Ethics and Politics of Collecting Cultural Artefacts* 33, 35–41 (Oxbow 2006).

[54] See, for example, the recent comments of John Boardman, *Who Owns Antiquities?*, Review of Jonathan Tokeley, *Rescuing the Past: The Cultural Heritage Crusade*, available online at <http://www.jonathantokeley.com/default> (visited Apr 21, 2007) (stating that "it is arguable that as much or more progress in understanding our past has been made by study of objects, excavated or not, than by excavation alone"); Randy Kennedy and Hugh Eakin, *Met Chief, Unbowed, Defends Museum's Role*, NY Times E1 (Feb 28, 2006) (quoting Philippe de Montebello, the director of the Metropolitan Museum of Art, who stated, "the information that is lost [when an object is looted] is a fraction of the information that an object can provide. . . . How much more would you learn from knowing which particular hole in—supposedly Cerveteri—[the Euphronios krater] came out of? . . . Everything is on the vase."). This approach can be identified with the "cultural internationalist" view first propounded by John Henry Merryman. John Henry Merryman, *Two Ways of Thinking about Cultural Property*, 80 Am J Intl L 831 (1986). However, this so-called "cultural internationalist" view of cultural property is not really internationalist and should more appropriately be termed a free market approach. As Kersel wrote, "The term internationalist conjures up positive connotations, providing access to all. Rather than being internationalist in approach the free-market position, in this context, advocates for the unfettered movement of cultural material in the marketplace—those who can afford to purchase the artifacts are allowed access. . . . The international exchange of free-market proponents is primarily a flow of objects from less-developed nations to collectors usually with a much higher per capita income. And the exchange is usually financial, not intellectual." Kersel, *License to Sell*, at 5 n 13, 10–11 (citations omitted) (cited in note 12). These proposals also generally fail to recognize the harm that the international market can do to individual objects to make them more appealing and more

looting and market demand.⁵⁵ While accepting that the country of origin has the right to criminalize the looting of sites, these proposals reject the holding of the *McClain* and *Schultz* decisions—that antiquities taken in violation of a national ownership law are stolen property in the destination countries, such as the US and England.⁵⁶ If such objects are regarded as legal, rather than stolen, then the number of legal objects available to be traded on the international market will expand considerably.⁵⁷

Those who reject the characterization of looted antiquities as stolen property argue that criminalizing the trade in looted antiquities has created a black market.⁵⁸ If the trade in looted artifacts were no longer criminalized, then the black market would largely disappear. This is, of course, correct, but it would not deter the looting of sites—the true harm caused by the trade in undocumented artifacts and the underlying detrimental conduct. If the looting of sites and the trade in stolen artifacts were decriminalized, the result would be more looting, not less, as there would no longer be any reason for restraint. Without national ownership laws, buried antiquities would be regarded as having no owner, or it would be impossible to prove who the true owner is. In a variation on the paradigmatic "tragedy of the commons,"⁵⁹ the first finder (that

---

saleable, in addition to the loss of context and knowledge. One may refer, as examples, to the damage done to the Kanakaria mosaics by the dealer's resetting of the mosaic tiles, Catherine Sease and Danae Thimme, *The Kanakaria Mosaics: The Conservators' View*, in Tubb, ed, *Antiquities Trade or Betrayed* 122, 124–27 (cited in note 8), and the looting and recutting of Neo-Assyrian reliefs to make them more attractive for the market, John Malcolm Russell, *The Final Sack of Nineveh* 48 (Yale 1998). They also fail to recognize that it does not have to be a choice between excavation and objects—when objects are properly excavated, the objects remain available to be studied, curated, and displayed in museums.

55   James Cuno, the director of the Art Institute of Chicago, has written that, "when an antiquity is offered to a museum for acquisition, the looting, *if indeed there was any*, has already occurred.... Museums are havens for objects that are already, *and for whatever reason*, alienated from their original context. Museums do not alienate objects." James Cuno, *View from the Universal Museum*, in John H. Merryman, ed, *Imperialism, Art and Restitution* 15, 29 (2006) (emphasis added). Cuno's use of the passive voice and the doubt he attempts to cast on the question of whether an undocumented artifact may be the product of looting indicate his denial of any link between a museum's acquisitions (and the funds it puts into the market) and the looting. See also Mackenzie, *Going, Going, Gone* at 142–45 (cited in note 37) (quoting from dealers' comments on the relationship between looting and market demand).

56   John Henry Merryman, *A Licit International Trade in Cultural Objects*, 4 Intl J Cultural Prop 13, 25–30 (1995).

57   Id at 30 (stating that "by enlarging the number and variety of cultural objects that could be licitly acquired, the suggested redefinition of a licit trade can divert trade from the black market and reduce the material, social and economic harm it causes").

58   John Henry Merryman, *Cultural Property Internationalism*, 12 Intl J Cultural Prop 11, 23 (2005).

59   In the classic problem of the "tragedy of the commons," overexploitation of a resource leads to economic inefficiency. "In a commons, by definition, multiple owners are each endowed with the privilege to use a given resource, and no one has the right to exclude another. When too many

is, the looter) would be able to gain and transfer title to looted artifacts. Looters would therefore have a greater incentive to take as much and as quickly as possible. Decriminalization would encourage, rather than discourage, more looting.

Other proposals that rely on decreased regulation of the market proffer that by decreasing regulation and moving toward a managed but less strictly regulated market in antiquities, demand for illegal objects will decrease and site looting will be deterred.[60] According to this argument, by providing a stream of properly excavated and legitimately obtained artifacts, the legitimate market would drive out the market for illegal and looted artifacts,[61] as buyers would presumably prefer to buy legal, rather than illegal, objects. However, the experiences of several countries with a managed market indicate that the managed market system will not deter site looting because of several intractable difficulties that the managed market poses. The difficulties that a managed market raises include: from where would these legitimate objects come, whether buyers will prefer these over looted objects, and whether the managed market will be sufficiently regulated to prevent newly-looted objects and those that have not been legitimately placed in the market from entering the legitimate market.

In a managed market, the legitimate artifacts would be those that are properly excavated and documented, and, once this process is completed, those that a country does not want to keep. Countries that are rich in archaeological resources would sell off less important or "duplicate" artifacts that are presumed to be stored in museums and storage depots.[62] Yet many countries are unlikely to sell off their antiquities and there is no realistic mechanism by which a

---

owners have such privileges of use, the resource is prone to overuse—a tragedy of the commons." Michael A. Heller, *The Tragedy of the Anticommons: Property in the Transition from Marx to Markets*, 111 Harv L Rev 621, 623–24 (1998). The solution to the problem of overexploitation is the creation of private property rights, including rights to exclude others and rights based on constructive possession. The analogy in the case of antiquities is the vesting of ownership of antiquities in the nation, which can then regulate the "exploitation" of archaeological sites through the awarding of excavation permits to those who are adequately trained in studying the past so that the full potential (non-economic) benefit of the sites can be realized. Preservation of sites can also bring sustainable economic benefits to the local population through archaeo-tourism and other forms of exploitation that do not harm our ability to understand the past.

[60] O'Keefe, *Trade in Antiquities* at 66–69 (cited in note 52).

[61] Merryman, 12 Intl J Cultural Prop at 23 (cited in note 58).

[62] Id. One of the difficulties with this proposal is determining which artifacts are unimportant, "duplicates," or "redundant." Those favoring this proposal believe that countries and museums should sell off those artifacts that are similar to each other or those that are of low market value. Merryman, 4 Intl J Cultural Prop at 36–37 (cited in note 56); O'Keefe, *Trade in Antiquities* at 69–75 (cited in note 52).

country can be forced to do so.[63] While the market determines the significance of an object by its monetary value, nations do not necessarily take this same approach.[64] Therefore, nations may not perceive that they have an "excess" of antiquities to sell on the international market.[65] Finally, there is some evidence that there is an insufficient number of antiquities in storerooms to satisfy market demand.[66]

Furthermore, a managed market is not likely to deter the looting of sites. Looted artifacts fill a variety of market niches, ranging from the relatively low-priced artifacts that are found in many similar forms to the high-priced "museum quality" piece. Even if a nation were to place the low-end objects on the market for sale, the desire of high-end collectors and some museums to acquire the "museum quality" pieces would not be satisfied through permitted sales.[67] The looting of sites would therefore continue in the search to satisfy the high-end demand, while artifacts of low economic value become the by-product of the looting. In fact, the availability of large numbers of cheaper artifacts on the market may encourage more people to enter the market and therefore increase, rather than decrease, demand.[68]

Examples of several nations that currently permit some form of a legal market or have done so in the past demonstrate that the looting of sites persists despite the availability of legally obtained artifacts on the market. Israel permits the legal sale of artifacts found on private land before enactment of its national ownership law in 1978 so long as the artifacts have been registered.[69] However,

---

[63] It is not for members of the market community to force a market-based solution on other countries. It is an inherent attribute of sovereignty for a nation to determine where to draw the line between public and private property and to determine how it wishes to conserve or dispose of its resources. For a general discussion, see Joseph W. Singer, *Sovereignty and Property*, 86 Nw U L Rev 1, 41–42, 47 (1991).

[64] Tubb and Brodie, *From Museum to Mantelpiece* at 108 (cited in note 39).

[65] O'Keefe points out that no one knows whether there are "excess" artifacts in museum storage and that there are reasons for keeping artifacts from a single site together since they serve as an archive from which further research can be conducted. O'Keefe, *Trade in Antiquities* at 71, 73 (cited in note 52). He also states that if museums are to be required to sell off objects in storage, then this principle should be applied equally to museums in all countries and not in a discriminatory manner that distinguishes between collections in the archaeologically rich nations and those in the market nations. Id at 73.

[66] Kersel, *License to Sell* at 13 (cited at note 12) (stating that studies indicate that the sale of artifacts from the storerooms of the Israel Antiquities Authority would deplete the storerooms in less than a year).

[67] Id (stating that high-end collectors and museum are not interested in acquiring duplicate or surplus objects); O'Keefe, *Trade in Antiquities* at 69 (cited in note 52).

[68] O'Keefe, *Trade in Antiquities* at 68 (cited in note 52).

[69] Kersel, *License to Sell* at 88–94 (cited in note 12).

because merchants swap registration numbers and exploit other loopholes in the law, many of the artifacts sold on the market do not come from the legal stock;[70] rather, the looting continues because a fresh stream of looted artifacts can enter the legitimate market.[71] There is even evidence of looting to obtain specific artifacts to satisfy market demand.[72] Cyprus has allowed the export of antiquities in the past, yet the looting of sites was not deterred.[73] The US permits a legal trade in antiquities found on private land,[74] but again sites in the US are still looted.[75] Canada and England permit private ownership and sale of antiquities found on private land and their markets are controlled only through an export licensing system.[76] Yet the presence of a managed market in privately owned and legally obtained artifacts does not seem to satisfy market demand and thereby deter the looting of archaeological sites.[77] The inescapable conclusion is that site looting is not deterred through a solution that encourages, rather than discourages, the market. Proposals that advocate less regulation of the market

---

[70] Id at 162–67.

[71] Id at 55–58.

[72] Id at 184–86.

[73] Ellen Herscher, *Destroying the Past in Order to "Save" It: Collecting Antiquities from Cyprus*, in Neil Asher Silberman and Ernest S. Frerichs, eds, *Archaeology and Society in the 21st Century: The Dead Sea Scrolls and Other Case Studies* 138, 146 (Israel Expl Soc 2001) (stating that "there is no indication that the availability of antiquities for legal export nor the opportunity for museums to obtain a share of the finds by licensed archaeological excavations had any impact on deterring rampant looting throughout the island").

[74] The Archaeological Resources Protection Act applies only to sites located on federally owned or controlled land. 16 USC § 470cc(a) (2000) (restricting excavation and removal of archaeological resources found on federal or Indian lands). State statutes that are similar to ARPA apply only to state-owned land. Patty Gerstenblith, *Identity and Cultural Property: The Protection of Cultural Property in the United States*, 75 BU L Rev 559, 596–601 (1995) (citing state statutes). Approximately half of the states have laws that apply to burials found on private land, but burials on private land in the other states and settlement sites on private land are generally not protected by statute. For a list of state statutes applying to burials on private land, see Patty Gerstenblith, *Protection of Cultural Heritage Found on Private Land: The Paradigm of the Miami Circle and Regulatory Takings Doctrine after Lucas*, 13 St Thomas L Rev 65, 101–03 (2000).

[75] Veletta Canouts and Francis P. McManamon, *Protecting the Past for the Future: Federal Archaeology in the United States*, in Brodie, Doole, and Renfrew, eds, *Trade in Illicit Antiquities* 97, 100–02 (cited in note 12).

[76] For the Canadian export licensing system, see the Canada Cultural Property Export and Import Act, RSC 1985, c C-51, § 37. For a description of the British export licensing system, see Sara E. Bush, *The Protection of British Heritage: Woburn Abbey and the Three Graces*, 5 Intl J Cultural Prop 269, 277–81 (1996).

[77] See, for example, the case of the Icklingham bronzes looted from a scheduled archaeological site in England and acquired by New York collectors Shelby White and Leon Levy. John Browning, *A Layman's Attempts to Precipitate Change in Domestic and International 'Heritage' Laws*, in Tubb, ed, *Antiquities Trade or Betrayed* 145 (cited in note 8).

provide a veneer of respectability that encourages trading in artifacts that are likely to be the product of contemporary site looting.

B. INCREASING REGULATION OF THE MARKET IN ANTIQUITIES

The alternative to a less regulated market is a more regulated market with the goal of decreasing demand for undocumented antiquities. There are several ways in which more regulation can be achieved. Direct regulation relies on methods by which the government imposes direct consequences on market participants. Market participants can achieve regulation through voluntary self-regulation. Indirect regulation is accomplished through the granting or denial of government benefits that are aimed at encouraging individuals and institutions to avoid acquiring undocumented artifacts.

1. Increasing Direct Regulation of the Market in Antiquities

There are several means by which direct regulation of the market in antiquities could be increased. As Mackenzie has pointed out, for the deterrent effect of the legal regime to be most effective, the risk of detection and the certainty and severity of punishment must be high.[78] The most obvious way to increase direct regulation would be to reverse the burden of proof so that the current possessor of an antiquity would carry the burden of proving the legitimate origin of the antiquity in civil forfeiture actions, private replevin claims, and criminal prosecutions. In June 2003, in fulfillment of its obligations under UN Security Council Resolution 1483, the UK adopted Statutory Instrument 2003 No 1519, which reverses the burden of proof in a criminal prosecution of individuals dealing in Iraqi cultural property illegally removed after August 6, 1990.[79] There is evidence from market statistics that this criminal provision is depressing the London market in Mesopotamian cylinder seals.[80]

---

[78] As Mackenzie states, "Just as justice must not only be done but be seen to be done, so antiquities must not only be licitly excavated and traded, but must be seen to be licitly excavated and traded." Mackenzie, *Going, Going, Gone* at 21 (cited in note 37).

[79] Iraq (United Nations Sanctions) Order, Statutory Instrument 2003 No 1519, available at <http://www.hmso.gov.uk/si/si2003/20031519.htm> (visited Apr 21, 2007). Section 8 (3) states, "Any person who deals in any item of illegally removed cultural property [from Iraq] shall be guilty of an offence . . . unless he proves that he did not know and had no reason to suppose that the items in question was illegally removed Iraqi cultural property." See also Kevin Chamberlain, *The Iraq (United Nations Sanctions) Order 2003—Is It Human Rights Compatible?*, 8 Art, Antiquity and Law 357, 361–68 (2003) (discussing whether this reversal of the burden of proof is compatible with European human rights law and concluding that it is).

[80] Brodie, *The Plunder of Iraq's Archaeological Heritage* at 217–18 (cited in note 48). The vast majority of Mesopotamian cylinder seals come from Iraq. Id at 215.

However, such a reversal of the burden of proof, particularly in criminal cases, would likely be unconstitutional in the US.

Another method of increasing direct regulation is to broaden the availability of criminal prosecution and increase the severity of punishment for those who have been convicted. One way of broadening the availability of criminal prosecution would be to make the knowing, intended, or attempted import of cultural materials in violation of an import restriction enacted pursuant to the CPIA a criminal violation.[81] The possibility of criminal prosecution, rather than simple civil forfeiture, should have a greater deterrent effect.

The Cultural Heritage Resource Crimes Sentencing Guideline ("Sentencing Guideline"), promulgated in 2002, significantly increases the criminal penalties available for those who have been convicted of a broad range of cultural heritage resource crimes, including trading in stolen antiquities.[82] In particular, the Sentencing Guideline has, as one of its goals, reducing reliance on market value to determine the severity of a sentence and focusing reliance, instead, on the harm done to the historical and archaeological record.[83] However, it is clear that this new guideline is not yet adequately understood by federal prosecutors and federal judges, as demonstrated by the way in which the author Joseph Braude, who smuggled into the US three cylinder seals stolen from the Iraq Museum in Baghdad in 2003, was charged, and the light sentence he was given.[84]

---

[81] St. Hilaire has argued that a knowing violation of a CPIA import restriction would constitute a criminal violation under 18 USC § 545, which states: "Whoever fraudulently or knowingly imports or brings into the United States, any merchandise contrary to law, or receives, conceals, buys, sells, or in any manner facilitates the transportation, concealment, or sale of such merchandise after importation, knowing the same to have been imported or brought into the United States contrary to law [shall be subject to criminal penalties]." St. Hilaire, *International Antiquities Trafficking* at 4 (cited in note 21).

[82] 18 USC Appx § 2B1.5 (2000).

[83] The US Sentencing Commission said, among the reasons for the new guidelines, that "[b]ecause individuals, communities, and nations identify themselves through intellectual, emotional, and spiritual connections to places and objects, the effects of cultural heritage resource crimes transcend mere monetary considerations. Accordingly, this new guideline takes into account the transcendent and irreplaceable value of cultural heritage resources and punishes in a proportionate way the aggravating conduct associated with cultural heritage resource crimes." Reason for Amendment, 18 USC Appx § 2B1.5. See Paula J. Desio, *Crimes and Punishment: Developing Sentencing Guidelines for Cultural Heritage Resource Crimes*, in Jennifer R. Richman and Marion P. Forsyth, eds, *Legal Perspectives on Cultural Resources* 61 (AltaMira 2004). The US Supreme Court's decision in *United States v Booker*, 543 US 220 (2005), has rendered the status of all sentencing guidelines uncertain.

[84] Braude was not even charged with violations of the National Stolen Property Act, despite the fact that the cylinder seals still had their Iraq Museum registration numbers partially visible. He was charged only with three counts of smuggling and making false statements in violation of 18 USC §

Mackenzie has proposed a radical shift in the way in which the criminal law could operate to deter trafficking in recently looted archaeological materials by instituting clearer legal prohibition with the consequence of higher risk of criminal conviction and more severe punishment. The essence of Mackenzie's proposal is that nations should adopt a legal rubric based on the registration of all antiquities that are currently held in collections (whether museums, private collections, or dealer and auction house inventory).[85] All antiquities currently in collections could be freely registered and this would, admittedly, launder title to these objects, regardless of whether they were obtained legitimately or not.[86] However, for any antiquity to be registered after this system was enacted, the owner would have to demonstrate clear legitimate title and excavation history.[87] Trading in any unregistered antiquities would be a criminal offense.

The trade-off of legitimating antiquities currently in collections might be worthwhile, if we could thereby assure that all antiquities looted in the future would become unmarketable and the legal consequences to those who trade in such antiquities would be sure, swift, and severe. However, before such a system could be seriously considered, we must recognize the difficulties in creating a foolproof registration system. Can antiquities (other than major pieces) be sufficiently identified in a registry so that recently looted artifacts could not be switched for others that were previously known and registered? Could we assure, even with modern technology, that no new artifacts would enter the legitimate market? It is not likely that this system would be workable and foolproof. Kersel's study of the registration system of antiquities in Israel demonstrates the difficulties in enforcing such a system.[88] It requires the devotion of government and law enforcement resources as well as the voluntary cooperation of dealers—elements that are clearly not present in the Israeli system. It also requires the technological ability to uniquely identify each artifact. There is no reason at this time to believe that a registration system would be reliably administered and enforced, technologically feasible, and cost effective.

2. Increasing Regulation through Voluntary Self-Regulation

Controlling the market through voluntary self-regulation is another way of reducing demand for looted antiquities. While some scholars participate in the

---

545. Braude was sentenced to six months of house arrest and two years of probation. See US Immigration and Customs Enforcement, *Press Release* (cited in note 47).

85 Mackenzie, *Going, Going, Gone* at 237–46 (cited in note 37).

86 Id at 240.

87 Id.

88 Kersel, *License to Sell* at 162–67 (cited in note 12).

trade by authenticating undocumented artifacts[89] and by collecting, professional organizations, such as the Archaeological Institute of America ("AIA") and the Society for American Archaeology ("SAA"), have codes of ethics that prohibit activities by their members that enhance the value of undocumented artifacts, including prohibitions on direct involvement in the trade, authentication, and appraisal of artifacts,[90] and the publication or presentation at their scholarly meetings of undocumented artifacts.[91]

Dealers' associations have adopted codes of ethics that regulate the conduct of their membership.[92] However, the codes of dealers' associations rarely address the specifics of the trade in antiquities or are ambiguous in doing so.[93] Only the Code of Practice for the Confédération Internationale des Négociants en Oeuvres d'Art specifies that members should not trade in "an imported object that was acquired dishonestly or illegally from an official excavation site or monuments or originated from an illegal, clandestine or

---

[89] Brodie, *The Plunder of Iraq's Archaeological Heritage* at 217–18 (cited in note 48).

[90] The AIA's Code of Ethics states that "members of the AIA should: ... [r]efuse to participate in the trade in undocumented antiquities and refrain from activities that enhance the value of such objects." The Code applies to both lay and professional members of the Institute. *AIA Code of Ethics*, available online at <http://www.archaeological.org/pdfs/AIA_Code_of_EthicsA5S.pdf> (visited Apr 21, 2007). The SAA's Principles of Archaeological Ethics states, "Whenever possible [archaeologists] should discourage, and should themselves avoid, activities that enhance the commercial value of archaeological objects . . . ." SAA, *Principles of Archeological Ethics*, available online at <http://www.saa.org/aboutSAA/committees/ethics/principles.html> (visited Apr 21, 2007).

[91] The AIA's Code of Ethics defines "undocumented antiquities" as "those which are not documented as belonging to a public or private collection before December 30, 1970, the date when the AIA Council endorsed the 1970 UNESCO Convention, or which have not been excavated and exported from the country of origin in accordance with the laws of that country." AIA Code of Ethics (cited in note 90). The AIA's policy for its publications states that they "will not serve for the announcement or initial scholarly presentation of any object in a private or public collection acquired after December 30, 1973, unless its existence is documented before that date, or it was legally exported from the country of origin." AIA, *Publications Policy for the AJA and Archaeology*, available online at <http://www.archaeological.org/webinfo.php?page=10040> (visited Apr 21, 2007). A similar policy pertains to papers presented at the AIA's Annual Meeting; see, for example, AIA, *Open Session Submission Form*, available online at <http://www.archaeological.org/formmaker.php?page=10178> (visited Apr 21, 2007).

[92] Merryman, 12 Intl J Cultural Prop at 27 (cited in note 58); O'Keefe, *Trade in Antiquities* at 47–51 (cited in note 52).

[93] Brodie notes that Article 2 of both the Antiquities Dealers Association's Code of Ethics and the Code of Ethics of the International Association of Dealers in Ancient Art say that their members should not trade in antiquities stolen from excavations. However, Brodie interprets the use of the phrase "stolen antiquities" as referring only to antiquities looted from known or designated archaeological sites or from private land. Brodie, *The Plunder of Iraq's Archaeological Heritage* at 218–19 (cited in note 48).

otherwise unofficial site."[94] In 1999, UNESCO promulgated an International Code of Ethics for Dealers in Cultural Property, which states in Article 1 that "[p]rofessional traders in cultural property will not import, export or transfer the ownership of this property when they have reasonable cause to believe it has been stolen, illegally alienated, clandestinely excavated or illegally exported."[95] While some but not all of these codes address the particular problems of the trade in undocumented antiquities, there is little evidence that these codes are internally enforced, and therefore they seem to have little impact on the actual conduct of the trade.[96]

Individual museums and the museum organizations have policies that regulate their acquisitions. The Code of Ethics for Museums of the International Council of Museums ("ICOM") requires that acquisitions be in full compliance with the laws of the country of origin of artifacts, transit countries, and the country where the museum is located.[97] On the other hand, the two major American museum associations do not take as clear a position. The Code of Ethics of the American Association of Museums says little about the particular problems of the acquisition of antiquities,[98] while the Association of Art Museum Directors' guidelines, adopted in June 2004, on the acquisition of ancient art and antiquities have numerous loopholes.[99] In contrast, several

---

[94] Code of Practice for the Control of International Trading in Works of Art, reprinted in 7 Intl J Cultural Prop 203 (1998).

[95] International Code of Ethics for Dealers in Cultural Property, available online at <http://www.unesco.org/culture/legalprotection/committee/html_eng/ethics1.shtml> (visited Apr 21, 2007).

[96] O'Keefe, *Trade in Antiquities* at 50–51 (cited in note 52). The UNESCO Code refers to professional traders and therefore includes both dealers and auction houses. There does not seem to be any other code of conduct that includes auction houses, but both Christie's and Sotheby's maintain their own internal rules of compliance. However, other than references to these compliance rules, the rules themselves are not publicly available. There is only one association of private collectors, and it has no code of conduct. Id at 44.

[97] ICOM, *Code of Ethics for Museums*, 2006, art 2.3, available online at <http://icom.museum/code2006_eng.pdf> (visited Apr 21, 2007).

[98] The Code states: "acquisition, disposal, and loan activities are conducted in a manner that respects the protection and preservation of natural and cultural resources and discourages illicit trade in such materials." American Association of Museums, *Code of Ethics for Museums*, available online at <http://www.aam-us.org/museumresources/ethics/coe.cfm> (visited Apr 21, 2007).

[99] Association of Art Museum Directors, *Report of the AAMD Task Force on the Acquisition of Archaeological Materials and Ancient Art*, available online at <http://www.mta-hq.org/pdf/Assem06_AAMD_Hdt.pdf> (visited Apr 21, 2007). For more detailed analysis of the AAMD guidelines, see Patty Gerstenblith, *Collecting Antiquities in the International Market: Philosophy, Law and Heritage*, in Sherry Hutt, ed, *Yearbook of Cultural Property Law 2007* (Left Coast forthcoming 2007).

individual museums, such as the Field Museum of Natural History in Chicago[100] and, more recently, the Getty Museum[101] and the Indianapolis Museum of Art,[102] have adopted policies that prohibit the acquisition of antiquities that are not documented before 1970 or that do not have an export license from the country of origin. Such policies assure that these museums will not be contributing, either directly or indirectly, to the funding of the contemporary looting of sites. However, most actively acquiring art museums do not make their acquisitions policies public and so it is not possible to determine what standards they follow.

While codes of ethics and practice could be a useful source of restraint on the market in undocumented antiquities, these codes seem not to be numerous, are often vague or ambiguous in referring to the particular problems of looted artifacts, and are often not enforced within the association. Without some external inducement to encourage the promulgation of codes that address the problems of undocumented antiquities, transparency of the codes' provisions, and adherence to them, it is difficult to assess their efficacy. To the extent that market participants are private individuals or corporations, it is also difficult to imagine what would provide this inducement other than greater direct regulation of the market.

3. Increasing Indirect Regulation of the Market in Antiquities

While most of the participants in the market are private actors (dealers, auction houses, and private collectors), museums are public institutions and they receive a significant amount of financial subsidy from federal, state, and local governments. They are therefore susceptible to various forms of indirect governmental regulation.[103] Most museums in the US are incorporated as

---

[100] The Field Museum's policy on accessions states that "the museum and staff 'shall be in full compliance with laws and regulations, both domestic and foreign, governing transfer of ownership and movement of materials across political boundaries.'" Willard L. Boyd, *Museums as Centers of Cultural Understanding*, in Merryman, ed, *Imperialism, Art and Restitution* 47, 50 (cited in note 55).

[101] See The J. Paul Getty Trust, *Policy Statement, Acquisitions by the J. Paul Getty Museum*, available online at <http://www.getty.edu/about/governance/pdfs/acquisitions_policy.pdf> (visited Apr 21, 2007).

[102] See Press Release, *IMA Declares Moratorium on Acquisition of Archaeological Objects Lacking Adequate Provenance*, available online at <http://www.ima-art.org/pressrelease.asp?sectionid=174> (visited Apr 21, 2007).

[103] The Native American Graves Protection and Repatriation Act requires museums that receive federal funding to create inventories and summaries of Native American cultural items in their collections and to make these available for restitution to lineal descendants and culturally affiliated tribes under various circumstances. 25 USC § 3001(8) (2000) (defining "museum" as "any institution or State or local government agency... that receives Federal funds...."). These

charitable organizations and receive their favored tax-exempt status under section 501(c)(3) of the Internal Revenue Code on the basis that they serve an educational or scientific purpose.[104] They therefore have a legal obligation to make this scientific or educational purpose paramount in their practices and functions and must give priority to the preservation of the cultural and historical record. American museums, as educational institutions, have a particular role to play in diminishing the demand for undocumented artifacts. Museums violate their educational or scientific purpose when they contribute, even if indirectly, to the looting of archaeological sites and the destruction of knowledge.

Museums in the US are, in many senses, the collectors of last resort due to both their highly visible leadership role among museums throughout the world and the US tax structure that encourages donations of art works, thereby reducing the cost of antiquities to the American purchaser.[105] However, if a museum accepts as a gift or bequest artifacts to which the museum is not receiving title, then the museum is receiving nothing of value and the American public is subsidizing the trade in undocumented artifacts. The IRS should be taking into consideration the certainty of title in determining whether to permit a collector to take a deduction for a gift of antiquities so as to eliminate this additional subsidy to the acquisition of undocumented antiquities.[106] In determining certainty of title, the burden of proving the artifact's legitimate

---

requirements could not have been directly imposed but were imposed in exchange for the benefit of federal funding.

[104] Section 501(c)(3) defines those organizations that qualify as charitable organizations as "corporations, and any community chest, fund, or foundation, organized and operated exclusively for religious, charitable, scientific, testing for public safety, literary, or educational purposes." 26 USC § 501(c)(3). Charitable organizations are exempt from the payment of taxes on any profits they earn, like other nonprofit organizations, but donations made to a § 501(c)(3) organization are eligible as deductions from the income of the donor (both individuals and corporations) under § 170, subject to certain limitations and so long as the organization is not classified as a private foundation. Section 642(c) allows a comparable deduction from the income of an estate or trust and section 2055 gives a similar deduction in the valuation of an estate for estate tax purposes. For a general discussion, see Patty Gerstenblith, *Acquisition and Deacquisition of Museum Collections and the Fiduciary Obligations of Museums to the Public*, 11 Cardozo J Intl & Comp L 409, 413 (2003).

[105] Shelby White, the owner of one of the largest private collections of antiquities in the US, wrote that the extent of public subsidy when art works are donated to museums from larger estates is approximately one-fourth of the art's fair market value. Shelby White, *Building American Museums: The Role of the Private Collector*, in Kate Fitz Gibbon, ed, *Who Owns the Past? Cultural Policy, Cultural Property, and the Law* 165, 174 (Rutgers 2005).

[106] When a donor donates art that is valued at more than $5,000, an appraisal must be obtained; if the artwork is worth more than $20,000, then the appraisal must be filed with the tax return. See IRS, *Instructions for Form 8283*, available online at <http://www.irs.gov/pub/irs-pdf/i8283.pdf> (visited Apr 21, 2007). In such cases, the IRS Art Advisory Panel reviews the valuation. However, the Panel considers only fair market value of the work and not the question of whether the museum is receiving good title. For a similar proposal, see Atwood, *Stealing History* at 245–46 (cited in note 12).

background should be placed on the donor. If a collector knows that he or she may not be able ultimately to donate an antiquity to a museum because the artifact's legitimate background cannot be affirmatively established, then the collector is more likely to avoid purchasing the undocumented artifact. This could have a significant impact on the prices that American collectors are willing to pay for undocumented antiquities and this should, in turn, discourage the market for such antiquities.

The state attorney general could also take a more active role in enforcing museum trustees' fiduciary obligations. When a museum purchases antiquities of undocumented background and the museum later returns them to the proper owner, this constitutes waste of the museum's assets and a violation of the fiduciary obligation of care.[107] The large numbers of artifacts returned to Italy and Greece in the past year alone by the Metropolitan Museum of Art, the Boston Museum of Fine Arts, and the Getty all represent, to the extent that these objects were purchased, funds that were wasted. The state attorney general should hold the museums' trustees responsible for such breaches of their obligations and impose personal liability for the waste of museum assets.

Museums also receive a considerable amount of direct funding from federal, state, and local governments, such as grants and funds for their operating budgets, and they often receive indirect subsidies such as free or below market leases on the land on which they are located.[108] In exchange for these subsidies, museums could be required to make public their acquisitions policies and their acquisitions with their ownership history.[109] In this way, the public would be able to determine how the museums are conducting themselves and whether they are acquiring undocumented antiquities. Indirect regulation of museums holds significant potential for reducing the demand for undocumented antiquities and thereby helping to diminish the looting of archaeological sites.

IV. CONCLUSION

The buying of undocumented antiquities that are the likely product of contemporary looting of archaeological sites contributes significantly to the destruction of our cultural heritage, a nonrenewable, finite resource, by providing a financial incentive for this looting. The destruction of sites imposes a harm on society and should be curtailed through a combination of efforts

---

[107] On the fiduciary duty of care of museum trustees, see Gordon H. Marsh, *Governance of Non-Profit Organizations: An Appropriate Standard of Conduct for Trustees and Directors of Museums and Other Cultural Institutions*, 85 Dickinson L Rev 607, 610–11 (1980–81).

[108] See Gerstenblith, 11 Cardozo J Intl L & Comp L at 415–16 (cited in note 104).

[109] The new Getty policy on acquisitions states that information concerning acquisitions will be made available to the public. *Acquisitions by the J. Paul Getty Museum* ¶ 6 (cited in note 101).

encompassing more vigorous enforcement of the laws that currently exist, more flexible approaches to the international and national legal regimes, indirect regulation of museum acquiring practices through compliance and transparency requirements for acquisitions in exchange for receipt of financial benefits from federal, state, and local governments, increased supervision of museum boards of trustees, and curtailment of the tax deduction available to donors of undocumented ancient works of art and antiquities. Increased regulation of the market should be realized through a combination of expansion of legal rules and law enforcement, greater observance of codes of practice with more precise prohibitions on participation in the trade in undocumented antiquities, and more regulation of American museums. These solutions are premised on the recognition that a loosely regulated market is a major contributor to the problem of site looting and not the source of a solution. While there has been considerable progress over the past twenty-five years, more progress is needed if our heritage will be preserved and future generations will be able to continue to enjoy and learn from the past.

[16]

The Protection of Cultural Property in Times of Armed Conflict: The Practice of the International Criminal Tribunal for the Former Yugoslavia

Hirad Abtahi[*]

I. INTRODUCTION

Destruction constitutes an inherent component of armed conflict. No war has been fought without damaging private or public property at least collaterally. In numerous conflicts, however, belligerents have tried to obtain psychological advantage by directly attacking the enemy's cultural property without the justification of military necessity. Such was the case during the conflict in the former Yugoslavia. In the same way that rape became an instrument to destroy the adversary's identity, cultural aggression, i.e., the destruction and pillage of the adversary's non-renewable cultural resources, became a tool to erase the manifestation of the adversary's identity. Both rape and damage to cultural property represented forms of "ethnic cleansing."

In the Croatian city of Vukovar, for example, Serb-controlled Federal troops vandalized ancient and medieval sites as well as the eighteenth-century Eltz Castle, which contained a museum.[1] The same troops attacked a complex of Roman villas in Split[2] and inflicted damage on the sixteenth-century Fortress of Stara Gradiška overlooking the Sava River.[3] In Dubrovnik, retreating Federal troops targeted the Renaissance arboreta, St. Ann Church, and the old city center, which is included on the World Heritage list.[4] The perpetrators in other cases have not yet been identified. The As-

---

[*] Diplôme d'Etudes Approfondies de Droit International, Strasbourg University, France; Associate Legal Officer, Chambers, International Criminal Tribunal for the former Yugoslavia (ICTY), The Hague, The Netherlands. The views expressed in this Article are those of the author in his personal capacity and not necessarily those of the ICTY or the United Nations.

1. Karen J. Delting, *Eternal Silence: The Destruction of Cultural Property in Yugoslavia*, 17 MD. J. INT'L L. & TRADE 41, 66–67 (1993) (citation omitted).
2. *Id.* at 66.
3. *Id.*
4. *Id.* at 67–68.

sumption and St. Dimitrius churches in Osijek were attacked.[5] In Bosnia-Herzegovina, Baščaršija and Stari Most, the historic centers of Sarajevo and Mostar respectively, were targeted.[6] In Croatia, the Jasenovac memorial complex fell under attack.[7]

These events illuminate the psychology behind the systematic destruction of cultural property both in the former Yugoslavia and in other conflicts where the destruction of cultural property is not merely collateral damage. By inflicting cultural damage on present generations, the enemy seeks to orphan future generations and destroy their understanding of who they are and from where they come. Degrading victims' cultural property also affects their identity before the world community and decreases world diversity. History has witnessed the poignant fate of many nations and peoples following brutal and intensive cultural mutilation. Some have ceased to exist while others have had their identity deeply and irreversibly altered.

The present study examines the various avenues available for prosecuting the destruction of cultural property through the statute and case law of the International Criminal Tribunal for the former Yugoslavia (ICTY). Although the ICTY has prosecuted and punished crimes relating to cultural property, it has encountered a number of psychological and legal challenges. Because the conflict in the former Yugoslavia centered on ethnicity and religion, most of the crimes against cultural property related to religious or educational targets. For a long time, existing indictments did not clearly cover other types of cultural property, such as institutions dedicated to science or works of science. Very recent practice shows the Tribunal's willingness to issue indictments charging crimes against more secular components of cultural property. In addition to finding a *prima facie* case, an international tribunal must consider these components important enough to address in an indictment.[8]

The ICTY must also deal with the impact that the prosecution and punishment of crimes against cultural property may have on the traditional distinction between crimes against property and crimes against persons. The

---

5. *Id.* at 67.
6. Delting, *supra* note 1, at 68.
7. *Id.*
8. On February 22, 2001, shortly before this Article went to press, the ICTY issued an indictment concerning the attacks on Dubrovnik, Croatia. Although five days later the confirming judge issued an order limiting public disclosure of the indictment, an ICTY press release said,

> several individuals have been charged with grave breaches of the Geneva Conventions of 1949 and with violations of the laws or customs of war arising from attacks made by the Yugoslav Peoples' Army on the Dubrovnik region between 1 October and 31 December 1991. The specific offences charged in the indictment include murder, cruel treatment, attacks on civilians, *devastation not justified by military necessity, unlawful attacks on civilian objects, destruction of historic monuments, wanton destruction of villages, and plunder of public and private property.*

Press Release, ICTY Office of the Prosecutor, Prosecutor Carla Del Ponte Issues Dubrovnik Indictment, P.H./P.I.S./569-E (Mar. 1, 2001), *at* http://www.un.org/icty/pressreal/p569-e.htm (emphasis added). This indictment is significant because, although the content of the indictment is under seal, "destruction of historic monuments" probably encompasses secular components of cultural property.

anthropocentric approach of law psychologically confines crimes against cultural property to a less visible position than other crimes.[9] Even when crimes against cultural property are addressed, it is because the perpetrators' objective was to harm the population whom the cultural property represented. For example, the ICTY addresses crimes involving the destruction of a mosque because they harmed the Muslim population. The same reasoning applies to the destruction of a Catholic monastery, which injured the Croat population, or of an Orthodox church, which harmed the Serb population. These anthropocentric and ethnocentric approaches require the establishment of a link between cultural property and the group of individuals that it represents. As a result, in the hierarchy of international crimes, there is often a tendency to place crimes against cultural property below crimes against persons. Although no one can deny the difference between the torture or murder of a human being and the destruction of cultural property, it remains important to recognize the seriousness of the latter, especially given its long-term effects.

This study will analyze how and when the ICTY gives crimes against cultural property adequate weight. Part II presents the definition of armed conflict and a tentative definition of cultural property. This study then analyzes the provisions of the ICTY Statute and judgments that are likely to apply to the protection of cultural property. Parts III and IV respectively analyze the direct and indirect protection of cultural property while Part V analyzes the protection *a posteriori*. The Article concludes by considering ways to increase protection for cultural property in the future.

II. Definitions

This Part defines the two key elements of this study, namely "armed conflict" and "cultural property."

A. *Armed Conflict*

In response to the atrocities that occurred during the armed conflicts surrounding the collapse the Socialist Federal Republic of Yugoslavia (SFRY) in the 1990s, the UN Security Council, pursuant to UN Charter Chapter VII, established the "International Tribunal for the Prosecution of Persons Responsible for Serious Violations of International Humanitarian Law Committed in the Territory of the Former Yugoslavia since 1991."[10] Its Statute

---

9. For this reason, most ICTY judgments referred to in this study involve cases where cultural property was not at stake. Some of the legal findings of the Chambers in these cases, however, can be applied to crimes involving cultural property by analogy. At the time of writing, other cases more directly related to cultural property lie dormant because the accused has not been arrested (and consequently no trial has been initiated) or the case is at the pre-trial stage or the trials are ongoing. Finally, it must be borne in mind that some of the judgments referred to in this study come from the first instance stage and are waiting the final judgment of the ICTY Appeals Chamber.

10. S.C. Res. 827, U.N. SCOR, 3217th Meeting, U.N. Doc. S/RES/827 (1993).

gives the ICTY jurisdiction to prosecute natural persons (competence *ratione personae*)[11] for grave breaches of the Geneva Convention of 1949, violations of the laws or customs of war, crimes against humanity, and genocide (competence *ratione materiae*).[12] These crimes must have occurred in the territory of the former Yugoslavia, including its land surface, airspace, and territorial waters (competence *ratione loci*) on or after January 1, 1991 (competence *ratione temporis*).[13]

Operating within the framework of the specific series of armed conflicts that had taken place in the former Yugoslavia since 1991, the ICTY had to define the term "armed conflict." According to the *Tadić Jurisdiction Decision*, "an armed conflict exists whenever there is a resort to armed force between States or protracted armed violence between governmental authorities and organized armed groups or between such groups within a State."[14] This definition encompasses both international and internal armed conflicts. With regard to geography, if an armed conflict took place within a given region, then the Tribunal does not need to establish the existence of the conflict in each territorial component of that region.[15] With regard to temporal scope, the *Tadić Jurisdiction Decision* held that it "applies from the initiation of . . . armed conflict and extends beyond the cessation of hostilities until a general conclusion of peace is reached," in the case of international armed conflict, or "a peaceful settlement is achieved," in the case of non-international armed conflict.[16]

Inseparable from the occurrence of armed conflict is the body of law that governs it.

> [T]he expression *international humanitarian law applicable in armed conflict* means international rules, established by treaties or custom, which are specifically intended to solve humanitarian problems directly arising from international or non-international armed conflicts and which, for humanitarian reasons, limits the right of Parties to a conflict to use the methods and means of warfare of their choice or protect persons and property that are, or may be,

---

11. *Report of the Secretary-General Pursuant to Paragraph 2 of the Security Council Resolution 808*, Annex, at 38, U.N. Doc. S/25704 (1993) [hereinafter *Report of the Secretary-General*] (including the text of the ICTY Statute in the Annex). *See also id.* at 14 (differentiating between "juridical persons, such as an association or organization" and "natural persons").
12. *Id.* at 36–38.
13. *Id.* at 39.
14. The Prosecutor v. Duško Tadić (Decision on the Defence Motion for Interlocutory Appeal Jurisdiction), No. IT-94-1-AR72, para. 70 (ICTY 1995), *available at* http://www.un.org/icty/tadic/appeal/decision-e/51002.htm [hereinafter *Tadić Jurisdiction Decision*].
15. *See* The Prosecutor v. Tihomir Blaškić (Trial Judgment), No. IT-95-14-T, para. 64 (ICTY 2000), *available at* http://www.un.org/icty/blaskic/trialc1/judgement/index.htm [hereinafter *Blaškić Trial Judgment*].
16. *Tadić Jurisdiction Decision*, No. IT-94-1-AR72, para. 70.

affected by conflict. The expression ... is often abbreviated to *international humanitarian law* or *humanitarian law*.[17]

This definition raises two issues. First, international humanitarian law consists of two major components: Geneva law, which protects war victims, and Hague law, which regulates the "methods and means of conducting hostilities."[18] Geneva law is much more developed than Hague law because of states' very cautious approach to constraints on their means of waging effective warfare.[19]

The definition also suggests a link between this body of law and the geographic nature of the armed conflict. While international humanitarian law is applicable to both international and non-international conflicts, the body of law for the former is much more developed because of the doctrine of state sovereignty.[20] Non-international armed conflicts, such as civil wars, were traditionally considered internal matters, which gave a state primary responsibility for the resolution of its conflict unless it requested the help of other states or international organizations. With a few exceptions during the Cold War,[21] this doctrine prevented a detailed elaboration of humanitarian law applicable to non-international armed conflicts. Since the early to mid-1990s, however, with the power vacuum created by the Soviet Union's collapse and the events in northern Iraq, the SFRY, Somalia, and Rwanda, the international community has acquired wider latitude to intervene—on an extremely selective basis—in places where either non-international armed conflicts or a combination of international and non-international armed conflicts occur. The issue of conflict classification remains important, however, because it determines which body of law governs the conflict; this is especially true in the case of the former Yugoslavia, which, depending on the time and place, experienced conflicts of a mixed nature.[22]

B. Cultural Property

The Statute of the ICTY does not use the term "cultural property." Article 3(d) provides some insight into its definition when it refers to "institutions dedicated to religion, charity and education, the arts and sciences, historic monuments and works of art and science." The absence of explicit reference to cultural property, however, correlates to the lack of a uniform

---

17. CLAUDE PILLOUD ET AL., INT'L COMM. OF THE RED CROSS, COMMENTARY ON THE ADDITIONAL PROTOCOLS OF 8 JUNE 1977 TO THE GENEVA CONVENTIONS OF 12 AUGUST 1949, at xxvii (Yves Sandoz et al. eds., 1987) [hereinafter COMMENTARY ON THE ADDITIONAL PROTOCOLS].
18. W.J. Fenrick, *Humanitarian Law and Criminal Trials*, 7 TRANSNAT'L L. & CONTEMP. PROBS. 23, 27 (1997).
19. *See id.*
20. *Id.* at 25.
21. The 1967–70 Biafran conflict in Nigeria offers an example.
22. *See* Fenrick, *supra* note 18, at 26.

definition of this concept in international instruments.[23] Two questions present obstacles to defining this concept: (1) What does "culture" encompass? (2) What type of property qualifies as "cultural"? Rather than formulating a precise definition of the concept, this section will seek to clarify it by reviewing the relevant international instruments in order to single out a common denominator comprised of those components of cultural property that are referred to by all the instruments.

1. *International Instruments Referring to the Components of Cultural Property*

Most international instruments relating to armed conflict refer to the components of cultural property, not to cultural property explicitly. For example, Article 56 of the Hague Convention (IV) Respecting the Laws and Customs of War on Land of 18 October 1907 (Hague Convention (IV)) and the Regulations annexed thereto (Hague Regulations) provides:

> The property of municipalities, that of institutions dedicated to religion, charity and education, the arts and sciences, even when State property, shall be treated as private property.
>
> All seizure of, destruction or wilful damage done to institutions of this character, historic monuments, works of art and science, is forbidden, and should be made the subject of legal proceedings.[24]

Article 3(d) of the ICTY Statute enumerates identical components for cultural property. Article 27 of the Hague Regulations provides for the protection of "buildings dedicated to religion, art, science, or charitable purposes, historic monuments, hospitals, and places where the sick and wounded are collected" as long as they are not used for military purposes.[25] The reference to cultural property together with places where the sick and wounded are collected represents an early recognition of the significance of cultural property.

The 1935 Roerich Pact aimed exclusively to protect cultural property. Article 1 of the Pact provides for the neutrality and protection of "historic monuments, museums, scientific, artistic, educational and cultural institu-

---

23. The Convention Concerning the Protection of the World Cultural and Natural Heritage, Nov. 16, 1972, 27 U.S.T. 37, 1037 U.N.T.S. 151, uses the term "cultural heritage." According to some writers, the difference between the two terms is that while cultural property comprises tangible movable and immovable property of cultural significance, cultural heritage "includes intangible heritage, such as crafts, folklore, and skills." Theresa Papademetriou, *International Aspects of Cultural Property: An Overview of Basic Instruments and Issues*, 24 INT'L J. LEGAL INFO. 270, 271–73 (1996).

24. Hague Convention Respecting the Laws and Customs of War on Land (Hague IV) and the Regulations annexed thereto, Oct. 18, 1907, Annex, art. 56, 36 Stat. 2277, 2309 [hereinafter Hague Convention (IV) and Regulations]. The Annex to Hague Convention (IV) is referred to as the Hague Regulations.

25. *Id.* Annex, art. 27, at 2303; *see also* Hague Convention Respecting Bombardment by Naval Forces in Time of War (Hague IX), Oct. 18, 1907, art. 5, 36 Stat. 2351, 2364.

tions."[26] The Pact, however, has a more limited geographic scope because it was concluded under the auspices of the regional Pan-American Union, the predecessor of the Organization of the American States.

Adopted on July 17, 1998, Article 8 of the International Criminal Court (ICC) Statute adopts the same approach as its precursors. Articles 8(2)(b)(ix) and 8(2)(e)(iv) refer to, among other serious violations of the laws of war, intentional attacks on cultural and religious institutions.[27] Like Article 27 of the Hague Regulations, it includes hospitals in the same list as cultural property.

These instruments encompass almost identical components of cultural property and illustrate the approach adopted by the majority of international instruments related to armed conflicts over the past century. A more limited number of international instruments refer to cultural property per se. They all have come into existence in the second half of the twentieth century.

2. International Instruments Referring to Cultural Property Per Se

After the Second World War wreaked havoc on the cultural heritage of Europe, an international breakthrough occurred that increased the protection of cultural property during armed conflicts. Signed on May 14, 1954, the Convention for the Protection of Cultural Property in the Event of Armed Conflict (1954 Hague Convention)[28] became the first armed conflict-related instrument to use the term "cultural property."[29] Article 1 provides:

> For the purposes of the present Convention, the term "cultural property" shall cover, irrespective of origin or ownership:
>
> (a) movable or immovable property of great importance to the cultural heritage of every people, such as monuments of architecture, art or history, whether religious or secular; archaeological sites; groups of buildings which, as a whole, are of historical or artistic interest; works of art; manuscripts, books and other objects of artistic, historical or archaeological interest; as well as scientific collections and important collections of books or archives or of reproductions of the property defined above;
>
> (b) buildings whose main and effective purpose is to preserve or exhibit the movable cultural property defined in sub-paragraph (a) such as museums, large libraries and depositories of archives, and

---

26. Treaty on the Protection of Artistic and Scientific Institutions and Historic Monuments (Roerich Pact), Apr. 15, 1935, 49 Stat. 3267, 3268, 167 L.N.T.S. 289, 290.
27. Rome Statute of the International Criminal Court, at 7–10, U.N. Doc. A/CONF.189/9 (1998) [hereinafter ICC Statute].
28. Convention for the Protection of Cultural Property in the Event of Armed Conflict, May 14, 1954, 249 U.N.T.S. 240 [hereinafter 1954 Hague Convention].
29. The same term is used by the 1970 UNESCO Convention on the Means of Prohibiting and Preventing the Illicit Import, Export and Transfer of Ownership of Cultural Property, Nov. 14, 1970, S. Exec. Doc. B, 92-2 (1972), 823 U.N.T.S. 231.

refuges intended to shelter, in the event of armed conflict, the movable cultural property defined in subparagraph (a);

(c) centres containing a large amount of cultural property as defined in sub-paragraphs (a) and (b), to be known as "centres containing monuments."[30]

Including significant buildings, objects, and depositories, this definition of cultural property is one of the most comprehensive ever provided in an international instrument, especially one related to armed conflict.

Almost a quarter of a century later, Article 53 of Additional Protocol I followed the example of the 1954 Hague Convention and referred to cultural property per se, although not in its heading ("Protection of cultural objects and of places of worship").[31] It built on the 1954 Hague Convention, providing that:

Without prejudice to the provisions of the Hague Convention for the Protection of Cultural Property in the Event of Armed Conflict of 14 May 1954, and of other relevant international instruments, it is prohibited:

(a) to commit any acts of hostility directed against the historic monuments, works of art or places of worship which constitute the cultural or spiritual heritage of peoples.[32]

The language, however, differed on one point. Article 1 of the 1954 Hague Convention referred to property that is "of great importance to the cultural heritage,"[33] while Article 53 of Additional Protocol I, for the same purpose, refers to objects that "constitute the cultural or spiritual heritage."[34] According to the Commentary on the Additional Protocols, "despite this difference in terminology the basic idea is the same."[35] Although "the adjective 'cultural' applies to historic monuments and works of art while the adjective 'spiritual' applies to places of worship,"[36] there are instances where the two may be interchangeable. For example, a temple may have cultural value, and a historic monument or work of art may have spiritual value.[37] When it is

---

30. 1954 Hague Convention, *supra* note 28, at 242.
31. Protocol Additional to the Geneva Conventions of 12 August 1949, and relating to the Protection of Victims of International Armed Conflicts, June 8, 1977, 1125 U.N.T.S. 3, 27 [hereinafter Additional Protocol I]. *See also* Protocol Additional to the Geneva Conventions of 12 August 1949, and relating to the Protection of Victims of Non-International Armed Conflicts, June 8, 1977, S. TREATY DOC. NO. 100-2 (1987), 1125 U.N.T.S. 609.
32. Additional Protocol I, *supra* note 31, at 27 (citation omitted).
33. 1954 Hague Convention, *supra* note 28, at 242.
34. Additional Protocol I, *supra* note 31, at 27.
35. COMMENTARY ON THE ADDITIONAL PROTOCOLS, *supra* note 17, para. 2064.
36. *Id.* para. 2065.
37. *Id.*

difficult to categorize an object, the Commentary gives extra weight to the views of the people who see it as part of their heritage.[38]

The above analysis reveals a common denominator among these instruments with regard to cultural property, namely "institutions dedicated to religion, charity and education, the arts and sciences, historic monuments and works of art and science," as described in Article 3(d) of the ICTY Statute.[39] If an item does not fit one of these components, this study will include it in the general protection provided to civilian objects.[40]

C. *Typology of ICTY Protective Measures*

Having defined the territorial and temporal scope of both armed conflict and humanitarian law and having clarified the concept of cultural property, this study now analyzes the ICTY Statute's relevant provisions and their application by the Chambers. Many ICTY indictments deal with the concept of property. Some, which will not be addressed in this study, focus on private property in the form of personal belongings.[41] Others deal with cultural property, charging crimes, cumulatively or alternatively, under three counts: (1) grave breaches of the Geneva Conventions of 1949, (2) violations of the laws or customs of war, and (3) crimes against humanity, particularly persecution on political, racial, and religious grounds. A crime targeting an institution dedicated to religion, for example, may be charged under a combination of these three counts.

Violations of these statutory provisions can lead to prosecution and punishment. The United Nations created the ICTY in order to punish those persons responsible for the commission of war atrocities in Yugoslavia. To this end, the ICTY Statute had to formulate norms and establish ways to protect them. It did so by criminalizing certain behaviors. Because the war was ongoing, the Tribunal also sought to deter future atrocities. The incorporation of norms in its Statute demonstrated the seriousness of the crimes and their condemnation by the international community as a result of its failure to protect them. The following sections of this Article analyze three types of protective measures for cultural property that can be identified in the ICTY Statute and case law: direct protection (Part III), indirect protection (Part IV), and protection *a posteriori* (Part V).

---

38. *Id.* ("In case of doubt, reference should be made in the first place to the value or veneration ascribed to the object by the people whose heritage it is.").
39. *Report of the Secretary-General, supra* note 11, at 37.
40. *See infra* Part IV.
41. *See* The Prosecutor v. Goran Jelisić (Indictment), No. IT-95-10, para. 36, Count 44 (ICTY 1998), *available at* http://www.un.org/icty/indictment/english/jel-2ai981019e.htm; The Prosecutor v. Zejnil Delalić "Čelebići" (Indictment), 1996 ICTY Y.B. 149, No. IT-96-21, para. 37, Count 49, *available at* http://www.un.org/icty/indictment/english/cel-ii960321e.htm; The Prosecutor v. Dragoljub Kunarac (Amended Indictment), No. IT-96-23-PT, Count 13 (ICTY 1999), *available at* http://www.un.org/icty/indictment/english/kun-3ai991201e.htm.

III. Direct Protection—Article 3(d) of the Statute: Violations of the Laws or Customs of War

A number of ICTY indictments alleging violations of the laws or customs of war refer explicitly to the components of cultural property. They charge "destruction or wilful damage done to institutions dedicated to religion,"[42] "destruction or wilful damage to institutions dedicated to religion or education,"[43] and "seizure, destruction or wilful damage done to institutions dedicated to religion."[44] These phrases all refer to Article 3(d) of the Statute, which provides:

> The International Tribunal shall have the power to prosecute persons violating the laws or customs of war. Such violations shall include, but not be limited to: . . .
>
> (d) seizure of, destruction or wilful damage done to institutions dedicated to religion, charity and education, the arts and sciences, historic monuments and works of art and science.[45]

Article 3(d) punishes the most direct violations of cultural property envisioned by the ICTY and makes explicit reference to the "common denominator" components of cultural property.[46]

A. Scope and Conditions of Applicability

ICTY case law has determined the scope and conditions of applicability of the Statute's Article 3. According to the *Tadić Jurisdiction Decision*, Article 3 applies to both internal and international armed conflicts.[47] In addition, as established by the *Čelebići* and *Blaškić Trial Judgments*, a nexus between the alleged crimes and the armed conflict must exist in order to charge under

---

42. The Prosecutor v. Radovan Karadžić (Indictment), 1995 ICTY Y.B. 204, 215, No. IT-95-5, Count 6, *available at* http://www.un.org/icty/indictment/english/kar-ii950724e.htm [hereinafter *Karadžić Indictment*]; The Prosecutor v. Radoslav Brđanin (First Amended Indictment), No. IT-99-36, Count 12 (ICTY 1996), *available at* http://www.un.org/icty/ind-e.htm.

43. The Prosecutor v. Tihomir Blaškić (Second Amended Indictment), No. IT-95-14-T, para. 11, Count 14 (ICTY 1997), *available at* http://www.un.org/icty/indictment/english/bla-2ai970425e.htm [hereinafter *Blaškić Indictment*]; The Prosecutor v. Dario Kordić (First Amended Indictment), No. IT-95-14/2, paras. 57, 58, Counts 43, 44 (ICTY 1998), *available at* http://www.un.org/icty/indictment/english/kor-1ai980930e.htm [hereinafter *Kordić Indictment*].

44. The Prosecutor v. Mladen Naletilić (Indictment), No. IT-98-34-I, Count 22 (ICTY 1998), *available at* http://www.un.org/icty/indictment/english/nal-ii981221e.pdf [hereinafter *Naletilić Indictment*].

45. *Report of the Secretary-General*, *supra* note 11, at 37.

46. Article 3(d) constitutes *lex specialis* because it explicitly enumerates a number of components of cultural property. For aspects of cultural property that are not mentioned in Article 3(d), reference may be made to those provisions of the ICTY Statute that constitute *lex generalis*, i.e., Articles 3(b), 3(c), and 3(e), Article 2(d) (although only for occupied territories), and Article 5(h). *See* Parts IV.A, IV.B, and IV.C *infra*.

47. *See Tadić Jurisdiction Decision*, No. IT-94-1-AR72, para. 137 (ICTY 1995), *available at* http://www.un.org/icty/tadic/appeal/decision-e/51002.htm.

Articles 2 and 3 of the Statute.[48] The *Blaškić Trial Judgment* held, however, that the accused did not need to intend active participation in the armed conflict if the "act fits into the geographical and temporal context of the conflict."[49] This broad interpretation of intent does not require a sophisticated level of organization, such as a plan or direct policy, for commission of a crime. The alleged crimes need not be "part of a policy or of a practice officially endorsed or tolerated"[50] by the belligerents, "in actual furtherance of a policy associated with the conduct of war,"[51] or even in the actual interests of the belligerents.[52]

The violations of the laws or customs of war enumerated in Article 3 of the Statute do not constitute an exhaustive list[53] and thus allow for more protection of cultural property. The Hague Convention (IV), as interpreted and applied by the Nuremberg Tribunal (IMT), represents the basis for Article 3 of the Statute.[54] Because it applies to both international and non-international armed conflicts, Article 3 is broader than common Article 3 of the 1949 Geneva Conventions, which applies only to non-international armed conflicts.[55] The *Blaškić* Trial Chamber stated that Article 3 of the

---

48. *See* The Prosecutor v. Zejnil Delalić "Čelebići" (Trial Judgment), No. IT-96-21-T, paras. 193–98 (ICTY 1998), *available at* http://www.un.org/icty/celebici/trialc2/jugement/main.htm [hereinafter *Čelebići Trial Judgment*]; *Blaškić Trial Judgment*, No. IT-95-14-T, para. 65 (ICTY 2000), *available at* http://www.un.org/ icty/blaskic/trialc1/judgement/index.htm.
49. *Blaškić Trial Judgment*, No. IT-95-14-T, para. 71.
50. The Prosecutor v. Duško Tadić (Trial Judgment), No. IT-94-1-T, para. 573 (ICTY 1997), *available at* http://www.un.org/icty/tadic/trialc2/jugement-e/tad-tj970507e.htm#_Toc387417337 [hereinafter *Tadić Trial Judgment*]. *See also Čelebići Trial Judgment*, No. IT-96-21-T, para. 195.
51. *Tadić Trial Judgment*, No. IT 94-1-T, para. 573.
52. *See Tadić Trial Judgment*, No. IT-94-1-T, para. 573.
53. *Blaškić Trial Judgment*, No. IT-95-14-T, para. 168. According to the Report of the Secretary-General, the Geneva Conventions, Hague Convention (IV), the Convention on the Prevention of the Crime of Genocide of 9 December 1948, and the Charter of the International Military Tribunal of 8 August 1945 represent "the part of conventional international humanitarian law which has beyond doubt become part of international customary law." *Report of the Secretary General, supra* note 11, at 9.
54. *Report of the Secretary-General, supra* note 11, at 11.
55. *Id.*; *see also Tadić Jurisdiction Decision*, No. IT-94-1-AR72, para. 86 (ICTY 1995), *available at* http://www.un.org/icty/tadic/appeal/decision-e/51002.htm. Pursuant to common Article 2 of the Geneva Conventions, the Conventions apply to international armed conflicts, including cases of total or partial occupation by one state of the territory of another. *See* Geneva Convention for the Amelioration of the Condition of the Wounded and Sick in Armed Forces in the Field, Aug. 12, 1949, 75 U.N.T.S. 31, 32 [hereinafter Geneva Convention I]; Geneva Convention for the Amelioration of the Condition of the Wounded, Sick and Shipwrecked Members of Armed Forces at Sea, Aug. 12, 1949, 75 U.N.T.S. 85, 86 [hereinafter Geneva Convention II]; Geneva Convention relative to the Treatment of Prisoners of War, Aug. 12, 1949, 75 U.N.T.S. 135, 136 [hereinafter Geneva Convention III]; Geneva Convention relative to the Protection of Civilian Persons in Time of War, Aug. 12, 1949, 75 U.N.T.S. 287, 288 [hereinafter Geneva Convention IV]. Common Article 3 of the Conventions, by contrast, applies to non-international armed conflict and encourages belligerents in such conflicts to bring into force other provisions of the Conventions, either partially or totally. Geneva Convention I, *supra*, at 32–34; Geneva Convention II, *supra*, at 86–88; Geneva Convention III, *supra*, at 136–38; Geneva Convention IV, *supra*, at 288–90. In the *Tadić Jurisdiction Decision*, the Appeals Chamber indicated that "in the present state of development of the law, Article 2 of the Statute only applies to offences committed within the context of international armed conflicts," *Tadić Jurisdiction Decision*, No. IT-94-1-AR72, para. 84, and that it was not possible to prosecute violations of common Article 3 under the grave breach provisions of the Geneva Conventions, *see id.* para. 87. The Appeals Chamber, however, agreed with the prosecution's argument that Article 3 of

Statute also encompasses the provisions of Additional Protocol I in relation to unlawful attacks upon civilian targets.[56] Therefore, the Trial Chamber did not need to rule on the applicability of Additional Protocol I.[57] The ICTY can be guided by Articles 52, "General protection of civilian objects," and 53, "Protection of cultural objects and places of worship," of Additional Protocol I when dealing with offenses involving cultural property.[58] In conclusion, under Article 3 of the Statute, the ICTY can prosecute persons not only for the violations listed therein, but also for violations of customary international law norms, such as common Article 3 of the Geneva Conventions, and for violations of treaty law that was binding upon the parties at the time of the conflict.

Finally, Article 7 of the Statute imposes individual criminal responsibility for violations of Article 3 of the Statute.[59] More generally, the *Tadić Jurisdiction Decision* held that customary international law imposes criminal responsibility for serious violations of common Article 3.[60]

B. *Elements of the Offenses with Regard to Cultural Property*

The cultural property protection provided by Article 3(d) has three advantages. First, it has a wide scope because it applies to both international and non-international armed conflicts. Second, the element of intent is broadly interpreted. Third, unlike other provisions of the Statute, it refers directly to cultural property. Nevertheless, this type of protection encounters a number of obstacles, mainly due to the qualification of the sites relating to cultural property.

ICTY case law provides some guidelines for which types of sites constituting or sheltering cultural property may be protected under Article 3(d). The *Blaškić Trial Judgment* held that "the damage or destruction must have been committed intentionally to institutions which may clearly be identified

---

the ICTY Statute confers power to prosecute the violation of common Article 3 of the Geneva Conventions. *See id.* paras. 88 – 93. In fact, it regarded Article 3 of the Statute as a general clause covering all violations of humanitarian law not falling within Articles 2, 4, or 5 of the Statute. *Tadić Jurisdiction Decision*, No. IT-94-1-AR72, para. 89.

56. *See Blaškić Trial Judgment*, No. IT-95-14-T, para. 170.

57. *Id.* If the Trial Chamber had had to rule on the applicability of Additional Protocol I, it would have found it applicable because both Croatia and Bosnia and Herzegovina were parties to it as of January 1, 1993. M.J. BOWMAN & D.J. HARRIS, MULTILATERAL TREATIES: INDEX AND CURRENT STATUS 287– 88 (11th ed. Supp. 1995). *See also Tadić Jurisdiction Decision*, No. IT-94-1-AR72, paras. 98, 102, 134; *Tadić Trial Judgment*, No. IT-94-1-T, paras. 609–11 (ICTY 1997), *available at* http://www.un.org/icty/tadic/trialc2/jugement-e/tad-tj970507e.htm#_Toc387417337; *Ćelebići Trial Judgment*, No. IT-96-21-T, para. 301 (ICTY 1998), *available at* http://www.un.org/icty/celebici/trialc2/judgement/main.htm; The Prosecutor v. Jean-Paul Akayesu, No. ICTR-96-4-T, para. 608 (ICTR 1998), *available at* http://www.ictr.org/ENGLISH/cases/Akayesu/judgement/akay001.htm [hereinafter *Akayesu Trial Judgment*]; Military and Paramilitary Activities (Nicar. v. U.S.), 1986 I.C.J. 14, 114 (June 27).

58. *See, e.g., infra* Part IV.B.2.

59. *See Blaškić Trial Judgment*, No. IT-95-14-T, para. 176; *see also Report of the Secretary-General, supra* note 11, at 38.

60. *Tadić Jurisdiction Decision*, No. IT-94-1-AR72, para. 134.

as dedicated to religion or education."[61] Although the *Blaškić Indictment* dealt mainly with institutions dedicated to religion, when Article 3(d) is considered in its entirety, the same reasoning can be applied to institutions dedicated to charity, art, or science, historic monuments, and works of art and science. It could be argued, however, that Article 3(d) specifically limits protection to the sites enumerated in the provision and does not apply to other aspects of cultural property, such as those listed in Article 1 of the 1954 Hague Convention.[62] The *Blaškić Trial Judgment* also held that at the time of the acts, the sites must not have been "used for military purposes" or within "the immediate vicinity of military objectives."[63] Subjecting the direct protection of cultural property to the uncertain parameters of military necessity is a drawback added to the already burdensome requirement of establishing a nexus between the alleged crimes and the armed conflict.

IV. INDIRECT PROTECTION

Articles providing indirect protection mention neither cultural property per se nor its components. Rather, they afford protection through that provided to civilian objects[64] and through the more anthropocentric crime of persecution.[65]

A. *Article 2(d) of the Statute: Grave Breaches of the Geneva Conventions of 1949*

Indictments use a variety of language to allege a grave breach of the Geneva Conventions of 1949 with regard to crimes involving cultural property. Common phrases include: "destruction of property,"[66] "extensive destruction of property,"[67] "appropriation of property,"[68] and "unlawful and wanton extensive destruction and appropriation of property not justified by military necessity."[69] Article 2(d) itself states:

---

61. *Blaškić Trial Judgment*, No. IT-95-14-T, para. 185.
62. 1954 Hague Convention, supra note 28, at 242.
63. *Blaškić Trial Judgment*, No. IT-95-14-T, para. 185.
64. *See* discussion *infra* Parts IV.A and IV.B.
65. *See* discussion *infra* Part IV.C.
66. *Karadžić Indictment*, 1995 ICTY Y.B. 215, No. IT-95-5, Count 7, *available at* http://www.un.org/icty/indictment/english/kar-ii950724e.htm; The Prosecutor v. Ivica Rajić (Indictment), No. IT-95-1, Counts 2, 5 (ICTY 1995), *available at* http://www.un.org/icty/indictment/english/raj-ii950829e.htm [hereinafter *Rajić Indictment*].
67. *Blaškić Indictment*, No. IT-95-14-T, para. 10, Count 11 (ICTY 1997), *available at* http://www.un.org/icty/indictment/english/bla-2ai970425e.htm; *Kordić Indictment*, No. IT-95-14/2, paras. 55, 56, Counts 37, 40 (ICTY 1998), *available at* http://www.un.org/icty/indictment/english/kor-1ai980930e.htm; *Naletilić Indictment*, No. IT-98-34-I, Count 19 (ICTY 1998), *available at* http://www.un.org/icty/indictment/english/nal-ii981221e.pdf.
68. *Karadžić Indictment*, No. IT-95-5, para. 43, Count 8.
69. *Brđanin Indictment*, No. IT-99-36, Count 10, *available at* http://www.un.org/icty/ind-e.htm.

> The International Tribunal shall have the power to prosecute persons committing or ordering to be committed grave breaches of the Geneva Conventions of 12 August 1949, namely the following acts against persons or property protected under the provisions of the relevant Geneva Convention: . . .
>
> (d) extensive destruction and appropriation of property, not justified by military necessity and carried out unlawfully and wantonly.[70]

The language used by the indictments illustrates various ways to apply this article. Since Article 2(d) does not refer either to cultural property or its components, this section will analyze the general scope and conditions of applicability of Article 2(d) before examining its application to crimes relating to cultural property.

1. Scope and Conditions of Applicability

Unlike Article 3 which applies to both international and non-international armed conflicts, Article 2 applies only when the conflict is international.[71] After establishing the international character of a conflict, the court must look for a nexus between the alleged crimes and the armed conflict.[72]

Article 2(d) imports into the Statute one of the grave breaches enumerated in Article 147 of Geneva Convention IV.[73] The "grave breaches must be perpetrated against persons or property covered by the 'protection' of any of the Geneva Conventions of 1949."[74] Article 53 of Geneva Convention IV prohibits an occupying power from extensively destroying property without the justification of military necessity.[75] In keeping with the requirement that the conflict be international, this protection is restricted to property within

---

70. *Report of the Secretary-General, supra* note 11, at 36.
71. *See Tadić Jurisdiction Decision*, No. IT-94-1-AR72, paras. 79–84 (ICTY 1995), *available at* http://www.un.org/icty/tadic/appeal/decision-e/51002.htm; The Prosecutor v. Tadić (Appeal Judgment), No. IT-94-1-A, para. 80 (ICTY 1999), *available at* http://www.un.org/icty/tadic/appeal/judgement/main.htm [hereinafter *Tadić Appeal Judgment*].
72. *See supra* Part III.A.
73. Article 147 of Geneva Convention IV provides:
   Grave breaches to which the preceding Article relates shall be those involving any of the following acts, if committed against persons or property protected by the present Convention: wilful killing, torture or inhuman treatment, including biological experiments, wilfully causing great suffering or serious injury to body or health, unlawful deportation or transfer or unlawful confinement of a protected person, compelling a protected person to serve in the forces of a hostile Power, or wilfully depriving a protected person of the rights of fair and regular trial prescribed in the present Convention, taking of hostages except *extensive destruction and appropriation of property, not justified by military necessity and carried out unlawfully and wantonly.*
Geneva Convention IV, *supra* note 55, at 388 (emphasis added).
74. *Blaškić Trial Judgment*, No. IT-95-14-T, para. 74 (ICTY 2000), *available at* http://www.un.org/icty/blaskic/trialc1/judgement/index.htm.
75. *See id.* para. 148.

the occupied territory.[76] "In order to dissipate any misconception in regard to the scope of Article 53 it must be pointed out that the property referred to is not accorded general protection; the Convention merely provides here for its protection in occupied territory."[77] Applying this rule, the Trial Chamber in *Blaškić* agreed with the prosecution's submission that enclaves in Bosnia and Herzegovina that were dominated by Bosnian Croat armed forces (HVO, or Croatian Defense Council)[78] constituted an occupied territory and that the Republic of "Croatia played the role of Occupying Power through the overall control it exercised over the HVO."[79] For similar facts with the same time frame and geographic scope,[80] however, the *Kordić* Trial Chamber found that Croatia exercised overall control over the HVO in central Bosnia,[81] but the territory controlled by the HVO did not constitute occupied territory.[82] Having examined the general conditions under which

---

76. OSCAR M. UHLER ET AL., INT'L COMM. OF THE RED CROSS, THE GENEVA CONVENTIONS OF 12 AUGUST 1949: COMMENTARY IV 301 (Jean C. Pictet ed., Ronald Griffin & C.W. Dumbleton trans., 1958) [hereinafter COMMENTARY ON GENEVA CONVENTION IV]; *see also Blaškić Trial Judgment*, No. IT-95-14-T, para. 148. Since the Geneva Conventions do not define the term "occupied territory," the *Kordić* Trial Chamber referred to and accepted the definition provided by customary international law. Article 42 of the Hague Regulations provides that a "'[t]erritory is considered occupied when it is actually placed under the authority of the hostile army. The occupation extends only to the territory where such authority has been established and can be exercised.'" The Prosecutor v. Dario Kordić and Mario Čerkez (Trial Judgment), No. IT-95-14/2-T, paras. 338–39 (ICTY 2001), *available at* http://www.un.org/icty/kordic/trialc/judgement/index.htm [hereinafter *Kordić Trial Judgment*] (quoting Hague Convention (IV) and Regulations, *supra* note 24, Annex, art. 42, at 2306).
77. COMMENTARY ON GENEVA CONVENTION IV, *supra* note 76, at 301.
78. This indictment charged Colonel Blaškić, the Commander of the Central Bosnia Operative Zone of the HVO, on the basis of both individual and superior responsibilities (respectively Articles 7(1) and 7(3) of the ICTY Statute, *Report of the Secretary-General, supra* note 11, at 38–39) for serious violations of international humanitarian law against Bosnian Muslims in Bosnia and Herzegovina from May 1992 to January 1994. These violations included persecution (Count 1), unlawful attacks on civilians and civilian objects (Counts 2–4), willful killing and causing serious injury (Counts 5–10), destruction and plunder of property (Counts 11–13), destruction of institutions relating to religion (Count 14), and inhuman treatment, the taking of hostages, and the use of human shields (Counts 15–20). *See generally Blaškić Indictment*, No. IT-95-14-T (ICTY 1997), *available at* http://www.un.org/icty/indictment/english/bla-2ai970425e.htm.
79. *See Blaškić Trial Judgment*, No. IT-95-14-T, para. 149–50.
80. The *Kordić Indictment* charges politician Dario Kordić and military leader Mario Čerkez on the basis of individual and superior responsibilities (Articles 7(1) and 7(3) of the ICTY Statute respectively) for serious violations of international humanitarian law against Bosnian Muslims in Bosnia and Herzegovina between 1991 and 1994. Kordić served as Vice President of the Croatian Community of Herceg-Bosna and of the Croatian Republic of Herceg-Bosna and President of the Croatian Democratic Union of Bosnia and Herzegovina, and Mario Čerkez served as Commander of the HVO Viteška Brigade. *Kordić Indictment*, No. IT-95-14/2, paras. 9, 12 (ICTY 1998), *available at* http://www.un.org/icty/indictment/english/kor-1ai980930e.htm. The violations they were charged with included persecution on political, racial, or religious grounds (Counts 1–2); unlawful attacks on civilians and civilian objects (Counts 3–6); willful killing, murder, causing serious injury, inhuman acts, and inhumane treatment (Counts 7–20); imprisonment, inhuman treatment, taking of hostages, and the use of human shields (Counts 21–36); destruction and plunder of property (Counts 37–42); and destruction of institutions dedicated to religion or education (Counts 43–44). *See generally id.*
81. *Kordić Trial Judgment*, No. IT-95-14/2-T, para. 145.
82. *Id.* para. 808. This type of finding may have far reaching consequences. Based on its finding that the property destroyed was not located in occupied territory, the Trial Chamber found that the offenses of extensive destruction of property as a grave breach of the Geneva Conventions under Article 2(d) of the

Article 2(d) applies, this Article will now focus on its specific application to crimes against cultural property.

2. Elements of the Offenses with Regard to Cultural Property

Geneva Convention IV prohibits an occupying power from destroying movable and immovable property "except when such destruction is rendered absolutely necessary for military operations."[83] To constitute a grave breach under this provision, the destruction must be extensive, unlawful, wanton, and unjustified by military necessity.[84] The scope of "extensive" depends on the facts of the case. A single act, such as the destruction of a hospital, may suffice to characterize as an offense under Article 2(d).[85] It remains unclear, however, whether one can analogize cultural property to a hospital. Article 27 of the Hague Regulations and Articles 8(2)(b)(ix) and 8(2)(e)(iv) of the ICC Statute mention "hospitals and places where the sick and wounded are collected" together with the components of cultural property.[86] If cultural property were given weight equal to a hospital, as suggested by those articles, the destruction of a single piece of cultural property might also qualify as an offense under Article 2(d).

The *Kordić Trial Judgment* described two distinct situations where the extensive destruction of property constitutes a grave breach.[87] The first situation is "where the property destroyed is of a type accorded general protection under the Geneva Conventions of 1949,[88] regardless of whether or not it is situated in occupied territory." The second situation is "where the property destroyed is accorded protection under the Geneva Conventions of 1949,[89] on account of its location in occupied territory" but only if destruction is not justified by military necessity and occurs on a large scale.[90] While the general protection applies to health-related objects, cultural property, when con-

---

Statute were "not made out"; it found the defendants not guilty on Counts 37 and 40 of the Indictment. *Id.* para. 808 and Disposition.

83. COMMENTARY ON GENEVA CONVENTION IV, *supra* note 76, at 601.
84. *Id.*
85. *Id.*
86. *See supra* Part II.B.1.
87. In both situations, the perpetrator must have acted with the "intent to destroy the property in question or in reckless disregard of the likelihood of its destruction." *Kordić Trial Judgment*, No. IT-95-14/2-T, paras. 341 (ICTY 2001), *available at* http://www.un.org/icty/kordic/trialc/judgement/index.htm.
88. *See, e.g.*, Geneva Convention I, *supra* note 55, chs. 3, 5, 6, at 44, 52, 54 (protecting medical units, buildings and material, and vehicles and aircraft); Geneva Convention II, *supra* note 55, arts. 22, 38, at 100, 108 (protecting hospital and medical transport ships). Article 18 of Geneva Convention IV provides that "[c]ivilian hospitals organized to give care to the wounded and sick, the infirm and maternity cases, may in no circumstances be the object of an attack, but shall in all times be respected and protected by the Parties to the conflict." Geneva Convention IV, *supra* note 55, at 300.
89. Even with regard to this type of property, however, the Conventions identify circumstances where the general protection will cease. *See, e.g.*, Geneva Convention I, *supra* note 55, arts. 21, 33, 36, at 46, 53, 54 (medical units, buildings and material, and medical aircraft, respectively); Geneva Convention II, *supra* note 55, art. 34, at 104 (hospital ships).
90. *Kordić Trial Judgment*, No. IT-95-14/2-T, paras. 341, 808.

sidered a type of civilian object, receives the second, more limited kind of protection. If cultural property could be analogized to hospitals, as suggested above, it would be covered by a very high degree of protection. Even then, however, the question remains as to which aspects of the general protection would apply to the protection of cultural property. Would it be its territorial aspect (i.e., protection beyond occupied territories), its military necessity aspect (i.e., prohibition of destruction regardless of military necessity), or its scale of destruction aspect (i.e., destruction of a single piece enough for a grave breach)? This broader type of protection would most likely embrace at least the third aspect because each piece of cultural property is unique and therefore people protest the loss of even a single piece of cultural property.

In sum, Article 2(d) has limited scope and conditions of applicability. It remains subject to the definition of military necessity. Moreover, it only applies to an occupied territory in the context of international armed conflict if a nexus between the alleged crimes and the armed conflict exists.

B. Articles 3(b), 3(c), and 3(e) of the Statute: Violation of the Laws or Customs of War

A number of indictments refer to the protection provided to civilian objects and/or to unlawful methods of combat. They use phrases such as: "plunder of public or private property,"[91] "plunder of public or private property,"[92] "deliberate attack on the civilian population and wanton destruction of the village,"[93] "unlawful attack on civilian objects,"[94] "wanton destruction not justified by military necessity,"[95] "wanton destruction of cities, towns or villages, or devastation not justified by military necessity,"[96] and "devastation not justified by military necessity."[97] These indictments cite to sections (b), (c), and (e) of Article 3 of the Statute, which provide:

---

91. *Karadžić Indictment*, 1995 ICTY Y.B. 216, No. IT-95-5, para. 43, Count 9, *available at* http://www.un.org/icty/indictment/english/kar-ii950724e.htm; *Blaškić Indictment*, No. IT-95-14-T, para. 10 Count 13 (ICTY 1997), *available at* http://www.un.org/icty/indictment/english/bla-2ai970425e.htm; *Naletilić Indictment*, No. IT-98-34-I, Count 21 (ICTY 1998), *available at* http://www.un.org/icty/indictment/english/nal-ii981221e.pdf.
92. *Kordić Indictment*, No. IT-95-14/2, Counts 39, 42 (ICTY 1998), *available at* http://www.un.org/icty/indictment/english/kor-1ai980930e.htm.
93. *Rajić Indictment*, No. IT-95-1, Counts 3, 6 (ICTY 1995), *available at* http://www.un.org/icty/indictment/english/raj-ii950829e.htm.
94. *Blaškić Indictment*, No. IT-95-14-T, para. 8, Count 4; *Kordić Indictment*, No. IT-95-14/2, para. 40, 41, Counts 4, 6.
95. *Kordić Indictment*, No. IT-95-14/2, para. 55, 56, Counts 38, 41; *Naletilić Indictment*, No. IT-98-34-I, Count 20.
96. *Brđanin Indictment*, No. IT-99-36, Count 11, *available at* http://www.un.org/icty/ind-e.htm.
97. *Blaškić Indictment*, No. IT-95-14-T, para. 8, 10, Counts 2, 12.

> The International Tribunal shall have the power to prosecute persons violating the laws or customs of war. Such violations shall include, but not be limited to: . . .
>
> (b) wanton destruction of cities, towns or villages, or devastation not justified by military necessity;
>
> (c) attack, or bombardment, by whatever means, of undefended towns, villages, dwellings, or buildings; . . .
>
> (e) plunder of public or private property.

In order to examine the application of this article to the protection of cultural property in the former Yugoslavia, this study analyzes the scope and conditions of applicability of Article 3 as determined by the ICTY case law.

1. Scope and Conditions of Applicability

The scope and conditions of applicability of Articles 3(b), 3(c), and 3(e) are the same as those of Article 3(d), which provided direct protection for cultural property.[98] While also indirect, the protective measures implied in Articles 3(b), 3(c), and 3(e) have two advantages over Article 2(d), which dealt with grave breaches. First, they have a wide scope because they apply to both international and non-international armed conflicts. Second, their enumerated list of violations is not exhaustive. Despite their broader scope, however, Articles 3(b), 3(c), and 3(e) present the same difficulty as Article 2(d). They require the establishment of a nexus between the alleged crimes and the armed conflict.

2. Elements of the Offences with Regard to Cultural Property

Article 3(b) of the Statute prohibits the devastation of property not justified by military necessity. Under this rule, the destruction of property, which could include cultural property, is punishable if it was intentional or "the foreseeable consequence of the act of the accused."[99] Therefore, both military necessity and the perpetrator's intention, however broadly interpreted, limit the protection provided by Article 3(b).[100]

Article 3(c) forbids the attack or bombardment by any means of undefended towns, villages, dwellings, or buildings. It thus protects cultural property when it is an integral part of these sites. The provision makes a distinction between civilian objects, which cannot be attacked, and military

---

98. *See supra* Part III.A.
99. *Blaškić Trial Judgment*, No. IT-95-14-T, para. 183 (ICTY 2000), *available at* http://www.un.org/icty/blaskic/trialc1/judgement/index.htm (referring to Count 12 of the *Blaškić Indictment* which pertains to Article 3(b) of the Statute).
100. *See supra* Part III.A.

objectives. Unfortunately, the Geneva Conventions refer to but do not define "military objective."[101]

Other instruments offer guidance for making this distinction. Article 8(1) of the 1954 Hague Convention offers a partial definition, which provides that "a limited number" of cultural sites

> may be placed under special protection . . . provided that they:
> (a) are situated at an adequate distance from any large industrial centre or from any important military objective constituting a vulnerable point, such as, for example, an aerodrome, [etc.] . . .
> (b) are not used for military purposes.[102]

This definition has limited value because it merely provides examples, such as an aerodrome, of what can constitute a military objective. Additional Protocol I's Article 52(2), "General Protection of Civilian Objects," narrows the definition of military objectives to "those objects which by their nature, location, purpose or use make an effective contribution to military action and whose total or partial destruction, capture or neutralization, in the circumstances ruling at the time, offers a definite military advantage."[103] Finally, Article 52(3) establishes a presumption against finding ordinary civilian objects to be used for military purposes;[104] places that constitute or shelter cultural property must be presumed to serve civilian purposes. Thus the main challenge of Article 3(c) lies in distinguishing between civilian objects and military objectives, which are poorly defined in international instruments.

The notion of cultural property damage embraces not only its physical destruction, but also acts of plunder likely to lead to its illegal export and/or sale. The *Blaškić Trial Judgment* held that Article 3(e)'s "prohibition on the wanton appropriation of enemy public or private property extends to both isolated acts of plunder for private interest and to 'the organized seizure of property undertaken within the framework of a systematic economic exploitation of occupied territory.'"[105] The *Čelebići Trial Judgment* defined plunder as "all forms of unlawful appropriation of property in armed conflict for which individual criminal responsibility attaches under international law,

---

101. *See, e.g.*, Article 18 (on the "Protection of Hospitals") of Geneva Convention IV which, in its last paragraph, provides, "In view of the dangers to which hospitals may be exposed by being close to military objectives, it is recommended that such hospitals be situated as far as possible from such objectives." Geneva Convention IV, *supra* note 55, at 300.

102. 1954 Hague Convention, *supra* note 28, at 246.

103. *Id.*

104. *Id.* ("In case of doubt whether an object which is normally dedicated to civilian purposes, such as a place of worship . . . is being used to make an effective contribution to military action, it shall be presumed not to be so used.").

105. *Blaškić Trial Judgment*, No. IT-95-14-T, para. 184 (ICTY 2000), *available at* http://www.un.org/icty/blaskic/trialc1/judgement/index.htm.

including those acts traditionally described as 'pillage.'"[106] Whether isolated or organized, the plunder of cultural property is punishable.

C. *Article 5(h)—Persecution: A Crime Against Humanity*

Under the category of crimes against humanity, a number of indictments refer to "persecutions on political, racial [and/or] religious grounds"[107] in order to allege crimes involving damage to cultural property. In Article 5 of the Statute, the subcategory of persecution appears along with those of "murder," "extermination," "enslavement," "deportation," "imprisonment," "torture," "rape," and "other inhumane acts."[108] More specifically, Article 5(h) of the Statute states:

> The International Tribunal shall have the power to prosecute persons responsible for the following crimes when committed in armed conflict, whether international or internal in character, and directed against any civilian population: . . .
>
> (h) persecutions on political, racial and religious grounds.[109]

To examine how the crime of persecution can be linked to damage inflicted to cultural property is to determine the scope and the conditions of applicability of this crime.

---

106. *Čelebići Trial Judgment*, No. IT-96-21-T, para. 591 (ICTY 1998), *available at* http://www.un.org/icty/celebici/trialc2/judgement/main.htm.
107. The Prosecutor v. Duško Tadić (Indictment), No. IT-94-1, Count 1 (ICTY 1999), *available at* http://www.un.org/icty/indictment/english/tad-2ai951214e.htm [hereinafter *Tadić Indictment*]; The Prosecutor v. Blagoje Simić (Second Amended Indictment), No. IT-95-9, Count 1 (ICTY 1998), *available at* http://www.un.org/icty/indictment/english/sim-2ai981211e.htm; *Blaškić Indictment*, No. IT-95-14-T, para. 7, Count 1 (ICTY 1997), *available at* http://www.un.org/icty/indictment/english/bla-2ai970425e.htm; *Kordić Indictment*, No. IT-95-14/2, Counts 1, 2 (ICTY 1998), *available at* http://www.un.org/icty/indictment/english/kor-1ai980930e.htm; The Prosecutor v. Zoran Kupreškić (Amended Indictment), No. IT-95-16, Count 1 (ICTY 1998), *available at* http://www.un.org/icty/indictment/english/kup-1ai980209e.htm\ [hereinafter *Kupreškić Indictment*]; The Prosecutor v. Mitar Vasiljević (Indictment), No. IT-98-32, Count 2 (ICTY 1998), *available at* http://www.un.org/icty/indictment/english/vas-ii000125e.htm; The Prosecutor v. Radislav Krstić (Indictment), No. IT-98-33, Count 6 (ICTY 1998), *available at* http://www.un.org/icty/indictment/english/krs-ii981102e.htm; *Naletilić Indictment*, No. IT-98-34-I, Count 1 (ICTY 1998), *available at* http://www.un.org/icty/indictment/english/nal-ii981221e.pdf; *Brđanin Indictment*, No. IT-99-36, Count 3, *available at* http://www.un.org/icty/ind-e.htm; The Prosecutor v. Slobodan Milošević (Indictment), No. IT-99-37, Count 4 (ICTY 1999) *available at* http://www.un.org/icty/indictment/english/mil-ii990524e.htm; The Prosecutor v. Momčilo Krajišnik (Indictment), No. IT-00-39-I, Count 7 (ICTY 2000), *available at* http://www.un.org/icty/indictment/english/kra-1ai000321e.htm.
108. *Report of the Secretary-General*, *supra* note 11, at 38.
109. *Id.*

1. Scope and Conditions of Applicability

Unlike Article 5 of the Statute, other international instruments, such as the Report of the Secretary-General, Article 3 of the International Criminal Tribunal for Rwanda (ICTR) Statute, and Article 7 of the ICC Statute do not require the existence of an armed conflict as an element of the definition of a crime against humanity.[110] According to the *Blaškić Trial Judgment*, however, while the ICTY does not include armed conflict in its definition of a crime against humanity, it makes it a condition for punishment by the Tribunal.[111] The *Tadić Appeal Judgment* states, "the armed conflict requirement is a *jurisdictional* element, 'not a substantive element of the *mens rea* of crimes against humanity.'"[112] Thus, while the requirement that there be an armed conflict is a condition for charging under Articles 2 and 3 of the Statute, which enumerate war crimes, it simply constitutes a condition for jurisdiction under Article 5.[113] Crimes against humanity may occur outside the context of an armed conflict, but the ICTY must find a nexus with armed conflict in order to have jurisdiction to prosecute.

a. Elements Common to All Crimes Against Humanity: The Widespread or Systematic Attack Against Any Civilian Population

Article 3 of the ICTR Statute,[114] Article 7 of the ICC Statute,[115] and the case law of both ad hoc Tribunals[116] all require an attack to be "widespread or systematic." According to the International Law Commission (ILC), "systematic" means "pursuant to a preconceived plan or policy. The implementation of this plan or policy could result in the repeated or continuous commission of inhumane acts."[117] The *Blaškić Trial Judgment* identified four elements that establish the systematic character of an act: (1) the existence of a political objective, plan, or ideology that aims to "destroy, persecute, or weaken" a community; (2) the commission of a large-scale crime against a civilian group or of repeated and continuous inhumane acts that are related

---

110. *Id.* at 13. *Cf. Akayesu Trial Judgment*, No. ICTR-96-4-T, paras. 563–84 (ICTR 1998), *available at* http://www.ictr.org/ENGLISH/cases/Akayesu/judgement/ akay001.htm; The Prosecutor v. Clément Kayishema, No. ICTR-95-1-T, paras. 119–34 (ICTR 1999), *available at* http://www.ictr.org/ENGLISH/cases/KayishemaRuzindana/judgement/index.htm [hereinafter *Kayishema Trial Judgment*].
111. *See Blaškić Trial Judgment*, No. IT-95-14-T, para. 66 (ICTY 2000), *available at* http://www.un.org/icty/blaskic/trialc1/judgement/index.htm.
112. *Tadić Appeal Judgment*, No. IT-94-1-A, para. 249.
113. *See Tadić Jurisdiction Decision*, No. IT-94-1-AR72, para. 140.
114. S.C. Res. 955, U.N. SCOR, 3452d mtg., Annex, at 4, U.N. Doc. S/RES/955 (1994).
115. ICC Statute, *supra* note 27, at 5.
116. *See Tadić Trial Judgment*, No. IT-94-1-T, para. 648 (ICTY 1997), *available at* http://www.un.org/icty/tadic/trialc2/judgement-e/tad-tj970507e.htm#_Toc387417337; *Akayesu Trial Judgment*, No. ICTR-96-4-T, paras. 579–81 (ICTR 1998), *available at* http://www.ictr.org/ENGLISH/cases/Akayesu/judgement/akay001.htm; *Kayishema Trial Judgment*, No. ICTR-95-1-T, para. 123 (ICTR 1999), *available at* http://www.ictr.org/ENGLISH/cases/KayishemaRuzindana/judgement/index.htm.
117. Report of the International Law Commission on the Work of Its Forty-Eighth Session, U.N. GAOR, 51st Sess., Supp. No. 10, at 94, U.N. Doc. A/51/10 (1996) [hereinafter 1996 ILC Report].

to each other; (3) reliance on significant public or private, military or non-military resources; and (4) the involvement of political and military leaders in the creation of a plan.[118] This plan need be neither "conceived at the highest level of the State,"[119] nor declared expressly or clearly.[120] It may be presumed from the occurrence of a series of events, such as significant acts of violence or "the destruction of non-military property, in particular, sacral sites."[121]

The "widespread" character of a crime against humanity, generally a matter of quantity, depends on the scale of the acts perpetrated and on the number of victims. The ILC considers acts "large-scale" if they are "directed against a multiplicity of victims."[122] This definition seems to exclude from crimes against humanity "an isolated inhumane act committed by a perpetrator acting on his own initiative and directed against a single victim."[123] Nevertheless, a crime may be considered widespread or committed on a large scale if it has "the cumulative effect of a series of inhumane acts or the singular effect of an inhumane act of extraordinary magnitude."[124] It is impossible to define the quantitative criterion since no threshold test has been developed to determine whether an act qualifies as "widespread or systematic."

Relying on the practices of both ad hoc Tribunals,[125] the Report of the Secretary-General,[126] Article 7(1) of the ICC Statute,[127] and the work of the ILC,[128] the *Blaškić Trial Judgment* asserted that the criteria of scale and systematic character "are not necessarily cumulative." In practice, however, they are often inextricably linked, because the combination of a widespread at-

---

118. *Blaškić Trial Judgment*, No. IT-95-14-T, para. 203 (ICTY 2000), *available at* http://www.un.org/icty/blaskic/trialc1/judgement/index.htm; *Report of the Secretary-General*, *supra* note 11, at 13. *See also Tadić Trial Judgment*, No. IT-94-1-T, para. 648; *Akayesu Trial Judgment*, No. ICTR-96-4-T, para. 580; *Kayishema Trial Judgment*, No. ICTR-95-1-T, para. 123.
119. *See Blaškić Trial Judgment*, No. IT-95-14-T, paras. 204, 205; *Tadić Trial Judgment*, No. IT-94-1-T, para. 654; *Kayishema Trial Judgment*, No. ICTR-95-1-T, para. 126; *Akayesu Trial Judgment*, No. ICTR-96-4-T, para. 580; 1996 ILC Report, *supra* note 117, at 93.
120. *See Blaškić Trial Judgment*, No. IT-95-14-T, para. 204; *Tadić Trial Judgment*, No. IT-94-1-T, para. 653.
121. *See Blaškić Trial Judgment*, No. IT-95-14-T, para. 204.
122. 1996 ILC Report, *supra* note 117, at 94–95.
123. *Id.* at 95.
124. *Id.*
125. *Blaškić Trial Judgment*, No. IT-95-14-T, para. 207, *citing* The Prosecutor v. Mile Mrkšić (Review of the Indictment Pursuant to Article 61 of the Rules of Procedure and Evidence), No. IT-95-13-R61, para. 30 (ICTY 1996); *Tadić Trial Judgment*, No. IT-94-1-T, paras. 646–47; *Akayesu Trial Judgment*, No. ICTR-96-4-T, para. 579; *Kayishema Trial Judgment*, No. ICTR-95-1-T, para 123.
126. *Blaškić Trial Judgment*, No. IT-95-14-T, para. 207, *citing Report of the Secretary-General*, *supra* note 11, para. 48.
127. *Blaškić Trial Judgment*, No. IT-95-14-T, para. 207, *citing* Article 7(1) of the ICC Statute, *supra* note 27, at 5.
128. *Blaškić Trial Judgment*, No. IT-95-14-T, para. 207, *citing* 1996 ILC Report, *supra* note 117, at 94–95.

tack and a large number of victims generally requires a certain amount of planning or organization.[129]

Finally, crimes against humanity are committed not only against civilians but also against former combatants who have ceased to participate in hostilities at the time of the crimes.[130] An intentionally targeted civilian population continues to qualify as such even if soldiers are present within that population.[131]

b. Elements Specific to the Crime of Persecution

i. Actus Reus

Although the Statutes of the IMT and both ad hoc Tribunals sanction political, racial, and religious persecution under crimes against humanity, they fail to define this subcategory. The *Kupreškić Trial Judgment* defines persecution as "the gross or blatant denial, on discriminatory grounds, of a fundamental right, laid down in international customary or treaty law, reaching the same level of gravity as the other acts prohibited in Article 5."[132] This broad definition could encompass acts prohibited under other parts of Article 5 and other articles of the Statute as well as acts of "equal gravity and severity" not covered by the Statute.[133] The crime of persecution includes acts "of a physical, economic, or judicial nature that violate an individual's basic or fundamental rights."[134] As a result, it covers attacks against persons and property, including cultural property, which will be discussed in detail below.[135] In the context of Article 5(h), attacks against property often involve the destruction of towns, villages, and other public or private property belonging to a given civilian population or extensive devastation not justified by military necessity and carried out unlawfully, wantonly, and discriminatorily. Attacks against property may also result in the plunder of property, which the court defines as "the unlawful, extensive, and wanton appropriation of property belonging to a particular" entity, such as an individual, state, or "quasi-state" public collective.[136] While often encompassing

---

129. *See Blaškić Trial Judgment*, No. IT-95-14-T, para. 207.
130. *See Akayesu Trial Judgment*, No. ICTR-96-4-T, para. 582 (ICTR 1998), *available at* http://www.ictr.org/ENGLISH/cases/Akayesu/judgement/akay001.htm; *Blaškić Trial Judgment*, No. IT-95-14-T, para. 214.
131. *See* The Prosecutor v. Zoran Kupreškić (Trial Judgment), No. IT-95-16-T, para. 549 (ICTY 2000), *available at* http://www.un.org/icty/kupreskic/trialc2/judgement/index.htm [hereinafter *Kupreškić Trial Judgment*]; *Tadić Trial Judgment*, No. IT-94-1-T, para. 643 (ICTY 1997), *available at* http://www.un.org/icty/tadic/trialc2/judgement-e/tad-tj970507e.htm#_Toc387417337; *Akayesu Trial Judgment*, No. ICTR-96-4-T, para. 582; *Blaškić Trial Judgment*, No. IT-95-14-T, para. 214.
132. *Kupreškić Trial Judgment*, No. IT-95-16-T, para. 621.
133. *Id.* paras. 617, 619.
134. *Id.* para. 616.
135. *See* Part IV.C.2 *infra*.
136. *Blaškić Trial Judgment*, No. IT-95-14-T, para. 234.

a series of acts,[137] persecution may be a single act if it occurs as part of a widespread and systematic attack against a civilian population and there is "clear evidence of the discriminatory intent" described in Article 5(h) of the Statute.[138]

From the text of Article 5 and the *Tadić Appeal Judgment*, it appears that the requirement of discriminatory purpose applies only to persecution.[139] According to the *Tadić Trial Judgment*, discrimination on "political, racial, and religious grounds" (read disjunctively) constitutes a crime against humanity.[140] The *Kupreškić Trial Judgment* finds that persecution may have an identical *actus reus* to other crimes against humanity but distinguishes persecution as "committed on discriminatory grounds."[141] Since some acts alone may not be serious enough to constitute a crime against humanity, discriminatory acts charged as persecution must be examined in context and weighed for their cumulative effect.[142]

ii. Mens Rea

The crime of persecution requires a mental element specific to crimes against humanity in addition to the required criminal intent.[143] "The perpetrator must knowingly participate in a widespread or systematic attack against a civilian population" with the intent to discriminate on political, racial, or religious grounds.[144] Neither Article 5 of the ICTY Statute[145] nor Article 3 of the ICTR Statute[146] defines the *mens rea* of a crime against humanity. Only Article 7 of the ICC Statute requires that criminal acts be perpetrated "with knowledge" of the "widespread or systematic attack."[147] As evident in the ad hoc Tribunals' case law, however, the *mens rea* of crimes against humanity has two parts: the accused must have knowledge of "the general context in which his acts occur" and of the nexus between his action and that context.[148]

---

137. *Kupreškić Trial Judgment*, No. IT-95-16-T, para. 615(d) ("persecution is commonly used to describe a series of acts rather than a single act.").
138. *Id.* para. 624. *See also Report of the Secretary-General, supra* note 11, at 38.
139. *See Tadić Appeal Judgment*, No. IT-94-1-A, paras. 697, 710 (ICTY 1999), *available at* http://www.un.org/icty/tadic/appeal/judgement/main.htm.
140. *Tadić Trial Judgment*, No. IT-94-1-T, paras. 711–13 (ICTY 1997), *available at* http://www.un.org/icty/tadic/trialc2/judgement-e/tad-tj970507e.htm#_Toc387417337.
141. *See Kupreškić Trial Judgment*, No. IT-95-16-T, para. 607.
142. *See id.* at 622.
143. *See Blaškić Trial Judgment*, No. IT-95-14-T, para. 244.
144. *Id.* para. 244.
145. *Report of the Secretary-General, supra* note 11, at 38.
146. S.C. Res. 955, *supra* note 114, at 4.
147. ICC Statute, *supra* note 27, at 5.
148. *See Kayishema Trial Judgment*, No. ICTR-95-1-T, para. 133 (ICTR 1999), *available at* http://www.ictr.org/ENGLISH/cases/KayishemaRuzindana/judgement/index.htm ("[T]o be guilty of crimes against humanity the perpetrator must know that there is an attack on a civilian population and that his act is part of the attack . . ."); *Blaškić Trial Judgment*, No. IT-95-14-T, para. 247; *Tadić Appeal Judgment*, No. IT-94-1-A, para. 248 (ICTY 1999), *available at* http://www.un.org/icty/tadic/appeal/judgement/main.htm; *Tadić Trial Judgment*, No. IT-94-1-T, para. 656 (ICTY 1997), *available at* http://www.

With regard to the second component of the *mens rea*, the *Blaškić Trial Judgment* held that it is not necessary for the accused to "have sought all the elements of that context."[149] The case law of both ad hoc Tribunals requires only knowledge by the accused of the criminal policy or plan.[150] As indicated in the *Blaškić Trial Judgment*, the *mens rea* for a crime against humanity simply requires that the agent "knowingly [take] the risk of participating in the implementation of the ideology, policy, or plan" in the name of which mass crimes are perpetrated. Even if an agent takes a "deliberate risk in the hope that the risk does not cause injury," his conduct equals knowledge.[151] The court can infer the defendant's knowledge of the political context from such factors as "the historical and political circumstances"; "the functions and responsibilities of the accused within the political or military hierarchy"; the scope, gravity, and nature of the crimes; and "the degree to which they are common knowledge."[152]

2. Elements of the Offenses with Regard to Cultural Property

Whether attacks on property constitute persecution depends on the type of property involved. In the *Flick* case, pursuant to the Allied Control Council for Germany's Law No. 10, the American military tribunal held that the compulsory taking of industrial property, even on discriminatory grounds, did not constitute persecution.[153] By contrast, the IMT stated that the per-

---

un.org/icty/tadic/trialc2/judgement-e/tad-tj970507e.htm#_Toc387417337 ("The perpetrator must know of the broader context in which his act occurs.").

149. The accused's knowing participation in a particular context can be inferred from his willingness to take "the risk of participating in the implementation" of a larger plan. *Blaškić Trial Judgment*, No. IT-95-14-T, para. 251. With regard to the commander's responsibility, the Trial Chamber held that the responsibility of questioning the "malevolent intentions of those defining the ideology, policy or plan" that resulted in the commission of a mass crime is incumbent upon the commander who participated in that crime. *Id.* para. 253.

150. *Tadić Trial Judgment*, No. IT-94-1-T, para. 657; *Tadić Appeal Judgment*, No. IT-94-1-A, para. 248; *Kayishema Trial Judgment*, No. ICTR-95-1-T, para. 133. The *Blaškić Trial Judgment*, however, allowed for "indirect malicious intent" (where the perpetrator could predict the outcome although he did not seek it) and "recklessness" (where the perpetrator foresaw the outcome as a probable or possible but not inevitable consequence). *Blaškić Trial Judgment*, No. IT-95-14-T, para. 254.

151. *Id.* paras. 254, 257.

152. *Id.* para. 259. In the *Kordić Trial Judgment*, the Trial Chamber held that
  In practice, it is hard to imagine a case where an accused somehow has the objective knowledge that his or her acts are committed in the context of a widespread or systematic attack against a civilian population, yet remains ignorant of the [discriminatory] grounds on which the attack was launched.
In that case, "any distinction between persecutions and any other crimes against humanity [would] collapse[ ]." *Kordić Trial Judgment*, No. IT-95-14/2-T, para. 218 (ICTY 2001), *available at* http://www.un.org/icty/kordic/trialc/judgement/index.htm. The Trial Chamber also found that "in order to possess the necessary heightened mens rea for the crime of persecution, the accused must have shared the aim of the discriminatory policy: 'the removal of those persons from the society in which they live alongside the perpetrator, or eventually from humanity itself.'" *Id.* para. 220 (quoting the *Kupreškić Trial Judgment*, No. IT-95-16-T, para. 634 (ICTY 2000), *available at* http://www.un.org/icty/kupreskic/trialc2/judgement/index.htm).

153. *See* U.S. v. Flick, 6 Nurenberg Military Tribunals 1215 (1949).

secution of the Jews was particularly apparent in, for example, the burning and demolishing of synagogues. The court convicted Alfred Rosenberg of war crimes and crimes against humanity for his involvement with "a system of organized plunder of both public and private property throughout the invaded countries;"[154] following Hitler's orders, Rosenberg established the *Einsatzstab Rosenberg*, which looted museums and libraries and stole collections and masterpieces of art.[155] Defendant Julius Streicher was found guilty of crimes against humanity, including the demolition of the Nuremberg synagogue.[156] In the *Eichmann* case many years later, the Jerusalem District Court held that the systematic destruction of synagogues manifested persecution of the Jews.[157] The 1991 and 1996 ILC reports similarly asserted that persecution may encompass the "systematic destruction of monuments or buildings representative of a particular social, religious, cultural or other group" when committed in a systematic manner or on a mass scale.[158]

With regard to Article 5(h), ICTY case law has had the opportunity to deal with crimes against property in general and crimes against cultural property in particular. The *Kupreškić Trial Judgment* held that comprehensive home and property destruction may have inhumane consequences identical to those of forced transfer or deportation and, if done discriminatorily, may constitute persecution.[159] The *Blaškić Trial Judgment* pointed out that persecution may take the form of "acts rendered serious not by their apparent cruelty but by the discrimination they seek to instill within humankind."[160] Thus the crime of persecution encompasses both crimes against persons ("bodily and mental harm and infringements upon individual freedom") and crimes against property ("acts which appear less serious, such as those targeting property") as long as the perpetrators selected victims on political, racial, or religious grounds.[161] In the *Blaškić Indictment*, persecution took "the form of confiscation or destruction" by Bosnian Croat forces of "symbolic buildings ... belonging to the Muslim population of Bosnia-Herzegovina."[162] The Muslim village of Ahmići, for example, not only had "no strategic importance,"[163] but also had "particular significance for the

---

154. United States v. Göring (Rosenberg Judgment), 1 International Military Tribunal: Trial of the Major War Criminals 293, 295 (1946).
155. *Id.*
156. United States v. Göring (Streicher Judgment), 1 International Military Tribunal: Trial of the Major War Criminals 301, 302 (1946).
157. Attorney-General of the Government of Israel v. Adolf Eichmann, 361 I.L.R. 5, para. 57 (Dist. Ct. of Jerusalem 1961) (Isr.).
158. Report of the International Law Commission on the Work of Its Forty-Third Session, U.N. GAOR, 46th Sess., Supp. No. 10, at 268, U.N. Doc. A/46/10 (1991).
159. *Kupreškić Trial Judgment*, No. IT-95-16-T, para. 631 (ICTY 2000), *available at* http://www.un.org/icty/kupreskic/trialc2/judgement/index.htm.
160. *Blaškić Trial Judgment*, No. IT-95-14-T, para. 227 (ICTY 2000), *available at* http://www.un.org/icty/blaskic/trialc1/judgement/index.htm.
161. *Id.* para. 233.
162. *Id.* para. 227.
163. In its findings, the *Kordić* Trial Chamber held that "the HVO deliberately targeted mosques and

Muslim community in Bosnia. Many imams and mullahs came from there. For that reason, Muslims in Bosnia considered Ahmići to be a holy place. In that way, the village of Ahmići symbolised Muslim culture in Bosnia."[164] The Trial Chamber used these factors to establish the discriminatory nature of the attack.

Discussing the destruction of institutions dedicated to religion in that village, the Trial Chamber established a link between the cultural and religious character of the newly built mosque in the hamlet of Donji Ahmići. It noted that the "inhabitants of Ahmići had collected the money to build it and were extremely proud of its architecture."[165] The Trial Chamber further concluded that "[t]he methods of attack and the scale of the crimes committed against the Muslim population or the edifices symbolising their culture sufficed to establish beyond reasonable doubt that the attack was aimed at the Muslim civilian population."[166] The Trial Chamber then quoted a witness according to whom: "apart from the systematic destruction and the religious edifices that had been dynamited, what was most striking was the fact that certain houses remained intact, inhabited even, and one wondered how those islands had been able to survive such a show of violence."[167] By taking into account this testimony, the Trial Chamber emphasized the discriminatory character of the attacks on cultural property.

In its analysis of the events in the central Bosnian municipality of Kiseljak, the *Blaškić* Trial Chamber established the systematic and massive nature of the attacks, which were part of an organized plan approved "at a highlevel of the military hierarchy."[168] A number of events occurred together, such as the systematic looting, damage, and destruction of Muslims' places of worship in most villages.[169] The attacks were also massive and targeted at least ten Muslim villages in the Kiseljak municipality.[170]

Finally, in the "dispositions" of the *Blaškić* and *Kordić* Trial Judgments, the Trial Chambers found defendants Tihomir Blaškić, Dario Kordić, and Mario Čerkez guilty of Counts 1 and 2 of their respective indictments. Accordingly, the Trial Chamber convicted Blaškić of having ordered a crime against humanity, namely persecutions against the Muslim civilians of Bosnia, *inter alia*, through attacks on towns and villages and the destruction and plunder of property and in particular of institutions dedicated to religion and educa-

---

other religious and educational institutions [including] the Ahmići mosque which ... was *not* used for military purposes but was deliberately destroyed by the HVO." *See Kordić Trial Judgment*, No. IT-95-14/2-T, para. 809 (ICTY 2001), *available at* http://www.un.org/icty/kordic/trialc/judgement/index.htm. In the Vitez municipality, four mosques and one Muslim junior seminary were destroyed. *Id.* para. 807(ii).

164. *Blaškić Trial Judgment*, No. IT-95-14-T., para. 411.
165. *Id.* para. 419.
166. *Id.* para. 422.
167. *Id.* para. 425.
168. *See id.* para. 624.
169. *See Blaškić Trial Judgment*, No. IT-95-14-T, para. 625.
170. *See id.* para. 626.

tion.[171] Convicting Kordić and Čerkez, the Trial Chamber held that the persecution of Bosnian Muslims by the Community of Herzeg-Bosna and the HVO "took the form of the most extreme expression of persecution, i.e., of attacking towns and villages with the concomitant destruction and plunder, killing, injuring and detaining of Bosnian Muslims."[172]

Finding an accused guilty of damages inflicted on cultural property under Article 5(h) gives high symbolic value to the protection of cultural property. Such crimes inflicted on cultural property constitute persecution, which is the subcategory of crimes against humanity closest to genocide in terms of *mens rea*. The ILC specifies that its provision on the definition of persecution "would apply to acts of persecution which lacked the specific intent required for the crime of genocide."[173] As stated in the *Kupreškić Trial Judgment*:

> the *mens rea* requirement for persecution is higher than for ordinary crimes against humanity, although lower than for genocide .... Persecution as a crime against humanity is an offence belonging to the same *genus* as genocide .... In both categories what matters is the intent to discriminate .... [F]rom the viewpoint of *mens rea*, genocide is an extreme and most inhuman form of persecution. [W]hen persecution escalates to the extreme form of wilful and deliberate acts designed to destroy a group or part of a group, it can be held that such persecution amounts to genocide.[174]

This analysis demonstrates how close are the boundaries between the crimes of persecution and genocide in terms of the element of intent.

While the parallel between persecution and genocide has the advantage of attaching symbolic value to the protection of cultural property, it also brings the problem of the high threshold for the presentation of evidence relating to both the *actus reus* and *mens rea* of the crime of persecution. For damages inflicted to cultural property to qualify as persecution, the attacks must be directed against a civilian population, widespread or systematic, and done on discriminatory grounds. This definition depends on an anthropocentric view of cultural property. Cultural property is protected not for its own sake, but because it represents a particular group of people.

V. Protection *A Posteriori*

While the direct and indirect protections discussed above relate to the ICTY's subject matter jurisdiction, protection *a posteriori* appears in the judgment and penalties part of the Statute and deals with the results of the

---

171. *See id.* Part VI Disposition.
172. *Kordić Trial Judgment*, No. IT-95-14/2-T, para. 827 (ICTY 2001), *available at* http://www.un.org/icty/kordic/trialc/judgement/index.htm.
173. 1996 ILC Report, *supra* note 117, at 98.
174. *Kupreškić Trial Judgment*, No. IT-95-16-T, para. 636 (ICTY 2000), *available at* http://www.un.org/icty/kupreskic/trialc2/judgement/index.htm.

theft or illegal export of cultural property. The ICTY Statute does not directly address the problem of restitution of stolen or illegally exported cultural property that has been plundered and pillaged. If the term "property" is interpreted broadly, however, then the following provisions could apply to the restitution of cultural property as well.

This protection is *a posteriori* because it goes beyond the punishment mandated by the Statute and aims for restitution of the property. Article 24(3) of the Statute provides: "In addition to imprisonment, the Trial Chambers may order the return of any property and proceeds acquired by criminal conduct, including by means of duress, to their rightful owners."[175] Rule 98 *ter* (B) (on Judgment) of the Rules of Procedure and Evidence (Rules) complements Article 24(3). It provides that:

> If the Trial Chamber finds the accused guilty of a crime and concludes from the evidence that unlawful taking of property by the accused was associated with it, it shall make a specific finding to that effect in its judgment. The Trial Chamber may order restitution as provided in Rule 105.[176]

Article 24(3) of the Statute, as complemented by Rules 98 *ter* (B) and 105, provides for the return of property to its rightful owners. With regard to cultural property, this principle raises the question of who is the rightful owner of stolen cultural property: the state from where it was stolen, the municipality, or the village, in the case of those objects important only for the local inhabitants? Furthermore, what if individuals belonging to the ethnic majority of a state stole cultural property from a minority that no longer lives in the state because it was ethnically cleansed? In such a case, what entity can represent the displaced minority efficiently, or in other words, to whom should the restitution be addressed?

The above provisions, especially Rule 105(A), also raise the issue of preservation of property. Their utility has yet to be tested for dealing with stolen and/or illegally exported cultural property, but in such a case, their effectiveness should not be in doubt. In the face of substantial damage to cultural

---

175. *Report of the Secretary-General, supra* note 11, at 45. *See also id.* at 28.
176. *See also* Rule 105 of the Rules of Procedure and Evidence on "Restitution of Property," which provides:

(A) After a judgement of conviction containing a specific finding as provided in Sub-rule 98 *ter* (B), the Trial Chamber shall, at the request of the Prosecutor, or may, *proprio motu*, hold a special hearing to determine the matter of the restitution of the property or the proceeds thereof, and may in the meantime order such provisional measures for the preservation and protection of the property or proceeds as it considers appropriate.

(B) The determination may extend to such property or its proceeds, even in the hands of third parties not otherwise connected with the crime of which the convicted person has been found guilty.

RULES OF PROCEDURE AND EVIDENCE, BASIC DOCUMENTS OF THE INTERNATIONAL CRIMINAL TRIBUNAL FOR THE FORMER YUGOSLAVIA, at 132, U.N. Doc. IT/32/REV.13, U.N. Sales No. E/F-98-III-P-1 (1998), *available at* http://www.un.org/icty/basic/rpe/IT32_rev18con.htm.

property, however, the utility of these provisions becomes extremely limited. Even if rebuilding a private house may not be an insurmountable task, the restoration of ancient frescoes that were intentionally blown up is a significantly harder undertaking.[177]

As analyzed in this Part, the ICTY Statute addresses the problem of stolen and illegally exported cultural property, but through a skeletal body of law instead of a comprehensive set of provisions. The most significant challenges that the ICTY faces are the identification of property's rightful owners and the actual restoration of damaged cultural property.

VI. CONCLUSION

The insertion in the ICTY Statute of crimes pertaining to cultural property, whether directly or indirectly, was a major step toward strengthening previous international instruments' protection of cultural property in times of armed conflict. The inclusion in ICTY indictments of criminal charges addressing damages to cultural property concretized this step. Finally, the ICTY's conviction of defendants for crimes involving cultural property was a remarkable achievement because it demonstrated the importance of the protection of cultural property in times of armed conflict. The *Blaškić* and *Kordić Trial Judgments* are the ICTY's most comprehensive judgments for offenses concerning cultural property because of the scale of the armed conflict and the allegations contained in the corresponding indictments.[178] The judgments' dispositions cover—and condemn—the violations of both direct and indirect protections reviewed in the present study.[179] While the ICTY has been successful in prosecuting and punishing crimes related to cultural

---

177. The current techniques for restoring art damaged in armed conflicts were developed in Italy in the post–World War II period. The first and most extensive campaign of restoring frescoes lasted from 1944 to 1958 and concerned the fourteenth- to fifteenth-century fresco cycle in the Camposanto (burial ground) in Pisa, which had been seriously damaged during a fire in July 1944. *See generally* CLARA BARACCHINI & ENRICO CASTELNUOVO, IL CAMPOSANTO DI PISA 201–12, ill. 88–91 (1996). By 1957, the fragments of the fifteenth-century *Tabernacolo di Mercatale* in Prato, Tuscany, which had been destroyed during an aerial bombardment in March 1944, had also been reassembled. *See* CESARE BRANDI ET AL., SAGGI SU FILIPPINO LIPPI 18, 92, ill. 41 (1957).

178. *See supra* note 78 and 80.

179. The Trial Chamber found Tihomir Blaškić guilty of persecution for, *inter alia*, "attacks on towns and villages . . . [and] the destruction and plunder of property and, in particular, of institutions dedicated to religion or education." The Trial Chamber also found Blaškić committed a grave breach under Article 2(d) for extensive destruction of property and violations of Article 3 for unlawful attack on civilian objects, Article 3(b) for devastation not justified by military necessity, Article 3(e) for plunder of public or private property, and Article 3(d) for destruction or willful damage done to institutions dedicated to religion or education. *See Blaškić Trial Judgment*, No. IT-95-14-T, Part VI Disposition (ICTY 2000), *available at* http://www.un.org/icty/blaskic/trialc1/judgement/index.htm. The *Kordić* Trial Chamber found both Dario Kordić and Mario Čerkez guilty of persecution under Article 5(h), a violation of the laws or customs of war under Article 3 for unlawful attack on civilian objects, a violation of the laws or customs of war under Article 3(b) for wanton destruction not justified by military necessity, a violation of the laws or customs of war under Article 3(e) for plunder of public or private property, and a violation of the laws or customs of war under Article 3(d) for destruction or willful damage to institutions dedicated to religion or education. *See Kordić Trial Judgment*, No. IT-95-14/2-T, Part IV Disposition (ICTY 2001), *available at* http://www.un.org/icty/kordic/trialc/judgement/index.htm.

property, a problem remains when one goes beyond punishment and tries to ensure restitution and restoration of cultural property.

The ICTY's prosecution of cultural property crimes is also significant because it blurred the traditional distinction between crimes against persons and crimes against property. The ICTY equates a crime against property to a grave breach of the Geneva Conventions of 1949, a violation of the laws or customs of war, and especially the crime against humanity of persecution. This practice of the ICTY may collapse in the long term the distinction between those two categories of crimes, at least for religious cultural property. Due to the nature of the conflict in the former Yugoslavia, religious symbols constituted the main targets of attacks on cultural property. Very recently, the ICTY demonstrated its willingness to issue indictments charging crimes against other forms of cultural property.[180] The admirable endeavor of making attacks on cultural property a primary crime also has political limits; it might exacerbate the reluctance of great military powers, such as the United States, to ratify the ICC because the fragile nature of cultural property makes it always subject to damage at least collaterally.[181]

The ultimate step, which has yet to be taken by international criminal justice, would be adopt a less anthropocentric approach with regard to cultural property and to indict solely on the basis of damage inflicted on cultural property. This study suggests "less anthropocentric" instead of "not anthropocentric" because cultural property is the product of humans and receives its cultural value from humans. The new type of indictments would depend on two *sine qua non* conditions. First, an international criminal court (either the ICC or another court) would have to find a *prima facie* case of ac-

---

180. *See supra* note 8 and accompanying text. *See also* Press Release, UNESCO, Director-General Welcomes Tribunal's Indictment on Destruction of Heritage in Dubrovnik, No.2001-40 (Mar. 13, 2001), *at* http://www.unesco.org/opi/eng/unescopress/2001/01-40e.shtml. UNESCO Director-General Koïchiro Matsuura "welcomed" the ICTY's inclusion of the destruction of historic monuments in its Dubrovnik indictment. He said,
> This sets a historic precedent as it is the first time since the judgements of the Nürnberg and Tokyo tribunals that a crime against cultural property has been sanctioned by an international tribunal. This indictment concerns a breach of the 1954 Hague Convention for the Protection of Cultural Property in the Event of Armed Conflict . . . . It shows that the international community will not sit idly by and condone crimes against cultural property.

Id. When he stated that "it is the first time since the judgements of the Nürnberg and Tokyo tribunals that a crime against cultural property has been sanctioned by an international tribunal," the Secretary-General probably meant a crime against cultural property registered under the 1954 Convention because, as this Article has shown, the ICTY has already condemned crimes against cultural property for sites not registered under the 1954 Hague Convention.

181. Thus, if a missile hits a target, the risk and amount of damage inflicted collaterally on a cultural site located in the vicinity are higher than to a concrete building situated at the same distance. *See, e.g.,* Michel Bessaguet, *Ravages et Dommages*, GÉO, May 1991, at 213, 217; David A. Meyer, *The 1954 Hague Cultural Property Convention and Its Emergence into Customary International Law*, 11 B.U. INT'L L.J. 349, 376–77 (1993) (explaining that, during Operation Desert Storm, despite the Coalition's care, an ancient temple in Ur, the Biblical city of the prophet Abraham, was collaterally damaged by a Coalition bombing campaign conducted against military targets located in the vicinity). *See also id.* at 365 (explaining that during the 1980–88 Iran-Iraq war the eleventh-century Jomeh (or Jameh) Mosque, located in the Iranian city of Isfahan, was damaged following the explosion of Iraqi Scud missiles).

tual damage inflicted on cultural property. Second, the court would have to perceive the damage as serious enough to be addressed per se for what cultural property is—the memory of humanity.

[17]

The Obligation to Prevent and Avoid Destruction of Cultural Heritage: From Bamiyan to Iraq

Francesco Francioni and Federico Lenzerini

INTRODUCTION

Throughout history, destruction and loss of cultural heritage have constantly occurred as a consequence of fanatic iconoclasm or as "collateral" effects of armed conflicts. As early as 391 A.D., the Roman Emperor Theodosius ordered the demolition of the Temple of Serapis in Alexandria to obliterate the last refuge of non-Christians. In 1992, Indu extremists were intent on the destruction of the sixteenth century Babri Mosque.[1] In more recent times, the Balkan wars have offered us the desolate spectacle of the devastation of Bosnia's mosques, libraries, and the ancient city of Dubrovnik. Extensive looting and forced transfer of cultural objects have accompanied almost every war, including the recent Iraqi war.[2] Aerial bombardments during the Second World War and in the more than one hundred armed conflicts that have plagued humanity since 1945 have contributed to the destruction and disappearance of much cultural heritage of great importance for the countries of origin and for humanity as a whole.

The violent destruction of the great rock sculptures of the Buddhas of Bamiyan by military and paramilitary forces of the Taliban government of Afghanistan in March 2001 could be seen as an ordinary example in this history of cultural infamy. At closer scrutiny, however, the violent acts themselves and the perverse modalities of their execution present various features that are new in the pathology of state behaviour toward cultural heritage.

First, unlike traditional war damage to cultural heritage, which affects the enemy's property, the demolition of the Buddhas of Bamiyan concerns heritage that belonged to the Afghan Nation. They were located in its territory and belonged to its ancient pre-Islamic past.

Second, the purpose of the destruction was not linked in any way to a military objective, but was inspired by the sheer will to eradicate any cultural manifestation of religious or spiritual creativity that did not correspond to the Taliban view of religion and culture.

Third, the modalities of the execution differed considerably from similar destruction that took in the course of recent armed conflicts. For instance, during the Balkan war of the 1990s and during the Iraq – Iran war in the 1980s, extensive destruction of cultural property occurred as a result of wanton bombardment, as in the case of Dubrovnik, or under the impulse of ethnic hatred. In the case of the Afghan Buddhas, the demolition was carefully planned, painstakingly announced to the media all over the world, and cynically documented in all its phases of preparation, bombing, and ultimate destruction.

Fourth, to the knowledge of these writers, the episode in point is the first one of planned, deliberate destruction of cultural heritage of great importance as an act of defiance toward the United Nations (UN) and the international community. It is not a mystery that the Taliban's decision to destroy the Buddhas of Bamiyan came in the wake of the sanctions adopted in 1999 and 2000 against the Afghan government because of their continuing sheltering and training of terrorists and planning of terrorist acts.[3]

Fifth, the destruction of the Buddhas and of other significant collections of pre-Islamic Afghan art took place as an act of narcissistic self-assertion against the pressure of the Director General of UNESCO, Ambassador Matsuura; his special envoy to Kabul, ambassador LaFranche; and the UN Secretary General, Kofi Annan, who all pleaded with the Taliban to reconsider their disgraceful decision to proceed with the destruction of all the statues in the country.[4]

Because of these elements, it is understandable that UNESCO and the international community as a whole

---

[1] See Saikal A. and Thakur R., "Vandalism in Afghanistan and No One to Stop it," in *The International Herald Tribune*, 6 March 2001, available at <http://www.unu.edu/hq/ginfo/media/Thakur38.html>.

[2] See the rich documentation provided by Boylan P., *Review of the Convention for the Protection of Cultural Property in the Event of Armed Conflict*, UNESCO, Paris, 1993.

This chapter is derived from a larger study undertaken by the authors on request by UNESCO in view of the development of an international instrument capable of clarifying in which circumstances deliberate destruction of cultural heritage constitutes a violation of international law (such instrument was finally adopted by the UNESCO General Conference on 17 October 2003 as *Declaration Concerning the Intentional Destruction of Cultural Heritage*). An earlier version of this study was published under the title "The Destruction of the Buddhas of Bamiyan and International Law" in the *European Journal of International Law*, vol. 14, 2003, p. 619–52.

[3] See, in particular, UN Security Council Resolution 1267(1999) of 15 October 1999; Resolution 1333(2000), adopted on 19 December 2000 with only the abstention of Malaysia and China (which provides for the strong condemnation of "the continuing use of the areas of Afghanistan under the control of [...] Taliban [...] for the sheltering and training of terrorists and planning of terrorist acts"); see also Resolution 1363(2001) of 30 July 2001.

[4] See also the appeal issued by ICOMOS and ICOM on 1 March 2001, where it is stated that the act of destruction "[...] would be a total cultural catastrophe. It would remain written in the pages of history next to the most infamous acts of barbarity." For a chronology of international efforts to dissuade the Taliban from carrying out their destructive plan see the Report of the Bureau of the World Heritage Committee, 25th Session, 25–30 June 2001, doc. WHO-2001/CONF.205/10.

reacted to the destruction of the Buddhas with shock.[5] There was great concern for the moral degradation shown by the authors of such acts, and a certain anxiety regarding the role of international law in preventing and suppressing such form of cultural vandalism which, in the words of the UNESCO Director General, can constitute a "crime against culture." This chapter is especially concerned with the latter point. It particularly addresses the question whether and to what extent contemporary international law protects cultural heritage of great importance for humanity against deliberate destruction perpetrated by a State in whose territory such heritage is located.

THE DESTRUCTION OF THE BUDDHAS OF BAMIYAN IN CONTEXT

The Taliban ("The Seekers") was formed in 1994 by a group of graduates of Pakistani Islamic colleges on the border with Afghanistan. The members of the group were led by *Mullah* (village-level religious leader) Mohammed Omar, a man who is said to have lost one of his eyes fighting the Soviets during their occupation of Afghanistan.[6] The Taliban advocated an "Islamic Revolution" in Afghanistan, aimed at the re-establishment of the unity of the country in the framework of the Islamic law *Sharia*.[7] Immediately after their rise, the Taliban were supported by most of the civilian population, which was frustrated by the situation of civil war persisting in the country since the end of 1970s. In particular, Afghan peoples were seduced by the hope of stability and restoration of peace promised by the Taliban, who seemed to be successful in stamping out corruption and improving living conditions.[8] For this reason, from 1994, the Taliban advance to gain effective power over Afghanistan had progressively intensified. At the critical date of the destruction of Buddhas, the Islamic Emirate of Afghanistan, established by the Taliban, covered some ninety to ninety-five percent of the Afghan territory, including the capital, Kabul. The rest of the territory, concentrated in the far northeast of the country, was still under the power of the Islamic State of Afghanistan, headed by the National Islamic United Front for the Salvation of Afghanistan ("United Front" or "Northern Front") that was led by B. Rabbani.[9]

Although at the end of the 1990s, the Taliban movement had gained effective control of the greatest part of the Afghan territory, this control was perceived by the international community as not being sufficient to confer on the Islamic Emirate of Afghanistan the attributes of legitimacy. Only a very small group of states (*i.e.*, Pakistan, Saudi Arabia, and the United Arab Emirates) had recognized the Taliban militia as the legitimate government of Afghanistan. The Afghan UN seat was still retained by the delegation of the Islamic State of Afghanistan,[10] which also retained control of most of the country's embassies abroad. President Rabbani continued to be acknowledged by most members of the international community, including Iran and Russia, as the rightful leader of Afghanistan.

War operations had intensified since June 2000 with the Taliban and the United Front receiving support, respectively, from Pakistan on the one side, and Iran, Russia, and some other former Soviet Republics on the other.[11] Nongovernmental organizations (NGOs) have reported both warring factions as systematically violating international humanitarian law and basic rights of individuals by burning houses, raping women, torturing, and executing peoples suspected of supporting the opposite faction.[12] For this reason, on 23 January 2001, *Amnesty International* urged the United States to support the establishment of an international tribunal for Afghanistan to investigate massacres perpetrated by the warring factions.[13] Afghanistan was estimated to have been at war for more than twenty years as of 2001. One of the worst effects of the conflict is the contamination of the Afghan territory with landmines. The Mine Action Programme for Afghanistan coordinated by the United Nations estimated that a known state area of 715 square kilometres was contaminated by landmines. Of this area, 333 square kilometres are considered as having a vital role for the accomplishment of basic social and economic human activities.[14]

Moreover, according to Human Rights Watch, during the war period, Afghanistan has lost a third of its population, with some 1.5 million peoples estimated to have died and another

---

[5] See, from a general point of view, the condemnation expressed by the UN General Assembly, in its Resolution 55/254 of 11 June 2001, on the protection of religious sites, with regard to "all acts or threat of violence, destruction, damage or endangerment, directed against religious sites as such, that continue to occur in the world."

[6] See "Who is Mullah Mohammad Omar?" at <http://www.afghan-web.com/politics/omar.html>.

[7] See UNHCR, "Background Paper on Refugees and Asylum Seekers from Afghanistan," Geneva, June 1997, at <http://www.unhcr.ch/refworld/country/cdr/cdrafg.htm>, at 2.4.

[8] See "Analysis: Who are the Taleban?" BBC News, 20 December 2000, at <http://news.bbc.co.uk/hi/english/world_south_asia.newsid_144000/144382.stm>.

[9] See Human Rights Watch, "Fueling Afghanistan's War" HRW World Report 2001: Asia Overview, at <http://www.hrw.org/backgrounder/asia/afghanistan/afghbk.htm>.

[10] See, at last, the UN General Assembly First Report of the Credentials Committee of the General Assembly Fifty-fifth session, UN Doc. A/55/537, 1 November 2000, at 6–8. See also Identical letters dated 14 September 2001 from the Permanent Representative of Afghanistan to the United Nations addressed to the Secretary-General and the President of the Security Council, UN doc. A/56/365–S/2001/870 of 17 September 2001.

[11] See Human Rights Watch, *cit.*, note 9.

[12] See Human Rights Watch, *cit.*, note 9; Clark K., "UN accuses Taleban of massacre" BBC News, 20 January 2001, at <http://www.afghan-politics.org>; UN Economic and Social Council, "Question of the Violation of Human Rights and Fundamental Freedoms in Any Part of the World," Report on the Situation of human rights in Afghanistan submitted by Mr. Kamal Hossain, Special Rapporteur, UN Doc. E/CN.4/2001/43, 1 February 2001, at 3 ff. and 41–4.

[13] See "Amnesty International Seeks US Support for Afghanistan International Tribunal," at <http://www.afghan-politics.org>.

[14] See UN General Assembly, "Emergency international assistance for peace, normalcy and reconstruction of war-stricken Afghanistan," Report of the Secretary-General, UN Doc. A/55/348, 31 August 2000, at 46. For a comprehensive survey on the effects of landmines on Afghan people see UN General Assembly, "Situation of human rights in Afghanistan," Note by the Secretary-General, UN Doc. A/55/346, 30 August 2000, at 42–7.

5 million fled as refugees to foreign countries.[15] Despite the promises made by the Taliban, Afghanistan managed in 2001 to reach the world's lowest life expectancy and, together with Somalia, was one of the two hungriest countries in the world.[16]

The persistence of war operations had induced, in the late 1990s, a large monetization of economic and social relations, combined with hyperinflation and the destruction of most of the subsistence economy.[17] Such sudden change produced abject poverty and the transformation of the internal economy into a system where, until recently, a significant part of the national income was obtained by the production of and trade in opium.[18] It may be supposed that by banning production of opium nationwide, the Taliban regime had tried to mitigate its international isolation by meeting one of the main requirements most often reiterated by the community of states. Similarly, the Taliban tried to take steps with regard to the discriminatory policy on grounds of gender, by relaxing the strict ban on female education previously imposed and by reinstituting the celebration of International Women's Day on 8 March.[19] However, this kind of measure, although welcomed, was nearly insignificant in a general context in which the conditions of women in the territories subjected to Taliban domination were of institutionalized virtual slavery.

Gender discrimination, together with a generally dramatic disregard of basic human rights,[20] was one of the consequences of extreme religious intolerance that characterized the Taliban regime. Such intolerance included absolute lack of freedom of expression and a total ban of pictures.[21] It is in this context of obscurantism that a decree promulgated by Mullah Omar on 8 January 2001 applied death penalty to Afghans who converted from Islam to Judaism or Christianity.[22]

Religious extremism and intolerance were not extraneous to the Taliban's decision to promote international terrorism. They hosted and supported Saudi Arabian dissident Osama Bin Laden in his fight against "imperialism of Western countries," especially by making Afghan territory available for hosting his training camps for terrorists.[23] This support was at the origin of the UN Security Council's decision to impose wide economic sanctions against the Taliban[24] and the concomitant downgrading of diplomatic relations between Afghanistan and Saudi Arabia, which, following the Afghan refusal to extradite Bin Laden, recalled its *charge d'affairs* from Kabul.[25] The Taliban leaders' response was that they would not take action against Bin Laden, who was considered a guest in their countries, and that any attempt to "try to change our ideology with economic sanctions will never work, because for us our ideology is first. The sanctions do have an effect, but exactly the wrong effect. The people are suffering."[26]

Even before the adoption of sanctions by the Security Council, the situation in Afghanistan had been the object of discussion within UNESCO with regard to the increasing threats to the cultural heritage of the country. Already in December 1997, the World Heritage Committee, the governing body of the 1972 UNESCO Convention on the protection of world cultural and natural heritage,[27] at its Naples meeting (under the Chairmanship of Professor Francioni) had adopted a resolution expressing concern at the reports about threats by the Taliban regime with regard to the Buddhist statues of Bamiyan. The resolution, unanimously adopted on a proposal by Italy, after having stressed that "the cultural and natural heritage of Afghanistan, particularly the Buddhist statues in Bamiyan [...] for its inestimable value, [has to be considered] not only as part of the heritage of Afghanistan but as part of the heritage of humankind," reads as follows:

"The *World Heritage Committee* [...] 1. *Reaffirms* the sovereign rights and responsibilities, towards the International Community, of

---

[15] See Human Rights Watch, *cit.*, note 9; UNHCR, "Background Paper on Refugees and Asylum Seekers from Afghanistan," *supra*, note 7, at 1.2, according to which, in 1996, the refugee population from Afghanistan was the largest in the world, standing at 2,628,550, whereas the number of internally displaced in Afghanistan reached 1,200,000 as of 31 December 1996. See also UN General Assembly – Security Council, "The situation in Afghanistan and its implications for international peace and security," Report of the Secretary-General, UN Doc. A/55/393–S/2000/875, 18 September 2000, at 39–42; UN General Assembly, "Situation of human rights in Afghanistan," Note by the Secretary-General, UN Doc. A/55/346, 30 August 2000, at 33–7; UN Doc. E/CN.4/2001/43, at 36–9; Finkel D., "The Road of Last Resort," in Washington Post, 18 March 2001, p. A01; Suarez R., "Afghanistan's Agony," *Online NewsHour*, 29 March 2001, at <http://www.afghan-politics.org>.

[16] See Human Rights Watch, *cit.*, note 9. According to World Food Program officials, in 2001, 3.8 million Afghan were facing severe shortage or absolute lack of food (See Suarez, *cit.*, note 15; see also UN Doc. E/CN.4/2001/43, at 53, according to which, in the past two years, Afghanistan's grain production has fallen by more than fifty percent, and now satisfies less than half of the whole national grain requirement); it was estimated that in 2001 the internal food production deficit amounted to 2.3 million tonnes, more than double the figure for 1999 (see UN Doc. A/55/346, at 29). Even before the beginning of the civil war, Afghanistan was among the world's poorest countries, but it did not experience the grinding poverty typical of ex-colonial societies characterized by a foreign economic dependence that generally magnifies social and economic disparities. In fact, it was characterized by a rural society in which human relationships were based on a system of solidarity and mutual help among social groups, which, in principle, maintained a fair distribution of resources (see Rubin B. R., "The Political Economy of War and Peace in Afghanistan," Sweden, 21 June 1999, available at <http://www.afghan-politics.org>, p. 3 f.).

[17] See Rubin, *cit.*, note 16, p. 6.

[18] Afghanistan is estimated to produce seventy-five percent of the world's raw opium, with a harvest estimated at 2,800 tons in 1998 (see Suarez, *cit.*, note 15; Rubin, *cit.*, note 16, p. 10). For the first time, on 27 July 2000, the Taliban supreme leader Mohammed Omar issued a decree imposing a complete ban on opium poppy cultivation in the controlled territory of Afghanistan (see UN Doc. A/55/393–S/2000/875, at 45).

[19] See UN Doc. A/55/346, at 53–54; UN Doc. E/CN.4/2001/43, at 50.

[20] See, in general, UN Doc. A/55/346 and UN Doc. E/CN.4/2001/43.

[21] See UN Doc. E/CN.4/2001/43, at 48.

[22] *Id.*, at 56.

[23] See, *supra*, note 3 and corresponding text.

[24] See UN Security Council Resolution 1333, *cit. supra*, note 3, paras. 4–7; see also UN Press Release SC/6979.

[25] See British Immigration & Nationality Directorate, "Afghanistan Assessment," October 2000, <http://www.ind.homeoffice.gov.uk/default.asp?pageId=162>, at 5.4.34.

[26] These words have been pronounced by the Taliban leader Sayed Rahmatullah Hashimi; see Suarez, *cit.*, note 15.

[27] See *infra*, note 38.

Image 1. Afghan Buddha before the destruction by the Taliban [© 2001 CNN], downloaded from <http://www.institute-for-afghan-studies.org/images/buddha_b1.jpg> (last checked on August 1, 2003).

Image 2. Destruction of Afghan Buddha by the Taliban [© 2001 CNN], downloaded from <http://www.institute-for-afghan-studies.org/images/buddha_d1.jpg> (last checked on August 1, 2003).

each State for the protection of its own cultural and natural heritage; 2. *Calls upon* the International Community to provide all the possible assistance needed to protect and conserve the cultural and natural heritage of Afghanistan under threat; 3. *Invites* the authorities in Afghanistan to take appropriate measures in order to safeguard the cultural and natural heritage of the country; 4. *Further invites* the authorities in Afghanistan to co-operate with UNESCO and the World Heritage Committee with a view to ensuring effective protection of its cultural and natural heritage [...]."[28]

THE TALIBAN'S "CULTURAL TERRORISM"

Unfortunately, the concern expressed by the World Heritage Committee at the Naples meeting proved to be well-founded.

In March 2001, the Taliban regime defiantly announced its decision to put into practice its new form of symbolic politics consisting of the deliberate destruction of cultural heritage representing religious and spiritual tradition different from Islam. Much to the shock of the international community, such decision culminated in the destruction of two ancient Buddha statues, which were carved in sandstone cliffs in the third and fifth centuries A.D. in Bamiyan, about ninety miles West of Kabul.[29] The statues, which stood fifty-three and thirty-six metres tall respectively, probably represented the most important Afghan cultural treasures. According to press agencies, the destruction of the two Buddhas began on

---

[28] See UNESCO, Report of the XXI Session of the World Heritage Committee, Naples, Italy, 1–6 December 1997, doc. WHC-97/CONF.208/17 of 27 February 1998, par. VII.58.

[29] See Hammond N., "Cultural Terrorism," in *The Wall Street Journal*, 5 March 2001, available at <http://hss.fullerton.edu/comparative/wsj_bamian.htm>.

Thursday 1 March 2001.[30] Images 1 and 2, which show one of the two statues before and during smashing operations, remain as historical witness of such outrageous acts against the heritage of humanity.

According to the Taliban themselves, the destruction of the two giant statues was perpetrated in pursuance of an edict issued by their supreme leader *Mullah* Mohammed Omar on 26 February 2001,[31] proclaiming that

"In view of the fatwa (religious edict) of prominent Afghan scholars and the verdict of the Afghan Supreme Court it has been decided to break down all statues/idols present in different parts of the country. This is because these idols have been gods of the infidels, and these are respected even now and perhaps maybe turned into gods again. The real God is only Allah, and all other false gods should be removed."[32]

After the issuance of the order, Mohammed Omar declared that it was to be done for "the implementation of Islamic order."[33] Nevertheless, according to a major expert of Islamic religion, Egyptian Fahmi Howeidy, the Taliban edict was contrary to Islam, given that "Islam respects other cultures even if they include rituals that are against Islamic law."[34] However, despite the difficulties met by Afghan troops in destroying the solid rock carved statues,[35] the Taliban Ambassador in Pakistan, Abdul Salam Saif, confirmed on 6 March 2001 that the destruction of all statues, including the two Buddhas, was being completed.[36]

In addition, according to the Online Center of Afghan Studies, there is clear evidence that the destruction of the two Buddhas was not an isolated incident, but was the peak of a systematic plan, pursued by the Taliban regime, for the complete eradication of the whole Afghan ancient cultural heritage.[37]

After the 11 September terrorist attacks on the United States and the Taliban's refusal to extradite Bin Laden and the suspected terrorists, virtually no country has continued to support the Taliban regime. The antiterror campaign launched by the United States, with the support of many other countries, has led to extensive aerial bombardment of the Taliban military and logistic infrastructure and to their final demise in December 2001. At the time of this writing, a coalition government composed of the various factions opposed to the Taliban has been formed under the presidency of H. Karzai. Although this is a welcome development, it does not absolve the past regime from crimes connected to complicity in mass terrorism and crimes against culture perpetrated by the deliberate destruction of pre-Islamic heritage in Afghanistan.

As has already been pointed out in section 1, the acts of systematic and deliberate destruction of cultural heritage perpetrated by the Taliban raise the question whether such acts are internationally wrongful acts notwithstanding the fact that they are aimed at objects located within the territory and the effective jurisdiction of the acting government. We shall try to address such questions in the following section.

THE DELIBERATE DESTRUCTION OF THE BUDDHA STATUES AS A VIOLATION OF INTERNATIONAL LAW

The evolution of the international protection of cultural heritage that has taken place in the last decades has built upon the idea that cultural heritage is an element of the general interest of the international community. By destroying Afghan cultural heritage, the Taliban regime breached, indeed, a number of international obligations, existing on the basis of both conventional and customary international law. First of all, such destruction gave rise to a breach of duties lying on Afghanistan for its membership to the 1972 World Heritage Convention.[38] According to the Preamble of this Convention,

"deterioration or disappearance of any item of [...] cultural [...] heritage constitutes an harmful impoverishment of the heritage of all the nations of the world."

It is important to point out that, although at the relevant time there were no Afghan properties inscribed on the World Heritage List,[39] article 12 of the Convention expressly states that

"[t]he fact that a property belonging to the cultural or natural heritage has not been included in either of the [World Heritage List or the list of World Heritage in Danger] shall in no way be construed to mean that it does not have an outstanding universal value for purposes other than those resulting from inclusion in these lists."

---

[30] See "Afghan Taliban Have Begun Smashing Statues," *Reuters* agency, Thursday, 1 March 2001, 5:08 A.M. EDT, available at <http://www.afghan-politics.org>.

[31] See "Taliban: Statues Must Be Destroyed," *Associated Press* agency, Monday, 26 February 2001, 6:14 P.M. ET, available at <http://www.afghan-politics.org>.

[32] The text of the edict is available at <http://www.afghan-politics.org> (*Associated Press* source).

[33] See "Kabul defends plan to break statues," *France Press* agency, 27 February 2001, available at <http://www.afghan-politics.org>.

[34] See "Taliban gathers explosive to destroy renowned Buddha statues," *Reuters* agency, Friday, 2 March 2001, 4:18 P.M., available at <http://www.afghan-politics.org>.

[35] See "Taliban gathers explosive to destroy renowned Buddha statues," *supra*, note 34.

[36] See "Taliban stop destruction of the Buddha-Statues," *Reuters* agency, Tuesday, 6 March 2001, 23:05, available at <http://www.afghan-politics.org> (on 6 March 2001, the destruction was suspended for celebrating an Islamic celebration).

[37] See the "Communiqué By the Online Center of Afghan Studies Regarding the Destruction of Afghan National and Archeological Treasures" of 28 February 2001, available at <http://www.afghan-politics.org>.

[38] For the text of the World Heritage Convention (1972 *UNESCO Convention Concerning the Protection of the World Cultural and Natural Heritage*) see the UNESCO Web site, at <http://www.unesco.org/whc/world_he.htm>. Afghanistan ratified the Convention on 20 March 1979 (see <http://www.unesco.org/whc/sp/afg.htm>).

[39] After the destruction of the Buddhas of Bamiyan, the World Heritage Committee inscribed in the List the Minaret and Archaeological Remains of Jam in 2002 (see <http://whc.unesco.org/pg.cfm?cid=31&id_site=211>) and the Cultural Landscape and Archaeological Remains of the Bamiyan Valley (just the one in which the two Buddhas were located) in 2003 (see <http://whc.unesco.org/pg.cfm?cid=31&id_site=208>).

This provision must be read in connection with article 4, which points out that

"the duty of ensuring the [...] protection, conservation, presentation and transmission to future generations of the cultural [...] heritage [...] situated on [the] territory [of each State Party to this Convention], belongs primarily to that State,"

The joint reading of these provisions makes it clear that membership in the World Heritage Convention binds States Parties to conserve and protect their own cultural properties even if they are not inscribed in the World Heritage List. As for the Bamiyan Buddhas, there is no doubt that they were to be considered as included in the concept of cultural heritage relevant to the Convention.[40] Regardless of whether they met the text of "outstanding universal value" set forth in article 1, the Buddhas were certainly "works of monumental sculpture" of generally recognized historical importance. There can be no doubt that the deliberate, wanton destruction of the great Buddhas is inconsistent with the letter and spirit of the 1972 Convention. The World Heritage Committee, in the already cited resolution adopted in 1997, had considered the statues of "inestimable value" and "not only part of the heritage of Afghanistan but as part of the heritage of humankind."[41] In a gesture laden with symbolic value this characterization was confirmed by the World Heritage Committee's decision, in July 2003, to inscribe the remains of the two giants Buddhas and the area of Bamiyan in the World Heritage List, as cultural heritage of outstanding universal value pursuant to the World Heritage Convention. The Committee justified such inscription by reference to the value of the Bamiyan valley as, *inter alia*, an exceptional testimony to the interchange of different cultures and to a cultural tradition that has disappeared, and the statues themselves, although actually destroyed, were to be considered an outstanding representation of Buddhist art.[42]

Because Afghanistan was, at the time of the destruction of the Buddhas of Bamiyan, actually perturbed by a civil war,[43] the present inquiry must turn now to the relevant norms on the protection of cultural heritage during armed conflicts.[44] Several conventional instruments, pertaining both to the protection of cultural heritage and *iure in bello* or humanitarian law, are applicable in this context.[45]

First, the protection of cultural properties was included in the conventions on the laws and customs of war concluded in The Hague between the end of the nineteenth and the beginning of the twentieth century. In particular, article 27 of the Regulations annexed to the Convention IV of 1907[46] provided that

"[i]n sieges and bombardments all necessary steps must be taken to spare, as far as possible, buildings dedicated to religion, art, science, or charitable purposes, historic monuments, hospitals, and places where the sick and wounded are collected, provided they are not being used at the time for military purposes."[47]

The Hague conventions on the laws and customs of war are applicable only to international armed conflicts,[48] and only in the case that *all* belligerent States are parties to the conventions themselves (so-called *si omnes* clause). However, the aforementioned provision demonstrates that, at the time of their adoption, the protection of cultural heritage already constituted a common concern of the international community.[49]

The aforementioned limitations, which greatly impaired the effectiveness of the Hague conventions, were excluded from the 1954 UNESCO Convention for the Protection of Cultural Property in the Event of Armed Conflicts.[50] In

---

[40] See article 1 of the World Heritage Convention (*supra*, note 45). The fact that the Bamyan Buddhas are included in the concept of cultural heritage as protected by the Convention is also demonstrated by the inclusion in the World Heritage List of a similar site, that is the Chinese *Mt. Emei and Leshan Giant Buddha*, inscribed by the World Heritage Committee in 1996 (see UNESCO Doc. WHC-96/CONF. 201/21 of 10 March 1997).

[41] See *supra*, note 28 and corresponding text.

[42] See *supra*, note 39. The Committee inscribed the valley of Bamiyan on the basis of the following criteria: *Criterion (i):* The Buddha statues and the cave art in Bamiyan Valley are an outstanding representation of the Gandharan school in Buddhist art in the Central Asian region. *Criterion (ii):* The artistic and architectural remains of Bamiyan Valley, and an important Buddhist centre on the Silk Road, are an exceptional testimony to the interchange of Indian, Hellenistic, Roman, Sasanian influences as the basis for the development of a particular artistic expression in the Gandharan school. To this can be added the Islamic influence in a later period. *Criterion (iii):* The Bamiyan Valley bears an exceptional testimony to a cultural tradition in the Central Asian region that has disappeared. *Criterion (iv):* The Bamiyan Valley is an outstanding example of a cultural landscape that illustrates a significant period in Buddhism. *Criterion (vi):* The Bamiyan Valley is the most monumental expression of the western Buddhism. It was an important centre of pilgrimage over many centuries. Because of their symbolic values, the monuments have suffered at different times during their existence, including the deliberate destruction in 2001, which shook the whole world.

[43] See *supra*, section 2.

[44] Generally on this issue see Nalhik S. E., "La protection internationale des biens culturels en cas de conflit armé," in *Recueil des Cours*, vol. 120, 1967/I, p. 65 ff.; Panzera A. F., *La tutela internazionale dei beni culturali in tempo di guerra*, Torino, 1993; Francioni F., "Patrimonio culturale, sovranità degli Stati e conflitti armati," in Feliciani G. (ed.), *Beni culturali di interesse religioso*, Bologna, 1995, p. 149 ff.; Gioia A., "La protezione dei beni culturali nei conflitti armati," in Francioni F., Del Vecchio A., and De Caterini P. (eds.), *Protezione internazionale del patrimonio culturale: interessi nazionali e difesa del patrimonio comune della cultura*, Milano, 200, p. 71 ff.

[45] On the protection of cultural heritage by international humanitarian law see Nahlik S. E., "Protection des biens culturels," in AA. VV., *Les dimensions internationales du droit humanitaire*, Paris, 1986, p. 237 ff.

[46] See *Convention (IV) respecting the Laws and Customs of War on Land and its annex: Regulations concerning the Laws and Customs of War on Land*. The Hague, 18 October 1907, available at <http://www.icrc.org/ihl.nsf>.

[47] The same principle is also expressed by article 56 of the Regulation annexed to the Hague Convention IV (*supra*, note 46) and article 5 of the *Convention (IX) concerning Bombardment by Naval Forces in Time of War* (available at <http://www.icrc.org/ihl.nsf>).

[48] See Ronzitti N., *Diritto internazionale dei conflitti armati*, Torino, 1998, p. 94 ff.

[49] This circumstance was confirmed in 1935 by the so-called *Roerich Pact* (*Treaty on the Protection of Artistic and Scientific Institutions and Historic Monuments*, Washington, 15 April 1935, available at <http://www.icrc.org/ihl.nsf>), a regional treaty concluded between the United States and other American states, the Preamble of which states that "immovable monuments [...] form the cultural treasure of peoples."

[50] The full text of the Convention and of its 1954 and 1999 Protocols is available in the UNESCO Web site, at <http://www.unesco.org/culture/laws>.

particular, according to article 19 of this Convention, states parties must apply the provisions that relate to respect for cultural property even in case of noninternational armed conflicts. The preamble of the Convention also affirms the relevance of the protection of cultural heritage as a global value pertaining to the international community as a whole, proclaiming that

"damage to cultural property belonging to any people whatsoever means damage to the cultural heritage of all mankind, since each people makes its contribution to the culture of the world,"

and that

"the preservation of the cultural heritage is of great importance for all peoples of the world and [...] it is important that this heritage should receive international protection."[51]

Unfortunately Afghanistan was not party to the Hague Convention at the relevant time, and its provisions are thus not applicable as conventional norms to the case of the destruction of cultural goods perpetrated by the Taliban.[52] The same conclusion can be reached with regard to the 1977 Protocol II to the Geneva Conventions of 12 August 1949 on humanitarian law,[53] article 16 of which, entitled "Protection of Cultural Objects and of Places of Worship," states that

"[w]ithout prejudice to the provisions of the Hague Convention for the Protection of Cultural Property in the Event of Armed Conflict of 14 May 1954, it is prohibited to commit any acts of hostility directed against historic monuments, works of art or places of worship which constitute the cultural or spiritual heritage of peoples, and to use them in support of the military effort."

Although, according to article I, this provision would be, in principle, applicable to the Afghan situation,[54] such an application is prevented by the fact that Afghanistan was not a party to the Protocol at the time of the destruction of the Buddhas.[55]

However, the absence of specific treaty obligations – except those deriving from the 1972 Convention – does not relieve the Taliban regime from international responsibility deriving from the destruction of the Buddhas of Bamiyan, under general norms of customary international law. Indeed, such responsibility may arise as a consequence of the breach of at least two customary norms that have been formed as a consequence of the international practice in the field of protection of cultural heritage.

In this sense, it is to be emphasized, at the general level, that the reconstruction of relevant customary international law is not simply an academic exercise; where such law is found to exist, it has practical implications. First of all, unlike treaty law, customary international law is *ex se* of binding character for all the countries of the world because it needs no formal acceptance by governments, whereas treaties must be ratified or acceded to by the state concerned in order to produce any binding effect for such a State. In practical terms, this means that the international community (*i.e.*, states and international organizations) may lawfully claim (and eventually enforce through the adoption of appropriate counter measures) respect for the relevant customary provisions *vis-à-vis* any government, irrespective of its formal acceptance of the relevant obligation. In addition, customary international law may generally be invoked before national courts as law applicable in the state concerned. For example, the U.S. Supreme Court has proclaimed since 1815 that courts are "bound by the law of nations, which is part of the law of the land,"[56] thus instructing national judges to routinely enforce customary international law. In a recent judgment, a District Court of New York applied such principle by stating that "Congress's failure to ratify [an international treaty] is not sufficient to exempt the United States from the obligation to respect] the customary international law principles contained in and underlying [such a] treaty,"[57] thus confirming the assumption that, when a customary norm actually exists, states are bound to respect it irrespective of whether or not they have ratified the existing international conventions proclaiming the rule that corresponds to the content of the customary norm itself.

The first of the two customary norms banning the intentional destruction of cultural heritage is to be found in the principle according to which such heritage constitutes part of the general interest of the international community as a whole. This principle belongs to the general category of norms establishing *erga omnes* obligations, a category enunciated by the International Court of Justice in the well-known *Barcelona Traction* case.[58] In this case, the Court distinguished between norms that create bilateral obligations of reciprocal character, binding upon individual states *inter sé*, and norms that create international obligations *erga omnes*, or obligations owed to the generality of states in the public interest. This category comprises the norms concerning the prohibition of force, the protection of basic human rights, or the protection of the general environment against massive degradation. In our view, the prohibition of acts of willful and systematic destruction of cultural heritage of great importance for humanity also falls in the category of *erga omnes* obligations. There are several manifestations of international practice that confirm the existence of such obligation. As early as 1907, the Hague Conventions on land warfare and naval bombardment proclaimed the principle that historic

---

[51] Generally on the 1954 Convention, see Nalhik, *cit.*, note 44, p. 120 ff.; Panzera, *cit.*, note 44, p. 30 ff. and 72 ff.; Gioia, *cit.*, note 44, p. 76 ff.
[52] For the updated list of the parties to the 1954 Convention, see the UNESCO Web site, at <http://www.unesco.org/culture/laws>.
[53] See *Protocol Additional to the Geneva Conventions of 12 August 1949, and Relating to the Protection of Victims of Non-International Armed Conflicts (Protocol II)*, UNTS, vol. 1125, p. 609.
[54] See article I of the Protocol II, *cit. supra*, note 53.
[55] For the updated list of the parties to the Protocol II to the Geneva conventions on humanitarian law see the United Nations High Commissioner on Human Rights Web site, at <http://www.unhchr.ch>.

[56] See *The Neriede*, 13 U.S. 388, 423 (1815). See also *The Paquete Habana*, 175 U.S. 677, 700 (1900).
[57] See *Beharry v. Reno*, 183 F. Supp. 2d 584 (E.D.N.Y. 2002), p. 29.
[58] See *Barcelona Traction, Light and Power Co.* case, *ICJ Rep.*, 1970, 3, p. 33–4.

monuments and buildings dedicated to art and science ought to be spared by military violence.[59] The *Roerich* Pact of 1935 went further to proclaim the principle that museums, monuments, and scientific and cultural institutions are to be protected as part of "common heritage of all people."[60] UNESCO has systematically restated this principle since the early 1950s. One can cite, among the several pertinent UNESCO recommendations,[61] the 1956 Recommendation on International Principles Applicable to Archeological Excavations,[62] and the Preamble, as well as Article 4, of the 1954 Hague Convention on the Protection of Cultural Property in the Event of Armed Conflicts.[63] More specifically, the idea of an international public interest in safeguarding cultural heritage is expressed by the 1972 World Heritage Convention, the Preamble of which states that

"the existing international conventions, recommendations and resolutions concerning cultural and natural property demonstrate the importance, for all the peoples of the world, of safeguarding this unique and irreplaceable property, to whatever people it may belong [...] [P]arts of the cultural or natural heritage are of outstanding interest and therefore need to be preserved as part of the world heritage of mankind as a whole."

A duty to preserve, and *a fortiori* not to deliberately destroy cultural heritage is also contemplated by the 1972 UNESCO Recommendation concerning the Protection, at National Level, of The Cultural and Natural Heritage.[64] The Preamble of this Recommendation states that

"every country in whose territory there are components of the cultural [...] heritage has an obligation to safeguard this part of mankind's heritage and to ensure that it is handed down to future generations."

and that

"knowledge and protection of the cultural [...] heritage in the various countries of the world are conducive to mutual understanding among the peoples."

If one considers the very high rate of ratification to the World Heritage Convention,[65] as well as the authoritative character of UNESCO recommendations, which really represent the near totality of the nations of the world that participate in the General Conference, it is not possible to deny that a general *opinio juris* exists in the international community on the binding character of the principles prohibiting deliberate destruction of cultural heritage of significant importance for humanity. This conclusion is reinforced by the fact that protection of cultural heritage as a matter of public interest, and not only as part of private property rights, is recognized in most of the mature domestic legal systems of the world. No civilized state, in the sense of article 38(c) of the Statute of the International Court of Justice, recognizes the right of the private owner of an important work of art to destroy it as part of the exercise of a supposedly unlimited right of private property. Catalogues and inventories of national treasures are generally intended to limit such private rights in view of safeguarding the public interest to the conservation and transmission of the cultural patrimony to future generations.[66] In the case of the Buddhas of Bamiyan, the injury to the international public interest, which consisted in the conservation of the monuments and in the prevention of their destruction, was all the more apparent because: (a) the destruction was motivated by invidious and discriminatory intent; (b) it was systematic; and (c) it was carried out in blatant defiance of the appeals coming from UNESCO, the UN,[67] ICOMOS, and many individual states.

The second customary principle pertinent to the present inquiry relates to the prohibition of acts of violence against cultural heritage in the event of armed conflicts.[68] Such a principle may be based on a consistent and unambiguous practice, which is demonstrated by the developments of international law in this field subsequent to the Hague conventions on the laws and customs of war. Besides the 1954 Hague Convention cited earlier,[69] one must consider the provision of article 53 of the 1977 Protocol I to the Geneva Conventions of 12 August 1949, relating to international armed conflicts, which states that

"[w]ithout prejudice to the provisions of the Hague Convention for the Protection of Cultural Property in the Event of Armed Conflict

---

[59] See respectively articles 27 and 56 of the Regulations annexed to The Hague Convention IV and article 5 of the Convention (IX) concerning Bombardment by Naval Forces in Time of War, *supra*, note 46.

[60] See *supra*, note 49.

[61] For a detailed examination of the relevant part of these recommendations, see Francioni, *cit.*, note 44, p. 152 f.; id., "Principi e criteri ispiratori per la protezione internazionale del patrimonio culturale," in Francioni, Del Vecchio, and De Caterini (eds.), *cit.*, note 44, p. 14 f. (the author notes that the relevance of these recommendations, for the formation of a customary norm in the field, is given by their reiterate repetition and by the fact that they are adopted by the UNESCO General Conference, which represents almost all members of the international community).

[62] 1956 UNESCO *Recommendation on International Principles Applicable to Archeological Excavations*, available in the UNESCO Web site, at <http://www.unesco.org/culture/laws/archaeological/html_eng/page1.shtml> (see, in particular, the fourth sentence of the Preamble).

[63] See *supra*, note 50.

[64] 1972 UNESCO *Recommendation concerning the Protection, at National Level, of The Cultural and Natural Heritage*, available at the UNESCO Web site, at <http://www.unesco.org/culture/laws/national/html_eng/page1.shtml>.

[65] The 1972 World Heritage Convention has been ratified by 178 states (updated 1 May 2004); see <http://www.unesco.org/whc/nwhc/pages/doc/main.htm>.

[66] See Sax J. L., *Playing Darts with a Rembrandt: Public and Private Rights in Cultural Treasures*, Ann Arbor, 1999.

[67] See *supra*, note 5.

[68] See Nahlik, *cit.*, note 44, pp. 89 and 145; Frigo M., *La protezione dei beni culturali nel diritto internazionale*, Milano, 1986, p. 62 ff.; Francioni, *cit.*, note 61, p. 13 ff.; Carducci G., "L'obligation de restitution des biens culturels et des objectes d'art en cas de conflit armé: droit coutumier et droit coventionel avant et après la Convention de La Haye de 1954," *RGDIP*, 2000, p. 289 ff.

[69] The 1954 Convention for the Protection of Cultural Property in the Event of Armed Conflicts has been ratified by 103 States, the 1977 Protocol II to the 1949 Geneva Conventions on humanitarian law by 152, and the 1977 Protocol I (see *infra*, note 70), by 159; see <http://www.icrc.org/ihl.nsf> (last checked on 7 August 2002).

of 14 May 1954, and of other relevant international instruments, it is prohibited: (a) to commit any acts of hostility directed against the historic monuments, works of art or places of worship which constitute the cultural or spiritual heritage of peoples; (b) to use such objects in support of the military effort; (c) to make such objects the object of reprisals."[70]

In addition, the acts of "seizure of, destruction or wilful damage done to institutions dedicated to religion, charity and education, the arts and sciences, historic monuments and works of art and science" are included by article 3(d) of the Statute of the International Criminal Tribunal for the Former Yugoslavia (ICTY) among the violations of the law or customs of war.[71] A similar approach is followed by the Statute of the International Criminal Court, whose articles 8(b)(IX) and 8(c)(IV), concerning, respectively, international and non-international armed conflicts, qualify as war crime any intentional attack directed, *inter alia*, against buildings dedicated to religious, educational, artistic, or humanitarian purposes, or historical monuments.[72] Finally, article 20(e)(iv) of the 1996 International Law Commission *Draft Code of Crimes Against the Peace and Security of Mankind* includes among war crimes all acts of "seizure of, destruction of or willful damage done to institutions dedicated to religion, charity and education, the arts and sciences, historic monuments and works of art and science."[73]

The customary character of the prohibition of destruction of cultural heritage (more precisely "destruction or willful damage to institutions dedicated to religion") during armed conflicts has been expressly confirmed by the ICTY in a recent judgment, in which both defendants, Dario Kordic and Mario Cerkez, have been found guilty of such a crime against cultural property because of their deliberate, armed attacks on ancient mosques of Bosnia Herzegovina.[74] According to the Tribunal, the act in point,

"when perpetrated with the requisite discriminatory intent, amounts to an attack on the very religious identity of a people. As such, it manifests a nearly pure expression of the notion of 'crimes against humanity', for all of humanity is indeed injured by the destruction of a unique religious culture and its concomitant cultural objects [...] [thus] amount[ing] to an act of persecution."[75]

The Hague Tribunal thus holds that this kind of crime may amount to an act of persecution included in the concept of "crimes against humanity" provided for by article 5(h) of the Statute.[76] In doing so, the Tribunal confirmed what it had already stated in one of its earlier judgements.[77] The same conclusion had been previously reached by the Nuremberg International Military Tribunal[78] and the International Law Commission.[79]

In addition, with regard to the shelling of the old town of Dubrovnik performed by the Yugoslav Forces on 6 December 1991, the ICTY held that

"the crime of destruction or wilful damage done to institutions dedicated to religion, charity, education, and the arts and sciences, and to historic monuments and works of art and science [...] represents a violation of values especially protected by the international community,"[80]

adding that

"the shelling attack on the Old Town was an attack not only against the history and heritage of the region, but also against the cultural heritage of humankind[81] [...] since it is a serious violation of international humanitarian law to attack civilian buildings, it is a crime of even greater seriousness to direct an attack on an especially protected site, such as the Old Town."[82]

There is a strong argument to hold that the description of the crime against culture as persecution, given by the ICTY in *Prosecutor v. Dario Kordic and Mario Cerkez*,[83] should also fit the factual situation with the case of the destruction of the Afghan cultural heritage perpetrated by the Taliban. In such a case, the discriminatory intent of destroying all signs of religions different from Islamism was declared by the Taliban themselves.[84]

We are aware that two objections may be raised with regard to our characterization of the destruction of the Buddhas of Bamiyan as an internationally wrongful act. The first stems from the circumstance that the practice cited earlier, especially the case law of the ICTY, relates to *individual criminal liability* and not to state responsibility. This is true. However, the objection is not persuasive, because, quite apart from

---

[70] See *Protocol Additional to the Geneva Convention of 12 August 1949, and relating to the Protection of Victims of International Armed Conflicts (Protocol I)*, UNTS, vol. 1125, p. 5.

[71] The text of the Statute is available at <http://www.un.org/icty/basic/statut/statute.htm>.

[72] For the text of the Statute see *ILM*, 1998, p. 999 ff.

[73] The text of the Draft Code is available at <http://www.un.org/law/ilc/texts/dcode.htm>.

[74] See *Prosecutor v. Dario Kordic and Mario Cerkez*, judgement of 26 February 2001 (Trial Chamber), available in the ICTY Web site, at <http://www.un.org/icty> (see also the judgement of the Appeals Chamber of 17 December 2004, available at <http://www.un.org/icty/kordic/appeal/judgement/cer-aj041217e.pdf>); see, in particular, par. 206, in which the Trial Chamber states that the act of destruction or wilful damage to institutions dedicated to religion "has [...] already been criminalised under customary international law."

[75] *Id.*, par. 207.

[76] See *supra*, note 71.

[77] See *Prosecutor v. Tihomir Blaskic*, judgement of 3 March 2000, par. 227, available in the ICTY Web site, <http://www.un.org/icty>.

[78] See *Nuremberg Judgement*, pp. 248 and 302, quoted by the ICTY in *Prosecutor v. Dario Kordic and Mario Cerkez*, cit., note 74, par. 206, note 267.

[79] See *Report of the International Law Commission on the work of its 43rd session*, 29 April–19 June 1991, doc. A/46/10/Suppl.10, p. 268, according to which the "systematic destruction of monuments or buildings representative of a particular social, religious, cultural or other group" is included in the concept of persecution.

[80] See *Prosecutor v. Miodrag Jokic*, judgment of 18 March 2004, available at <http://www.un.org/icty>, par. 46 (emphasis added).

[81] *Id.*, par. 51 (emphasis added).

[82] *Id.*, par. 53. The Old Town of Dubrovnik is inscribed in the UNESCO World Heritage List since 1979 (see <http://whc.unesco.org/sites/95.htm>).

[83] See *supra*, text corresponding to note 75.

[84] See *supra*, text corresponding to note 32.

the position one takes on the controversial problem whether individual criminal liability is an aspect of state responsibility or is totally autonomous,[85] it is clear that, in the case of the destruction of the Buddhas, the individual acts and the state conduct are one and the same, and form the inseparable elements of a single criminal design. The second possible objection could be that the alleged applicability of the prohibition of intentional destruction of cultural heritage is limited to international wars, to situations of military occupation of foreign territory, and should not be applicable to noninternational armed conflicts. This objection also is unfounded. The universal value of cultural heritage seems to exclude such a conceptual discrimination. In the last decades, international practice has extended the application of all main principles of humanitarian law, originally provided for international armed conflicts, to civil wars, ethnic conflicts, and conflicts of a noninternational character. This is apparent in the text of the 1999 Second Protocol to the 1954 Hague Convention[86] as well as in the recent statutes of international criminal tribunals.[87] The customary character of international rules protecting cultural heritage in internal armed conflicts has also been expressly confirmed by the ICTY in the foremost *Tadic* case, specifically referring to "Article 19 of the Hague Convention for the Protection of Cultural Property in the Event of Armed Conflict of 14 May 1954."[88]

If customary prohibition of deliberate destruction of cultural heritage of great significance for humanity exists in the event of internal conflicts, it would, indeed, be nonsense to maintain that similar intentional acts of destruction are permitted in times of peace.[89]

To conclude, the willful and discriminatory destruction of the great Buddhas of Bamiyan perpetrated by the Taliban in March 2001 constitutes a breach of the customary international law forbidding wanton destruction of cultural heritage. Additionally, the destruction in point entailed a specific breach of the World Heritage Convention commitment to ensure protection of cultural heritage situated in the territory of parties.[90]

Because international norms applicable to cultural heritage consider the destruction of any nation's cultural property as a loss and an injury to the collective patrimony of humankind's civilization, the deliberate devastation of cultural heritage of great significance for humanity entails a violation of an international obligation having *erga omnes* character. In the Afghan case, the *erga omnes* character of such obligation was confirmed by the fact that, although there was no directly and materially injured third state, because the act of violence was committed in the territory and against a value pertaining to the transgressor state as such, there was unanimous protest by the international community, including foreign governments and international organizations, against the destruction of the Buddhas. The customary obligation in point has the scope of limiting the power that the territorial state has over assets located within the sphere of its sovereignty, and it exists toward the international community as a whole, and thus, *a fortiori*, toward all states.

Such principle has been confirmed by the text and the spirit of the *Declaration Concerning the Intentional Destruction of Cultural Heritage*, adopted by the UNESCO General Conference on 17 October 2003, precisely as a reaction to the destruction of the two giant Buddhas of Bamiyan.[91] The first sentence of the Preamble affirms that the destruction of the Buddhas "affected the international community as a whole."[92] The sixth sentence reiterates, "one of the fundamental principles of the Preamble of the 1954 Hague Convention for the Protection of Cultural Property in the Event of Armed Conflict," according to which "damage to cultural property belonging to any people whatsoever means damage to the cultural heritage of all mankind." Article I affirms the recognition by the international community of "the importance of the protection of cultural heritage," and its commitment "to fight against its intentional destruction" in view of ensuring its transmission to "the succeeding generations." To this end, Article III recommends States to take "all appropriate measures to prevent, avoid, stop and suppress acts of intentional destruction of cultural heritage, *wherever such heritage is located*";[93] such duty is to be complied both in peacetime[94] and in the event of armed

---

[85] For a thorough discussion of this problem, with different conclusions, see Dupuy P. M., "International Criminal Responsibility and the Individual and International Responsibility of the State," in Cassese A., Gaeta P., and Jones J. R. W. D., *The Rome Statute of the International Criminal Court: A Commentary*, Oxford, 2002, p. 1085 ff.; Maison R., "La Responsabilité individuelle pour crime d'État en droit international public," thesis at the University of Paris, 2 January 2000, *passim*.

[86] *Second Protocol to the Hague Convention of 1954 for the Protection of Cultural Property in the Event of Armed Conflict*, in *ILM*, 1999, p. 769, particularly article 22.1.

[87] See, for example, the statutes of the International Criminal Tribunal for the Former Yugoslavia (*supra*, note 71), the International Criminal Tribunal for Rwanda (available at <http://www.ictr.org>), and the International Criminal Court (*supra*, note 72). See also the case law of the ICTY, especially the definition of armed conflict given by the Tribunal in *Prosecutor v. Dusko Tadic* (Appeal Chamber, 2 October 1995), in 35 *ILM* 1996, p. 32, paragraphs 66–70.

[88] See *Prosecutor v. Dusko Tadic, cit.*, note 87, par. 98.

[89] See Lenzerini F., "The UNESCO Declaration Concerning the Intentional Destruction of Cultural Heritage: One Step Forward and Two Steps Back," in 13(2003) *Italian Yearbook of International Law*, 2005, p. 131 ff.

[90] See the Preamble, article 4 and article 12 of the World Heritage Convention, *supra*, note 38.

[91] The full text of the Declaration is available in the UNESCO Web site, at <http://www.unesco.org>; for a critical comment see Lenzerini, *cit.*, note 89, *passim*.

[92] The very first sentence of the Preamble reads as follows: "[r]ecalling the tragic destruction of the Buddhas of Bamiyan that affected the international community as a whole." As already noted, the first version of the present chapter was elaborated, on a request of UNESCO, as a report having the purpose of investigating the status of international law concerning the matter of the deliberate destruction of cultural heritage in view of defining, at a preliminary stage, the possible content of an international instrument condemning such a kind of act; the 2003 UNESCO Declaration is actually that instrument.

[93] Emphasis added.   [94] See Article IV.

conflict ("in conformity with customary international law"), including the cases of internal wars and occupation.[95] The Declaration also affirms the responsibility of every State that "intentionally destroys or intentionally fails to take appropriate measures to prohibit, prevent, stop, and punish any intentional destruction of cultural heritage of great importance for humanity,"[96] as well as individuals who perform or order to be committed acts of deliberate destruction of such heritage.[97]

The deliberate and systematic destruction of cultural properties of pre-Islamic Afghanistan and, more particularly, of the Bamiyan Buddhas, in so far as this heritage constituted a representation of both a religious belief and the cultural identity of a people, could finally be envisaged as a violation of certain human rights; namely, the right to the preservation of one's own culture and the right to practice and obtain respect of one's own religion.[98] The destruction of religious symbols certainly is inconsistent with the obligation to respect cultural diversity and with religious toleration. These arguments remain valid, for even if the Buddhas of Bamiyan were no longer actively functional to the practice of religious rights, they nevertheless embodied an important testimony of past religious traditions and of cultural exchange among the peoples of Asia.

THE DUTY TO "PREVENT" AND "AVOID" DEVASTATION OF CULTURAL HERITAGE: OCCUPYING FORCES AND IRAQI CULTURAL TREASURES

As pointed out in the previous section, Article III of the UNESCO Declaration Concerning the Intentional Destruction of Cultural Heritage affirms the duty of States to, *inter alia*, prevent and avoid acts of intentional destruction of cultural heritage, irrespective of where such heritage is located. Article V then adds that such a duty exists also in the case of military occupation.

In this respect, the case of the devastation of the Iraqi National Museum of Baghdad and the arson of the Iraqi National Library, perpetrated in April 2003 after the entry of the U.S. forces in the city, is worth mentioning.[99] Absolutely priceless cultural treasures were conserved in such institutions, such as irreplaceable artifacts of Sumerian, Akkadian, Babylonian, Assyrian, and Arab art, including the Uruk vase (dating from 3500 B.C.) and artifacts excavated from the ancient Sumerian city of Ur, as well as thousands of Islamic ancient manuscripts. Many of these treasures have probably been irremediably lost as a result of the devastation of the National Museum and National Library. Although, properly speaking, the case of the Iraqi National Museum was a case of looting and not exactly of intentional destruction as such, it had, nevertheless, the actual effect of a severe loss of cultural treasures which, given their outstanding value, should be preserved in the interest of humanity as a whole. One may argue that such loss is equivalent to destruction both in terms of similar ideological condemnation and in terms of intolerability of the effects produced. It is thus not illogical to maintain that the legal regime provided for the cases of destruction of cultural heritage also extends to failure to prevent looting or any other form of annihilation of such heritage. As for the arson of the National Library, there is no doubt that it is precisely included in the concept of destruction of cultural heritage dealt with by the UNESCO Declaration.

Having this in mind, the core legal problem related to the devastation of the Iraqi cultural heritage consists of ascertaining whether and to what extent the occupying military forces can be considered responsible for such devastation according to relevant international law, as illustrated in the previous paragraph. In this regard, the obligation of occupying forces to preserve the integrity of local heritage derives not only from international principles applicable to intentional destruction, but also from the law concerning the protection of cultural heritage in the event of armed conflict. In particular, article 4, par. 3, of the 1954 Hague Convention imposes upon states parties the obligation of prohibiting, preventing, and putting a stop "to any form of theft, pillage or misappropriation of, and any acts of vandalism directed against, cultural property."[100] Although the United States is not party to the Hague Convention,[101] the content of the provision just reproduced corresponds to an obligation existing under customary international law.[102] This is confirmed by the treatment that U.S. war manuals reserve to these obligations as part of customary law.[103] If this is correct, then the question arises

---

[95] See Article V.
[96] See Article VI. The provision specifies that such responsibility exists irrespective of the fact that the cultural heritage concerned "is inscribed on a list maintained by UNESCO or another international organization."
[97] See Article VII (containing the same specification included in Article VI; see the previous note).
[98] The freedom of religion, which includes the right to freely manifest one's own religion in worship, observance, practice, and teaching, is stated by the main international conventional instruments on human rights; see, *inter alia*, article 18(1) of the 1966 *International Covenant on Civil and Political Rights* (UNTS, vol. 999, p. 171 ff.), article 9(1) of the 1950 *European Convention on Human Rights* (*European Treaty Series*, No. 5), and article 12(1) of the 1969 *American Convention on Human Rights* (*O.A.S. Treaty Series* No. 36). See also article 18 of the *Universal Declaration of Human Rights* and the UN *Declaration on the Elimination of All Forms of Intolerance and of Discrimination Based on Religion and Belief* (General Assembly res. 36/55 of 25 November 1981, available at <http://www.unhchr.ch/html/menu/3/b/d_intole.htm>).

[99] On this case see Francioni F., "Guerra e patrimonio culturale," in *Il Giornale dell'Arte*, June 2003, p. 1; Phuong C., "The Protection of Iraqi Cultural Property," in 53 *ICLQ*, 2004, p. 985 ff.
[100] See *supra*, note 50.
[101] See <http://erc.unesco.org/cp/convention.asp?KO=13637&language=E> (updated 17 November 2004).
[102] See Phuong, *cit.*, note 100, p. 987.
[103] Incidentally, the U.S. Government not only has signed the 1954 Hague Convention, but has also expressed the intention to proceed to its ratification by transmitting its text to the Senate, where consent to ratification has been pending for a while.

whether the United States' conduct, at the relevant time, involved a breach of its duty to prevent the looting to Iraqi cultural heritage. On the other hand, one must ask whether inaction of U.S. forces in preventing the devastation of Iraqi cultural heritage could be excused, thus excluding responsibility, in consideration of the possibility that the fighting taking place in Iraq at the relevant time could be so severe to materially preclude the U.S. army from having the chance of ensuring protection of cultural institutions in Baghdad. In this context, one must consider that U.S. forces did not arrive at the National Museum until 16 April 2003, whereas its looting took place between 8 and 12 April.[104] Was this attributable to negligence or to the actual impossibility of reaching the museum in time for preventing its devastation? This is a problem of fact on which there is disagreement. According to some sources, the American soldiers arrived in the place where the museum is located after many journalists were already there;[105] others maintain that the museum was being used by the Iraqi forces as a military position.[106] Of course, if the first set of facts is true, the United States could be considered responsible for failing to prevent the devastation of Iraqi cultural institutions because they actually had the means and material chance of preventing the pillaging and destruction of cultural treasures by swifter action and failed to do so. If on the other the museum was used by the Iraqi army for military defense,[107] then it is difficult to hold the United States responsible for negligent conduct since Iraqi resistance rendered impossible a timely advance to prevent the devastation of Iraqi cultural heritage: an outright attack on the museum and other cultural institutions if in fact such institution supported belligerent activities would have only worsened the degree of such devastation.

CONCLUSION

Destruction and dispersion of cultural heritage in recent years have caused not only shock and condemnation within the international community, but also a progressive development of pertinent international law. Individual states; international organizations, such as the United Nations and UNESCO; religious authorities, including some of the most influential Islamic authorities; NGOs; and people all over the world have called for international mobilisation against such acts of barbarity and religious intolerance such as the bombing of the Buddhas of Bamiyan. Is this sufficient to render such acts contrary to contemporary international law? This chapter has tried to provide a preliminary assessment of this question in light of contemporary international practice: the conclusion reached is rather promising. As in the area of fundamental human rights, first, and in the area of environmental protection, later, states may no longer invoke their sovereignty and domestic jurisdiction in order to justify acts of deliberate destruction of cultural heritage of great importance for humanity as a whole. Our analysis has tried to demonstrate also that, when such destruction is associated with the intent to discriminate or annihilate another religion and its forms of cultural expression, then the act amounts also to an attack on the very identity of the targeted people and religion and thus on the dignity and fundamental rights of its members. As the ICTY recently confirmed, such discriminatory destruction "[...] manifests a nearly pure expression of the notion of 'crimes against humanity', for all of humanity is indeed injured."[108] It is therefore rather evident that deliberate destruction of cultural heritage is a matter of concern not only for the people who own that heritage, but for humanity as a whole, and its perpetration entails a violation of an *erga omnes* obligations that each state is bound to respect *vis-a-vis* any other country and the international community as a whole.

QUESTIONS FOR DISCUSSION

1. Why should international law prohibit a state from destroying cultural property that is disliked or disapproved (see the destruction of monuments memorializing oppressive dictators, racism, or slavery)?

2. What is the status of customary international law concerning the intentional destruction of cultural heritage?

3. Why is it important that intentional destruction of cultural heritage is prohibited by customary international law besides international conventions?

4. Which objections could be raised with regard to the characterization of the destruction of the Buddhas of Bamiyan as an internationally wrongful act?

5. In what sense may the state obligation of refraining from and preventing destruction of cultural heritage of universal value be considered as having *erga omnes* character?

6. Which conditions should be satisfied in order to consider the occupying military forces responsible of the devastation of Iraqi cultural heritage?

---

[104] See Phuong, *cit.*, note 100, p. 985.
[105] See Hassan G., "The Pillage of Iraq," 7 July 2004, at <http://www.countercurrents.org/iraq-hassan070704.htm>, and the sources cited therein; in particular, according to the Middle East correspondent Robert Fisk, who witnessed the pillage himself, "US troops [...] did nothing to prevent looters from destroying priceless treasures of Iraq's history in the Baghdad Museum and in the museum in the northern city of Mosul, or from looting three hospitals," showing concern only for "the Ministry of Interior, of course – with its vast wealth of intelligence information on Iraq – and the Ministry of oil."
[106] See Phuong, *cit.*, note 100, p. 987.
[107] See Francioni, *cit.*, note 100, who emphasizes the fact that this possibility is not so implausible, given the reiterated practice of the Iraqi government led by Saddam Hussein to systematically place military objectives in the proximity of protected places such as hospitals as well as religious and cultural institutions.

[108] See *supra*, text corresponding to note 75.

USEFUL WEB SITE LINKS

http://portal.unesco.org/en/ev.php-URL_ID=12024&URL_DO=DO_TOPIC&URL_SECTION=201.html
(UNESCO Legal Instruments: International Conventions, Recommendations and Declarations concerning the protection of cultural heritage)

http://whc.unesco.org
(World Heritage Committee's home page)

http://whc.unesco.org/pg.cfm?cid=31&id_site=208
(World Heritage List: Cultural Landscape and Archaeological Remains of the Bamiyan Valley's page)

http://www.icrc.org/ihl
(International Committee of the Red Cross Treaty Database on International Humanitarian Law: all relevant treaties in full text, including ratification lists and search engine)

http://www.un.org/icty
(Web site of the International Criminal Tribunal for the Former Yugoslavia, including full text of judgements concerning destruction of cultural heritage)

[18]
Post-conflict Heritage and Tourism in Cambodia: The Burden of Angkor

Tim Winter

The World Heritage Site of Angkor is enduring one of the most crucial, turbulent periods in its 1200-year history. Since the early 1990s over 20 countries have contributed millions of dollars to help safeguard and restore its temples. As one of Southeast Asia's premier destinations, Angkor has also seen a 10,000% growth in international tourist arrivals in just over a decade. The challenges arising from the intense convergence of these two paradoxical and unstable agendas—heritage conservation and tourism development—are greatly compounded by Cambodia's need to recover from war and turmoil. This paper explores the critical trends that have surfaced at Angkor and why the challenges posed by surging tourism have been inadequately addressed. It argues Angkor's dominant role within Cambodia's post-conflict heritage and tourism industries requires closer, more critical attention given recent events in the country. This article is the summary of Winter's book Post-conflict Heritage, Post-colonial Tourism *(Routledge 2007).*

Keywords: Angkor; Cambodia; Conflict; Development; Poverty; Tourism

Introduction

As the 1990s unfolded Cambodia would undergo a series of rapid and profound social transformations; from civil war to peace, from socialist-style authoritarianism to multi-party democracy, and from geographic isolation to a free-market economy. After more than two decades of violent conflict and social turmoil, the country needed at once to restore its cultural, economic and political infrastructures. The speed at which Cambodia embraced modernity and globalisation during this period grossly exaggerated the paradoxes inherent to these two transformative processes. A real energy to develop, to move forward, modernise and depart from the revolutionary, socialist politics of the recent past, was partnered by an intense desire to look back, to reclaim, and to retrieve what was lost.

Tim Winter, University of Sydney. Correspondence to timwinter@me.com

It was widely recognised that a key focal point for these interweaving agendas would be the World Heritage Site of Angkor in the north-west of the country (Figure 1). It was a recognition, however, that looked beyond the actual temples themselves, and towards Angkor's role in the emergence of two key industries: heritage and tourism. The development of a 'cultural heritage' industry promised the restoration of identity, history, cultural sovereignty and national pride. International tourism promised much needed socio-economic development. As one of Southeast Asia's most important cultural heritage landscapes, there was little doubt Angkor would stand in the foreground of both these industries in the coming years. This paper examines this situation, tracing the ways in which the site has been conceptually framed and managed over the last 15 years. It also situates Angkor within the wider social, political and economic contexts of a post-conflict, postcolonial Cambodia. It will be argued that, given Cambodia's recent past, more critical attention needs to be paid to the powerful role Angkor plays in the country's heritage and tourism industries.

Figure 1 Traffic congestion at South Gate of Angkor Thom. *Source*: T. Winter.

A Brief Guide to Angkor

Covering an area of just over 400 square kilometres, the World Heritage Site of Angkor is comprised of four main elements: tropical forest, areas of cultivated land, a number of rural communities, and some of the largest and most elaborate architectural structures ever created. Recent NASA satellite imagery and research by the University of Sydney has revealed, however, that the Angkor region stretched far beyond the boundaries of the area designated as a World Heritage space, covering an area in the order of 1,000 square kilometres.[1] Held up by some scholars as the largest pre-modern urban space on the planet, the greater Angkor region thus fully absorbs its modern and ever expanding neighbour: the nearby town of Siem Reap, which today acts as the gateway for temple bound tourists.

The dozens of elaborately carved temples dotted across the landscape are testimony to what is historically Southeast Asia's most powerful and expansive kingdom—a territory which, at its height, stretched from central Laos in the north to central Thailand in the south, and from the Mekong delta in the west to the borders of Pagan in the east. It is commonly accepted today that the Angkorean period spanned from 802 to 1431 CE.[2] As each new king took the throne, the temple complexes they built became more ambitious, time consuming and dependent upon ever-greater amounts of labour. In Angkor Wat, the Angkorean period has also given us the largest religious building on the planet. Unlike the Egyptian pyramids, Khmer architecture combined immense scale with intricate ornamental detail. It was an architectural programme that would culminate in the highly extravagant Angkor Thom city complex; the ruins of which dominate the landscape today. Not surprisingly, the demands of such extensive construction schedules have been cited by historians as a major contributory factor to Angkor's eventual decline.[3]

Sacked by the Siamese c.1431, and with regional power shifting towards Siam, Angkor's much reduced population distilled into a collection of rural villages focused around Theravada Buddhist monastic communities. No longer the seat of Southeast Asia's greatest military power, Angkor's architectural landscape steadily succumbed to the tropical climate and surrounding forest.[4] The cumulative effect of intense heat, rain and pernicious vegetation over a number of centuries not only attacked Angkor's stone temples but also destroyed any wooden structures not maintained by the few villages living nearby. Although a number of Spanish, Portuguese and Asian travellers visited the region after Angkor's demise, the late nineteenth-century travel diaries of French botanist Henri Mouhot became pivotal in awakening interest in Europe.[5] Encountering a labyrinth of monumental structures entangled with tree roots and lichen in 1860, Mouhot's account was read as if Angkor had been 'discovered' as a 'lost', even dead, civilisation.[6] Despite the presence of numerous local villages, a powerful mythology surrounding loss and rediscovery was reinforced by the very aesthetics of Angkor's seemingly abandoned, wild and ruinous landscape.[7] A mythology that endures today.

A language of rediscovery and restitution would come to play a crucial role in legitimising the subsequent political and cultural construction of the French administrative territory of *Indochine*. The restoration of Angkor by the French would serve as a powerful metaphor for their assistance in restoring a once glorious, but now 'languid' Khmer culture and civilisation.[8] The scholarly pursuits of the Ecole Française d'Extrême Orient (EFEO) would be instrumental in defining Angkor's monumental landscape as a once glorious, but now lost, cultural and national heritage.[9] As a consequence, during an era of colonialism spanning just over 90 years the temples emerged as the keystone to a Cambodian national, cultural and ethnic identity.[10] Crucially, once independence from the French was secured in 1954, Angkor remained an immensely important symbolic site for this young, forward-looking nation.[11] However, as Cambodia became embroiled in the Vietnam–America war, efforts to conserve and restore Angkor ceased and tourism dwindled. Indeed under the Khmer Rouge regime, Cambodia would effectively isolate itself from the world with devastating consequences. Although never explicitly targeted for destruction throughout a conflict lasting more than two decades, the temples would suffer from neglect and damage.

In 1991, bolstered by the momentum created by the Paris Peace Accords, the country would begin its turbulent transition towards political stability and a free-market economy after a period of history defined by genocide, civil war and a decade long occupation by Vietnam.[12] As we shall see shortly, the formidable task of reconstructing its cultural, social and economic foundations would be heavily shaped by an extraordinary growth in tourism. However, with many of its social and physical infrastructures destroyed, the country's heritage and tourism industries would be characterised by distinct geographic and historical imbalances.

Cultures of Heritage

The addition of Angkor to the World Heritage list in 1992 stemmed from a need to protect, restore and help develop one of Southeast Asia's most important cultural landscapes. In the nomination process however, the discourse of 'value' centred on the site's monumental and archaeological remains.[13] Damage, looting and deterioration had to be urgently addressed and reversed wherever possible. The reconstruction of Angkor's temples was understandably regarded as the most potent symbol and demonstration of a country in recovery. The ties between monumental restoration and socio-political reconstruction—a cultural, political dyad first forged during the colonial period, as noted above—were now about to reappear. However, the traumatic events of recent decades combined with a vision of Angkor as a unifying marker of modern cultural, national and ethnic identity to greatly intensify the expectation that cultural heritage would give momentum to a wider socio-cultural recovery.

Previous events had left Cambodia with wholly inadequate governmental, administrative and legal structures. The country also lacked expertise in monumental conservation, archaeology, community development, tourism, urban planning or forestry. In recognition of these challenges UNESCO created an administrative body, the International Coordinating Committee for the Safeguarding and Development of Angkor (ICC).[14] The organisation would focus specifically on the newly listed World Heritage Site and its environs, including the nearby town of Siem Reap. Further protection would come from a Zoning and Environmental Management Plan (ZEMP).[15]

Enforced by Royal Decree, ZEMP would prove an effective mechanism for insulating the region from its challenging social context. To complement these initiatives, the World Heritage Committee also called for the establishment of a Cambodian-run management body. To this end the Authority for the Protection and Safeguarding of the Angkor Region (APSARA), was created in 1994. In the short term APSARA would act as an organisational bridge between the attendant international community and the domestic government. Although the ICC was generally expected to remain in attendance for in excess of a decade, it was hoped that APSARA, as a self-funded, independent and autonomous Cambodian management authority, would fill the void left by the eventual withdraw of international partners.

Angkor's immense historical importance, along with its global prestige, led to an unprecedented influx of international assistance. Since the early 1990s more than 20 countries—including France, Japan, China, India, America, Germany, Italy and Australia—have together donated millions of dollars to help safeguard the temples.[16] Working under the umbrella of the ICC, teams have been guided by various internationally ratified charters, including the 1954 Hague Convention and the 1972 World Heritage Convention. Guidance has also come from the former experiences of EFEO. The immense institutional knowledge EFEO built up during 70 years of research presented the ICC with a uniquely valuable archive of reports, scholarly publications, fieldwork diaries and thousands of photographs, maps and drawings. Although it was recognised mistakes had been made, and that strategies had evolved over decades of research, EFEO's expertise was crucial to steering the various teams now involved, many of which had little, or no, prior experience of Khmer architecture. EFEO's vast body of knowledge in epigraphy, architectural conservation, art history and to a lesser degree archaeology represented an invaluable resource for modern scholars. On the flip side however, the pre-eminence of EFEO meant that a representation of Angkor—one that neglected vernacular, social histories in favour of the material heritage of a 'high', regal culture—would be re-invoked and re-authenticated through a late twentieth-century framework of world heritage.

Lying at the heart of this process would be an understanding of culture grounded in rational science. The international nature of the ICC demanded a language capable of being shared across the table, universally applied and unequivocally valued by all. Rational science would provide the solution; a unifying medium through which a Khmer temple previously restored by French conservators could be rebuilt by a Japanese team supported by experts from Italy, Germany and the UK. The foundations for this approach can be traced back to the 1972 Protection of the World Cultural and Natural Heritage Convention, which, as Hitchcock points out, was conceived at a time when policies were geared towards the scientific management of tangible heritage.[17] As the 1990s progressed annual conferences and symposiums held in Siem Reap would be dedicated to the engineering technicalities of structural foundations, the mineral composition of sandstone carvings, or the load-bearing capacities of arches and precariously tilting columns. Similarly, annual reports and publications rarely departed from discussing cultural heritage as a language of technology and scientific enquiry.[18] While the dilapidated state of Angkor's ruins undoubtedly demanded such efforts, a heritage discourse rooted in a 'logical positivism', to use Laura Jane Smith's term, raises important questions that warrant closer attention.[19] The critique offered by Smith of such cultural heritage frameworks centres around their application of 'technical procedures and science to conflicts over material culture [which] de-politicize issues through the employment of its expertise'.[20] In essence, the ICC's orientation towards architectural restoration and archaeology 'stress[ed] objectivity and technical rigor' to define its authoritative position as the arbitrator of Angkorean history.[21] In essence, science would provide the ontological foundations for a universally shared definition of 'authenticity'.

This scientific orientation towards cultural heritage has meant the extensive attention paid to the evolution of construction styles and the reappropriation of buildings by later kings has significantly contrasted with a lack of interest in histories of ancestral spirit cults, oral traditions or contemporary temple ritual practices.[22] With few projects guided by anthropologists, historians or sociologists there has been little to counter the positivist, and universalising, language of rational science. In an environment characterised by a quest for objectivity and ontological 'truths' ideas such as historical relativism, plurality or multi-vocality have remained firmly on the margins. Beyond the temples themselves, this situation has had important implications for the park's villages and monastic communities (Figure 2). Some of Cambodia's oldest and most important Buddhist monasteries are situated within the Angkor area. And yet research within the ICC on Angkor as a living heritage, a place of vernacular, religious practices has been limited to the modestly budgeted efforts of a small APSARA team of young anthropologists. Although UNESCO successfully intervened to overturn plans to relocate a number of these monasteries outside the park in 2001, the ICC has otherwise engaged little with the revival of the Buddhist or animist traditions of local residents. Recent publications by Ang and Harris remind us of the importance of these shortcomings.[23] Together, these authors show how Cambodia's Buddhism operates as a socially and politically engaged religion and that the rejuvenation of Cambodia's monastic community (*sangha*) is essential to a broader cultural and societal revivalism. As we have seen, however, such areas have often been overlooked within a vision of architectural splendour and pristine glory that essentially rests upon the cultural binaries of regal/vernacular, classical/non-classical and modern/traditional first introduced in the late nineteenth century.

Cambodia's Post-conflict National Heritage

The lack of historians, social anthropologists or even more phenomenologically inclined archaeologists within the ICC has also contributed to Angkor's emergence as an atomised island of research, demarcated as a rural museum of art and architectural glories. In the face of weak legislative, executive and judicial branches of Cambodia's transitional government, it was critical that UNESCO protected the Angkor–Siem Reap region with strong legal and spatial boundaries. While such policies have been largely successful, the isolation of Angkor combined with the influx of international assistance to the region has ensured the site remains a 'phantasmagoria' of Cambodian

Figure 2 Cambodians Lighting Incense inside Angkor Wat. *Source*: T. Winter.

history, to use Norindr's term, and the apogee of a tri-focal historical narrative which devalues the less illustrious 'pre' and 'post' Angkorean periods.[24] With Angkor's temples securing a large share of the funds that enter the country to help protect and 'rebuild' Cambodia's cultural heritage we have to look further afield to fully appreciate the implications of this situation.

As part of an analysis of twentieth-century Cambodian performance art, Turnbull argues that cultural heritage grants since the early 1990s have principally been directed towards 'the country's architectural and archaeological patrimony rather than its equally fragile intangible legacy'.[25] Looking back to 1960 he reminds us Phnom Penh was home to 30 performance art theatres, and that Cambodians enjoyed performances from around 50 theatre companies. Today there are only two commercially run theatres for the entire country. Destroyed by fire in 1994, the ruinous Suramarit theatre in Phnom Penh—once the icon of a vibrant culture of independence—symbolises the political, economic inertia surrounding this sector of the country's cultural heritage.[26] While Turnbull welcomes recent efforts by UNESCO, various non-governmental organisations and the Royal University of Fine Arts to restore shadow puppetry and classical and non-classical dance forms, he concludes 'while Cambodians appear to cling determinedly to the fundamentals Khmer of identity... their connection to the nation's intangible culture has been more tenuous'.[27] Turnbull's account of a neglected modern heritage is relevant here because it reveals the priorities of the state's cultural enterprise, and its desire to source cultural markers such as classical dance which have a seemingly indisputable provenance.

This quest for a homogeneous ethno-national identity has been further demonstrated by Dahles and ter Horst in their analysis of Cambodia's silk industry. The revival of silk production and designs 'celebrates ethnic Khmer dominance' in part through a genealogical link with the courts of Angkor.[28] International tourism has played a crucial role here. As they state, by connecting 'the weaving of traditional silk garments for royal and religious ceremonies... [with Angkor]... these garments cannot be anything but traditionally and authentically Khmer.[29] In a similar way, and as I have shown elsewhere, the 'Apsara dance' has sought its provenance in the royal courts of the Angkorean period in order to become the obligatory 'cultural experience' for foreign tourists.[30]

Finally here, the 'Angkor National Museum', which opened in Siem Reap in December 2007, vividly illustrates the ongoing centrality of monumental architecture to the construction of a national history. The museum houses eight galleries dedicated entirely to the display of artefacts and statues from the pre-, post- and Angkor periods. As the exhibition unfolds, this Angkorean history is once again conflated with the story of a Khmer 'national' identity.[31] Despite being called a National Museum, no space is given to the country's ethnic and religious minorities, vernacular cultural forms or the country's transition from colonialism to independence. As a reflection of the omnipotence of carved sandstone in the socio-cultural landscape of Cambodia's heritage industry, the museum reinforces the idea that the country has few personalities, engineering triumphs or distinctive cultural industries to complement its achievements in stone.

Seen together, the examples of silks, performing arts and the new Angkor National Museum begin to illustrate what role, direct and indirect, Angkor plays in the restoration of Cambodia's cultural heritage. They also point towards the impact of tourism on such processes. Given that recent history has severely weakened the country's public sphere, debates and critiques about the relationships between identity and culture, tradition and modernity remain limited. An episode of profound turmoil has understandably given rise to a deep-seated anxiety over what constitutes Khmer and Cambodian identity. As the country has reopened its borders such concerns have also been driven by a desire for difference within a highly connected region. A classical, culturally and historically pure Angkor represents an important resource for a fragile identity. It is suggested, however, that an idealised Angkor undergoing reconstruction has once again become the basis of a state nationalism rooted in a static, if not timeless, vision of a glorious past. Angkorean centric heritage and tourism industries are simultaneously advancing and restraining the parameters of the country's social and cultural revival. Dominated by architectural glories, these two industries significantly increase the risk of the country trapping itself in a mono-cultural, mono-ethnic national identity.[32] When considered alongside events in recent Cambodian history, most notably the xenophobic nationalism of the Khmer Rouge, this situation becomes a cause for considerable concern.

Poverty, Inequalities and Development

In 1994, around 8,000 foreign tourists visited Angkor. Just over a decade later, in 2005, over 830,000 international tourists visited the site, an increase of 10,000% in just over a decade.[33] While this growth curve appears staggering in both real and relative terms, it was widely anticipated given Angkor's global prestige and its central location within Southeast Asia's highly interconnected regional tourism industry. When the Angkor–Siem Reap region was added to the World Heritage list in 1992, conservation and socio-economic development were identified as two halves of a long-term sustainable management plan. Understandably, the ICC viewed the impending arrival of an international tourism industry as a force that would threaten Angkor's long-term survival. Fearful of rampant and uncontrolled development, UNESCO stated in 1996 that tourism 'threatens to damage this Khmer cultural legacy far more swiftly and decisively than did any ancient invaders, or even the clandestine raiders of today'.[34] Such warnings and caution were wholly understandable. However, as the 1990s progressed the issue of development would be largely overlooked in a programme principally oriented towards archaeology and the protection and restoration of the site's temple architecture. Within this conservation paradigm, development, tourism and the generation of capital were all perceived as threats, impending dangers and issues to be resisted. Rather than embracing the complexities of this new era, the international community overseeing Angkor rarely engaged with the issue of tourism and the consequences it would hold.

Like the rest of Cambodia, the Angkor–Siem Reap region was suffering from major 'deficiencies in infrastructure and human resources'.[35] Yet within an ICC managerial framework principally composed of experts in architecture, archaeology, engineering and stone conservation such challenges rarely received the attention they deserved. In the committee's annual reports for the crucial five-year period after the region's listing as a World Heritage Site less than 10 pages out of 400 were dedicated to tourism.[36]

With international efforts firmly centred on architectural conservation, responsibility for urban development and tourism would lie with the Cambodian-run APSARA Authority. To this end the organisation was founded with three principal departments: *Culture and Monuments, Urban Development and Tourism Development*. APSARA's struggle towards operational stability, along with its severe lack of resources, meant that efforts were directed towards maintaining a supportive relationship with the international community.[37] It was a situation that resulted in resources being largely directed towards the Department of Culture and Monuments. In addition to successfully operating as a coordinating hub for numerous international projects, the department undertook the task of building a Cambodian pool of expertise. Real successes were achieved in training young Cambodian scholars in the areas of temple conservation, archaeology, Geographic Information Systems (GIS) and temple management.

By implication however, the other two sides of APSARA's organisational triangle—the departments of Urban Development and Tourism—received less support and finance. Even as the 1990s came to a close, the directors of two these departments could each only call upon the support of less than five trained staff. As part of their report into the Angkor–Siem Reap region, the New Zealand consultants, Miskell and Thomas, concluded that for both departments 'resources and budget provisions are inadequate for the tasks required'.[38] While there is little doubt that Angkor's fragile temples warranted urgent and sustained attention, the neglect of tourism (Figure 3), and its social, economic consequences, would have deleterious consequences.

Equally surprisingly, tourism was also overlooked by a foreign aid industry assisting with Cambodia's socio-economic development. Throughout the 1990s multilateral banks such as the World Bank and Asian Development Bank (ADB), along with governments from Australia, France, Japan and the US, were influential in mapping the parameters of Cambodia's socio-economic recovery and plan for national reconstruction. The implementation of a three-year structural adjustment programme, lasting between 1993 and 1996, would principally focus on the more 'traditional' industries of agriculture and manufacturing, and the export of natural resources like timber and rubber.[39] Within such a framework, the role of culture, and associated tertiary industries like tourism, were only given a passing acknowledgement. Similarly, only a broad recognition of tourism's 'future potential' would appear in the Royal Government's *First Socioeconomic Development Plan* produced in 1996. Despite identifying tourism as one of the country's 'main opportunities for rebuilding its economy', the document's account of reform and economic progress offered few details of how this potential would be realised.[40]

In essence, with tourism lying at the margins of both the cultural heritage and developmental sectors, an institutional and intellectual void concerning the relationship between culture, tourism and development emerged within, and across, the various bodies involved in Cambodia's reconstruction. By the beginning of the 2000s rapid tourism growth had become an important reality. The town of Siem Reap was witnessing a construction boom, not only in the hotel and restaurant sectors, but also in a housing industry catering to the ever-growing numbers of Cambodians now migrating to the area. The election victory of the Cambodian People's Party as the sole ruling

Figure 3 Tourists at Angkor Wat During Khmer New Year Festival. *Source*: T. Winter.

party in 1998 also proved an important turning point in Angkor's development. For a number of government officials Angkorean tourism now offered significant economic benefits. The country's precarious political and economic climate also meant initiatives towards development were invariably short term in their outlook. In a few short years Angkor had become one of the state's most important economic assets.

In response to this new era, the APSARA authority and UNESCO jointly hosted a number of workshops and conferences on 'Cultural Tourism' in Siem Reap and Phnom Penh. Driven by a concern for steering Angkor's development away from the more destructive forms of 'mass tourism', these initiatives focused on site protection and the provision of 'high quality' tourist facilities. In terms of site protection, it was becoming evident that hundreds of thousands of domestic and international visitors each year were eroding and damaging the temples. With many travel agents operating copycat itineraries the site's most iconic temples were suffering from extreme peaks and tourist surges on a daily basis. For UNESCO and the ICC tourism was rapidly becoming unsustainable. Although these workshops highlighted a numbers of common goals, the discussion revealed that the international heritage community and the Royal Government were on different paths and held contrasting visions concerning Angkor's future. In an attempt to accommodate these rapidly diverging agendas, the ICC moved towards a language of 'sustainable development'. Accordingly, the 2003 Paris Declaration on Angkor noted that 'sustainable ethical tourism in the Siem Reap/ Angkor region [should be used] as a tool in the fight against poverty'.[41] Recognising the previous lack of attention given to this area, it was recommended that 'development projects in the province of Siem Reap/Angkor be discussed in all their aspects, particularly economic, social and environment, within the framework of the periodic meetings of the ICC'.[42] This declaration has ensured that issues such as sewerage, water management, forestry and urban planning have received far greater attention within workshops, consultancy reports and government initiatives. Better communication channels have also opened up between the ICC, the Royal Government and the various Non-Governmental Organisations (NGOs) working on community development programmes in the region.

However, the speed of tourism growth in the Angkor–Siem Reap region continues to outpace these policy responses. Ensuring tourism can be better channelled to overcome the major economic and social inequalities that have emerged both within, and around, the town of Siem Reap in the last decade remains a major challenge. For those with language and service industry skills, tourism has proved a lucrative industry to work in. After tips, commissions and bonuses, the monthly income for head chefs, tour guides and hotel management staff often exceeds 1,000 US dollars. The personal income of entrepreneurial business owners has been many times more. While a number of NGOs have worked successfully to bolster rural employment and grassroots development through tourism related initiatives, the industry has created major imbalances in the region's economy. Indeed, beyond the pockets of wealth created by tourism, the salaries of school teachers, manual labourers, nurses, or market traders remains in the region of 30 to 40 US dollars per month. Although such inequalities are a common feature to places undergoing rapid tourism development, it is suggested here that in the case of Siem Reap, such problems have been exacerbated by a combination of policy frameworks of cultural tourism and sustainability primarily concerned with limiting tourism's detrimental impact on the Angkor archaeological park, coupled with the government's desires to draw the region into its top-down, state-centric model of development. The ongoing, long-term growth of tourism suggests the need for more community-oriented policies capable of improving the equitable distribution of tourism related capital across the region.[43] In a country that now has the highest levels of extreme poverty in Southeast Asia, Siem Reap province continues to languish as the country's third poorest.[44]

In looking to the future, Ministry of Tourism efforts to promote coastal destinations, along with eco-tourism in the northeast of the country and around the great lake Tonle Sap will undoubtedly help these regions to emerge as tourist destinations. The Khmer Rouge, remembered at places like Anlong Veng, Pol Pot's final resting place, will continue to draw visitors. Casino and sex tourism will also grow, with Phnom Penh and the border town of Poipet acting as the main centres of commerce. It is highly likely, however, that these regionalised developments will continue to be outpaced by the ongoing expansion of tourism at Angkor. With the annual number of foreign tourists visiting Angkor expected to exceed the three million mark by 2010, tourism will further exacerbate regional imbalances and major wealth inequalities both within and across communities, and across the country as a whole.

In this respect, Cambodia exemplifies Aihwa Ong's description of economic globalisation whereby places of hyper-growth like Angkor become surrounded by zones of abandonment.[45] Historically unprecedented levels of tourism have transformed the site's temples into an immensely important resource for capital accumulation. There is little doubt that an annual income of millions of dollars has been instrumental in steadying Cambodia's GDP growth, and that the industry has been the driving force for investments in both social and physical infrastructures. Equally however, the flows and distribution of wealth have been hugely disproportionate. It is thus argued here that the degree to which a tourism industry dominated by Angkor has contributed to nation-wide economic and political stability remains open to question.

Conclusion

The situation surrounding Angkor today is a stark example of a phenomenon common to many countries attempting to recover after periods of conflict or political turmoil. Reconciliation, cultural rejuvenation and economic rehabilitation are urgent and simultaneous demands. Heritage and cultural tourism are widely regarded as effective tools for protecting past histories, that can simultaneously provide the economic fuel for societal modernisation. In essence, heritage tourism looks in both directions: restoring and promoting the past while promising future prosperity. Almost inevitably however, the convergence of these agendas spawns contestation and various unexpected and paradoxical outcomes. Post-conflict Cambodia epitomises this situation. There is little doubt that heritage and tourism are contributing to, and providing substantial momentum for, the reconstruction of the country's cultural, social and physical infrastructures. As the keystone to this fragile recovery, Angkor stands as a beacon of strength, historical power and aesthetic grandeur. International tourism is also proving to be an abundant and seemingly ever expanding source of income. But as the number of conservation projects and annual visitor totals continue to grow, this highly symbolic site finds itself caught in an increasingly intense web of competing agendas.

There is little doubting that the protection and conservation of Angkor's architectural structures and the archaeological research conducted since the early 1990s have been worthy and important enterprises. It has been argued here, however, that such efforts have created a world heritage framework that re-solidifies the problematic binaries of regal/vernacular, classical/non-classical and modern/traditional first introduced in the late nineteenth century. This has meant the ways in which Cambodians value Angkor as a lived space, a landscape in constant flux and a shared heritage of everyday, inter-generational traditions have been marginalised within a discourse of monumental grandeur and classical antiquity. In a context where ideas of a national identity and Khmer culture are being welded onto a vision of lost, timeless glories the Cambodian heritage industry has emerged as a rigid framework which defines the 'authentic' or 'traditional' in narrow, absolutist ways. Heritage and tourism risk Cambodia once again trapping itself in a mono-cultural, mono-ethnic, nationalism.

The re-emergence of international tourism in Cambodia has also transformed the town of Siem Reap into an enclave of imbalanced wealth and development, and a micro-economy beyond which lies sustained rural poverty. Angkorean tourism is thus fuelling the country's ever increasing concentrations in wealth and sub-national inequalities. As Calavan et al. warn us, these economic imbalances, by implication, drastically reduce the chances of much needed social and political reforms being achieved.[46] As the case of Angkor shows, heritage and tourism can have far reaching social consequences in the developing world. This brief paper has argued that if we are to better understand and critically challenge these consequences, sustained and rigorous attention needs to be given to the broader political, economic and socio-cultural processes that shape heritage and tourism in countries like Cambodia today.

Notes

[1] See, for example, Pottier, 'Carte Archéologique de la Région d'Angkor. Zone Sud' and University of Sydney, *Greater Angkor Project*, http://acl.arts.usyd.edu.au/projects/externalprojects/urbanangkor.html [accessed 1 May 2007].
[2] Jacques and Freeman, *Angkor: cities and temples*
[3] See for example Higham, *The Civilization of Angkor*.
[4] Ibid.
[5] See Dagens *Angkor: heart of an Asian empire*.
[6] See Norindr, *Phantasmatic Indochina*.
[7] Winter, *Post-Conflict Heritage, Postcolonial Tourism*.
[8] Edwards, *Cambodge: the cultivation of a nation 1860–1945*
[9] As a product of late nineteenth-century European historiography, the vision of a Cambodian nation was largely moulded around French colonial agendas. For a detailed account of the politicised relationship between race, nation and culture within the French construction of Cambodge, see Ibid.
[10] See Winter, op. cit.
[11] See Edwards, op. cit.
[12] See Chandler, *A History of Cambodia*.
[13] Wager, *Developing a Strategy for the Angkor World Heritage Site*, 515–23.
[14] For further details see UNESCO, *Safeguarding and Development of Angkor*.
[15] Wager, op. cit., 515–23
[16] Winter, op. cit.
[17] Hitchcock, *Afterword*, 181–86.
[18] Winter, op. cit.
[19] Smith, *Archaeological Theory and the Politics of Cultural Heritage*.
[20] Ibid., 37
[21] Ibid., 10
[22] This neglect of traditions and temple usage by the international heritage community forms part of Miura's PhD thesis, which focuses on the impact world heritage enlistment has had on one particular village within the park. See Miura, 'Contested Heritage: People of Angkor'.
[23] Ang, 'The place of animism within popular Buddhism in Cambodia', and Harris, *Cambodian Buddhism*.
[24] Norindr, *Phantasmatic Indochina*.
[25] Turnbull, 'A burned out Theater', 139.

[26] According to Turnbull 'Of the three million dollars on average that the government spends annually on performance culture—a mere 0.25 per cent of Cambodia's national budget—much of it is allocated to a bloated network of around 3,000 administrators.' Ibid., 139.
[27] Ibid., 140.
[28] Dahles and Ter Horst, 'Weaving into Cambodia', 124.
[29] Ibid., 130.
[30] Winter, 'When Ancient "Glory" Meets Modern "Tragedy"', 37–53.
[31] For further details, see http://www.angkornationalmuseum.com [accessed 10 February 2008].
[32] Partly in response to such concerns, UNESCO assisted with the production of an *Inventory of Intangible Cultural Heritage of Cambodia*. Published in 2004, this inventory provides an important foundation for the cultivation of cultural policies that seek to create more pluralistic and vernacular connections between the past and the present.
[33] Ministry of Tourism/UNDP/WTO, *National Tourism Development Plan For Cambodia*. These figures do not include domestic tourists.
[34] UNESCO/APSARA, *Angkor: Past, Present and Future*, 166–67.
[35] Ministry of Planning, *First Socioeconomic Development Plan 1996–2000*, 157.
[36] Winter, *Post-Conflict Heritage, Postcolonial Tourism*, 74.
[37] For more details, see UNESCO/APSARA, *Angkor: Past, Present and Future*.
[38] Miskell and Thomas, *Angkor Forest Rehabilitation and Landscape Enhancement Project*, 2/36.
[39] Winter, *Post-Conflict Heritage, Postcolonial Tourism*, 68.
[40] Ministry of Planning, *First Socioeconomic Development Plan 1996–2000*, 156.
[41] UNESCO, *Paris Declaration*, 4.
[42] Ibid.
[43] See, for example, Ball, 'Tourism No Help to Siem Reap's Poorest', 1.
[44] Asian Development Bank, *Key Indicators 2004*, 40.
[45] Ong, *Neoliberalism as Exception*.
[46] Calavan et al., *Cambodian Corruption Assessment*.

References

Ang, C. 'The Place of Animism Within Popular Buddhism in Cambodia: the Example of the Monastery.' *Asian Folklore Studies*, no. 47 (1988): 35–41.
Asian Development Bank. *Key Indicators 2004: Poverty in Asia: Measurement, Estimates and Prospects*. Asian Development Bank, Manila, 2004.
Ball, M. 'Tourism No Help to Siem Reap's Poorest'. *Cambodia Daily*, 17 December 2002, 1.
Calavan, M., Briquets, S. and O'Brien, J. *Cambodian Corruption Assessment*, USAID, Phnom Penh, 2004.
Chandler, D. *A History of Cambodia*, Colorado, USA: Westview Press, 2000
Dagens, B. *Angkor: Heart of an Asian Empire*. London: Thames and Hudson, 1995.
Dahles, H. and J. Ter Horst. 'Weaving into Cambodia: Negotiated Ethnicity in the (Post)Colonial Silk Industry'. In *Expressions of Cambodia: the Politics of Tradition, Identity and Change*, ed. L. Ollier and T. Winter, 119–132. London: Routledge, 2006.
Edwards, P. *Cambodge: the Cultivation of a Nation 1860–1945*. Honolulu: University of Hawaii Press, 2007.
Harris, I. *Cambodian Buddhism; History and Practice*. Honolulu: University of Hawaii, 2005.
Higham, C. *The Civilization of Angkor*, London: Weidenfeld & Nicolson, 2001
Hitchcock, M. 'Afterword'. In *The Politics of World Heritage; Negotiating Tourism and Conservation*, ed. D. Harrison and M. Hitchcock. Clevedon: Channel View Publications, 2005: 181–186.
Jacques, C. and M. Freeman. *Angkor: Cities and Temples*. London: Thames & Hudson, 1997: 181–186.
Ministry of Planning. *First Socioeconomic Development Plan, 1996–2000*. Phnom Penh: Royal Government of Cambodia.

Ministry of Tourism/UNDP/WTO. *National Tourism Development Plan For Cambodia*. Phnom Penh: Ministry of Tourism, 1996.

Miura, K. 'Contested Heritage: People of Angkor'. Unpublished Ph.D Thesis, London: School of Oriental and African Studies, 2004.

Norindr, P. *Phantasmatic Indochina: French Colonial Ideology in Architecture, Film, and Literature.* London: Duke University Press, 1996.

Ong, A. *Neoliberalism as Exception: Mutations in Citizenship and Sovereignty.* Durham, NC: Duke University Press, 2006.

Pottier, C. 'Carte Archéologique De La Région D'Angkor. Zone Sud'. Universite Paris III—Sorbonne Nouvelle (UFR Orient et Monde Arabe), 1999.

Smith, L. *Archaeological Theory and the Politics of Cultural Heritage.* London: Routledge, 2004.

Turnbull, R. 'A Burned Out Theatre: the State of Cambodia's Performing Arts'. In *Expressions of Cambodia: the Politics of Tradition, Identity and Change*, ed. L. Ollier and T. Winter, 133–149. London: Routledge, 2006.

UNESCO. *Paris Declaration: Adopted at Second Intergovernmental Conference for the Safeguarding and Sustainable Development of Angkor and Its Region.* 14–15 November 2003, Paris: UNESCO..

———. *Safeguarding and Development of Angkor.* Tokyo: UNESCO, 1993.

——— and APSARA. *Angkor: Past, Present and Future.* Phnom Penh: APSARA, 1996.

——— and Ministry of Culture and Fine Arts. *Inventory of Intangible Cultural Heritage of Cambodia.* Phnom Penh: UNESCO/Ministry of Culture and Fine Arts, 2004.

Wager, J. 'Environmental Planning for a World Heritage Site: Case Study of Angkor Wat, Cambodia.' *Environmental Planning and Management* 38, no. 3 (1995): 419–434.

Winter, T. *Post-Conflict Heritage, Postcolonial Tourism: Culture, Politics and Development at Angkor.* London: Routledge, 2007

———. 'When Ancient "Glory" Meets Modern "Tragedy": Angkor and the Khmer Rouge in Contemporary Tourism'. In *Expressions of Cambodia: the Politics of Tradition, Identity and Change*, ed. L. Ollier and T. Winter, 37–53. London: Routledge, 2006.

Part IV
Future Directions in Cultural Heritage Rights Law

[19]

Changing Climate, Changing Culture: Adding the Climate Change Dimension to the Protection of Intangible Cultural Heritage

Hee-Eun Kim*

Abstract: This article explores the interplay between climate change and cultural heritage, in particular the intangible aspects of cultural heritage, in international legal frameworks, either existing or under development. The prime focus of the current climate change regime of the United Nations Framework Convention on Climate Change (UNFCCC) is the reduction of greenhouse gas emissions, leaving certain aspects of cultural heritage rather on the sidelines of debate and policy. However, where climate change combines with generally weak law and policy for culture and traditions, countries vulnerable to climate change may face significant cultural loss in the years to come.

In its inventory of present and contemplated legal protection options, this article draws particular attention to policymaking directed at shaping a "rights-based" system in the form of sui generis rights, to complement any existing intellectual property based protection. If adequately motivated, indigenous people have a key role to play not only in observing change, but also in developing adaptive models to cope.

INTRODUCTION

The Intergovernmental Panel on Climate Change (IPCC), an international scientific body organized to assess the risks of climate change, has found that the "unequivocal warming of the climate system" as observed in the increase of global average temperature, melting of glaciers and sea level rise is "very likely due to

---

*Stanford Law School. Email: hkim1121@gmail.com

ACKNOWLEDGEMENTS: I wish to thank Professor John H. Merryman of Stanford Law School for his inspiring support and the reviewers and the editors of IJCP for their helpful suggestions.

anthropogenic" (i.e., originating in human activity) greenhouse gas concentration.[1] Consistent with this finding, the prime focus of the current climate change regime led by the United Nations Framework Convention on Climate Change (UNFCCC) is the reduction of greenhouse gas emissions.[2]

The UNFCCC's utilitarian focus leaves certain aspects of cultural heritage on the sidelines of debate and policy. To what extent does climate change influence cultural heritage? Capturing a causal link between climate change and ever-changing cultural heritage presents a serious challenge. The distinction between normal climatic variability and anthropogenic causes adds complexity to such a determination. Recent observations that climate change increasingly makes people move appear to provide an existential foundation for linking climate causes and cultural heritage effects. As discussed in the following text, experts warn that one of the gravest effects of climate change concerns human mobility.[3] In other words, a significant number of people are likely to be forced to, or to voluntarily leave their homeland because of, for example, shoreline erosion, coastal flooding, and agricultural disruption.[4] Countries with populations on the verge of such displacement note that the impact of climate change concerns their survival and security, and "the cultural identity of an entire nation is under threat."[5]

So far, the adverse effects of climate change on cultural heritage tend to be considered primarily in connection with tangible or physical cultural properties, such as buildings, monuments, or archeological sites destroyed by extreme weather events.[6] Conversely, the effects of climate change on less tangible cultural heritage such as the loss of oral tradition and languages have been receiving less attention.[7]

While the interaction between climate change and cultural heritage has a range of tangible and intangible dimensions, the present article focuses on the "intangible aspects of cultural heritage"[8] as affected by climate change. It explores legal and policy options to place climate change considerations in the context of ongoing efforts to protect intangible cultural heritage within the relevant international legal frameworks.

The second section of the article provides some factual background on climate change-driven migration in and from countries such as the Small Island Developing States (SIDS).[9] Where climate change combines with generally weak law and policy for culture and traditions, some SIDS may face significant cultural loss in the years to come. To support this assessment, this section also presents selected statistics and data relevant to climate change displacement and cultural heritage in these regions.

Against this background of climate change displacement and vulnerability of cultural heritage, the third section of the article looks at several existing climate change-related international legal frameworks applicable to the protection of intangible cultural heritage. In terms of the relationship between climate change and cultural heritage, the climate change regime under the UNFCCC primarily recognizes the *usefulness* of traditional knowledge in the context of climate change adaptation. This acknowledges the role of local knowledge systems in the way in which local communities understand and adapt to changes in climate.[10] This section also touches on the risk management approach of UNESCO and principles under international refugee law to protect cultural rights of refugees.

The fourth section of the article draws attention to lessons from policymaking efforts on shaping a sui generis rights-based system for protecting "traditional cultural expressions" or "expressions of folklore"[11] complementing any existing intellectual property-based protection through the World Intellectual Property Organization (WIPO) and certain regional intellectual property authorities. On the basis of those efforts, this section explores certain law and policy options to enhance the protection of intangible cultural heritage against cultural loss triggered by climate change displacement.

BACKGROUND: CLIMATE CHANGE DISPLACEMENT AND CULTURAL HERITAGE

Climate Change Makes More People Move

The frequency and severity of certain hazards combined with vulnerability have been generally attributed to climate change.[12] The IPCC, which assesses scientific, technical, and socioeconomic information relevant to the understanding of climate change,[13] notes migration as one of the likely key consequences of climate change,[14] without asserting any "monocausal relationship."[15] International agencies concerned with migration and displacement observe that "gradual and sudden environmental changes are already resulting, with anywhere between 50 and 200 million people moving as a result [of rising sea levels, floods, droughts, famine and hurricanes] by the middle of the century, either within their countries or across borders, on a permanent or temporary basis."[16] (However, in the absence of a harmonized definition of climate change displacement[17] and baseline information on levels of climate change causing displacement,[18] such estimates may vary.)

To answer basic qualitative and quantitative questions,[19] the Inter-Agency Standing Committee (IASC), a mechanism for inter-agency coordination of humanitarian assistance among key United Nations (UN) and non-UN humanitarian organizations,[20] set up an expert group in 2008. Taking an existing categorization for internally displaced persons as a basis, this expert group developed a typology classifying causes of movement, nature of movement, and existing legal frameworks for those moving within or beyond borders.[21]

The first category is "sudden-onset disaster displacement"[22] such as floods and storms: for example, 36 million people in 2008 (including 15 million in the Sichuan earthquake in China alone).[23] The second category is "slow-onset disaster displacement"[24] such as drought.[25] The third category, singled out from the second, is displacement linked to sea-level rise.

Climate change displacement linked to sea-level rise is predicted to grow exponentially,[26] particularly in SIDS, Africa,[27] the Asian mega deltas, and the polar regions.[28] Four relocation cases are often dubbed as "the climate canaries"[29] heralding such trends: the Cartaret islands in Papua New Guinea,[30] the Lateu village in Vanuatu,[31] the Shishmaref village on Sarichef island in Alaska,[32] and the submerged Lohachara island in India's Hooghly River.[33]

While in many cases climate change-displaced persons remain within their country, some may cross borders, into an uncertain legal status.[34] In particular, SIDS have been considering the prospect of international climate change relocation. For example, in 2008 the president of the Maldives announced that the government would begin to divert a portion of the country's tourist revenue to buying a new homeland as an insurance policy against climate change.[35] He says Sri Lanka and India are regarded as suitable destinations because of their similar cultures, cuisines, and climates; and Australia is under consideration because of its vast unoccupied land.[36]

Kiribati is also looking to acquire land elsewhere so as to relocate communities in danger of being uprooted by rising sea levels.[37] Its government has been trying to secure enhanced labor migration options such as nursing, with an initial target of about 1,000 citizens annually to work in Australia and New Zealand.[38] Through remittances, such migrants can support their extended family members remaining in Kiribati.[39]

It should be noted that relocation between islands or abroad is increasingly common for Pacific islanders. For instance, Tuvalu is a small coral atoll nation—0.1 times the size of Washington, DC—with the highest point reaching only 16 feet above average sea level.[40] It is often depicted as one of the areas most vulnerable to climate change.[41] It had an estimated population of 10,000 as of July 2010.[42] A significant number of additional Tuvaluans have left, including some 3,000 to New Zealand, 300 to Australia, and others to the United States.[43] Such migration reportedly is motivated by environmental concerns, such as sea-level rise, tidal flooding, and salinity of limited arable land, in addition to other economic, political, and social reasons.[44]

The Vulnerability of Cultural Heritage to Climate Change Displacement

When climate change causes migration, what does this mean for the cultural heritage of the land left behind? It has been observed that refugee camps generally show a high level of cultural activity.[45] This phenomenon has been explained as "an empowering way of securing continuity and some semblance of stability" while "enabling [the refugees] to experiment with" new identities, strategies for adaptation and survival.[46] Indeed, maintaining cultural values and traditions on a longer-term basis after settling in a foreign country poses a significant challenge.

A survey of the Tuvaluan community in New Zealand observes that, "although community-based culture is still evident through their church activities, island celebration functions and sports events, they are not as strong as back home in the islands."[47] Reported reasons include the changes in lifestyle and financial conditions that come with living in New Zealand.[48] Naturally, the traditional Tuvaluan culture blends with that of New Zealand, with the dispersed nature of Tuvaluan settlement in the country further diluting the community-based culture.[49]

Not only those who have left, but also those still on the islands experience "a deep sense of 'loss' or at least an expectation of inevitable looming 'loss' of place of the home islands which form the very core of their identities."[50] The loss of their culture and traditions is mentioned as one of the biggest concerns of South Pacific islanders preparing to move.[51] Such feelings of "losing ground" are hardly surprising, because the relationship of indigenous peoples to their land is particularly important to their sovereignty and identity: Will they be able to maintain their culture on foreign soil?[52]

Few available statistics specifically document the extent of climate change-related vulnerabilities of cultural heritage.[53] Within the limits of this article, it may be useful to review certain indicators pertaining to SIDS: for example, whether or not a country is a member of UNESCO; the extent of UNESCO-listed cultural heritage; and the number of languages in the SIDS. Partial and secondary as some of these data may be, they do suggest that protecting the SIDS' cultural heritage from the effects of climate change is more than an academic concern.[54]

In terms of natural and tangible cultural heritage protection, all of the 38 SIDS that are UN members have also joined the UNFCCC and UNESCO. With five exceptions (Bahamas, Nauru, Singapore, Timor-Lesté, and Tuvalu),[55] they are also members of UNESCO's World Heritage Convention. Although the number of actually inscribed World Heritage properties is relatively small, SIDS members of the convention count 28 items on the World Heritage List (whereas Belize's Barrier Reef Reserve System[56] also features on the list of World Heritage in Danger).

Another illustration of protectable culture is provided by the Convention for the Safeguarding of Intangible Cultural Heritage (the ICH Convention)[57] established in 2003, together with the Representative List of the Intangible Cultural Heritage of Humanity.[58] Out of a total of 232 listed items, only six relate to SIDS: "Language, Dance and Music of the Garifuna" in Belize; "La Tumba Francesa" in Cuba; "The Cocolo Dance Drama Tradition" and "The Cultural Space of the Brotherhood of the Holy Spirit of the Congos of Villa Mella," both in the Dominican Republic; "The Maroon Heritage of Moore Town" in Jamaica; "The Lakalaka, Dances and Sung Speeches of Tonga"; and "Vanuatu Sand Drawing."[59]

The Vanuatuan item exemplifies the intangible heritage involved, its vulnerability, and safeguarding efforts. Proclaimed a Masterpiece of the Oral and Intangible Heritage of Humanity by UNESCO in 2003,[60] Vanuatu's sand drawings are artful geometric patterns produced directly on the ground to transmit traditional knowledge about local history, indigenous rituals, kinship systems, natural phenomena, and farming techniques.[61] Sand drawing also represents a means of communication among the members of various language groups in the north of the Vanuatu archipelago.[62] Expert sand drawers possess intimate knowledge of the numerous graphic patterns and a deep understanding of their complex layers of meaning.[63]

To help preserve the practice and meaning of Vanuatu sand drawing, Vanuatu's National Cultural Council, a representative body of cultural policy, initiated a National Action Plan for the Safeguarding of Sand Drawing in 2000.[64] Sponsored by UNESCO and Japan Funds-in-Trust for the Preservation and Promotion of Intangible Cultural Heritage, the National Action Plan consisted of two components: revitalization, transmission, and promotion; and legal protection, income generation, and inventory-making.[65] One project outcome is the National Sand Drawing Festival established in 2004.[66]

A further indicator of vulnerable cultural diversity are the local languages in SIDS.[67] Statistics show SIDS' rich linguistic heritage. For example, Papua New Guinea is one of the most linguistically diverse and complex areas in the world, with close to 850 indigenous languages spoken,[68] and at least as many traditional communities, among a population of about 6 million.[69] Among these languages,

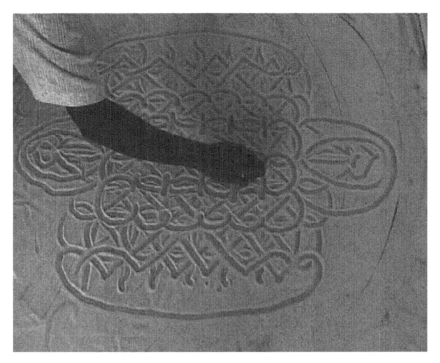

FIGURE 1. Vanuatu Sand Drawing (© *Vanuatu National Cultural Council*).

CHANGING CLIMATE, CHANGING CULTURE

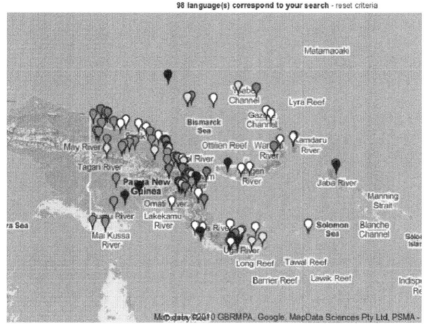

FIGURE 2. UNESCO Atlas of the World Languages in Danger—Papua New Guinea. (© UNESCO, http://www.unesco.org/culture/en/endangeredlanguages/atlas)

UNESCO's *Atlas of the World Languages in Danger* identifies at least 98 as vulnerable, endangered, or even extinct.[70] See Figure 2.

Vanuatu, a much smaller country with a population of 240,000, still has 110 languages, 46 of which are considered to be at critical risk.[71] Efforts to revitalize such languages notwithstanding,[72] such findings appear to reflect a general trend. Table 1 lists the aforementioned selected indicators of protectable cultural heritage in SIDS, together with the net migration rate per country.

CLIMATE CHANGE-RELATED INSTRUMENTS AND INTANGIBLE CULTURAL HERITAGE

The Climate Change Regime Focuses on the Utility of Traditional Knowledge

Historically, traditional knowledge[76] has been an important source of local innovation to provide solutions for adjusting to the conditions of nature. In this sense, the use of traditional knowledge is often discussed in the context of knowledge

Table 1
Selected Indicators of Protectable Cultural Heritage in Small Island Developing States

Small Island Developing States (SIDS)	Parties to the Intangible Cultural Heritage (ICH) Convention	Parties to the Cultural Diversity Convention	Number of World Heritage Properties Inscribed	Number of Representative Intangible Heritage Listed	Number of Languages (Extant/Extinct)[73]	Net Migration Rate per 1,000 Persons (2010 est.)[74]
Antigua and Barbuda			0	0	2 (2/0)	2.35
Bahamas			0	0	3 (2/1)	0.00
Bahrain			1	0	3 (3/0)	0.00
Barbados	✓	✓	0	0	2 (2/0)	−0.30
Belize	✓		1*	1	8 (8/0)	0.00
Cape Verde			1	0	2 (2/0)	−0.67
Comoros			0	0	6 (6/0)	0.00
Cuba	✓	✓	9	1	3 (3/0)	−1.56
Dominica	✓		1	0	3 (3/0)	−5.44
Dominican Republic	✓	✓	1	2	4 (4/0)	−2.04
Fiji	✓	✓	0	0	10 (10/0)	−7.37
Grenada	✓	✓	0	0	3 (3/0)	−3.67
Guinea-Bissau		✓	0	0	22 (22/0)	0.00
Guyana		✓	0	0	17 (16/1)	−15.83
Haiti	✓	✓	1	0	3 (3/0)	−9.75
Jamaica	✓	✓	0	1	3 (3/0)	−5.52
Kiribati			1	0	2 (2/0)	−2.87
Maldives			0	0	1 (1/0)	−12.60
Marshall Islands			1	0	2 (2/0)	−5.30
Mauritius	✓	✓	2	0	6 (6/0)	−0.03
Micronesia (Federated States of)			0	0	18 (18/0)	−21.01
Nauru			0	0	3 (3/0)	−16.08

(*continued*)

Table 1 Continued

Small Island Developing States (SIDS)	Parties to the Intangible Cultural Heritage (ICH) Convention	Parties to the Cultural Diversity Convention	Number of World Heritage Properties Inscribed	Number of Representative Intangible Heritage Listed	Number of Languages (Extant/Extinct)[73]	Net Migration Rate per 1,000 Persons (2010 est.)[74]
Palau			0	0	4 (4/0)	0.86
Papua New Guinea	✓		1	0	841 (830/11)	0.00
Samoa			0	0	2 (2/0)	−11.52
São Tomé and Príncipe	✓		0	0	4 (4/0)	−9.52
Singapore			0	0	21 (21/0)	4.79
St. Kitts and Nevis			1	0	2 (2/0)	1.26
St. Lucia	✓		1	0	2 (2/0)	−3.93
St. Vincent and the Grenadines	✓	✓	0	0	2 (2/0)	−11.36
Seychelles	✓	✓	2	0	3 (3/0)	1.04
Solomon Islands			1	0	74 (71/3)	−1.94
Suriname			2	0	17 (17/0)	0.00
Timor-Lesté			0	0	~19[75]	0.00
Tonga	✓	✓	0	1	3 (3/0)	0.00
Trinidad Tobago	✓	✓	0	0	6 (6/0)	−7.11
Tuvalu			0	0	2 (2/0)	−7.07
Vanuatu	✓		1	1	110 (108/2)	0.00
Total of SIDS	18	11	28	7	N/A	Average: −4.01

*In the World Heritage in Danger.

dissemination and technology transfer for climate change adaptation. For example, the UN Convention to Combat Desertification (UNCCD)[77] documented the practical relevance of traditional knowledge in member countries[78] for sustainable management of dryland ecosystems.[79] The UNFCCC, too, acknowledges the importance of using traditional knowledge in climate change adaptation[80] and aims to promote its dissemination in developing countries. Local knowledge systems can help communities understand and adapt to change in climate.[81]

Conversely, given the primary concern with the reduction of greenhouse gas emissions under the UNFCCC and the Kyoto Protocol, aspects of cultural heritage less utilitarian for the purpose of greenhouse gas reduction, such as traditional cultural expressions (TCEs) or expressions of folklore, hardly figure in the ongoing climate change discussion. For instance, the Kyoto Protocol's Clean Development Mechanism (CDM) projects allow developed countries to invest in greenhouse gas emission reduction projects in developing countries, and in return they receive credit for the remission reduction or removal achieved.[82] Not surprisingly, there is no current CDM project directly involving the protection of TCEs or expressions of folklore, or indeed of cultural heritage in a broader sense.[83]

The National Adaptation Program of Action (NAPA), intended to address the urgent adaptation needs of Least Developed Countries under the auspices of the UNFCCC,[84] also seems to neglect projects directly related to the protection of cultural heritage. A few SIDS—Samoa, the Solomon Islands, and Vanuatu—have submitted NAPA projects in relation to their tourism industry,[85] but without express reference to the protection of cultural heritage.

UNESCO's Risk Management Approach for Climate Change Adaptation: The ICOMOS Position

The UNESCO World Heritage Centre, in its report on climate change and World Heritage,[86] recognizes climate change as one of a range of factors affecting our natural and cultural heritage. Set out in the following text is UNESCO's itemization of principal climate change risks and their impact on cultural heritage.[87]

Noting that conservation of World Heritage is essentially about "the management of change" and that the climate is one such area of change, UNESCO recommends a three-part strategy for safeguarding World Heritage against the emerging climate conditions:[89]

- Preventive actions: monitoring, reporting and mitigation of climate change effects through environmentally sound choices and decisions at a range of levels: individual, community, institutional and corporate.
- Corrective actions: adaptation to the reality of climate change through global and regional strategies and local management of plans.

- Sharing knowledge: including best practices, research, communication, public and political support, education and training, capacity building, networking, etc.[90]

Taking a similar approach, the International Council on Monuments and Sites (ICOMOS) concludes that

> climate change adaptation for cultural heritage should be mainstreamed into the existing methodologies for preservation and conservation of sites, buildings, settlements, landscapes, movable objects and the living traditions and that appropriate standards and protocols should be developed for the purpose. Equally cultural heritage needs and concerns should be mainstreamed into institutional processes and policies for disaster reduction.[91]

Skeptical about such risk management approaches, some scholars observe that, in the climate change regime, cultural heritage struggles to compete against an "avalanche of other urgent resource-demanding concerns."[92] Part of the problem, they assert, is the cultural heritage regime itself paying little attention to the "cultural heritage values"[93] for mankind. The human and cultural dimension of climate change implies "the need to consider how the loss of tangible heritage places, sites and structures will affect communities and the intangible aspects of culture, or on finding locally appropriate response to this potential loss."[94] Such understanding of how climate change jeopardizes entire cultures and ways of life is viewed as a catalyst for action.[95] For example, if adequately motivated,[96] indigenous people have a key role not only in observing change, but also in developing adaptive models to cope.[97]

Emerging Climate Change Refugee Policy Proposals and Cultural Heritage

Current international refugee law incorporates the principles of nondiscrimination and national treatment. According to the Convention Relating to the Status of Refugees (the 1951 Refugee Convention),[98] the host country must not discriminate refugees on race, religion, or country of origin.[99] Also, the host country is required to provide treatment "at least as favorable as that accorded to their nationals with respect to freedom to practice their religion and freedom as regards the religious education of their children."[100]

The latter principle of national treatment is also applied to the protection of industrial property and of rights in literary, artistic, and scientific works. A refugee must be accorded in the country in which he or she has his habitual residence the same protection as is accorded to the nationals of that country.[101] In addition, the 1951 Refugee Convention provides for "intergenerational transmission and the

Table 2
UNESCO: Principal Climate Change Risks and Impacts on Cultural Heritage[88]

Climate Indicator	Climate Change Risk	Physical, Social, and Cultural Impacts on Cultural Heritage
Atmospheric moisture change	• Flooding (sea, river) • Intense rainfall • Changes in water-table levels • Changes in soil chemistry • Ground water changes • Changes in humidity cycles • Increase in time of wetness • Sea salt chlorides	• pH changes to buried archeological evidence • Loss of stratigraphic integrity caused by cracking and heaving from changes in sediment moisture • Data loss preserved in waterlogged/anaerobic/anoxic conditions • Eutrophication accelerating microbial decomposition of organics • Physical changes to porous building materials and finishes caused by rising damp • Damage caused by faulty or inadequate water disposal systems; historic rain-water goods incapable of handling heavy rain and often difficult to access, maintain, and adjust • Crystallization and dissolution of salts caused by wetting and drying affecting standing structures, archaeology, wall paintings, frescos, and other decorated surfaces • Erosion of inorganic and organic materials caused by flood waters • Biological attack of organic materials by insects, molds, fungi, and invasive species such as termites • Subsoil instability, ground heave, and subsidence • Relative humidity cycles/shock causing splitting, cracking, flaking, and dusting of materials and surfaces • Corrosion of metals • Other combined effects (e.g., increase in moisture combined with fertilizers and pesticides)
Temperature change	• Diurnal, seasonal, extreme events (heat waves, snow loading) • Changes in freeze-thaw and ice storms, and increase in wet frost	• Deterioration of facades due to thermal stress • Freeze-thaw/frost damage • Damage inside brick, stone, or ceramics that has gotten wet and frozen within material before drying • Biochemical deterioration • Changes in *fitness for purpose* of some structures. • Inappropriate adaptation to allow structures to remain in use

(*continued*)

Table 2 Continued

Climate Indicator	Climate Change Risk	Physical, Social, and Cultural Impacts on Cultural Heritage
Sea-level rise	• Coastal flooding • Sea-water incursion	• Coastal erosion/loss • Intermittent introduction of large masses of *strange* water to the site, which may disturb the metastable equilibrium between artifacts and soil • Permanent submersion of low-lying areas • Population migration • Disruption of communities • Loss of rituals and breakdown of social interactions
Wind	• Wind-driven rain • Wind-transported salt • Wind-driven sand • Wind gusts and changes in direction	• Penetrative moisture into porous cultural heritage materials • Static and dynamic loading of historic or archeological structures • Structural damage and collapse • Deterioration of surfaces caused by erosion
Desertification	• Drought • Heat waves • Fall in water table	• Erosion • Salt weathering • Impact on health of population • Abandonment and collapse • Loss of cultural memory
Climate and pollution acting together	• pH precipitation • Changes in deposition of pollutants	• Stone recession by dissolution of carbonates • Blackening of materials • Influence of biocolonialization
Climate and biological effects	• Proliferation of invasive species • Spread of existing and new species of insects (e.g., termites) • Increase in mold growth • Changes to lichen colonies on buildings • Decline of original plant materials	• Collapse of structural timber and timber finishes • Reduction in availability of native species for repair and maintenance of buildings • Changes in the natural heritage values of cultural heritage sites • Changes in appearance of landscapes • Transformation of communities • Changes the livelihood of traditional settlements • Changes in family structures as sources of livelihood become more dispersed and distant

non-interference of this transmission,"[102] a right of association,[103] and freedom of movement.[104]

One limitation of national treatment or most-favored nation clauses is that, if the host country does not offer its nationals adequate protection of cultural identity or heritage per se, *climate change refugees* can hardly expect better protection. Considering that international refugee law does not yet cater to issues specifically associated with climate change displacement,[105] some are advocating the creation of a treaty covering climate change refugees.[106] Proponents of such an agreement argue that as climate change refugees' intangible cultural heritage "is no longer preserved by the laws and institutions of their home state, the legal protection of [climate change refugees'] cultural autonomy may be regarded as a mechanism of preservation, . . . and safeguarding intangible cultural heritage can further support the relocation of entire population and social groups."[107] Further, some argue that environmental refugees should be given a right to "constitute themselves collectively and maintain their collective identity."[108]

LESSONS FROM RIGHTS-BASED PROTECTION OF TRADITIONAL CULTURAL EXPRESSIONS

A wide range of public considerations underlies ongoing efforts to protect intangible cultural heritage.[109] While the 2003 UNESCO Convention does not provide a separate definition of *protection* as such,[110] the 2005 UNESCO Convention on the Protection and Promotion of the Diversity of Cultural Expressions (the 2005 UNESCO Convention) defines it as "the adoption of measures aimed at the preservation, safeguarding and enhancement of the diversity of cultural expressions."[111] The 1985 UNESCO-WIPO Model Provisions for National Laws on the Protection of Expressions of Folklore against Illicit Exploitation and Other Prejudicial Actions (the 1985 UNESCO-WIPO Model Provisions) states inter alia that "protection should be against any improper utilization of expressions of folklore [or traditional cultural expressions], including the general practice of making profit by commercially exploiting such expressions outside their originating communities without any recompense to such communities."[112]

For practical purposes, protection of intangible cultural heritage needs to focus on two goals: to prevent "misappropriation" by third parties without prior informed consent; and, especially relevant in the context of climate change, to prevent *loss* as such.[113] Increasingly, it is thought that both of these goals can be served by according specific rights to holders of intangible cultural heritage and that tailored rights can motivate them to preserve, practice, and promote their traditional assets even after they leave their homeland. In this regard, this section of the article briefly describes the soft-law making process for the protection of traditional cultural expressions at WIPO and other intergovernmental institutions and situates the climate change dimension in that process.

Rights-Based Mechanisms in Some South Pacific Countries

It has been noted that, for South Pacific islanders,

> the concept of ownership (either by individuals, families or communities) of songs, dances and other forms of traditional knowledge and custom has been well-established for a long period of time ... and the knowledge [of such traditional cultural expressions] was a commodity exchanged between local groups in the past.[114]

To decide ownership disputes, courts often relied on customary law.[115] An example is *In the Matter of the Nagol Jump*, in which case a group of applicants tried to prevent others from performing the Nagol jump on the island of Santo (the Nagol jump is a traditional ceremony, similar to bungee jumping, from the island of Pentecost).[116] The Supreme Court of Vanuatu decided the case on "substantial justice" and "in conformity with custom", finding that the Nagol jumping should "return" to its origins in Pentecost.[117]

In recent years, a growing number of South Pacific countries have been formally integrating the protection of traditional cultural expressions into existing intellectual property law[118] and, additionally, have been developing a sui generis protection system generally based on the Secretariat of Pacific Community's 2002 Model Law on Traditional Knowledge and Expression of Culture ("South Pacific Model Law").[119] Administration and advancement of the South Pacific Model Law are now in the hands of the Pacific Island Forum Secretariat, which has further established the Traditional Knowledge Implementation Action Plan,[120] with the aim of assisting the Cook Islands, Fiji, Kiribati, Palau, Papua New Guinea, and Vanuatu in their implementation of traditional knowledge and traditional cultural expressions protection. Similar activities address the needs of other SIDS such as Niue, Samoa, and the Solomon Islands.[121]

Major Components of Sui Generis Protection

International efforts to provide a sui generis basis for the protection of traditional cultural expressions have focused primarily on instruments of soft law, such as the aforementioned 1985 UNESCO-WIPO Model Provisions.[122] In 2000 the WIPO General Assembly created the WIPO Intergovernmental Committee on Intellectual Property and Genetic Resources, Traditional Knowledge and Folklore (IGC) to negotiate appropriate protection mechanisms.[123] In 2006 the IGC developed draft objectives, principles, and substantive provisions for the protection of traditional cultural expressions/expressions of folklore (IGC Draft).[124] While the IGC work has progressed to a stage of text-based expert meetings,[125] regional developments saw not only the creation of the South Pacific Model Law, but also the adoption by the African Regional Intellectual Property Organization (ARIPO) of the Swakopmund Protocol on the Protection of Traditional Knowledge and Expression of Folklore within the Framework of ARIPO.[126] The principal elements of these instruments may be summarized as follows.

Subject Matter and Scope of Protection

As defined in the IGC Draft, "traditional culture expressions" or "expressions of folklore" are any forms, whether tangible or intangible, in which traditional culture and knowledge are expressed, appear or are manifested, and comprise forms of expressions or combinations that are verbal, musical, by action, or tangible.[127] Such expressions should be protected against acts of misappropriation.[128]

The South Pacific Model Law recognizes concepts of "traditional cultural rights" and "moral rights" to traditional knowledge or expressions of culture. Moral rights thereby refer to the right of attribution of ownership,[129] the right against derogatory treatment,[130] and the right to equitable benefits from derivative works with commercial nature.[131]

Traditional cultural rights are described as encompassing rights in relation to cultural expressions to authorize or prevent their reproduction, publication, public performance or display, broadcast, translation, adaptation, arrangement, transformation, modification, fixation (such as by making a photograph, film, or sound recording), making available online, creation of derivative works, making, using, offering for sale, selling, importing, exporting, or use in any other material form.[132]

Exceptions and Limitations

The IGC Draft foresees exceptions and limitations to these rights for teaching and learning, noncommercial research or private study, criticism or review, reporting news or current events, use in the course of legal proceedings, the making of recordings and other reproductions of traditional cultural expressions for purposes of their inclusion in an archive or inventory for noncommercial cultural heritage safeguarding purposes, and incidental uses.[133] Interestingly, the South Pacific Model Law limits the teaching exception to "face to face" teaching[134] and does not provide exceptions for the making of recordings for purposes of archiving.[135]

Beneficiaries

The beneficiaries are the indigenous people and traditional and other cultural communities in whom the custody, care, and safeguarding of the traditional cultural expressions are entrusted in accordance with their customary law and practice; and who maintain, use, or develop the traditional cultural expressions as being characteristic of their cultural and social identity and cultural heritage.[136]

Term of Protection

The South Pacific Model Law states that traditional cultural rights as well as moral rights continue in perpetuity, are inalienable, and cannot be waived or transferred.[137] Conversely, the IGC Draft foresees protection as long as traditional cultural expressions remain registered or notified according to any rules on formalities; and for secret traditional cultural expressions, as long as they remain secret.[138]

Formalities

As a general rule, the protection as such of traditional cultural expressions is not dependent on any formality.[139] However, registration or notification systems may be envisaged.[140]

In terms of user procedures, the South Pacific Model Law identifies two contractual avenues for a prospective user of traditional cultural expression for noncustomary purposes to seek prior informed consent: (1) applying to a 'Cultural Authority' in charge of identifying beneficiaries and acting as a liaison between prospective users and the beneficiaries; or (2) directly dealing with the beneficiaries.[141]

Sanctions, Remedies and Exercise of Rights

The IGC Draft states that accessible, appropriate, and adequate enforcement and dispute-resolution mechanisms, border measures, sanctions, and remedies, including criminal, civil, and administrative remedies should be available in case of breach of protected traditional cultural expressions.[142] In addition, the South Pacific Model Law specifically refers to public apology, alternative dispute resolution (ADR), and customary law options.[143]

Relationship with Intellectual Property Protection and Other Forms of Protection

The IGC Draft provides that the envisaged sui generis protection does not replace, but is complementary to, protection under intellectual property laws and programs for the safeguarding, preservation, and promotion of cultural heritage, and other available legal and nonlegal measures.[144] Likewise, the South Pacific Model Law affirms that traditional cultural rights do not affect any rights existing under intellectual property law or other national law.[145] It may thereby be noted that while creators of works derived from traditional cultural expressions benefit from intellectual property protection, under the South Pacific Model Law such third parties would also be subject to obligations to the original right holders.[146]

International and Regional Protection

In dealing with the "technical question of how rights and interests of foreign holders" in traditional cultural expressions should be recognized in national laws,[147] the IGC Draft takes the notion of national treatment[148] as a starting point and proposes to supplement it with mutual recognition, reciprocity or assimilation.[149] The South Pacific Model Law refers to enforcement through reciprocal arrangement.[150]

Adding the Climate Change Dimension

Building on the principal components of sui generis protection of traditional cultural expressions cited as an example, this final part adds three brief and diverse considerations that might usefully figure in negotiation and implementation of these instruments, with a view to safeguarding intangible cultural heritage in the face of climate change and climate change displacement.

Cross-Border Protection

The cross-border aspect of climate change displacement lends weight to the international dimension of protection of intangible cultural heritage. Acknowledging such international protection as priority,[151] the IGC in its norm-setting process for traditional cultural expressions explored, inter alia, whether it should seek to determine at the international level how their misappropriation and use should be suppressed, and through what kind of legal instruments.[152] Taking the existing international protection of copyright as an example, the Berne Convention prescribes minimum standards of protection that are binding on all member states. However, with views differing among participants in the IGC process on the desirable degree of protection for traditional knowledge or traditional cultural expressions, and its relation to the existing international intellectual property rights system, the IGC Draft eventually opted for "a neutral form so as not to preempt the policy choices."[153]

National treatment is helpful where the host country provides sufficient protection for the intangible cultural heritage of its nationals. Likewise, reciprocal arrangements, such as those adopted in the South Pacific Model Law, are useful if the host country and the country of origin share an effective standard of protection of such rights. The challenge is how to accommodate national self-determination in this regard while ensuring international protection. Further awareness of the cultural impact of climate change migration might stimulate the development of a minimum standards approach coupled with an international registration system, perhaps somewhat comparable maybe to the system for appellations of origin established by the Lisbon Agreement.[154]

More Funding Initiatives

Legal protection alone cannot maintain intangible cultural heritage. Funding is essential, for example to support education, promotion, recording and archiving. One of the first initiatives in this direction is the WIPO Voluntary Fund for Accredited Indigenous and Local Communities, launched in 2010.[155] One year earlier, the 2005 UNESCO Convention[156] created the International Fund for Cultural Diversity (IFCD). The purpose of the IFCD is to promote sustainable development and poverty reduction in developing countries through support for projects and activities aiming to foster the emergence of a dynamic cultural sector.[157] The first batch of funding requests has been received, but only few came from SIDS and none were related to climate change.[158] Here again, further awareness of the threat that climate change poses to intangible cultural heritage may improve the financial basis for giving effect to legal protection.

Training, Good Practices, National Policies: It Takes a Village

A 2007 survey of practices and protocols regarding the safeguarding of cultural heritage and related intellectual property issues revealed a strong interest on the part of museums, libraries, and archives in South Pacific countries in receiving training on such issues and developing good practices and guidelines.[159]

To respond to such needs, WIPO operates the Creative Heritage Project,[160] which aims to offer practical training to local communities, museums, and archives in developing countries on recording, digitizing, and disseminating their creative cultural expressions as well as on intellectual property issues.[161] A pilot program undertaken with a Maasai community and National Museums of Kenya confirmed the introduction of intellectual property rights management as a useful tool for promoting the safeguarding and legal protection of intangible heritage.[162]

Becoming increasingly aware of their cultural interests, some South Pacific countries are taking the lead in researching the impact of climate change on their cultural heritage. For example, Vanuatu has adopted a cultural research policy[163] under which the Vanuatu National Cultural Council approves research projects consistent with the country's research priorities, such as language documentation, cultural and historic site documentation, documentation of indigenous histories, and case studies of contemporary social change. Research projects must substantially involve indigenous communities, scholars and students,[164] and commercial proceeds of any research products are to be shared between the council and the researcher.[165]

CONCLUSION

The impact of climate change on cultural heritage hardly figures in current climate change policymaking, with its dominant focus on greenhouse gas emissions and their direct consequences. Likewise, the conventional perspective of cultural heritage risk management concerns especially the loss of tangible heritage sites and structures, and to a lesser extent how such loss will affect communities and the intangible aspects of culture. However, as climate change displacement materializes, these human dimensions will demand increasing attention.

One perspective on cultural property is as part of "the cultural heritage of all mankind,"[166] whatever the place of origin or present location.[167] Another view of cultural property is as "a national cultural heritage" invoking in nations or communities a special interest to attribute unique character to their cultural objects and to legitimize demands for retaining cultural property.[168]

The emergence of international climate change issues in cultural heritage, intangible as well as tangible, could complicate such distinction of interests. Accommodation may need to be made for climate change-related regulation, international human rights law concerning climate change refugees, and intellectual property rights or sui generis rights relevant to the protection and promotion of traditional knowledge and traditional cultural expressions, especially in terms of cross-border protection.

ENDNOTES

1. IPCC, *Climate Change 2007*, 30.
2. United Nations Framework Convention on Climate Change, article 2, opened for signature 9 May 1992, S. Treaty Doc. No. 102-38, 1771 U.N.T.S. 107 (hereinafter UNFCCC).
3. See for example, Norwegian Refugee Council (NRC), *Climate Changed: People Displaced*, 5. Animals are also forced to leave their homelands. An interview by Yale Environment 360 with Stephanie Pfirman (geologist) describes how an ice refuge zone could become a key habitat for polar bears, ringed seals, and other ice-dependent Arctic creatures.
4. Myers and Kent, *Environmental Exodus*, 134.
5. H.E. Apisai Ielemia, Prime Minister of Tuvalu, General Debate at the 63rd UN General Assembly. See also O'Neil, *Culture Change*, which explains that even in the absence of climate change, cultural identity in modern times is vulnerable to change because of challenges such as globalization and technological development.
6. See for example, European Commission, *Cultural Heritage—Environment—Research*, which states that the European Commission's research efforts "focus on better assessing and understanding the mechanisms by which damage to cultural heritage occurs, and on finding the best possible measures and means to ensure that tangible cultural heritage is protected."
7. See for example, Brinicombe, Lucy. Oxfam. "Cancún Climate Change Conference: Indigenous Voices Gather Strength." Guardian.co.uk Environmental Blog ⟨guardian.co.uk/environmenta/blog⟩ 8 December 2010 (accessed), which comments that despite indigenous people such as native American and Inuit communities being among those most influenced by climate change, "up until today, their voice has been but a whisper." ⟨http://www.guardian.co.uk/environment/blog/2010/dec/08/cancun-climate-change-conference-indigenous⟩
8. According to Article 2 of the Convention for the Safeguarding of the Intangible Cultural Heritage, intangible cultural heritage means

> the practices, representations, expressions, knowledge, skills—as well as the instruments, objects, artifacts and cultural spaces associated therewith—that communities, groups and, in some cases, individuals recognize as part of their cultural heritage. This intangible cultural heritage, transmitted from generation to generation, is constantly recreated by communities and groups in response to their environment, their interaction with nature and their history, and provides them with a sense of identity and continuity, thus promoting respect for cultural diversity and human creativity.... Intangible cultural heritage is manifested *inter alia* in the following domains: (a) oral traditions and expressions, including language as a vehicle of the intangible cultural heritage; (b) performing arts; (c) social practices, rituals and festive events; (d) knowledge and practices concerning nature and the universe; and (e) traditional craftsmanship.

See the Convention for the Safeguarding of the Intangible Cultural Heritage, art. 2, 17 October 2003, in force 20 April 2006 2368 U.N.T.S. 1 [hereinafter 2003 UNESCO Convention].
9. The United Nations Department of Economic and Social Affairs (UN DESA) lists 52 small island developing states, 32 UN Members and 14 non-UN Members or Associate Members of the Regional Commissions.
10. Colette, *Climate Change and World Heritage*, 30.
11. According to Article 1(a) of the WIPO Revised Draft Provisions for the Protection of Traditional Cutltural Expressions/Expressions of Folklore, *traditional cultural expressions* or *expressions of folklore* are any forms, whether tangible and intangible, in which traditional culture and knowledge are expressed, appear or are manifested, and comprise the following forms of expressions or combinations thereof:

1. verbal expressions, such as stories, epics, legends, poetry, riddles and other narratives; words, signs, names, and symbols;
2. musical expressions, such as songs and instrumental music;
3. expressions by action, such as dances, plays, ceremonies, rituals and other performances, whether or not reduced to a material form; and,
4. tangible expressions, such as productions of art, in particular, drawings, designs, paintings (including body painting), carvings, sculptures, pottery, terra-cotta, mosaic, woodwork, metalware, jewelry, baskets, needlework, textiles, glassware, carpets, costumes; handicrafts; musical instruments; and architectural forms; which are:

   a. the products of creative intellectual activity, including individual and communal creativity;
   b. characteristic of a community's cultural and social identity and cultural heritage; and
   c. maintained, used or developed by such community, or by individuals having the right or responsibility to do so in accordance with the customary law and practices of that community.

See WIPO, *Revised Draft Provisions*, 11. The terms *traditional cultural expressions* and *expressions of folklore* can be used interchangeably. For further discussion about traditional cultural expressions, see the fourth section of the article.

Cf. The 2005 Convention on the Protection and Promotion of the Diversity of Cultural Expressions defines *cultural expressions* broadly as "cultural expressions are those expressions that result from the creativity of individuals, groups and societies, and that have cultural content." See Convention on the Protection and Promotion of the Diversity of Cultural Expressions, 20 October 2005, U.N. Doc. CLT-2005/CONVENTION DIVERSITE-CULT REV., art. 4(1) [hereinafter 2005 UNESCO Convention].

12. Norwegian Refugee Council (NRC), *Climate Changed: People Displaced*, 5, which states that, for example, "the overall trend shows that the number of recorded natural disasters has doubled from approximately 200 to over 400 per year over the past two decades" (citing Emergency Events Database ⟨http://www.em-dat.be⟩) (accessed 25 November 2010).

13. Intergovernmental Panel on Climate Change (IPCC) ⟨http://www.ipcc.ch⟩.

14. See generally IPCC, *First Assessment Report (1999)*; also IPCC, *Fourth Assessment Report (2007)* and IPCC, *Climate Change 2007: Synthesis Report*.

15. See for example, UNHCR et al., *Forced Displacement*, 2, which states that "there is no monocausal relationship between climate change and displacement.... However, ... there is a clear link between the effects of climate change and displacement".

16. IOM et al., *Climate Change, Migration*, 1, noting, however, the absence of "scientifically verified estimates of climate change-related displacement or of overall population flows triggered by the effects of climate change." See also Kang, *Climate Change, Migration and Human Rights*, 3–4, citing *the Stern Report on the Economics of Climate Change*, 56. See also Docherty and Giannini, "Confronting a Rising Tide," 353–54, which states that estimates of the number of climate refugees vary depending on the definition of the class of the displaced and the source of the data, and that while some research urges caution in attempting to predict a number, other studies present figures ranging from 50 million to 200 million displaced persons before 2100.

17. Docherty and Giannini, "Confronting a Rising Tide," 353–54.

18. Norwegian Refugee Council (NRC), *Climate Changed: People Displaced*, 6.

19. Norwegian Refugee Council (NRC), *Climate Changed: People Displaced*, 6.

20. Inter-Agency Standing Committee (IASC) ⟨http://www.humanitarianinfo.org⟩.

21. Informal Group on Migration/Displacement and Climate Change of the IASC, "Climate Change, Migration and Displacement," 1–4. A fourth category, "armed conflict/violence over shrinking natural resources," falls outside the scope of this article.

22. Norwegian Refugee Council (NRC), *Climate Changed: People Displaced*, 5–7.

23. Norwegian Refugee Council (NRC), *Climate Changed: People Displaced*, 5–7.

24. Norwegian Refugee Council (NRC), *Climate Changed: People Displaced*, 5–7, which points out that, although some 26.5 million were reported to have been affected by 12 droughts in 2008,

estimates for displacement are not readily available because of the complexity in determining the element of force and ascribing causation.

25. See for example, Myers, "Environmental Refugees," 609–11, stating that

> out of the 25 million environmental refuges in 1995 around the world, there were roughly 5 million in the African Sahel, where a full 10 million had fled from droughts, only half returning home.... In other parts of Sub-Saharan Africa, 7 million people had been obliged to migrate in order to obtain relief food.

26. Norwegian Refugee Council (NRC), *Climate Changed: People Displaced*, 5–7.

27. See for example, Annan, *Keynote Speech at the Global Conference*, 4 November 2010, highlighting that "feeding Africa, at a time of climate change, is one of the major development challenges of our time" and "without concerted action, we will see many more people forced to leave their land, increased famines, tensions and instability."

28. Norwegian Refugee Council (NRC), *Climate Changed: People Displaced*, 7.

29. IOM, *Migration and Climate Change*, 25–26, commenting that the world's media have been competing to find the "first conclusive 'victim' of climate change—who, like a miner's canary, will mark the beginning of a period of irreversible climate impacts."

30. IOM, *Migration and Climate Change*, 25–26, stating that "in 2005, it was officially decided to evacuate the 1,000 residents of the Carteret Islands, a group of small and low-lying coral atolls administered by Papua New Guinea, to the larger island of Bougainville, 100 kilometers away."

31. IOM, *Migration and Climate Change*, 25–26, noting that "about a hundred residents of Lateu, on the island of Tegua on Vanuatu, were relocated farther inland, following storm-damage, erosion and salt damage to their original village."

32. IOM, *Migration and Climate Change*, 25–26, explaining that "a combination of melting permafrost and sea-shore erosion at a rate of up to 3.3 meters a year have forced the inhabitants to relocate their village several kilometers to the south."

33. IOM, *Migration and Climate Change*, 25–26, stating that

> Lohachara island in the Hooghly river delta, once home to 10,000 people, and which had first started flooding 20 years ago, had finally been entirely submerged. One of a number of vanishing islands in the delta, the loss of the islands and other coastal land in the delta has left thousands of people homeless.

34. Biermann and Boas, "Preparing for a Warmer World," 60–67, addressing the need of a global governance system regarding "climate change refugees" or "climate refugees." These refugees can be defined as "people who have to leave their habitats, immediately, or in the near future, because of sudden or gradual alterations in their natural environment related to at least one of three impacts of climate change: sea-level rise, extreme weather events, and drought and water scarcity." For further discussions on "climate change refugees," see Docherty and Giannini, "Confronting a Rising Tide"; and Hodgkinson *et al.*, *The Hour When The Ship Comes In*.

35. See for example, Randeep Ramesh. "Paradise Almost Lost: Maldives Seek to Buy a New Homeland," *Guardian*, 10 November 2008, 1.

36. Ramesh, Randeep. "Paradise Almost Lost," *Guardian*, 10 November 2008, 1.

37. "Kiribati Seeks Relocation as Climate Change Sets In," *Solomon Times Online*, 16 February 2009, ⟨http://www.solomontimes.com/news.aspx?nwID=3584⟩ (accessed 8 November 2010); see also UNHCR News Stories, *Pacific Islanders Face the Reality of Climate Change . . . and of Relocation* ⟨http://www.unhcr.org/print/4b264c836.html⟩ (14 December 2009) accessed.

38. Norwegian Refugee Council (NRC), *Climate Changed: People Displaced*, 15.

39. Loughry and McAdam, "Kiribati—Relocation and Adaptation," 51–52.

40. Central Intelligence Agency (CIA), *The World Factbook 2009*.

41. See for example, Fauvre and Stanley, "Five Takes on Climate," 306, introducing five documentaries about climate and cultural change in Tuvalu: "The Disappearing of Tuvalu: Trouble in Paradise," "Paradise Drowned: Tuvalu, The Disappearing Nation," "Tuvalu: That Sinking Feeling," "Before the Flood," "Time and Tide."

42. Fauvre and Stanley, "Five Takes on Climate," 306. By comparison, the population of the Maldives was 395,650 and that of Kiribati 99,485.

43. Gemenne and Shen, *Environmental Change and Forced Migration*.

44. Gemenne and Shen, *Environmental Change and Forced Migration*.

45. See for example, Conquergood, "Health Theater in a Hmong," 174–80, opening with a description of a Hmong woman in a refugee camp in Thailand singing about the loss of her husband, children, house, farm, animals, and country in the traditional form of a Hmong folk song.

46. Conquergood, "Health Theater in a Hmong," 180.

47. Gemenne and Shen, *Environmental Change and Forced Migration*, 21–23.

48. Gemenne and Shen, *Environmental Change and Forced Migration*, 21–23.

49. Gemenne and Shen, *Environmental Change and Forced Migration*, 21–23; watch also Panos Pictures, "Tuvalu—Island on the Frontline.".

50. Henry and Jeffrey, "Waterworld: The Heritage Dimensions," 13–14, provide an interview of locals in the Federated States of Micronesia.

51. Loughry, "Climate Change: The Tipping Point," 2.

52. See for example, von Lewinski, *Indigenous Heritage and Intellectual Property*, 508, citing Felicia Sandler, "Music of the Village."

53. See for example, UNESCO Institute for Statistics, *Measuring the Diversity*, which discusses the difficulties of measuring the diversity of cultural expressions in one country or among countries and providing a number of related working documents. But also see for example, UNESCO Institute for Statistics, *The 2009 Framework*, which proposes the use of an industry classification system for this purpose.

54. On the impacts of climate change on SIDS and their vulnerabilities, see Barnett and Campbell, *Climate Change and Small Island*; Intergovernmental Panel on Climate Change, *Fourth Assessment Report (2007)* (analyzing key future impacts and vulnerabilities category by category e.g., water resources, coastal systems and resources, agriculture, fisheries and food security, biodiversity, human settlement and well-being, economic, financial and sociocultural impacts, and infrastructure and transportation); United Nations Framework Convention on Climate Change (UNFCCC), *Vulnerability and Adaptation*; UN DESA, *SIDS Network* ⟨http://www.sidsnet.org⟩; IPCC, *Climate Change 2007: Synthesis Report*.

55. States Parties to the World Heritage Convention number 187 as of June 2010.

56. See for example, Shane D. Williams, "Oceana Celebrates GOB's Ban on Trawling," *Guardian.bz* (9 December 2010) ⟨http://www.guardian.bz/all-news/59-other-news/2648-oceana-celebrates-gobs-ban-on-trawling⟩. Williams discusses the government of Belize's banning of trawling, a method of fishing in which a huge net is dragged under water by one or more boats. Trawling has contributed to the destruction of Belize's barrier reef, the second largest in the world.

57. States Parties to the 2003 Convention number 133 as of July 2010.

58. Details of UNESCO's safeguarding projects, including recording and training, can be found at ⟨http://www.unesco.org/culture/ich/en/lists⟩.

59. The term *sandroing* is also used, which is in Bislama, the local language.

60. See UNESCO, *Vanuatu Sand Drawings* and also UNESCO's "Vanuatu Sand Drawings" video.

61. Vanuatu National Cultural Council, *The National Action Plan*.

62. Vanuatu National Cultural Council, *The National Action Plan*.

63. Vanuatu National Cultural Council, *The National Action Plan*.

64. Vanuatu National Cultural Council, *The National Action Plan*.

65. Vanuatu National Cultural Council, *The National Action Plan*.

66. UNESCO, *Vanuatu Sand Drawings*.

67. See for example, UNESCO World Report, 11–22, identifying languages, education, cultural contents on media, crafts markets and tourism as "key vectors of cultural diversity."

68. For more on the languages of Papua New Guinea, see Aikhenvald and Stebbins, "Languages of New Guinea," 239–66.

69. Central Intelligence Agency (CIA), *The World Factbook 2009*.

70. Moseley, *Atlas of the World's Languages*.

71. Moseley, *Atlas of the World's Languages*.
72. See for example, Max Planck Institute for Psycholinguistics, *Dokumentation Bedrohter*, including a documentation project of "Vera'a", one of the endangered languages of Vanuatu, with less than 300 speakers.
73. Language data are based on Lewis, *Ethnologue: Languages of the World*. In Table 1, "extant" languages include both "living languages" and "languages being spoken as a second language without mother-tongue speakers," and "extinct" languages means no known speakers exist.
74. Central Intelligence Agency (CIA), *The World Factbook 2009*, defines the net migration rate as "the difference between the number of persons entering (+) and leaving (−) a country during the year per 1,000 persons, based on midyear population," and stating that "[t]he net migration rate indicates the contribution of migration to the overall level of population change. It does not distinguish between economic migrants, refugees, and other types of migrants nor does it distinguish between lawful migrants and undocumented migrants."
75. The Central Intelligence Agency (CIA), *The World Factbook 2009*, states that, in addition to Portuguese, Indonesian, and English, there are about 16 indigenous languages. Among those indigenous languages, Tetum, Galole, Mambae, and Kemak are spoken by significant numbers of people.
76. See generally, Taubman and Leistner, "Traditional Knowledge," 59–173; and Taubman, "Saving the Village," 521–564.
77. United Nations Convention to Combat Desertification in Those Countries Experiencing Serious Drought and/or Desertification, Particularly in Africa, opened for signature 17 June 1994 33 I.L.M. 1328 (hereinafter UNCCD).
78. Articles 17, 18, and 19 of UNCCD.
79. See generally, UNCCD, *Promotion of Traditional Knowledge*, on a wide range of traditional knowledge regarding for example, control of wind or water erosion, water conservation, improvement of soil fertility, plant protection, forestry, social structures, and housing architecture.
80. See generally, UNFCCC, *Technologies for Adaptation*.
81. Colette, *Climate Change and World Heritage*, 30.
82. Kyoto Protocol to the UNFCCC, art. 12, adopted 10 December 1997, 37. I.L.M. 22 (entered into force 16 February 2005) [hereinafter Kyoto Protocol]. The Kyoto Protocol states that the purpose of the clean development mechanism is "to assist Parties not included in Annex I in achieving sustainable development and in contributing to the ultimate objectives of the Convention, and to assist Parties included in Annex I in achieving compliance with their quantified emission limitation and reduction commitments under Article 3 [of the Kyoto Protocol]."
83. UNFCCC, *CDM in Numbers*.
84. Article 4(9) of UNFCCC.
85. UNFCCC, *NAPA Tourism*.
86. Colette, *Climate Change and World Heritage*, 10–11; World Heritage Committee, 30th Sess., Vilnius, Lithuania, 8–16 July 2006, Decision 30COM 7.1 Issues Related to the State of Conservation of World Heritage Properties: the Impacts of Climate Change on World Heritage Properties, WHC-06/30.COM/19 (23 August 2006).
87. Colette, *Climate Change and World Heritage*, 10–11.
88. Colette, *Climate Change and World Heritage*, 10–11.
89. Colette, *Climate Change and World Heritage*, 10–11.
90. Colette, *Climate Change and World Heritage*, 10–11.
91. International Council on Monuments and Sites (ICOMOS), *Resolution at the International Workshop*.
92. Christoff, "Places Worth Keeping?" 43, opines that "the belief that current policies and institutions are sufficient to deal with the challenges of mitigation and adaptation is bolstered by unwillingness to visualize and conceive of the enormity of the potential changes we face even at low levels of global temperature increase …"
93. Pearson, "Climate Change Its Impacts," 40.
94. McIntyre-Tamwoy, "The Impact of Global," 8.

95. Christoff, "Places Worth Keeping?" 44.
96. See for example, Alivizatou, *Curating Intangible Cultural Heritage*, citing the Vanuatuan politician Ralph Regenvanu's remarks that

> tourism can distort cultural expressions. The question, however, is if the community who is the bearer and practitioner of the tradition decides to alter the tradition for the purpose of making money, is that a distortion? Or maybe is the intervention of UNESCO, museums and anthropologists saying that they can't do that the real distortion?

97. See for example, Rowland, "Saving the Past from the Future," 21.
98. Convention Relating to the Status of Refugees, opened for signature 28 July 1951, 189 U.N.T.S. 150 [hereinafter 1951 Refugee Convention].
99. Article 3 of the 1951 Refugee Convention.
100. Article 4 of the 1951 Refugee Convention.
101. Article 14 of the 1951 Refugee Convention.
102. Hodgkinson *et al.*, *The Hour When The Ship Comes In*, 44–45.
103. Article 15 of the 1951 Refugee Convention.
104. Article 26 of the 1951 Refugee Convention.
105. See for example, Docherty and Giannini, "Confronting a Rising Tide," 353–54; Biermann and Boas, "Preparing for a Warmer World," 60–67; Hodgkinson *et al.*, *The Hour When The Ship Comes In*, 44–45.
106. See for example, IOM *et al.*, *Climate Change, Migration*, 1.
107. See for example, Hodgkinson *et al.*, *The Hour When The Ship Comes In*, 44–45.
108. Hodgkinson *et al.*, *The Hour When The Ship Comes In*, 44–45 (citing Julien Betaillle et al., Draft Convention on the International Status of Environmentally-Displaced Persons, 4 Revue Europeenne de Droit de L'Environment 395 [2008]).
109. Cf. Torsen, "Intellectual Property and Traditional," 201, observing that "[t]o some extent, the very goal of any eventual instrument is not entirely clear", but that WIPO, WTO, and the World Bank are "providing opportunities to wrestle with these and other issues."
110. But the 2003 UNESCO Convention defines *safeguarding* as "measures aimed at ensuring the viability of the intangible cultural heritage, including the identification, documentation, research, preservation, protection, promotion, enhancement, transmission, particularly through formal and non-formal education, as well as the revitalization of the various aspects of such heritage."
111. Article 4(7) of the 2005 UNESCO Convention.
112. UNESCO and WIPO, Model Provisions for National Laws on the Protection of Expressions of Folklore Against Illicit Exploitation and Other Prejudicial Actions with a Commentary, 4 (1985).
113. See for example, WIPO, *Climate Change and the Intellectual Property System*, 40–45.
114. Forsyth, "Intellectual Property Laws," states that rights to certain songs and carvings were protected by *tabu* and often magic and could be purchased with payments of food, mats and other forms of currency; Kalinoe, "Ascertaining the Nature," 27, and "Promulgating Traditional Knowledge," 6; and Marahare, "Towards an Equitable Future," 2.
115. Forsyth, "Intellectual Property Laws."
116. Forsyth, "Intellectual Property Laws."
117. Forsyth, "Intellectual Property Laws." *Cf.* The Vanuatu Cultural Centre, the institution mandated to regulate commercial filming of cultural subjects in Vanuatu, has declared "a moratorium or ban on all commercial filming by foreign film companies of the Nagol jump on Pentecost effective from January 1, 2006," in response to "growing concerns about the increasing distortion of this traditional ceremony due to growing commercialization." See Vanuatu Cultural Centre, *Moratorium on Commercial Filming of Nagol*.
118. WIPO, *Legislative Texts on the Protection*, indicates that, for example, Fiji, the Federated States of Micronesia, Papua New Guinea, Samoa, and Vanuatu have incorporated the protection of traditional cultural expressions in their copyright laws and Palau in its Historical and Cultural Preservation Act of 1995. However, opinion is divided as to whether the intellectual property system offers

optimal protection of traditional cultural expressions. See Marra, "IP & Traditional Cultural," who describes how, during a side event of the 17th Session of WIPO IGC on 8 December 2010, some indigenous communities expressed reluctance to accept copyright protection of their traditional cultural expressions because copyright affords only temporary protection, instead of the perpetual protection to which they feel their culture is entitled.

119. Secretariat of the Pacific Community (SPC), *Regional Framework for the Protection* (hereinafter, "South Pacific Model Law").

120. Pacific Islands Forum Secretariat (PIFS), *Traditional Knowledge*, provides that the Action Plan consists of two components: first, to develop a national system of protection setting out new rights and obligations in traditional knowledge that will complement existing forms of protection for intellectual property; second, to develop cultural industries to promote the commercialization of traditional knowledge.

121. E-mail from Douveri Henao, Trade Policy Officer, PIFS, 12 December 2010; see also UN Secretary-General, *Five-year Review*, 34, noting that several SIDS have undertaken initiatives to protect traditional knowledge, skills, and cultural expressions.

122. UNESCO and WIPO, *Model Provisions*.

123. WIPO General Assembly, 26th Sess. (12th Extraordinary Sess.), at 23, WIPO Doc. WO/GA/26/10 (3 October 2000). See also WIPO General Assembly, 26th Sess. (12th Extraordinary Sess.), *Matters Concerning Intellectual Property and Genetic Resources, Traditional Knowledge and Folklore*, WIPO Doc. WO/GA/26/6 (25 August 2000).

124. See generally, WIPO, *Revised Draft Provisions*.

125. See for example, most recently, WIPO IGC, 17th Sess., 6–10 December 2010, Decisions of the Seventeenth Session of the Committee, WIPO Doc. WIPO/GRTKF/IC/17 (10 December 2010).

126. Adopted by the Diplomatic Conference of the African Regional Intellectual Property Organization (ARIPO) in Swakopmund, Namibia on 9 August 2010; see also WIPO, "Director General Welcomes."

127. IGC Draft, Article 1.
128. IGC Draft, Article 3.
129. South Pacific Model Law, Article 13.
130. South Pacific Model Law, Article 12.
131. South Pacific Model Law, Article 12.
132. South Pacific Model Law, Article 7.
133. IGC Draft, Article 5.
134. South Pacific Model Law, Article 7(4).
135. See generally, WIPO, *Intellectual Property and the Safeguarding*.
136. IGC Draft, Article 2.
137. South Pacific Model Law, Articles 9, 10 and 13(4).
138. IGC Draft, Article 6.
139. IGC Draft, Article 7. See also *Explanatory Memorandum for the South Pacific Model Law*, 1–3.
140. IGC Draft, Article 7.
141. South Pacific Model Law, Articles 20, 21, 22, 23, and 24. See also *Explanatory Memorandum for the South Pacific Model Law*, 1–3.
142. IGC Draft, Article 8.
143. South Pacific Model Law, Article 31.
144. IGC Draft, Article 10.
145. South Pacific Model Law, Article 11.
146. South Pacific Model Law, Article 12.
147. IGC Draft, Article 11.
148. See for example, the Berne Convention for the Protection of Literary and Artistic Works, art. 5(1), 9 September 1886, as last revised at Paris, 24 July 1971, S. Treaty Doc. No. 99-27 (1986) [hereinafter Berne Convention], which states that

[a]uthors shall enjoy, in respect of works for which they are protected under this Convention, in countries of the Union other than the country of origin, the rights which their respective laws do now or may hereafter grant to their nationals, as well as the rights specially granted by this Convention.

149. See for example, WIPO, *Revised Draft Provisions*, 48.

150. South Pacific Model Law, Article 39, commentary explains that country A may enter into a reciprocal arrangement with country B whereby A agrees to extend the same protection to traditional cultural expressions originating from B (but present in A) and vice versa. Under such arrangement, an expression of culture such as a sculpture which was brought from B to A for an exhibition for the duration of its stay in A would be protected in the same way as a sculpture is normally protected in A.

151. See for example, WIPO IGC, 7th Sess., 6–10 June 2010, *Practical Means of Giving Effect to the International Dimension of the Committee's Work*, WIPO Doc. WIPO/GRTKF/IC/8/6 (Apr. 4, 2005).

152. WIPO, *Practical Means*, 3.

153. WIPO, *Practical Means*, 13.

154. See WIPO, *Lisbon System for the International Registration*.

155. WIPO, "IGC Makes Significant Progress."

156. As of June 2010, there are 116 ratifications of the 2005 Convention.

157. See UNESCO, *Measuring the Diversity*.

158. Intergovernmental Committee for the Protection and Promotion of the Diversity of Cultural Expressions Fourth Ordinary Session Paris, UNESCO Headquarters 29 November–3 December 2010, Item 10A of the Provisional Agenda: Implementation of the International Fund for Cultural Diversity (IFCD).

159. Talakai, *Intellectual Property and Safeguarding*, 10.

160. The WIPO *Creative Heritage Project* provides project descriptions including: "IP Management by Museums, Libraries and Archives," "IP and Handicrafts," "Creative Heritage Gateway," "Community Cultural Documentation," and "IP Management related to Arts Festivals."

161. Wendland, "Seeking Tangible Benefits," 129.

162. Wendland, "Seeking Tangible Benefits," 129 (while pointing out challenges with regard to policies, ownership issues, local politics, sustainability, and scalability).

163. Vanuatu National Cultural Council, *Vanuatu Cultural Research Policy*, at art. 3.

164. Vanuatu Cultural Research Policy, Article 7.

165. Vanuatu Cultural Research Policy, Article 12.

166. Convention for the Protection of Cultural Property in the Event of Armed Conflict, 14 May 1954, 249 U.N.T.S. 240 [hereinafter 1954 Hague Convention].

167. Merryman, "Two Ways of Thinking," 837.

168. Merryman, "Two Ways of Thinking," 832; see also Merryman, *Thinking About The Elgin Marbles*, 82–109.

BIBLIOGRAPHY

Aikhenvald, Alexandra Y., and Tonya N. Stebbins. "Languages of New Guinea." In *The Vanishing Languages of the Pacific Rim*, edited by Osahito Miyaoka, Osamu Sakiyama, and Michael E. Krauss, 239–66. Oxford: Oxford University Press, 2007.

Alivizatou, Marilena. "Curating Intangible Cultural Heritage: The Case of the Vanuatu Cultural Centre," *2009 Lamphun Field School: Intangible Cultural Heritage and Museums* (25 August 2009): 44, http://www.sac.or.th/databases/fieldschool/wp-content/uploads/2009/ppt/Curating-ICH-Case-of-Vanuatu-Cultural-Centre_Alivizatou_Aug-25.pdf (2009) accessed 14 December 2010.

Annan, Kofi A. "Feeding Africa at a Time of Climate Change—a Major Development Challenge of Our Era" (keynote speech, the Global Conference on Agriculture, Food Security and Climate Change, the Hague, the Netherlands, 4 November 2010)⟨http://www.agra-alliance.org/content/news/detail/1227⟩ accessed 4 December 2010.

Barnett, Jon, and John Campbell. *Climate Change and Small Island States: Power, Knowledge and the South Pacific*. London: Earthscan, 2010.

Biermann, Frank, and Ingrid Boas. "Preparing for a Warmer World: Towards a Global Governance System to Protect Climate Refugees." *Global Environmental Politics* 10, no. 1 (February 2010): 60–67, doi:10.1162/glep. 2010.10.1.60.

Central Intelligence Agency (CIA). *The World Factbook 2009*. ⟨https://www.cia.gov/library/publications/the-world-factbook/index.html⟩ (2011) accessed 14 December 2010.

Christoff, Peter. "Places Worth Keeping? Global Warming, Heritage and the Challenges to Governance." *Historic Environment* 21, no. 1 (2008): 41–44.

Colette, Augustin, ed. *Climate Change and World Heritage: Report on Predicting and Managing the Impacts of Climate Change on World Heritage and Strategy to Assist State Parties to Implement Appropriate Management Responses*. Paris: UNESCO World Heritage Centre, 2007.

Conquergood, Dwight. "Health Theater in a Hmong Refugee Camp: Performance, Communication, and Culture." *The Drama Review* 32 (Autumn 1988): 174–80.

Docherty, Bonnie, and Tyler Giannini. "Confronting a Rising Tide: A Proposal for a Convention on Climate Change Refugees." *Harvard Environmental Law Review* 33 (2009): 353–54.

European Commission. *Cultural Heritage—Environment—Research*. ⟨http://ec.europa.eu/research/environment/index_en.cfm?pg=cultural⟩ (3 September 2010) accessed 7 December 2010.

Farrell, Ben. *Pacific Islanders Face the Reality of Climate Change ... and of Relocation*. ⟨http://www.unhcr.org/print/4b264c836.html⟩ (14 December 2009) accessed 1 October 2010.

Fauvre, Anne, and Keith Stanley. "Five Takes on Climate and Cultural Change in Tuvalu." *The Contemporary Pacific* 19 no. 1 (Spring 2007): 306.

Forsyth, Miranda. "Intellectual Property Laws in the South Pacific: Friend or Foe?" *Journal of South Pacific Law* 7 (2003). ⟨http://www.paclii.org/journals/fjSPLvol07no1/8.shtml⟩ accessed 14 December 2010.

Gemenne, François, and Shawn Shen. *Environmental Change and Forced Migration Scenarios (EACH-FOR): Specific Targeted Project Scientific Support to Policies—SSP: Tuvalu and New Zealand Case Study Report (Ref. No. D 2.3.2.3.)*. ⟨http://www.each-for.eu⟩ (2007) accessed 25 November 2008.

Henry, Rosita, and William Jeffrey. "Waterworld: The Heritage Dimensions of 'Climate Change' in the Pacific." *Historic Environment* 21 (2008): 13–14.

Hodgkinson, David, Tess Burton, Heather Anderson, and Lucy Young. *The Hour When The Ship Comes In': A Convention for Persons Displaced by Climate Change*. ⟨http://www.hodgkinsongroup.com/documents/Hour_When_Ship_Comes_In.pdf⟩ (23 December 2009) accessed 8 December 2010.

Ielemia, H. E. Apisai. *General Debate at the 63rd United Nations General Assembly* (26 September 2008). ⟨http://www.un.org/ga/63/generaldebate/pdf/tuvalu_en.pdf⟩ accessed 31 August 2010.

Informal Group on Migration/Displacement and Climate Change of the IASC. "Climate Change, Migration and Displacement: Who Will Be Affected?" (Working Paper, October 2008). ⟨http://www.unfccc.int/resource/docs/2008/smsn/igo/022.pdf⟩ (28 November 2008) accessed 27 November 2010.

Intergovernmental Panel on Climate Change. *Climate Change 2007: Synthesis Report (2007)*. IPCC, Core Writing Team, R.K. Pachauri, and A. Reisinger (eds.), *Climate Change 2007: Synthesis Report*. Geneva: IPCC, 2008. http://www.ipcc.ch/publications_and_data/publications_ipcc_fourth_assessment_report_synthesis_report.htm (accessed 8 November 2010).

———. IPCC First Assessment Report 1990 (FAR). Geneva: IPCC, 1990. http://www.ipcc.ch/ipccreports/1992%20IPCC%20Supplement/IPCC_1990_and_1992_Assessments/English/ipcc_90_92_assessments_far_overview.pdf (accessed 8 November 2010).

———. *First Assessment Report (1999)*.

International Council on Monuments and Sites (ICOMOS). *Resolution at the International Workshop on Impact of Climate Change on Cultural Heritage*, New Delhi (22 May 2007).

International Organization for Migration (IOM). *Migration and Climate Change*. IOM Migration Research Series No. 31 (2008): 25–26.

IOM, Office of the United Nations High Commissioner for Refugees (UNHCR), the United Nations University (UNU) *in cooperation with* the Norwegian Refugee Council (NRC) and the Representative of the Secretary General on the Human Rights of Internally Displaced Persons (RSG on the HR of IDP), *Climate Change, Migration, and Displacement: Impacts, Vulnerability, and Adaptation Options*, submitted to the 5th Session of the Ad-Hoc Working Group on Long-Term Cooperative Action under the UNFCCC, 29 March–8 April 2009, 1 (6 February 2009).

Kalinoe, Lawrence. "Ascertaining the Nature of Indigenous Intellectual and Cultural Property and Traditional Knowledge and the Search for Legal Options in Regulating Access in Papua New Guinea." *Melanesian Law Journal* 27 (January 2000). ⟨http://www.paclii.org/journals/MLJ/2000/1.html⟩ accessed 9 December 2010.

———. "Promulgating Traditional Knowledge Sensitive IPR Legislation in Papua New Guinea and Related Developments in Pacific Island Countries: A Reflection on the Past Three Years." *Melanesian Law Journal* 27 (January 2000). ⟨http://www.paclii.org/journals/MLJ/2000/6.html⟩ accessed 9 December 2010.

Kang, Kyung-wha. *Climate Change, Migration and Human Rights, at the Conference on Climate Change and Migration: Addressing Vulnerabilities and Harnessing Opportunities* (19 February 2008). ⟨http://www.ohchr.org/EN/NewsEvents/Pages/DisplayNews.aspx?NewsID=9162&LangID=E⟩ (accessed 16 October 2011).

Kim, Hee-Eun. *The Role of the Patent System in Stimulating Innovation and Technology Transfer for Climate Change (Including Aspects of Licensing and Competition Law)*. Baden-Baden: Nomos, 2011.

Lewis, M. Paul, ed. *Ethnologue: Languages of the World*, 16th ed. Dallas: SIL International, 2009.

Loughry, Maryanne. "Climate Change: The Tipping Point." *Link (A Newsletter for Friends of the Jesuit Refugee Service Australia)* 10 no. 4 (Summer 2010): 2.

Loughry, Maryanne, and Jane McAdam. "Kiribati—Relocation and Adaptation." *Forced Migration Review* 31 (October 2008): 51–52.

Marahare, Don. "Towards an Equitable Future in Vanuatu: The Legal Protection of Cultural Property." *Journal of South Pacific Law* 8 (2004): 2. ⟨http://www.paclii.org/journals/fJSPL/vol08no2/6.shtml⟩ accessed 12 September 2010.

Marra, Kaitlin. "IP & Traditional Cultural Expressions: An Unnatural Alliance?" *Intellectual Property Watch*. ⟨http://www.ip-watch.org/weblog/2011/01/05/ip-traditional-cultural-expressions-an-unnatural-alliance/⟩ (5 January 2011) accessed 16 October 2011.

Max Planck Institute for Psycholinguistics. *Dokumentation Bedrohter Sprachen* (DoBeS) [Documentation of Endangered Languages]. ⟨http://www.mpi.nl/DOBEs⟩ (2006) accessed 12 October 2010.

McIntyre-Tamwoy, Susan. "The Impact of Global Climate Change and Cultural Heritage: Grasping the Issues and Defining the Problem." *Historic Environment* 21 (2008): 8.

Merryman, John H. "Two Ways of Thinking About Cultural Property." *American Journal of International Law* 80 (1986): 832–37.

———. *Thinking About The Elgin Marbles: Critical Essays on Cultural Property, Art and Law*. Alphen aan den Rijn: Kluwer Law International, 2009.

Moseley, Christopher, ed. *Atlas of the World's Languages in Danger*. Paris: UNESCO Publishing, 2010. ⟨http://www.unesco.org/culture/languages-atlas/en/atlasmap.html⟩ accessed 16 October 2011.

Myers, Norman. "Environmental Refugees: A Growing Phenomenon of the 21st Century." *Philosophical Transactions of the Royal Society Biological Sciences* 357 (2001): 609–11.

Myers, Norman and Jennifer Kent. *Environmental Exodus: An Emergent Crisis in the Global Arena*. ⟨http://www.climate.org/PDF/Environmental%20Exodus.pdf⟩ (1995) accessed 23 September 2011.

Norwegian Refugee Council (NRC). *Climate Changed: People Displaced* (2009): 5–15. ⟨http://www.nrc.no/?did=9448676⟩ (8 December 2009) accessed 25 November 2010.

O'Neil, Dennis. *Culture Change: An Introduction to the Processes and Consequences of Culture Change*. ⟨http://anthro.palomar.edu/change/⟩ (2008) accessed 30 November 2010.

Pacific Islands Forum Secretariat (PIFS). *Traditional Knowledge Implementation Action Plan*. ⟨http://www.forumsec.org.fj/resources/uploads/attachments/documents/Traditional Knowledge Action Plan 2009.pdf⟩ (21 December 2010) accessed 24 November 2010.

Panos Pictures. "Tuvalu—Island on the Frontline of Climate Change." *VIMEO* (4 June 2009). ⟨http://www.vimeo.com/4997847⟩ accessed 16 October 2010.

Pearson, Michael. "Climate Change and Its Impacts on Australia's Cultural Heritage." *Historic Environment* 21 (2008): 40.

Pfirman, Stephanie, interview by Yale Environment 360. "As the Arctic Ocean Melts, A Refugee Plan for the Polar Bear," 22 December 2010. ⟨http://e360.yale.edu/feature/as_the_arctic_ocean_melts_can_refuge_save_polar_bears/2355/⟩ (22 December 2010) accessed 16 October 2011.

Rowland, Mike. "Saving the Past from the Future." *Historic Environment* 21 (2008): 21.

Sandler, Felicia. "Music of the Village in the Global Market Place: Self-Expression, Inspiration, Appropriation, or Exploitation?" PhD diss., Ann Arbor: University of Michigan, 2001.

Secretariat of the Pacific Community (SPC). *Explanatory Memorandum for the South Pacific Model Law*, in Regional Framework for the Protection of Traditional Knowledge and Expressions of Culture (2002): 1–3, http://www.wipo.int/wipolex/en/text.jsp?file_id=184651 (last modified 14 October 2011) accessed 16 October 2011.

Talakai, Malia. *Intellectual Property and Safeguarding Cultural Heritage: A Survey of Practices and Protocols in the South Pacific*. ⟨http://www.wipo.int/tk/en/culturalheritage/surveys.html⟩ (September 2007) accessed 24 November 2010.

Taubman, Antony. "Saving the Village: Conserving Jurisprudential Diversity in the International Protection of Traditional Knowledge." In *International Public Goods and Transfer of Technology Under a Globalized Intellectual Property Regime*, edited by Keith E. Maskus and Jerome H. Reichman, 521–64. Cambridge: Cambridge University Press, 2005.

Taubman, Antony, and Matthias Leistner. "Traditional Knowledge." In *Indigenous Heritage and Intellectual Property: Genetic Resources, Traditional Knowledge and Folklore*, 2nd ed., edited by Silke von Lewinski, 59–173. Alphen aan den Rijn: Kluwer Law International, 2008.

Torsen, Molly. "Intellectual Property and Traditional Cultural Expressions: A Synopsis Of Current Issues." *Intercultural Human Rights Law Review* 3 (2008): 201.

Torsen, Molly and Jane Anderson, WIPO. *Intellectual Property and the Safeguarding of Traditional Cultures: Legal Issues and Practical Options for Museums, Libraries and Archives*. ⟨http://www.wipo.int/tk/en/publications/1023.pdf⟩ (December 2010) accessed 17 October 2011

UNESCO. *Intergovernmental Committee for the Protection and Promotion of the Diversity of Cultural Expressions*, Fourth Ordinary Session Paris, UNESCO Headquarters 29 November 29–3 December 3 2010 Item 10A of the Provisional Agenda: Implementation of the International Fund for Cultural Diversity (IFCD). ⟨http://www.unesco.org/new/fileadmin/MULTIMEDIA/HQ/CLT/pdf/Conv2005_4IGC_decisions_en_10_12_10.pdf⟩ (last modified 10 June 2010) accessed 12 October 2010.

———. UNESCO World Report: Investing in Cultural Diversity and Intercultural Dialogue (2009): 11–22.

———. *Vanuatu Sand Drawings*. ⟨http://www.unesco.org/culture/ich/en/RL/00073⟩ (2010) accessed 16 September 2011.

———. "Vanuatu Sand Drawings." *YouTube* video (28 September 2009). ⟨http://www.youtube.com/watch?v=nJociHoB-t8⟩ accessed 10 December 2010.

UNESCO Institute for Statistics. *Measuring the Diversity of Cultural Expressions*. ⟨http://www.uis.unesco.org/ev.php?ID=7061_201&2=DO_TOPIC⟩ (2009) accessed 8 December 2010.

UNESCO and WIPO, *Model Provisions for National Laws on the Protection of Expressions of Folklore Against Illicit Exploitation and Other Prejudicial Actions with a Commentary*, 4 (1985). http://www.wipo.int/export/sites/www/tk/en/documents/pdf/1982-folklore-model-provisions.pdf (last modified 1 February 2010) accessed 30 November 2010.

———. *The 2009 UNESCO Framework for Cultural Statistics*. ⟨http://www.uis.unesco.org/Culture/Pages/cultural-diversity.aspx⟩ (2009) accessed 16 September 2011.

United Nations Framework Convention on Climate Change (UNFCCC). *CDM in Numbers*. ⟨http://cdm.unfccc.int/Statistics/index.html⟩ (2011) accessed 14 December 2010.

———. *NAPA Priorities Database*. ⟨http://unfccc.int/files/adaptation/application/pdf/napa_tourism.pdf⟩ (September 2008) accessed 12 December 2010.

———. *Technologies for Adaptation to Climate Change* (2006). ⟨http://www.unfccc.int/ttclear/pdf/tech_for_adaptation.pdf⟩ (2006) accessed 12 December 2010.

———. *Vulnerability and Adaptation to Climate Change in Small Island Developing States: Background Paper for the Expert Meeting on Adaptation for Small Island Developing States* (2007).

UNHCR, in cooperation with NRC, RSG on the HR of IDP and UNU. *Forced Displacement in the Context of Climate Change: Challenges for States under International Law*, ⟨http://unfccc.int/resource/docs/2009/smsn/igo/049.pdf⟩ (19 May 2009) accessed 27 November 2010. Submitted to the 6th Session of the Ad Hoc Working Group on Long-Term Cooperative Action under the UNFCCC, 1–12 June 2009 ⟨http://unfccc.int/meetings/sb30/items/4842.php⟩ (June 2009) accessed 27 November 2010.

United Nations Convention to Combat Desertification (UNCCD). *Promotion of Traditional Knowledge: A Compilation of UNCCD Documents and Reports from 1997–2003* (2005). ⟨http://www.unccd.int/publicinfo/publications/docs/traditional_knowledge.pdf⟩ (last modified 19 September 2011) accessed 16 October 2011.

UN Secretary-General. *Five-year Review of the Mauritius Strategy for the Further Implementation of the Programme of Action for the Sustainable Development of Small Island Developing States*, 34, U.N. Doc. A/65/115 (6 July 2010).

Vanuatu Cultural Centre. *Moratorium on Commercial Filming of Nagol.* ⟨http://www.vanuatuculture.org/site-bm2/research/20051122_pentecost_land_dive.shtml⟩ (22 November 2005) accessed 6 December 2010.

Vanuatu National Cultural Council. *The National Action Plan for the Safeguarding of Sand Drawing, a UNESCO Masterpiece of the Oral and Intangible Heritage of Humanity.* ⟨http://www.vanuatuculture.org/site-bm2/sand/050627_sanddrawing.shtml⟩ (last modified 10 August 2011) accessed 17 October 2011.

———. *Vanuatu Cultural Research Policy.* ⟨http://www.vanuatuculture.org/site-bm2/research/050520_culturalresearchpolicy.shtml⟩ (2004) accessed 17 December 2010.

von Lewinski, Silke, ed. *Indigenous Heritage and Intellectual Property: Genetic Resources, Traditional Knowledge and Folklore*, 2nd ed. Alphen aan den Rijn: Kluwer Law International, 2008.

Wendland, Wend B. "Seeking Tangible Benefits from Linking Culture, Development and Intellectual Property." *International Journal of Intangible Heritage* 29 (2009): 129.

WIPO. *Revised Draft Provisions for the Protection of Traditional Cultural Expressions/Expressions of Folklore: Policy Objectives and Core Principles.* ⟨http://www.wipo.int/export/sites/www/tk/en/consultations/draft_provisions/pdf/tce-provisions.pdf⟩ (2006) accessed 30 November 2010.

———. *Climate Change and the Intellectual Property System: What Challenges, What Options, What Solutions?* ⟨http://www.wipo.int/export/sites/www/patentscope/en/lifesciences/pdf/ip_climate.pdf⟩ (14 November 2008) accessed 30 November 2010.

———. *Creative Heritage Project: Strategic Management of IP Rights and Interests.* ⟨http://www.wipo.int/tk/en/culturalheritage⟩ (2010) accessed 17 October 2011.

———. "Director General Welcomes Moves to Enhance Protection of Traditional Knowledge & Folklore in Africa," press release, 31 August 2010, WIPO Press Release PR/2010/654.

———. "IGC Makes Significant Progress, Sets the Stage for Working Groups on GRs and TK," press release, 10 December 2010. WIPO Press Release PR/2010/675/ ⟨http://www.wipo.int/pressroom/en/articles/2010/article_0051.html⟩ accessed 14 December 2010.

———. *Lisbon System for the International Registration of Appellations of Origin.* ⟨http://www.wipo.int/lisbon/en/⟩ (13 January 2011) accessed 17 October 2011.

———. *Legislative Texts on the Protection of Traditional Cultural Expressions (Expressions of Folklore) (TCEs).* ⟨http://www.wipo.int/tk/en/laws/folklore.html⟩ (4 April 2011) accessed 17 October 2011.

[20]

The UNESCO Convention on the Protection and Promotion of the Diversity of Cultural Expressions: Building a New World Information and Communication Order?*

RACHAEL CRAUFURD SMITH
University of Edinburgh

The UNESCO Convention on the Protection and Promotion of the Diversity of Cultural Expressions was adopted in October 2005. This article explores the Convention's objectives and the contribution that the Convention is likely to make to their realisation in the future. In its final form the Convention is considerably less ambitious than many of its promoters had wished: key provisions are expressed in aspirational terms, the Convention's dispute resolution procedures are consensual and the Convention explicitly states that it does not modify the rights or obligations of its Parties under pre-existing international agreements. The extensive support that the Convention received from the international community at the time of its adoption, with one hundred and forty eight countries voting in its favour, nevertheless affords it considerable political weight. The Convention may consequently play a role in the interpretation of existing international agreements, including the WTO agreements, and in negotiations over their future development. The article also suggests that there may be more scope than is initially apparent for the Convention to be used as a basis for evaluating state measures, not only in relation to international trade, but also regarding the domestic treatment of cultural minorities. For such review to become meaningful, however, active support will be necessary not only from civil society organisations, which played a key role in the Convention's initial development, but also from contracting states and the various Convention organs.

Rachael Craufurd Smith: r.c.smith@ed.ac.uk
Date submitted: 2006-09-29

An earlier version of this paper was presented at a conference on *Communication Technology and Social Policy: Expanding Access, Redefining Control*, organized by the Annenberg Schools for Communication at the University of Pennsylvania and the University of Southern California, funded by the Annenberg Foundation Trust at Sunnylands, in Palm Springs in April 2006.

* Europa Institute, University of Edinburgh. I would like to thank the two anonymous reviewers of this article, together with Prof. Bruno de Witte and Sean Smith, who read and provided helpful comments on an earlier draft. Part of the research for this article was undertaken while studying on a Jean Monnet Fellowship at the European University Institute, Florence, and I would like to thank the Institute for its generous assistance during that time. Most importantly, this article would not have been written without the support and encouragement of the USC Annenberg Center and, in particular, Professor Larry Gross.

During the '70s and early '80s, a number of developing, non-aligned countries promoted within UNESCO the idea of a 'New World Information and Communication Order' (NWICO), entailing a more equitable exchange of information between rich and poor nations.[1] The debates which raged over the NWICO revealed not only fundamental disagreements concerning the legitimacy of state intervention in media markets to promote objectives such as cultural diversity, but also the power and influence wielded by certain communications industries, particularly the print and audiovisual media industries in the United States. Dissatisfaction by the U.S. with the general thrust and outcome of the NWICO debates was instrumental in its decision to leave UNESCO in 1984, shortly followed by the UK. The subsequent growth in global communications, spurred on by digitisation and convergence among previously distinct sectors, has not resolved, and in some cases has exacerbated, these tensions. The Internet, for example, though greatly enhancing opportunities for the exchange of information and ideas is currently dominated by a handful of languages. In consequence, many states, comprising both developed and developing countries such as Canada and Senegal, continue to argue that the system of global mass communications threatens the survival of particular languages and cultures. They also argue that international trade rules, in particular those agreed within the WTO, could in the future constrain their ability to respond to such threats with measures such as quotas, subsidies and foreign ownership limits, designed to support their domestic industries.

With the new millennium the international community returned to these issues, launching two major initiatives to explore whether action should be taken to address these concerns and, if so, what form it should take. Firstly, UNESCO has acted as the forum for further consideration of the impact of international trade on cultural diversity. This led to the drafting of a Convention on the Protection and Promotion of the Diversity of Cultural Expressions (the 'Convention'), which was adopted in October 2005.[2] Secondly, the World Summit on the Information Society (WSIS), sponsored by the International Telecommunications Union (ITU), met for its final session in Tunis in November 2005. Major objectives of the WSIS were to widen, and render more equitable, access to information and communication technologies and to evaluate the existing system of internet governance. The WSIS led to the agreement of the Geneva Declaration of Principles and Plan of Action and the Tunis Agenda for the Information Society.[3]

This paper focuses on the first of these initiatives, the UNESCO Convention, and considers what contribution it is likely to make to the promotion of cultural diversity in the future, particularly in the

---

[1] Their concern over 'cultural imperialism' was also shared by certain developed countries such as Canada, France and Finland. For a historical overview see Cate, F. H. (1989-1990) The First Amendment and the International "Free Flow" of Information. Virginia Journal of International Law. 30, 372-420 and International Commission for the Study of Communication Problems (1980). Many Voices One World. Paris: UNESCO, at 40-43.

[2] UNESCO, *Convention on the Protection and Promotion of the Diversity of Cultural Expressions*, CLT-2005/CONVENTION DIVERSITE-CULT REV (20 October 2005) available at: http://portal.unesco.org/culture/en/ev.php-URL_ID=30855&URL_DO=DO_TOPIC&URL_SECTION=201.html (accessed 28/08/06).

[3] For information on WSIS, its documents and follow-up initiatives see the website at: http://www.itu.int/wsis/index.html (accessed 28/08/06).

communications sector. Before setting out the underlying aims and structure of the UNESCO Convention, a couple of general observations might be made. Firstly, although the Convention was primarily a response to concerns relating to the trade in media goods and services it does not single the media out for special attention. Its main focus is consequently hidden behind a more general ambition to protect cultural diversity. Media goods and services are just a distinct category within the wider field of 'cultural expressions,' which the Convention seeks to promote. On the other hand, recital 19 to the Convention notes that the flow of communications between countries also creates a 'challenge for cultural diversity, namely in view of risks of imbalances between rich and poor countries.' Communications media thus have a dual status within the Convention: seen as both distinct forms of expression deserving of protection in their own right and as powerful vectors of ideas and information, capable of destabilising the production of authentic cultural expressions, if not kept in check or subjected to countervailing measures.

Secondly, although centrally concerned with the mass media and communications, the Convention does not attempt to establish communication rights along the lines mapped out by the CRIS organization.[4] Indeed, despite the European Commission's claim that the Convention introduces 'a series of rights and obligations, at both national and international levels, with a view to the protection and promotion of cultural diversity,' it establishes no rights at all for media organisations, journalists, or the communicating public at large.[5] Rather, the Convention confirms the entitlement/rights of *states* to introduce culturally motivated measures and it is therefore through state action, if at all, that these interests are to be realised under the Convention.[6] At first reading, therefore, the Convention appears both rather oblique and lacking in substance, though closer examination reveals that there is potential for the Convention to play a more significant role than this suggests in shaping the future communications environment.

The UNESCO Convention was adopted on the 20th October 2005.[7] One hundred and forty eight countries voted for the Convention, four countries abstained - Australia, Honduras, Nicaragua and Liberia, and two countries opposed it - the U.S. and Israel. A commitment by UNESCO to take on board the drafting of such a convention dates back to October 2003,[8] but experts working on the project for

---

[4] See Communication Rights in the Information Society ('CRIS') (2005). Assessing Communication Rights: A Handbook, available at: http://www.crisinfo.org/ (accessed 30/11/06).

[5] European Commission, *Proposal for a Council Decision on the Conclusion of the UNESCO Convention on the Protection and Promotion of the Diversity of Cultural Expressions*, COM(2005), at 3. Recital 12 of the Convention does, however, emphasise the role which freedom of thought, expression and information, as well as media diversity, can play in fostering cultural expression.

[6] UNESCO Convention, n. 2 above, Article 1(h).

[7] For discussion on the negotiations see Mazzone, G. (2005). A Battle Worth Fighting. Diffusion online. 36, 2-5, available at: http://www.ebu.ch/en/union/diffusion_on_line/ (accessed 28/08/06).

[8] Resolution 32 C/34, adopted on the report of Commission IV at the 21st plenary meeting of the UNESCO General Conference on 17 October 2003. The initial formal request for UNESCO to consider adoption of a cultural diversity convention was made by Canada, France, Germany, Greece, Morocco, Mexico, Monaco, and Senegal. A number of key NGOs, such as the International Network for Cultural Diversity ('INCD') and Campaign for Communication Rights in the Information Society ('CRIS'), played an extremely active role in shaping the Convention, and regular reports on their involvement were published in the Media Trade

UNESCO did not have to start from scratch in that three separate organisations had already drafted quite detailed proposals. These organisations - the Cultural Industries Sectoral Advisory Group (SAGIT), a committee composed of representatives from the culture industries that advises the Canadian Government;[9] the International Network for Cultural Diversity (INCD), a network of artists and cultural groups founded in 2000;[10] and the International Network on Cultural Policy (INCP), a group of over 40 culture ministers which has met regularly since 1998[11] - are all backed and supported by Canada, which has taken a leading role in promoting the Convention. In addition to the preparatory work carried out by these organisations, UNESCO itself has produced a wide variety of conventions and declarations in the cultural field, many concerned with very similar issues, on which the drafters could draw for inspiration.[12] The Convention will come into force three months after it has been ratified by thirty states.[13]

A. Why was the UNESCO Convention adopted?

Those countries which supported the UNESCO Convention had four main objectives: Firstly, an overarching objective, to promote and protect cultural diversity. Secondly, to identify those measures which states and public bodies may legitimately take to safeguard cultural diversity. Thirdly, to ensure, as far as possible, that international trade rules do not prevent such intervention. Fourthly, through a process of international cooperation, to assist developing countries, as well as smaller cultural and linguistic regions, to preserve and fully exploit their cultural heritage. These objectives are clearly interlinked and the containment of international trade rules and support for cultural initiatives in developing countries may be viewed as distinct means to achieve the convention's primary objective of promoting and preserving cultural diversity.

For some participants in the drafting process the Convention was seen as filling 'a legal vacuum in world governance' in the cultural sphere.[14] Pascal Lamy, while European Commissioner for Trade in 2001, noted that the 'complete lack of standards relating to culture at international level is an untenable situation, just as it would be in relation to the environment, health, organized crime or finance.'[15] It

---

Monitor at: http://www.mediatrademonitor.org/ (accessed 30/11/06). The INCD website can be found at: http://www.incd.net/ (accessed 30/11/06).

[9] SAGIT, in its February 1999 Report entitled 'Canadian Culture in a Global World, New Strategies for Cultures and Trade,' was the first of the groups to propose a separate convention on cultural diversity. The report is available at: http://www.dfait-maeci.gc.ca/tna-nac/canculture-en.asp. For its subsequent draft proposal see: http://www.dfait-maeci.gc.ca/tna-nac/sagit_paper-en.asp.

[10] INCD, *Proposed Convention on Cultural Diversity* (15 January 2003).

[11] INCP, *Draft International Convention on Cultural Diversity* (29 July 2003).

[12] See below at text accompanying n. 16.

[13] The European Community has now put in place the necessary mechanisms to formally accede to the Convention and has called on its Member States to take measures to ratify the Convention, n. 5 above. If all 25 members of the EU comply then this, on its own, would bring the Convention close to being operational.

[14] European Commission, n. 5 above, at 3.

[15] Lamy, P. (2005). Strategy and Negotiating Position. Diffusion online. 36, 6-7, at 6, available at: http://www.ebu.ch/en/union/diffusion_on_line/ (accessed 28/08/06).

would, however, be wrong to see the Convention as breaking entirely new ground, in that there are already in force a number of international agreements on cultural matters, many adopted in the last five years. The particular focus of the present Convention on international trade in cultural goods and services and the role of culture in development is certainly distinctive, but it is not unique, and the Convention clearly draws on the various implementation techniques adopted in these earlier documents.

Firstly, it is possible to point to a number of documents which seek to establish cultural rights either in general or for particular groups. These include the 1948 *Universal Declaration of Human Rights*,[16] the 1966 *International Covenant on Economic, Social and Cultural Rights*,[17] the 1966 *International Covenant on Civil and Political Rights*,[18] which in Article 27 provides for the rights of 'ethnic, religious or linguistic minorities...to enjoy their own culture, to profess and practise their own religion, or to use their own language' in common with other members of their group, and the 1995 *Council of Europe Framework Convention on National Minorities*,[19] which sets out rights for national minorities to participate in public life, use their own language, and gain access to education and the media. Those drafting the UNESCO Convention clearly did not want to stray into the controversial field of specific cultural rights which could have alienated many of its ultimate supporters and such issues are consequently dealt with only indirectly.[20]

Other agreements, such as the 1971 *Universal Copyright Convention*, deal with intellectual property rights, a controversial issue that is also avoided in the present Convention.[21] The Convention is closer to large group of international treaties and declarations designed to protect cultural heritage, either generally or in specific fields. These agreements include the 1972 *Convention Concerning the Protection of the World Cultural and Natural Heritage*,[22] the 2000 *European Landscape Convention*,[23] and the 2003

---

[16] UN, *Universal Declaration of Human Rights*, 1948, at: http://www.un.org/rights.

[17] UN, *International Covenant on Economic, Social and Cultural Rights*, 1966, at: http://untreaty.un.org/.

[18] UN, *International Covenant on Civil and Political Rights*, 1966, at: http://untreaty.un.org/.

[19] *Council of Europe Framework Convention on National Minorities*, Strasbourg 1995, European Treaty Series no. 157.

[20] See also text accompanying n. 56 below.

[21] UNESCO, *Universal Copyright Convention*, 1971 at: http://portal.unesco.org/en/ev.php-URL_ID=12025&URL_DO=DO_TOPIC&URL_SECTION=-471.html (accessed 28/08/06). The US had attempted to introduce more than 15 clauses into the Convention with the objective of linking stronger intellectual property rights to cultural diversity. These were effectively opposed by Brazil, whose negotiators worked closely with NGOs, in particular the CRIS. As a result all explicit references to intellectual property were removed from the body of the Convention, though recital eight notes that traditional knowledge may be a 'source of intangible and material wealth,' Mazzone, n. 7 above.

[22] UNESCO, *Convention Concerning the Protection of the World Cultural and Natural Heritage*, Paris 1972 at: http://portal.unesco.org/en/ev.php-URL_ID=12025&URL_DO=DO_TOPIC&URL_SECTION=-471.html (accessed 28/08/06).

[23] Council of Europe, *European Landscape Convention*, 2000, European Treaty Series (ETS) no. 176.

Convention for the Safeguarding of the Intangible Cultural Heritage[24]. The present Convention shares the central concern of these documents over the fragility of our cultural heritage, but goes beyond them to consider more generally not only how our cultural heritage can be preserved but also how cultural creation can be stimulated in the future.

The most direct international precursors of the Convention are, however, a small group of documents which deal explicitly with the relationship between trade and culture. These include the 1950 *Florence Agreement* and accompanying 1976 *Nairobi Protocol*[25] and two more recent declarations, the *Council of Europe Declaration on Cultural Diversity*, adopted in December 2000,[26] and the UNESCO *Universal Declaration on Cultural Diversity*, adopted in November 2001[27]. The *Florence Agreement* and *Nairobi Protocol* seek to remove customs charges on the importation of certain educational, scientific and cultural materials and prohibit the imposition, again in relation to specific cultural goods, of discriminatory internal charges. With regard to a limited category of cultural goods, therefore, the international community recognised early on the importance of free trade and the unacceptability of discriminatory charges. The Florence Agreement also contains an early example of a 'cultural preservation' clause. The reservation to the Agreement allows, solely in relation to trade between the US and another party, either side to suspend the operation of the Agreement where the scale of imports under the Agreement threatens 'serious injury to the domestic industry ... producing like or directly competitive products.'[28]

Although the 2001 UNESCO *Universal Declaration on Cultural Diversity* places considerable emphasis on the importance of cultural rights, and thus has close links with the first category of agreements, it also focuses on the opportunities and threats which economic and technical development pose for cultural diversity and the importance of international co-operation in addressing the impact of world trade. These preoccupations underpin the 2000 Council of Europe Declaration and go to the heart of the present Convention.

The two UNESCO and Council of Europe declarations consequently intersect with the Convention in important respects, but have had relatively little impact in practice owing to their purely exhortatory status. The declarations were unlikely to be sufficient on their own to address a loss of cultural diversity, a fact explicitly acknowledged in the Action Plan accompanying the UNESCO Declaration, which noted the commitment of Member States to considering whether they should adopt a further international legal

---

[24] UNESCO, *Convention for the Safeguarding of the Intangible Cultural Heritage*, 2003, available at: http://portal.unesco.org/en/ev.php-URL_ID=12025&URL_DO=DO_TOPIC&URL_SECTION=-471.html (accessed 28/08/06).

[25] UN, *Agreement on the Importation of Educational, Scientific and Cultural Materials* ('Florence Agreement') 1950, and Nairobi Protocol, 1976, available at: http://www.unesco.org/culture/laws/florence/html_eng/page4.shtml.

[26] Council of Europe, *Declaration on Cultural Diversity*, 2000, available at: http://cm.coe.int/ta/decl/2000/2000dec2.htm.

[27] UNESCO *Universal Declaration on Cultural Diversity*, 2001, available at: *http://portal.unesco.org/culture/en/ev.php-URL_ID=2977&URL_DO=DO_TOPIC&URL_SECTION=201.html*.

[28] Protocol annexed to the Florence Agreement, n. 25 above.

instrument in this field (para. 1). Introduction of a binding Convention was thus seen as ratcheting up the status of cultural diversity as a matter of international concern, just as international agreements on the environment and health have helped to underline the importance of these considerations in other international fora such as the WTO.[29]

As a carefully constructed package, based round the four objectives indicated above and avoiding such controversial areas as cultural rights, the Convention ultimately gained support from an extensive coalition of developing and developed countries. Inevitably, however, those states which approved the Convention had different priorities and interests. The main driving force behind the Convention was Canada, which worked to build up support within the various culture industries and state departments. Canada's colonial past, high levels of immigration and the presence of a significant aboriginal population led to an early commitment to multicultural policies.[30] Its cultural and geographic proximity to the U.S., one of the world's major exporters of cultural goods and services, has sensitised Canada to concerns over the impact of foreign trade on domestic culture and national identity.[31] But Canada not only produces for the domestic market, it is increasingly a major exporter of cultural products. It consequently promoted the Convention on two grounds, which at first sight appear to be in tension: firstly, it sought to clarify the legitimacy in international law of the extensive array of measures it has adopted to protect its domestic cultural industries; secondly, it sought to ensure continued access for its cultural goods and services to foreign markets.[32]

Other developed states that supported the Convention had a different mix of preoccupations. France, for example, does not share Canada's overt multiculturalism but was equally committed to supporting the French language and resisting what it sees as American 'cultural imperialism,' particularly in the media sector.[33] The European Community, which joined the debate at a relatively late stage in the

---

[29] European Commission, n. 5 above, at 3. For discussion of the influence of environmental and human rights considerations on the interpretation of the WTO agreements see Marceau, G. (2001). Conflicts of Norms and Conflicts of Jurisdiction: the Relationship between the WTO Agreement and MEAs and Other Treaties. Journal of World Trade. 35/6, 1081-1131.

[30] Canada was the first developed democratic country to officially adopt a policy of multiculturalism in 1971, on which see Kymlicka, W. (2001). Politics in the Vernacular: Nationalism, Multiculturalism and Citizenship. Oxford: Oxford University Press, at 154; and Acheson, K. and Maule, C. (2002). Cultural Issues in Trade Agreements: Multiculturalism, Liberalism and the NICD Initiative. Carleton Economic Paper, CEP 02-07, 1-33, at 16-24.

[31] See the 1999 SAGIT Report, n. 9 above for details of Canadian measures designed to protect indigenous culture industries. Statistics on US trade in core cultural goods and services are contained in UNESCO (2005). International Flows of Selected Cultural Goods and Services, 1994-2003. Montreal: UNESCO Institute for Statistics.

[32] The 1999 SAGIT Report, n. 9 above, notes that the Canadian government saw the purpose as setting out 'clear ground rules to enable Canada and other countries to maintain policies that promote their culture while respecting the rules of the international trading system and ensuring markets for cultural exports.'

[33] Although India makes more films annually than the USA, U.S. films dominate the international market and around eighty-five per cent of all films which have a world-wide screening are produced in Hollywood:

proceedings, not only sought to maintain its ability to promote Europe's cultural industries through quotas and subsidies but was also interested in underlining to its own Member States the competence that it now enjoys in the cultural field.[34]

Developing countries share some of these concerns, though their participation in the trade in cultural goods and services is markedly less than that of high-income countries. The value of core cultural goods exported by 90% of low-income countries in 2002 was, for example, less than U.S. $10 million. Notable exceptions were India, with U.S. $284.4 million, and Indonesia, with U.S. $112.3 million.[35] Clearly there are significant variations within this group, but the low and middle income countries broadly saw the Convention as a forum in which to argue for a more equitable balance in the flow of cultural goods and services between countries, and for greater freedom of movement for their artists and performers. They also sought a greater commitment from developed countries to provide technical and financial assistance to support their fledgling cultural industries.

On the question of 'cultural imperialism,' developing, just as developed, countries differ in their perception of how threatening imported goods and services are to their indigenous cultures. As the European Commission has noted '[t]he conditions for preserving and promoting cultural diversity in Europe and the world depend not only on economic conditions, but also on a multitude of other structural factors.'[36] In the media context, for example, some countries, particularly those with large domestic markets, have been able to develop relatively strong, integrated media companies such as the Televisa group in Mexico or TV Globo in Brazil. Though the field of high cost, high risk, film production and distribution is dominated internationally by the U.S., these companies show that it is possible for certain middle income countries to develop flourishing television production and distribution companies with significant foreign exports – in the case of Televisa to the Spanish speaking population in the U.S.[37]

Countries with smaller populations and lower GDP cannot expect to mirror such developments and their demand for audiovisual goods and services are often met by high quality, comparatively cheap, US productions. But though the threat of 'cultural imperialism' may here seem more real, it is not inevitable that U.S. goods and services will dominate. In the Latin American context, for example, Hernán

---

figures taken from UNESCO, Culture, Trade and Globalisation: Questions and Answers, available at: http://www.unesco.org/culture/industries/trade/html_eng/question2.shtml (accessed 28/08/06).

[34] The European Community has exclusive responsibility for the common commercial policy and its policies in relation to development, the European internal market, competition and the protection of intellectual property have significant cultural implications. See European Commission, n. 5, at the commentary in Annex 1b, and Ferri, D., (2005). EU Participation in the UNESCO Convention on Protection and Promotion of the Diversity of Cultural Expressions: Some Constitutional Remarks. European Diversity and Autonomy Papers. 3, 5-34. For criticism of Community intervention see INCD, Statement on the Position of the European Union in the Negotiations on the Convention on the Protection of the Diversity of Cultural Contents and Artistic Expression, at: http://www.incd.net/incden.html (accessed 30/08/06).

[35] UNESCO, n. 31 above at 27.

[36] European Commission, n. 5 above, at 2.

[37] Galperin, H. (1999). Cultural Industries Policy in Regional Trade Agreements: the Cases of NAFTA, the European Union and MERCOSUR. Media Culture and Society. 21/5, 627-648.

Galperin notes that the inflow of American television programmes to Paraguay and Uruguay began to decrease steadily from the 1980s, with television stations gradually buying in programmes with a closer cultural connection to their audience from Argentina and Brazil.[38] Regional identities, language and historical ties all have an important impact on patterns of cultural exchange and interaction.

In order to assess whether the Convention is likely to transcend the preceding declarations on cultural diversity and meet the four main objectives of those countries which voted for it – to promote cultural diversity; to clarify which culturally motivated state measures are legitimate; to prevent international trade rules undermining domestic cultural policies; and to co-ordinate international support for developing countries and threatened cultures - it is necessary to take a closer look at the Convention's provisions in each of these areas. But before doing so, the paper briefly examines what the Convention understands by cultural diversity and why its preservation is thought to be important.

B. What Kind of Cultural Expressions are Covered by the Convention and Why is Cultural Diversity Important?

The overarching objective of the Convention is 'to protect and promote the diversity of cultural expressions' (Art. 1(a)) and although the Convention also lists a further eight objectives and eight principles, these primarily offer guidance as to how this diversity might be realised and what it might look like in practice. Cultural expressions are defined as 'those expressions that result from the creativity of individuals, groups and societies, and that have cultural content' (Art. 4.3). 'Cultural content' is said to refer 'to the symbolic meaning, artistic dimension and cultural values that originate from or express cultural identities' (Art. 4.2). This is in line with a number of international declarations and resolutions, in particular the 2001 *Universal Declaration on Cultural Diversity*, which reaffirms that 'culture should be regarded as the set of distinctive spiritual, material, intellectual and emotional features of society or a social group, and that it encompasses, in addition to art and literature, lifestyles, ways of living together, value systems, traditions and beliefs.'[39]

It is clear, therefore, that the Convention adopts a broad approach to its subject matter, encompassing not just artistic expressions but all expressions that reflect distinct cultures. It consequently covers film and television programmes, classic cinema and tacky game shows, web logs and websites, as well as man-made landscapes, food and culinary practices, sport and other forms of recreation. Although the Convention does not attempt to define 'culture,' it does not limit its field of operation to 'high' culture, to those cultural goods and practices which are thought to have an 'improving' or 'civilising' nature, or which can be identified according to their refinement or other aesthetic qualities. A 'narrow' approach of this latter kind often exhibits a backward-looking perspective, with a focus on those buildings, literary and

---

[38] *Ibid.*, at 641.

[39] UNESCO *Universal Declaration*, n. 27 above, at recital five. This draws on the Final Declaration of the World Conference on Cultural Policies held in Mexico in 1982 which defined culture to be 'the whole complex of distinctive spiritual, material, intellectual and emotional features that characterize a society or social group. It includes not only the arts and letters, but also modes of life, the fundamental rights of the human being, value systems, traditions and beliefs.'

artistic works considered to be the high points of a particular society's past endeavours and to constitute its 'cultural heritage.'

The central objective of the Convention is to support state measures designed to prevent the loss, or extinction, of distinct cultural expressions and to foster environments in which different cultures can flourish. The concern over cultural extinction may at first sight seem relatively unproblematic. Parallels are sometimes drawn with biodiversity, with the implicit suggestion that when one distinctive cultural practice is lost there is the risk that a wide range of related and mutually dependent cultural forms, interwoven into larger cultural ecosystems will also be destroyed.[40] But what evidence is there for such claims? And should we be concerned when any cultural practice or artefact is consigned to the scrap heap, as the biodiversity parallel would suggest, or only when certain types of cultural goods or practices disappear and then only in specific circumstances? The case for state intervention to address a potential reduction in cultural diversity is explored in more detail below.

UNESCO has for some time now been highlighting various forms of cultural depletion, thought to be caused, in large part, by processes associated with 'globalisation.' These processes, according to Ulrich Beck, are those 'through which sovereign national states are criss-crossed and undermined by transnational actors with varying prospects of power, orientations, identities and networks.'[41] Rapid transportation and communication systems now mean that capital, persons, goods and services can flow with relative ease and speed around the world. As Pascal Lamy notes there has been 'a simultaneous contraction of space and time': a century ago it would have taken twenty four hours for information to pass from London to Bombay, now it takes five seconds, and the pace of economic development in countries such as China is unprecedented.[42]

As more states follow the path of economic development, the exposure of their citizens to imported cultural goods and services, together with the values embedded in them, inevitably increases. There is evidence that economic development and growing urbanisation leads to a certain convergence in values and outlook and it is hard to think of a developed country that has not lost many of its traditional customs, dialects or languages in the face of enhanced communications and intra as well as inter national trade.[43] UNESCO estimates that one language is lost on average every two weeks and that over 50 per

---

[40] European Commission, n. 5 above, at 3.

[41] Beck, U. (2000). What is Globalization? Cambridge: Polity Press, at 11. For an early statement of concern over the potential impact of exposure to foreign media on domestic culture, see International Commission for the Study of Communication Problems in its Many Voices One World report, n. 1 above, at 30-31. For subsequent commentary see World Commission for Cultural Development (1997). Our Creative Diversity. New Delhi: Oxford and IBH, chapter 4, and the Human Development Report (2004). Cultural Liberty in Today's Diverse World. New York: United Nations Development Programme, at 10-11 and 97-99.

[42] Lamy, P., 'The WTO in the Archipelago of Global Governance,' speech to the Institute of International Studies, Geneva, 14 March 2006 at: http://www.wto.org/English/news_e/sppl_e/sppl20_e.htm.

[43] Inglehart, R. and Baker, W. E. (2000). Modernization, Cultural Change and the Persistence of Traditional Values. American Sociological Review. 65, 19-51. See also DiMaggio, P., Culture and Economy, in

cent of the world's 6,000 languages are currently endangered.[44] Cultural practices or beliefs which have no tangible record are particularly vulnerable and even where a written record remains the culture may be impossible to recreate, once lost, in any authentic sense.[45] It is consequently possible to point to an objective loss of certain cultural expressions and this loss is likely to be most apparent in countries undergoing rapid urbanisation and economic development.

But although it is possible to chart in certain sectors and in certain countries processes of cultural depletion, the endpoint may not be cultural standardisation or homogenisation. The 'global homogenisation scenario' is just one of a number of potential outcomes of globalisation that can be envisaged. Ulf Hannerz, for example, posits a competing scenario of 'peripheral corruption' in which the periphery first adopts ideas and knowledge from the centre and then corrupts them,[46] while the term 'glocalization' has been coined to refer to the way in which global and local cultures interact and influence each other.[47] Core aspects, or 'deep structures,' of a culture may be difficult to shift and reconfiguration, when it occurs, is likely to be a gradual and negotiated process.[48] Within industrialised societies there remains considerable cultural variation, with religious traditions, in particular, still exerting a marked influence. Inglehart and Baker conclude, for example, that industrializing societies are not, in general, becoming like the U.S., which they categorise as something of a 'deviant case.'[49] Given that it is precisely the developed countries which have had most exposure to U.S. cultural goods and services, the thesis that this leads ineluctably to the adoption of American values and aspirations begins to look decidedly shaky. As Galperin's study of the South American media discussed above indicates, cultural depletion and development are influenced by a wide range of economic, social, geographic and historical factors.[50]

Certain, mainly urban, areas are also becoming increasingly diverse and cosmopolitan. At a subjective level, therefore, more people may be experiencing more cultural diversity than ever before. But this subjective experience of increasing cultural diversity is no answer to the objective loss of certain cultures and their particular manifestations. The UNESCO Convention is not interested in balancing the

---

Smelser, N. J. and Swedberg, R. (eds.) (1994). The Handbook of Economic Sociology. Princeton: Princeton University Press. 27-49.

[44] UNESCO website on endangered languages at:
http://portal.unesco.org/culture/en/ev.php@URL_ID=8270&URL_DO=DO_TOPIC&URL_SECTION=201.html (accessed 28/08/06).

[45] The vulnerability of the intangible heritage was recognised in the 2003 UNESCO, *Convention for the Safeguarding of the Intangible Cultural Heritage*, n. 24 above.

[46] Hannerz, U., Scenarios for Peripheral Cultures, in King, A. D. (1997). Culture, Globalization and the World-System. Contemporary Conditions for the Representation of Identity. Minneapolis: University of Minnesota Press. 107-128.

[47] Robertson, R., Glocalization: Time-space and Homogeneity-Heterogeneity, in Featherstone, M., Lash, S. and Robertson, R. (eds.)(1995). Global Modernities. London: Sage Publications, at 25-44; Beck, n. 41 above, at 45-50.

[48] Morris, N. (2002). The Myth of Unadulterated Culture Meets the Threat of Imported Media. Media, Culture and Society. 24/2, 278-289, at 283.

[49] Inglehart and Baker, n. 43 above, at 31.

[50] Galperin, n. 37 above.

concrete loss of a language or a distinct practice in country or region A with the experience of enhanced diversity for residents of cities X, Y, or Z.

If we accept that processes of cultural depletion are at work, albeit in a patchy and uneven fashion, is this ultimately problematic? On a liberal view, an increase or decrease in cultural diversity is not in and of itself something to be welcomed or deplored; what is relevant is the process of cultural change and, in particular, the degree of autonomy of the individuals who shape that process.[51] Thus, a move to a more homogenous world culture, leading to the loss of distinct cultural communities and forms of expression, should not be seen as detrimental if consequent on free and informed decisions by those involved. Those adopting such a way of life do so because they consider such a move, on balance, to be beneficial to them. This is so, even though 'choice' may seem a rather esoteric concept when one is dealing with individuals on the poverty line who are offered the possibility of economic advancement. The situation is different where those who wish to maintain a particular culture are prevented from doing so by coercive state measures. Where, for example, the state prohibits a community from using traditional hunting techniques or speaking a particular language in schools.[52]

The Convention engages with this argument on a number of fronts. Firstly, it holds that cultural diversity 'creates a rich and varied world, which increases the range of choices and nurtures human capacities and values' (3rd recital). Cultural diversity can thus make our lives more textured and interesting, opening up alternative perspectives and lifestyles. Those who employ the concept of individual choice to question the inherent value of cultural diversity, have to address the problem that cultural choices made by individuals at point A may limit the options open to others at point B. Thus, a majority of Canadians may prefer to watch U.S. over Canadian drama and entertainment television programmes, even though some still value the Canadian versions.[53] Left to market forces, Canadian production in such circumstances could dwindle to such a level that it becomes unsustainable. Once an industry and its infrastructure have folded, regeneration is extremely difficult. At this point Canadians will have lost the opportunity to choose whether to watch Canadian or U.S. programmes.

Because they convey values and reflect identities, cultural goods and services cannot simply be substituted in the way that a car from one country can be substituted for a car from another. If a country ceases to be able to produce its own films or television programmes as a result of competition from a neighbouring country that enjoys certain demographic, linguistic or first mover advantages, it loses the

---

[51] For discussion of liberal views on diversity see Acheson, K. and Maule, C., n. 30 above, at 6-8; Kymlicka, W., Liberal Theories of Multiculturalism, in Meyer, L. H., Paulson, S. L. and Pogge, T. W. (eds.)(2003), Rights, Culture, and Law; Themes from the Legal and Political Philosophy of Joseph Raz. Oxford: OUP, 229-273, and Waldron, J., Minority Cultures and the Cosmopolitan Alternative, in Kymlicka, W. (ed.) (1995). The Rights of Minority Cultures. Oxford: OUP, 93-121.
[52] Will Kymlicka (2003) notes that representations by states that they are 'ethnoculturally neutral' are often misleading. Such states may in fact pursue policies designed to promote the use of particular languages or cultural practices in a process of 'nation building,' thereby consolidating the position of certain dominant cultural groups, n. 51 above at 237-238.
[53] Hitchens, L. (1997/8). Preparing for the Information Society: Lessons from Canada. Yearbook of Media and Entertainment Law. III, 98-146, at 125.

ability to explore, through these particular media, its own values, idiosyncrasies and pre-occupations.[54] And though foreign and domestic films and television programmes may raise many similar issues, foreign products are less likely to engage with these issues in as relevant or resonant a way as those directly addressing the home population. They can provide valuable alternative viewpoints and perspectives but are unlikely to be simple substitutes. The Convention explicitly recognises this distinctive quality of cultural activities, goods and services, which constitute 'vehicles of identity, values and meaning' (Art.1(g)).[55]

On this view, measures taken by states to ensure the continuing viability of their domestic cultural industries in the face of international competition should be accommodated within the international trading system as legitimate restraints on trade. In providing support for Canadian film and television production, Canada is not mandating that its citizens adopt certain lifestyles or values, but is seeking to ensure that Canadians are informed about and can engage critically with their own cultures. The Convention consequently does not reject the importance of individual choice, rather it affords it central importance and seeks to maintain it over both the short and long term.

Other arguments for the preservation of cultural diversity can be identified in the Convention. Recital four, for example, ambitiously suggests that those practices of toleration and respect which foster cultural diversity will also facilitate 'peace and security at the local, national and international levels.' Cultural diversity may also provide rather more direct and immediate benefits. On the one hand, cultural goods and services constitute an increasingly important component of world trade, but it is a trade dominated by a handful of developed countries. The Convention thus seeks to assist all countries in fully exploiting their cultural heritage. In particular, recital eight notes that traditional knowledge may be a 'source of intangible and material wealth,' of benefit to indigenous communities through its contribution to sustainable development. On the other, when a culture ceases to exist as a living practice we lose with it specific human insights and skills, often developed over centuries. These could provide unique answers to present or future problems, problems that we currently may not even envisage. Cultural diversity is consequently regarded by the Convention as offering material benefits not only to specific countries but also to mankind in general (recital two).

---

[54] See Morris, N., n. 48 above, at 286, and Baker, C. E. (2002). Media, Markets and Democracy. Cambridge: Cambridge University Press. Baker argues that domestic communications industries are important not only on democratic grounds, as more likely to provide essential information about ones own country, its internal policies and external relations, but also on 'dialogic' grounds, because they enable citizens to discuss and engage actively with their own cultures.

[55] A central concern of those countries that pushed for adoption of the UNESCO Convention was that the existing WTO trade agreements fail to recognise the distinctive nature of cultural goods and services. The US in its 2000 *Communication on Audiovisual and Related Services* to the WTO Council for Trade in Services did not deny that audiovisual services had unique characteristics because of their cultural content, but rather concluded that this should not automatically take them outwith the ambit of the trade agreements. Other goods and services, it observed, have distinct qualities and these can be adequately accommodated within the framework of the GATS. Paper S/CSS/W/21 of the 18 December 2000, available from the WTO website at: http://www.wto.org/english/docs_e/docs_e.htm (accessed 28/08/06).

C. What Measures, If Any, Does The Convention Require States To Take To Promote Cultural Diversity?

What obligations do states undertake when they sign up to the Cultural Diversity Convention? Initial examination of the Convention suggests that it is essentially permissive and imposes relatively few positive obligations on Contracting Parties to promote or maintain cultural diversity. Although the Convention states that 'cultural diversity can be protected and promoted only if human rights and fundamental freedoms, *such as...the ability of individuals to choose cultural expressions*, are guaranteed' (Art. 2.1, emphasis added) and recognises the 'equal dignity of...all cultures, including the cultures of persons belonging to minorities and indigenous peoples' (Principle 3 and see also Art. 7), it does not, unlike the 2001 *UNESCO Declaration on Cultural Diversity* or the *European Framework Convention on National Minorities*, list specific cultural rights regarding, for example, language use or access to education, which states must respect.[56]

Instead, the Convention reaffirms 'the *sovereign rights of States* to maintain, adopt and implement policies and measures *that they deem appropriate*' in order to preserve cultural diversity (Art. 1(h) italics added). State sovereignty in the cultural field is included as one of the eight guiding principles which underpin the Convention (Art. 2(2) and see also Art. 5). Key figures in the drafting process saw the Convention as an essentially declaratory instrument and although the Convention in Article 6 sets out a list of measures which Parties may take to promote cultural diversity, they are not obliged to do so.[57]

The Convention is at its most directional in relation to education, co-operation with civil society organisations, support for developing countries (considered in more detail in section G below) and reporting requirements. Thus, Article 10 provides that 'Parties shall encourage and promote' understanding of cultural diversity 'through educational and greater public awareness campaigns,' while Article 11 requires them to 'encourage the active participation of civil society' in their efforts to achieve the objectives of the Convention. These provisions are not at all constraining, given the open-ended way in which they have been phrased ('encourage,' 'promote' etc.), and it would seem enough for a Party merely to undertake some initiatives in these general areas, however ineffective. Parties are also required to provide, every four years, 'appropriate information' to UNESCO, detailing the measures they have taken to promote cultural diversity at the domestic and international levels, and to generally share and exchange information in this regard (Arts. 9 and 19).

Reporting requirements can perform a number of useful functions and have been widely used in international agreements in the cultural field.[58] They enable compliance with specific obligations to be evaluated; impose political pressure on states to improve their performance in a given area, even when there are no formal sanctions; and enable comparisons to be drawn between different regulatory techniques, good practice to be identified, and guidance for future action developed. When combined with clear obligations, effective external monitoring and sufficient publicity, reporting requirements can

---

[56] See text accompanying note 20 above.
[57] See the 31 May report from Garry Neil, INCD Executive Director, in the INCD (2005) Newsletter 6/1at: http://www.incd.net/docs/NewsletterMay2005.htm (accessed 14/02/06).
[58] See, for example, the *Council of Europe Framework Convention on National Minorities*, n. 19 above.

influence state behaviour, particularly where the state accepts the underlying objectives of the regulation in question.[59]

Where, however, important competing interests are at play it is unlikely that reporting requirements will have much of an effect. Thus, the requirement in Article 4.3 of the EU 'Television Without Frontiers Directive' that Member States report to the European Commission the percentage of European programmes broadcast by television stations under their jurisdiction has undoubtedly encouraged Member States to monitor whether their broadcasters comply with the European content quota.[60] This, however, is in a context in which they could potentially be fined if they fail to return reports and, even here, states continue to omit inconvenient information. Italy, for example, has regularly refused to provide data concerning the percentage of European programmes on its domestic satellite channels.[61]

As previously noted, Article 9 of the Convention merely requires Parties to report every four years on those measures they *have taken* 'to protect and promote the diversity of cultural expressions within their territory and at the international level.' There is thus no obligation to report generally on their countries' state of cultural diversity and, if a state does nothing to protect or enhance diversity, there will simply be nothing to report. In particular, Parties are not obliged to report any measures which decrease cultural diversity and are unlikely to wish to publicise such measures where they have been adopted. The Convention does not provide for sanctions where states fail to file reports.

Without effective follow up and investigation from an independent body, there is a real risk that the reporting process in the Convention will result in partial or misleading information. If adopted as originally drafted, the Convention would have set up a world cultural observatory and a permanent group of experts to oversee and support the implementation of the Convention, but these provisions were removed from the text at an early stage of deliberations on the basis that they were 'overly ambitious.'[62] In terms of collating information on good practice and analysing developments in the cultural field, UNESCO now undertakes to use 'existing mechanisms within the Secretariat' for this purpose and to develop a data bank in order to complement information collected through the formal reporting process (Art. 19). Absent additional resources, however, this does not appear to be much of an advance on the existing position.[63]

---

[59] For discussion of the effectiveness of reporting requirements see Sunstein, C. (1999). Public Broadcasting and the Public Interest: Notes Towards a "Third Way". Chicago Law and Economics Working Papers. 65, 1-71, available at: http://www.law.uchicago.edu/Lawecon/workingpapers.html (accessed 28/08/06).

[60] Directive 89/552/EEC (1989) OJ L298, as amended by Directive 97/36/EC (1997) OJ L202.

[61] See, for example, European Commission, *Sixth Communication on the application of Articles 4 and 5 of Directive 89/552/EEC, as amended by Directive 97/36/EC, for the period 2001-2002*, COM (2004) 524 final, at 10.

[62] Mazzone, n. 7 above.

[63] The Fund for Cultural Diversity, which could be used for this purpose, has no guaranteed source of finance, on which see text accompanying n. 111 below.

With regard to review of the country reports, these are to be sent to the Intergovernmental Committee, a body to be composed, at least initially, of representatives of 18 Parties, elected for four year terms (Art. 23). The Committee is required to summarize and comment on the reports before passing them on to the Conference of Parties, the Convention's supreme regulatory organ (Art. 23.6(c)). The Intergovernmental Committee has power to invite public and private organisations, or individuals, to participate in its meetings in order to consult on specific issues (Art. 23.7) so that there is some scope for the Committee, given sufficient drive and adequate administrative backing, to inject a degree of political bite into the reporting procedure.

Even less constraining are those articles in the Convention which require Parties simply to 'endeavour' to achieve certain things. Article 7, for example, provides that parties 'shall endeavour to create in their territory an environment that encourages individuals and social groups ... to create, disseminate, distribute and have access to their own cultural expressions,' and to 'diverse cultural expressions from within their territory as well as from other countries of the world.' A similar formulation can be found in Article 12, which seeks to promote 'bilateral, regional and international cooperation,' and in a number of articles relating to support for developing countries.[64]

Even an autocratic state that does nothing to support cultural diversity might consequently consider signing up to the Convention a relatively unproblematic exercise. It requires Parties to do very little in terms of concrete action and, at worst, could result in a state being criticised by the Intergovernmental Committee or Conference of Parties for failure to take sufficient measures to promote or protect cultural diversity, on the basis of the state's own four yearly reports. It is not impossible that such a state might find itself involved in a dispute with another Party regarding the interpretation or application of the Convention under Article 25. This might, for example, relate to whether the state had complied with its 'duty' under Article 7 to 'endeavour to' create an environment in which social groups have access to their own and each others' cultures. But State Parties are unlikely to challenge other Parties concerning their compliance with the Convention unless their own nationals or an emigrant community are affected and the Convention's dispute settlement procedures are not open to individuals or non-governmental organisations.

Moreover, the Convention's dispute settlement procedures, though potentially administratively irksome for a state, are not legally constraining. If negotiation fails and the Parties cannot agree to refer the matter to mediation, or mediation does not resolve the issue, a Party can then set in motion a process of conciliation. But Parties can opt out of conciliation altogether by virtue of Article 25.4, and those that do accept the procedure know that this will not expose them to binding rulings. Rather, the five member Conciliation Commission is empowered simply to make 'proposals' for the resolution of a dispute and Parties are required to 'consider' the terms of these proposals 'in good faith.'[65] Perhaps most importantly, there is no provision for formal sanction in circumstances where a Party ignores the Conciliation Commission's recommendations and retains the contested measures.

---

[64] See further section G below.
[65] Convention, Annex, Article 5.

Ultimately, the effectiveness of the Convention is likely to depend on how the UNESCO Secretariat, civil society organisations, and the Intergovernmental Committee set up by the Convention use the political leverage afforded them, for example through comments on the country reports, to put pressure on State Parties to modify their behaviour.[66]

D. Does the Convention Clarify Those Measures That States Are Permitted To Take Under International Law To Promote and Protect Cultural Diversity?

A key objective of those who pressed for adoption of the Convention was to obtain clarification as to the type of domestic measures that states may legitimately adopt in order to enhance cultural diversity. How successful is the Convention likely to be in meeting this objective?

Though the Convention imposes only the most limited obligations on Parties to take action to promote cultural diversity, it confers extensive rights on states to introduce measures with this end in view. The Convention adopts here an 'all inclusive' approach: its object is to endorse forms of market intervention rather than preclude them. Thus, Article 6, headed 'rights of parties at the national level,' contains a non-exhaustive list of measures that Parties 'may adopt' and this list is framed in such open ended terms that it is difficult to envisage a form of state support that would not be covered. The first sub-paragraph of Article 6.2 is particularly broad, in that it refers to all regulatory measures which have as their underlying *objective* the protection of cultural diversity. Given this provision it is questionable whether further specification was needed, but the Convention goes on to list, *inter alia*, measures 'that provide opportunities for domestic cultural activities, goods and services ... including provisions relating to the language used'; that assist independent cultural industries gain access to the means of production, dissemination and distribution; that provide public finance; and that support public institutions and 'artists and others involved in the creation of cultural expression.[67] The Convention also explicitly mentions measures designed to enhance media diversity, in particular through support for public service broadcasting.[68]

The Convention consequently endorses assistance for both public and private bodies and can be read as covering the whole gamut of often controversial support measures which states employ in the audiovisual context, such as transmission quotas, financial subsidies, tax relief, preferential access to distribution facilities or advertising resources, and investment or ownership restrictions. What is immediately striking is that there is no attempt in Article 6 to provide guidance as to the respective merits of the measures it enumerates or how states might reduce the trade distorting effects of such measures. In particular, the Convention makes no express reference to principles such as proportionality or effectiveness, which could guide the application of these measures and serve to prevent more blatant

---

[66] For further discussion see Bernier, I., in collaboration with Ruiz Fabri, H. (2006). La Mise en Oeuvre et le Suivi de la Convention de l'Unesco sur la Protection et la Promotion de la Diversité des Expressions Culturelles. Quebec: Government of Quebec, available online at:
http://mcc.quebectel.qc.ca/sites/mcc/ClinStat.nsf/ce5e08c8e9d9f012852570c8001493ee/49a54fb3750f3a418525713b00714b1e!OpenDocument (accessed 28/09/2006).
[67] Convention, Article 6.2 (a)-(g).
[68] Convention, Article 6.2 (h).

forms of protectionism. The closest Article 6.2 comes to this is in the requirement that measures adopted under sub paragraphs (b) and (f) be 'appropriate.' It is thus hardly surprising that a key concern voiced by the U.S. over the Convention was that it could be used to justify protectionism: Louise Oliver, the U.S. ambassador to UNESCO, stated that it was 'too open to misinterpretation and too prone to abuse for us to support it.'[69] The ability to generate effective guidance over time as to the appropriate exercise by Parties of their rights under Article 6 will thus be essential if the Convention is to have any credibility.

In relation to 'ranking,' the U.S. has, for example, taken the view that subsidies are a preferable form of intervention to, say, quotas, which constitute a more direct restriction on foreign goods and services. In its 2000 *Communication on Audiovisual and Related Services* to the WTO Council for Trade in Services the U.S. stated that '[t]here is a precedent in the WTO for devising rules which recognize the use of carefully circumscribed subsidies for specifically defined purposes, all the while ensuring that the potential for trade distortive effects is effectively contained or significantly neutralized.'[70] It suggested that a specific understanding on subsidies might be developed which would take into account cultural considerations.[71] The U.S. has also adopted a more tolerant attitude to subsidy regimes in its recent Free Trade Agreements with countries such as Singapore and Australia than it has to other access restrictions in the audiovisual sector.[72]

One might conclude that this is merely a cynical assessment on the part of the U.S. of the actual impact on its own communications industry of foreign subsidies. Although the scale of public subsidies can be substantial, and in Europe up to sixty per cent of cinema funding comes from the public sector,[73] they are unlikely to compensate for major structural disadvantages, such as a restricted linguistic market. Indeed, film production within Europe remains fragmented and fragile, with very few European films distributed outside their country of production.[74] Subsidies may consequently not be sufficient to shore up a failing industry and states vary in their ability to provide financial assistance for their cultural industries. Moreover, public subsidies can stifle innovation and result in poor quality products. Given these complexities it is not surprising that there is no attempt in the Convention to rank the various measures

---

[69] Cited in Diderich, J. (2005). U.S. Isolated as UNESCO Approves Pact Aimed at Protecting Cultural Diversity. Associated Press. October 20. Available in the online version of the New Mexican at http://www.freenewmexican.com/news/33993.html (accessed 10/25/2005).

[70] See n. 55 above at para. 10(iii).

[71] *Ibid.*

[72] Wunsch-Vincent, S. (2006). The WTO, the Internet and Trade in Digital Products. Oxford: Hart Publishing, at 212-213 and 230; and Wunsch-Vincent, S. (2003), The Digital Trade Agenda of the U.S.: Parallel Tracks of Bilateral, Regional and Multilateral Liberalization. *Aussenwirtschaft.* 58. Jahrgang (2003), Heft I, Zurich:Ruegger, 7-46 at 11.

[73] IMCA (2003). Identification and Evaluation of Financial Flows within the European Cinema Industry by Comparison with the American Model. Study no. DG EAC/34/01.

[74] For a recent evaluation of the impact of EU support programmes see Henning, V. and Alpar, A. (2005). Public Mechanisms in Feature Film Production: the EU MEDIA Plus Programme. Media, Culture and Society. 27/2, 229-250. The new Community MEDIA 2007 programme was agreed in *Decision no. 1718/2006/EC...concerning the implementation of a programme of support for the audiovisual sector* [2006] OJ L 327/12. See also the IMCA study at n. 73 above.

that states can introduce to support their cultural industries, and the adoption of a range of different initiatives may be the most effective way to stimulate domestic production. Further study in this area is, however, clearly needed. With the demise of proposals for a world observatory and standing body of experts, guidance is most likely to be provided by the UNESCO Secretariat under Article 19, or the Intergovernmental Committee when acting on a request from the Conference of Parties to prepare operational guidelines for the implementation and application of the Convention' provisions under Article 23.6(b).

Another area which requires clarification is whether states can adopt measures under Article 6 which directly discriminate against foreign goods, services or persons on grounds of nationality. Although it is unlikely that the Parties to the Convention would accept a reading of Article 6 which entirely excludes such measures - many states, for example, restrict foreign ownership of their media on diversity grounds —restrictions of this type may go beyond what is necessary to protect the cultural interests at stake. In the context of the EU, Member States are not permitted to justify directly discriminatory trade barriers on cultural grounds, though such a justification may be put forward to support a measure that, on its face, is non-discriminatory but which renders it difficult for foreign goods or services to access the domestic market.[75] In principle, therefore, the imposition by a Member State of the EU of a broadcast quota framed in terms of domestic production would be illegal, whereas a quota for programmes that reflect domestic culture or language might well be justifiable because such a quota does not automatically exclude foreign companies from the domestic market. It is striking, however, that at the pan-European level, the European Community mandates European programme quotas based precisely on the participation of European producers and artists.[76] For the EU, therefore, films and television programmes made outside the EU are not cultural substitutes for programmes made within it, even when they focus on European issues.[77]

Finally, there is no mention in Article 6, or indeed more generally in the Convention, of the principle of proportionality. The principle has been incorporated into a wide range of international agreements on, among other things, human rights and trade.[78] At its most exacting it can be used to ensure that state measures pursue legitimate objectives and do not go beyond what is strictly necessary to attain those objectives. Less intensively, it can be used to test the 'reasonableness' or appropriateness of a measure, affording the state greater latitude.

---

[75] See Katsirea, I. (2003). Why the European Broadcasting Quota Should be Abolished. European Law Review. 28/2, 190-209. Some scope for direct discrimination is, however, accepted in the context of domestic aid for the cinema industry in the light of Article 87.3(d) of the European Community Treaty.

[76] Articles 5 and 6 of the EC Television Without Frontiers Directive, n. 60, above.

[77] For helpful discussion of industrial and cultural objectives underlying the quota and its practical impact see Katsirea, I., n. 75 above. For consideration of similar issues in the context of an Australian/New Zealand dispute see *Project Blue Sky v Australian Broadcasting Authority* [1998] HCA 28, particularly Brennan CJ at para.12.

[78] Consider, for example, the requirement in Articles 8, 9, 10 and 11 of the European Convention on Human Rights that limitations on certain freedoms be 'necessary in a democratic society' and the requirement in Article XX of GATT and XIV GATS that restrictions on trade covered by those Articles should not constitute 'a means of arbitrary or unjustifiable discrimination.'

A good example of a rigorous application of the principle in the cultural sphere is provided by the ruling of the European Court of Justice in the *Familiapress* case.[79] *Familiapress* concerned an Austrian prohibition on the sale of newspapers and periodicals that included puzzles, such as crosswords, for which there were money prizes. The objective behind this prohibition was to prevent powerful newspaper groups winning over readers for their papers by means of financial incentives, rather than through the quality of their reporting. Austria feared that smaller independent newspapers would be unable to offer similar inducements and could be squeezed out of the market. The European Court of Justice held that it was legitimate for Austria to seek to protect media pluralism but carefully considered whether there were other less restrictive measures that might have been adopted, capable of achieving a similar result. Rather than prohibit the sale of foreign newspapers, published in countries where such prizes are allowed, Austria could have required foreign newspapers to 'black out' their promotions or indicate to purchasers that they were not available to people resident in Austria. In addition, the Court of Justice called on the domestic court to establish whether newspapers offering cash prizes were in fact in competition with publications produced by the smaller presses, and whether consumers were actually swayed in their purchasing decisions by the prospect of a prize.[80] The rigorous approach adopted by the Court in this case was undoubtedly influenced by the free speech issues at stake, in that the Austrian law prevented its citizens from obtaining information from other countries.

It is probable that those drafting the Convention decided to avoid express mention of any concept such as proportionality that could open up domestic cultural policies to potentially searching review of this type. Such review would undermine the 'sovereign rights of States to maintain ... policies and measures *that they deem appropriate* for the protection and promotion' of cultural diversity, affirmed in Article 1(h) of the Convention.[81] Moreover, proportionality tends to be employed in international agreements to exert a brake on state action that could curtail key rights or freedoms that it is the object of the agreements to protect. Here, the object of the Convention is precisely to assert the rights of states to take measures to protect cultural diversity, so that the introduction of a proportionality requirement in this context could have appeared inappropriate. Yet the *Familiapress* case illustrates how proportionality can play a valuable role in encouraging states to research carefully the economic and behavioural assumptions on which their cultural policies are based and to consider the availability of alternative, less restrictive, measures. Though the existence of such alternatives should not necessarily invalidate state measures, and the exacting version of the proportionality test applied in *Familiapress* is arguably unduly restrictive in this context, states should nevertheless be able to show that their measures are capable of promoting or protecting domestic cultural expression, that there is a need for such intervention, and that the impact on the importation of foreign cultural goods and services is not excessive given the likely benefits to domestic competitors. Without such a principle, American concerns over the Convention's capacity to endorse

---

[79] Case C-368/95, *Vereinigte Familiapress Zeitungsverlags-und vertriebs GmbH v Heinrich Bauer Verlag* [1997] ECR I-3689.
[80] *Ibid.*, para. 28.
[81] Italics added. In the WTO context Scott Sinclair has argued that application of the test of necessity 'has repeatedly failed to provide an adequate defence for challenged regulations': Sinclair, S. (2006, June). Crunch Time in Geneva. Canadian Centre for Policy Alternatives, 1-30, at 19: http://www.policyalternatives.ca/reports_studies/index.cfm (accessed 7/09/2006).

protectionism would appear to be well founded and all Parties may ultimately find themselves to be the losers.

The principle of proportionality, or some principle akin to it such as 'reasonableness' or 'appropriateness,' the latter of which finds a toe-hold in Article 6.2, may, however, be brought in through the back door by two of the three constraints which the Convention imposes on state discretion in the cultural field: compliance with fundamental rights and compliance with the principles and objectives set out in the Convention. The third constraint is that measures taken by Parties to promote cultural diversity must not contravene obligations that they have undertaken in other international agreements. Although the Convention at first sight appears to afford states considerable latitude in developing their cultural policies, this latitude is consequently not unbounded, and the potential impact of these limitations is discussed in more detail below.

E. Ultimate Constraints on State Action: Fundamental Rights and the Convention's Overarching Principles

The Convention requires that all measures taken by Parties to promote cultural diversity conform to 'universally recognized human rights instruments' (Articles 5.1 and 2.1). Just as the European Court of Justice took into account the importance of fundamental rights in the *Familiapress* case when assessing the Austrian press restrictions, so Parties must consider fundamental rights when framing their domestic regulations. Universally recognized human rights instruments, such as the Universal Declaration of Human Rights or the European Convention on Human Rights, do allow for derogations in specific circumstances which may be broad enough to cover cultural objectives. In order to justify these derogations states are required to establish that their restrictions are necessary and proportionate. Whenever a state restricts cultural expression it is likely also to restrict a fundamental right, such as the right to freedom of expression or information, and a proportionality test will consequently be brought into play. Thus, if country A, a Party to the Cultural Diversity Convention, decides to impose an 80 per cent domestic content quota on its radio and television broadcasters, country B, also a Party to the Convention, could seek to test out the legitimacy, and thus proportionality, of this restriction on freedom of expression or economic rights using the dispute settlement procedures in Article 25.

The second constraint on domestic cultural policy stems from Article 5.2, which requires that all measures adopted under the Convention should be consistent with the Convention's other provisions, including its overarching objectives and principles. The Convention sets out nine objectives and eight guiding principles in Articles 1 and 2, which primarily offer guidance on how cultural diversity might be realised and what it might look like in practice. Perhaps the most important principles in this regard are those which require 'equal dignity and respect for all cultures...including the cultures of...minorities and indigenous peoples'; 'equitable access,' which includes access to cultures from all over the world and 'access of cultures to the means of expression and dissemination'; and 'openness and balance,' which again calls on states to 'promote, in an appropriate manner, openness to other cultures of the world' (principles 3, 7 and 8). The first of these could be used to challenge state measures that repress or discriminate against particular cultures, while the latter principle precludes Parties from seeking to insulate their citizens from exposure to alternative cultures. The principle of 'equitable access' introduces a balancing criterion not entirely unlike the principle of proportionality and the requirement in Article 20 that

Parties should perform their obligations under the Convention in 'good faith' might also be interpreted as establishing a general principle of reasonableness.[82] Although State Parties may prove unwilling to directly question other Parties for failure to respect these principles, the explicit recognition of these principles in the Convention provides a tool for interest groups and non governmental organisations to bring culturally destructive or unduly restrictive state measures to the attention of the Convention organs.

Whether the Convention can move beyond a mere endorsement of state practice and provide meaningful guidance as to how and when the various measures listed in Article 6 should be implemented, will, as noted above, depend very much on the dynamism of the UNESCO Secretariat and the Intergovernmental Committee as well as the integrity of the Conference of Parties. Key functions of the Intergovernmental Committee are to monitor the application of the Convention, to review the country reports, and, *at the request of the Conference of the Parties, to prepare and submit operational guidelines on the implementation and application of the Convention's provisions.*[83] More generally, it is empowered to make recommendations concerning situations which the Parties themselves bring to its attention.[84] Clarification on particular Convention provisions might also be obtained through Party recourse to the dispute resolution procedures in Article 25. There is thus scope for a range of different bodies to begin to flesh out the vague and over-general articles that make up the bulk of the Convention's text. In particular, specific guidance could be given as to the economic conditions which would warrant the introduction of subsidies or quotas, as well as the procedures which states should adopt to monitor and review such measures. This is guidance which the WTO has so far been unable to provide and constitutes one of the main rationales for a separate cultural convention. Whether or not such steps are taken will reveal whether the Parties to the Convention see it simply as a means to endorse their own cultural practices, or as a genuine attempt to further cultural diversity.

F. The Relationship Between The Convention And Other International Instruments

The third constraint which the Convention imposes on its Parties is that they should perform in good faith their obligations under all other treaties to which they are party (Art. 20). Although the Convention states that Parties may adopt measures to promote cultural diversity under Article 6, this apparent freedom is consequently limited by their other international obligations, not merely those in the field of human rights. For this reason also, the abstract list in Article 6 is misleading: the simple fact that a measure falls within the scope of Article 6 provides no guarantee that a state is entitled to adopt it. This will depend in every case on the measure's compliance with fundamental rights, the Convention's principles and objectives, and the state's other international commitments.

Article 20, which deals with the relationship between the Convention and other treaties, proved to be one of the most controversial provisions to draft. Some states wanted the Convention to modify pre-existing international agreements, at least where pressing cultural matters were at stake. A major

---

[82] 'Good faith' is considered a general principle of international law that prohibits the abusive or unreasonable exercise by a state of its rights, see Van den Bossche, P. (2005). The Law and Policy of the World Trade Organization: Text, Cases and Materials. Cambridge: Cambridge University Press, at 58.
[83] Convention, Article 6(a), (b) and (c).
[84] Convention, Article 6(d).

criticism made by the EU and Canada of GATT and GATS is that they do not contain a general cultural derogation.[85] Although the 'positive list' approach adopted in GATS, which enables states to gradually make liberalising commitments, has so far allowed states to shield their cultural services from foreign competition, this is not an option in the context of GATT, which is considerably more prescriptive.[86] International trade rules are thus broad enough to cut down certain domestic cultural policies, as the *Canada Periodicals* case, discussed below, illustrates.

Article 30.4(b) of the 1969 *Vienna Convention on the Law of Treaties* (the 'Vienna Convention') addresses those situations where there are two treaties but not all members of the first treaty are members of the second. Article 30.4(b) provides that a treaty will only govern the mutual rights and obligations of states when they are both parties to it. Since the U.S. has indicated its fundamental opposition to the UNESCO Convention, and is unlikely to ratify it, its relations with Parties to the Convention under other international agreements, such as GATT and GATS, or bilateral free trade agreements, remain unaffected.

What about relations between two countries that have both ratified an earlier treaty and the UNESCO Convention? In this case, Article 30.3 of the Vienna Convention indicates that the UNESCO Convention should take precedence over any earlier agreements to which they are both parties. An earlier agreement will take effect only to the extent that its provisions 'are compatible' with the later agreement. This, however, is subject to any contrary provision in the later treaty, in that Article 30.2 of the Vienna Convention provides that '[w]hen a treaty specifies that it is subject to, or that it is not to be considered as incompatible with, an earlier or later treaty, the provisions of that other treaty prevail.' The UNESCO Convention does contain such a provision in Article 20.1, which states that Parties are to 'perform in good faith their obligations under this Convention and all other treaties to which they are Parties.' This is further confirmed in Article 20.2 which states that '[n]othing in this Convention shall be interpreted as modifying rights and obligations of the Parties under any other treaties to which they are parties.'

This was not an inevitable outcome and at one point the drafters of the UNESCO Convention put forward two distinct versions of what is now Article 20. The first of these provided simply that the Convention would not affect the rights and obligations of its Parties under other existing international instruments, while the second contained the proviso 'except where the exercise of those rights and obligations would cause serious damage or threat to the diversity of cultural expressions.'[87] It was the first of these that was ultimately adopted, without the restriction to 'existing' treaties. In consequence, there

---

[85] For a history of the dispute over the accommodation of cultural interests within the WTO see De Witte, B., Trade in Culture: International Legal Regimes and EU Constitutional Values, in de Búrca, G. and Scott, J. (eds.)(2001). The EU and the WTO: Legal and Constitutional Issues. Oxford: Hart; Pauwels, C. and Loisen, J. (2003). The WTO and the Audiovisual Sector: Economic Free Trade vs Cultural Horse Trading? European Journal of Communication. 18/2, 291-313, and Footer, M. E. and Graber, C. B. (2000). Trade Liberalization and Cultural Policy. Journal of International Economic Law. 3/1, 115-144.

[86] Luff, D. (2004). Telecommunications and Audio-visual Services: Considerations for a Convergence Policy at the World Trade Organization Level. Journal of World Trade. 38/6, 1059-1086, at 1071-1072.

[87] See the preliminary draft of the UNESCO Convention detailed at document CLT/CPD/2005/CONF.203/6, at 36.

would appear to be little, if any, scope for a Party to rely on its 'right' to adopt measures to protect cultural diversity under the UNESCO Convention in defence to a claim that it is in breach of obligations under a prior agreement such as GATT or GATS.[88]

Joost Pauwelyn has argued that most of the obligations undertaken by parties to the WTO agreements are of a 'reciprocal' rather than 'integral' nature.[89] Their reciprocal nature means that it is possible for them to be modified by the parties among themselves, provided this does not lead to the rights of third parties being infringed. This is not to say that the new agreement can form the basis of a claim before a WTO panel or that such a panel must judicially enforce its terms, but the new agreement may be considered part of the applicable law before a WTO panel, and thus provide, according to Pauwelyn, a legal defence to a claim of a WTO breach.[90] On this, admittedly controversial, view, the Convention might be able to modify the Parties' existing obligations under the WTO obligations. But the Convention does appear to have expressly excluded any such eventuality and it is doubtful whether a Party could be said to be 'performing in good faith' its obligations under the WTO agreements, according to Article 20.1 of the UNESCO Convention, if it were to try to use the Convention to avoid them.

Parties to both the WTO agreements and the Convention may, however, prefer to resolve their disputes using the less confrontational and constraining dispute resolution procedures in the Convention. In particular, the Convention might be thought to offer a more conducive forum than the WTO for the articulation and working through of disputes concerning cultural matters. It is arguable that recourse to the Convention rather than WTO dispute resolution procedures by WTO Members could constitute an infringement of their obligation under Article 23.1 of the WTO's *Understanding on Rules and Procedures Governing the Settlement of Disputes* (DSU).[91] This requires Members, when they seek 'the redress of a violation of obligations or other nullification or impairment of benefits under the covered agreements,' to have recourse to the rules and procedures of the DSU. Similar questions concerning the appropriate forum could also arise where a dispute calls into question the compatibility of Party's measures with international human rights instruments under Articles 2.1 and 5. Article 62 of the European Convention on Human Rights, for example, provides that Parties, 'except by special agreement...will not avail themselves of treaties, conventions or declarations in force between them for the purpose of submitting...a dispute arising out of the interpretation or application of this Convention to a means of settlement other than those provided for in this Convention.'

Whether recourse by a Party to dispute settlement under the Convention is held to constitute an infringement of its obligations under existing treaties not to use alternative fora could well depend on the way in which its complaint is framed. A Party is unlikely to expose itself to a challenge of this kind by arguing directly that measures adopted by another Party under the Convention infringe GATT or GATS or a

---

[88] Voon. T. (2006). UNESCO and the WTO: A Clash of Cultures? International and Comparative Law Quarterly. 55/3, 635-652 at 650.
[89] Pauwelyn, J. (2003). Conflict of Norms in Public International Law: How WTO Law Relates to Other Rules of International Law. Cambridge: Cambridge University Press, particularly at 69-88.
[90] *Ibid.* Marceau, n. 29 above, at 1100-1108, suggests that in such circumstances it may be possible for the WTO panel to decline jurisdiction on the basis that the WTO provisions have been 'superseded.'
[91] For helpful discussion on this point see Voon, n.88 above, at 642-644.

particular human rights treaty. Instead, it is more likely to complain that such measures have not been adopted 'in good faith,' as required by Article 20,[92] or are not 'appropriate' or sufficiently 'aimed' at preserving cultural diversity within Article 6, because they are excessive or disproportionate. Such a question then turns on the fitness for purpose of the cultural measure rather than whether it accords with standards established in other treaties. As section E above indicates, however, this latter issue may well be at the root of a dispute and the line between those complaints that should or should not be resolved under the UNESCO Convention may be difficult to draw in a convincing fashion. Where a dispute is brought before a WTO panel, which raises issues that properly fall within the scope of a WTO agreement, it is unlikely that the panel would refuse to hear the complaint because cultural considerations are at play.[93]

Tania Voon has also suggested that the Convention's dispute settlement procedures lack transparency, in that a party to another international agreement, such as GATT or GATS, could be unaware that a dispute has been mutually resolved in this way or its outcome.[94] Although Article 20 of the Convention calls on Parties 'to foster mutual supportiveness' between the Convention and other international agreements to which they are parties, it is not impossible that ultimate resolution of a dispute under the Convention could conflict with the provisions of other treaties.

Although Article 20 of the Convention provides that the Convention is not to override other international agreements to which its members are parties, it may have an indirect effect on their operation. Firstly, the Convention could influence the interpretation of existing agreements, and, secondly, it is likely to be deployed as a political tool to influence the content of future agreements. This latter point is particularly important, in that a number of countries which supported the Convention primarily saw it as a mechanism to forestall any evolution of the WTO rules that might restrict their ability to pursue cultural objectives in the future. They view with concern the recent free trade agreements entered into by the U.S. with Chile, Singapore, CAFTA, Morocco, the Dominican Republic and Bahrain.[95] These agreements adopt a 'negative list' approach in the field of services, requiring states to establish a definitive list of restrictions rather than enabling them to gradually make market opening concessions. The U.S. has throughout sought to ensure minimal restrictions are maintained or can be imposed in relation to electronically delivered services and 'digital products.'

This approach is not acceptable to a number of the Convention's core supporters. In the EU context, for example, the European Community is currently considering the adoption of an Audiovisual

---

[92] See n. 82 above.

[93] See Marceau, 29 above, at 1117, and at 1108-1115 for a more general discussion on the principles which could be used to determine the appropriate forum when conventions overlap.

[94] Voon, n. 88 above, at 645.

[95] For detailed analysis see Wunsch-Vincent (2006), n. 72 above, chapter 7, and Bernier, I. (2004). The Recent Free Trade Agreements of the United States as Illustration of their New Strategy Regarding the Audiovisual Sector. 1-21. Available at: www.mcc.gouv.qc.ca/diversite-culturelle/eng/pdf/conf_seoul_ang_2004.pdf (accessed 28/09/06).

Media Services Directive.[96] The proposal is intended to respond to the new ways in which audiovisual material is transmitted and consumed, and includes measures which apply to audiovisual content, whatever its means of delivery (analogue or digital) and whether provided as part of a scheduled or on-demand service. The scope of the proposed directive is consequently wider than the existing Television Without Frontiers Directive, which applies solely to television broadcasting.[97] Although the proposal does not attempt to extend the existing European content quota across the whole spectrum of electronic media services, it does call on Member States 'to ensure that media service providers under their jurisdiction promote, where practicable and by appropriate means, production of and access to European works.'[98] The EU thus clearly wishes to retain its competence to introduce culturally motivated measures across the electronic communications field – and does not accept the U.S. 'standstill' agenda.

For some states, therefore, the Convention will be seen to be a success if it strengthens their hand in fending off further liberalisation within the WTO.[99] This is particularly important in the context of GATS, which requires Members to enter into successive rounds of negotiations with a view to progressive liberalisation in the service sectors.[100] Article XIX.2 provides, however, that service liberalisation is to 'take place with due respect for national policy objectives' and the Convention will undoubtedly be deployed by states wishing to retain their ability to impose trade restrictive measures on cultural grounds. Although trade talks under the DOHA development agenda were suspended in July 2006, a final agreement, incorporating extensive liberalisation in the field of services, cannot be ruled out. The attempt to push forward liberalisation by establishing benchmarks for assessing state commitments, by introducing plurilateral alongside established bilateral negotiations, and by entering into negotiations over new rules governing non-discriminatory domestic regulations under Article VI:4 of GATS, could have significant implications for state competence in the cultural sphere.[101]

But despite Article 20.1(b) of the Convention, which states that Parties, when entering into other international obligations, 'shall take into account the relevant provisions of this Convention,' it is unlikely that the Convention will have much of an impact on the existence or nature of future bilateral agreements. Although developed countries with established cultural industries, such as Canada or France, may be unwilling to restrict their competence in the cultural field, and the Convention provides an additional

---

[96] European Commission, *Proposal for a Directive...amending Council Directive 89/552/EEC on the coordination of certain provisions laid down by law, regulation or administrative action in Member States concerning the pursuit of television broadcasting activities*, COM(2005) 646 final.

[97] Directive 89/552/EEC, as amended by Directive 97/36/EC, n. 60 above.

[98] European Commission, *Proposal for a Directive...amending Council Directive 89/552/EEC*, n. 96 above, at Article 1(6), introducing a new Article 3f(1).

[99] Leaving Members such as the EU free to concentrate in trade negotiations on other intractable issues such as agricultural subsidies, see Mazzone, G., n. 7 above at 5.

[100] GATS, Article XIX.

[101] Sinclair, S., n. 81 above, who notes that plurilateral requests have been put forward in relation to audiovisual services, *ibid*. p. 15.

justification for such a stance, many states will consider the economic benefits of bilateral trade deals, particularly with the U.S., to outweigh any potential prejudice to their cultural industries in the future.[102]

Turning to the Convention's potential influence on the way in which other treaties are interpreted or applied, Article 20.1(b) requires that Parties, when interpreting or applying other treaties to which they are parties, take into account relevant provisions of the Convention. But in the context of agreements such as GATT and GATS, which have their own dispute resolution organs, final determination of what the agreement ultimately requires rests not with the parties but with those organs. WTO panels and the Appellate Body are, however, required to interpret the provisions of the WTO agreements taking into account all relevant rules of international law.[103] Article 31.3 (c) of the Vienna Convention provides that, in interpreting treaties, '[t]here shall be taken into account together with the context: (c) any relevant rules of international law applicable in the relations between the parties.' Gabrielle Marceau has noted that 'in most cases the proper interpretation of the relevant WTO provisions...should lead to a reading of the WTO provisions so as to avoid conflict with other treaty provisions.'[104]

Even if the Convention does not directly override provisions in the WTO agreements it could, therefore, potentially affect their interpretation. This could be important, for example, when determining the scope of the various exceptions provided for in the agreements, or whether certain goods should be considered 'like' goods for the purposes of paragraph 4 of Article III GATT, which requires that products be 'accorded treatment no less favourable than that accorded to like products of national origin.' The Convention might in such circumstances lead to greater weight being afforded to the cultural dimensions of a product.

That this may not always be possible, however, is illustrated by the *Canada Periodicals* case.[105] This concerned a Canadian excise tax that targeted U.S. magazines, or periodicals, transmitted into Canada in electronic form to avoid Canadian import duties and then printed in Canada prior to distribution. If the periodical was altered in its Canadian version to include Canadian advertising it potentially became classified as a 'split-run edition' and was subject to a swinging excise tax, amounting to 80 per cent of the value of all advertisements contained in the edition. The tax had been introduced to support magazine production in Canada in the face of strong U.S. competition. The provision in GATT that ultimately outlawed the Canadian tax was the second sentence of Article III.2. This precludes taxes on imported goods that are in competition with, or substitutable for, domestic goods, where this affords protection to domestic production. Although Canada argued before the Appellate Body that split run and domestic

---

[102] That attitudes vary across both the developed and developing world is evidenced by the *Joint Statement on the Negotiations on Audiovisual Services of the 30 June 2005, made by Hong Kong China, Japan, Mexico, the separate customs territory of Taiwan, Penghu, Kinmen and Matsu, and the United States*, which emphasises the economic benefits to be gained from further liberalisation in the audiovisual sector: WTO TN/S/W/49. See also materials cited at n. 95 above.

[103] Marceau, n. 29 above; Pauwelyn, n. 89 at 251-256, Van den Bossche, n. 82 at 63-64, Voon, n. 88 at 645-647.

[104] Marceau, n. 29 above, at 1082.

[105] *Canada – Certain Measures Concerning Periodicals* (WT/DS31/AB/R) adopted 30 July 1997, available at: http://www.wto.org/english/tratop_e/dispu_e/cases_e/ds31_e.htm.

magazines were not comparable because they were created for different markets – they were not 'substitutable information vehicles' – the Appellate Body preferred the arguments of the U.S., which pointed out that advertisers were prepared to buy space in split run editions thereby indicating that such editions could command a domestic market and compete with domestic magazines.[106] The focus here on market competition and substitutability, on whether readers will buy a foreign product even if culturally distinct from a domestic one, provides no scope for cultural considerations to be taken into account. Certain GATT or GATS provisions may simply not be open, therefore, to interpretation in a Convention-friendly manner, and it will be sufficient for one such provision to be applicable to invalidate a culturally motivated trade restriction. Furthermore, even in areas where the Convention could come into play as an interpretative tool there is no guarantee that it will be applied in the way that a Party desires.

The Convention could also influence how GATT and GATS are understood to interact. This is important because there may be cases where a culturally motivated regulation affects the provision of both goods and services. In the context of services, states can refrain from making national treatment commitments under article XVII of GATS, whereas there is no such scope under GATT. In *Canada Periodicals* the excise tax was analysed as a restriction on trade in goods and held to violate Article III.2 of GATT, even though it also had implications for the provision of advertising services. In this case the tax was specifically designed to protect domestic periodicals, so that the application of GATT appears justifiable, but it is also possible to envisage instances where a domestic regulation directly affects trade in services but also has a secondary, indirect, impact on the sale of goods. For example, a requirement that radio stations broadcast a certain percentage of songs in the national language, which restricts the provision of services, could also have a negative impact on the sale of foreign compact discs, classified as goods.[107] To invalidate the measure on the basis of GATT could undermine the freedom that states currently retain under GATS to pursue cultural objectives. In such instances the UNESCO Convention might lead a WTO panel or the Appellate Body to give precedence to GATS over the GATT.[108]

More fundamentally, the Convention could influence whether a product is classified as a 'good' or 'service.' The U.S. has, for example, been pressing for electronic downloads of music and films over the internet to be considered goods, in effect online versions of compact or digital video discs, which are undoubtedly goods. If such a question were to be referred to a WTO dispute body, it would be open to a party to argue that the download should be classified as a service on the basis that this would afford

---

[106] *Ibid.*, 24-26.

[107] An example discussed by Weber, O. From Regional to Global Freedom of Trade in Audio-visual Goods and Services? A Comparison of the Impact on the Audio-visual Sector of the Preferential Trade Zones Established by the European Communities and the World Trade Organization, in Craufurd Smith, R., (ed.)(2004). Culture and EU Law. Oxford: OUP, at 353-381. Such a restriction could also affect the sale of electronic downloads of music over the internet, on which see text accompanying n.108 below.

[108] For helpful discussion of this issue see Pauwelyn, n. 89 above, at 403-405. In *Canada Periodicals*, n. 105 above, the Appellate Body (at IV) held, however, that GATT and GATS 'do not override' each other and concluded that it was not necessary, given the way in which the complaint had been framed, to consider whether there was any potential conflict between the two. See also *EC-Bananas III*, WT/DS27/R at para. 221.

greater scope for states to retain culturally motivated regulations recognised to be legitimate under the Convention.

In conclusion, although the UNESCO Convention, once in force, will not directly shield its Parties from actions for infringement of their obligations under other international agreements, most notably under GATT and GATS, it could influence in important respects the interpretation and operation of these agreements. The Convention's essentially co-operative dispute resolution procedures may also prove attractive for the resolution of culture-related disputes, leading to the development of principles to manage the trade-culture interface. More importantly, the extensive support displayed by the international community for the Convention at the time of its adoption strengthens the position of those states who wish to prevent any further encroachment by international trade rules into their competence in the cultural domain.

G. The Convention and Developing Countries

The UNESCO Convention gained support from developing countries, as well as smaller cultural and linguistic regions, through its commitment to assist them in their efforts to preserve and fully exploit their cultural heritage.[109] In particular, Article 13 of the Convention recognises the importance of culture for sustainable development and calls on Parties to integrate culture into their development policies at all levels. The Convention is uncharacteristically specific in listing a number of concrete ways in which Parties are required to 'endeavour' to support sustainable development. This includes strengthening developing countries' production and distribution capacities through facilitating access to domestic markets and international distribution networks for their cultural goods and services; facilitating the mobility of cultural workers from developing countries; and encouraging collaboration between developed and developing countries in areas such as music and film (Art.14). Developed countries are additionally called on to undertake exchanges with developing countries, offering preferential access to their cultural workers, goods and services (Art.16). The Convention could play a valuable role here in helping to re-orient domestic development policies. In the EU context, for example, a recent study for the European Commission indicated that EU Member States mainly seek to project and promote their own cultures through co-operation agreements with third countries, rather than sustain the cultures existing within those countries.[110]

A second strand of support is to take the form of 'capacity building' through the exchange of information and expertise in order to develop management capacities, policy development and implementation, use of technology, and skills development and transfer (Art.14.2). Parties are required to 'encourage' the formation of partnerships between the private and public sectors and non-profit organisations working in the cultural field (Art.15). The Convention also calls for the transfer of technology and know-how, especially with regard to cultural industries and enterprises (Art.14.3).

---

[109] See, in particular, Articles 1(a) and (b) and 2.6.

[110] Ernst and Young (2004) Study of External Cooperation of the European Union and its Member States in the Culture and Audiovisual Sectors. See in particular p. 6.

Finally, Parties are to 'endeavour' to provide financial assistance through the establishment of an International Fund for Cultural Diversity, official development assistance and other forms of support, such as low interest loans and grants (Art. 14.4). An earlier draft of the Convention had envisaged that Parties to the Convention would be required to contribute to the Fund but, under the Convention as adopted, contributions are to be voluntary. These may be supplemented by funds appropriated by the General Conference of UNESCO and contributions or gifts from other states, organisations or individuals.[111] The precise use to which the Fund is to be put is to be determined by the Intergovernmental Committee, following guidelines determined by the Conference of Parties.

It is too early to say whether the Convention will have much, if any, impact in the development field once it enters into force. Although the provisions on development employ the undemanding 'shall endeavour/facilitate/encourage' terminology, there is greater specificity as to the type of action which is envisaged and this, coupled with the reporting requirement in Article 9, could encourage concrete action and a redirection of existing policies in this area. But, as with other aspects of the Convention, much is left to the good will and enthusiasm of the Parties. In the absence of any formal sanction for 'non-compliance,' and without assured funding or adequate administrative resources, this may simply not be enough to bring the Convention's development agenda to life.

H. Conclusion

Can the UNESCO Convention usher in a new world communications order and is it likely to realise the objectives of those who voted for it? With the Convention not yet in force it is risky to make predictions, but the answer to the first question is fairly clearly 'no,' and to the second, 'yes, in part.' Arguably, the Convention was never intended by its promoters to be an innovative measure; it was primarily designed to maintain the status quo in the field of trade and culture. In particular, developed countries such as Canada and France promoted the Convention on the basis that it would provide high level political endorsement for their culturally motivated trade restrictions. It serves to justify not only their existing measures but also their refusal to make commitments in new and developing communications sectors in the future. But for the Convention to be influential politically it needs to attract wide support from across the international community, from developed and developing countries. The result is a document that evades controversy, which establishes general objectives and frames them in purely exhortatory terms. As a political manifesto, with little legal substance, it is hardly an advance on the international declarations on cultural diversity which preceded it.

Even as a political tool the influence of the Convention may prove to be quite limited. The U.S. is unlikely to ratify the Convention in the foreseeable future, and with trade talks stalled at the WTO level, the U.S. is turning to bilateral agreements in order to liberalise international trade in goods and services. It is no coincidence that Korea halved its existing screen quota for domestic films, a continuing source of irritation for the U.S. despite its legality under GATT, days before the U.S. announced that it was launching trade talks with Korea early in 2006.[112] Nor does the Convention enable parties to 'clawback'

---

[111] Convention, Article 18.

[112] See the open letter of the 24 March 2006 to the US trade representative from INCD and the Free Press organisation calling for the US to 'propose an unrestricted and unlimited exemption for cultural goods and

their existing WTO or bilateral free trade commitments, though it may influence the interpretation and operation of such international agreements in the future. It is, however, far from clear what impact the Convention will have on the resolution of some of the fundamental uncertainties that currently exist in the context of GATT and GATS, notably whether electronic communications products should be classified as goods or services, and the approach to be adopted where both GATT and GATS apply to a particular measure.

For developing countries or minority groups the Convention offers nothing by way of concrete entitlement. Given that cultural diversity may be threatened as much, if not more, by forces operating internally within states, the underlying pre-occupation of the Convention with inter-state relations and international trade represents a clear limitation.[113] Although Article 7 of the Convention recognizes that all peoples, including indigenous peoples and minority groups, should be able to create, disseminate and have access to their own cultures, it falls short of framing such interests in terms of rights and imposes merely an obligation of endeavour, rather than result, on State Parties to promote such interests. Its dispute resolution procedures are closed to individuals and interest groups, most likely to take up such cases, and its use of the term 'interculturality' rather than 'multiculturalism' appears designed to diffuse potential tensions with Parties over their internal policies of integration or assimilation. The Convention focuses, then, on affirming state rights and defines these rights in extremely open ended terms, giving real ground for concern that this, as the U.S. suggests, could turn into a protectionist's charter.

The Convention does, however, introduce a number of constraints which come into play once a state takes action to promote or protect cultural diversity, namely, respect for fundamental rights and the Convention's overarching principles and objectives. These principles could be used to challenge not only repressive or discriminatory measures but also to introduce a test of proportionality or reasonableness, thereby adding a much needed element of rigour to what is a highly permissive document. Although one of the criticisms that can be levelled at the Convention is that its dispute settlement procedures are extremely weak, the largely consensual processes of negotiation, mediation and conciliation which it maps out could ultimately encourage states to engage with one another and address cultural issues constructively. Though the appropriate relationship between the Convention and other fora when a dispute combines culture with trade or human rights issues has yet to be resolved, the Convention's dispute resolution procedures could, paradoxically, prove to be one of its more significant assets.

As to bringing about change on a more general level, the system of country reports, though far from perfect, could highlight difficulties being encountered by certain cultural groups, particularly if interest groups and non-governmental organisations co-ordinate effectively with the Convention bodies. The Convention emphasises the role of civil society organisations and calls on Parties to encourage their participation in realising the Convention's objectives. Given the active role played by non-governmental organisations, such as the INCD and CRIS, in shaping the Convention, their ongoing commitment to monitoring its ultimate implementation is not surprising.[114] Indeed, the passage of the Convention itself

---

services from the terms of the free trade agreement with the Republic of Korea': http://www.incd.net/ (accessed 28/09/06).

[113] See the Human Development Report (2004), n. 41, above, at 73-84.
[114] See n. 8 above.

stimulated the development of international networks of individuals and groups committed to the protection and promotion of cultural diversity. For the country reports to be meaningful, however, they must be subjected to informed and independent scrutiny. It is thus important that the Intergovernmental Committee and those involved with the operation of the Convention, such as the UNESCO Secretariat, have adequate funds and administrative resources to carry out their tasks, even with the support of civil society organisations. The inability of the Convention's promoters to reach agreement on mandatory contributions to the International Fund for Cultural Diversity, the introduction of a world cultural observatory and a standing committee of experts, could here prove a major impediment.

Finally, there is scope for the Intergovernmental Committee, at the request of the Conference of Parties, to draw up guidelines as to the application of the Convention's provisions and to make recommendations on situations brought to its attention. These guidelines, together with the statistics and information that the UNESCO Secretariat is committed to compiling under Article 19, could provide an invaluable basis for the evaluation of domestic measures in the cultural field in the future. In consequence, although the UNESCO Convention appears on its face singularly unambitious, there is scope for it to be influential at both international and domestic levels. But for this potential to be realised, states must not only ratify the Convention but also actively pursue its goals of preserving and promoting cultural diversity in the future.

[21]
The Human Genome as Common Heritage: Common Sense or Legal Nonsense?

Pilar N. Ossorio

"If there is an obvious component of the common heritage of mankind, indeed, more obvious than the resources of the sea-bed itself, it is the human genetic system."[1]

"It would be prejudicial for scientists to adopt a generalized system of patenting knowledge about the human genome....Such a development would be ethically unacceptable. A patent should not be granted for something that is part of our universal heritage."[2]

In the opening years of the 21st century, it became fashionable to describe the human genome as belonging to the common heritage of humanity.[3] The United Nations, in its Universal Declaration on the Human Genome and Human Rights,[4] now identifies the human genome as part of the common heritage, as does the international Human Genome Organization (HUGO) and the Council of Europe.[5] The common heritage concept has played a prominent role in arguments against patenting the human genome or portions thereof.[6] This essay considers whether the common heritage designation will advance the political and legal goals of its proponents.

From a pre-doctrinal perspective, it seems eminently sensible to think of the human genome as part of our common heritage. Human genes are literally passed between generations; they unite each person with her or his forebears, descendants, and siblings, and they represent a connection among all human beings as members of the "human family." The human genome both reflects human evolution and is the substrate for further evolution. Even people who do not hold genetic reductionist or determinist views may feel that something deeply important is reflected or embodied in our genomes. Many people can accept the plausibility of claims that all human beings have a profound interest in the human genome – that all people have a significant stake in how and whether the human genome is manipulated, and in what principles would guide its commercial exploitation. But are these profound interests adequately addressed by designating the genome as part of humanity's common heritage?

This essay begins with a brief discussion of the concept of public property in general, because common heritage doctrines may create a form of public property. Next, the essay examines the political and legal history of the common heritage (CH) concept and identifies

---

Pilar N. Ossorio, Ph.D., J.D., *is an Associate Professor of Law and Bioethics at the University of Wisconsin-Madison and Program Faculty for the Graduate Program in Population Health.*

two somewhat distinct lineages or approaches. These two approaches are examined to determine whether CH-related jurisprudential and governance principles developed in other contexts can usefully be applied to the human genome. The essay then considers what the common heritage designation contributes to assessments of the permissibility of patenting human DNA sequences.

I. Public Property
A. Theories of Public Property
Designating a resource, region, or artifact as a part of the common heritage of humanity marks it as public property, or as a publicly accessible resource. Historically, several mechanisms have allowed land or resources to be owned by, or held on behalf of, the public. Land and resources have occasionally been made publicly accessible, or maintained for particular public purposes, even when the public had no formal property right.[7] Because the common heritage is only one form of public property, it is useful to have a very brief overview of the different types of public property. This overview may provide us with conceptual tools that aid in determining whether the human genome should be public property, what form that property might take (i.e., what bundle of rights would be associated with that property), and what justifications for the genome as public property, or publicly accessible resource, seem most and least plausible.

Three general categories of public property are *res communis*, *res nullius*, and *res publicae*.[8] *Res communis* is property owned by all (literally, a "common possession"), or at least accessible to all. *Res communis* lands and resources are generally managed for the benefit of the public, either by law or custom, and may be referred to as a commons property or resource. The common heritage is a recent politico-legal construct and is probably a form of *res communis*.

Res nullius, on the other hand, refers to things owned by none. *Res nullius* territories or resources are public by default; they are public because nobody has yet appropriated or laid claim to them. *Res nullius* refers to wastelands or "no man's lands," and little if any *res nullius* still exists on earth. The lands and resources beneath the high seas were *res nullius* until 1982 when they were claimed as the common heritage of humanity under the Convention on the Law of the Sea.[9]

In addition to the CH, other forms of *res communis* include lands and resources in the public domain. The government owns lands in the public domain, but they may be used by the public and may be privately appropriated in accordance with applicable statutes. Ideas can also be in the public domain if they are not protected by some form of intellectual property, such as patents, copyrights, or trade secrets. Ideas in the public domain may be used by anybody without obtaining permission or paying royalties.

Another interesting contemporary form of public property is the public trust. Public trust is a relatively ill-defined legal doctrine, whose very name conveys "intimations of guardianship, responsibility, and community."[10] Generally speaking, public trust doctrine requires that state governments use trust property for public purposes, hold trust property available for use by the general public, and maintain the property for certain types of public use.[11] Public trust doctrine may also imply certain procedural requirements, such as the requirement that governmental decisions concerning trust property be well informed and reflect public participation.[12] Although sometimes referred to as *res communis*, items subject to contemporary doctrines of the public trust were considered *res publicae* under Roman law.[13]

The public trust doctrine traditionally applied to lands under navigable waters and to shorelines. Recently, it has also been applied to wild animals that depend on tide lands[14] and to public park land,[15] and commentators have suggested widening its scope to other areas of resource management where diffuse public interests must be protected against focused, private interests (i.e., the public choice justification).[16] Under U.S. law, a state government is the "trustee" for public trust property. Public trust property can be sold in some U.S. jurisdictions; however, courts tend to interpret such grants narrowly, and have held that the state has trustee obligations that it may not lawfully divest.[17]

The conceptual underpinnings of public trust doctrine include beliefs that (1) "certain interests are so intrinsically important to every citizen that their free availability tends to mark the society as one of citizens rather than of serfs";[18] (2) certain benefits derive so directly or particularly from nature that they should be available to the entirety of the populace; and (3) certain uses of property are of a particularly public nature, or have value only to the extent that they are public.[19] Public trust doctrine can be viewed as a usufruct – a right to use a property belonging to the state without destroying or damaging it – or easement, as against the state or against private owners of properties that abut navigable waterways or other public trust lands. One commentator has urged that the CH should be viewed as providing a use right to the public, rather than a common property right.[20]

At least one commentator has explicitly argued that the human genome should be held in public trust.[21] This proposal has some appeal, particularly insofar as the conceptual underpinnings of public trust doctrine

> While many people now perceive human genetic material as a rich resource, one must remember that this "resource" resides in the bodies of all people. This fact raises numerous questions concerning how a trustee would "manage" the resource for the good of the public at large without impinging on people's autonomy and their procreative and other liberty interests.

are consistent with widely held beliefs that knowledge of human genetics is of great intrinsic importance to all people, and that benefits deriving directly from human biology should be available to all people. The public choice justification is also apropos: in evaluating policy decisions concerning human DNA, some commentators express the view that the well-focused and clearly articulated financial interests of the biotechnology industry will overcome the diffuse and difficult-to-articulate social and moral interests of the world's majority. The conception of public trust as a procedural mandate also resonates with views held by many commentators and advocates, who believe that genetics policy should incorporate broad public input and a robust deliberative process.

However, designating the human genome as a public trust may generate several problems. For example, while many people now perceive human genetic material as a rich resource, one must remember that this "resource" resides in the bodies of all people. This fact raises numerous questions concerning how a trustee would "manage" the resource for the good of the public at large without impinging on people's autonomy and their procreative and other liberty interests. What would it mean to hold the trust property available for public use if the property resides, in part, in every person's body? Any theory of the genome as public property, or publicly accessible resource, must confront similar issues, and I return to these topics in greater detail below when discussing the genome as common heritage.

Another problem arises from the fact that human genetic material is a resource that transcends state and national boundaries. Currently, public trust law in the U.S. is a state law doctrine, not a doctrine of international or even federal law. Scholars and policymakers often consider it advantageous for states to conduct different legal experiments on a particular policy problem, so differences in state law are not always perceived as problematic. However, a patchwork of different state and national doctrines governing the permissibility of particular forms of genetics research or product development would be economically inefficient. And a patchwork of different state laws would likely not satisfy people who have moral objections to some genetics research or to commodification of the human genome. One solution would be to promulgate a new international law doctrine of the public trust, in which an organization such as the United Nations would become the trustee of the human genome.

B. *Common Heritage and Common Ownership*
Numerous treaties designate territory or resources as part of humanity's common heritage, including those that govern the following: activities on the floor of the deep sea, activities in outer space, activities in Antarctica, the use of seeds, preservation of historical artifacts, and conservation of environmental wonders.[22] International law doctrines on the CH reflect some of the same underlying principles and motivations as the public trust doctrine. My analysis of the legal instruments and historical texts suggests that the CH concept is embodied in two separate legal lineages that developed from different historical and political antecedents. For the remainder of this article, these doctrines will be designated as the Common Heritage Property Doctrine (CHPD) and the Common Heritage Duties Doctrine (CHDD).[23]

The CHPD vests all people or all nations with equal *property* interests in a territory or resource. For instance, the Convention on the Law of the Sea states that "[a]ll rights in the resources of the Area are vested in mankind as a whole, on whose behalf the Authority shall act."[24] This property-oriented CH doctrine is also reflected in multilateral agreements concerning Antarctica and resources in outer space.[25]

The CHPD embodies four general principles: (1) no single entity can have sovereignty over, or unilaterally appropriate, the resource or territory in question; (2) all countries will share in a management authority of some sort, which will manage the resource or territory for the "benefit of all humanity"; (3) benefits from the exploitation of the territory or resource will be actively shared among nations; and (4) the area will be used only for peaceful purposes.[26] Thus far, the doctrine has only been applied to lands that were formerly *res nullius*, such as extraterrestrial territory and resources, or territory and resources beneath the deep sea.

The CHPD originated during the late 1960s[27] and arose from the equity concerns of less-industrialized and southern hemisphere nations. Representatives of these nations noted that traditional economic theories did not take into account the power imbalance between them and the wealthier, industrialized, northern nations. Less-industrialized nations argued that this power imbalance is concretized in the frameworks of international legal agreements, so that the distribution of benefits and burdens deriving from resource exploitation inevitably favors more-industrialized nations.[28] This distribution is created for reasons that are largely independent of need, desert, talent, or other morally relevant criteria. Thus, representatives of the less-industrialized nations argued that international agreements should explicitly compensate for uneven distributions of power through various redistributive strategies such as taxes and technology transfers.[29] In addition, governance institutions for the management of CH resources should be structured so as to offset the wealth and power concentrated in the hands of the industrialized nations. Because of its particular history, the CHPD emphasized the distribution of benefits rather than the distribution of burdens or duties that might be associated with maintaining a CH resource.

The Convention on the Law of the Sea[30] has been described as "the only fully-fledged development of the [CH] concept."[31] This Convention exemplifies the equity concerns underlying the CHPD, and it calls for activities in the deep sea to be carried out "for the benefit of mankind as a whole...taking into particular consideration the interests and needs of developing States and of peoples who have not attained full independence or other self-governing status...."[32] It calls for "equitable sharing of financial and other economic benefits" derived from activities carried out in the deep sea, for technology transfers, and for the conduct of activities in a manner that promotes "balanced growth of international trade."[33] The sea bed and its resources will be managed democratically by an international authority that includes members from all countries, with each country having one vote.[34] This one-country-one-vote approach to governance represents an explicitly majoritarian strategy to offset the minority's concentrated power and interests.

Economists and policymakers from the industrialized nations have generally opposed CHPD treaties. They believe that public property leads to waste and mismanagement of resources in most cases.[35] Furthermore, they argue that lack of clearly defined, individualized property rights discourages the private sector investment necessary to find and develop resources.[36] The fruits of deep sea mining or moon mining are not stored in a warehouse waiting for distribution; rather, resources must be sought out, extracted, transported, and transformed into useful products. These activities require the investment of money, time, and technology development, and firms or nations will not have any incentive to make such investments if they cannot be recouped. Industrialized countries argue that if firms are forced to transfer their own technology for deep sea mining, then the transfer recipients (developing countries and their firms) will gain a competitive advantage – a version of the free-rider problem. Firms are thought to be unwilling to invest where free-riders may prevent the developer or discoverer from recouping its investment or obtaining reasonable rents (i.e., profit).

Tensions between the more- and less-industrialized countries concerning the CHPD still have not been fully resolved. No nation or firm is yet in position to engage in industrial mining of the deep sea or any celestial body, and so these tensions have been allowed to simmer. In contrast, human genome research is well underway, and many people perceive the genome as a very accessible natural resource that is already being profitably exploited through the development of new treatments and products based on human genetic knowledge.

Commentators who feel that the human genome should be a form of public property may find the CHPD appealing in some aspects but troubling in others. The CHPD approach responds to the perception of some less-industrialized nations and indigenous peoples that the transfer of biological resources, and wealth derived from such resources, has been unidirectional. Some commentators argue that indigenous plants, animals, knowledge, and human bodily materials have flowed from rain forests, villages, and reservations to the industrialized countries and large corporations, but little if anything of value has flowed the other direction. This type of activity and relationship has been labeled bioprospecting or, more pejoratively, biopiracy and biocolonialism.[37] Many scholars and activists are concerned that human DNA and human cells have become the new exploitable resource, that people will be mined for "genetic gold" by scientists from industrialized countries and large corporations. Commentators and advocates express concern that people from less-industrialized societies may be too poor to benefit from products produced using their own DNA. And many indigenous rights supporters believe that scientists are far more interested in the survival of indigenous DNA and tissue samples than in the survival of indigenous people.[38]

Objections to biopiracy are not necessarily deep objections to genetics research itself, but rather to researchers' methods of obtaining biological materials or indigenous knowledge, and to the distribution of benefits deriving from that research.[39] The redistributive aspects of the CHPD may, therefore, appeal to scholars and advocates concerned about biopiracy. The CHPD provides legal mechanisms and governance structures to promote the bidirectional flow of knowledge, resources, and technologies, and to help ensure that people from whom resources are taken receive comparable benefits. In addition, if a resource management authority for the human genome operated according to a one-country-one-vote principle, then the CHPD could help ensure that the concerns, interests, and values of less-industrialized nations influenced the goals and projects of human genome research.[40]

The CHPD raises several concerns, however. Application of this doctrine will not satisfy people who believe that it is simply wrong to commodify or commercialize the human genome or products derived from it. No codification of the CHPD prevents economic exploitation of the CH resources; nothing in the CH designation prevents the moon or the deep sea bed from being mined. Rather, the CHPD ensures that all nations and all peoples have access to the resource and share the benefits derived from it.

Though the CHPD would not prevent commercial exploitation of human DNA per se, it might provide the impetus for a governance framework under which economically disadvantaged populations would be more likely to benefit from genome derived knowledge or products. This benefit could be accomplished through technology transfers. Alternatively, countries or firms that profit most from genome science and technologies could be taxed on their profit, and revenue from this tax could be used to pay for beneficial genome-derived products for populations that otherwise could not afford them.[41]

The CHPD will, however, be viewed as antithetical to the outlook of many people who express the belief that nobody should own the human genome, because the CHPD would vest all people with a property right in the genome. Some scholars who oppose human DNA patenting base this belief on the proposition that nobody should "own" human genetic material – that it should be *res nullius*. Many indigenous people hold this belief as well.[42] If one believes that nobody should own the genome, then one is unlikely to be satisfied with a doctrine holding that everybody owns the genome.

Although *res nullius* and *res communis* may be seen as functional equivalents ("the thing is owned by nobody and therefore it is owned by everybody"), there are distinct differences between these two forms of property. In particular, *res communis* is managed for the common good, whereas *res nullius* is essentially unmanaged, left wild and untrammeled by human intervention or intention. Designating the human genome as our common heritage invokes the specter of an international management authority for the human genome and human genome research.

Under CHPD treaties to date, the peoples' rights are to be vindicated through governmental representatives who participate in an authority that manages the resource for the common good. What would it mean to manage the human genetic resource for the common good when that resource resides, at least in part, in the bodies of all people? What goals and values would be pursued through this management, and how would management be conducted without interfering with procreative liberty and personal privacy? Lifelong legal prohibitions on reproduction or marriage would violate U.S. constitutional rights, but restrictions on some types of in vitro, reproductive, or genetic manipulations might not present constitutional problems. Management of human genetic resources is not a new concept, but one that has a distinctly dishonorable history as the underpinning for some repressive and deadly eugenicist political regimes.[43]

On the other hand, without some form of international management, it is not clear how the CHPD goals of benefit redistribution and maximization of the common good could be achieved. What mechanism would be employed to decide which genetics research and which uses of the genome were for the benefit of all humanity? Who would decide, and without a management authority, to whom would appeals be brought when a use of the genome was contested? Is the concept of benefit to all of humanity simply empty rhetoric without such an authority?

Those who would conceive of the human genome as our common heritage must seriously consider the consequences of creating a property right for all people in a resource that resides within the bodies of all people. Treaties that embody the CHPD generally conceive of the resource in question as an undivided whole in which all people own a stake. This conception is sensible for resources that are external to people's bodies and that were previously *res nullius*, such as the resources of the deep sea or the moon. But, a human genetic resource resides, at least in part, in the bodies of autonomous persons who possess interests, values, projects, and legal rights. The notion of a property right in a constituent part of other people's bodies could lead to policies and practices that are antithetical to commonly held beliefs about self-ownership and autonomy.

One might argue that the CHPD should be applied to the human genome, but that the associated rights would comprise only a very "thin" bundle. Perhaps the collective property rights under the CHPD would provide no more than a claim that people refrain from engaging in certain genetic interventions that could adversely affect offspring and impose great costs on society at large. Of course, implementation of such a claim would require international consensus on the question of what constitutes an adverse effect. The thin bundle of rights might also (or instead) confer a collective claim on people to donate genetic material for research purposes. Even this thinner bundle would raise constitutional issues, however.

People may have religious or political reasons for not participating in at least some genetics research. In theory, the proposition that the CH doctrine requires all people to contribute bodily material for genetic research does not entail that each person must contribute to any or all research. But a regime that attempted to catalog each and every person's detailed preferences regarding which types of research she would or would not participate in, or to which institutions and researchers she wanted her DNA provided, might

> While the focus of the CHDD is on the duties associated with preservation, this doctrine also incorporates assumptions that the benefits of exposure to cultural and natural heritage objects will be widely distributed, or at least available to people without regard to nationality or generation.

prove unwieldy and impracticable. Furthermore, a doctrine that would give researchers a claim to people's genetic material may be viewed with great suspicion by people who understand themselves as having been exploited by researchers and the pharmaceutical or biotechnology industry in the past. Indigenous people around the world, and perhaps many other people, may view even a thin bundle of rights and obligations under the CHPD as yet another expression of disrespect and another justification for scientific thievery.

One might argue that the CHPD inheres in human genetic information, or in products derived using knowledge from the human genome, rather than in the genetic material residing in people's bodies. To make such a claim plausible, however, a proponent must explain why all people would have rights to the information or genome-derived products generated by the labor and ingenuity of a few people. The Convention on the Law of the Sea calls for equitable sharing of benefits derived from activities carried out in the deep sea.[44] The justification for redistributing the fruits of a few people's labor in the sea bed is that the *underlying resource* being exploited belongs equally to everybody. If an underlying genome resource does not belong equally to all people, then one must develop a distinct rationale for why information derived from specific people's genomes, developed through the labor and investments of particular scientists and entrepreneurs, belongs equally to all people.

C. *The Other Common Heritage Doctrine*
A second and lesser recognized CH doctrine may have some applicability to the concept of the human genome as a form of public property. This doctrine, which I refer to as the Common Heritage Duties Doctrine (CHDD), reflects the rare situation in which a public resource is composed of incremental, individual holdings. This incarnation of the common heritage doctrine addresses all nations' duties to preserve certain highly significant cultural artifacts and natural wonders. The CHDD originated in nationalist preservationist movements in Europe and England and in the laws of war.[45]

In association with international cultural preservation, the common heritage language was first codified in the Convention for the Protection of Cultural Property in the Event of Armed Conflict (hereinafter Hague 54), and later in the Convention for the Protection of the World Cultural and Natural Heritage (hereinafter World Heritage Convention).[46]

The animating insight of the CHDD is stated in the preamble of Hague 54: "...damage to cultural property belonging to any people whatsoever means damage to the cultural heritage of all mankind, since each people makes its contribution to the culture of the world...."[47]

The CHDD does not recognize an explicit property right for all nations or people in other's cultural or natural heritage. Rather, this doctrine articulates a special, portentous *interest* of all people in certain cultural and natural objects, and a *duty* to help preserve them. The World Heritage Convention states, "Whilst fully respecting the sovereignty of the States on whose territory the cultural and natural heritage mentioned [above] is situated, and without prejudice to property rights provided by national legislation, the States Parties to this Convention recognize that such heritage constitutes a world heritage for whose protection it is the duty of the international community as a whole to co-operate."[48]

Principles underlying the CHDD include the following beliefs: (1) that the greatness and goodness of a people can be encapsulated or represented in individual objects of creation; (2) that awe-inspiring artifacts are important for fostering creative efforts among members of present and future generations; and (3) that living people have obligations to future generations. The value of stewardship is clearly manifest in this doctrine.[49] And the doctrine reflects the normative stance that interdependence – among human beings and between humans and the non-human natural world – ought to be recognized and nurtured in national and international policy.

Rather than focusing on the fair distribution of benefits, the CHDD emphasizes the fair distribution of duties and burdens. The CHDD emphasizes the fiduciary duties of possessors to preserve cultural treasures/natural wonders, to promote scientific investigation of the heritage, and to promote education concerning the heritage. The owner of cultural or natural heritage property should use and preserve it for the benefit of all humanity. While the focus of the CHDD is on the duties associated with preservation, this doctrine also incorporates assumptions that the benefits of exposure to cultural and natural heritage objects will be widely distributed, or at least available to people without regard to nationality or generation.

International assistance to uphold the CH preservation duty should be sought and granted only as needed.[50] No CHDD-type of treaty has created a right of nations to intervene in the sovereignty of other nations for the purpose of protecting cultural or natural heritage. The CHDD incorporates a still unresolved tension between the values of sovereignty and stewardship.[51]

The CHDD is an intriguing doctrine for those interested in the human genome as a form of public resource. This doctrine avoids the problems of creating a property right in a resource that resides within all individuals; in this regard it is more of a *res publicae* than *res communis* doctrine. The CHDD also avoids the problem of resource management by an international agency or administrative authority. It does, however, leave open the possibility that a national authority attempting to preserve human genomes (or some of them) would intervene in people's behavior in ways that violated rights of privacy, procreation, or other liberties.

Several interesting and, perhaps, enlightening parallels exist between cultural property and human genomes. For instance, both possess a peculiarly dual nature. Cultural property can be both private and public at the same time. Individuals may own historically important objects, but individuals cannot own the quantum of history that inheres in the objects. Cultural property may have a value that can be recognized and captured through private ownership, but it has another "heritage" value that may be protected by society-at-large through preservation laws. The public may have some claims for the use of cultural property, in the form of demands for such property to be displayed in museums or otherwise available for public viewing. Although the individual or state ownership interests and the international cultural heritage interests are often consonant, at times private ownership may be in conflict with or not fully protective of the heritage value.[52]

Human genomes also have a complex, dual nature. Each person's total genome is unique to her (unless she is a monozygotic twin), and the information contained therein is importantly about her. Yet each of us shares parts of our genomes with parents, siblings, and other family members. Because parts of our genomes are identical to the genomes of our relatives, one person's genetic information also constitutes information about family members. One person's genetic test may disclose health risks for other family members and/or ancestry information that pertains to other family members. For these reasons, family members may have at least a moral claim to access each other's genetic information in some cases. Intrafamilial conflicts may arise concerning the distribution of genetic test results, or their functional implications. Some guidelines for adjudicating these intrafamilial conflicts have been formulated.[53]

The duality of genetic information goes beyond its relevance for immediate family members. Some genetics research generates information about frequencies of DNA variants within and between groups of people; such information characterizes populations rather than individuals.[54] Thus, an individual's genome may be of great interest to members of the public whose recent ancestry is similar to that individual's. Like heritage property, genomes and genetic information have both private/personal and communal/public characteristics.

The CHDD is still very much a developing doctrine, and mechanisms to adjudicate conflicts between private or state ownership interests and international heritage interests have yet to be articulated. The potential for conflicts to arise among nations in the cultural heritage context parallels the potential for conflicts to arise among individuals and family members or communities over human genetic information.

The preservationist underpinning of the cultural heritage notion captures another important value relating to the human genome – one that is not so clearly evident in the CHPD. While difficult to articulate precisely, it could be called the value of nonintervention, or the value of respect for natural genomes. Some people feel that the naturally evolved human genome should be preserved and protected for future generations. For instance, members of the Council of Europe have argued that human rights to life and dignity entail the right to inherit a genome that has not been artificially altered.[55] This belief is generally based on the perception that humans do not possess enough wisdom to intercede so directly in our species' biological future. Attempts to intervene in the genomes of those who will be born reflect dangerous hubris and are bound to end badly. People holding such beliefs will not necessarily be satisfied with a CHPD approach, which may allow for a substantial amount of genetic manipulation so long as there is equitable sharing of any benefits derived. The CHDD, with its focus on preservation and future generations, would provide a better framework within which to express these noninterventionist concerns.

Another interesting parallel between cultural heritage and the human genome is that both are abstract concepts. No one particular object constitutes "the cultural heritage." No one piece of cultural property embodies the entire history or identity of a nation, but each piece is important because cumulatively they represent and define the cultural identity of a people. Cultural heritage is an abstract concept, yet it is almost universally acknowledged to be both worthy and capable of protection.

The human genome is also an abstract concept in that no particular, singular, natural object is the referent of the phrase "the human genome."[56] Parents do not pass on just one single human genome to their children. Rather, each person receives a unique genome (unless she is a monozygotic twin) created by the combination of chromosomes inherited from each parent. The international Human Genome Project[57] constructed a representative sequence of human DNA by piecing together information from many different individuals. This reference human genome sequence is not "The Human Genome"; it is simply a human genome.

Although each human being possesses a human genome, human individuals do not posses a single particular object in common that no other species or entity possesses. For this reason, it is not self-evident that possessing a human genome gives each of us an interest in some common biological resource. The intuitively obvious idea that the human genome should be designated as CH because "the human genome is an even more integral part of humankind than the traditional [objects to which] the Common Heritage concept [applies]..."[58] becomes much less obvious after careful consideration. Furthermore, "if the human genome is an abstraction and not a natural object, people's worries about preserving its integrity for future generations become concerns about the future of an idea, not a natural resource."[59]

Although the human genome is an abstraction, one might understand this abstraction as being embodied in the genomes of all of the people who exist and all who will exist. One might think of the human genome as a kind of cumulative record, in which each piece plays an important role in creating the whole, and together they represent something more significant than merely the sum of their parts. After all, people value discrete objects that together compose the cultural heritage, and the existence of treaties for the preservation of humanity's cultural heritage suggests that attempting to preserve particular embodiments of an abstract concept is neither entirely novel nor implausible.

However, attempts to preserve the human genome do raise a series of questions that have not been adequately addressed in ethics discussions to date – what exactly would one attempt to preserve, and why would one attempt to preserve it? Some reasons for preserving cultural property include venerating and memorializing genius, obtaining inspiration from models of human greatness, and promoting communal self-definition. The reasons for preserving natural wonders include a concept of responsible stewardship of nature, a belief that our abilities and inclinations to alter nature bring certain responsibilities to other living creatures and ecosystems, a sense of self-preservation, and a desire to preserve objects that engender awe and inspire humility. The preservation ethos applied to cultural and natural heritage concerns resources that can be extinguished or annihilated.

But what of the human genome? Ought the human genome be preserved or protected as an awe-inspiring work of nature? Does this urge to preserve reflect a certain inappropriate hubris regarding the centrality of human beings in the grand scheme of things? Are not other creatures' genomes similarly awe-inspiring works of nature? Does a desire to protect the human genome indicate an over-inflated belief in the power of DNA to determine personal identity? Before national or international governing bodies enact policies that venerate the human genome, reasons for placing more significance on human genomes than on other biological or physiological substances ought to be carefully delineated. To the extent that "the human genome" is concretized in each human being as a particular genome, the human genome will exist so long as human beings exist. Its continued existence does not depend on special, genome-directed policies or legal doctrines.

Policymakers, scientists, and ethicists must query what it would mean to protect or preserve the human genome, and how one would determine whether the endeavor was succeeding. New genetic variants continuously arise through mutation and DNA rearrangement. Existing genetic variants are lost through natural selection and by chance. Any particular human genome might only be seen once in this world, and with each generation, nature creates new genomes. In fact, many theorists argue that the great evolutionary importance of sexual reproduction is to provide mechanisms for rearranging genes and chromosomes, for creating new combinations of genetic variants.[60] In the stock of all human genes, referred to as the gene pool, the nature and frequency of genetic variants is constantly shifting.[61] Given the fluid, protean nature of the human gene pool, what ought to be preserved?

What does it mean to preserve something that is constantly changing? One could take DNA samples from each person and store them. But this approach probably would not affirm many of the values that people seek to affirm by attaching the common heritage label to the human genome. If people are concerned about the effects of genetic manipulation on future generations, then merely preserving genomes in vitro will not address the perceived problems. Furthermore, some people have religious reasons to oppose projects that would preserve their DNA, because they do not want any part of their bodies, or copies of molecules from their bodies, surviving after they have died.

Some commentators argue for a right of future generations to inherit untampered-with genomes. However, proponents of this right do not oppose every possible genetic alteration that could be passed on to future generations; they make exceptions for medical genetic interventions that would prevent people from being born with "serious diseases."[62] Thus, they cannot be committed to preserving all naturally occurring genomes. The proposed right may reflect fear that genetic tampering will lead to painful or deadly mistakes. Proponents may also fear that inheritable genetic alterations could lead to novel properties or capacities in future generations, to the loss of important human properties or capacities, or to other changes that could create "post human" offspring who have somehow separated from the rest of the species.

The desire to avoid genetic alterations that create "post-human" individuals might be consistent with a CHDD approach to genome policy. Countries and cultures need not preserve every human creation as part of the cultural heritage, and likewise, people might not be required to preserve every human genome or every variant of a human gene. However, the prospect of preserving some but not all genomes raises thorny questions about which genomes or gene variants would be preserved, who would choose which ones to be preserved, and what criteria would be used to make such a choice? A policy of preserving only some people's genomes, or only some genes and gene variants, would lend itself to choices guided by ignorance, prejudice, or corruption.

Problems would also arise with attempts to preserve only a portion of people's genomes, either in vitro or in vivo. This approach might result in attempts to assign the essence of humanity, or the unifying properties of the human species, to a particular set of DNA sequences. Such a policy likely would place too much importance and value on DNA. Furthermore, finding the genetic essence of humanity is probably an impossible task, even if some group of people could agree on what constitutes the essence of humanity.

The elements of any international law doctrine are constituted through treaty negotiations, through the wording of international agreements, through the creation of institutions based on the treaties, and through later adjudicative interpretations of the agreements. Although several treaties use the CH as an underlying principle, these treaties and the institutions for which they call have barely been implemented and have never been litigated, so the preceding discussion has been based on treaty language, and on various academic analyses of the CH treaties.

Because the CH concept is still nebulous, designating the human genome as part of the common heritage of humanity does not specify any particular normative approach to human genome research or product development. Rather, the difficult work of generating international agreement on applicable legal and ethical standards remains to be accomplished. At this juncture, the primary benefit of describing the human genome as belonging to the common heritage of humanity may be to motivate international discussion in a spirit of inclusion and cooperation.

II. Patents, Ownership, and the Common Heritage

The CH notion is often invoked as a basis for opposing patents on human DNA. The preceding discussion in section I ought to demonstrate that designating the human genome, or some part of it, as the common heritage of humanity would not settle questions regarding whether human DNA sequences, genes, or genomes should be patented. At the very least, a successful argument against patenting human DNA must show that patenting is antithetical to rules or norms embodied in the CH designation. For many people, the CH-related argument against patenting seems startlingly obvious, and it could be formulated as follows:

1. The human genome is part of the common heritage of humanity.

2. The common heritage is composed of things owned by all people; therefore,
3. The human genome is owned by all people.
4. Something owned by all people cannot be appropriated by or owned by one person or firm because this would be theft or conversion; therefore,
5. The human genome cannot be appropriated or owned by any individual person or firm because that would be theft or conversion.
6. Patents on the human genome allow patent holders to appropriate or own or appropriate human DNA; and therefore,
7. Patents on the human genome are antithetical to the rules or norms of the CH designation.

In summary, if everybody owns the genome, then one scientist or firm cannot own it by patenting it.

Unfortunately, the argument above embodies misconceptions about CH doctrines. For instance, proposition 2 is incorrect when applied to the CHDD because the CHDD does not provide for a common property interest in the human genome. The CHDD, which provides rights that are more in the nature of *res publicae* than *res communis*, is entirely compatible with the notion that private individuals, firms, or single states could own components or embodiments of the common genome heritage, just as private individuals can own artwork or buildings that comprise the cultural heritage.

Proposition 4 – something owned by all people cannot be appropriated by or owned by one person or firm because this would be theft or conversion – is not true with respect to the CHPD. Treaties that exemplify the CHPD allow firms or states to extract CH resources, to convert those resources into economically more valuable and private forms of property, and to sell the resulting property. The CHPD envisions the transfer of some common heritage property from everybody to a few people. If done in accordance with the relevant treaty and legal rules, such a transfer would not constitute theft, conversion, or a violation of CHPD norms. CHPD resources can be privatized and commodified, so long as the resulting benefits are properly shared. If the CH designation is to prevent all appropriation or private ownership of DNA sequences, it will have to do so under some new and different form of the doctrine, justified by arguments that remain to be elaborated.

The argument above also contains mistaken understandings of the patent law. Proposition 6 states that patents confer ownership of things covered by the patent; however, patent rights do *not* grant ownership of patented items or processes.[63] Patents only confer the right to *exclude* others from making, using, selling, offering for sale, or importing, without authorization, items covered by the patent.[64] A patent does not confer positive rights of possession or use, important rights in the "bundle of rights" typically associated with ownership of real or personal property. A patent holder may possess some DNA covered by the patent, but that possession is not a right granted by her patent.

Thus, it should be clear that proposition 6 in the argument above is incorrect. One could, perhaps, construct a valid CH-based argument against certain *uses* of human DNA patents by focusing on ways in which those uses contravene underlying principles or norms (whether explicit or implicit) of the CH concept. An access or sharing norm imbues both the CHPD and the CHDD, and so might best support arguments against certain uses of human DNA patents. Because patents confer a right to exclude, they can be used in ways that prevent widespread access to any item that incorporates something covered by the patent or that derives from patented products or processes.

Although patents confer the right to exclude others from making, using, or selling an item without authorization, patentees often sell items covered by their patents. An unconditional sale extinguishes the patentee's rights in that embodiment of the patented invention, and the buyer attains all use and resale rights (subject to other laws, of course). Through licensing agreements, patentees often authorize others to make, use, and/or sell items covered by their patents. The mere fact that a DNA sequence is patented does not preclude many people from accessing/using that sequence, so patenting need not violate the CH's access norms.

Furthermore, by legal convention patents on human DNA sequences do not confer on the patentee any control over DNA as it occurs naturally inside of a person's body.[65] A patentee could not exclude people from "using" their own inherited DNA to replicate cells or to reproduce. Patents on DNA can only be used to exclude others from manufacturing, using, or selling copies of the DNA sequence(s) covered by the patent. Typically, non-natural human DNA sequences are extracorporeal. Designating the genome as a form of CH would not necessarily entail a significant interest of all people in artificially or industrially constructed, extracorporeal copies of human DNA. Therefore, even if the patentee exercised her exclusionary right to prevent others from making, using, or selling important DNA sequences or DNA-derived treatments, it is not entirely clear that the patentee would violate access norms associated with the CH doctrines.

In constructing an argument regarding CH doctrines and access to or use of human DNA, one should acknowledge the difference between the referents for the words "genome," "gene," and "DNA." Genomes contain genes, and both genomes and genes consist of DNA. Even if the common heritage conferred some property or use rights in a person's entire individual genome, or in some abstract human genome, it is not clear that such a right would attach to any particular human gene or DNA fragment. A right or interest in the whole of something does not necessarily entail a right or interest in each component part of the thing. For instance, although nucleotides are the building blocks of humanity's purported genomic heritage, individual nucleotides, or nucleotide sequences that are not found in humans, may have little significance to the majority of people. Proponents of designating

Many such treatments will be "down stream" inventions that do not incorporate human DNA sequences. These treatments will have derived from years of labor and millions of dollars of investment by private individuals, firms, and states.

Some strategic uses of patents likely would run counter to the CH rights of accessibility, so long as those rights reached particular human genes, gene products (proteins), or genome-derived products. For instance, an inventor could obtain a patent on a DNA sequence and the protein encoded by that sequence and then refuse to manufacture and market the sequence or protein. She could also employ her patent right to refuse others the opportunity to manufacture

A legal regime that would treat the human genome as *res publicae* may be the least difficult to implement and the most amenable to fulfilling the goals of common heritage proponents. The rules of such a regime would be directed towards uses of genomes and human genetic technology, but would not afford all of humanity with a property right in the human genome (in the abstract) or in any particular human genome.

the human genome as humanity's CH probably would not support the claim that humanity has a CH interest in individual nucleotides, or in each and every sequence that could be constructed from nucleotides.

To formulate convincing arguments concerning the genome as a CH, one must specify in some detail what will be included as the heritage *res* and what reach-through would be accorded to CH rights. If the CH does not confer some universal property right in particular genes, a right to use or access particular genes, or a right to use information about particular genes, then the CH might not preclude patentees from blocking access to most genome-derived products. The human DNA sequence patents granted to date confer exclusionary rights with respect to particular genes or short DNA fragments, not to entire human genomes. Beneficial products may be several steps removed from the entire human genome.

As discussed in the preceeding section, if the CH designation confers rights to "the human genome," then clear arguments must be constructed to explain how far CH rights and interests can reach. To what derivatives of the genome ought such rights and interests attach? Developing such arguments is crucial because the crux of objections to patents on humanity's common genetic heritage is that they could be used to block or diminish access to (sometimes lifesaving) genome-derived treatments and medicines.

and market the product. Refusal to manufacture products or to license others to do so probably is not widespread, perhaps because this behavior would usually prevent the patentee from recouping research costs on the patented invention. However, patents are occasionally used to prevent competitors from entering a market rather than as a more direct means of generating income for an individual or company. Because this strategic behavior would mean that no product covered by the patent would be made available to the public during the patent term, this use would likely violate public access norms of both CH doctrines.

Creative governance and regulatory approaches could be used to overcome conflicts that might arise between the patentee's exclusionary rights and the public's access rights granted under a CH doctrine. Patentees or licensees who "sat on" their patented technology, neither continuing research on the invention nor producing a product that incorporated the invention, could be required by law to license their patents to a university/firm that would develop and market the technology.[66] Patentees could be required by law to license genome-derived products on a sliding scale, perhaps one based on a recipient country's per capita expenditure for medical research or health care.

A different approach would designate some international governance agency as the assignee and trustee of all human DNA patents. This agency could choose whether and how to enforce each patent so as to promote knowledge generation and widespread access to essential inventions.[67] Depending on the particulars, this solution could conflict with some current U.S. law, and it probably could not be retroactively applied to the thousands of existing human DNA patents that are already licensed. Alternatively, tax policy could be used to generate incentives for firms to make genome-derived products accessible. Or taxes could be used to redistribute genome-derived wealth in ways that helped to ensure access to essential inventions.[68] In developing creative governance approaches, policymakers should bear in mind that the extreme complexity of the rules developed to enact the common heritage concept in the Convention on the Law of the Sea probably contributed to many countries' reluctance to sign or ratify the Convention.[69]

Note that the entire economic foundation of the patent system rests on the assumption that privatization of knowledge through intellectual property laws ultimately will lead to the availability of the maximum number of products and the maximum generation of publicly accessible knowledge. Assuming that the maximum number of products results in the maximum number of beneficial, health-promoting products, a proponent of the patent system could argue that patents are entirely consistent with common heritage values. A proponent might also argue that patents are more consistent with CH values than would be a policy that put most genome-based inventions in the public domain. Whether or not patent protection actually maximizes the quantity of beneficial products is an empirical question that is very difficult to test.[70]

The idea that we should privatize new knowledge to make inventions more available may seem counterintuitive. One commentator states that it is *prima facie* irrational for a society to grant exclusionary rights over something that all could use at once, and thus intellectual property faces a special burden of justification.[71] The justification for intellectual property stems from the concept of market failure for public goods. Knowledge is a public good – competition for knowledge is non-rivalrous because knowledge has the properties of inexhaustibility and non-excludability. Inexhaustibility means that a unit of the good can be consumed without detracting in the least from the consumption opportunities available to others.[72] Non-excludability means that many people can use the thing at the same time and not interfere with each other.

Non-rivalrous competition may lead to market failure because multiple second users of the new knowledge may prevent those who invest in the production of new knowledge from recouping their research and development costs. To prevent failure in the knowledge production market, the patent system grants inventors a limited monopoly which allows them to control latecomers' manufacture, use, or sale of the invention.[73]

When the patent term expires, the public gains the right to freely use information contained in the patent – the information goes into the public domain. Currently, the U.S. patent term runs from the date of issue until 20 years from the date of filing.[74]

During the patent term, a product covered by the patent may be on the market, but unavailable to many who need it because of prices set far above competitive rates. The prospect that some or many members of a society could be priced out of luxury goods or widgets strikes many people as unproblematic. The patent system's trade off, the promise of generating more products over the long term by conferring private benefit to inventors in the short term, holds appeal when the goods in question are not basic necessities of life.

On the other hand, non-competitive pricing strikes many people as completely untenable when the product in question is a lifesaving medical treatment. For individuals who could die from lack of AIDs drugs, or entire societies that could perish for want of these drugs, the patent system holds only the empty and mocking promise that many more AIDs drugs will be available after they are gone. Commentators who press for designating the human genome as humanity's CH may be focusing primarily on the importance of access to the life-enhancing and life-saving inventions that will derive from genetic knowledge. To date, however, it is unclear what proportion of genome-associated inventions will be lifesaving or health improving, what proportion will be beneficial but not essential, and what proportion will be frivolous.

Conclusion

This essay argues that the common heritage concept derives from two different historical and political trends, and is embodied in two quite different lineages of international law. The Common Heritage Property Doctrine reflects the interests of less-industrialized countries in attaining equal access to resources and technologies. This doctrine provides for a property right of all people or all nations in things that are designated as part of our common heritage. A second doctrine, the Common Heritage Duties Doctrine, derives from nationalist movements for the preservation of cultural artifacts and the promotion of national identity. This doctrine does not create a property right in the common heritage; rather, it creates a duty of preservation and, perhaps, rights of access to the common heritage.

Both doctrines address some concerns associated with human genetic research and genome-derived products. However, the Common Heritage Property Doctrine also raises significant constitutional and ethical problems because applying it to the human genome would mean creating a property right to a resource that resides, at least in part, in all of our bodies. The Common Heritage Duties Doctrine is better suited to promote some important values underlying the move to designate the human genome as a form of public property. However, the Common Heritage Duties Doctrine may inappropriately reify the genome and attribute too much significance to human DNA as a mark of, or bearer of, our humanity.

The normative implications of designating the human genome as our common heritage are far fewer than most proponents of the common heritage language probably realize. Following this designation, or as part of any international agreement attaching the designation, the international community would still have to agree on the content of our rights and duties with respect to the human genome and to products derived from it. The international community would also have to develop governance institutions and enforcement mechanisms. A legal regime that would treat the human genome as *res publicae* may be the least difficult to implement and the most amenable to fulfilling the goals of CH proponents. The rules of such a regime would be directed towards uses of genomes and human genetic technology, but would not afford all of humanity with a property right in the human genome (in the abstract) or in any particular human genome.

A common heritage designation would not rule out the patenting of human DNA. However, patentees' rights to exclude others from manufacturing or selling an invention could be used in ways that contradict the important value of public access embodied in both common heritage doctrines. If access to essential inventions is the *conditio sine qua non* of the move to designate the human genome as common heritage, then proponents may be better served by focusing on policies that advance basic human rights throughout the world. Although some genome-derived inventions will contribute to important medical treatments, many inventions or the products that incorporate them will be relatively trivial, such as inventions used in cosmetics. Human kind's portentous interests in the human genome, whatever they may be, probably do not extend to interests in every genome-related patent or product. And many of humanity's most important problems, including medical ones, can be addressed using existing knowledge and products that have little to do with human genetic knowledge or technologies.

Acknowledgement
The author thanks Nam Dao for assistance with research for this article.

References
1. E. Aguis, "Germ-Line Cells – Our Responsibilities for Future Generations," in S. Busuttil et al., eds., *Our Responsibilities towards Future Generations* (Valletta, Malta: Foundation for International Studies, 1990): 133-143.
2. H. Curien, "The Human Genome Project and Patents," *Science* 254, no. 5039 (1991): 1710-1712.
3. B. M. Knoppers, "Biobanking: International Norms," *Journal of Law, Medicine & Ethics* 33, no. 1 (2005): 7-14, at 11 ("At the international level, there is increasing recognition and confirmation that, at the level of species, the human genome is the common heritage of humanity, and that human genetic research databases are global public goods.")
4. UNESCO, "Universal Declaration on the Human Genome and Human Rights," Resolution 152, United Nations General Assembly, 53rd Session, U.N. Doc. A/53/635/Add.2, 1998, available at <http://portal.unesco.org/en/ev.php-URL_ID=13177&URL_DO=DO_TOPIC&URL_SECTION=201.html> (last visited June 26, 2007), reprinted in N. Lenoir, "Universal Declaration on the Human Genome and Human Rights: The First Legal and Ethical Framework at the Global Level," *Columbia Human Rights Law Review* (1999): 537-587.
5. The Human Genome Organization, "Statement on the Principled Conduct of Genetics Research," *Eubios Journal of Asian and International Bioethics* 6, no. 3 (1996): 59-60; The Human Genome Organization, *Statement on Benefit Sharing*, April 9, 2000, available at <http://www.hugo-international.org/Statement_on_Benefit_Sharing.htm> (last visited June 19, 2007) [hereinafter cited as Benefit Sharing]; Council of Europe (Parliamentary Assembly), *Recommendation 1512, Protection of the Human Genome by the Council of Europe*, 2001, available at <http://assembly.coe.int/Documents/AdoptedText/ta01/erec1512.htm> (last visited June 25, 2007).
6. See, e.g., M. L. Sturges, "Who Should Hold Property Rights to the Human Genome? An Application of the Common Heritage of Humankind," *American University International Law Review* 13 (1997): 219-261; see Curien, *supra* note 2; L. J. Demaine and A. X. Fellmeth, "Reinventing the Double Helix: A Novel and Nonobvious Reconceptualization of the Biotechnology Patent," *Stanford Law Review* 55 (2002): 303-462, at 442: "Scores of eminent scientists and many foreign governments have taken the position that the human genome and other naturally occurring genomes are res communis – the common heritage and inheritance of mankind – and, therefore, should not be subject to patents"; D. S. Karjala, "Biotech Patents and Indigenous Peoples," *Minnesota Journal of Law, Science & Technology* 7 (2006): 483-527.
7. C. M. Rose, "The Comedy of the Commons: Custom, Commerce, and Inherently Public Property," *University of Chicago Law Review* 53, no. 3 (1986): 711-781; C. M. Rose, "Takings, Public Trust, Unhappy Truths, and Helpless Giants: A Review of Professor Joseph Sax's Defense of the Environment through Academic Scholarship: Joseph Sax and the Idea of Public Trust," *Ecology Law Quarterly* 25 (1998): 351-362.
8. These categories derive from ancient Roman law. J. A. Bovenberg, "Mining the Common Heritage of Our DNA: Lessons Learned from Grotius and Pardo," *Duke Law & Technology Review* 8 (2006): paragraphs 9-12, available at <http://www.law.duke.edu/journals/dltr/articles/2006dltr0008.html> (last visited June 25, 2007).
9. United Nations, "Convention on the Law of the Sea," U.N. Document A/Conf.62/122, reprinted in *International Legal Materials Treaties and Agreements* 21 (1982): 1261-1354.
10. See Rose (1998), *supra* note 7.
11. J. L. Sax, "The Public Trust Doctrine in Natural Resource Law: Effective Judicial Intervention," *Michigan Law Review* 68 (1970): 471-566.

12. *Id.*; see also Rose (1998), *supra* note 7.
13. *Res publicae* referred to streams and ports. See Bovenberg, *supra* note 8, at paragraph 9; see also, *National Audubon Society et al. v. Dept. of Water and Power of the City of Los Angeles*, 33 Cal. 3d 419 (1983) (en banc, rehearing denied) ("'By the law of nature these things are common to mankind – the air, running water, the sea and consequently the shores of the sea.' [Institutes of Justinian 2.1.1.] From this origin in Roman law, the English common law evolved the concept of the public trust, under which the sovereign owns 'all of its navigable waterways and the lands lying beneath them as trustee of a public trust for the benefit of the people,'" at 433-434) [hereinafter cited as National Audubon Society].
14. *Id.* (National Audubon Society).
15. See *Friends of Van Cortlandt Park v. City of New York*, 95 N.Y.2d 623 (2001).
16. See Sax, *supra* note 11.
17. *Id.*; see also National Audubon Society, *supra* note 13, at 438-439.
18. *Id.*
19. See Rose (1986), *supra* note 7; Sax, *supra* note 11.
20. K. Baslar, *The Concept of the Common Heritage of Mankind in International Law* (The Hague/Boston/London: Martinus Nijhoff, 1998): at 85-91.
21. B. Looney, "Should Genes Be Patented? The Gene Patenting Controversy: Ethical and Policy Foundations of an International Agreement," *Law and Policy in International Business* 26 (1994): 231-272.
22. Reviewed in Baslar, *supra* note 20, at 108-109, chap. 5, 6, and 7.
23. To some degree, the distinction between the CHPD and the CHDD correlates with a distinction made by Baslar between the CH as applied to lands and resources found in extranational spaces (places beyond national boundaries, such as the deep sea or the moon) and the CH as applied to lands and resources found within the boundaries of sovereign states. See Baslar, *supra* note 20, at 110-111, chap. 8.
24. See Convention on the Law of the Sea, *supra* note 9.
25. The Antarctica Treaty System includes the Antarctic Treaty of 1969, measures enacted under the 1969 treaty, and associated multilateral and bilateral instruments. See Baslar, *supra* note 20, at chap. 7; United Nations, *Agreement Governing the Activities of States on the Moon and Other Celestial Bodies - U.N. Doc. A/AC.105/L.113/Add. 4*, reprinted in *Houston International Law Journal* 2, no. 3 (1979): 3-33.
26. G. H. Reynolds and R. P. Merges, *Outer Space: Problems of Law and Policy* (San Francisco: Westview Press, 1989); C. M. Vernon, "Common Cultural Property: The Search for Rights of Protective Intervention," *Case Western Reserve Journal of International Law* 26 (1994): 435-478.
27. The first use of the "common heritage" concept in a contemporary legal context is attributed to Arvid Pardo, a Maltese Ambassador to the United Nations, who used the term in an address on deep sea mining before the United Nations General Assembly in 1967. See Baslar, *supra* note 20, at 31-37.
28. V. Shiva, "Biotechnology Development and the Conservation of Biodiversity," in V. Shiva and I. Moser, eds., *Biopolitics: A Feminist and Ecological Reader on Biotechnology* (London and New Jersey: Zed Books, 1995): 193-213; see Reynolds and Merges, *supra* note 26, at 7.
29. For an extensive review of the economic arguments and excerpts from the literature, see Reynolds and Merges, *supra* note 26.
30. See Convention on the Law of the Sea, *supra* note 9.
31. See Baslar, *supra* note 20, at 206.
32. Convention on the Law of the Sea, *supra* note 9, at Article 140.
33. *Id.*, at Article 140, 144, 150.
34. *Id.*, at Article 156, 159.
35. G. Hardin, "The Tragedy of the Commons," *Science* 162, no. 3859 (1968): 1243-1248.
36. See Reynolds and Merges, *supra* note 26.
37. See, e.g., D. Harry et al., *Declaration of Indigenous Peoples of the Western Hemisphere Regarding the Human Genome Diversity Project*, signed by 18 organizations on February 19, 1995, available at <http://ankn.uaf.edu/IKS/declaration.html> (last visited June 29, 2007); B. J. Crieger, "The West Knows Best?" *The Hastings Center Report* 26, no. 2 (1996): 50; see Shiva, *supra* note 28; L. A. Whitt, *Biocolonialism and the Commidification of Knowledge*, paper prepared for the North American Conference on Genetic Research and Native Peoples: Colonialism through Biopiracy, 1998 (paper on file with author); J. Reardon, "The Human Genome Diversity Project: A Case Study in Coproduction," *Social Studies of Science* 31, no. 3 (2001): 357-388; L. Rohter, "In the Amazon, Giving Blood But Getting Nothing," *New York Times National Edition*, June 20, 2007, at A1.
38. See, e.g., B. Tokar, *The Human Genome Diversity Project: Indgenous Communities and the Commercialization of Science* (Plainfield, Canada: The Edmonds Institute, 1998).
39. Discussed in Karjala, *supra* note 6.
40. A problem with the one-country-one-vote model is that it provides a mechanism for ratifying the interests of national governments, but it does not necessarily provide a mechanism for identifying or responding to the interests of minority groups within nation states. In designing a governance structure, one ought not to expect that national governments are equally effective at representing the interests of all people within their jurisdictions. Furthermore, some indigenous communities have a sovereign or quasi-sovereign status within larger nation-states, and it is not clear that governments of nation-states can or ought to represent these indigenous communities. How would American Indian tribes be represented in the governance of a CH property?
41. A related solution has been suggested by Bovenberg, *supra* note 8, at paragraph 31.
42. See Vernon, *supra* note 26; Shiva, *supra* note 28; *id.*
43. E. T. Juengst, "Should We Treat the Human Germ-Line as a Global Human Resource?" in E. Agius and S. Busuttil, eds., *Germ-Line Intervention and Our Responsibilities to Future Generations* (Great Britain: Kluwer Academic Press, 1998): 85-102.
44. See Convention on the Law of the Sea, *supra* note 9.
45. J. H. Merryman, "Two Ways of Thinking About Cultural Property," *American Journal of International Law* 80 (1986): 831-853; J. L. Sax, "Is Anyone Minding Stonehenge? The Origins of Cultural Property Protection in England," *California Law Review* 78 (1990): 1543-1567 [hereinafter cited as Stonehenge]; J. L. Sax, "Heritage Preservation as a Public Duty: The Abbe Gregoire and the Origins of an Idea," *Michigan Law Review* 88 (1990): 1142-1168.
46. United Nations, "Convention Concerning the Protection of the World Cultural and Natural Heritage," *U.S. Treaties and Other International Agreements*, Paris, 1972 [hereinafter cited as World Heritage Convention]; UNESCO, "Convention for the Protection of Cultural Property in the Event of Armed Conflict," *United Nations Treaties Series* 249 (1954): 215-240, available at <http://untreaty.un.org/English/acess.asp> (last visited June 12, 2007). As of May 2005, there were 115 states party to this Convention; the United States signed in May 1954, and the treaty was submitted to the U.S. Senate on January 6, 1999, as Treaty Doc. 106-1. To date, the Senate has not held any hearings on this Treaty. Discussed in P. E. Hagen, "Treaty Priority List for the 110th Congress," *American Law Institute - American Bar Association Continuing Legal Education* SM 083 (2007): 189-197, at 192.
47. *Id.* (1954 Convention).
48. See World Heritage Convention, *supra* note 46.
49. See Baslar, *supra* note 20, at 117-158.
50. See World Heritage Convention, *supra* note 46.
51. See Baslar, *supra* note 20, at 117-158.
52. See Merryman, *supra* note 45; Sax (Stonehenge), *supra* note 45.
53. ASHG Statement, "Professional Disclosure of Familial Information," *American Journal of Human Genetics* 62, no. 3 (1998): 474-483.

54. See, e.g., C. Dennis, "The Rough Guide to the Genome," *Nature* 425, no. 6960 (2003): 758-759; The Human Genome Structural Variation Working Group, "Completing the Map of Human Genetic Variation," *Nature* 447, no. 7141 (2007): 161-165; P. N. Ossorio, "About Face: Forensic Genetic Testing for Race and Other Visible Traits," *Journal of Law, Medicine & Ethics* 34, no. 2 (2006): 277-292; M. W. Smith and N. Patterson et al., "A High Density Admixture Map for Disease Gene Discovery in African Americans," *American Journal of Human Genetics* 74, no. 5 (2004): 1001-1013; R. A. Kittles and K. M. Weiss, "Race, Ancestry, and Genes: Implications for Defining Disease Risk," *Annual Review of Genomics and Human Genetics* 4 (2003): 33-67.
55. Council of Europe, *Texts Adopted, Recommendation 934 on Genetic Engineering, P.A. 33rd Sess., Pt. III*, 1982, available at <http://assmbly.coe.int/Main.asp?link=/Documents/AdoptedText/ta82/EREC934.htm> (last visited June 12, 2007) (recommendation 4.a."the rights to life and human dignity protected by Articles 2 and 3 of the European Convention on Human Rights imply the right to inherit a genetic pattern which has not been artificially changed.")
56. See Juengst, *supra* note 43.
57. International Human Genome Sequencing Consortium, "Finishing the Euchromatic Sequence of the Human Genome," *Nature* 431, no. 7011 (2004): 931-945; R. Cook-Deegan, *The Gene Wars: Science, Politics, and the Human Genome* (New York: W. W. Norton, 1994); D. J. Kevles and L. Hood, eds., *The Code of Codes: Scientific and Social Issues in the Human Genome Project* (Cambridge: Harvard University Press, 1992).
58. See Sturges, *supra* note 6, at 224.
59. See Juengst, *supra* note 43.
60. N. H. Barton and B. Charlesworth, "Why Sex and Recombination," *Science* 281, no. 5385 (1998): 1986-1989.
61. J. V. Neel, *Physician to the Gene Pool: Genetic Lessons and Other Stories* (New York: James Wiley & Sons, Inc., 1994).
62. See Council of Europe, *supra* note 55; B. M. Knoppers, *Human Dignity and Genetic Heritage* (Ottowa: Law Reform Commission of Canada, 1991): at 93.
63. P. N. Ossorio, "Legal and Ethical Issues in Biotechnology Patenting," in J. Burley and J. Harris, eds., *A Companion to Genethics: Philosophy and the Genetic Revolution* (Oxford: Blackwell Publishers, Ltd., 2002): 408-419.
64. "Contents and term of patent," *United States Code*, Title 35, section 154 (a)(1) (2007) ("Every patent shall contain a short title of the invention and a grant to the patentee..., of the right to exclude others from making, using offering for sale, or selling the invention throughout the United States or importing the invention into the united states....")
65. See Ossorio, *supra* note 63.
66. This approach would be similar to the march-in right currently granted under U.S. law to federal agencies that fund research resulting in patented inventions. "March-in rights," *United States Code*, Title 35, Chapter 18, section 203 (2007). No federal agency has ever exercised the march-in right.
67. This approach bears some relation to proposals that biobanks should act as trustees for individuals whose samples and information are included in the bank. See D. E. Winickoff and R. N. Winickoff, "The Charitable Trust as a Model for Genomic Biobanks," *New England Journal of Medicine* 349, no. 12 (2003): 1180-1184.
68. For proposals for sharing the benefits of biomedical research through taxation see, see Bovenberg, *supra* note 8, at paragraph 31; Benefit Sharing, *supra* note 5; J. A. Bovenberg, "Whose Tissue Is It Anyway?" *Nature Biotechnology* 23, no. 8 (2005): 929-933.
69. See Bovenberg, *supra* note 8, at paragraph 29.
70. M. A. Heller and R. S. Eisenberg, "Can Patents Deter Innovation? The Anticommons in Biomedical Research," *Science* 280, no. 5377 (1998): 698-701; R. S. Eisenberg, "Patents and the Progress of Science: Exclusive Rights and Experimental Use," *University of Chicago Law Review* 56 (1993): 1017-1086.
71. N. Hettinger, "Patenting Life: Biotechnology, Intellectual Property, and Environmental Ethics," *Boston College Environmental Affairs Law Review* 22 (1995): 267-304.
72. R. Cornes and T. Sandler, *The Theory of Externalities, Public Goods, and Club Goods* (New York: Cambridge University Press, 1986).
73. Note, however, that patents do not necessarily create true economic monopolies. If products not covered by the patent can compete in the same market as the patented item, and the patentee cannot control pricing in that market, then the patent has not conferred a true monopoly. Numerous patented drugs, such as cholesterol lowering statins, have sold in markets in which several different patented drugs, or various patented and unpatented drugs, competed.
74. "Contents and Term of Patent," *United States Code*, Title 35, section 154 (a)(2) (2007) ("such grant shall be for a term beginning on the date on which the patent issues and ending 20 years from the date on which the application for the patent was filed in the United States..."). Determining the actual date on which a patent expires is not always straightforward. The date of filing can be earlier than the date of the application on which the patent issues, and there are statutory provisions that allow for the terms of some patents to be extended.

[22]

SOCIAL THOUGHT & COMMENTARY

Cultural Heritage Rights:
From Ownership and Descent to Justice and Well-being

Ian Hodder
Stanford University

Abstract
The protection of cultural heritage sites is normally evaluated in terms of universal and scholarly significance criteria, although increasingly the contributions of sites and monuments to the economic and social well-being of communities have been recognized. Human rights discourse, despite its many problems and limitations, offers a possible mechanism for evaluating heritage in terms of social justice and well-being. A cultural heritage right based on descent is particularly problematic and cannot be supported by archaeological, historical, and anthropological theories. A cultural heritage right based on whether people are in practice able to participate in sites and objects in such a way as to fulfill their capabilities is an alternative, as long as it also includes responsibilities to other communities with conflicting interests. However, few archaeologists and heritage managers have the training and expertise to work out short- and long-term economic and social benefits of artifacts, sites, and monuments, and they have limited experience in facilitating human capabili-

Cultural Heritage Rights: From Ownership and Descent to Justice and Well-being

ties through heritage beyond scholarship, aesthetics, and identity politics.
[Keywords: Heritage, human rights, well-being, rights and duties, cultural affiliation, descent]

Discussion of the value of global heritage has focused on estimating the universal value of monuments. This universalist position is clear in UNESCO (United Nations Educational, Scientific and Cultural Organization) statements on the duties of nation states to protect heritage of outstanding value for the sake of humanity as a whole. In 1972, UNESCO agreed on a World Heritage Convention that states, "The cultural and natural heritage is among the priceless and irreplaceable assets, not only of each nation, but of humanity as a whole. The loss, through deterioration or disappearance, of any of these most prized assets constitutes an impoverishment of the heritage of all the peoples of the world. Parts of that heritage, because of their exceptional qualities, can be considered to be of 'outstanding universal value' and as such worthy of special protection against the dangers which increasingly threaten them."

"Outstanding universal value" is identified by UNESCO if a monument is an outstanding example of a particular phase or culture or society or civilization—in other words it is an outstanding example of a type of site. The monument also has to be "authentic"—for example, really from the period in question. It also has to have "integrity"—the monument should not be built upon, developed, be very eroded, partial. The focus is all on the thing (Labadi 2007, Lafrenz Samuels 2008).

Such a definition of universal value is also closely linked to the expertise of archaeologists and historians who can evaluate a monument in relation to other monuments (Byrne 1991). It is dependent on the knowledge of categories of object, on previous research that has defined types of site and architecture, and on expert evaluation of particular examples in relation to others known. "Outstanding" is defined by the scientist, by the archaeology specialist evaluating evidence in objective terms. Science and cultural value here are hand in hand.

The danger with such estimations, however scientific and objective they may appear to be is that they derive from a western tradition of scholarship (Byrne 1991). The monuments are evaluated in terms of objective and abstract knowledge about cultural variation, types, and norms. The heritage is surrounded in expert knowledge, or rather it is defined through practices of expertise that have a distanced universalizing character. Valuation of heritage in these terms cannot deal with the different claims on the past that are today made by a wide variety of diverse communities. Today non-western indigenous groups stake claims to ownership of their pasts (Liebmann and Rizvi 2008). These claims evaluate cultural heritage in very different terms—as ritual objects, signs of the ancestors, icons of identity, objects of social power, sources of income.

All societies destroy their heritage. Drive around Britain or the United States and one can see houses being knocked down to make new estates, roads being torn up so that new high-speed highways can be built, forests cleared, old barns left to rot, industrial chimneys destroyed, and disused power stations dismantled. But, of course, some of these monuments from the past are saved, and even power stations can be made into art galleries (the Tate Modern in London, for example). We keep and protect only a selection of what is past. We preserve what is of value to us. Both at national and international levels, the values are arrived at objectively, through scholarly discourse (Gerstenblith 2002).

Increasingly today, however, such evaluations have to be balanced against the views of a variety of stakeholders (McNiven and Russell 2005, Silliman 2008). Regional, national, and international heritage managers recognize that a wide range of other interests and values may pertain (Lowenthal 1985, Cleere 1989, Bernbeck and Pollack 1996). Heritage management increasingly takes note of issues such as economic and development value, religious sensitivities, and the role of heritage in identity formation. In other words, matters of justice and well-being are being considered alongside the scholarly estimation of outstanding cultural value for humanity as a whole (Colwell-Chanthaphonh and Ferguson 2008). To talk of social justice and well-being is to take the discourse on cultural heritage closer to the discourse on human rights.

My question in this paper is whether it is possible to move beyond the evaluation of heritage in terms of outstanding value—defined largely in terms of the scholarly evaluation of things—towards a system of evaluation in terms of well-being and social justice (Lilley and Williams 2005). In the UNESCO process, "outstanding universal value" is evaluated in terms of the quality, rarity, and diversity of things. These are abstract categorizations based on nothing except Western values. They are Western components of art appreciation rolled out onto the universal stage. They are not grounded in social values and are bound to be contested. So the attraction of rights talk is that it may be a mechanism for widening the debate about cultural heritage to focus on social justice.

The archaeological process of excavation destroys the very contextual information that it seeks to explore, but archaeology also has an important productive role. By clearing away the soil from monuments and artifacts, it also brings things into the public domain. Perhaps more than any other social science it produces a material outcome that has a public place. Archaeology is "place making" and it is "history making"—it produces places and temporalities. The things and monuments protrude into social life—in that sense archaeologists also produce social relations in the world around them. When they make places and histories, they produce artifacts and monuments that people have to deal with and cope with. The resulting interactions can be both positive and negative. They can lead to healing or pain. They can be productive or destructive. There is a duty, then, to think about the rights of those affected.

At the end of this paper, I will discuss how a focus on well-being, rather than on the universal value of artifacts, might be an effective strategy in claims for the protection of human rights in the case of the destruction of Hasankeyf by the Ilisu Dam project in southeast Turkey (Kitchen and Ronayne 2001). But I wish first to consider whether human rights discourse might be an effective mechanism for evaluating heritage in terms of social justice and well-being, and to consider what such a cultural heritage right might look like.

Limits of Human Rights Discourse

It is not difficult to critique the discourse on human rights. A strong international discourse on human rights emerged after World War II in parallel with the great genocides of the 20th century. It is not at all clear that the various UN declarations on human rights have been effective in arresting or even limiting the violence and inhumanity we increasingly see around us. Many of the declarations are non-binding and many states have not signed them. There is little opportunity for enforcement. "Rights" seems to be a discourse which allows us to talk about something we do nothing to stop. Rights are increasingly concerned with legal language rather than with moral and social injustice. It is a language through which states criticize each other, but not themselves. Thus, for example, the US refuses to support the International Criminal Court until there is a provision excepting its own citizens from prosecution by the Court.

There have been many criticisms of rights discourse as a western perspective imposed on non-western countries (Stacy 2009). There is a longstanding multicultural or contextualist critique that notes the variations in the ways that rights are construed in different cultures and societies (e.g., Duquette 2005). Another problem with the rights discourse is that the legal discussion of rights often seems to fail to differentiate between different types of rights; thus, the right to life seems very different from the right to leisure, education, or the enjoyment of cultural life.

The human rights debate often seems removed from underlying issues of inequality and injustice. This gap was, according to Ivison (2008:182), foreseen by Marx in his essay "On the Jewish question," where he distinguishes between political and human emancipation. People may achieve political freedom, the right of expression, and the vote (political emancipation), without achieving resolution of deeper forms of alienation and inequality (human emancipation).

Foucault too was a critic of the human rights discourse. For Foucault (1977), rights exist within relations of power, instead of being external to and opposed to them (as is so often claimed). A language describing the rights of free individuals in relation to the sovereign state is a discourse masking the spread of disciplinary power. Governmentality (a linking of government and rationality) is a mode of power in which populations are governed through a specific rationality in which the notion of individual rights is central. The discourse of rights becomes a form of disciplinary power. It is difficult to deny the validity of this critique in relation to cultural heritage. When UNESCO or Western institutions persuade the global community about the right way to approach heritage, they impose new forms of governance and power (Byrne 1991).

Perhaps most fundamentally, legal discourse about rights immediately places social negotiation within a straitjacket (Ivison 2008, Stacy 2009). The focus is on whether individuals or groups do or do not have certain rights. The determination of rights tends to pit people against each other in an adversarial setting. Issues that might be dealt with through collaboration and negotiation become oppositional. For this and the other reasons listed above, I am not convinced that the introduction of a rights discourse will solve problems regarding claims on cultural heritage. I do not believe that rights are the answer, but I do have one hope. Human rights talk is really a dialogue that is going on within the international community. When engaging in rights talk, people work out what they think about our global responsibilities to each other. The talk is part of gradually changing values regarding "global justice." So the discussion of rights in relation to cultural heritage is useful in my view, not because I expect legally binding cultural heritage rights to be enforced any time soon, but because rights talk may promote a broader, people-based dialogue about the values that are important in the evaluation of claims about the past. The discourse is an ongoing process of working it out as a global community—seeing what we feel and what is fundamentally important about heritage for all of us.

Thus if people come to see a certain behavior (such as female circumcision or the death penalty) as negative, so that behavior will enter into the discourse of rights. If they see something as positive (such as protecting the heritage of indigenous groups), so too it will become an issue of rights. These and other causes are continually being debated, and as a global community we change our ideas about killing seals, hunting for ivory, the definition of torture, wearing headscarves, and so on. There is continual flux as to whether we think certain behaviors violate human rights. The debate is not about absolutes, but about social negotiation, nowadays at the global scale, over what is right and wrong in the particular historical contexts in which we find ourselves. It is important that cultural heritage be evaluated in this same arena. Even if legislative change is not the result, the debate may lead to change in the climate regarding what is seen as acceptable behavior. At the very least, heritage rights talk takes us away from discussing heritage in terms of the universal outstanding value of things as defined by the academy.

Cultural Heritage and Human Rights

How has heritage been involved in human rights? The brief answer is, not very much (Silverman and Ruggles 2008, though see Prott 1996 in relation to cultural rights as human rights). But we shall see that in so far as cultural heritage has been involved in human rights discourse, the focus has often been on rights in relation to ownership and descent. It has been assumed that descent from cultural groups in the past endows groups and persons in the present with the ownership and thus care of cultural heritage.

In the universal declarations dealing with human rights, we see very little reference to heritage or cultural heritage. UNESCOs Constitution calls upon the Organization to give "fresh impulse...to the spread of culture, assuring the conservation and the protection of the world's inheritance of books, works of art and monuments of history and science.." (UNESCO 1970:9). The 1948 "Universal Declaration of Human Rights" does not refer to cultural heritage, but it does, in Article 27, refer to the right to participate in the cultural life of the community. One could argue that, for example, the right to work in the Declaration could be interpreted as referring to the right to benefit from heritage employment, and the right to education could be used to refer to the right to know about the past, and the right to leisure could be used to refer to the right to visit heritage sites, but there is no specific reference to cultural heritage.

The UN's 1966 "International Covenant on Economic, Social and Cultural rights," Article 15, again refers to the right of everyone to take part in cultural life (e.g., see Stavenhagen 1998). The UN "International Covenant on Civil and Political Rights" says that minorities should not be denied the right "to enjoy their own culture" (Article 27). In 1970, UNESCO published a discussion of cultural rights as human rights. The volume presents the deliberations of a group of politicians and academics, including Ernest Gellner, participating in their personal capacities, on topics including the relationships between local cultures and the international community. The document appears to have had little impact. The UN's 1992 "Declaration on the Rights of Persons Belonging to National or Ethnic, Religious and Linguistic Minorities" still has little that refers to cultural heritage, although Article 4 calls upon states to enable persons belonging to minorities to develop their culture.

It is of interest, and telling, that the most explicit reference in these early statements of universal rights occurs in Article 29 of the 1989 UN "Convention on the Rights of the Child." This states that "the education of the child shall be directed to the development of respect...for his or her own cultural identity, language and values, for the national values of the country in which the child is living, the country from which he or she may originate, and for civilizations different from his or her own."

One can already see a tension in these statements between the universal value of heritage for all and the value for particular groups, whether nations or minorities. The focus on the rights of separate groups has become of greater importance as part of postcolonial processes of separation and identification. We have seen the recognition of minority rights most clearly in archaeology in the World Archaeological Congress code of ethics which acknowledges the role of indigenous groups in the control over their own heritage (the World Archaeological Congress First Code of Ethics and the Vermillion Accord - Fforde, Hubert, and Turnbull 2004). It is thus of interest that the UN declaration that does discuss cultural heritage at some length is the "Declaration on the Rights of Indigenous Peoples" adopted by the UN General Assembly in 2007, but not ratified by a number of key states. In Article 5, there is reference to the right of indigenous peoples to maintain and strengthen their distinct political, legal, economic, social and cultural institutions. In Article 8, indigenous people and individuals have the right not to have their culture destroyed.

But it is Article 11 that is most worthy of quoting in full in this context:

1. Indigenous peoples have the right to practise and revitalize their cultural traditions and customs. This includes the right to maintain, protect and develop the past, present and future manifestations of their cultures, such as archaeological and historical sites, artefacts, designs, ceremonies, technologies and visual and performing arts and literature.

2. States shall provide redress through effective mechanisms, which may include restitution, developed in conjunction with indigenous peoples, with respect to their cultural, intellectual, religious and spiritual property taken without their free, prior and informed consent or in violation of their laws, traditions and customs.

Throughout such declarations (for other UN discussions about culture and rights see Schmidt 1996) there is a silence about how one defines "my," "our," "their" culture or cultural heritage. The problem emerges right at the start. Article 27 in the 1948 Declaration states that, "everyone has the right freely to participate in the cultural life of the community." There is a tension between everyone and community. Which community, and does everyone have the right to participate in everyone's community? And what happens if there are overlapping definitions of "the community?" There is a tension between the universal access of all to know about global cultural heritage and its diversity, and the right of nations and indigenous groups and minorities to control "their own" past and gain restitution.

IAN HODDER

Rights by Descent

What is meant by this notion of "ownership" of the past, and how does this "ownership" confer rights? In most of the UN declarations, ownership of heritage is vested in the sovereign nation state and, in the more recent declarations, rights of protection and use, if not ownership, are given to descendant communities. Certainly within the NAGPRA (Native American Graves Protection and Repatriation Act) process in the United States, for example, repatriation of skeletal remains and cultural artifacts depends on the evaluation of affiliation and descent (Fine-Dare 2002).

This focus on ownership by bounded groups in the cultural heritage discourse has also been influenced by the debate about looting and trade in antiquities. As Schmidt (1996) notes for the plundering of Africa's past, the links that are now being made between the rights discourse and cultural heritage often start from anger and social alienation associated with the physical removal of material remains to somewhere else. The desire to "get it back" has fueled discussions of rights worldwide (Schmidt 1996, Prott 1996).

The notion that culture is a bounded entity related to and owned by groups that exist through time is at the heart of NAGPRA and other claims processes in relation to cultural heritage. Many of those at the forefront of discussions of the relationships between rights and cultural heritage focus on the importance of ownership. Thus Peter Schmidt (In press:88) argues, "we need to address taken-for-granted practices and ethical lapses that violate human rights to a cultural past, including ownership of history about others' pasts. We need to ensure that ownership remains in the hands of indigenous peoples." This focus on the ownership of the past perhaps derives from the longer assumption that nation states have sovereign control of the heritage within their own borders. The discourse is so pervasive that we have perhaps turned a blind eye to the uncomfortable evidence from anthropology and history about the difficulties of making links between cultures and people. Culture is now seen as hybrid, flexible, in process, contextually changing, and transforming. Is this simply a post-modern, Western perspective that seeks to undermine the importance of tradition and descent to subject peoples? Clearly, people often feel very strongly about identities and even invented traditions may provide shelter and a resource. I will describe the force of these relationships below in terms of well-being. Archaeologists have great difficulty demonstrating any theoretical or other basis for following identities back into the archaeological past as there simply are no grounds for arguing

869

that pots and peoples coincide through time—as Childe (1952) argued long ago (also see Hodder 1978 and Jacobs 2009 in relation to NAGPRA).

The notion that groups (nation states, regional groups such as the Kurds, language groups such as Bantu speakers, indigenous groups) have an inherent right to the culture from which they are descended rests on grounds that archaeologists and anthropologists have rejected—that peoples and cultures "descend" together. Claims to the past based on fixed boundaries and close associations between people and cultures are contradicted by the evidence that culture is passed down through complex and fluid channels, heritage is continually being reproduced and reinterpreted, human groups and cultures are in the long term open and in flux (Geertz 1973, Hodder 1978, Jacobs 2009, Sahlins 1976, Turner 1967).

The notion that the past is owned by someone is also necessarily conflictual. To claim an origin is always to exclude others, it is always to determine in-groups and out-groups. It is always about dividing populations. The past is a limited good from which multiple descents can be claimed (Jacobs 2009). Thus the identification of Moundbuilders in the prehistory of the Americas excluded native Americans from their heritage. The claim by colonial invaders of a *terra nullius* in Australia or South Africa excluded those of African descent. The claim of a Germanic Lausatia excluded a Polish and Slavic presence. The claim of an original homeland for the Jews in Palestine supports the exclusion of Palestinians (Meskell 1998, Ucko 1987, Lowenthal 1985, Shennan 1994).

Placing ownership at the heart of cultural heritage rights also does not take into account the many different nuances in the notion of ownership. Much cultural heritage is not owned in the way that an individual or a corporation owns land. Heritage ownership is often collective, and it is often more spiritual than pecuniary, more about identity and less about control. Although we are used to saying that heritage is partly a construction of the present, it is not "invented" by anyone and so differs from "intellectual property" (see, however, McGuire 2004). There are numerous ways in which people interact with heritage. They may want access, they may want to use it for education or have a voice in what is written and projected about it, they may want to use it in healing, reconciliation and restitution, make money out of it, put it in a museum, repatriate it, loan it, hide it, destroy it. It is difficult to use "ownership" as a term to encompass all these nuances of meaning. Below I will use alternative terms such as well-being and the ability to participate.

IAN HODDER

A further difficulty with the ownership basis for cultural heritage rights is that it traps people into categories from which they may have difficulty escaping. People may be attracted by the income to be gained from performing "their own" cultural heritage. Heritage managers and developers may ask that local residents make craft products, or live in houses that are traditional. People may become identified with the categories placed upon them, encapsulated in the past, or rather in the past as we would want it to be. People may be forced to claim rights as members of some past entity constructed in the present—as Classic Maya or Machu Picchu Inca (Castaneda 1996, Silverman 2002).

Finally, notions of ownership and descent do not deal well with the ways in which heritage works in the contemporary globalized world. In 2003, the government of Australia made claims to Turkey that Gallipoli, the site of the battle by ANZAC (Australia and New Zealand Army Corp) forces against Ottoman forces in 1915, should be listed as part of Australian heritage. There are many dimensions of heritage that overlap and cannot be described in any simple way as "ownership." Many claims to cultural heritage are transnational, including religious rights for access to Lourdes and Mecca, rights of diasporic groups to their homelands, rights to cemeteries of those that have fallen in wars abroad. It is widely recognized today that heritage management is best achieved through multiple partnerships and dialogues across a dispersed and multi-centered world (Meskell 2009).

From Descent to Well-being

The task seems to be then, to develop a notion of heritage rights that focuses on social justice (rather than solely on the universal value of the objects and monuments themselves) without the entitlement to that justice being based on the assumption of exclusionary descent. A starting definition of cultural heritage rights might then be: *Everyone has a right to participate in and benefit from cultural heritage.* The key phrase I have left out here is "his or her own" in front of "cultural heritage." What this definition does is focus on the right that we all have to participate in and benefit from cultural heritage. This is the right described in Article 27 of the 1948 UN Declaration, but it avoids the notion that we benefit only from "our own" heritage and it avoids the difficulty of having to relate the right to descent.

Cultural Heritage Rights: From Ownership and Descent to Justice and Well-being

This definition of the right leaves open the many ways in which cultural heritage might be defined. It leaves open the many ways in which people participate in the past. A person may feel connected to past artifacts and monuments in terms of co-presence (I or my people were or are there), production (I or my people made it), ownership (I or my people owned it), religious belief (I or my people believe in it), aesthetics (I or my people think it is beautiful), and so on. There may be sentimental, historical, economic, or ritual associations with heritage. These are all forms of association that lead to claims for different forms of participation in the present with a particular heritage.

But the definition glosses difficult issues. If the focus of heritage rights claims is to be participation rather than ownership, are not the claims of minorities undermined? Does it not become possible for anyone to claim association (through donations of funds, expertise) and override the interests of local groups?

Given that a particular group is closely associated with a cultural heritage which is central to its well-being, it has a right, under the formulation presented here, to participate and benefit from that heritage. So the emphasis has shifted from demonstrating that a person really is descended from a cultural group and has moved to the question of whether a person has the capacity to participate in heritage. The question becomes whether a person is able to participate in cultural heritage so as to enhance that person's well-being.

In turning cultural heritage towards well-being, the capability and functioning approach to human rights as advocated by Martha Nussbaum and Amartya Sen is of value. In their approach to comparing the well-being of people and nations, the focus is not on how many resources people have or on how satisfied they feel, but on what they are actually able to do (Sen 1993, Nussbaum 1997). The approach makes no assumptions about commensurability: it is not argued that there is a single metric of well-being. It is argued that the pursuit of capabilities is irreducibly plural. In the heritage field, the capabilities might include having attachments to things and people outside oneself. According to this view, people should have the capability to pursue heritage even if they do not pursue this capability into functioning behavior. A heritage capability might allow other aspects of well-being—to be employed, to have good health, to think, feel, imagine. Thinking about rights in this way allows us to ask whether people are really able to attain diverse forms of well-being

IAN HODDER

through heritage. Considering heritage in this way allows us to examine whether people are in practice able to participate in sites, objects, identities in such a way as to fulfill their capabilities.

In competing claims over heritage, there will of course be different claims, from different standpoints, that the past enhances well-being and allows different persons and groups to achieve their capabilities. In such contexts, there is a need for dialogue and collaboration, as is widely recognized today, in order to come to an understanding of the different positions and to reach some conclusion. Collaboration and dialogue are now the hallmarks of heritage management (Colwell-Chanthaphonh and Ferguson 2008; Habu, Fawcett, and Matsunaga 2008; McNiven and Russell 2005; Silliman 2008), but they need to include broader questions than cultural value, descent, and ownership. They need to deal with the ways in which cultural heritage enhances the well-being and capacities of individuals and groups.

At any particular historical moment, some rights are seen as so basic and fundamental to life that they "trump" other rights. Ivison (2008) describes the way some rights are like cards that trump all others on the table. In my view, the right to heritage in terms of basic subsistence trumps an academic interest, unless an alternative subsistence can be found. Involvement in cultural heritage may be so fundamental for local groups that the interests of cultural tourists or archaeological scholars may rightly be seen as secondary. There may be widespread agreement about the evaluation of needs—which rights trump others. If such is the case in a particular instance, the ranking of rights, implicitly or explicitly, may provide a mechanism for distinguishing between competing claims. As noted in the UNESCO (1970:105) discussion referred to above, "the first task of life is to live and one of the principal functions of culture is to enable people to maintain and perpetuate life."

In these ways, the right to cultural heritage is not seen as an absolute, "God-given" right, but as something dependent on and relative to particular practical contexts. Thus, for example, for many native American groups, identity and well-being have become very entangled in cultural heritage. In such a context, the past matters at the level of fundamental human rights. The same may be said for some immigrant groups in the United States, but for an Englishman in New York participation in Native American and African American pasts is not fundamental although there may be value in knowledge and study. The right to cultural heritage is specific to historical conditions.

873

So we can add to our identification of a cultural heritage right: *Everyone has a right to participate in and benefit from cultural heritage that is of consequence to their well-being.*

Rights and Duties

As Clapham (2007:21-22) notes, the American rights rhetoric is near silent on responsibility. The rights bearer is seen as a lone autonomous individual. "The language of rights is too often understood exclusively in terms of the advantages it confers on individuals claiming them. Rights confer advantages but they also impose duties, and no system of rights is complete without an account of how and why they do so" (Ivison 2008:64). Certainly many of the originators of our current discourse on rights linked rights to duties. According to Locke, for example, rights are derived from our duties to God and, though him, to each other.

The "Universal Declaration of Human Rights" (1948) talks of the duties owed by an individual to a community and links these duties to securing the rights of others, but, on the whole, in most discussions of human rights, the rights of the rights bearer are linked to the duties of a rights giver—normally the state (Macleod 2005). Thus, as Ivison puts it, following Wesley Hohfeld, "if D has a right with respect to H to perform X, then H has a duty not to interfere with D in X-ing" (Ivison 2008:11). Some would prefer that we talk about responsibility and community rather than right entitlement (Clapham 2007).

The "Declaration on the Rights of Indigenous Peoples" adopted by the UN General Assembly in 2007 quoted above has paired the rights of indigenous peoples with the duties of the State to protect those rights. But there is no mention of the duty of indigenous groups to protect the interests of other indigenous groups or other participating groups in that heritage.

Shyllon (1998, see also Schmidt 1996) refers to a distinctly African take on cultural rights. In the Banjul "African Charter on Human and Peoples' Rights" (adopted by the Assembly of Heads of State of the Organization of African Unity held in Nairobi in 1981—Umozurike 1983) there is a strong focus on shared collective rights, but also on a duty to share and promote "African culture." The Preamble states, "enjoyment of rights and freedoms also implies the performance of duties on the part of everyone."

In the "Universal Declaration of Human Rights," rights are linked to the duties of the State to protect those rights. But there is little discussion there or in much of the rights literature of the notion that rights are conditional on the responsibilities of the rights bearer as part of a social contract (Ivison 2008). In practice, however, most fundamental human rights are conditional and limited by law. Thus in the United States a person has a right to life and liberty only in so far as that person respects the life and liberty of others: to take a life, is to lose the right to life. A person has a right to work in so far as that person does not work by stealing the products of labor from others. A person has a right to health in the United States, only if that person makes insurance or Social Security payments. And so on. Rights are often defined as claims that are made simply by virtue of being a human adult, but in practice they are closely linked to the duties we have to each other in specific historical contexts (Clapham 2007, Turner 2006). Rights are conditional on normative behavior (doing the right thing), systems of values (what is the right thing), and exchanges of public and private good.

The linking of rights and duties is dangerously conservative if it implies that rights are only given if duties are fulfilled. People may not have the means to fulfill their duties or they may not see the duties in the way conceived of by dominant groups or by society at large. So rights are related to, but separated from duties. People may have a right to X even if they cannot fulfill their duties with respect to X. If the inability to fulfill duties is a matter of resources, then others (e.g., the state) have the duty to provide the means of fulfillment. If it is a matter of disagreement about rights and duties, then it remains the case that rights to X are related to the duty to acknowledge other forms of participation in X.

As Turner (2006:67-68) notes in a general evaluation of human rights discourse, "one criticism of human rights is that there has been little effort to develop a notion of human duties. Through the notion of cosmopolitan virtue, it is possible to develop a theory of human obligation that recognizes care and respect for other cultures and ironic doubt about the claims of one's own culture. These obligations are sequential: recognition, respect, concern, care, and irony. An ethic of care is compatible with human rights and is logically necessary for the development of cultural rights. Care for the safety and security of other communities and cultures rests on our recognizing the precariousness of cultures in a global environment. An ironic distance from one's own culture remains a condition for recognizing the mutual vulnerability of humans."

The notion that rights to heritage can be linked to duties towards other interests is seen in attempts to share the past or to involve it in post-conflict reconciliation and healing. For example, Israelis and Palestinians have undertaken joint projects to conserve and put on display sites and monuments that are of importance to different communities such as Crusader castles with earlier (Jewish) and later (Islamic) levels (Scham and Yahya 2003). If archaeologists in such a context can come together to work on a shared past (Scham and Yahya 2003), however difficult and however limited the results, then it must be possible for all of us to recognize the legitimate interests of others in relation to cultural heritage. The legitimacy of these interests should not, in my view, be based on who was here first, who came from where, who is descended from whom. Rather, as noted above, the legitimacy is based on the undoubted fact that for both Israelis and Palestinians, for example, their heritage matters to them in pursuing their most fundamental capacities. But recognition of this legitimacy does not preclude responsibility to others to benefit. Indeed, in the Palestinian and Israeli collaboration, it is recognition of the right to participation that has inspired working together. In post-conflict situations in South Africa or the Balkans, reconciliation and healing may be mediated through recognition of conflicting interests and mutual benefits in restoring and caring for heritage (Meskell 2009; see also African American heritage—LaRoche 2005)

So my focus is to relate rights to duties to others. I wish to define a right to cultural heritage as *"Everyone has a right to participate in and benefit from cultural heritage that is of consequence to their well-being, and everyone has a duty towards others with respect to that right."*

So the question is not about descent, but about the extent to which people participate in heritage, or rather, how much they have the capability to participate in it (in terms of access, education, performance, appreciation, religious experience, employment, and so on). And it is a question of recognizing that others have capabilities that may require access to the same monuments. I have tried to set cultural heritage in the frame of our rights and duties towards each other. I have tried to move away from the notion that it is the care for the object that is the duty, and to say that the duty is towards other participants.

Conclusions and Practices

The history of the discourse on human rights has been dominated by authors such as Hobbes, Locke, Kant, and Hegel, all of whom understood rights as referring to the fundamental status of human beings, a status perhaps given by God, perhaps deriving from some inherent dignity of persons (that is male persons), perhaps given in a social contract. I have argued in this paper that when such a notion of inherent rights is linked to the notion that persons derive their rights to heritage by descent, the result is a dangerous conception of cultural heritage as basic, fundamental, God-given, absolute. In fact, we know that cultural identities are endlessly mixed, fluid, contested, shared. Especially in the contemporary globalized world, rights to heritage are argued from many perspectives and angles. I have tried, therefore, to describe a definition of cultural heritage rights that is attuned to this more complex world. Rather than cultural heritage rights as statuses based on universal values, I have related them to the specific needs of persons in their search for well-being.

But is this a dangerously utilitarian perspective? What does this definition of cultural heritage rights mean for the view that some heritage is of such skill, beauty, quality, uniqueness that it just deserves preservation—regardless of whether it does anyone any good? What happens to the idea that cultural heritage of outstanding universal value should be preserved? It seems to me that, in the long run, heritage that has no social value will not continue to be funded and preserved. Indeed, it will probably cease to be defined as heritage. But the very fact that we identify an object or monument as of high quality, implies that it has meaning for people at some level. Artifacts of great aesthetic value contribute to cultural life and, thus, under the various UN declarations and conventions, they matter and they enhance well-being. But, under the formulation presented here, they are not protected because they are of aesthetic value. They are protected because our valuation of them as aesthetic entangles them in a particular social context in which they are of consequence to well-being.

And what happens, from this utilitarian perspective, to the notion of abstract and obscure scientific and academic knowledge? We might identify a particular artifact or monument as a good example of a particular type and base its protection on that categorization. This and other forms of scientific knowledge about the past do enhance well-being in that they contribute to cultural life. They contribute to knowledge and education. In these ways, the information is of consequence. When stacked up against competing claims to control and interpret a particular artifact and monument, this scientific knowledge may well be trumped by other needs and values more fundamental to basic human rights. But scientific knowledge about the past has numerous forms of social value and enhances many human rights.

And what of the right of antiquities dealers and collectors to control the licit artifacts that they have paid a good price for? Should they not have the right to control them, and trade and sell them in the way they see best (Merryman 2005)? The traded artifacts can be seen as objects of high cultural value that have great social importance for individuals, however elite they may be. Surely traded artifacts are of consequence to the well-being of dealers and collectors? Under the formulation argued here, the rights of collectors and museums are related to their obligations to others for whom the collections are of consequence. In fact, most museums today and many collectors are engaged in some form of access, sharing, loaning, repatriation that recognizes the legitimate interests of claimant groups (McNiven and Russell 2005, Liebmann and Rizvi 2008). In my view, debates about repatriation and return need to be evaluated less in terms of decisions about histories and dates of legislation, and more in terms of the degree to which the artifacts matter to participating groups—the degree to which human rights might be better served by return or repatriation rather than by being kept in a private glass case or in a museum basement. There is no doubt in my mind that to keep a deeply religious object or one that is of great importance to a cultural group locked up in this way denies fundamental human rights to others.

I would like to end with an example of how a focus on well-being, rather than on the universal value of artifacts, might be an effective strategy in claims for the protection of human rights. In southeast Turkey, there has been a recent proliferation of human rights NGOs dealing with the displacement of people as a result of the series of dams built there since the 1960s (the GAP Güneydoğu Anadolu Projesi or Southeastern Anatolian Project). The increase in this human rights activism since 2000 has partly resulted from Turkey's EU accession process, but it has also resulted from the rise to power of the AK (Justice and Development) Party which seems supportive of some form of recognition of the Kurds in the region. Since the international outcry over the damage to the Roman mosaics at Zeugma as a result of the dam building, cultural heritage issues have been part of the political activism in the southeast; thus there are "Stop Ilisu Dam" and "Save Hasankeyf" NGOs (Kitchen and Ronayne 2001). Hasankeyf is a site in the GAP region with a mixture of Christian and Islamic monuments that will be lost if the dams are constructed as planned.

The "Save Hasankeyf" movement uses the rhetoric of universal cultural value to make its case. This argument is pitted against the rhetoric of the state GAP project and the European dam construction companies which emphasizes the jobs, agriculture and future well-being of people that will follow from the dam construction. At the time of writing, European governments have withdrawn their export credit guarantees for the Ilisu Dam project, citing Turkey's failure to deal with human rights claims concerning the environment and cultural heritage. The Turkish government may go ahead anyway with the dam and it is clear that much of the argument about human rights in this case centers on well-being—employment, history, environment. It might be argued then that the "Save Hasankeyf" NGO would be more successful adding to their talk of the universal value of cultural things a focus on the well-being that could be obtained from the archaeological sites if saved and restored as an income generating heritage. Prominent artists like Nobel Prize winning writer Orhan Pamuk and pop singer Tarkan have joined the campaign to stop the Ilisu Dam and make Hasankeyf a World Heritage Site. But rather than promoting the universal discourse of object values, an alternative strategy would be to demonstrate the different forms of well-being that could be attained by saving Hasankeyf. This would be to use the arguments of the GAP project (that the Dam will provide jobs and agriculture) against itself. But heritage managers and archaeologists are not used to work out the long-term sustainable economic benefits of sites, as well as the values gained from education, identity and dignity. Unless archaeologists are willing to work out the benefits in clear terms, over short and long terms, it will remain difficult to protect heritage that allows people to achieve their capabilities. As archaeologists and heritage managers, we have for too long been focused on objects rather than people.

ACKNOWLEDGEMENTS

I am very grateful to Lynn Meskell, as well as to Helen Stacy, Richard Leventhal, Brian Daniels, Duncan Ivison, and Neil Brodie for the discussions that led to this paper.

REFERENCES

Bernbeck, Reinhard and Susan Pollack. 1996. "Ayodhya, Archaeology and Identity." *Current Anthropology* 37 (Supplement):S138-142.

Byrne, Denis. 1991. "Western Hegemony in Archaeological Heritage Management." *History and Anthropology* 5:269-276.

Castaneda, Quetzil. 1996. *In the Museum of Maya Culture: Touring Chichen Itza.* Minneapolis: University of Minnesota Press.

Childe, V. Gordon. 1952. *New Light on the Most Ancient East.* London: Routledge and Paul.

Clapham, Andrew. 2007. *Human Rights: A Very Short Introduction.* Oxford: Oxford University Press.

Cleere, Henry, ed. 1989. *Archaeological Heritage Management in the Modern World.* London: Unwin Hyman.

Colwell-Chanthaphonh, Chip and T.J Ferguson, eds. 2008. *Collaboration in Archaeological Practice. Engaging Descendant Communities.* Lanham: Altamira Press.

Duquette, David. 2005. "Universalism and Relativism in Human Rights." In D.A. Reidy and M.N.S. Sellers, eds. *Universal Human Rights: Moral Order in a Divided World*, 59-78. Lanham: Rowman and Littlefield.

Fforde, Cressida, Jane Hubert, and Paul Turnbull, eds. 2004. *The Dead and their Possessions: Repatriation in Principle, Policy and Practice.* London: Routledge.

Fine-Dare, Kathleen S. 2002. *Grave Injustice: The American Indian Repatriation Movement and NAGPRA.* Lincoln: University of Nebraska Press.

Foucault, Michel. 1977. *Discipline and Punish.* London: Penguin.

Geertz, Clifford. 1973. *The Interpretation of Culture.* New York: Basic Books.

Gerstenblith, Patty. 2002. "Cultural Significance and the Kennewick Skeleton: Some Thoughts on the Resolution of Cultural Heritage Disputes." In E. Barkan and R. Bush, eds. *Naming the Stones, Claiming the Bones*, 162-197. Los Angeles: Getty Research Institute.

Habu, Junko, Clare Fawcett, and John M. Matsunaga, eds. 2008. *Evaluating Multiple Narratives. Beyond Nationalist, Colonialist, Imperialist Archaeologies.* New York: Springer.

Hodder, Ian. 1978. *The Spatial Organization of Culture.* London: Duckworth.

Ivison, Duncan. 2008. *Rights.* Montreal: McGill Queens University Press.

Jacobs, Jordan. 2009. "Repatriation and the Reconstruction of Identity." *Museum Anthropology* 32 (2): 83-98.

Kitchen, W. and M. Ronayne. 2001. "The Ilisu Dam in Southeast Turkey: Archaeology at Risk." *Antiquity* 75:37-38.

Labadi, Sophia. 2007. "Representations of the Nation and Cultural Diversity in Discourses on World Heritage." *Journal of Social Archaeology* 7:147-170.

Lafrenz Samuels, Kathryn. 2008. "Value and Significance in Archaeology." *Archaeological Dialogues* 15:71-97.

LaRoche, Cheryl J. 2005. "Heritage, Archaeology, and African American History." Society of American Archaeology *Archaeological Record* 5(2):34-37.

Liebmann, Matthew and Uzma Z. Rizvi. 2008. *Archaeology and the Postcolonial Critique.* Lanham: Altamira Press.

Lilley, I. and M. Williams. 2005. "Archaeological Significance and Indigenous Knowledge: A View from Australia." In C. Mathers, T. Darvill and B. Little, eds. *Heritage of Value, Archaeology of Renown: Reshaping Archaeological Assessment and Significance*, 227-257. Gainesville: University Press of Florida.

Lowenthal, David. 1985. *The Past is a Foreign Country.* Cambridge: Cambridge University Press.

Macleod, Alistair M. 2005. "The Structure of Arguments for Human Rights." In D.A. Reidy and M.N.S. Sellers, eds. *Universal Human rights: Moral Order in a Divided World*, 17-36. Lanham: Rowman and Littlefield.

McGuire, Randall H. 2004. "Contested Pasts: Archaeology and Native Americans." In L. Meskell and R.W. Preucel, eds. *A Companion to Social Archaeology*, 374-395. London: Blackwell.

McNiven, Ian and Lynette Russell. 2005. *Appropriated Pasts: Indigenous Peoples and the Colonial Culture of Archaeology*. Walnut Creek: Altamira Press.

Merryman, John Henry. 2005. "Cultural Property Internationalism." *International Journal of Cultural Property* 12:11-39.

Meskell, Lynn, ed. 1998. *Archaeology under Fire. Nationalism, Politics and Heritage in the Eastern Mediterranean and Middle East*. London: Routledge.

_____. 2009. *Cosmopolitan Archaeologies*. Durham and London: Duke University Press.

Nussbaum, Martha C. 1997. "Capabilities and Human Rights." *Fordham Law Review* 66:273-300.

Prott, Lyndel V. 1996. "Saving the Heritage. UNESCO's Action against Illicit Traffic in Africa." In P. Schmidt and R. J. McIntosh, eds. *Plundering Africa's Past*, 29-44. Bloomington: Indiana University Press.

Sahlins, Marshall. 1976. *Culture and Practical Reason*. Chicago: University of Chicago Press.

Scham, Sandra A. and Adel Yahya. 2003. "Heritage and Reconciliation." *Journal of Sociology* 3:339-416.

Schmidt, Peter. 1996. "The Human Right to a Cultural Heritage: African Applications." In P. Schmidt and R. J. McIntosh, eds. *Plundering Africa's Past*, 18-28. Bloomington: Indiana University Press.

_____. In press. "Human Rights, Culture, and Dams: A New Global Perspective." In S.A. Brandt and F.A. Hassan, eds. *Damming the Past: Dams and Cultural Heritage Management*. Lanham, MD: Lexington Books.

Sen, Amartya. 1993. "Capability and Well-being." In M. Nussbaum and A. Sen, eds. *The Quality of Life*, 30-31. Oxford: Oxford University Press.

Shennan, Stephen, ed. 1994. *Archaeological Approaches to Cultural Identity*. London: Routledge.

Shyllon, Folarin. 1998. "The Right to a Cultural Past: African Viewpoints." In H. Niec, ed. *Cultural Rights and Wrongs*, 103-119. Paris and London: UNESCO and the Institute of Arts and Law.

Silliman, Stephen W., ed. 2008. *Collaborative Indigenous Archaeology at the Trowel's Edge: Explorations in Methodology, Education and Ethics*. Tucson: University of Arizona Press.

Silverman, Helaine. 2002. "Touring Ancient Times: The Present and Presented Past in Contemporary Peru." *American Anthropologist* 104(3):881-902.

Silverman, Helaine and D. Fairchild Ruggles, eds. 2008. *Cultural Heritage and Human Rights*. Heidelberg: Springer.

Stacy, Helen. 2009. *Human Rights for the 21st Century: Sovereignty, Civil Society, Culture*. Stanford: Stanford University Press.

Stavenhagen, Rudolfo. 1998. "Cultural Rights: A Social Science Perspective." In H. Niec, ed. *Cultural Rights and Wrongs*, 1-20. Paris and London: UNESCO and the Institute of Arts and Law.

Turner, Bryan S. 2006. *Vulnerability and Human Rights*. Philadelphia: The Pennsylvania State University Press.

Turner, Victor. 1967. *The Forest of Symbols*. Ithaca, NY: Cornell University Press.

Ucko, Peter. 1987. *Academic Freedom and Apartheid: The Story of the World Archaeological Congress*. London: Duckworth.

Umozurike, U.O. 1983. "The African Charter on Human and Peoples' Rights." *The American Journal of International Law* 77(4):902-912.

United Nations Educational, Scientific and Cultural Organization. 1970. Cultural Rights as Human Rights. Paris: UNESCO.

_____. 1972. "Convention Concerning the Protection of the World Cultural and Natural Heritage." Accessed from http://whc.unesco.org/en/conventiontext on January 1, 2010.

United Nations General Assembly. 1948. "Universal Declaration of Human Rights." Accessed from http://www.un.org/en/documents/udhr/ on January 1, 2010.

_____. 1966. "International Covenant on Economic, Social and Cultural Rights." Accessed from http://daccess-ddsny.un.org/doc/RESOLUTION/GEN/NR0/005/03/IMG/NR000503.pdf?OpenElement on September 20, 2010.

_____. 1966. "International Covenant on Civil and Political Rights." Accessed from http://www.un.org/millennium/law/iv-4.htm on September 20, 2010.

_____. 1989. "Convention on the Rights of the Child." Accessed from http://www.un.org/millennium/law/iv-10.htm on 20 September, 2010

_____. 1992. "Declaration on the Rights of Persons Belonging to National, Ethnic, Religious, Linguistic Minorities." Accessed from http://www.un.org/documents/ga/res/47/a47r135.htm on September 10, 2010.

_____. 2007. "Declaration on the Rights of Indigenous Peoples." Accessed from http://www.un.org/esa/socdev/unpfii/en/drip.html on January 1, 2010.

Name Index

Abtahi, Hirad xv, xvii, 375–406
Ahmed, M.A. 61
Aikawa (Aikawa-Faure), Noriko 65, 262, 294
Albro, R. 61
Allen, V. 142
Alsop, J. 168
Amend, S. 126
Amend, T. 126
Anaya, J. xvi
Anderson, J. 73
Anderson, R. 315, 316
Andolino, R. 61
Ang, C. 426
Annan, Kofi 407
Antons, Christoph 71, 276
Appadurai, A. 68, 141, 150
Appiah, K. 73
Aragon, L.V. 72
Arantes, Antonio 299
Aylwin, N. 61, 69

Baines, G. 155
Baird, Melissa F. xvii, xxi, xxii, xxiii, xxv, xxvi, xxviii, xxix, 149, 156, 311–24
Baker, W.E. 481
Balandier, Georges 155
Balliger, R. 72
Bandarin, F. 138
Bannister, K.P. 64
Barsh, Russel L. 241
Bator, Paul 164, 167, 186, 198
Bebbington, A. 61, 62, 68
Beck, Ulrich 480
Belgrave, M. 314
Belisarius 6
Bell, C. 67
Bell, Jonathan S. xvii, xxviii, 79–98
Beltrán, J. 127
Bender, B. 312
Bendix, Regina 65, 302
Bernbeck, Reinhard 521
Bin Laden, Osama 409

Blake, Janet xvi, xvii, xviii, xxiii, xxviii, 33–57, 280, 289, 299, 301
Blaškić, Tihomir 401
Bøås, M. 268, 269
Boast, R. 315
Bonaparte, Napoléon 6–9 11
Bortolotto, Chiara 304
Boyle, A.E. 52
Bramley, C. 69
Braude, Joseph 358, 366
Breglia, Lisa 64, 65, 322
Brodie, Neil 537
Brown, Michael F. xvii, xxv, xxix, 62, 68, 144, 146, 235–56
Brown, Wendy 248
Buergin, R. 134
Buggey, S. 64
Burri-Nenova, M. 60, 71
Bush, George W. 241
Busse, M. 66
Byrne, Denis 520, 523
Byrne-Sutton, Quentin 24

Calavan, M. 434
Campese, J. 128
Canetti, Elias 266
Carman, J. 312
Carpenter, K.A. 73
Carter, Howard 90
Carter, Jennifer 291
Castaneda, Quetzil 529
Castells, Manuel 60, 237
Čerkez, Mario 401, 402, 415
Chagall, Marc 328
Chan, A. 68
Chardin, Jean-Baptiste-Siméon 343
Childe, V. Gordon 528
Chippindale, Christopher 350
Chirikure, S. 147
Christen, K. 60
Chuzi, Wang 162, 163, 170, 199
Cicero 5, 6

Clapham, Andrew 532, 533
Clark, A.K. 60
Clarke, G. 68
Cleere, Henry 521
Clifford, J. 61
Coffey, M.K. 60
Coggins, Clemency 166
Coleman, E.B. 60, 71
Collier, S.J. 149
Collins, J. 149
Colwell-Chanthaphonh, Chip 521, 531
Comaroff, John L. 73
Comaroff, Jean 73
Conlin, M.V. 142
Coombe, Rosemary J. xvi, xvii, xviii, xxiii, xxv, xxviii, xxix, xxxi, 59–78, 156, 242, 245, 275–309
Coombes, A.E. 140
Cooper, F. 140, 155
Cowen, Tyler 238, 242
Croke, Alexander 8, 9
Craufurd Smith, Rachael xvii, 471–502
Cruikshank, B. 147

Daes, Erica 280
Dahles, H. 428
Dailoo, Shabnam Inanloo xvii, xix, 101–23
Dalai Lama 169
Daniels, Brian 537
Davis, M. 139, 141
Davis, Michael H. 248
De Cesari, C. 150
de Quincy, Quatremère 7–9
de Vattel, Emer de 6, 8
Delang, C.O. 134
Denhez, M. 263
Denon, Vivant 84
Dervyttere, A. 61
deSouza, M. 60
Dommann, Monika 71
Dromgoole, Sarah xvii, 201–34
du Cros, Hilary 83
Dudley, N. 132
Duquette, David 523
Dutfield, Graham 241, 247
Dutra, Michael L. xvii, xxix, 161–99

Edelman, M. 61
Ellis, R. 147, 149

Elyachar, J. 61, 154
Ensor, J. 61
Escobar, A. 62
Esterhuysen, A. 146

Fabian, J. 149
Farchakh, Joanne 358
Fathy, Hassan 86
Fawcett, Clare 531
Feldmann, Arthur 341
Ferguson, J. 150
Ferguson, T.J. 521, 531
Fforde, Cressida 526
Filbo, C.F. 60
Fillippucci, P. 68
Fine-Dare, Kathleen S. 527
Fischer-Lescano, A. 72
Fitch, James Marston 81
Forbes, Susan 313, 318, 320
Forrest, Craig 278
Foucault, Michel 523
Francioni, Francesco xv, xvii, 407–19
Friedman, S. 155
Frigo, M. 60

Galperin, Hernán 478, 479, 481
Geertz, Clifford 528
Geismar, Heidi 66, 67
Gentry, K. 314, 315
Gerstenblith, Patty xvii, xxix, 347–73, 521
Gibson, N.C. 151
Gill, David W.J. 350
Girsberger, M. 71, 276
Giuliani, Rudolph 148
Glass, A. 65
Goering, Hermann 11
Goodale, M. 60
Goodman, J. 71
Gow, D. 60, 61
Goytisolo, Juan 257, 260–66, 269
Graber, C.B. 71, 72
Grace, Lawrence 314
Green, G.L. 72
Greene, S. 61
Greiber, T. 130, 133
Griffer, Jan 342
Grotius, Hugo 5, 6, 8, 9

Haber, A. 149

Habu, Junko 531
Hale, C.R. 60
Halleck, Henry Wager 9
Hallman, Robert 3
Handler, R. 61, 72
Hannerz, Ulf 481
Harris, I. 426
Harrison, Simon 61, 238
Hart, H.L.A. xxxi
Harvey, David 60, 62
Hawass, Zahi 89, 91
Hay, Robert 85, 89
Hayashi, M. 227
Hayden, Dolores 82
Hecht, Robert 347
Hegel, Georg Wilhelm Friedrich 534
Helfer, L. 61
Henare, A. 313, 314
Herzfeld, M. 149
Hirst, David 341
Hirtz, F. 60
Hitler, Adolf 11, 14, 400
Hobbes, Thomas 534
Hodder, Ian xvii, 519–40
Hoffman, B.T. xxiii, xxvi
Hohfeld, Wesley 532
Holdgate, Martin W. 321
Hoo, S.K. 146
Höpperger, M. 68
Howeidy, Fahmi 411
Hristov, J. 60
Hubert, Jane 526
Huchzermeyer, M. 148
Humphrey, C. 60

Inglehart, R. 481
Ivison, Duncan 319, 523, 531–3, 537

Jacobs, Jordan 528
Jennings, Ron 156
Jolliffe, L. 142
Jopela, Albino Pereira de Jesus 147, 156
Jovanovic, M.A. 61
Jung, C. 60

Kamenka, E. 49
Kaneff, D. 61
Kansa, E.C. 60
Kant, Immanuel 534

Karzai, H. 411
Kawharu, M. 312–14
Kaye, Lawrence 329
Kearney, Amanda 302, 305
Kempf, E. 127
Kerr, Rose 168
Kersel, Morag 367
Kiedzelski-Eichner, Nora 3
Kim, Hee-Eun xvii, xxii, xxv, 439–70
King, A.D. 61
Kingsbury, B.W. 61
Kirsch, S. 61
Kirshenblatt-Gimblett, B. 312
Kirsten, J.F. 69
Kiss, A-C. 43
Kitchen, W. 522, 536
Kordić, Dario 401, 402, 415
Kothari, A. 126
Kreps, C. 67
Kruse, K.M. 139, 140

Labadi, Sophia 156, 520
LaFranche, Ambassador 407
Lafrenz Samuels, Kathryn 520
Lamy, Pascal 474, 480
LaRoche, Cheryl J. 534
Larsen, P.B. 128
Larson, J. 69
Lasgorceix, A. 126
Laurie, N. 61
Leach, James 72, 242
Lele, S. 126
Lennon, Jane 300
Lenzerini, Federico xv, xvii, 407–19
Leventhal, Richard 537
Li, T. 62
Lieber, Francis 9
Liebmann, Matthew 521, 536
Lilley, I. 521
Locke, John 532, 534
Long, D.L. 312
Long, S. 312
Loulanski, T. xxiii, 64
Lowenthal, David xix, 36, 41, 81, 521, 528
Lowrey, K. 61
Lund, Carsten 203

Mackenzie, S.M.R. 356, 357, 359, 365, 367
Macleod, Alistair M. 532

Macmillan, Fiona 61, 71, 72
Magliocco, Sabina 246
Maharaj, B. 148
Manetsi, Thabo 156
Marceau, Gabrielle 497
Marcellus 6
Marr, C. 314, 315
Marrie, Henrietta 296
Marschall, S. 150
Marx, Karl 523
Masuku van Damme, L.S. 147
Matisse, Henri 14
Matsunaga, John M. 531
Matsuura, Ambassador 407
Matunga, H. 313, 314
Maxmin, Jody 3
Mbembe, A. 140, 155
Mbhekiseni, Mavuso 156
McAffee, K. 70
McCarthy, C. 312–14
McCully, M. 314
McGuire, Randall H. 528
McKenzie, John 315
McKercher, Bob 83
McNeill, D. 268, 269
McNiven, Ian 521, 531, 536
Meinke, Hans 260
Memmott, P. 312
Merryman, John Henry xvii, xviii, xxviii, xxix, 3–31, 165, 167, 196, 236, 244, 536
Meskell, Lynn 64, 83, 91, 147, 149, 156, 312, 528, 529, 534, 537
Miraftab, F. 148
Mitchell, N. 64
Mitchell, Timothy 91, 92
Mngqolo, Sephai 142, 143
Morris, David 156
Müller, Benny 276
Munjeri, D. 63
Murray, N. 139
Mutu, M. 314

Nafziger, James 333
Nahlik, S.E. 12
Nakamura, Carolyn 156
Nakht 89
Ndlovu, N. 147
Ndoro, W. 148
Neil, Garry 298

Nicholas, G.P. 64–6
Niezen, R. xvi
Noble, Brian 67
Noko, David 145
Nussbaum, Martha 530
Nuttall, S. 140, 155

O'Keefe, P.J. xviii, 35, 216, 217
Oliver, Louise 488
Omar, Mohammed 408, 411
Omar, Mullah 408
Ong, Aihwa 149, 433
Ossorio, Pilar N. xvii, 503–17
Oviedo, Gonzalo xvi, xvii, xix, 125–36

Pamuk, Orhan 537
Pannekoek, Frits xvii, xix, 101–23
Parry, B. 60
Paterson, Robert K. xvii, xxiii, xxv, 327–46
Peck, J. 148
Perreault, T. 60, 61
Philips, Adrian 104
Pithouse, R. 151
Pol Pot 432
Pollack, Susan 521
Polonius 16
Polybius 5, 6
Posey, Darrell 241
Prakash, G. 139, 140
Prott, Lyndel V. xviii, 35, 36, 38, 50, 54, 524, 527
Puschkarsky, Tatjana xvi, xvii, xix, 125–36
Pwiti, G. 148

Qin Shi Huang, Emperor 195, 197

Rabbani, B. 408
Radcliffe, Sarah A. 61, 68
Rajak, Dina 147
Rao, V. 141
Reigl, Alois 81
Rhind, Alexander Henry 85
Rhoades, R.E. 61
Rizvi, Uzma Z. 521, 536
Robbins, Bruce 240
Rogerson, C.M. 144
Romer, Isabella Frances 85
Ronayne, M. 522, 536
Rose, D.B. 312
Rosenberg, Alfred 11, 400

Roy, A. 141
Ruggles, D. Fairchild xx, 138, 524
Ruru, J. 314–16
Ruskin, John 79
Russell, Lynette 521, 531, 536

Sahlins, Marshall 71, 528
Salem Saif, Abdul 411
Sauer, Carl O. 82, 103, 104
Saugestad, S. 61
Scafidi, Susan 245
Scham, Sandra A. 534
Scheermeyer, C. 149
Scher, Philip 72, 307
Schmidt, Peter 526, 527, 532
Schmitt, Thomas M. xvii, xxii, xxix, 257–73
Schubert, Ruth 262
Scott, J.C. 138
Sen, Amartya 530
Shennan, Stephen 528
Shepherd, N. 149
Shyllon, Folarin 532
Silliman, Stephen W. 521, 531
Silverman, Helaine xx, 524, 529
Simone, A.M. 140
Sissons, J. 313
Smith, Laurajane xxi, 62–4, 82, 287, 312, 322, 426
Sobukwe, Robert 142, 143
Solomon 112
Solomon, M. 314
Speed, S. 60
Stacy, Helen 523, 537
Stamatopoulou, Elsa 240
Stavenhagen, Rudolfo 525
Stewart-Harawira, M. 61
Stokes, J. 315
Strang, V. 312
Strathern, Marilyn 241, 248
Streicher, Julius 400
Sunder, Madhavi 69
Swanepoel, S. 142
Sylva, P. 126
Sylvain, R. 60
Symonides, J. 61

Taiepa, T. 311
Tapsell, Paul 313, 314
Tarkan 537

Te Heuheu Tukino IV, Horonuku 311, 314, 315, 320
ter Horst, J. 428
Teubner, G. 72
Theodosius, Emperor 407
Thutmose IV 89
Titchen, Sarah 317, 318, 320
Tittila 6
True, Marion 347
Tsing, A. 62
Tsosie, Rebecca 276
Tumu te Heuheu 315, 316
Turcotte, Joseph F. xvi, xvii, xviii, xxiii, xxv, xxviii, xxix, 275–309
Turnbull, Paul 526
Turnbull, R. 428
Turner, Bryan S. 533
Turner, Victor 528

Ucko, Peter 528
Umozurike, U.O. 532
Urice, Stephen 3

van der Merwe, C. 144, 145
van Gogh, Vincent 14
van Oers, R. 138
Verdery, K. 60
Vézina, Brigitte 276
von Benda-Beckmann, F. 73

Waterton, E. 312
Watts, M. 60
Weber, Max 249
Weismantel, M. 60
Weiss, Lindsay M. xvii, xxii, xxvi, xxxi, 137–59
Wendland, W.B. 71
Whatmore, S. 60
Wheaton, Henry 8, 9
Williams, M. 521
Williams, R. 46
Winer, M. 312
Winter, Tim xvii, xxii, xxvi, xxviii, xxix, 421–36
Wong, T. 134
Wylie, A. 65, 66

Yahya, Adel 534
Yang Buzhi 195
Yang Pengyue 195
Yang Zhifa 195

Yu, P. 61
Yudice, G. 60

Zedong, Mao 168, 199

Zikode, Sibusiso Innocent 150, 152, 153, 156
Zitong, Jin 180
Žižek, Slavoj 139
Zarazoga, Federico Mayor 260